TOWARDS A NEW COLD WAR

Other titles by Noam Chomsky available from The New Press

American Power and the New Mandarins:
Historical and Political Essays

For Reasons of State

On Language: Chomsky's Classic Works Language and Responsibility *and*
Reflections on Language *in One Volume*

Problems of Knowledge and Freedom

Understanding Power: The Indispensable Chomsky
(edited by Peter R. Mitchell and John Schoeffel)

TOWARDS A NEW COLD WAR

*U.S. Foreign Policy
from Vietnam to Reagan*

NOAM CHOMSKY

THE NEW PRESS

NEW YORK
LONDON

First published as *Towards a New Cold War: Essays on the Current Crisis and How We Got There* by Pantheon Books, a division of Random House, Inc., New York, 1982
This edition published in the United States by The New Press, New York, 2003
Distributed by W. W. Norton & Company, Inc., New York

ISBN 1-56584-859-4 (pbk.)
CIP data available

The New Press was established in 1990 as a not-for-profit alternative to the large, commercial publishing houses currently dominating the book publishing industry. The New Press operates in the public interest rather than for private gain, and is committed to publishing, in innovative ways, works of educational, cultural, and community value that are often deemed insufficiently profitable.

The New Press
38 Greene Street, 4th floor
New York, NY 10013
www.thenewpress.com

In the United Kingdom:
6 Salem Road
London W2 4BU

Composition by dix!

Printed in Canada

10 9 8 7 6 5 4 3 2 1

CONTENTS

TOWARDS A NEW COLD WAR

TOWARDS A NEW COLD WAR

FOREWORD BY JOHN PILGER

"To confront a mind that radically alters our perception of the world," wrote James Peck in *The Chomsky Reader*, "is one of life's most unsettling yet liberating experiences. Unsettling because it can undercut carefully constructed rationales and liberating because at last the obvious is seen for what it is."[1]

For me, Noam Chomsky has been liberating the "obvious" since I first read him while reporting from the United States on the American war in Vietnam. Without Chomsky's rare marshalling of evidence and critique of American power, the truth, the "obvious" about that war, might not have been told: nor the truth about so many human upheavals of our time. If Chomsky is regarded as a phenomenon, it is because he has given millions of people an insight into how their lives, and the lives of others, are influenced and often distorted by unaccountable forces. He has encouraged us to look at political life from the ground up, not from the vantage point of power, where elites, such as the corporate media, have their stands. He is, as Edward Said wrote, "an agent of people." That is why this new edition of *Towards a New Cold War* is so welcome; its truths, its revelations of the "obvious," have the same force today as when the collection was first published.

In this introduction, however, I would like to seize an opportunity and offer some personal thoughts on the author, and describe something of my last encounter with him. I owe him much, as my own work as a reporter and filmmaker in many countries has also sought to breach walls of Orwellian "truth" that often conceal the machinations of power in our "free" societies and the source of suffering of those throughout the world who pay for our "freedom." For countless others, his disclosures and clarity exemplify Milan Kundera's aphorism that the "struggle of people [against power] is the struggle of memory against forgetting."[2]

Chomsky's work on the Vietnam war is an important case in point. He demonstrated that, far from being a "noble cause" whose execution was a "tragic mistake," as it was so often misrepresented (and still is), the war was a logical exercise in imperial power, and that the United States, in furthering its strategic interests in the region, had invaded a small peasant country, systematically devastating its environment and killing its people, communist and non-communist. That truth played a critical part in galvanizing the movement that opposed the war and in raising people's awareness about "other Vietnams." Without a similar body of opposition in the United States, Ronald Reagan might well have invaded Nicaragua with American troops. The same is true of the recent attack on Iraq; without massive worldwide opposition, of which Chomsky's work was a wellspring, the United States might well have gone further and used weapons of mass destruction, even "limited" nuclear weapons.

What Chomsky has made vivid is the truth that western political leaders, respectable people whose "moderation" contains not a hint of totalitarianism, can, at great remove in physical and cultural distance, kill and maim people on a scale comparable with the accredited monsters of our time. Thus, John Kennedy terror-bombed Vietnam; and Gerald Ford and Jimmy Carter backed genocide in East Timor; and George Bush conducted a slaughter in Iraq in 1991, called the Gulf war, and his son finished the job in 2003, both of them calling their crimes a "moral crusade."

Of course, in identifying such truths, Chomsky has got himself into a great deal of trouble. One of the roots of the hostility towards him is that he strikes at the heart of America's libertarian self-image, distinguishing between liberals and conservatives only to illuminate their common ground. His first two political works, "The Responsibility of Intellectuals" (1967) and *American Power and the New Mandarins* (1969), were frontal assaults on American intellectuals and journalists whose liberalism, he maintained, served to mask their role as "ideological managers" of a lawless, imperial system whose lethal consequences were reported at home as acts of benevolence or as "mistakes" for which media redemption was guaranteed.

Like the dissident writers of the former Soviet empire, he returns in most of his work to a fundamental theme of morality: that Americans, and by implication those of us living within the American orbit, are subject to "an ideological system dedicated to the service of power" which has no notion of conscience, and requires "apathy and obedience [so as] to bar any serious challenge to elite rule."[3] Alternative views are marginalised by a "device of historical amnesia and tunnel vision cultivated in intellectual circles."[4] He refers to American academics and journalists as a "secular priesthood" to whom America's "manifest destiny," its "right" to attack and coerce small nations, is seemingly God-given.[5]

He unnerves and shames and often enrages these liberals; for he not only identifies liberalism as an *ideology*, so often reactionary and violent, he demonstrates the very intellectual independence claimed by his liberal critics. On Zionism—still one of the great American taboos—he wrote in *The Culture of Terrorism* that the relationship of American liberal intellectuals with the Israeli state compared with their predecessors' flirtation with Stalinist Russia in the 1930s. They are fellow-travellers, he wrote, with "protective attitudes towards the Holy State and the effort to downplay in its repression and violence, to provide apologetics for it. . . ."[6]

A fine example of this was a recent veiled diatribe in the *New Yorker* (March 31, 2003) by Larissa MacFarquhar. Chomsky's thinking, she wrote, "has grown simplistic and rigid . . . he is stuck in the past. . . ." How dare he compare the motives for America's invasion of Vietnam, with America's subsequent rapacious actions! How dare he trace a clear historical pattern; how dare he suggest that the deaths of large numbers of human beings caused by American policies and missiles elsewhere in the world—in Africa, for God's sake—bear comparison with "our" deaths on September 11. The former were, of course, "mistakes." Applying the pseudo-psychotherapy with which some liberal commentators like to cover their own reactionary motives, the writer berated Chomsky for "always refus[ing] to talk about motives in politics." That must be a different Chomsky from the one I have read and heard over the years. What upset her, I suspect, was his refusal to jettison or even trim his principles and to have the same "change of heart" enjoyed by one of his warmongering critics she quotes. He is therefore "isolated." Indeed, "For those who doubt the consensus of the nineties and the war on terrorism, Chomsky is almost the only voice there is." No, there are many other voices; but a liberal writer who describes a "consensus" on "the war on terrorism" without using inverted commas, will never hear them, let alone acknowledge them; one famous heretic is more than enough.

What has infuriated Chomsky's enemies is that he is almost impossible to pigeon-hole. Although he describes himself as a libertarian socialist, he supports no ideology. He is not a Marxist; while admiring Marx as a philosopher, he sees no point in beatifying him. Indeed, his political stands seem oddly untheoretical for one who has made his name as a theorist, in linguistics. He believes revolutions bring violence and suffering and he argues that "one who pays some attention to history will not be surprised if those who cry most loudly that we must smash and destroy are later found among the administrators of some new system of repression." If he has a faith it is in "the commonsense of the ordinary people . . . ever since I had any political awareness I was always on the side of the loser." [7] The essayist Brian Morton wrote that "many Americans are no longer convinced that our government has the right to destroy any country it wants—and Chomsky deserves much of the credit." [8] Although written prior to September 11, 2001, those words remain as true today: as Americans begin to stir from perhaps the most virulent period of brainwashing in their history and fear, not only terrorism, but the designs of their own government.

He is an internationalist of the Bertrand Russell kind. He was against the manipulations of both sides in the old Cold War, believing that the superpowers were actually united in suppressing the aspirations of small nations. It is characteristic of him that, while many chose to celebrate the end of the Cold War, he was cautious. He describes as an American nightmare "the dominance of the Eurasian land mass by one unified power"— Europe; and that what we are seeing today "is a gradual restoration of the trade and colonial relationship of Western Europe with the East." He believes "the big growing conflict is between Europe and the United States. It's been true for years . . . They [the US establishment] really want to stick it to the Europeans." [9]

I corresponded with Noam Chomsky for years before I met him. In 1989, I went to hear him speak in a packed suburban town hall in London and, to my surprise, found not an accomplished orator but a gentle, self-effacing man with an endearing dash of anarchy about him. He could barely be heard past the third row and was much concerned with responding to the convoluted interruptions of a heckler. His commitment to the principle of free expression, "the voice of all the people being heard," has often gotten him into difficulty. The man haranguing him, and whose right to be heard Chomsky defended, had neo-fascist views. At that awkward moment, Chomsky struck me as a morally courageous person.

Certainly, his gentleness belies the analytical hell-raiser, reminding us of Norman Mailer's description of him in *The Armies of the Night* (they shared a prison cell in 1967 following the march on the Pentagon), as "a slim, sharp-featured man with an ascetic expression, and an air of gentle but absolute moral integrity." [10] He is also very funny; his use of farce and irony, often miscast as sarcasm, allows him to turn officialspeak on its head.

I asked him about this, specifically the power of common political shorthand like "moderates" and "extremists." He said, "In educated circles, they're taken very seriously. No journalist, no intellectual, no writer can simply express the truth about the Vietnam war that the United States *attacked* Vietnam. That isn't being moderate. . . . In the 1930s, the American government described Hitler as a moderate, standing between the extremists of the left and right; there we had to support him. Mussolini was a moderate. In the mid-1980s, Saddam Hussein was a moderate, contributing 'stability' to the region. General Suharto of Indonesia is described regularly as a moderate. From 1965, when he came to power, slaughtering maybe 700,000 people, the *New York Times* and other journals described him as the leader of the Indonesian moderates." [11]

In 2003, on the eve of the American attack on Iraq, I asked him about the parallels that are increasingly drawn between the unelected Bush cabal and historical neo-fascism (defined by Benito Mussolini as the "merger between the state and corporatism"). He replied that one striking difference with the rise of German fascism in the 1930s was that, unlike the United States in the era of George W. Bush, there was plenty of discontent and opposition among intellectuals. [12]

"You are sometimes described as an extremist," I said. "Sure, I *am* an extremist," he replied, "because a moderate is anyone who supports Western power and an extremist is anyone who objects to it. Take for example, George Kennan [the American Cold War strategist]. He was one of the leading architects of the modern world and is at the soft or dovish end of the U.S. planning spectrum. When he was head of the policy planning staff, he quite explicitly said—in internal documents, not publicly of course—that we must put aside vague and idealistic slogans about human rights, democratisation and the raising of living standards and deal in straight power concepts if we want to maintain the disparity between our enormous wealth and the poverty of everyone else. But it's rare that someone is that honest." [13]

I said, "You've had some spectacular rows. The historian Arthur Schlesinger accused you of 'betraying the intellectual tradition.' " His reply was quintessential Chomsky. "That's true; I agree with him," he said. "The intellectual tradition is one of servility to power, and if I didn't betray it, I'd be ashamed of myself."

Chomsky's attacks are mainly aimed at the United States and he often refers to the "dark side of America." Although he rejects the myth of a Chosen People that has bewitched so many Americans, he acknowledges that America is (or was, until George W. Bush's Patriot Act) one of the freest society in history. Wasn't there a fundamental contradiction there? "No," he replied. "[Freedom in America] was not a gift; it's not because it was written in the Constitution. Up to the 1920s, the United States was very repressive, probably more so than England. The great breakthrough was in 1964 when the law of seditious libel was eliminated. This, in effect, made it a crime to condemn authority. It was finally declared unconstitutional in the course of the civil rights struggle. Only popular struggle protects freedom. . . .

"Britain was one of the freest countries in the world in the nineteenth century and had a horrendous record of atrocities. There's simply no correlation between internal freedom and external violence. In fact, things are even more complex in the United States, which probably has the most sophisticated system of doctrinaire management in the world. You see, the basic idea which runs right through modern history and modern liberalism is that the public has got to be marginalised. [They] are viewed as no more than ignorant and meddlesome outsiders, a bewildered herd. And it's the responsible men who have to make decisions and to protect society from the trampling and rage of the bewildered herd. Now, since it's a democracy, they—the herd, that is—are permitted occasionally to lend weight to one or another member of the responsible class. That's called an election."

We talked about the incident in London when he defended the right of a neo-fascist to heckle him. I asked him, "Does that right extend to everybody?" "Yes," he replied, "if we don't believe in free expression for people we despise, we don't believe in it all."

Noam Chomsky doubtless pays a personal price for his dissidence, which I believe is heroic. "It makes me infuriated," he said. "I get angry. I'm a pretty mild guy. I don't throw plates around, but internally I am seething all the time. . . . A lot of my friends have burned out and I can understand that. It's very wearing and it's very frustrating."

Now in his seventies, he shows no sign of this "wearing"; and I salute him.

London
May 2003

INTRODUCTION

THE ESSAYS THAT FOLLOW are concerned primarily with the evolution of American foreign policy and ideology since the early 1970s. By that time, it was becoming clear that "the U.S. has suffered a severe erosion of hegemony . . . , the constellation of political, economic, and military strength that allows a great power to work its will on the rest of the world." It was equally apparent that "there is no easy way out of the dilemma imposed on U.S. policymakers by the loss of U.S. hegemony." [1] The preceding period has been aptly described by Samuel Huntington as one in which "the U.S. was the hegemonic power in a system of world order." [2] This period was bound to be transitory, as the rest of the industrial world recovered from the devastation of World War II and a measure of independence was achieved in the so-called Third World, and as the era of unconstrained consumption of natural resources began to draw to a close, giving rise to new forms of interdependence and conflict. The decline of American hegemony was hastened, and in some ways symbolized, by the failure of the United States to crush the resistance to its domination in Indochina. This enormously costly venture weakened the United States somewhat relative to its industrial rivals-allies, and constrained its ability "to work its will on the rest of the world."

The decline of U.S. hegemony is generally described in terms of the superpower conflict. When relations to other powers are considered, it is within this standard framework. Thus we read in the business press that "the U.S. is facing the threat of a slow disintegration of the alliance network erected after World War II to block Soviet expansion." West German Chancellor Helmut Schmidt "can go his own way [towards détente], because Carter is incapable of imposing U.S. policies on Bonn," and France can "take up its historic role as Russia's best friend in Western Europe." "Still more frightening for Washington policymakers, however, is the theme—voiced with increasing frequency by 'progressives' on both sides of the Atlantic—that 'détente is divisible,' " so that "if Washington insists on confrontation with the Soviet Union, in this view, Europeans and the Japanese might follow their own separate strategies." Meanwhile, "Central America and the Caribbean are in turmoil, and Communist ability to harass the U.S. is increasing apace." The Russians can "appeal to old European habits and games . . . to erode joint Western resolve," perhaps causing "the end of the Western alliance—and the 'Finlandization' of Western Europe."[3]

An elite Working Group of the Atlantic Council offers a similar diagnosis. The primary threat to world order is that "the Soviet Union has extended its reach to one of truly global proportions," a fact underlined by the Soviet invasion of Afghanistan. The most likely Soviet threat, however, "is going to be in the political arena"; "the prime mission of the Soviet armed forces, Soviet writers say, is to protect the system should a declining capitalist world be impelled to use force, and not to put the system at risk by moving against a strong adversary." Soviet strategy is "to foster the relaxation of tensions, not only with Western Europe, but originally with the United States as well" and to change the military balance by building up its own forces while "seeking to weaken the NATO military position through arms control talks and by exhorting and threatening the European allies over the risks connected with nuclear modernization," while at the same time, the Soviet Union is "following a policy of aggressive political and even military intervention in the Third World." With regard to the NATO alliance, "the highest priority Soviet policy goal . . . is the splitting of Europe and the United States." Many Europeans welcome détente "as both an inevitable step toward peaceful life on the European continent and a crucial counterpart to collective defense." The Europeans have "a tangible stake in maintaining the *status quo* and in decoupling their relations with the Russians from tensions and crises outside the NATO area," where "the projection of Soviet influence as well as indigenous threats to Western access to vital resources in the Third World—through arms aid, Cuban and East German surrogates, and Soviet forces—has greatly increased." The United States, however, "is inclined to view détente as indivisible, and to deplore a differential East-West posture that protects allied fruits of conciliation at the expense of conceding the Soviets a free hand outside the NATO area."[4] Correspondingly, U.S. policy is to evade arms control talks while making some gestures to pacify European opinion, and to maintain a high level of international tension by such moves as offering "lethal weapons" to China and others, to which I will return.[5]

Similar concerns are voiced in some circles on the other side of the Atlantic, for example, by the London *Economist*, which warns that "the relationship between western Europe and north America, alias the Atlantic alliance, is in the early stages of what could be a terminal illness," largely because of European unwillingness to take "a suitably larger share of the burden of the west's defences off the shoulders of the relatively declining American economy. . . ."[6]

Such analyses certainly do identify crucial elements of contemporary international affairs. Europe and Japan are increasingly tending to go their own way in economic policy and diplomatic initiatives, realizing long-standing fears and concerns of American planners. One aspect of this somewhat increased independence is the effort to lessen tensions and extend economic relations with the Soviet bloc; the Atlantic Council report observes that "Communist trade with European NATO countries is now about two-thirds of the current level of trade between the United States and its European partners." And independent European initiatives towards the Third World are also sure to proliferate. The same is true of Japan and, in fact, of newly industrializing states such as South Korea. Furthermore, while it is misleading to speak of a "threat to Western access to vital resources in the Third World," it is true that access on terms the West might prefer is threatened, more by "indigenous threats" than by Soviet power.

But the general framework of analysis in terms of superpower rivalry is deceptive. Loss of hegemony and relative economic decline are problems affecting the Soviet Union as well as the United States. The phrase "Communist ability to harass the U.S." conceals something quite different: the decline in the U.S. ability to impose its will. More generally, what has been declining is the Cold War system that proved so useful for both superpowers as a device for controlling their allies and mobilizing domestic support for the ugly and often costly measures required to impose the desired form of order and stability on their respective domains. And what is "increasing apace" is the ability of other states and combinations of states to exercise a degree of initiative in world affairs. These developments pose problems for U.S. state managers as well as for the transnational corporations that are closely linked to U.S. state power and that rely on it to maintain a world system in which they can expand and prosper. The military-bureaucratic elite that rules the USSR faces similar difficulties in its own narrower domain of influence and control.

That the Soviet government is a major threat to anyone within the reach of its power—including its own citizens—is hardly debatable. But this reach is far more restricted than Western ideologists have alleged over the years. The historical record, I think, is quite plain: The Soviet threat has been manipulated, over and over again, to justify the exercise of U.S. force against threats to U.S. dominance that are indigenous, though such indigenous forces may turn to the USSR for support when under U.S. attack. And the same remains true today. Once again, the behavior of the superpower enemy is symmetrical, in this regard.

When the Atlantic Council Working Group argues that "deterrence . . . has perforce become a world-wide responsibility in response to world-wide threats," based ultimately on Soviet power, some decoding is in order. The veil lifts when the group adds that "the Western hemisphere encompasses considerable poverty and discontent as problems of economic development and social justice confront most governments." In fact, what must be "deterred" in the Western hemisphere is not "Soviet-inspired Cuban activity," as the Working Group contends. Rather, "deterrence" is directed against indigenous attempts to overcome the poverty and discontent—for which the term "considerable" is something of an understatement—that have been the systematic consequence of U.S. intervention in the region and to attain a measure of social justice that is intolerable to the governments that the United States backs or has imposed in its own interests, or more accurately, in the interests of those who stand to gain from exploitation, oppression, and suffering.

Various measures have been undertaken by U.S. policymakers to arrest or reverse the decline of American hegemony: Nixonian neomercantilism and reliance on surrogate states to enforce order, "playing the China card," trilateralism, and currently, heightening of international tensions so that the allies will be compelled to shelter under the umbrella of American force— the one dimension along which the United States still retains the overwhelming dominance of earlier years. These measures have had at best limited success. One further task that had to be undertaken in the "post-Vietnam era" was to return the domestic population to a proper state of apathy and obedience, to overcome "the crisis of democracy" and the "Vietnam syndrome." These are the technical terms that have been devised to refer, respectively, to the efforts of formerly passive groups to engage in the political process, and to the general unwillingness of the population to bear the material costs and the moral burden of aggression and massacre. It has been the responsibility of the system of ideological control and propaganda to accomplish this dual task, and there is no doubt that, in part at least, the goals have been achieved. Throughout this period, it has been clear enough that when the time appeared to be ripe, there would be moves to reconstruct the capacity to intervene and subvert,[7] and with it, the Cold

War system along with its domestic counterpart, militarization of the economy. Such steps were being taken in the latter part of the Carter Administration (see Chapter 7), and constitute the central thrust of the Reagan program.

These topics are addressed from several points of view in the following essays. Throughout, two themes interweave: the evolution of policy, and the ways it is depicted by the media and scholarship over a fairly broad mainstream of articulate opinion. In studying any other society, past or present, we have little difficulty in considering—and generally establishing—the reasonable thesis that foreign policy reflects the distribution of domestic power, responding to the demands of those who are in a position to make the essential decisions as to how the society functions. Similarly, we expect to find—and do find—that those who accommodate to the needs of domestic power and serve its interests will tend to dominate the system of communication, education, and indoctrination. We find it particularly easy to adopt this quite rational stance in the case of official enemies. Discussing the Soviet Union, no reasonable person hesitates to entertain the possibility that its foreign policy is designed to enhance the power and privilege of the ruling military-bureaucratic elite, that the system of propaganda is committed to denying and concealing this fact, and that the pattern of repression and coercion that results from Soviet intervention reflects the perceived needs of this ruling group. Indeed, this is generally taken to be obvious truth, as it is, to a very good first approximation.

It is more difficult, and far more important, to adopt the same rational stance with regard to one's own society or its close allies or dependencies. In modern state capitalist societies such as our own, domestic decision-making is dominated by the private business sector in the political as well as the strictly economic arena. Its representatives largely staff the state executive, and more significantly, it sets limits on what the state can do. Actions that "erode business confidence" would lead to capital flight, investment cutbacks, and in general an intolerable deterioration of the social and economic climate, facts that state managers committed to significant reform could hardly disregard, in the unlikely event that they should attain political power. Furthermore, those who have a dominant position in the domestic economy command substantial means to influence public opinion. It would be surprising indeed if this power were not reflected in the mass media—themselves major corporations—and the schools and universities; if it did not, in short, shape the prevailing ideology to a considerable extent.

What we should expect to find is (1) that foreign policy is guided by the primary commitment to improving the climate for business operations in a global system that is open to exploitation of human and material resources by those who dominate the domestic economy, and (2) that this commitment is portrayed as guided by the highest ideals and by deep concern for human welfare. And this is indeed what we do find, again to a very good first approximation, though with a finer-grained analysis one finds conflicts between state managers and private corporate power, internal conflict within business circles, and an impact of ethnic and other pressure groups; and some critical discussion and analysis, along with intermittent accurate reporting. Some examples of such second-order phenomena will be discussed below, but I will concentrate on the major factors.

Improvement of the climate for business operations in under-developed societies is generally facilitated by destruction of unions and other popular organizations, undermining of programs devoted to domestic welfare (e.g., agricultural programs directed to local consumption rather than export crops), and considerable brutality if there is resistance to such measures. Investigating regions of the Third World that have been subjected to U.S. influence and control, we find a pattern of just this sort, and we find that it has regularly been enhanced by U.S. intervention.[8] We also should expect to discover, and do discover, that the general public is rarely exposed to the impact of the United States on the Third World, and that in the occasional discussion of sporadic examples (e.g., state terror in Guatemala), the U.S. role is generally suppressed. The suffering, starvation, murderous repression, and exploitation throughout the domains of U.S. influence and intervention are rarely perceived to be related to systematic U.S. policy initiatives guided by the interests of those with effective domestic power, in striking contrast to our interpretation of the systems dominated by official enemies.

It is currently fashionable to distinguish between "authoritarian" and "totalitarian" regimes. We oppose the latter, and there is debate over the stance we should adopt towards the former. Investigating particular cases, we can easily identify the feature that in practice distinguishes the two categories: A regime is "totalitarian," hence the essence of evil, if it restricts "economic freedom," a term that does not refer to the freedom of workers or communities to control production but rather to the freedom for private business—crucially, U.S.-based transnational corporations—to conduct its affairs without constraint. If it does not restrict the freedom to invest and exploit, a state is at worst "authoritarian." The distinction has little relation to the concern of the regime for the welfare of the population. The terror-and-torture states of Latin America, for example, are merely "authoritarian." We may deplore their practices (always ignoring our own role in laying the basis for them and enhancing them), but we do not subject them to embargoes, harassment, terrorism, subversion, or outright invasion. These measures are restricted to "totalitarian regimes"—though, in this case, we may attempt at times to wean them from their evil ways.[9] See note 67.

Jacobo Timerman asks why Argentina is regarded as "authoritarian"—hence basically a friend—while Poland is "totalitarian." "Do you imagine . . . in Argentina, a movement like Solidarity? Impossible. They would kill everybody, Lech Walesa, everybody."[10] The answer to his question was given by David Rockefeller, who explained to a group of bankers in New York in 1977, at the height of the savage atrocities of this Nazi-like regime, that "I have the impression that finally Argentina has a regime which understands the private enterprise system."[11] The Polish regime and its Soviet big brother do not share this understanding, however they may welcome Western trade, loans, and technology.

One may ask similar questions about the practices undertaken during the period when human rights was supposedly "the Soul of our foreign policy" (President Carter's phrase). During these years, Congress designated seven countries as such extreme human rights violators that they could not be recipients of U.S. aid: Vietnam, Laos, Cambodia, Cuba, Mozambique, Angola—and Uganda. No list would have been complete without Idi Amin, of course, though it is well to recall the U.S. contribution to keeping him in power to the end.[12] As for the other six, it does not seem overly difficult to identify the feature that distinguishes them from more acceptable regimes: They had recently engaged in the criminal behavior of extricating themselves from the "Free World." Apart from that distinguishing property, it is difficult to see on what basis Mozambique, for example, is more criminal than a long series of terror states supported by the United States.

Sanctions imposed on human rights violators in the domain of American influence during the "Human Rights era" barely changed the familiar pattern.[13] Consider, for example, the case of Chile. A recent review of Carter's sanctions after the decision by the Reagan Administration to lift them concludes that "there is little evidence that the sanctions ever had much bite anyway." The most serious sanction was the ban on Export-Import Bank financing for U.S. companies doing business with or in Chile, announced by the Carter Administration in November 1979 in reprisal for Chile's refusal to extradite three intelligence officers wanted by U.S. courts for their role in the assassination of Orlando Letelier and Ronni Moffit in Washington in 1976 (assassination in the U.S. capital is considered to be going too far). "Two weeks after Carter had made his announcement, the U.S. embassy in Santiago published its annual report on the Chilean economy, which specifically sought to encourage US investment." During the period of the cutoff of Ex-Im Bank finance, U.S. exports substantially increased (by about two-thirds), "the kind of improvement the US embassy's report had defined as a 'medium-run target.' " At the same time, U.S. banks lent Chilean institutions more than $1 billion, and major corporations undertook large-scale investment programs.[14] This is very much the normal pattern in the case of a state that "understands the private enterprise system."

The same basic principles explain the anti-Communism and selective anti-fascism and anti-imperialism of U.S. foreign policy. The so-called Communist regimes are invariably enemies—unless, of course, they can function as enemies of an even greater Communist enemy while being in part accommodated into the Western system—not because they are founded on coercion and terrorize their populations, but because they separate themselves from the U.S.-dominated world system and attempt to use their resources for their own development. The United States was opposed to Japanese fascism largely on the grounds that it was closing off U.S. access to China, and was willing to enter into an accommodation with Japan if this policy were changed.[15] The United States was strongly committed to dismantling the British imperial preference system, but, as the British Colonial Office correctly perceived, "The Americans are quite ready to make their dependencies politically 'independent' while economically bound to them and see no inconsistency in this." [16] The United States also opposed national capitalism in Europe after World War II on similar grounds, attempting and succeeding to integrate Western Europe within a U.S.-dominated global system,[17] though frictions always remained and are now becoming more significant with the decline of American hegemony. These are central themes of U.S. foreign policy to which I will return below in various contexts (particularly Chapters 2 and 7). They will remain so in the changing circumstances of the coming years.

Since much of the discussion below will be devoted to the ways in which the articulate intelligentsia deal with these topics, it may be appropriate to ask what we have a right to expect in a free society. What standards of evaluation does it make sense to impose? Obviously we demand a commitment to discover the truth, and beyond that, concentration on what is important: in short, that those who comment on contemporary affairs attempt to determine and tell the truth about matters of importance.

What is important? Reasonable people may differ about some cases, but others are clear, and suggest some useful guidelines. Consider, for example, two studies of human rights violations in the United States, one, a pamphlet put out in East Germany, the other, a petition submitted to the United Nations by church and civil rights groups in the United States.[18] Assuming the reports in each to be true, we know at once which document is important. We are little impressed by the DDR pamphlet, just as we are not impressed when the World Peace Council analyzes and condemns U.S. or U.S.-backed atrocities throughout much of the world. What they say may be true, but it is not important for their domestic and international audience; what is important for this audience is a discussion of the treatment of dissidents in the Soviet zone or Soviet terror bombing in Afghanistan. Their protests about human rights violations in or by the United States, apart from the evident hypocrisy, have a mixed effect. In part, the effects may be beneficial. International protest apparently played some part in mitigating the treatment of the Wilmington Ten, for example. Surely there was little protest or even awareness here, though attempts were made to elicit some comments from President Carter on this gross miscarriage of justice—in vain.[19] But the effects of even valid criticism of U.S. human rights practices from such sources may be harmful as well: namely, in buttressing domestic propaganda systems and thus laying the basis for oppression and atrocities—a comment which, though obvious and valid, will be ridiculed by conformist intellectuals of the state to which it is addressed.

The conclusion from such examples is evident. One index of importance is how information leads to action. What are its likely consequences for victims of oppression? The proper focus of concern for us lies in areas where we have a responsibility for what is happening and the opportunity to mitigate or terminate suffering and violence. This is particularly true in a democratic society, where policies can be influenced, often significantly so, by public opinion and action. Analysis and condemnation of the practices of official enemies is legitimate, provided that it is honest, and is sometimes worth undertaking, but it is often of little or no importance, by this reasonable standard.[20]

To ask serious questions about the nature and behavior of one's own society is often difficult and unpleasant: difficult because the answers are generally concealed, and unpleasant because the answers are often not only ugly—in foreign affairs, roughly in proportion to the power of the state—but also painful. To understand the truth about these matters is to be led to actions that may not be easy to undertake and that may even carry a significant personal cost. In contrast, the easy way is to succumb to the demands of the powerful, to avoid searching questions, and to accept the doctrine that is hammered home incessantly by the propaganda system. This is, no doubt, the main reason for the easy victory of dominant ideologies, for the general tendency to remain silent or to keep fairly close to official doctrine with regard to the behavior of one's own state and its allies and dependencies, while lining up to condemn the real or alleged crimes of its enemies. That this should be the pattern in states founded on violence and terror is not surprising; the costs of independence of mind are severe in the USSR, where the result may be imprisonment with brutal treatment, or in Guatemala, where it is likely to be "disappearance."[21] That the same pattern should be found in a society such as ours, where the personal costs are negligible in comparison,[22] is much more significant. The factors that lead to this consequence are more subtle, but they are very effective, as will be illustrated in the chapters that follow.

In some cases, the achievements of self-censorship are quite spectacular. Consider, for example, the following case. When the USSR invaded Afghanistan in December 1979, no one in the United States had the slightest difficulty in labeling the invasion as what it was: a Soviet invasion of Afghanistan. One can think of all sorts of complicating factors,[23] but the basic fact is clear, undeniable, subject to no dispute, and admitting no justification. Commenting on this matter, the London *Economist* observed that though one may conjure up complexities, "yet an invader is an invader unless invited in by a government with some claim to legitimacy."[24] Forthright and accurate.

Consider now a second case. In 1962, the United States invaded South Vietnam after years of failure in suppressing the former anti-French resistance through the medium of a murderous client government. In that year, U.S. warplanes began the large-scale bombardment of the South Vietnamese countryside, initiating a series of efforts to drive the rural population and mountain tribes into concentration camps ("strategic hamlets") where they could be "protected" from the South Vietnamese insurgents, who had returned to the guerrilla struggle in 1959 after the U.S.-organized violence of the late 1950s had virtually decimated the former Viet Minh.

Hundreds of thousands of montagnards and peasants were driven from their villages in these attacks,[25] which mounted in intensity in the following years, leading to the full-scale invasion and massive systematic bombardment of South Vietnam in 1965.[26] The U.S.-backed government had no claim to legitimacy; the Pentagon Papers analysts describe it accurately as "essentially the creation of the United States."[27] The contempt of the United States for its client was exhibited in the Diem coup of 1963 and the subsequent replacement of one government after another when they refused to follow U.S. orders, in the memoirs of U.S. Ambassador General Maxwell Taylor, and in many other U.S. government actions and statements.[28]

We may now apply the valid principle formulated by the *Economist:* "An invader is an invader unless invited in by a government with some claim to legitimacy." Yet almost twenty years after the U.S. military assault on the rural society of South Vietnam began, sixteen years after the full-scale invasion that followed with its well-known horrors, it is still impossible for mainstream U.S. scholarship or media to pronounce the dread words: "U.S. aggression in South Vietnam," "the U.S. invasion of South Vietnam." Perhaps one will be able to say the same about the USSR with reference to Afghanistan in 1998. A comparable record of submissiveness to the state religion would be regarded with considerable satisfaction by any dictator. In the United States, and much of the West, the success of the propaganda system, which is indeed spectacular, is particularly notable in that it has been achieved virtually without the use of force or coercion. Those who abide by the system—virtually everyone who writes about the subject in the mainstream press and scholarship—cannot claim, as can their counterparts in the Soviet Union, that they submit out of legitimate fear.

Suppose it were argued that there is some merit in the claim that the United States was not attacking rural South Vietnam (i.e., some 80 percent of the population in 1962) but was defending it from "aggression from the North," or "Chinese expansionism," or "the Russian drive for global domination" (or Martians). These claims are of the same order of validity as the Russian party line on Afghanistan, which also appears to be widely believed at home, judging by the reports of journalists and foreign visitors: that the USSR, responding to the call of the legitimate government, is defending the progressive regime from terrorists sponsored from abroad. Furthermore, even if one were to concede more merit to the claim than I do, this would not be relevant to the crucial point: the remarkable uniformity of the mainstream intelligentsia. Those who doubt this judgment might sample the voluminous record to determine how frequently the U.S. invasion of South Vietnam has been described as such.

I will return to the devices that are used to obscure the plain facts (see particularly Chapters 3 to 6). The refusal to recognize them is not restricted to American commentators. A senior editor of the respected West German journal *Die Zeit* refers to the "sobering" American experience in "the hapless, costly and society-rending intervention in Southeast Asia" (the reference is to the "rending" of American society, not of the societies of Indochina). In the same article, he describes the Soviet invasion of Afghanistan simply as "the Soviet invasion of Afghanistan." [29] In the case of Afghanistan, we sympathize with the victims; in the case of Indochina, with the aggressors. A British military historian writes: "However great the provocation, the transgression of internal law was blatant and had to be punished if it was not to be repeated"—referring to the Soviet invasion of Afghanistan. In the same issue of *Foreign Affairs*, two U.S. public opinion specialists inform us that while "many Americans came to feel that the force we applied in Vietnam was inconsistent with our claim to be a good people," nevertheless, "this matter remains controversial." No stern judgments here about punishing transgressions of international law.[30] Examples abound. In fact, the pattern is virtually exceptionless.[31]

Once it is understood that the category of "American aggression" cannot exist as a matter of doctrinal faith, no matter what the facts may be, one can begin to comprehend such strange phenomena as the debate over amnesty for those who recognized the truth and refused to take part in criminal aggression in Indochina (see Chapter 1). Thus Father Theodore Hesburgh, president of Notre Dame University, relates that as a member of President Ford's Amnesty Board, he was in favor of pardoning "Vietnam offenders." When asked to defend this extremist position, he explained that as a priest he is in the "pardoning business." [32] This is considered a deeply humane and thoughtful response in the United States. With a little mental effort, one can even comprehend the comment by CBS newsman Dan Rather, explaining why the United States is reluctant to aid Afghan rebels: "We tried to help in a situation like this in Vietnam, and we got our hands burned." [33] In the minds of the most helpless victims of official propaganda—on occasion, its purveyors, as in this case—the U.S. bombing of villages and defoliation missions in South Vietnam in 1962 and the huge massacre of the subsequent years are analogous to aiding Afghan guerrillas to defend themselves

against Soviet aggression. Since "we got our hands burned" trying to help
Vietnam, it is unreasonable to expect us to extend the same benevolent
assistance today.

One does read denunciations of the United Nations for failing to "protect
Afghanistan or Vietnam," one of its many sins (another being that it is "an
anti-Semitic organization")—but the reference is not to the inability of the
U.N. to protect Vietnam from American aggression; rather, to its failure to
protect Vietnam after 1975, when "genocide is being perpetrated" as the
leadership "is treading specifically in Hitler's footsteps, even adopting some
of his devices."[34] The U.N. was never charged with failure to protect Vietnam from American aggression, or even to denounce this aggression. In fact,
the concept "American aggression" is unthinkable, perhaps an oxymoron.
One may speak of "the Vietnam war (which we entered out of fear of Chinese expansionism)"[35] or describe our intervention as an unfortunate or
tragic error, but the well-documented facts have been effectively expunged
from official history.

To assess the performance of the free press in this regard, it is sometimes
useful to ask how we would react to similar pronouncements in the propaganda organs of our totalitarian enemies. Suppose, for example, that we
were to read the following complaint in some Communist party organ:

> For a segment of Western Europe's right, Afghanistan is a windfall. Ex-
> otic, blessedly far from home and potentially confirming a post-
> Czechoslovakia generation's notions of the misuse of Soviet power, the
> controversy over the war is packed with possibilities for simplistic por-
> trayal. It offers Europeans the luxuries of distance and vagueness. Also, it
> drowns out discomfort about Vietnam, distracts attention from El Sal-
> vador, and tends to confirm fond suspicions that superpowers behave
> alike.

Sickening, no doubt, but what can one expect from a controlled party press.
In fact, the passage is virtually a transposition of a passage on El Salvador in
the *New York Times*, with the obvious changes of names.[36] At about the
same time, we read in a *New York Times* editorial that the death squads in
El Salvador "have contributed as much as leftists to the murder of 10,000
people in the last year," as "the Reagan team, like the Carter Administration, seems to be trying to shore up a frail 'center'"; and in the news
columns, that "support for the Salvadoran Government in this country has

been weakened, however, by its seeming inability to crack down on right-wing groups that have carried out political assassinations."[37] Faithful to official truth, our newspaper of record could hardly be expected to be overly concerned with the fact that church groups in El Salvador attribute the overwhelming bulk of the massacres to the government itself and that the evidence is strong that the government cannot crack down on the assassins because it would be cracking down on its own army and police forces.[38]

"When a reputable newspaper lies, it poisons the community," a *New York Times* editorial proclaims grandly, condemning a *Washington Post* reporter for concocting an interview with a drug addict.[39] The most poisonous form of lying is distortion or suppression of the truth in the service of the state, particularly in concealing the role of the state in ongoing violence, massacre, and oppression. I think the evidence is overwhelming that this is a standard feature of the free press. Many examples will be discussed below; a great many more are presented elsewhere.[40]

This behavior is systematic, not sporadic. The critique extends as well to the examples that are offered as the "strongest case" by those who denounce the press for its "anti-government bias" (or praise it for its crusading zeal)—for example, Watergate and the allegedly critical attitude of the national press towards the Vietnam war—as will be discussed below.[41] If so, the thesis is established in its strongest form. But even short of such a demonstration, the abundant evidence that has been presented serves to construct a case that should be of much concern to people concerned with the state of American freedom.

The general subservience of the media to the state propaganda system does not result from direct government order, threats or coercion, centralized decisions, and other devices characteristic of totalitarian states, but from a complex interplay of more subtle factors.[42] A similar complex of inducements—access to privilege and prestige, class interest, penalties for straying beyond acceptable limits, and the like—produces a systematic bias in the scholarship that is concerned with foreign policy and its formation, serving to protect the basic system of social, economic, and political decision-making from scrutiny, a topic that goes beyond the scope of these essays, though illustrative examples will be discussed. It is by no means necessary to yield to these pressures, certainly in a society that lacks the forms of coercion and punishment found elsewhere. But the temptation to do so is considerable, and those who choose a different path often find that opportunities to do their work or reach more than a marginal audience are limited or excluded. To put it in the simplest terms, a talented young journalist or a student aiming for a scholarly career can choose to play the game by the rules, with the prospect of advancement to a position of prestige and privilege and sometimes even a degree of power; or to pursue an independent path, with the likelihood of a minor post as a police reporter or in a community college, exclusion from major journals, vilification and abuse,[43] or driving a taxi cab. Given such choices, the end result is not very surprising. Few options are open to isolated individuals in a basically depoliticized society lacking popular organizations that question the legitimacy of existing structures of domination and control, state or private.

Recall that I am speaking of significant prevailing tendencies. Exceptions do exist, sometimes important ones. Furthermore, the enormous mass of material that is produced in the media and books makes it possible for a really assiduous and committed researcher to gain a fair picture of the real world by cutting through the mass of misrepresentation and fraud to the nuggets hidden within.

All of these questions deserve careful examination. These essays fall far short of this goal, but they do attempt to add weight to the contention that the task is well worth undertaking.

To conclude these introductory remarks, I would like to outline briefly my own understanding of the evolution of policy that lies in the background of the specific cases discussed and issues addressed in the following chapters. I will consider five topics: (1) the range of policy options now under consideration among "foreign policy elites"; (2) the path that is being chosen by the Reagan Administration; (3) the reasons for this choice; (4) the historical background leading to it; and (5) the current scene and likely prospects, as I see them.

Three major turning points are generally recognized in U.S. foreign policy since World War II: adoption of the "containment policy" in the late 1940s, the turn towards détente in the early 1970s, and the current move towards a more "assertive" policy towards the Soviet Union today, allegedly in response to its violation of the spirit of détente and its global aggressiveness. This picture is partially accurate—one can, surely, identify these major shifts of policy—but it is quite misleading. It is conventional to describe U.S. foreign policy as defensive, a response to the aggressiveness of the superpower enemy (or earlier, China, when "Chinese expansionism" was a standard component of the propaganda system); Soviet analysts adopt a similar pose. As in the case of virtually any system of propaganda, there is an element of truth in this formulation, but it is largely pretense, in two major respects. First, U.S. policy can be regarded as "defensive" only if one regards much of the world as in effect an American possession, hence to be "defended" from indigenous elements or the intrusion of other powers that seek the kind of power and influence that the United States enjoys. Second, relations with the Soviet Union constitute only one element in the design and execution of policy, by no means always the major one. U.S. foreign policy is also concerned, and crucially so, with the industrial allies and rivals of the "First World"; with emerging powers and power blocs such as Brazil, OPEC, and ASEAN, as they gain a degree of independence; with the underdeveloped Third World countries that are the usual victims; and with another victim, the domestic population, which must be mobilized to support these policies. In the case of each of the turning points just noted, and others, one can identify the role of these factors. To a significant degree, the superpower enemy is invoked as the sole or dominant element in order to maintain the "defensive" image and to justify or conceal actions that are aimed in other directions, a major function of the Cold War system for both superpowers, as already noted.

As for topic (1), the range of foreign policy options now under consideration in elite circles is quite narrow (see Chapter 8). All are varieties of "containment," which, as in the 1940s, serves as a cover for global interventionism. The variants differ only in tactical assessments. By late 1978, the Carter Administration was moving towards a program of militarization of the economy, and the events of late 1979—the hostage crisis and the Russian invasion of Afghanistan—were exploited to help overcome the "Vietnam syndrome" and to lay the basis for a more aggressive and confrontationist stance (see Chapter 7), a fact that was noted with some dismay abroad. The *Manchester Guardian* expressed a fairly common European view when it downplayed the significance of the Soviet invasion in early 1980, proposing a "wiser approach" than American hysterics about a Russian march to the Gulf, a "European beginning" which is difficult to advance "whilst America remains so hyped on flamboyant militarism."[44] Reagan's program continues, and significantly accelerates, the tendencies that were manifest in the latter part of Carter's term.

The tendencies that were developing can be illustrated in the case of El Salvador, the first foreign policy crisis of the Reagan Administration. The United States backed the military coup of October 1979 that replaced the brutal Romero government[45] by a junta that contained some moderate and reformist military officers and civilians. By January, the junta had collapsed in the midst of rising state terrorism, and power shifted to the right-wing military. President Carter decided to send extensive military aid and three ten-man mobile training teams "aimed at averting indiscriminate repression and creating a 'clean' counterinsurgency force." [46] These decisions were made in defiance of the request from Archbishop Oscar Romero, who pleaded with President Carter to withhold military aid that would "without doubt intensify injustice and repression" because "the army command seems largely concerned with crushing leftist guerrilla and political groups. . . ." The Carter Administration's decision to provide military assistance "despite continuing repression of opposition groups here" is simple enough to explain: It "appears aimed at preventing at all costs 'another Nicaragua.'" [47]

In the case of Nicaragua, the Carter Administration had supported Somoza until virtually the end; in fact, Carter's message of support to Somoza in the midst of the massacre over which he was presiding may have been a factor precipitating the revolt,[48] much as Carter's adulatory comments about the Shah in Teheran apparently served as a stimulus to the revolution there by revealing the utter hypocrisy of the human rights rhetoric.[49] Only when it was evident that Somoza could not hold out against a virtually unified population, including even the business groups that are the natural allies of the United States, did Carter move to "mediate," too late to prevent a Sandinista victory. Furthermore, it is unlikely that the Israeli arms that were the major supplies for Somoza's murderous National Guard at the end were dispatched without U.S. approval; where it has chosen to do so, the United States has blocked the sale of Israeli arms in Latin America, and the relations of dependency between Israel and the United States are such that one can hardly doubt that this is always possible. The lesson of Nicaragua was that to maintain its control, the United States should have shifted earlier to supporting a less tyrannical and savage regime; hence the support for the October 1979 coup in El Salvador. The further lesson was that if this attempt fails, the United States should move quickly and forcefully to suppress popular resistance, the same lesson that American planners such as General Maxwell Taylor had drawn from the Vietnam experience by 1965.[50] This explains the decision to arm the right-wing military regime of El Salvador in early 1980, coupled with "reform measures" that have impressed the U.S. press, but few others; see below.

The Reagan Administration has pursued the same policy but with some new twists. While its predecessor treated El Salvador as a local problem of maintaining control of a client state, the Reagan Administration, while accelerating military assistance to the generals who were presiding over the massacre of the population, also sought to raise the El Salvador issue to the level of an international confrontation, presenting it as a Communist campaign orchestrated by the Soviet Union with the cooperation of Cuba, Ethiopia, and Vietnam to take over Central America. The transparent purpose of the propaganda campaign was to enflame war hysteria and to mobilize both the allies and the domestic population in "defense" against the Soviet drive to take over the world in the style of Hitler. This propaganda campaign was a dismal failure, both at home and abroad. The Reagan Administration also experimented with another device: "International terrorism," organized by the Soviet Union, is the key problem of the modern world and the mechanism by which the Soviet Union aims at global conquest. This act has also not been selling very well, and when it fails, some new venture will presumably be undertaken. I will return to some details in discussing the current scene.

Summarizing parts (1) and (2) of these remarks, the Reagan Administration is seeking to raise the level of international tension and to create a mood of crisis at home and abroad, seizing whatever opportunities present themselves. Turning to part (3), the reasons are not difficult to discern. They are implicit in the domestic policies that constitute the core of the Reagan Administration program: transfer of resources from the poor to the rich by slashing social welfare programs and by regressive tax policies, and a vast increase in the state sector of the economy in the familiar mode: by subsidizing and providing a guaranteed market for high-technology production, namely, military production.[51] This is in no sense a "conservative" program, as it is customarily mislabeled.

It is not surprising that the government should turn to armaments in an effort to deal with such problems as flagging productivity and a deteriorating industrial plant. There are many predecessors for the choice of arms production and bribery of the rich as a means for dealing with economic problems, most recently, the Kennedy Administration program to "get the country moving again" by the device of military Keynesianism and regressive tax measures to stimulate investment. Government policy must be designed so that it does not interfere too much with the prerogatives and power of private capital, as it would were the state to become directly involved in the production of useful goods that can be sold for profit, but rather enhances them. The natural choice, then, is to subsidize the production of waste. In an advanced industrial society, this must be high-technology waste, preferably rapidly obsolescing so that there is a continual need for more. Furthermore, the taxpayer must be induced to foot the bill. There are only so many times that people can be awed by the sight of a man setting foot on the moon, but fear of a powerful enemy can be an effective goad if the propaganda system is functioning smoothly. Furthermore, bribery of the rich—the only device to stimulate investment readily available in a state capitalist society—may lead to more consumption, real estate speculation, investment abroad, and so on, defeating the goal of "reindustrialization," unless a guaranteed market is provided. What is more, the goods produced should preferably not be total waste; optimally, they can be employed to help maintain a global order open to investment and exploitation. There is one obvious policy choice that satisfies these and similar requirements, and it is the one regularly undertaken: what is euphemistically called "defense." Any student of Orwell should have known what was coming when the War Department was renamed the "Department of Defense" in 1947.

The rulers of the Soviet Union march along a parallel path; they perceive their power to be enhanced by more tanks and missiles, not homes and consumer goods. This natural tendency was considerably strengthened when the Kennedy Administration adopted a program of massive rearmament under the stimulus of a faked "missile gap," and chose the policy of humiliation rather than diplomatic settlement at the time of the Cuban missile crisis in 1962. Each superpower provides a continually escalating threat, both real and convenient, to impel its partner to proceed in a direction that conforms to systematic internal pressures. While these are not laws of nature, there are compelling and mutually supportive factors that lead towards militarization of the economy. To alter the process will be no mean task.

Nevertheless, it is not an easy matter to sell to the general public a domestic program based on impoverishing a large part of the population for the benefit of the wealthy, destroying the environment, eliminating health and safety standards, and subsidizing the production of high-technology waste. There is a classic means for achieving this end: heightening international tensions and creating a war scare. In a time of crisis, the population may be willing to tighten their belts and follow orders. A mood of crisis will also facilitate the resort to global intervention, as in the "era of counterinsurgency" launched by the Kennedy Administration. And this may be required, perhaps not in Latin America, but quite possibly in the Middle East, a region more crucial for American power. While attention was focused on the dispatch of several dozen military advisers to El Salvador in early 1981, some 250 U.S. Army and Air Force communications experts were dispatched to Oman for a month of war games in March.[52] A mood of tension may also reduce the danger of independent initiatives by industrial rivals, who may have no choice but to fall into line if a real crisis develops.

What is more, the allies must also be induced to increase military production. If the United States diverts substantial resources to the production of waste, its already precarious position in international markets will be weakened (apart from arms exports, which are far from negligible) if its rivals do not destroy their capacity for useful production as well. An international crisis, it is hoped, may contribute to this end.

For such reasons as these, it was predictable that the Reagan Administration would search for ways to construct an atmosphere of international confrontation. The state of the world is such that opportunities to exploit should not be lacking, though it is interesting to observe that the early efforts have simply not worked.

Putting aside discussion of specifics until later, let us now turn to part (4) of these remarks, the historical backgrounds for current policy.

One of President Reagan's advisers on Latin American affairs, Roger Fontaine, recently stated that American policy in Central America should be modeled on what the United States did "in Greece in 1947 with the Truman Doctrine."[53] The allusion may be more apt than he is aware, judging by the context.[54] The specific motivation for the Truman Doctrine was, in fact, the situation in Greece, where Britain lacked the resources in 1946 to maintain the royalist regime it had imposed by force after the Germans had withdrawn, and the United States was intent on replacing British power to prevent a victory of Communist-led guerrillas that might set the dominoes toppling (see Chapter 7)—the threat, both to Greece and to the other dominoes, was an indigenous one, as has regularly been the case.

In the background planning for the Truman Doctrine two opposing views emerged. George Kennan, the author of the containment policy (though not in the form it assumed), objected to placing aid to the Greek government and to Turkey "in the framework of a universal policy rather than in that of a specific decision addressed to a specific set of circumstances." The wording of the Truman speech, in fact, reflected the "heavy ideological emphasis of the State Department's draft," which "appalled"

Kennan, as John Lewis Gaddis comments. He continues: Washington officials "present[ed] aid to Greece and Turkey in terms of an ideological conflict between two ways of life. . . ."[55] Perennial presidential advisor Clark
Clifford described Truman's speech as "the opening gun in a campaign to
bring people up to [the] realization that the war isn't over by any means,"
and a State Department information officer argued that "the only way we
can sell the public on our new policy is by emphasizing the necessity of
holding the line: communism vs. democracy should be the major theme."
"It was," Gaddis adds. He describes the Truman Doctrine as "a form of
shock therapy: it was a last-ditch effort by the Administration to prod Congress and the American people into accepting the responsibilities of the
world leadership which one year earlier, largely in response to public opinion, Washington officials had assumed by deciding to 'get tough with Russia.' "

Apart from the reference to the response to public opinion, which appears
to put the cart before the horse, the observation is accurate. The public was
in a pacifistic mood and had to be shocked into the realization that the war
was not over, so that the Administration could carry out its ambitious plans
for constructing a world system of the sort outlined in wartime planning,[56] a
global order that would be responsive to the needs of the American economy and those who controlled it. Truman himself said that he had wanted
for several months to "proclaim the new doctrine when a fitting moment
arose," the opportunity being the Greek crisis. Joseph Jones, the State Department official who drafted the speech, attributed to Secretary of State
George Marshall the view that "*all* barriers to bold action were indeed
down" (his emphasis). The *New York Times* proclaimed that with the Truman Doctrine, "the epoch of isolation and occasional intervention is ended"
and "is being replaced by an era of American Responsibility."[57]

Others should beware when a nation begins to speak of its "Responsibility." The first to bear its burden were the Greeks, who were subjected to a
reign of terror and violence as the United States proceeded "to support free
people who are resisting attempted subjugation by armed minorities or by
outside pressures," in the words of the Truman Doctrine (see Chapter 7).
Others were soon to be subjected to "bold action" of a similar sort. In Western Europe, industrial capitalism was reconstructed as part of a U.S.-domi-
nated world system, with benefits for many, including the U.S. businesses
that "prospered and expanded on overseas orders," "fueled initially by the
dollars of the Marshall Plan," and the U.S.-based transnational corporations

that flourished in the expanding European economies and elsewhere "under the umbrella of American power," in the words of *Business Week* (see Chapter 2). The Pacific was turned into an "American lake," very much as planners had anticipated.[58] In general, the widely held fears that there would be no outlet for U.S.-produced goods—the United States was producing "almost half of the real world gross national product" at the end of World War II,[59] and policymakers remembered well that the depression had been overcome only through wartime spending—were, in part, relieved.

I mentioned earlier that while foreign policy initiatives are generally described as defensive reactions to the Soviet threat, in reality they involve other dimensions—and the relation to the USSR has hardly been characteristically "defensive." The adoption of the "containment" policy in 1947 illustrates the general pattern. The alleged Soviet threat was invoked to shock the domestic population into accepting the Cold War framework for intervention in the Third World and measures for reconstructing industrial capitalism in ways that suited U.S. interests. While much has changed since, the same dimensions of policy are relevant for understanding the return to "moderate containment" or some more aggressive variant of it today (see Chapters 7 and 8). The Reagan Administration has attempted to exploit the threatened collapse of the military regime in El Salvador rather in the way that the Truman Administration exploited the inability of the British to repress popular forces in Greece in the mid-1940s, and may well continue to play this gambit with regard to Central America. In this respect, Fontaine's remark cited above has some merit, though not in its intended sense.

By 1950, the early postwar programs were flagging and the fears of depression, loss of export markets, and an independent course in Western Europe (what Fred Block calls "the nightmare for U.S. policy makers"[60]), were once again on the ascendant. These provide the background for NSC 68 (April 1950), a report to the National Security Council proposing a vast program of militarization of the economy.[61] The document calls for "a rapid and sustained build-up of the political, economic, and military strength of the free world," which can be achieved only if it is recognized "by this Government, the American people, and all free peoples, that the cold war is in fact a real war in which the survival of the free world is at stake." The exaggeration of the Soviet threat reaches almost hysterical proportions, though the use to which it is put is highlighted by the simultaneous recognition of Soviet weakness by the drafters. The document proposed to overcome domestic economic problems by the familiar device of military Keynesianism and "to overcome Western Europe's tendency to pursue an independent economic course by binding Western Europe to the U.S. with military ties" (Block). With regard to the Soviet Union, NSC 68 called for a "rollback" strategy, aiming "to hasten the decay of the Soviet system" from within and to "foster the seeds of destruction within the Soviet system." The United States "should take dynamic steps to reduce the power and influence of the Kremlin inside the Soviet Union and other areas under its control" through "convert means in the fields of economic warfare and political and psychological warfare with a view to fomenting and supporting unrest and revolt in selected strategic satellite countries," including support for national independence movements among the Russian peoples. Essentially the charges familiar in Communist propaganda.

We must undertake "the responsibility of world leadership," whatever the risks, and commit ourselves "to foster a world environment in which the American system can survive and flourish," the report continues. This should not be difficult, in the light of our "moral ascendency": "The essential tolerance of our world outlook, our generous and constructive impulses, and the absence of covetousness in our international relations are assets of potentially enormous influence" (or, we might add, would be so, if we could only somehow overcome the blindness of Latin Americans and others who, in their absurd and obtuse delusions, fail to perceive these fundamental elements of U.S. policies and actions). But "the excesses of a permanently open mind," "the excess of tolerance," and "dissent among us" can become a "vulnerability" of our society. In particular, we must be concerned over Soviet efforts to subvert "labor unions, civic enterprises, schools, churches, and all media for influencing opinion." Furthermore, "a large measure of sacrifice and discipline will be demanded of the American people" requiring "reduction of Federal expenditures for purposes other than defense and foreign assistance, if necessary by the deferment of certain desirable programs" and an end to "excessive or wasteful usage of our resources in time of peace." With improvement of internal security, massive rearmament here and in Western Europe, actions to undermine the USSR from within, and appropriate sacrifice and discipline, we may achieve a sufficient preponderance of strength so that we can "negotiate a settlement with the Soviet Union (or a successor state or states)."

Like the Truman Doctrine, this was a proposal awaiting the opportune moment for enactment. The moment arrived with the Korean War and the

Chinese intervention as MacArthur's army was marching on the Yalu River. The general tenor of the proposals is, again, strikingly similar to that of the current "Resurgent America" program of the Reagan Administration, both in the manipulation of the alleged Soviet drive for "world domination" and in the real domestic and international goals concealed by Cold War imagery and rhetoric.[62]

In fact, "rollback" attempts predated NSC 68. In September 1949, the CIA initiated a three-year program "to establish a network of active resistance movements behind Russian lines which the U.S. military hoped to use in the war everyone thought was coming"—where "everyone" excludes the CIA analysts who estimated the probability of war as "most unlikely," but includes the military, in particular Air Force intelligence, whose chief stated that "we can't accept" a paper denying the likelihood of a Russian attack on Western Europe or "we'll never get any budgets through," according to the member of the Board of National Estimates who was the paper's author. The program began with a flight by an American aircraft stripped of identifying markings which dropped two CIA-trained Ukrainian operatives into an area of the Ukraine "where a partisan army, once encouraged by Hitler's Germany, still maintained itself in the Carpathian mountains." The U.S. military believed that resistance movements in the USSR "might genuinely threaten Moscow's control if only the United States provided support," and the Joint Chiefs and CIA then proceeded to organize partisan armies, introducing hundreds of agents and military supplies to aid resistance groups "in Russian-occupied territory"; "in no way was this a reluctant or half-hearted effort." In the Ukraine, clandestine warfare continued until late 1952, after which "the only CIA penetration of Communist countries with armed men . . . was directed against China, where four-man agent teams were air-dropped at least until 1960," perhaps six teams a year.[63]

All of this provides an interesting backdrop to NSC 68, as do U.S. actions in Greece, Korea, and elsewhere in the late 1940s. One wonders, incidentally, what the reaction would have been to the discovery that the KGB was air-dropping agents and supplies to guerrilla movements that had been backed by Hitler and were fighting in the mountains of Colorado or Puerto Rico.

The Kennedy Administration a decade later adopted similar rhetoric and programs.[64] Again, the similarity to the Reagan programs of militarization and international confrontation and aggressiveness are striking, revealing how narrow is the actual political spectrum in the United States.

The following years were ones of varying success for American global policies. In the Western Hemisphere, the United States failed to overthrow Castro but did succeed, through embargo and extensive terrorism, in seriously hampering social and economic development, enhancing the repressive and totalitarian elements in the Cuban revolution, and driving Cuba into a relation of dependency with the Soviet Union (see below, pp. 52f.). Elsewhere in Latin America, however, the United States scored many more substantive successes. One crucial event was the U.S.-backed Brazilian coup of 1964, bringing into power a military regime which, with constant U.S. backing, subdued its own population with ample terror and reduced living standards for much of the population in the course of an "economic miracle" that was much admired here. Lincoln Gordon, Kennedy's ambassador to Brazil and later Assistant Secretary of State for Inter-American Affairs, described the 1964 "revolution" as "the single most decisive victory for freedom in the mid-twentieth century" and "one of the critical points of inflection in mid-twentieth century world history."[65] This decisive victory for freedom had a significant domino effect, helping to bring to power some of the most barbarous regimes of the modern world throughout the continent, with regular and crucial U.S. support.[66]

In Central America and the Caribbean, U.S. policy was also generally a success, particularly in the Dominican Republic, where a potentially dangerous democratic movement was prevented from attaining power by an American invasion, leading again to a regime of torture, terror, and ample rewards for American investors;[67] and in Guatemala, where as already noted (see note 21), U.S. contributions to counterinsurgency in the late 1960s maintained the rule of a collection of gangsters who rank high among claimants for awards for terrorism and savagery.[68]

In short, U.S. policy in the region generally achieved its aims, despite some setbacks, as "a plague of repression" perhaps without historical precedent settled over the continent.[69]

In the Middle East, U.S. foreign policy was generally a marked success in the 1960s. The fascist coup in Greece, which took place while the U.S. Sixth Fleet was riding anchor in the Port of Athens, headed off the perceived threat of leftist influence in a country that has always been regarded as an important base for U.S. operations in the eastern Mediterranean and the Middle East,[70] and also incidentally opened the doors wide to renewed American investment (see Chapter 7, note 23). The Israeli victory shortly after eliminated the threat posed by Nasserite radical nationalism to the oil producers of the Arabian peninsula and consolidated U.S. relations with a triumphant Israel that was believed at the time to rule supreme. The American position of dominance appeared to be firmly established in this crucial region (see Chapters 2, 11, and 12).

In Asia results were mixed, including notable successes, such as the incorporation of Indonesia into the Free World with the military coup of 1965, followed by freedom for investors and the massacre of several hundred thousand peasants, vindicating the U.S. stand in Vietnam in the eyes of liberal American scholars (see Chapter 13); and the Philippines, where the Marcos martial law regime provided a Latin American-style mixture of profits, torture, repression, starvation, and impoverishment, and where "analysts contend that Marcos is secure so long as he maintains the twin props of his rule—military support and foreign investment—particularly from the US."[71] But there were also failures. Despite enormous efforts, the U.S. attack on Indochina did not ultimately succeed, though it is important to bear in mind that it was only a partial failure.[72] The primary motive of the twenty-five-year U.S. intervention was not fear of "Chinese expansionism" or other similar fantasies of the media and much of scholarship, but rather concern over the potential "domino effect" of successful social and economic development under a nationalist-Communist leadership which, though eager for friendly relations with the United States and always— even at the height of the war—very wary of the intentions of its powerful neighbor to the north, would surely have taken an independent path rather than joining the Free World in the manner of Thailand, Indonesia, or the Philippines. But this threat has been eliminated, certainly for many years, as a result of the effectiveness of the U.S. attack in destroying the societies and even the land. Some reminders that would be regular media and school textbook fare in a truly free society may be useful.

British journalist John Pilger reports that

in Cu Chi, near Saigon, which I remember as thick forest, there is today a shimmering horizon of wilderness which has been poisoned, perhaps for generations. Eleven million gallons of the herbicide Agent Orange were dumped on Vietnam; its chief ingredient, dioxin, is estimated to be a thousand times more destructive than thalidomide. Blind and deformed babies are now common in those areas sprayed during Operation Hades, later re-named Operation Ranch Hand.[73]

Reporting on a visit to Vietnam, Ngo Vinh Long (see note 43) writes that in one central province, 7 million antipersonnel bombs and M-79 grenades had to be dislodged in order to reclaim the fields. In another, a million unexploded bombs and grenades remain in the ground and more than three thousand people have been killed since 1975. A third is largely "denuded by the bombing and shelling." Destruction of trees and vegetation have led to flooding and scorching winds that blow sand into the rice paddies. "Much of the land in central Vietnam had been destroyed by chemical defoliants, bombs and salt water which invaded the paddyfields after American forces destroyed the sea dikes and widened many rivers to accommodate their gunboats." [74]

In the Plain of Jars in Laos, where a completely defenseless peasant society was subjected to one of the most devastating attacks in the history of warfare, the land is littered with unexploded ordnance. The United States has refused to provide the technology to remove it. The U.S. government has even denied information to Mennonite representatives who have sought ways to help peasants who must clear the land by hand, with many casualties. [75]

There is ample reporting of the mass starvation that Vietnam is facing, but the fact that the United States made a certain contribution to this tragedy is often conveniently overlooked. For example, *Business Week* reports the "prospect of famine" in Vietnam, and the accompanying renewal of "the 'boat people' exodus," but the report has no word to suggest that the United States has ever had any involvement in Indochina, past or present. [76]

In fact, the involvement is present as well as past. Since the war's end, the United States has done what it could to ensure that its partial victory would endure. "There is a great deal of evidence," Martin Woollacott writes, "that the foot-dragging policy of the United States on diplomatic relations and on aid, whether or not it was tagged with the humiliating label of reparations, helped to close off the Yugoslavia option for Vietnam." [77] That is quite correct. A World Bank official observes that "since 1977, the US has constantly refused to make any accommodation with Vietnam, forcing it further and further into the Soviet camp." [78] This is a typical procedure when some area is "lost" to the Free World; compare the case of China, Cuba, and now Nicaragua. It is a procedure that may be reversed (as in the case of China) if it is recognized that "rollback" is not in the cards. [79] For the time being, however, the United States is committed to maximizing hardship and suffering in Vietnam. It has exerted effective pressure on the World Bank to withhold development aid,[80] and the Reagan Administration "has launched a vigorous, behind-the-scenes campaign at UN headquarters to cut UN humanitarian and development aid to Vietnam." [81] The present moment is particularly opportune because of the starvation conditions in Vietnam and the fact that "refugees recently leaving Vietnam are reported to be citing economic reasons far more than any other for their flight from the hard-pressed Southeast Asian nation." [82] Thus, cutting food aid has a double benefit: increasing misery, and increasing the refugee flow, so that Western humanitarians can then deplore the barbarian savagery of the Vietnamese leadership as illustrated by the tragic fate of the boat people. The United States and the European Economic Community have refused to respond to a UNICEF appeal for milk and food for the Vietnam emergency. The U.S. government also initially rejected an appeal from the Mennonite Central Committee to allow it to ship wheat to Vietnam, where, the committee's executive secretary for Asia points out, "drought in late 1979 and early 1980 was followed by typhoons and floods that caused heavy destruction to the rice crop in northern and central Vietnam." [83] At the same time, "prospects for loans from the Asian Development Bank and the World Bank are very bleak, since many donor countries, especially the US and Japan [which benefited substantially from the U.S. war as an offshore procurement base], are opposed to any assistance to Vietnam." [84]

The official reason for blocking international aid of any sort to Vietnam is to punish Vietnam for its illegal occupation of Cambodia. But this is pure fraud:

One moderate third-world ambassador makes a point echoed by many of his colleagues: "By attempting to stop UN agencies from providing assistance and relief to Cambodia and to Vietnam, the United States is really trying to apply sanctions of sorts against Vietnam for its illegal occupation of Cambodia. How is it then that the United States is so reluctant to apply sanctions against South Africa for its illegal occupation of Namibia? If the US were consistent it would have a stronger case, morally and politically." [85]

Furthermore, the United States has not attempted to "punish Indonesia for its illegal occupation of East Timor"; rather, it has provided accelerating military aid to Indonesia since 1975 to assist in this aggression and the accompanying massacre (see Chapter 13; no one accuses Vietnam of conducting a massacre in Cambodia[86]—on the contrary, the invasion may have helped to avert further massacres—nor can it be claimed that Timorese border attacks in collusion with a powerful ally were a threat to Indonesia). And the United States never suggested sanctions against Israel to punish it for its attacks on Jordan and Lebanon or its occupation of the West Bank, Gaza Strip, Golan Heights, and Sinai, or for the settlement policy on the West Bank, which the Carter Administration repeatedly described as "illegal" (see Chapter 9). The true character of the U.S. stand is, furthermore, revealed with utter clarity by the U.S. refusal to provide more than a trickle of aid to help overcome the ravages of the U.S. war in Laos, where there has also been widespread starvation.[87]

In fact, the goal of U.S. policy is clear enough. Not content with a partial victory of the sort just described, the United States wants to ensure the maximum possible suffering in countries that have been so ignoble as to resist American aggression, in the hope that sooner or later "Vietnam will crack," and the partial victory can be extended to a total one. Perhaps analogues can be found in the gloomy history of great-power cynicism, but offhand none come to mind. Again, it is noteworthy that protest is next to nonexistent, providing further insights into "Western humanism" and the real significance of the wringing of hands over human rights violations committed by official enemies.

By 1968 it had become evident to influential and powerful groups in the United States that the cost of subduing the Vietnamese was too great and was harming the position of the United States vis-à-vis its industrial allies, so that the enterprise should be reduced in scale or liquidated. Major business circles turned against the war, followed shortly after by segments of the media and the articulate intelligentsia, who previously had been generally antagonistic to antiwar activities (most remained so), tending to agree with the assessment of Senator Mike Mansfield, who denounced the "sense of utter irresponsibility" shown by demonstrators calling for an end to the bombing of North Vietnam and a negotiated settlement in October 1965.[88] Anthony Lewis wrote in the *New York Times* that "by 1969 it was clear to most of the world—and most Americans—that the intervention had been a disastrous mistake," despite our earlier "blundering efforts to do good,"[89] a position that many echoed. Nixon and Kissinger attempted to salvage victory in South Vietnam at least (see Chapters 3 and 6), but their efforts came to grief—partially, as noted.

It should again be stressed in this connection that opposition to the war among the articulate intelligentsia was restricted to rather narrow grounds (see Chapter 1, at note 31). At the left-liberal end of the spectrum, attitudes ranged generally from those expressed by Anthony Lewis (the argument against the war "was that the United States had misunderstood the cultural and political forces at work in Indochina—that it was in a position where it could not impose a solution except at a price too costly to itself") to those of Irving Howe ("We opposed the war because we believed, as Stanley Hoffman has written, that 'Washington could "save" the people of South Vietnam and Cambodia from communism only at a cost that made a mockery of the word "save" . . . ' ").[90] The argument against the war was either the cost to us or the cost to them—as we determine it. In contrast, we opposed the Russian invasions of Hungary, Czechoslovakia, and Afghanistan because aggression is wrong, whatever its costs to either party, and with no laments over "the complexities of history."

Another success of U.S. intervention was that, in large measure, only the more harsh and brutal elements could survive the onslaught. In South Vietnam, the National Liberation Front, which had called for neutralization of South Vietnam (along with Laos and Cambodia) and a broad-based government, was destroyed, the major achievement of the U.S. war. By 1970 it was reasonably clear that if the United States were finally to withdraw, there would be a northern takeover, because of the success of the United States in decimating the southern resistance,[91] offering Western hypocrites the opportunity to appeal to this consequence of U.S. aggression as justification for the claim that the United States was defending South Vietnam against "aggression from Hanoi" (see note 145; Chapter 4, note 7; Chapter 5). In Cambodia, the Khmer Rouge, who had only a marginal existence at the time of the U.S. "incursion" in 1970, were mobilized by the terror bombings.[92] One can only speculate about what might have been, but the consequences of the U.S. attack were in large measure predictable.

The basic success of U.S. intervention was clear from developments elsewhere in Southeast Asia: the "economic miracle" of the ASEAN countries, the rapid expansion of U.S. and Japanese investment, and the brutality and repression that are the familiar accompaniments.

By the early 1970s it was apparent that the quarter-century of American hegemony had come to an end, though the United States remained the world's most powerful state. The decline is illustrated by such measures as share of world product (see p. 22, above) and in many other ways. To cite one minor example, when the United States invaded Lebanon in 1958, sending ashore troops with atomic-armed rockets while nuclear weapons were deployed on offshore aircraft carriers and the Strategic Air Command was placed on a worldwide nuclear alert,[93] the Sixth Fleet calmly banned all commercial air traffic in the eastern Mediterranean.[94] It is doubtful that the United States could do the same if it determined to invade Lebanon today. Such examples help to explain the feelings of frustration and outrage expressed by many U.S. high officials, who feel that the United States has become a "pitiful helpless giant" in Nixon's words, unfairly treated by the lesser breeds.

The recognition of the limits of American power led to the acceptance of détente by Nixon and Kissinger. As always, this policy adjustment is conventionally described with reference to the superpower enemy, but it involved the other dimensions of foreign policy discussed earlier as well. With regard to the Third World, the Nixon Doctrine sought to enlist surrogate states to preserve stability and order regionally, notably Iran and Israel in the Middle East. There were also the beginnings of what was later called "trilateralism"—the collective management of global affairs by the United States, Western Europe, and Japan, though the seat of power was to remain in Washington, as Kissinger emphasized.[95] Détente as well was a move towards coordinated global management: China was to be incorporated within the Western system, in a sharp reversal of policy responding to Chinese initiatives,[96] and the Soviet Union was to be a junior partner, more or less in accordance with Stalin's concept, a policy that is held to have failed on the grounds that the Soviet Union insisted upon equality (see Chapter 8).

The domestic dimension was also relevant to the move towards détente. Not only was the United States then limited in its capacity for intervention, but more seriously, the "Vietnam syndrome" and the "crisis of democracy" had eroded the base of domestic support for intervention. And the ritual invocation of the Soviet drive for world domination had temporarily lost its efficacy. The efforts of the following decade to overcome this problem are discussed in the following chapters. One notable component of these efforts was the Human Rights Crusade, which is taken to have been a domestic success at least: "Thanks to Presidents Ford and Carter, the task of restoring our image of ourselves as good and decent people had been accomplished before the 1980 campaign,"[97] not an easy task, given the level of understanding of U.S. policy—which has little to do with "ourselves as good and decent people" except in the fantasies that perceive foreign policy as growing out of a

pluralist consensus—that had been attained by much of the general population by the early 1970s. The crusade, however, had its failings, and sometimes led to misunderstandings, as Carter's ambassador to Iran, William H.
Sullivan, pointed out in a July 1977 report to Washington:

> "The assumption appeared to be that we are opposed to monarchical sys-
> tems of government and seek to have them replaced by democracies,"
> Sullivan complained. This, he said, he had set straight.[98]

The domestic impact was generally as hoped, however, and it is currently
believed that the process has advanced sufficiently so that the alleged Russian effort "to impose its absolute authority over the rest of the world" (NSC
68) can once again be used to whip the population into line in support of the
classic measures of militarization of the economy, subversion, and intervention.

Despite the fundamental cynicism of the Human Rights Crusade, discussed below and in the references cited, it should not be overlooked that it
had beneficial effects to some degree, particularly in helping to reinforce
church and other groups in Latin America that were struggling to counter
the "plague of repression" that the United States had been instrumental in
spreading over much of the continent in the 1960s.[99]

Policies of the 1970s, both at home and abroad, are also discussed in the
essays that follow. By late 1978 the return to a more militant and aggressive
posture in world affairs, with the concomitant militarization of the domestic economy, was clear, and the process has been accelerated under the Reagan Administration as it tries to realize the program of "Resurgent
America" (see Chapters 7 and 8). Though as usual, the characterization of
policy ("containment," etc.) emphasizes the relation to the superpower
enemy, the policies must be understood along each of the dimensions already noted, including by now the new centers of power (e.g., OPEC) that
must be taken into account. The Soviet and domestic dimensions are again
closely related: The Soviet Union and its satellites, bent on world conquest,
threaten our destruction, so those who are not at the high end of the income
distribution must be willing to sacrifice for the cause, bearing the burden of
Reagan's domestic program. "Cuba has declared covert war on its neighbors—our neighbors," while building up Nicaragua "as a forward base of
operations with a large army and intelligence apparatus already in
place . . . ," we are informed by Thomas Enders, who formerly presided

over the destruction of Cambodia and is now Assistant Secretary of State for Inter-American Affairs: "The United States will join with them to bring the cost of that war back to Havana." [100] In fact, it is the United States that has declared war on the mass of the population of Central America while the Somozist National Guard prepares to invade Nicaragua from its bases in Honduras and Miami. [101] The rhetoric is familiar, and also its meaning.

The chief White House policy adviser, Edwin Meese, states that Cuba and the Soviet Union must "wake up to the fact" that the Reagan Administration "will take the necessary steps to keep the peace any place in the world," warning that "the President has said many times he would like potential or real adversaries to go to bed every night wondering what we will do the next day. I don't think we would rule out anything" [102]—a version of Nixon's "madman theory." The audience, however, is the American people more than the Russians and their satellites, and not only them. A conservative British commentator points out: "The alarmed audience consists of all those people in smaller countries who see more clearly than ever that the U.S. does not give a damn about their fate and would be prepared to bomb the hell out of them for the sake of denying territory to the Soviet Union"—or more realistically, denying their own territory to them. "The reality is, however, that it is American policy which is scaring the pants off most of the Conservative party [in England] and virtually the whole of Western Europe." [103]

The propaganda directed to the American people builds on the successes already achieved in overcoming the "Vietnam syndrome" and the "crisis of democracy." Prior to Reagan's acceleration of the rush towards militarization, the *New York Times* published a series of articles of which the first was headed "Nation's Military Anxiety Grows as Russians Gain." [104] The text is accompanied by a poll report that does support the first part of the headline, showing a steady increase in the proportion of the population that believes military expenditures to be too low, from 8 percent in early 1973, at the height of the "Vietnam syndrome," to 49 percent in January 1980. As for the Russian "gains," the picture is more murky, contrary to the headline's assertion, which is repeated as fact throughout the series despite the citation of expert opinion and evidence to the contrary. If the gains are supposed to be geopolitical, the assumption is dubious indeed; see Chapter 7. What the authors assert is that the Soviet military machine "now outspends the United States year after year to build installations and to buy guns, planes, tanks, ships and nuclear missiles." But they do not point out that this conclusion is based on CIA estimates that border on fraud, and that even by these estimates, which highly inflate the scale of Soviet military power, NATO outspends the Warsaw pact by a substantial margin,[105] putting aside the fact that China should be added as part of the anti-Soviet alliance and that a substantial part of Soviet military expenditures is devoted to the Chinese border.[106]

The new policy of "containment" and "Resurgent America" in part recapitulates earlier policies already reviewed, but there are differences. The crucial difference relates to Europe and Japan, which are now major economic rivals, increasingly likely to go their own way, realizing "the nightmare for U.S. policy makers" (see p. 22). Furthermore, as noted, the United States cannot maintain its position in world trade (arms sales apart) if resources are diverted from useful production here alone. Seymour Melman estimates that the ratio of military expenditures to fixed capital production is $46 to $100 in the United States, $18.90 to $100 in West Germany, and $3.70 to $100 in Japan: "The concentration of fixed capital in economically productive work has paid off richly in Germany and Japan," he notes.[107] Therefore it is necessary to induce our rivals-allies to waste their resources on a scale approximating our intentions here. Deputy Secretary of Defense Frank Carlucci is one of several U.S. officials who have delivered the message to the allies, with increasing persistence: Given that Western Europe's GNP actually exceeds that of the United States, the United States "cannot be expected to improve and strengthen U.S. forces in Europe unless other allies increase their own contribution to the combined defense effort. Nor can the United States, unaided, bear the burden of promoting Western interests beyond Europe." [108]

There are serious problems, however, in engaging the allies in promoting Western interests. One problem is that it is *their* interests that they will promote, and these increasingly conflict with those of the United States. In the Middle East, for example, the United States is not eager for European involvement; in fact, it has been positively opposed to it. During and after World War II, the United States succeeded in largely displacing its European rivals from the Middle East (see Chapter 2), and in more recent years U.S. diplomacy has aimed at blocking European initiatives such as the Euro-Arab dialogue and ensuring that the fate of this resource-rich region remains in the hands of the United States (see Chapters 11 and 12). The conflict has taken new forms in the 1970s, as the industrial societies seek to expand exports to the oil producers and obtain a larger share of the huge development projects there. The American Businessmen's Group in Saudi Arabia complains that the U.S. share is declining in both domains in the face of stiff competition from Europe, Japan, and others.[109] Most development contracts are now going to Europe, with both France and Germany apparently surpassing the United States in 1980, along with Japan and even South Korea.[110] The Europeans are also obtaining a larger share of military sales, one of the most effective means of recycling petrodollars and gaining a degree of control over the importing state. France, for example, obtained a naval contract amounting to over $3 billion with Saudi Arabia in 1980. Whatever fluctuations there may be in exports and development contracts, there is no question that European initiatives, whether diplomatic or economic (these being closely related), "could provoke a major policy clash with the United States in the region" and are a source of concern in Washington.[111]

A second problem is that the Europeans are less than enthusiastic about jumping on the Reagan bandwagon, a fact that has caused some irritation in the United States. One high State Department official complains, "We keep on hearing all this mooing and meowing on defense from Europeans, but we want to see some action, and now." [112] Polls taken by USICA (formerly, the U.S. Information Agency) in Europe indicate large-scale opposition to U.S. NATO proposals: stationing advanced missiles in Europe, deploying the neutron bomb, maintaining (let alone expanding) military spending, etc.[113] For Europe, détente has been a valuable development. Traditional East-West trade patterns have been reconstituted and in part expanded, particularly as Western Europe becomes more interdependent with the Soviet Union in development of energy resources. Recall the concerns of the Atlantic Council noted above (pp. 2–3). Efforts by the Reagan team to convince the Europeans that détente should be abandoned as a failure, that "détente is indivisible" (meaning that East-West trade ties should be weakened and tensions heightened as a consequence of Soviet actions in the Third World), and that military expenditures should be increased as part of a new activist "containment policy" are falling on deaf ears, to put it mildly.[114] The same is true of Japan, where the government almost collapsed in early 1981 when the prime minister used the term "alliance," suggesting that he might be committing Japan to military cooperation with the United States.[115] In Japan too, public opinion does not support a military build-up. A poll by *Asabi Shimbun* (more or less the Japanese *New York Times*) found in March 1981 that only 22 percent of the population advocated stronger military forces.[116] Like most Europeans, the Japanese are unwilling to adopt the Reagan Administration's thesis concerning the ominous Soviet military threat. One Japanese diplomat, referring to Secretary of State Haig's presentation at the ASEAN conference in Manila, states, "They kept telling us how imminent was the danger, but we frankly do not see the threat as so severe." Furthermore, "the deep-seated opposition of Japanese leaders to meeting what they view as impossible American demands on defense spending appears to have been fortified by the anti-American furor surrounding the right of US ships to carry nuclear weapons into Japanese ports." [117]

Reagan's emissaries have fared no better in the Middle East, apart from Israel, where Prime Minister Menahem Begin agreed that "it is not an artificial alarm. The free world is shrinking and is in permanent danger." Elsewhere, the typical response to Haig's mission was that of the Saudi Arabian foreign minister, who informed him that the kingdom regarded Israel, not the USSR, "as the principal cause of instability and insecurity in the region." [118] No doubt the well-known Egyptian journalist Mohammed Heikal expressed a fairly general feeling when he wrote in early 1980: "Any Arab leader who tried to stir his people's religious conscience by invoking the sanctity of Kabul to condemn an occupation that is 13 weeks old would only remind them of the occupation to which their holy city of Jerusalem had been subjected for 13 years." [119]

Similarly, it is not easy to convince a European audience that a "well-orchestrated international Communist campaign designed to transform the Salvadoran crisis from the internal conflict to an increasingly international confrontation is under way"—a precise characterization of Reagan Administration policy. Europeans are not limited to the U.S. press, and are well aware that while indeed "the source rests outside the target area," it does not rest in Moscow or Havana; and they are readily able to determine who is conducting "the disinformation programs under way in the U.S. and Europe." [120] Things were no easier closer to home, where Mexican President López Portillo drew an analogy between El Salvador and Poland, both "essentially internal conflicts, adding that efforts to explain them as the result of outside agitation—the United States charge in El Salvador and the Soviet contention in Poland—were 'an insult to intelligence.' " He went on to say that "in our continent, social injustice is the true womb of unrest and revolutionary violence. The theory that foreign subversion is the origin of our ills is unacceptable to the democratic nations of the area." The president of Venezuela, on a state visit, appeared to agree, stressing his opposition to "U.S. intervention in the area." [121]

Even in the United States, the attempt of the Reagan Administration to enflame the El Salvador issue to an international confrontation met with little success. Mail to the White House was reported to be "running 10 to 1 against the administration's new emphasis on military aid and advisers," and polls indicate very strong public opposition to economic or military aid or military advisers for the junta.[122] This fact is all the more significant in the light of the general media coverage of events in El Salvador, which, as usual, rarely departed from the official interpretation and gave only a sporadic indication of what was depicted in the foreign press on the basis of direct reporting or such sources as the Catholic Church in El Salvador.[123]

While there is no space here to give anything like an adequate review of the facts, some mention should be made of El Salvador, not only because of the role it played in the early stage of the Reagan Administration's efforts to produce an international confrontation—on the model of Greece in 1947 and many subsequent cases—but because the situation is so important, by the valid criterion discussed earlier (see p. 9). Often we are powerless to help when terrible things happen in the world: widespread starvation, millions of child slaves, torture, massacre, repression. Sometimes we can do a great deal: We can stop the horrors at the source rather than simply deploring the atrocities or perhaps giving a little aid to the victims. This is possible when it is our own government that is the primary cause of the atrocities. It is such cases as these that are of real importance in terms of human consequences, and that will engage the attention and efforts of people concerned with such consequences. The case of El Salvador is about as clear and striking an example as one could hope to find.

The general picture presented in the U.S. press as of early 1981 was that of the U.S. government: A moderate regime is attempting to carry out reforms in the face of left-wing violence ("a Pol Pot left," as Carter's Ambassador Robert White and others described the mixture of guerrillas, peasant organizations, unions, and church groups that stood in opposition to the government), unable to control the right-wing "death squads." [124] The picture presented by the foreign press was quite different.[125] Its coverage generally corresponds to the conclusions of church sources in El Salvador and of the Council on Hemispheric Affairs, whose 1980 Annual Human Rights Report found El Salvador and Guatemala to be the worst human rights violators in Latin America, replacing Argentina:

More people have died in El Salvador during the past year, largely as the result of government-condoned right-wing "death squad" killings, than in all other nations of Latin America combined. . . . The death toll . . . reached almost 10,000, with the vast majority of the victims falling prey to the right-wing terrorism sanctioned by key government officials. . . . [T]hese countless killings have gone unpunished and even uninvestigated as the government's own military and police forces are almost always involved in them. . . . [126]

As the year ended, Professor Jeane Kirkpatrick of Georgetown University, now head of the U.S. delegation to the U.N. stated: "And I think it's a terrible injustice to the Government and the military when you suggest that they were somehow responsible for terrorism and assassination." [127] And the *Washington Post* chimed in, "There is no real argument that most of the estimated 10,000 political fatalities in 1980 were victims of government forces or irregulars associated with them." [128]

If one wants to learn about what is happening in rural El Salvador, the best place to go is obviously to the Honduran border, where thirty-five thousand refugees, mostly women and children, are living in misery, dreadful squalor, and starvation in remote areas, trying to escape the raids of the Salvadoran army and ORDEN (the paramilitary forces of the government of El Salvador—see note 159), which cross the border to attack refugee camps to which they have driven the population, according to the U.N. High Commissioner for Refugees.[129] These refugees can tell the story of what is actually happening in the rural areas where reporters rarely can go except under government control.[130]

A U.S. congressional delegation visited the border areas on a fact-finding mission in January 1981 and submitted a report to Congress.[131] Members of the delegation interviewed many refugees along the border area, taperecording the interviews. The refugees

describe what appears to be a systematic campaign conducted by the security forces of El Salvador to deny any rural base for guerrilla operations in the north. By terrorizing and depopulating villages in the region, they have sought to isolate the guerrillas and create problems of logistics and food supply. . . . The Salvadoran method of "drying up the ocean" involves, according to those who have fled from its violence, a combination of murder, torture, rape, the burning of crops in order to create starvation conditions, and a program of general terrorism and harassment.

The report then presents sample interviews in which refugees describe bombing and burning of villages by the army, mass murder of fleeing civilians, shooting of defenseless peasants from helicopters, and extraordinary brutality (e.g.: mutilation; decapitation; "children around the age of 8 being raped, and then they would take their bayonets and make mincemeat of them"; "the army would cut people up and put soap and coffee in their stomachs as a mocking. They would slit the stomach of a pregnant woman and take the child out, as if they were taking eggs out of an iguana. That is what I saw"). With regard to the guerrillas, refugees report: "We don't complain about them at all," "they haven't done any of those kinds of things," "it's the military that is doing this. Only the military. The popular organization [i.e., the "Pol Pot left"] isn't doing any of this." As for the military: "They were killing everybody. They were looking for people to kill—that's what they were doing." [132] The delegation interviewed José Morales Ehrlich, the number-two civilian in the government, who informed them that "instead of putting military outlaws on trial, the worst of them have been assigned to desk jobs or given scholarships to study abroad"—these are the changes that have been made to correct "occasional mistakes from a human rights point of view" (summary of Ehrlich's remarks). The report concludes that the security forces of El Salvador, "operating independent of responsible civilian control . . . are conducting a systematic campaign of terrorism directed against segments of their own population." In fact, the government is effectively under right-wing military control, the reformist officers having been driven out of the governing junta. [133]

Several foreign journalists have visited the border areas. Édouard Bailby, in a lengthy report that appears to have received no coverage in the U.S. press, points out that journalists and international observers are not permitted to visit the regions where security forces operate, so that one must visit the Honduran border (as he did) to determine the facts from the refugees who have fled there since the Rio Sumpul massacre in May 1980. [134] He found that refugees hide in the forest "in fear of the killer-commandos who come from El Salvador." He gives a detailed report of massacres, brutality, mutilation, and terror on the part of the armed forces that are "a true repetition of the methods utilized by the SS during the second world war," since the Rio Sumpul massacre, when "the genocide began," at times with the assistance of the Honduran army. [135]

David Blundy of the *Sunday Times* (London) spent ten days in the border area a few months later, interviewing doctors, priests, Honduran soldiers,

Salvadoran refugees, and members of church aid groups, who "provided overwhelming evidence of atrocities of increasing brutality and repression by the Honduran army as well as the Salvadorans." The Salvadoran army, he writes, "is carrying out what can only be described as mass extermination of thousands of peasants living in the area" where the guerrillas are based in a "co-ordinated military campaign by the Salvadoran military, assisted by the Honduran army with—according to some Honduran sources—the support of the United States." Blundy reports refugee accounts of bombing, napalm attacks, destruction of villages, massacres, rape, torture by the Salvadoran and Honduran army forces, stories of "an existence of almost incomprehensible brutality." He also describes the Lempa River massacre of March 16, when thousands of refugees attempted to cross the river for two days under constant attack by the Salvadoran air force in cooperation with the Honduran army, who killed refugees with machetes and beat them to death with rifle butts, basing his account largely on the reports of priests who were present, attempting to save the victims.[136]

In the week before the Lempa River massacre (March 7–13), 798 people were killed, of whom 681 were peasants killed by bombing or helicopter gunships, according to the Legal Aid Office of the San Salvador Archdiocese.[137] Shortly after, the *New York Times* reported that "assassinations by government forces appear to be declining," a sign of President Duarte's success in curbing "extreme rightists" who are "losing influence" within the military.[138] On the day of the massacre, the *New York Times* story on El Salvador was headlined "For Salvador Peasants, Fruits of Change Seem Good," the second of a series on the great successes of the land reform program.[139] Shortly before, the *Times* reported the plight of the peasants, "vulnerable to both prowling guerrillas and trigger-happy soldiers"; only the depredations of the former are described, along with a description of "a small mob shouting for weapons with which to fight the guerrillas" and the testimony of "a paid vigilante in the service of the landowner" who explains that "here the terrorists do not come to propagandize. They attack and kill." "The exodus is greatest from rebel-controlled areas," Schumacher reports, "with the peasants leaving for either personal safety or political preference," safety from the guerrillas, one must assume, given the evidence reported.[140]

Those reporting from areas not under the control of the army of El Salvador—though not in the *New York Times*—find a somewhat different picture, as noted, even sometimes in the U.S. press; for example, in the *Los Angeles Times*, where the director of the Honduran office of the U.N. High

Commissioner for Refugees is quoted as saying, "The vast majority of these people are running from the armed forces."[141]

The reports from the Honduran border describe graphically the nature of the government that the United States is supporting, advising, training, and arming. There are other indications, also generally ignored by the U.S. media, though comparable sources are characteristically given wide and immediate publicity in the case of enemy crimes. The Legal Aid Office of the San Salvador Archdiocese (see note 137) provides a regular and detailed accounting of killings. According to its records, the killings are overwhelmingly the responsibility of the government security forces, secondarily the right-wing "death squads" that are closely tied to the military and probably commanded by them.[142] The situation is much the same in Guatemala, a more important domino (see notes 21 and 189; and Chapter 7). What the U.S. government has attempted to portray, with the general though not total collaboration of the media, is something quite different, as noted.

It may also be recalled that the government military forces that are conducting these massacre operations are U.S.-trained, as are many of those in the top positions of the military and security agencies, including the Treasury Police, who are sometimes accused of the worst atrocities. From 1957 to 1974, a U.S. public safety program was conducted under USAID to upgrade the "operational skills and effectiveness" of the Salvadoran security forces. Until 1963, it was directed mainly to the National Police, and afterwards, to the National Guard. When the program terminated in 1974, USAID analysts concluded that "the National Police . . . has advanced from a nondescript, *cuartel*-bound group of poorly trained men to a well-disciplined, well-trained, and respected uniformed corps. It has good riot control capability, good investigative capability, good records and fair communications and mobility. It handles routine law enforcement well."[143] The impact of U.S. training in El Salvador—which is quite typical of the Latin American scene—is useful to bear in mind when we read that the United States is sending military advisers to train the military forces of El Salvador or some other client regime with the aim of "averting indiscriminate repression and creating a 'clean' counterinsurgency force" (see above, p. 16).

The major propaganda effort of the U.S. government was the State Department White Paper, released with great fanfare on February 23, 1981.[144] As noted earlier, the campaign to convince the world on the basis of this collection of documents that the USSR was engaged in aggression in El Salvador through the medium of its proxies from Cuba to Vietnam was met with derision or disregard. But in the United States, the press reported the conclusions of the White Paper at face value, in accordance with the official interpretation, raising few serious questions. Many simply adopted the propaganda allegations as unchallengeable doctrine. *Business Week*, for example, stated flatly that "the most important question is whether Washington will deal with the ultimate source of aggression in the area—Cuba—because it is not only El Salvador that is under attack. . . . The decision in late February to send additional U.S. military advisers to El Salvador to help the junta repulse external aggression is likely to be only the first step in an escalation unless Washington persuades Fidel Castro and his Soviet sponsors to back off." A naval blockade is recommended, unless we want to relive the experience of Vietnam.[145]

Only one journalist, to my knowledge, immediately carried out a careful investigation of the actual documents, namely John Dinges. He discovered that the documents indicate that "only about 10 tons [of armaments] ever actually crossed the border," not the two hundred tons claimed in the accompanying government charges, and that the guerrilla representatives "encountered a cool reception in Moscow."[146] But his report was ignored, and the media generally just repeated what they were told. The conformism of the media did not go entirely unnoticed. Hodding Carter wrote that "the real story is that the administration's propaganda blitz went virtually unchallenged for several weeks" as the media "initially gave Washington's claims about the El Salvador civil war the kind of over-eager, over-credulous respect which warms the heart of every government flack," demonstrating "that big government sets the terms of public discussion about major issues far more often than the press likes to admit or the public understands."[147]

Carter claims that "many reporters did eventually start asking the hard questions." In fact, apart from Dinges, few "hard questions" were raised in the mainstream media[148] until June when the *Wall Street Journal* published an extensive critical commentary by Jonathan Kwitny that completely demolished the White Paper, revealing—despite the understated tone—that it was a tissue of fabrications and distortions. Jon D. Glassman of the State Department, who bears primary responsibility for the report, conceded that the figure of two hundred tons of supplies does not come from the documents at all, but from alleged "intelligence." "The only concrete instance of Soviet aid delivered to the Salvadoran rebels reported in the 19 documents was an airplane ticket from Moscow to Vietnam for one guerrilla," Kwitny observes. Robert White, who was U.S. ambassador at the time that the documents were allegedly found, expressed "incredulity at Mr. Glassman's story of the discovery" of one batch of documents, and notes that the documents Glassman claimed were found in the dramatic manner he describes were already known to the embassy before he arrived in El Salvador. White does believe that the documents are genuine, however. He says, "The only thing that ever made me think that these documents were genuine was that they proved so little." Kwitny adds, "Mr. Glassman even expresses an opinion very close to that of Mr. White—that the shortcomings of the documents indicate that they are genuine 'and disprove the fabrication argument.' " Documents are misrepresented, misidentified, and used as the basis for "extrapolations" that are completely meaningless. In short, the whole story fell apart, though another column the same day informs us that the State Department will try again, with another White Paper.[149]

The day after the *Wall Street Journal* critique appeared, the *Washington Post* published a skeptical article on the White Paper, giving many additional examples of "factual errors, misleading statements and unresolved ambiguities that raise questions about the administration's interpretation of participation by communist countries in the Salvadoran civil war."[150] The *New York Times* held the line, however, restricting itself largely to government defense of the basic thrust of the White Paper and to minor issues of detail.[151] With regard to arms shipments, the *Times* story conceded only that the documents "present a confusing picture" and "are even more unclear on the volume of arms reaching the rebels." The discussion by Dinges three months earlier is not mentioned (nor is it mentioned by the *Wall Street Journal* or the *Post*), nor the major discoveries of the *Journal* and *Post* investigations. On the timing of these critical studies, see note 169.

One intriguing element of Juan de Onis's State Department apologetics in the *Times* is his remark that "even" former Ambassador White, who has criticized the Reagan policies in El Salvador, "has not questioned the basic conclusion" of the White Paper. Naturally, since as de Onis adds, "while still Ambassador, Mr. White said during the January guerrilla offensive that at least 100 insurgents had entered El Salvador by sea from Nicaragua to join the uprising." De Onis did not see fit to add that White opened his testimony before the Senate Foreign Relations Committee on April 9 by saying that "I have become increasingly skeptical of the reality of that invasion," in which "no one was captured and no battle took place."[152] De Onis does not even take note of the serious doubts expressed in the pages of the *New York Times* at the time.[153] This report notes that Ambassador White "gave credibility" to the "unconfirmed reports" of the guerrilla landing from Nicaragua. As for evidence, the junta offered none, apart from the claim that "the boats were made of wood not available in El Salvador" and "that a major battle had ensued in which 53 rebels had died." "Reporters who visited the area, however, were told that the local garrison had been attacked by guerrillas on successive nights, with seven soldiers and two guerrillas killed. Three small boats had also been found near La Unión several days before the landing was reported." The Nicaraguan government denied the charge, and "United States officials appeared to retract their initial claim, conceding that 'our rush to believe what we were told was not totally warranted' and 'there was some over-statement in the beginning.' " The "rush to believe" was evidently still overwhelming de Onis four months later.

Meanwhile, the U.S. government announced that it had shipped 343 tons of arms to El Salvador in 1981.[154] The press has been silent on the important question of other sources of arms for the junta (cf. Chapter 8, note 26). Press reports indicate that these must be extensive. "I doubt if there are better-equipped infantrymen anywhere in Central America," Philip Jacobson writes in the *Sunday Times* (London): "The troops one sees now all carry the latest automatic rifles and grenade-launchers; they have good steel helmets and sturdy boots; above all, they have so much small-arms ammunition that they are given to blazing away whole magazines at the slightest excuse." In contrast, guerrilla caches exhibited to journalists show only a variety of weapons ranging from U.S. M-16s to "bolt-action rifles, ancient shotguns and home-made bombs." [155] In addition, there is the crucial matter of air power and heavy artillery.

A careful reading of press reports, with their references to West German assault rifles, French helicopters, Israeli machine guns, etc., indicates that arms must be arriving from many sources, and sometimes there is even a more direct hint. For example, Kenneth Freed reports in the *Los Angeles Times* that "although Venezuelan President Luis Herrera Campins will not disclose amounts, he reportedly has poured hundreds of millions of dollars into El Salvador to help Duarte and the junta maintain control" [156]—the money, like U.S. "economic aid," is presumably used to purchase armaments from U.S. allies.

Hodding Carter's observation on how the government sets the terms of public discussion is much to the point. It is well illustrated by the case of the El Salvador White Paper, and by many similar cases. The story is a very old one. A study of the first major government propaganda agency, the Committee on Public Information established during World War I (see Chapter 1), observes that "the CPI discovered in 1917–18 that one of the best means of controlling news was flooding news channels with 'facts,' or what amounted to official information." [157] While procedures may have become more sophisticated since that time, little of significance has changed, including the regular willingness of substantial segments of the articulate intelligentsia to accept the officially designated terms of public discussion, e.g., with regard to U.S. aggression in South Vietnam from the early 1960s (see above, pp. 10f.), and other cases that will be examined below.

Suppose, in fact, that we do take the government's claims in the White Paper at face value. Then it follows that from September 1980, the guerrillas began receiving supplies from the Communist countries—apparently the merest trickle. This was four months after the Rio Sumpul massacre when "the genocide began," according to Bailby, six months after the massive assault on the peasantry that coincided with the announcement of the land reform at a time when, according to President Duarte, "The masses were with the guerrillas." [158] How should we react to this momentous discovery?

One possible reaction is suggested by an account by T. D. Allman, one of the few U.S. reporters to have sought out people in the countryside apart from government guidance, describing his meeting with the remnants of a village near the town of Aguilares. The group had organized as a Catholic "grassroots congregation" (*comunidad de base*), devoted to Bible study, prayer, and nonviolent methods of self-help. "At first only their leaders were harassed, beaten, and tortured," but later, as one put it, "the strict repression began." They were driven from their homes. Men who sought work or appeared in town were killed. Women were then sent to the town for food and medicine, but they were killed. They then sent children instead; an eight-year old girl had just been killed. The murderers were government forces or ORDEN.[159] One of the men of the village told Allman that he "had heard that beyond the mountains where El Salvador becomes Honduras, beyond even the other sea on the other side of Honduras, there existed a country that might give them boots and uniforms and guns, called Cuba. But how could one get to that place? Even when one went to Aguilares to attend Mass, the Guardias took you, and tortured you, and killed you." An old man then asked Allman, "Can you tell us, please, sir, how we might contact these Cubans, to inform them of our need, so that they might help us?" [160]

But no such reaction as this to the White Paper is or could be expressed in the conformist American press.

Allman reminds us that the origins of Reagan's policies lie in the Human Rights Administration: "Even in the good old hard-nosed days of *entente cordiale* between Washington and Batista and Trujillo and Papa Doc and all the rest, it would have been difficult to find an instance of an American president standing quite so resolutely behind a regime that quite so shamelessly tortured peasants and castrated doctors of philosophy and disemboweled little children and raped nuns and shot archbishops dead while they celebrated Mass." He also observes, with reason, that what is happening now in El Salvador is *Matanza*, Part II, a replay of the vast slaughter of peasants in 1932 when privilege had once before been seriously threatened by the poor, that time without our assistance, hence without the need to invoke the "Soviet drive for world domination." [161]

Something else that we are supposed to believe is that the land reform is marching from strength to strength in accordance with the plans of the "reformist junta," undermining the appeal of the guerrillas, as reported by Edward Schumacher in the *Times* while the army was massacring fleeing peasants at the Lempa River (see above, p. 40). One way to assess the success of the land reform would be to ask the opinion of the director of the agrarian reform program, José Rodolf Viera. That possibility is excluded, however, because he was assassinated by right-wing elements on January 4, 1981. One can, however, inquire of his "former top assistant," Leonel Gómez, who "fled El Salvador after Mr. Viera's murder," the *New York Times* reports.[162] To say that Gómez fled after Viera's murder does not quite tell the whole story. In fact, we learn elsewhere, he fled when he "saw several dozen uniformed soldiers sealing off nearby streets" and realized that the "death squad" was coming for him, too, on January 13.[163] Gómez "thinks support for the terror and killings from within the officer corps is . . . virtually institutionalized," and that President Duarte has no real power. "The junta, he says, has virtually no support." "The Army is in control, according to Gómez, and the US is giving military aid to a 'killer government.' " [164]

Gómez, who comes from a landowning family and is quite critical of the civilians who resigned from the junta in January 1980 after a major outbreak of state terror, has had various things to say about the land reform program for which he was a top adviser in interviews and press conferences. He states that while the land reform program has seized large amounts of land from wealthy families, it "has distributed plots only to a relatively few peasants." The greatest success of the Salvadoran Institute in charge of land reform (ISTA), of which he was a deputy, was in investigating the military: "We found huge amounts of corruption." "We were finding that ISTA was buying land already in government hands. They were buying land nobody wanted as a favor to rich friends. All of this piles up a debt that has to be paid by the peasants." He also believes that the left is nowhere near as strong militarily as the United States claims, and hopes "they will learn from experience and become like the Sandinistas in Nicaragua." [165] Gómez states further that the agrarian reform has become a "gravy train" for the military. [166]

A subsequent co-authored article expands on this interpretation of the land reform. [167] Gómez and Cameron believe that "Phase I of the program, which breaks up the country's largest estates, has worked" and that Phase III, the "Land to the Tiller plan" is supported by the peasants and "has the potential to improve dramatically the lives of those receiving the land where they had previously worked as sharecroppers" (Phase II, which was to break up middle-sized farm holdings, including the bulk of the coffee plantations, will not be enacted, it is generally assumed). The land reform, they believe, has broken the power of the traditional oligarchy, but is replacing it by a new military oligarchy. The Christian Democrats "have not achieved anything substantial for the people of El Salvador" and their presence in the junta "gives only a respectable façade to a military dictatorship." They believe that support for the guerrillas is not great, though "the government enjoys even less popularity," and the brutal killings by the army "have succeeded in traumatizing the Salvadoran people into fearful passivity." The army "is held together by a vast network of corruption," which now extends to the nationalized banks and 15 percent of the country's best farmland. "The vast majority of killings occur in sweeps of the countryside by the armed forces or by death squads operating under the formal direction or informal sanction of regional military commanders." The general picture they paint is of a shift of power from the traditional oligarchy to a military oligarchy of extraordinary brutality and corruption.

An Oxfam study of the land reform program takes a still dimmer view, concluding that "the majority of the rural population—landless and poorest—are excluded from any potential benefits under the present land reform" (close to two-thirds of the rural population, the authors estimate) and that it will be a disaster for most of the others, confining them for thirty years to tiny plots of marginal land that cannot provide even subsistence and that will be exhausted after a few years planting. The reform was imposed by the United States without adequate planning and with no consultation by those who would allegedly benefit from it. Peasants in cooperatives believe "that they have simply changed *patronos*, that the agrarian reform does not represent a substantial change in their lives." Key Salvadoran officials regard its major component (Decree 207, the "Land to the Tiller" program) as a "misguided and U.S. imposed initiative" (in their own words). The land reform program "aggravates the most serious agrarian problems of El Salvador," the report concludes.

The authors also observe that the regions affected by Decree 207 "coincide almost identically with the areas of greatest repression against peasants by government security forces." Other reports strongly support their conclusion that the land reform had the effect of providing hard-line military with "the context in which they could pursue a counter-insurgency war," in the style already indicated.[168] The major repression against the peasantry was launched under the state of siege announced along with the land reform program.

As noted, the Reagan Administration basically pursued and extended the Carter program of support for repression and massacre in El Salvador, while attempting to exploit the tragedy, in the manner of earlier years, for the purposes of their domestic programs of militarization and alms for the wealthy. It is interesting that in spite of the massive propaganda campaign and the generally willing cooperation of the media, the attempt was as much a failure domestically as it was internationally (see p. 37, above). The Carter-Reagan initiatives in El Salvador succeeded in revitalizing the peace movement, adding to the impetus already provided by Carter's evident turn towards a more militaristic posture in the latter part of his term. By early 1981, the level of opposition that had developed—spontaneously, without leadership, and with very little interaction for the most part—was reminiscent of the 1960s. The "Vietnam syndrome" has not been overcome as successfully as elite groups had hoped. In fact, the 1970s were by no means as quiescent as is widely believed, as a great many people know from their personal experience, though there was little activity on a national scale on major issues of peace and war (there was much local activity, and there were national actions on other issues).

The popular response to the U.S. support for a collection of murderers in El Salvador is of interest in two important respects. In the first place, there was a perceptible impact on the government and the press. By spring, the government had drawn back from its attempt to create an international confrontation over the El Salvador issue. The policies of support for repression and massacre continued, but the rhetoric was much muted.[169] There is little doubt that the policy shift was a result of the domestic reaction combined with the international opposition that had developed. For the tortured people of El Salvador, the difference is not great, and will not become significant unless the popular opposition to the U.S. support for the military junta continues and intensifies. But what seemed the easiest path to implement Reagan's long-term program in the context of a national mobilization has been blocked, a fact that may prove significant as the implications of this program become clear in practice. This does not mean that there is no danger of direct U.S. military intervention, either in El Salvador or, more likely, elsewhere. But perhaps a barrier has been placed on the road towards such actions.

Secondly, the response reveals serious flaws in the widely held argument that there has been a great "conservative shift" in the country in the past years. U.S. involvement in El Salvador in early 1981 was more or less comparable to Vietnam in about 1960, when the program of domestic repression in South Vietnam was recognized to be failing and plans were being laid for the outright aggression that began in 1962. But the public reaction is vastly different. In 1960 there was virtually no detectable opposition to the U.S. intervention in Indochina (primarily South Vietnam and Laos, where the United States succeeded in subverting the relatively free elections of 1958 and installed its own military client). The reaction to the current policies towards El Salvador is more similar to what was happening in the United States in 1965–67, when hundreds of thousands of American troops were invading South Vietnam and the United States had brought North Vietnam into the war (much as planners anticipated) by the bombing of the North. The comparison reveals that in certain respects there has been a "shift to the left" (though I doubt that terms such as "left" and "right" are very meaningful with reference to the domestic U.S. scene). I will return shortly to the alleged Reagan "popular mandate."

As noted earlier, the Russian-sponsored Cuban aggression against El Salvador was only one element of a two-pronged propaganda offensive launched by the Reagan Administration to create the required mood of international crisis. The second prong was "international terrorism," another device by which Soviet planners are aiming to take over the world. The centerpiece of this campaign was the nicely timed book by Claire Sterling, *The*

Terror Network,[170] "which has caused much commotion in Washington." [171] The book claims to demonstrate both the Soviet campaign and the complicity of the Western governments, the CIA, and others in concealing it. It was given unusual publicity and is being widely circulated by the Reader's Digest press. The media blitz included articles by Sterling in several journals, notably the *New York Times Magazine*,[172] where she presented her major conclusions.

The book has also been widely and sometimes enthusiastically reviewed, a typical phenomenon in the case of books that provide a welcome message, however absurd their contents may be.[173] *Business Week* comments that although Sterling does not prove her case "totally" and although her evidence is necessarily circumstantial, nevertheless "it is overwhelmingly compelling in its logic." [174] In an unprecedented review signed by the editor in *Foreign Affairs*, the book is described as "a landmark book, breaking much new ground," with a case that is "powerful and persuasive" that the Soviet Union is "a central contributor" to international terrorism.[175] The *Business Week* reviewer, Ronald Taggiasco, was particularly impressed by the fact that "in Italy alone, 115 people were killed by terrorist violence last year, 85 of them in the bomb blast at Bologna's train station." Taggiasco forgot to mention that the Italian Communist party has been in the forefront of the antiterrorist campaign in Italy and that the Bologna bombing was a *right-wing* terrorist operation. These facts, which are presumably known to the Rome bureau chief of *Business Week*, do not deter him from concluding that Sterling has built an overwhelming case to show that international terrorism is a Soviet-inspired campaign, or from criticizing U.S. Administrations (prior to the Reagan Administration, which has finally seen the light) for "consistently deny[ing] that this widespread campaign of terrorism emanates from Moscow or that it follows a grand design aimed at bringing down Western democracies," of which the Bologna bombing is a notable example.

The actual source of the Bologna bombing, the major terrorist incident of the past years, was noted by other reviewers, farther from the mainstream, for example, Jonathan Marshall (note 173), who adds that the second-largest terrorist incident in Europe, when fifty-three people were killed at the Munich Oktoberfest in the same year (1980), was the work of neo-Nazis. Sterling's book opens with a reference to these incidents, and the comment that she will be concerned only "obliquely" with "Black terrorism." Marshall points out that Sterling claims that the "most atrocious terrorist act of the seventies in Europe" was a Palestinian attack on an airplane that took thirty-one lives, and that she does not mention at all the fact that "the most atrocious act outside of Europe in that decade was the bombing in 1976 by CIA-trained Cuban exiles of a Cuban passenger jet—killing all 73 aboard, including Cuba's gold medal-winning international fencing team." Note that the reference throughout is to individual terrorism, not state terrorism, for example, the shooting down of a civilian Libyan airliner by the Israeli air force with the loss of 102 passengers and 8 crewmen after it had over-flown Cairo in a sandstorm and was attempting to return to Cairo, a few minutes flight time away, in February 1973.[176] Not to speak of somewhat more notable acts of state terrorism during the decade of the 1970s.

The clinching argument for Sterling is this: "It is not happenstance that none of the major terrorist attacks have been directed against the Soviet Union or any of its satellites or client states"—such as South Yemen, the PLO, and Cuba, the main instruments of the Soviet-controlled "worldwide terror network aimed at the destabilization of Western democratic society." [177] This argument has much impressed reviewers. Walter Laqueur writes that she has provided "ample evidence" that terrorism occurs "almost exclusively in democratic or relatively democratic countries." [178] Daniel Schorr is more skeptical:

> As evidence of Soviet instigation, Mrs. Sterling refers to the apparent immunity of the Soviet world to terrorism, ignoring both the high risk in a police state and the fact that acts of terrorism that did occur might not be reported. But she makes no effort to explain how the United States, which should have figured as the principal target of a coordinated Communist campaign, has managed to remain relatively immune from Europe's terrorist nightmare.[179]

This decisive argument merits a few words of comment. Shortly before the media blitz began, the *New York Times* devoted twenty lines to a rocket attack on the South Yemen embassy in Paris: "Responsibility for the attack was taken by a group that said it was avenging the bombing of a Paris synagogue in the Rue Copernic four months ago, which took four lives." This was the first time that "military rockets" had been used in a terrorist action in Paris, according to the police. One imagines that the rocketing of the Israeli embassy might have been treated somewhat differently. On the Palestinians as victims of terrorism, see the references of note 176.

The major target of terrorist attacks for the past twenty years has undoubtedly been Cuba. The bombing of the Cubana airliner in October 1976
is only one example. In April of that year, two Cuban fishing vessels were attacked by boats coming from Miami, the main center of anti-Cuban terrorism, in which the CIA is heavily involved. A few weeks later, two persons
were killed in the bombing of the Cuban embassy in Portugal. In July, the
Cuban mission to the U.N. was bombed and there was a series of bombings
aimed at Cuban targets in the Carribean and Colombia, along with an attempted bombing of a pro-Cuban meeting at the Academy of Music in New
York. In August, two officials of the Cuban embassy in Argentina were kidnapped and Cubana airline offices in Panama were bombed. In October, the
Cuban embassy in Venezuela was fired upon (and Orlando Letelier and
Ronni Moffitt were assassinated in September in Washington, with the apparent involvement of Miami-based Cuban terrorists). In November, the
Cuban embassy in Madrid was bombed.[180]

This is only a small piece of the story. The Kennedy Administration
launched a major terrorist campaign against Cuba, which was going "full
blast" in 1963.[181] Many details of the Kennedy campaign are presented in a
memoir by Bradley Ayers, a Ranger officer assigned to the CIA for these operations.[182] These were under the direct control of Robert Kennedy, Ayers reports, citing his personal appearances to encourage the terrorists. Apart from
the attempts to assassinate Castro, which are well known, these terrorist actions included attacks on fishing boats and Cuban civilian installations, and
poisoning of crops and livestock—projects that were, in fact, very effective,
apparently requiring the destruction of half a million pigs after an outbreak
of African swine fever caused by U.S.-based terrorists in what the U.N. Food
and Agricultural Organization called the "most alarming event" of 1971.[183]

Further details of U.S. terrorism against Cuba during the Kennedy Administration, under the direct control of Robert Kennedy, are presented by
Taylor Branch and George Crile.[184] They estimate that the four-year "secret
war against Cuba" involved several thousand men and cost as much as $100
million a year. "As late as 1964 the Agency was landing weapons in Cuba
every week and sending up to fifty agents on missions to destroy oil refineries, railroad bridges, and sugar mills." During this period, "there were missions to Cuba almost every week," some of them "large-scale raids aimed at
blowing up oil refineries and chemical plants," including attacks on the
Texaco oil refinery and a sulfuric acid plant; also a diesel plant, a lumber-
yard, and mines. Attacks were launched against Russian ships in Oriente

Province and railroad bridges, where commandos "watched a train run off the ruptured tracks," then bombing a sugar warehouse. One attack was the shelling of the Blanquita Hotel in Havana, "inflicting heavy damages on the hotel." Another favorite device was economic sabotage. The CIA contaminated sugar cargoes sent out from Cuba, arranged to have "invisible, untraceable chemicals [poured] into lubricating fluids that were being shipped to Cuba," convinced a Frankfurt ball-bearing manufacturer "to produce a shipment of ball bearings off center," sabotaged buses from England, and so on.

All of this, of course, was illegal under American laws, but that was irrelevant. The "secrecy" was maintained with the willing cooperation of the press. As one agent explained, "The guys learn not to hurt you," and not only keep quiet about the facts but also run stories fed to them by the CIA. "American supervisors often accompanied their Cuban agents" on these raids.

Branch and Crile believe that "the secret war failed in all of its objectives," since it reinforced Cuban nationalism and forced Castro into alliance with the Soviet Union. But that is too narrow an interpretation. True, the Kennedy terrorism did not succeed in overthrowing the regime, but it did cause substantial damage to the Cuban economy and was a major factor— perhaps the major factor—impelling Cuba to a permanent state of military mobilization. The twenty years of terrorist attacks on Cuba carried out directly or abetted by the U.S. government helped to overcome the major danger posed by Cuba, namely, that successful independent development outside of U.S. control might have a "demonstration effect," always the essential core of the domino theory. Even the dependence on the Soviet Union is a net plus for the United States, for two reasons: It provides a propaganda cover for the regular U.S. assaults against Latin America (in "defense against Soviet-inspired Cuban threats," as in El Salvador); it is an *independent* Cuba that would threaten U.S. dominance in Latin America because of the potential domino effect.

But Cuba is immune to terrorist attack according to the Sterling thesis, the ultimate proof that the international terrorist conspiracy is hatched in Moscow.[185] The CIA annual report cited above (note 179) even states that 1980 "marked the first year that a large number of deadly terrorist attacks were carried out by national governments," referring to "the Libyan government's assassination campaign against dissidents living in Europe and the exchange of terrorist attacks on diplomats in the Middle East."[186]

The fact that the Sterling thesis about the immunity of Soviet clients from terrorist attack can even be mentioned without ridicule, that "international terrorism" can be discussed with no notice of the U.S. government's role in organizing and directing terrorist actions against Cuba, is still another example of the spectacular achievements of Western propaganda systems, though it does not attain the level of the masterful suppression of U.S. aggression in Indochina, discussed earlier.

Sterling does indeed mention Cuba in her *New York Times Magazine* article: "The revolutionary decade of the 1960's had been focused in Latin America as Fidel Castro preached his gospel of spontaneous, popular revolution," though later "the fulcrum of revolution had moved to the Middle East," as the international campaign orchestrated by Moscow shifted sights. It is surely appropriate to discuss Latin America in the decade of the 1960s and since in a report on terrorism. It was then that U.S.-inspired state terrorism in Latin America reached previously unknown heights,[187] quite apart from the large-scale terrorist attacks against one Latin American country carried out or backed by the United States.

If policy follows its normal course, Nicaragua will sooner or later become another Soviet client, as the U.S. imposes a stranglehold on its reconstruction and development, rebuffs efforts to maintain decent relations, and supports harassment and intervention—the pattern of China, Cuba, Guatemala's Arbenz, Allende's Chile, Vietnam in the 1940s and in the post-1975 period, etc. Then Nicaragua too will become involved in "international terrorism." Or perhaps it already is. As evidence, note that "right-wing Nicaraguan exiles here [in the Honduran capital], confident of the support of some sectors of the Honduran Army and hoping for a 'green light' from Washington, are preparing to invade their homeland to overthrow the 20-month-old Sandinist Government." A Nicaraguan exile leader asserts that his "freedom force" will soon be joined by thousands of sympathizers from Guatemala and Miami:

> Although "counterrevolutionary" bands have frequently attacked Sandinist border posts in recent months, Nicaragua, in building up its military strength, has apparently been prompted more by the fear that the exiles are backed by both the Reagan Administration and the military governments of the region. A 200,000-man popular militia is rapidly being trained to fight alongside the existing 40,000-strong Sandinist army and police.

So far, there is no clear evidence of United States support for the Nicaraguan exiles, although a few dozen have been receiving military training in camps run by Cuban exiles outside Miami. Some State Department officials are also known to favor a policy of first "strangling" the Sandinist Government economically and then, in the words of one American diplomat, "financing dissent groups." Asked about Pentagon or Central Intelligence Agency involvement with the exiles, [exile leader] Mr. Cardenal replied, "No comment." [188]

Here, surely, we have *prima facie* evidence of international terrorism, produced right in the midst of the great flurry of concern over this malady, which threatens to undermine Western civilization. Somehow, it escaped notice. Other examples do as well. The *New York Times* reported Secretary of State Haig's accusation that the Soviet Union is "training, funding and equipping" international terrorism; and in the next column reported that in Guatemala, "violent Government repression of leftist and moderate groups here is increasing at the very time that Reagan Administration officials are looking for a way to repair relations with the military regime of Maj. Gen. Romeo Lucas Garcia"—the inheritor of the legacy of earlier U.S. commitments to enhancing terrorism, violence, oppression, and starvation in Guatemala (see note 21 above and Chapter 7).[189] Is this terrorism, indeed, international terrorism, given the U.S. involvement over many years, the Israeli arms shipped to the murderers, etc? Does it become an even clearer example of international terrorism when the Reagan Administration, "in a maneuver circumventing the human rights considerations imposed by U.S. law, has approved the sale of 50 large military trucks and 100 jeeps to the military-dominated government of Guatemala"?[190] Not by the standards of the free press.

In fact, even putting aside the clear and obvious cases, such as Cuba, if one were to employ Sterling's curious logic one could show in other ways that the United States is the center of international terrorism. The international press has occasionally suggested links between the perpetrators of the Oktoberfest massacre and right-wing Christian militants in Lebanon,[191] who are armed and supported by Israel, which is unique as a recipient of U.S. economic and military aid and diplomatic support, as well as enjoying unprecedented intelligence ties with the United States.[192] Ergo, . . . Or, one may apply Sterling's logic to a 945-page criminal indictment against "587 leaders of the ultraconservative National Action Party, whose militant Gray

Wolves are blamed for many murders of leftists and liberals [694 political killings are charged] in the factional strife that led to last September's military coup," alleging ties to right-wing organizations in Western Europe, donations drawn on West German and American banks, etc.[193]

But let us put aside the Sterling-style logic that has so entranced reviewers, and keep to straight fact. Reviewing the susceptibility of Soviet clients to terrorist attack—in significant part, based in the United States with the direct involvement of the U.S. government—we can certainly perceive ample grounds to applaud Sterling's conclusion:

> What is needed is extensive public debate—in the media, at the universities, among intellectuals in general—cutting through old romantic concepts.

American intellectuals have, in fact, been much concerned over the rise of terrorism. "Four hundred intellectuals, warning that the Soviet Union is an increased danger to democratic societies, have announced the formation of an international committee to lead a 'struggle for freedom' " against "those who kidnap and throw bombs, many of whom are trained in the Soviet Union." Like Sterling, they are "concerned about a spreading practice of indulging in self-criticism to the point of condoning terrorism as being justified." [194] No further details are given on those who "condone terrorism," for example, against Cuba, or in Guatemala.

Perhaps the most cynical attempt by the media to put their resources to the service of the government propaganda campaign on international terrorism was the ABC Television "20/20" program on terrorism in the Middle East, aired on April 2, 1981. The program was devoted to "the alarming story of the Unholy War" being fought in the Middle East "between Soviet trained terrorists [the PLO] and the world's toughest Intelligence forces" (Israel). The PLO represents the Soviet Union while Israel represents the United States in this "relentless warfare": "America's vital interests are being threatened in this continuing conflict between the Soviet Union and the United States." With the conflict of Israel and the Palestinians framed in this fashion at the outset, anyone familiar with the standard techniques of a state propaganda service or its willing accomplices knows exactly what to expect, and there are no surprises.

The ABC "news report" begins by stating that "we're not going to talk about the profound issues underlying the fifty year [sic] war." Rather, what is presented is a starkly drawn black-and-white picture: on the one hand, Palestinian terrorists, fanatics belonging to an organization that states "openly that it fights by none of the rules," who like nothing better than killing women and children; on the other, tough, honorable "freedom fighters," defending their homes and families—and incidentally, Western civilization. The bloodthirsty Palestinian maniacs "have succeeded in forcing Israel into a profound moral dilemma. Stung by their attacks, she's lashed back at her enemies," attacking "PLO bases inside Lebanon . . . regardless of the fact that the PLO bases are situated in the midst of the civilian population." "Perhaps the most difficult aspect of fighting a war against terrorism is not allowing it to provoke a nation into sinking to the level of its enemy." An Israeli major laments that "when, when you kill someone . . . you just . . . lose something of your soul." Geraldo Rivera, who interviews him, is so impressed that he repeats this moving insight.[195] But the gallant Israelis have no choice, faced with implacable Russian-armed and -trained murderers.

"There's no headquarters in Russia of terrorism where the KGB tells the PLO or the Red Brigades or the Baader-Meinhof Gang where and who to hit next," Rivera states in closing:

> But the evidence is very clear that the Russians are financing, training and supplying groups that use the tactics of terror, and the Russians don't do anything out of the goodness of their hearts. They do it because every time the fabric of a democratic country is weakened by acts of terror, that serves the Soviet dream of world revolution. Three days after he took control of Russia—that was in 1917—Lenin said, "Let the people's terror begin." [196]

It is unnecessary to explore further the "profound issues underlying the fifty year war" between Jews and Palestinians, in presenting this melodrama.

There are several points to note in connection with this cheap propaganda exercise. The first, and most obvious, is the childishly silly effort to portray the Palestinian-Israeli conflict as a proxy struggle between the Soviet Union, aiming to undermine the West, and the United States, standing as ever for justice and freedom. The second is the portrayal of Palestinians as murderers and the Israelis as heroes, reluctantly resorting to force because they have no choice, faced with a profound moral dilemma in consequence. It is true that this shameful portrayal does not stray far from the clichés of the propaganda system that has been erected by American intellectuals (see, for example, Chapter 10; also Chapters 9 and 12). One might charitably assume that correspondent Geraldo Rivera and producer Barbara Newman, who prepared the documentary, simply didn't know any better—didn't know, for example, about Israeli state terrorism in the early 1950s, long before the PLO came into existence (see Chapters 9, 10, and 12). But that charitable assumption would be false. Barbara Newman, at least, certainly knew better. In fact, she was very well informed about the background of the conflict and about Israel's resort to terrorism and repression against Palestinians from the origins of the state, as well as the interplay of terrorism in the years before. The presentation can only be characterized as blatant deceit—on the part of whom, I do not know. If a comparable program—falsifying the picture in an equal and opposite direction—were aired on Soviet television, we would not hesitate to characterize it as an illustration of Soviet anti-Semitism and a sign of the obscene vulgarity of a totalitarian system of propaganda. A far more severe moral judgment is in order when this course is freely undertaken, as in this instance. But, of course, it all passes virtually without comment.

The devious means that the Soviet Union employs in its support for international terrorism are analyzed further by Charles Mohr, in the *New York Times*. He notes that "an ideological gap between the Soviet Union and international terrorists is being bridged." What is happening is that insurgent movements are turning towards "mass political action" in place of armed struggle, as "Soviet officials have succeeded in subjecting some terrorist and guerrilla movements to tighter discipline and closer adherence to orthodox revolutionary doctrine." [197] A new and more ominous chapter is opening in the frightening story of the inexorable Soviet surge towards world domination, with a promise of greater "global political violence" as insurgent groups turn away from violence under Soviet pressure. The Russians are so all-powerful that they have succeeded in overturning the canons of elementary logic, something that even the God of the medieval theologians was unable to do.

The campaign to exploit "international terrorism" has fared little better than the simultaneous efforts to frighten the West by tales of Soviet aggression in El Salvador, despite heroic efforts. Abroad, it appears to have been stillborn. In the United States, apart from inciting some intellectual circles, it also appears to have fallen on deaf ears, by and large. Something else will have to be found. There are many possibilities, given the many places where unpredictable crises are likely to erupt, but it will not be an easy task. American hegemony has indeed declined, along with the parallel decline in Soviet influence. Others simply have to be taken into account. The Reagan Administration might, for example, like to stir up an international confrontation over Angola, but it will face problems; the reaction of Nigeria, for example, cannot be discounted—or, for that matter, the reaction of American corporations that are happily doing business in this "Soviet satellite," which trades primarily with the West and is recognized by every Western country apart from the United States (see Chapter 7, note 9). Similar problems arise in connection with other potential targets of opportunity, for example, Libya.

In discussing the propaganda campaign waged in an effort to exploit El Salvador, in the style of Greece in 1947, to mobilize the domestic population in a New Cold War, I mentioned that the reaction indicates a significant shift away from what is commonly mislabeled "conservatism," but should more properly be termed "reactionary jingoism." If this is correct, how are we to interpret Reagan's "popular mandate"?

In the first place, there was no such "mandate," though Reagan had strong support among certain groups, primarily those who expected to benefit from his domestic program.[198] More than half the electorate did not vote for either of the major candidates, and of the slightly more than a quarter of the electorate who voted for Reagan, a good part were, in fact, voting against Carter. A *New York Times*/CBS poll found that only 11 percent of the Reagan voters chose him on grounds that "he's a real conservative."[199] If so, then a small fraction of the electorate constitutes the "popular mandate" for Reagan's programs. As for the defeat of congressional liberals, an analysis of the electoral returns shows that "the actual correlation between the liberalism score of the 247 House Democrats and their loss of electoral support between 1978 and 1980 is so low that statistically, degree of liberalism accounted for less than 1 percent of their loss of electoral support."[200]

There seems to be good reason to believe that the 1980 vote was really a vote "against." It may be interpreted in the light of the regular decline over the past years in the confidence that the population exhibits in institutions and professions, as polls have revealed; and more specifically, as Orren and Dionne argue, as "less a right turn than a turn-off to perceived government failures." The fact that current problems should be perceived as "government failures" is easy to understand. In part, it is true; but to a large extent it reflects the fact that private centers of power are so well protected from scrutiny in the American ideological system.[201] If things go wrong, it must be the government that is to blame. Therefore we must cut taxes (for the wealthy), "get government off our backs" (but not corporations), and generally develop welfare programs for the rich and the powerful.

When the domestic impact of the Reagan programs begins to hit home, there may be a sharp, perhaps even violent reaction; more so than, say, in Thatcher's England,[202] though the riots of summer 1981 in England may be a precursor of what lies ahead. In part, this is likely because the United States does not have such programs as National Health Insurance that Britain and other industrial democracies maintain, which can cushion the shock of unemployment and degradation of living standards. Another factor is that the United States is a more violent society, and also a more depoliticized one—there is no real political opposition nor popular structures through which alternative programs can be developed and pursued, and social and political debate is confined to a narrow spectrum as compared with other industrial democracies.

The situation offers many uncertainties. Perhaps there will be an evolution towards a Brazilian-style "capitalistic fascism," as Paul Samuelson predicts.[203] One can perceive the outlines of its potential mass base in some of the more mean-spirited, repressive, self-centered, and reactionary elements in American society. But the same circumstances may be conducive to more hopeful developments, which are also discernible on the current scene, for example, in the widespread opposition to a renewal of overt state violence. The "Vietnam syndrome" has, fortunately, not been cured, and the "crisis of democracy" that so troubles elite groups may yet intensify. Though an extrapolation of present tendencies leads to bleak forecasts, there are many opportunities for those who choose to work for a more just and more humane social order.

The essays that follow were written from 1973 through early 1981. Some are case studies dealing with particular episodes in the return to Cold War confrontation and militarization of American society, while others approach these topics from a more general point of view. Chapters 1 and 2 (1977, 1978) fall into the latter category; their focus is the stance that the intelligentsia tend to adopt towards state power, and more specifically, the phenomenon of "counterrevolutionary subordination"[204] during the post-World War II period in the United States. Chapter 3 through 8 trace the process of ideological reconstruction from 1973 to the present. Chapter 3 (1973) deals with the Paris Accords of January 1973, discussing the unconcealed commitment of the Nixon-Kissinger Administration to subvert the Paris peace treaty in order to achieve the aims of American aggression in South Vietnam, and the compliance of the media, which helped lay the basis for the intensification of the fighting and the breakdown of the settlement, largely at U.S.-Saigon initiative. Chapter 4 (1975) is concerned with the ways in which the ideological system came to terms with the failure of this effort, specifically, the intriguing system of apologetics for the American war in the retrospective assessments as it came to an end, and the obvious significance that this service to the state propaganda system would—and did—have for overcoming what was later to be called "the Vietnam syndrome." Chapter 5 (1978), written jointly with Edward S. Herman, is a review of one of the major works of apologetics for the American war in Vietnam, what has been called the "new revisionism,"[205] a highly misleading term since, as illustrated throughout these essays and elsewhere,[206] the mainstream of the intelligentsia rarely departed very far from the state propaganda system in their interpretation of the war, turning against it at about the same time, and for the same reasons, as leading business circles. Chapter 6 (1979) is a review of the first volume of Henry Kissinger's memoirs of his term in office. Chapter 7 (1980) treats the (by then, obvious) return to a Cold War posture in a more general way, while Chapter 8 (1981) turns to the options being considered by "foreign policy elites" at the outset of the Reagan Administration and the thinking that lies behind them.

Chapters 9 through 12 are concerned with the Middle East, a central focus of foreign policy since the Second World War, and indeed before, primarily because of its incomparable reserves of cheap energy. Chapter 11 (1977) and parts of Chapter 2 deal with U.S. petroleum strategy, and Chapter 12 (1978) considers U.S. policy towards Israel in this context, among other related topics. The Israel-Palestinian conflict is the primary focus of Chapter 9 (1974, with an Afterword updating the discussion to 1981), along with the role that Israel has come to play among American intellectuals since the U.S.-Israel relationship was solidified with the Israeli military victory of 1967. The latter topic is the subject of Chapter 10 (1977).

The final chapter (1980–81) is a case study of one of the many illustrations of the reality behind the "human rights" rhetoric that has been exploited so effectively in the process of ideological reconstruction in the

1970s,[207] namely, the case of the U.S. government role in one of the major massacres of the past years, in Timor, and the cooperative role of the media in this venture.

These chapters are slightly edited versions of the originals, sometimes with additions and corrections, and with some deletions to avoid redundancy. The notes are largely new, as will be evident from the dates of references cited, and in part incorporate material from other articles not included here. Sometimes, I have used an original unpublished version which differs somewhat from the texts cited here.

Chapter 1 was the Huizinga lecture delivered in Leiden in December 1977. It was published as a booklet in English and Dutch translation: *Intellectuals and the State* (Baarn, the Netherlands: by Internationale, Het Wereldvenster, 1978), and was reprinted in *Freedom* (Britain), April 15, 1978. Excerpts appeared in the United States under the title "The Secular Priesthood: Intellectuals and American Power," *Working Papers* (May–June 1979), and elsewhere, subsequently, in English and various translations.

Chapter 2 appeared as the first chapter of my *'Human Rights' and American Foreign Policy* (Nottingham: Spokesman Books, 1978); and in A. Edelstein, ed., *Images and Ideas in American Culture: Essays in Memory of Philip Rahv* (Hanover: University Press of New Hampshire, 1979), for which it was originally written.

Chapter 3 is based on a talk delivered at the Columbia University Seminar on the Political Economy of War and Peace, January 25, 1973, the day that the text of the January 24 peace treaty and the White House interpretation of it appeared in the press. It was published in *Social Policy* (September-October 1973). Sections had appeared in *Ramparts* ("Endgame: the Tactics of Peace in Vietnam"; April 1973), and some passages also appeared in the introduction to *The Backroom Boys* (London: Fontana, 1973), the British edition of part of the book that had appeared earlier under the title *For Reasons of State* (New York: Pantheon, 1973).

Chapter 4 was published in *Ramparts* (August-September 1975). Material on the *Mayagüez* incident is added from my "U.S. Involvement in Vietnam," *Bridge* (October 1975).

Chapter 5 (co-authored with Edward S. Herman) appeared in *Inquiry*, March 19, 1979, in a somewhat different form.

Parts of the original version of Chapter 6 appeared, somewhat edited, in *Inquiry*, April 7, 1980. The full original appeared in Spanish translation in

Bicicleta (Spain; April 1980), and in Italian translation in *Il Ponte* (August 1980).

Chapter 7 appeared in Japanese translation in my book *Intellectuals and the State* (Tokyo: TBS-Britannica) in 1981. The English text appears in *Philosophy and Social Action* (India), nos. 3–4 (1980), and in Spanish translation in *Bicicleta* (May–June 1980).

Chapter 8 appears in Spanish translation in *Bicicleta* (March 1981) and in Mexico in *Nexos* (May 1981), and in *Our Generation* (Canada), Summer 1981. A somewhat different English version appears in *Socialist Review* (July–August 1981).

Parts of Chapter 9 appeared in *Socialist Revolution* (now *Socialist Review;* June 1975), followed by a critical response by Fuad Faris and my response (April–June 1976). Parts appear in Uri Davis, A. Mack, and N. Yuval-Davis, eds., *Israel and the Palestinians* (London: Ithaca Press, 1975). The Afterword is new.

Chapter 10 appeared in the *New York Arts Journal* (Spring 1977), followed by a critical response by David Schoenbrun and my response (September–October 1977).

Chapter 11 appeared in French translation in *Le Monde diplomatique* (April 1977); and in English in *Seven Days,* April 11, 1977.

Parts of Chapter 12 appeared in the *Nation,* July 22, 1978; the rest in *Seven Days,* September 8, 1978. The entire review-article was published under the title "War after War" in *Gazelle Review of Literature on the Middle East* (London; 1978).

Chapter 13 was published as a pamphlet of the Asian Center (New York; 1980), and in *Southeast Asia Chronicle* (August 1980), under the title "A curtain of ignorance." The Afterword is new.

Chapter One

INTELLECTUALS AND THE STATE (1977)

THERE ARE TWO BASIC QUESTIONS that I would like to consider in these remarks, the first rather abstract, the second more topical.

First, I would like to discuss the roles that intellectuals often tend to play in modern industrial society, a topic that has been a lively one at least since the Dreyfus affair, when the term "intellectual" came into common usage as a committed group of intellectuals took an important stand on an issue of justice. In this context I also want to comment on the engagement of American intellectuals in the ideological battles relating to World War I, when a prominent group of liberal intellectuals including John Dewey, Walter Lippmann, and others described themselves as a new class, engaged for the first time in applying intelligence to the design of national policy.

Second, I want to turn to some of the contemporary contributions of the "new class"—specifically, their contribution to constructing the moral and ideological framework that will be appropriate to the tasks of the American state in the "post-Vietnam era." I will try to show that some rather striking features of contemporary ideology can be understood in the terms suggested in the preliminary, more general discussion.

Before proceeding, I would like to enter several caveats. In the second part of this talk I will concentrate on the United States—in part, because I know it better, but also because of its predominant influence in world affairs since World War II. But much of what I have to say has direct bearing, I think, on other industrial democracies. Furthermore, time being short, I am going to omit many important nuances and draw lines more sharply than the full range of complexity warrants, trying to isolate some "ideal cases" that can serve to organize and facilitate our understanding of more complex phenomena, much as one does in the natural sciences, for example. Though such an effort carries risks, it is indispensable if we hope to proceed beyond a kind of "natural history" to some understanding of what lies behind a confusing range of events, acts, and pronouncements. Finally, I will, reluctantly, have to omit the documentation that is certainly required to make a case that I will only sketch in outline. I have tried to do this elsewhere in books and articles.

What are the typical roles of the intelligentsia in modern industrial society? There is a classic analysis of this question in the works of Bakunin, about a century ago. He may have been the first to suggest the concept of a "new class" in reference to those who were coming to control technical knowledge. In a series of analyses and predictions that may be among the most remarkable within the social sciences, Bakunin warned that the new class will attempt to convert their access to knowledge into power over economic and social life.[1] They will try to create

> the reign of *scientific intelligence*, the most aristocratic, despotic, arrogant and elitist of all regimes. There will be a new class, a new hierarchy of real and counterfeit scientists and scholars, and the world will be divided into a minority ruling in the name of knowledge, and an immense ignorant majority. And then, woe unto the mass of ignorant ones.

Though a passionately committed socialist himself, Bakunin did not spare the socialist movement the force of his critique: "The organization and the rule of the society by socialist savants," he wrote, "is the worst of all despotic governments." The leaders of the Communist party will proceed "to liberate [the people] in their own way," concentrating "all administrative power in their own strong hands, because the ignorant people are in need of a strong guardianship . . . [the mass of the people will be] under the direct command of the state engineers, who will constitute the new privileged political-scientific class." For the proletariat, the new regime "will, in reality, be nothing but a barracks" under the control of a Red bureaucracy. But surely it is "heresy against common sense and historical experience" to believe that "a group of individuals, even the most intelligent and best-intentioned, would be capable of becoming the mind, the soul, the directing and unifying will of the revolutionary movement and the economic organization of the proletariat of all lands." In fact, the "learned minority, which presumes to express the will of the people," will rule in "a pseudo-representative government" that will "serve to conceal the domination of the masses by a handful of privileged elite."

As for liberal capitalism, it develops in the direction of increased state centralization, while the "sovereign people" will submit to the "intellectual governing minority, who, while claiming to represent the people, unfailingly exploits them." "The people," Bakunin wrote, "will feel no better if the stick with which they are being beaten is labelled 'the people's stick.'" Under either evolving system of governance—state socialist or state capitalist—"the shrewd and educated" will gain privileges while "regimented workingmen and women will sleep, wake, work, and live to the beat of a drum."

A century later, Bakunin's new class has become a grim feature of contemporary reality. State centralization has indeed proceeded in capitalist society, along with and always closely linked to centralization of ownership and control in the economic institutions that set many of the basic conditions for social life. By the turn of the century there were already close links in the United States between corporate ownership and control on the one hand, and university-based programs in technology and industrial management on the other, a development studied in recent work by David Noble.[2] And in more recent times there has been an increasing flow of technical intelligentsia through universities, government, foundations, management, major law firms that represent broad interests of corporate capitalism, and in general through the tightly linked network of planning and social control. Spokesmen for the new class never tire of telling us how the people rule, while concealing the real workings of power. The real and counterfeit scientists have been responsible for innumerable atrocities themselves and for the legitimation of many others, while wielding the people's stick.

I need not dwell on the performance of Bakunin's Red bureaucracy when they have succeeded in centralizing state power in their hands, riding to power on a wave of popular movements that they have proceeded to dismantle and finally destroy.

I might also mention in this connection the penetrating studies by the Dutch Marxist scientist Anton Pannekoek.[3] Writing in the late 1930s and then under the German occupation, he discussed "the social ideals growing up in the minds of the intellectual class now that it feels its increasing importance in the process of production: a well-ordered organization of production for use under the direction of technical and scientific experts." These ideals, he pointed out, are shared by the intelligentsia in capitalist societies and by Communist intellectuals, whose aim is "to bring to power, by means of the fighting force of the workers, a layer of leaders who then establish planned production by means of State-Power." They develop the theory that "the talented energetic minority takes the lead and the incapable majority follows and obeys." Their natural social ideology is some version of state socialism, "a design for reconstructing society on the basis of a working class such as the middle class sees it and knows it under capitalism"—tools of production, submissive, incapable of rational decision. To this mentality, "an economic system where the workers are themselves masters and leaders of their work . . . is identical with anarchy and chaos." But state socialism, as conceived by the intellectuals, is a plan of social organization "entirely different from a true disposal by the producers over production," true socialism, a system in which workers are "masters of the factories, masters of their own labor, to conduct it at their own will."

The emergence of a new class of scientific intelligentsia has been extensively discussed—though with a very different attitude towards the phenomenon described—by Western analysts of "postindustrial society"; for example, Daniel Bell, who believes that "the entire complex of social prestige and social status will be rooted in the intellectual and scientific communities," [4] or John Kenneth Galbraith, who holds that "power in economic life has over time passed from its ancient association with land to association with capital and then on, in recent times, to the composite of knowledge and skills which comprises the technostructure." [5] Both have expressed high hopes for the new "educational and scientific estate," Bakunin's new class, ruling in the name of knowledge. But I must emphasize that Pannekoek did not conclude that since the technical intelligentsia make decisions on behalf of others in capitalist democracy, they therefore hold power.

One may, I think, note a kind of convergence, in this regard at least, between so-called socialist and capitalist societies. Lenin proclaimed in 1918 that "*unquestioning submission* to a single will is absolutely necessary for the success of labour processes that are based on large-scale machine-industry . . . today the Revolution demands, in the interests of socialism, that the masses *unquestioningly obey the single will* of the leaders of the labour process" (emphasis in original); "there is not the least contradiction between soviet (i.e., socialist) democracy and the use of dictatorial power by a few persons." And two years later: "The transition to practical work is connected with individual authority. This is the system which more than any other assures the best utilization of human resources." [6]

Consider, in comparison, the following dictum:

> Vital decision-making, particularly in policy matters, must remain at the top. God—the Communist commentators to the contrary—is clearly democratic. He distributes brain power universally, but He quite justifiably expects us to do something efficient and constructive with that priceless gift. That is what management is all about. Its medium is human capacity, and its most fundamental task is to deal with change. It is the gate through which social, political, economic, technological change, indeed change in every dimension, is rationally spread through society . . . the real threat to democracy comes not from overmanagement, but from undermanagement. To undermanage reality is not to keep it free. It is simply to let some force other than reason shape reality . . . if it is not reason that rules man, then man falls short of his potential.

In short, reason demands submission to centralized management: This is true freedom, the realization of democracy. Apart from the reference to God, it would be hard to tell whether the quote is from Lenin, or—as indeed is the case—Robert McNamara, a typical example of the scientific and educational estate in state capitalist democracy.[7]

Science has also been called upon to explain the need for submission to the talented leadership of those whom Isaiah Berlin has called "the secular priesthood." For example, Edward Thorndike, one of the founders of experimental psychology and a person with great influence on American schools, solemnly explained in 1939 the following grand discovery:

> It is the great good fortune of mankind that there is a substantial positive correlation between intelligence and morality, including good will toward one's fellows. Consequently our superiors in ability are on the average our benefactors, and it is often safer to trust our interests to them than to ourselves. No group of men can be expected to act one-hundred percent in the interest of mankind, but this group of the ablest men will come nearest to the ideal.

Earlier he had explained that "the argument for democracy is not that it gives power to men without distinction, but that it gives greater freedom for ability and character to attain power,"[8] as we have repeatedly witnessed.

Think what this means in a capitalist democracy. Some complex of characteristics tends to enhance wealth and power (it also doesn't hurt to have rich parents), including political power, which is closely linked to success in the private economy. This collection of characteristics—some combination of avarice, lack of concern for one's fellows, energy and determination, a certain style of cleverness, etc.—is "nearest to the ideal," and democracy permits the people so endowed to rise to power, which is good, because they are our benefactors, given the correlation between intelligence and morality.

Suppose we add a standard assumption that is central to many of the modern justifications for meritocracy, and to much of economic theory as well: People labor only for reward; the natural state for humans is to vegetate. It then follows that talent should be rewarded, for the benefit of all, since otherwise the talented and moral (recall the correlation) will not bestir themselves to act as our benefactors. The message, for the great mass of the population, is straightforward: "You are better off if you are poor. Accept powerlessness and poverty for your own good." One might note the importance of this lesson when other techniques of social control fail, for example, the promise of endless growth, which has served for a long period to induce conformity and obedience.

The secular priesthood has noticed that democracy poses some problems for the realization of the rule of reason, in which everyone submits willingly to their benefactors. One problem is that in a democracy, the voice of the people is heard. Therefore, it is necessary to find ways to ensure that the people's voice speaks the right words. The problem was faced in an interesting essay by the well-known political scientist Harold Lasswell in the early 1930s.[9] He wrote that the rise of democracy—or, as he put it, "the displacement of cults of simple obedience by democratic assertiveness"—"complicated the problem of eliciting concerted action," a problem perceived early by "military writers." The spread of schooling "did not release the masses from ignorance and superstition but altered the nature of both and compelled the development of a whole new technique of control, largely through propaganda." With the rise of democracy, "propaganda attains eminence as the one means of mass mobilization which is cheaper than violence, bribery or other possible control techniques." Propaganda, he explained, "as a mere tool is no more moral or immoral than a pump handle." It may be employed for good ends or bad. "Propaganda is surely here to stay; the modern world is peculiarly dependent upon it for the coordination of atomized components in times of crisis and for the conduct of large-scale 'normal' operations." It is "certain that propaganda will in time be viewed with fewer misgivings." He went on to point out that "the modern conception of social management is profoundly affected by the propagandist outlook" in its task of eliciting "concerted action for public ends." The propagandist outlook respects individuality, but

> this regard for men in the mass rests upon no democratic dogmatisms about men being the best judges of their own interests. The modern propagandist, like the modern psychologist, recognizes that men are often poor judges of their own interests. . . . With respect to those adjustments which do require mass action the task of the propagandist is that of inventing goal symbols which serve the double function of facilitating adoption and adaptation.

Management must cultivate "sensitiveness to those concentrations of motive which are implicit and available for rapid mobilization when the appropriate symbol is offered." The modern propagandist "is able and anxious to apply the methods of scientific observation and analysis to the processes of society" and "to direct his creative flashes to final guidance in action," since in creating symbols he is "no phrasemonger but a promoter of overt acts."

It would seem to follow that no moral issue is posed when a benevolent authority manipulates "men in the mass" by appropriate forms of propaganda. This Leninist idea is a typical doctrine of the new class and is an example of the convergence of which I spoke earlier. (See note 23.)

In fact, in a capitalist democracy the pump handle will generally be operated by those who control the economy, and it comes as no great surprise to learn that they have fully comprehended this message, most notably in the "public relations" industry which has flourished ever since the potential for indoctrination was effectively demonstrated during the First World War. "Public relations," we learn from a leading spokesman for industry, "is nothing more than the mass production of personal good manners and good morals." [10] And a vast effort has been expended to ensure that Americans have both—as these are defined by our benefactors. [11]

The leading figure in the public relations field, Edward Bernays, has had interesting things to say about these matters. [12] "Leaders . . . of major organized groups, . . . with the aid of technicians . . . who have specialized in utilizing the channels of communication, have been able to accomplish . . . scientifically what we have termed 'the engineering of consent,' " he explained in the *Annals of the American Academy of Political and Social Sci-*

ence in 1947—at a time when a vast propaganda campaign was undertaken by government and industry, which has not flagged since. The phrase "engineering of consent," [13] Bernays continues,

> quite simply means the application of scientific principles and tried practices to the task of getting people to support ideas and programs. . . . The engineering of consent is the very essence of the democratic process, the freedom to persuade and suggest. . . . A leader frequently cannot wait for the people to arrive at even general understanding . . . democratic leaders must play their part in . . . engineering . . . consent to socially constructive goals and values.

Once again, it is business and its representatives in government who will, in practice, judge what is "socially constructive."

Who has this freedom to persuade and to suggest, which is the essence of the democratic process? Evidently, it is not evenly distributed—nor should it be, given the correlation between intelligence and morality. One estimate of how the freedom to persuade is distributed appeared in the leading business journal *Fortune* in 1949, where it was claimed that "nearly half of the contents of the best newspapers is derived from publicity releases; nearly all the contents of the lesser papers . . . are directly or indirectly the work of [public relations] departments." The editors went on to make the now familiar point that "it is as impossible to imagine a genuine democracy without the science of persuasion as it is to think of a totalitarian state without coercion." [14] Indoctrination is to democracy what coercion is to dictatorship—naturally, since the stick that beats the people is labeled "the people's stick."

With such insights as these we begin to gain a better picture of one major role of the intelligentsia in a capitalist democracy. Contrary to the illusions of the postindustrial theorists, power is not shifting into their hands—though one should not underestimate the significance of the flow of trained manpower from university to government and management for many decades. But the more significant function of the intelligentsia is ideological control. They are, in Gramsci's phrase, "experts in legitimation." They must ensure that beliefs are properly inculcated, beliefs that serve the interests of those with objective power, based ultimately on control of capital in the state capitalist societies. The well-bred intelligentsia operate the pump handle, conducting mass mobilization in a way that is, as Lasswell observed, cheaper than violence or bribery and much better suited to the image of democracy.

I have been speaking so far only of those who are sometimes called the "responsible intellectuals," those who associate themselves with external power or even try to share in it or capture it. There are, of course, those who combat it, try to limit it, to undermine and dissolve it, to help clear the way for an effective democracy which, in my view at least, must incorporate the leading principles that Pannekoek outlined. There is a revealing analysis of these several roles in the major publication of the Trilateral Commission, a private organization of elites of the United States, Western Europe, and Japan founded at David Rockefeller's initiative in 1973, which achieved some notoriety when its members captured the posts of President, Vice-President, National Security Adviser, Secretaries of State, Defense, and Treasury, and a host of lesser offices in the 1976 U.S. presidential elections.

This study, called *The Crisis of Democracy*, is the work of scholars from the three trilateral regions.[15] The crisis of democracy to which they refer arises from the fact that during the 1960s, segments of the normally quiescent masses of the population became politically mobilized and began to press their demands, thus creating a crisis, since naturally these demands cannot be met, at least without a significant redistribution of wealth and power, which is not to be contemplated. The trilateral scholars, quite consistently, therefore urge more "moderation in democracy."

The lesson is similar to one offered to the underdeveloped world by another distinguished political scientist, Ithiel de Sola Pool, who explained in 1967 that

> in the Congo, in Vietnam, in the Dominican Republic, it is clear that order depends on somehow compelling newly mobilized strata to return to a measure of passivity and defeatism from which they have recently been aroused by the process of modernization. At least temporarily, the maintenance of order requires a lowering of newly acquired aspirations and levels of political activity.

This is not mere dogma, but what "we have learned in the past thirty years of intensive empirical study of contemporary societies."[16] The trilateral scholars are proposing, in essence, that the same lesson be applied in the centers of industrial capitalism as well.

Earlier precedents come to mind at once—for example, medieval attitudes towards the third estate. The "qualities which bring credit to 'this low estate of Frenchmen' " are "humility, diligence, obedience to the king, and docility in bowing 'voluntarily to the pleasure of the lords' "—Huizinga's characterization, citing the chronicler Chastellain.[17] Correspondingly, on the underdeveloped periphery of modern civilization, the natural state of passivity and defeatism must be restored. And at home, in the version of democracy expounded by the trilateral theorists, the commoners may petition the state, but with moderation. It is unnecessary for these scholars to stress that other social groups, somewhat better placed, will not temper their demands, though the American contributor does recall, with a trace of nostalgia perhaps, that before the crisis of democracy had erupted, "Truman had been able to govern the country with the cooperation of a relatively small number of Wall Street lawyers and bankers," a happy state to which we may return if the commoners cease their indecent clamor.

It is in this context that the Trilateral Commission study turns to the intelligentsia, who, according to their analysis, come in the familiar two varieties: (1) the "technocratic and policy-oriented intellectuals," responsible, serious, and constructive; (2) the "value-oriented intellectuals," a sinister grouping who pose a serious danger to democracy as they "devote themselves to the derogation of leadership, the challenging of authority, and the unmasking and delegitimation of established institutions"—even going so far as to delegitimate the institutions that are responsible for "the indoctrination of the young"—while sowing confusion and stirring dissatisfaction in the minds of the populace.

Speaking of our enemies, we despise the technocratic and policy-oriented intellectuals as "commisars" and "apparatchiks," and honor the value-oriented intellectuals as the "democratic dissidents." At home, the values are reversed. Ways must be found to control the value-oriented intellectuals so that democracy can survive, with the citizenry reduced to the apathy and obedience that become them, and with the commisars free to conduct the serious work of social management. The intellectual backgrounds of all of this, I have already discussed.

It is interesting that the term "value-oriented" should be used to refer to those who challenge the structure of authority, with the implication that it is improper, offensive, and dangerous to be guided by such values as truth and honesty: The trilateral scholars nowhere attempt to show that the value-oriented intellectuals they so fear and disdain are wrong or misguided in their conclusions. It is also striking that subservience to the state and its doctrines is not regarded as "a value," but merely the natural commitment of the intelligentsia, or at least their more honorable representatives.

At the outset I mentioned the Dreyfusards and the liberal American intellectuals who rallied to the state during the First World War. It is fair, I think, to regard these two groups as early variants of the two categories of intellectuals distinguished in the Trilateral Commission study.

Those who denounced the injustice of the state at the time of the Dreyfus affair by no means dominated French intellectual life, as Henk Wesseling reminds us in a recent study.[18] They typify the "value-oriented intellectuals" who have always been such a trial to their more sober colleagues.

Consider, in contrast, the group of liberal pragmatists in John Dewey's circle during World War I.[19] In December 1916, the editor of the *New Republic* wrote to President Wilson's leading adviser, Colonel House, that their most fervent wish was "to back the President up in his work" and "be the faithful and helpful interpreters of what seems to be one of the greatest enterprises ever undertaken by an American president." At the time, Wilson was calling for "peace without victory"—and a few months later, for victory without peace. By then, his leading enterprise was to guide a divided nation into the European war. The intellectuals proved to be faithful and helpful interpreters of this great enterprise. According to their own estimate, which is no doubt exaggerated, "the effective and decisive work on behalf of the war has been accomplished by . . . a class which must be comprehensively but loosely described as the 'intellectuals' " (*New Republic*, April 7, 1917). The nation entered the war "under the influence of a moral verdict reached after the utmost deliberation by the more thoughtful members of the community"—the secular priesthood, the technocratic and policy-oriented intellectuals, the commissars. The latter term is in fact rather apt. The techniques of propaganda described by later scholars were developed and applied with much success during World War I and led to the explosive growth of the public relations field shortly after—though for accuracy, I should add that "the more thoughtful members of the community" were as much the victims of the highly effective British propaganda machine, with its manufacture of "Hun atrocities," as they were purveyors of war propaganda, proceeding (in their own words) to "impose their will upon a reluctant or indifferent majority."

It would only be fair to commend the BBC for returning the favor in October and November of 1977, with its presentation on the Third Programme of a series entitled "Many Reasons Why: The American Involvement in Vietnam." [20] Demonstrating its taste for symmetry, the BBC has concocted an account that is certain to delight the American propaganda services no less than the response of the more thoughtful members of the American intellectual community must have warmed the hearts of such men as Sir Gilbert Parker, who headed the American section of the British propaganda bureau in World War I, and who was able to gloat about "the permeation of the American Press by British influence" in his secret reports to the British Cabinet.[21]

The services rendered to the state by the academic professions during World War I are surveyed in a recent work by Carol Gruber.[22] Historians were particularly keen to be mobilized. A National Board for Historical Service (NBHS) was founded by a group of historians "to bring into useful operation, in the present emergency, the intelligence and skill of the historical workers of the country," so one of them (A. C. McLaughlin) wrote in *The Dial* in May 1917. One of the founders of the NBHS, Frederic L. Paxson, later described its activity as "historical engineering, explaining the issues of the war that we might the better win it"—an early example of "the engineering of consent." The press was also mobilized. An NBHS study of the German press concluded that the "voluntary co-operation of the newspaper publishers of America resulted in a more effective standardization of the information and arguments presented to the American people, than existed under the nominally strict military control exercised in Germany." The main government commission (Creel Commission) established to direct wartime propaganda made effective use of the services of American scholars. Among its achievements was a pamphlet entitled *The German-Bolshevik Conspiracy*, which employed documents generally regarded as forgeries in Europe (and shown to be forgeries forty years later by George Kennan) to "demonstrate" that the Bolsheviks were paid agents of the German General Staff, who had materially aided them in coming to power. In later years too, historians were to advocate "historical engineering" in the war against the Bolshevik menace. In his presidential address to the American Historical Association in 1949, Conyers Read explained that

> we must clearly assume a militant attitude if we are to survive. . . . Discipline is the essential prerequisite of every effective army whether it march under the Stars and Stripes or under the Hammer and Sickle. . . . Total war, whether it be hot or cold, enlists everyone and calls upon every-

one to assume his part. The historian is no freer from this obligation than the physicist. . . . This sounds like the advocacy of one form of social control as against another. In short, it is.

The long, sorry record has been surveyed in an important unread monograph by Jesse Lemisch.[23]

Not all of the scholars who lent their services during World War I were acclaimed. Thorstein Veblen, for example, "prepared a report demonstrating that the shortage of farm labor in the Midwest could be met by ending the harassment and persecution of the members of the Industrial Workers of the World (IWW)," Carol Gruber points out, but "he also, however, together with his assistant, was fired for his pains" from his position as statistical expert for the Food Administration.

Then too there were "value-oriented intellectuals" who did not see the light. Randolph Bourne is the best-known case. We may recall how he was dropped by the *New Republic,* and forced out of an editorial position on *The Dial* by John Dewey, one indication of his displeasure over Bourne's penetrating criticism of the liberal intellectuals who were working to sell the war, Bourne felt, in the interests of "an opportunist programme of state-socialism at home"—with the secular priesthood in command—"and a league of benevolently-imperialistic nations abroad."

Clarence Karier goes on to observe that John Dewey had much contempt for the "pacifists" who, in his words "wasted rather than invested their potentialities when they turned so vigorously to opposing entrance" into the war instead of working for attainable goals within the growing chauvinist consenus (July 1917). In a more abstract discussion of "force and coercion," Dewey had expressed his view that if pacifists "would change their tune from the intrinsic immorality of the use of coercive force to the comparative inefficiency and stupidity of existing methods of using force, their good intentions would be more fruitful." Continuing, Dewey explained:

Squeamishness about force is the mark not of idealistic but of moonstruck morals. . . . The criterion of value lies in the relative efficiency and economy of the expenditure of force as a means to an end. With advance of knowledge, refined, subtle and indirect use of force is always replacing coarse, obvious and direct methods of applying it. This is the explanation to the ordinary feeling against the use of force. What is thought of as brutal, violent, immoral, is a use of physical agencies which are gross, sensational and evident on their own account, in cases where it is possible to employ with greater economy and less waste means which are comparatively imperceptible and refined.

His general point was that "the only question which can be raised about the justification of force is that of comparative efficiency and economy in its use." [24] This in April 1916. A good, sober, pragmatic evaluation, which we have heard in other contexts since, without Dewey's qualifications.

Not surprisingly, Dewey felt that the war had taught valuable lessons in this regard. He wrote that "the one great thing that the war has accomplished, it seems to me, of a permanent sort, is the enforcement of a psychological and educational lesson. . . . It has proved now that it is possible for human beings to take hold of human affairs and manage them, to see an end which has to be gained, a purpose which must be fulfilled, and deliberately and intelligently to go to work to organize the means, the resources and the methods of accomplishing those results." Now that this lesson had been learned, "the real question with us will be one of effectively discerning whether the intelligent men of the community really want to bring about a better reorganized social order." [25] The war had revealed the possibilities of intelligent administration, and it is now the responsibility of the intelligent men of the community to rise to the occasion, organizing intelligence for the design of a more benign state capitalist social order, with the economical and refined use of force to achieve socially desirable ends.

I have so far been discussing the first of my two topics, the roles played by intellectuals, focusing on the role of commissar versus dissident, technocratic and policy-oriented versus value-oriented intellectual. Now I would like to apply these remarks to the contemporary world. First, however, a few general comments, to set the stage, as I see it.

The United States emerged from World War II with unparalleled wealth and power. Quite naturally, state power was employed to construct an international order—extensive, though not all-encompassing—that would satisfy the needs of the masters of the domestic economy. Equally naturally, this is not what one reads in most history books, though the basic facts are, I believe, well established, and the business press is often quite straightforward about the matter. [26]

In general, the postwar global enterprise was a stunning success, though there were reversals—the most dramatic in Southeast Asia. In the course of a "limited war," which proved quite costly, U.S. power declined somewhat relative to its industrial rivals. A major task of the state and its propagandists has been and remains to reconstruct the domestic and international order that was bruised, though never undermined, by the bloody events in Indochina. I will concentrate here only on the reconstruction of the ideological system, since that is the province of the intelligentsia; more central tasks are delegated elsewhere.

In the United States, the prevailing version of the "white man's burden" has been the doctrine, carefully nurtured by the intelligentsia, that the United States, alone among the powers of modern history, is not guided in its international affairs by the perceived material interests of those with domestic power, but rather wanders aimlessly, merely reacting to the initiatives of others, while pursuing abstract moral principles: the Wilsonian principles of freedom and self-determination, democracy, equality, and so on. Responsible controversy proceeds within a narrow spectrum: At one extreme, there are those who laud the United States for its unique benevolence; at the other, we find the "realist" critics—George Kennan and Hans Morgenthau, for example—who deplore the foolishness of American policy and believe that we should not be so obsessively moralistic but should pursue the national interest in a rational way.

The work of the realist critics gives the deepest insight into the dominant ideology and dramatically reveals the extent of its penetration. In the early 1960s, Hans Morgenthau—who was near the outer limits of responsible criticism and, to his credit, passed beyond them a few years later—could write that the United States has a "transcendent purpose," namely, "the establishment of equality in freedom in America," and indeed throughout the world, since "the arena within which the United States must defend and promote its purpose has become world-wide." "America has become the Rome and Athens of the Western world, the foundation of its lawful order and the fountainhead of its culture," though "America does not know this." [27]

To be sure, Morgenthau recognizes certain defects both at home and abroad—in Central America and the Philippines, for example. But he chides those critics who rely on the ample historical record to deny the "transcendent purpose" of America and who claim that the United States is very much like every other power—what is often described (though not by Morgenthau) as a "radical critique," a revealing choice of words. Such critics, according to Morgenthau, are guilty of a simple error of logic: "To reason thus is to confound the abuse of reality with reality itself." It is the unachieved "national purpose," revealed by "the evidence of history as our minds reflect it," which is the reality; the actual historical record is merely the abuse of reality.

The theological overtones are apparent, and Morgenthau is not unaware of them. He remarks that the critics, who mistake the real world for reality, have fallen into "the error of atheism, which denies the validity of religion on similar grounds." The comment is apt. There is indeed something truly religious in the fervor with which responsible American intellectuals have sought to deny plain fact and to secure their dogmas concerning American benevolence, the contemporary version of the "civilizing mission."

But the doctrines of the state religion were not able to survive the war in Vietnam, at least among large parts of the population. The result was an ideological crisis. The institutional foundations for the repeated counterrevolutionary intervention of the postwar years remained unshaken, but the doctrinal system that had served to gain popular support for the crusade against independent development had collapsed. The problem of the day has been to reconstruct it. It is a serious problem, since imperial intervention carries costs, both material and moral, which must be borne by the population. I would now like to survey some of the methods by which this problem is being faced by the secular priesthood.

The first task is to rewrite the history of the American war in Vietnam. This is relatively easy, since the press and academic scholarship have consistently held to the required mythical history, to which I will return.

A more difficult task is to shift the moral onus of the war to its victims. This seems a rather unpromising enterprise—rather as if the Nazis had attempted to blame the Jews for the crematoria. But undaunted, American propagandists are pursuing this effort too, and with some success. Things have reached the point where an American President can appear on national television and state that we owe "no debt" to the Vietnamese, because "the destruction was mutual." [28] And there is not a whisper of protest when this monstrous statement, worthy of Hitler or Stalin, is blandly produced in the midst of a discourse on human rights. Not only do we owe them no debt for having murdered and destroyed and ravaged their land, but we now may stand back and sanctimoniously blame them for dying of disease and malnutrition, deploring their cruelty when hundreds die trying to clear unexploded ordnance by hand from fields laid waste by the violence of the American state, wringing our hands in mock horror when those who were able to survive the American assault—predictably, the toughest and harshest elements—resort to oppression and sometimes massive violence, or fail to find solutions to material problems that have no analogue in Western history perhaps since the Black Death.

The only unresolved issue is the remains of American pilots missing in action, not American responsibility to help rebuild what they destroyed, if this is even possible. Worse yet, we refuse to allow others to aid them. India tried to send one hundred buffalo to Vietnam to help replenish the herds decimated by American terror, a necessity of survival for this primitive agricultural economy. This tiny gift had to be channeled through the Red Cross to avoid American retribution—cancellation of "Food for Peace" aid, in this case.[29] In Indochina peasants pull plows because the animal herds were destroyed by American bombardment. And the *Washington Post*, which concealed and supported that aggression, publishes photographs of Cambodian peasants pulling plows as an illustration of Communist atrocities. In fact, the photographs in this case are probable fabrications of Thai intelligence, so clumsy that they were rejected even by the right-wing English-language Thai press—though the European press has been less discriminating in this regard. The *Post* knew this, and knew its account of the source of the photographs to be a falsehood, but refused to publish a letter giving the documented facts that it knew to be true, let alone publicly retract its fabrications—one small example of the stream of misrepresentation that has disfigured the American (indeed Western) press with regard to postwar developments in Indochina. A good deal of this is documented elsewhere, and I will not review it here.[30] The crucial point here is the truly obscene character of the attempt to blame the victims, the denial of American responsibility, and the startling success of this campaign; and still more, the refusal to meet the elementary responsibility to offer massive reparations to help overcome the carnage.

Another task for the intelligentsia is to reduce the "lessons of the war" to the narrowest possible terms. Again, this is not very difficult, since the intellectuals always tended to construe the issues in an entirely unprincipled fashion. There is a study by a Columbia University sociologist, Charles Kadushin, that gives a good deal of insight into the facts, which are rather different from what is generally assumed.[31] He investigated attitudes of a group that he called "the American intellectual elite" in 1970, at the very peak of active opposition to the war, when colleges were closed down in opposition to the invasion of Cambodia and demonstrations swept the country. Much of his study was devoted to the war in Vietnam. The "intellectual elite" opposed the war, almost without exception. But the grounds for their opposition deserve careful attention. Kadushin identified three categories of opposition—what he called "ideological," "moral," and "pragmatic" grounds. Under "ideological" opposition to the war he includes the belief that aggression is wrong, even when conducted by the United States. Opposition on "moral" grounds is based on deaths and atrocities: The war is too bloody. "Pragmatic" opposition to the war is grounded on the feeling that we probably can't get away with it: The war is too costly; the enterprise should be liquidated as no longer worthwhile.

There are two points of interest about this analysis. First, the terminology itself. No doubt the group surveyed would have been unanimous in deploring Russian aggression in Czechoslovakia. But on what grounds? Not on "pragmatic" grounds, since it was quite successful and not very costly. Not on "moral" grounds, since casualties were few. Rather, on "ideological" grounds: that is, on grounds that aggression is wrong, even if it is relatively bloodless, costless, and successful. But would we ever refer to this as an objection on "ideological" grounds? Surely not. It is only when one challenges the divine right of the United States to intervene by force in the internal affairs of others that such sinister terms as "ideological" are invoked.

More interesting, however, is the distribution of responses. Opposition on "ideological" grounds of opposition to aggression was very limited. More objected on "moral" grounds. But to an overwhelming degree, objections were "pragmatic." Recall that this survey was taken at the height of popular opposition to the war, when, in contrast to the "intellectual elite," substantial segments of the unwashed masses had come to oppose the war on grounds of principle and even to act on their beliefs, much to the horror of more delicate souls who now explain that their sense of irony and the complexities of history kept them removed from such vulgar display. As for the survey itself, my guess would be that a similar study in Germany in 1944 might have produced comparable results.

Similar attitudes are revealed in the debate over "amnesty" for those referred to as "draft dodgers." The more compassionate feel that they should be granted absolution for their crimes, though others sternly object that they must bear some punishment at least. That the real question is the granting of "amnesty" to those who conducted the war, or the intellectual claque that supported them until it became too costly, is an observation that far transcends the limits of "responsibility" within the reigning doctrinal system. It is commonly alleged that the "draft dodgers," and the student movement on the whole, opposed the war out of fear. They were unwilling to face the terrors of the war. In fact, the leading initiative in the American resistance, which was unprecedented in scale and character, was taken by young men who could have easily escaped combat—not very difficult at the time for privileged groups—but who chose to face great risk, long imprisonment or exile, out of simple moral commitment. Similar comments apply rather generally to desertion, the resistance of the underprivileged. The common claim that student opposition to the war collapsed because of the termination of the draft, though comforting to ideologues, is also false. In fact, certain more "politicized" elements in the student movement had (foolishly in my view) come to regard opposition to the war as relatively unimportant long before the draft was ended; and mass opposition to the war quite closely reflected the degree of overt American involvement, independently of the draft. But the ideological system cannot tolerate the fact that there was a principled opposition to the war, primarily among the young, conducted with great courage, conviction, personal cost, and considerable effectiveness. Therefore it is necessary to pretend that the serious and meaningful opposition was led by sober-minded intellectuals and heroic politicians, those "thoughtful members of the community" who, like their predecessors, reached a verdict "after the utmost deliberation" and acted with dispatch to restore national policy to its proper channels.

The rewriting of this history too deserves serious attention—more than I can give it here. To illustrate with just one case, consider the current (December 10, 1977) issue of the *New Republic*, still more or less the official journal of the liberal intelligentsia. The lead editorial, entitled "The McCarthy Decade," is an ode to Eugene McCarthy, who "changed the landscape of American politics" when he challenged Lyndon Johnson in the 1968 presidential campaign. The McCarthy campaign, the editors allege, "seeded the political system with men and women schooled in dissent" and introduced "a streak of unpredictable idealism" into American political life. "The most obvious postscript to the McCarthy campaign was the ending of the Vietnam war," as McCarthy "and his cohort established a consensus on the need to end that war." The editors quote with approval John Kenneth Galbraith's statement on the aforementioned BBC program that McCarthy is "the man who deserves more credit than anybody else for bringing our involvement in the war to an end," and they proceed to laud

McCarthy for his modesty in refusing the mantle of hero. McCarthy, they conclude, "has insured that no President ever will feel again that he can carry on a war unaffected by the moral judgment of the people."

Compare this analysis with the facts. By late 1967, the mass popular movement against the war had reached a remarkable scale. Its great success was that the government had been unable to declare a national mobilization. The costs of the war were concealed, contributing to an economic crisis which, by 1968, had brought leading business and conservative circles to insist that the effort to subdue the Vietnamese be limited. The Pentagon Papers reveal that by late 1967 the scale and character of popular opposition was causing great concern to planners.[32] The Tet offensive, which shortly after undermined government propaganda claims, enhanced these fears. A Defense Department memorandum expressed the concern that increased force levels would lead to "increased defiance of the draft and growing unrest in the cities," running the risk of "provoking a domestic crisis of unprecedented proportions." Mass popular demonstrations and civil disobedience were a particular concern, so much so that the Joint Chiefs of Staff had to consider whether "sufficient forces would still be available for civil disorder control" if more troops were sent to crush the Vietnamese.

The unanticipated growth of protest and resistance was largely leaderless and spontaneous. It took place against a background of considerable hostility in the media and the political system, and of occasional violence and disruption. One can identify deeply committed activists—Dave Dellinger, for example—who worked with tireless devotion to arouse and organize the public to oppose American aggression, with its mounting and ever more visible atrocities. There were some, like Benjamin Spock, who supported the young resisters, and even a few who joined them; for example, Father Daniel Berrigan, who offered "our apologies, good friends, for the fracture of good order, the burning of paper instead of children," when he and six others destroyed draft files in Catonsville, Maryland. But one will search in vain for the contribution of Eugene McCarthy to "establishing a consensus" against the war or arousing opposition to it. In the difficult early period, he did not even rise to the level of insignificance. There were a few political figures—Ernest Gruening and Wayne Morse, for example—who condemned the escalation of the American war. McCarthy never joined them.

After the Tet offensive of January 1968, it was generally recognized that the United States must shift to a more "capital intensive" effort, relying on technology rather than manpower. The American expeditionary force was beginning to collapse from within. The American command was coming to learn a familiar lesson of colonial war: A citizen's army cannot be trusted to conduct the inevitable atrocities; such a war must be waged by professional killers. After 1968, the war dragged on for seven long years, with unspeakable barbarism and major massacres, such as Operation SPEEDY EXPRESS in the Mekong Delta in 1969. Popular opposition peaked in the early 1970s, and continued, despite press efforts to conceal U.S. initiatives, until the very end. Throughout this period, too, there was barely a whisper from Eugene McCarthy.

Why then has McCarthy been elevated to the liberal Pantheon? The reason is simple. His brief appearance in 1968 symbolizes quite accurately the opposition to the war on the part of the liberal intelligentsia. Riding to national prominence on the wave of mass opposition to the war, McCarthy slipped silently away after failing to gain the Democratic nomination at Chicago in August 1968. He did succeed, briefly, in diverting popular energies to political channels, and came close to gaining political power by exploiting the forces of a movement that he had played no part whatsoever in mobilizing. His utter cynicism was revealed with great clarity by his behavior after he lost the nomination. Had he been even minimally serious, he would have made use of his undeserved prestige as a "spokesman" for the peace movement that he had so shamelessly exploited, to press for an end to the American war. But little more was heard from McCarthy, who demonstrated by his silence that he cared as little for the issue of the American war as he did for his youthful supporters who were bloodied by police riots in the streets of Chicago as he was attempting to win the Democratic candidacy, through their efforts on his behalf. He is, in short, a proper figure for canonization by the liberal intelligentsia.

The general attitudes of this group are reflected in the material now being produced on the "lessons of the war." To cite just one of many examples, the well-known Asian specialist Edwin Reischauer of Harvard writes that

> the real lesson of the Vietnam war is the tremendous cost of attempting to control the destiny of a Southeast Asian country against the cross-currents of nationalism. Southeast Asia simply is not open to external control at a cost that would make this a feasible proposition for any outside power.[33]

The clear implication is that if the costs were less, the effort to impose "external control" would be quite legitimate—if exercised by the United States, that is; obviously not by China or Russia. The United States, in short, is once again unique: The obligations of the U.N. Charter, though part of "the supreme law of the land," do not apply to a state devoted with such selflessness and honor to the Wilsonian principles of freedom and independence.

Reischauer proceeds as well to repeat familiar fantasies about the origins of the American intervention in the alleged belief that Ho Chi Minh was "merely the front-line agent" of a unified international Communism. To him, "the tragedy of U.S. involvement in Vietnam is that this picture was never really correct," not the consequences of this "involvement" for the people of Indochina, a lesser tragedy. As is standard, he chooses to ignore the substantial documentary record which reveals that planners had full awareness of the nationalist commitment of the Viet Minh and that after they had decided on intervention they sought long and hard, without success, for some evidence to establish what they needed to justify that decision: that Ho Chi Minh was a puppet of outside forces. This documentary record is plainly unacceptable, therefore eliminated from the record of sober scholarship. "Error" and "ignorance," however, are socially neutral categories, and are available for use by critics among the secular priesthood.

These examples illustrate some rather important general points about propaganda and the intelligentsia. In a totalitarian society, the mechanisms of indoctrination are simple and transparent. The state determines official truth. The technocratic and policy-oriented intellectuals parrot official doctrine, which is easily identified. In a curious way, this practice frees the mind. Internally, at least, one can identify the propaganda message and reject it. Overt expression of such rejection carries a risk; how serious the risk, and over how broad a range, depends on just how violent the state actually is.

Under capitalist democracy, the situation is considerably more complex. The press and the intellectuals are held to be fiercely independent, hypercritical, antagonistic to the "establishment," in an adversary relation to the state.[34] The trilateral analysts, for example, describe the press as a new source of national power, dangerously opposed to state authority. Reality is a little different. True, there is criticism, but a careful look will show that it remains within narrow bounds. The basic principles of the state propaganda system are assumed by the critics. In contrast to the totalitarian system, the propaganda apparatus does not merely stake out a position to which all must conform—or which they may privately oppose. Rather, it seeks to determine and limit the entire spectrum of thought: the official doctrine at one extreme, and the position of its most vocal adversaries at the other. Over the entire spectrum, the same fundamental assumptions are insinuated, though rarely expressed. They are presupposed, but not asserted. According to the press, the hawks and doves share a commitment to the fundamental unspoken principle that the United States has a legitimate right to exercise force and violence, where it chooses to do so (see Chapter 4). And the "realist" criticism of American foreign policy, which marked the outer limits of respectable controversy until the impact of the student movement forced the doors of academia to open slightly, adopts the basic assumption that U.S. foreign policy is one of benevolence—misplaced benevolence, the critics say. Across the entire spectrum of debate it is presupposed that the United States, alone in modern history, acts out of a commitment to abstract moral principles rather than rational calculation by ruling groups concerned for their material interests.

There are many other examples. The democratic system of thought control is seductive and compelling. The more vigorous the debate, the better the system of propaganda is served, since the tacit, unspoken assumptions are more forcefully implanted. An independent mind must seek to separate itself from official doctrine, and from the criticism advanced by its alleged opponents; not just from the assertions of the propaganda system, but from its tacit presuppositions as well, as expressed by critic and defender. This is a far more difficult task. Any expert in indoctrination will confirm, no doubt, that it is far more effective to constrain all possible thought within a framework of tacit assumption than to try to impose a particular explicit belief with a bludgeon. It may be that some of the spectacular achievements of the American propaganda system, where all of this has been elevated to a high art, are attributable to the method of feigned dissent practiced by the responsible intelligentsia.

A final task of the propaganda system is to restore the faith in our transcendent purpose. It is not enough to demonstrate the evil of our enemies, and to transfer to them the responsibility for the atrocities committed against them. It is also necessary to reestablish our own moral purity. Here, events have proceeded with an almost mythic quality. I do not suggest that it was planned; merely that the propaganda system rose magnificently to the presented occasions.

The drama unfolded in two acts: Act One may be entitled "Catharsis"; Act Two, "Rebirth," or "Spiritual Regeneration."

In Act One, the evil was personalized and expelled. Richard Nixon had a point when he claimed that the press was mounting an unfair campaign against him, but he failed to comprehend the role he was playing in the unfolding drama. In fact, the charges against Nixon were for behavior not too far out of the ordinary, though he erred in choosing his victims among the powerful, a significant deviation from established practice.[35] He was never charged with the serious crimes of his Administration: the "secret bombing" of Cambodia, for example. The issue was indeed raised, but it was the secrecy of the bombing, not the bombing itself, that was held to be the crime. Again, the crucial, tacit assumption: The United States, in its majesty, has the right to bomb a defenseless peasant society—but it is wrong to mislead Congress about the matter. The secrecy of the bombing was indeed remarkable. I have been privately informed by a high military officer who was involved in planning the Cambodian "incursion" in April 1970 that even top commanders were denied photo-reconnaissance intelligence, apparently because the government was unwilling to reveal to these officers the devastation from American bombing in the countryside that they would soon traverse. But any criticism of the Nixon Administration on these grounds remains within the permissible bounds of tactical debate.

We might ask, incidentally, in what sense the bombing was "secret." Actually, the bombing was "secret" because the press refused to expose it. Like the bombing of northern Laos before it, the American attack on neutral Cambodia must have been known to the press. A few days after the Nixon-Kissinger "secret bombing" began, Prince Sihanouk—whose government was recognized by the United States—called upon the international press to denounce American attacks on peaceful villages and the murder of defenseless peasants. There was no outcry, because the press was committed to secrecy, exactly as in earlier years, when the peasants of northern Laos were mercilessly bombed, hundreds of miles from the nearest zone of combat or even supply routes. It was years later, when open season was declared on Richard Nixon, that the press had the gall to accuse him of having imposed a veil of secrecy over these atrocities—which are rarely recognized as atrocities, since even now (1977) the press prefers to believe that the attacks were directed against North Vietnamese and Viet Cong military targets.[36]

In these and other ways, Act One was successfully completed and the evil, now identified and localized, was expunged. Next the curtain rose on Act

Two: "Rebirth," the discovery of Human Rights, our new transcendent purpose. As Arthur Schlesinger explained in the *Wall Street Journal*, "In effect, human rights is replacing self-determination as the guiding value in American foreign policy." [37]

In a perverse sense he is right. That is, to the exact extent that self-determination was the guiding value in the past—in the era of Nicaragua and Cuba, Guatemala and Iran, Vietnam and Laos and Cambodia, the Dominican Republic and Chile—to exactly that extent, human rights will be our guiding value tomorrow. The fact that such sentiments can be seriously expressed, and greeted with respect, is itself a remarkable indication of the intellectual and moral degeneration that accompanies the triumph of the awesome propaganda system.

There is much more to say about these achievements, and I have not even mentioned domestic analogues that are certainly required to complete the story. But I think it is fair to say that the secular priesthood, relying on the method of feigned dissent characteristic of democratic propaganda systems, has very largely succeeded, within only a few years, in destroying the historical record and supplanting it with a more comfortable story, transferring the moral onus of American aggression to its victims, reducing the "lessons" of the war to the socially neutral categories of error, ignorance, and cost, and reconstructing a suitable doctrine of the civilizing mission of the West, with America in the lead.

To appreciate fully the range of these accomplishments, we may conduct a simple *Gedankenexperiment* along lines already suggested. Imagine that World War II had ended in a stalemate, with the Nazis driven from France and the Low Countries but remaining a major world power, intact among the ruins. Imagine that a stratum of dissenting intellectuals had emerged who criticized Hitler for his errors in attempting to wage a two-front war, destroying a valuable source of labor power with the death camps, reacting with too much brutality to the intolerable burdens placed on Germany at Versailles, and so on. How might they have proceeded to reinterpret the contemporary scene? Perhaps like this.

First, they would have explained the historic need for German power to be resurrected, perhaps invoking Martin Heidegger's theory that Germany alone can defend the classic values of humanistic civilization from the barbarians of East and West, not to speak of the hordes of Asia and Africa. They might then have turned to the situation in what they would have called "occupied Europe"; say, France, calm and peaceful until the Anglo-

American invasion of 1944 abetted by Communist-led terrorists within, and now under American occupation: Recall that Eisenhower had "supreme authority" and the "ultimate determination of where, when and how civil administration . . . shall be exercised by French citizens" under a directive from Roosevelt issued with Churchill's approval.[38] They would have observed with horror that before and during this occupation the terrorists of the resistance carried out a great massacre of collaborators, amounting to a minimum of thirty to forty thousand murders within a few months, according to the assessment of the French historian of the resistance, Robert Aron, basing himself on a detailed analysis of the French gendarmerie, and amounting to no less than 7 million killed, according to the detailed studies of Pleyber-Grandjean, whom Aron calls a "victim of the Liberation."[39] Appalled by these monstrous events, the German dissidents might even have produced a judgment not unlike that of the editor of the *New Republic*, who explained recently that "the American collapse [in Indochina] will read in history as among the ugliest of national crimes" (June 11, 1977)—not what the United States did, but its failure to persist, is criminal. Comparably, the Nazi failure to withstand the Anglo-American invasion—a foreign invasion from abroad, not a general uprising within[40]—will read in history as the ugliest of crimes, as attested by the millions of helpless victims; we may assume that the "7 million victims" story would have prevailed within the domains of Nazi influence. Continuing, these analysts might have observed with dismay the terrible suffering of the people of France and England— not to speak of Russia—in the fierce winter of 1946–47, with production stagnating and the United States unwilling even to grant a loan except under conditions that reduce Britain to American vassalage, while the massive atrocities in Greece supervised by the conquerors (see Chapter 7) would have roused them to impotent rage. Perhaps, as moral men, they might have objected to an annual reenactment of the events at Auschwitz, as indecent, much as some Americans feebly protest the annual reenactment of the Hiroshima bombing, by the pilot of the Enola Gay, for example, in October 1977 in a Texas air show, before an audience of twenty thousand admiring spectators.[41]

What we have witnessed in the United States and the West generally in the past few years is in some ways a grim parody, in the real world, of this invented nightmare. It has proceeded with little articulate protest—again, a testimony to the effectiveness of the institutions of propaganda and ideology and the notable commitment of large segments of the intelligentsia to established power, even as they occasionally combat its excesses.[42]

I mentioned before that ruling groups throughout the First World of industrial capitalism require a system of beliefs that will justify their dominance. The "North-South" conflict will not subside, and new forms of domination will have to be devised to ensure that privileged segments of Western industrial society maintain substantial control over global resources, human and material, and benefit disproportionately from this control. Thus it comes as no surprise that the reconstitution of ideology in the United States finds echoes throughout the industrial world, sometimes in surprising places. To cite only one minor example, the outstanding foreign correspondent Martin Woollacott of the *Manchester Guardian* expresses his dismay and astonishment that the Cambodian Marxists who studied in Paris never absorbed the "essential humaneness of French life and thought."[43] How this "humaneness" expressed itself in Indochina under French rule I need not discuss—those interested might turn to a gripping study by Ngo Vinh Long.[44] Nor is there any need to speak of the humaneness of Western imperialism elsewhere, or the humaneness of European civilization itself, culminating in two mass slaughters. I have already mentioned the humaneness of the Paris where these Cambodian Marxists studied, as World War II came to a bloody end; and I could have gone on to describe its humaneness a few years before, as French authorities were vigorously rounding up Jews for shipment to death camps.[45] But it is an absolute requirement for the Western system of ideology that a vast gulf be established between the civilized West, with its traditional commitment to human dignity, liberty, and self-determination, and the barbaric brutality of those who for some reason—perhaps defective genes—fail to appreciate the depth of this historic commitment, so well revealed by America's Asian wars, for example.

Over twenty years ago, a rare study of the political economy of American foreign policy was published by a group sponsored by the National Planning Association and the Woodrow Wilson Foundation.[46] They observed, quite accurately, that the primary threat of Communism is the economic transformation of the Communist powers "in ways which reduce their willingness and ability to complement the industrial economies of the West." It is the recognition of this threat that has inspired American counterrevolutionary intervention in the Third World, though the specter of Russian or Chinese aggression in Western Europe, Asia, the Middle East, Africa, and Latin America has been dangled before the public as a more acceptable threat. The problem remains, and will continue to evoke Western antagonism to independent development, which is often led by a state socialist leadership that follows the model of Bakunin's Red bureaucracy. In an era of growing material shortages and resource competition, the "North-South" conflict may lead to new forms of still unimagined horror, while those who preside over stagnating economies in the industrial societies that are unable to absorb a superfluous class of workers without appropriate skills, concerned over popular opposition to the international terrorism they organize and support, will search for ways to implement the proposals of the trilateral analysts as to how to impose passivity and obedience in the interests of something called "democracy."

Those who may be concerned about unemployment for intellectuals need not worry too much, I believe. Under circumstances such as these, there should be considerable need and ample opportunity for the secular priesthood.

Chapter Two

FOREIGN POLICY AND
THE INTELLIGENTSIA (1978)

So it would seem that our repeated interventions, covert and overt, in Latin
America and elsewhere, our brutal assault on the Vietnamese people, not to
mention our benign inattentiveness to the abolition of democracy in Greece by a
few crummy colonels wholly dependent on American arms and loans, are all
mere accidents or mistakes perhaps.

—Philip Rahv, *New York Review of Books,*
October 12, 1967

I F W E H O P E to understand anything about the foreign policy of any
state, it is a good idea to begin by investigating the domestic social
structure. Who sets foreign policy? What interests do these people represent? What is the domestic source of their power? It is a reasonable surmise that the policy that evolves will reflect the special interests of those
who design it. An honest study of history will reveal that this natural expectation is quite generally fulfilled. The evidence is overwhelming, in my
opinion, that the United States is no exception to the general rule—a thesis
that is often characterized as a "radical critique," in a curious intellectual
move to which I will return.

Some attention to the historical record, as well as common sense, leads to
a second reasonable expectation: In every society there will emerge a caste
of propagandists who labor to disguise the obvious, to conceal the actual
workings of power, and to spin a web of mythical goals and purposes, utterly
benign, that allegedly guide national policy. A typical thesis of the propaganda system is that *the nation* is an agent in international affairs, not special groups within it, and that *the nation* is guided by certain ideals and
principles, all of them noble. Sometimes the ideals miscarry, because of

error or bad leadership or the complexities and ironies of history. But any horror, any atrocity will be explained away as an unfortunate—or sometimes tragic—deviation from the national purpose. A subsidiary thesis is that the nation is not an active agent, but rather responds to threats posed to its security, or to order and stability, by awesome and evil outside forces.

Again, the United States is no exception to the general rule. If it is exceptional at all, its uniqueness lies in the fact that intellectuals tend to be so eager to promulgate the state religion and to explain away whatever happens as "tragic error" or inexplicable deviation from our most deeply held ideals. In this respect the United States is perhaps unusual, at least among the industrial democracies. In the midst of the worst horrors of the American war in Vietnam, there was always a Sidney Hook to dismiss "the unfortunate accidental loss of life" or the "unintended consequences of military action"[1] as B-52s carried out systematic carpet bombing in the densely populated Mekong Delta in South Vietnam, or other similar exercises of what Arthur Schlesinger once described as "our general program of international good will" (referring to United States Vietnam policy in 1954).[2] There are many similar examples.

Here is one case, not untypical. William V. Shannon, liberal commentator for the *New York Times*, explains how "in trying to do good, we have been living beyond our moral resources and have fallen into hypocrisy and self-righteousness."[3] A few passages convey the flavor:

> For a quarter century, the United States has been trying to do good, encourage political liberty, and promote social justice in the Third World. But in Latin America where we have traditionally been a friend and protector and in Asia where we have made the most painful sacrifices of our young men and our wealth, our relationships have mostly proved to be a recurring source of sorrow, waste and tragedy.... Thus through economic assistance and the training of anti-guerrilla army teams we have been intervening with the best of motives [in Latin America]. But benevolence, intelligence and hard work have proved not to be enough. Chile demonstrates the problem [where with the best of motives] by intervening in this complicated situation, the C.I.A. implicated the United States in the unexpected sequel of a grim military dictatorship that employs torture and has destroyed the very freedom and liberal institutions we were trying to protect.

deviation from the doctrines of the state religion. Of the two categories, the latter are probably far more effective in inculcating attitudes of obedience and in "socializing" the public.

A personal experience may be relevant at this point. Like many others who have been involved in writing and actions opposed to state policy, I am frequently asked for comments on current affairs or social and political issues by press, radio, and television in Canada, Western Europe, Japan, Latin America, and Australia—but almost never in the United States. Here, commentary is reserved for professional experts, who rarely depart from a rather narrow ideological range; as Henry Kissinger has accurately commented, in our "age of the expert" the "expert has his constituency—those who have a vested interest in commonly held opinions; elaborating and defining its consensus at a high level has, after all, made him an expert."[18] The academic profession has numerous devices to ensure that professional expertise remains "responsible," though it is true that this system of control was partially threatened in the 1960s. Since the media in the United States, in part perhaps from naiveté, conform virtually without question to the cult of expertise, there is little danger that dissident analyses will be voiced, and if they are, they are clearly labeled "dissident opinion" rather than dispassionate, hard, political analysis. This is another example of "American exceptionalism" within the world of industrial democracies.

To return to the main theme: The United States, in fact, is no more engaged in programs of international good will than any other state has been. Furthermore, it is just mystification to speak of the nation, with its national purpose, as an agent in world affairs. In the United States, as elsewhere, foreign policy is designed and implemented by narrow groups who derive their power from domestic sources—in our form of state capitalism, from their control over the domestic economy, including the militarized state sector. Study after study reveals the obvious: Top advisory and decision-making positions relating to international affairs are heavily concentrated in the hands of representatives of major corporations, banks, investment firms, the few law firms that cater to corporate interests,[19] and the technocratic and policy-oriented intellectuals who do the bidding of those who own and manage the basic institutions of the domestic society, the private empires that govern most aspects of our lives with little pretense of public accountability and not even a gesture to democratic control.

Within the nation-state, the effective "national purpose" will be articulated, by and large, by those who control the central economic institutions,

And so on. He concludes that we must observe Reinhold Niebuhr's warning that "no nation or individual, even the most righteous, is good enough to fulfill God's purposes in history"—not even the United States, that paragon of righteousness and selfless benevolence, which has been a friend and protector for so long in Nicaragua and Guatemala and had made such painful sacrifices for the peasants of Indochina in the preceding twenty-five years. We must therefore be more constrained in our efforts to "advance our moral ideals," or we will be trapped in "ironic paradoxes" as our efforts to fulfill God's purposes lead to unexpected sequels.

Had these words been written twenty years earlier, they would have been disgraceful enough. That they should appear in September 1974 surpasses belief, or would do so were it not that such depraved submissiveness to the state propaganda system is so typical of substantial segments of the liberal intelligentsia as virtually to go unnoticed.

It is commonly believed that an adversary relationship developed between the government and the intelligentsia during the Vietnam war. We read, for example, that "most American intellectuals have since Vietnam come to believe that the exercise of American power is immoral" and that a new "convergence is emerging now around [a new] objective: the dismantling of American power throughout the world."[4] This is sheer myth, akin to the belief that the media have become a "notable new source of national power," opposed to the state.[5] In fact, through the war and since, the national media remained properly subservient to the basic principles of the state propaganda system, with a few exceptions,[6] as one would expect from major corporations. They raised a critical voice when rational imperialists determined that the Vietnam enterprise should be limited or liquidated, or when powerful interests were threatened, as in the Watergate episode.[7]

As for the intellectuals, while it is true that an articulate and principled opposition to the war developed, primarily among students, it never passed quite limited bounds. Illusions to the contrary are common, and are fostered often by those who are so frightened by any sign of weakening of ideological controls that they respond with hysteria and vast exaggeration. Critics of new initiatives in strategic weapons development are commonly denounced for their "call for unilateral disarmament." Correspondingly, the call for a "pragmatic" retreat from the exuberant interventionism of earlier years is transmuted into a demand for "the dismantling of American power throughout the world."[8]

A typical version of the dominant "pragmatic" position is presented by columnist Joseph Kraft, commenting on Kissinger's diplomacy and the reaction to it:

> The balance-of-power approach was acceptable as long as it worked. More specifically, while the Vietnam war lasted, particularly while chances of an indecisive or happy end seemed open, the Kissinger diplomacy commanded general approval. But the debacle in Vietnam showed that the United States has broken with its traditional policy of selflessly supporting the good guys. It demonstrated that American policymakers had used all the dirty tricks in the game on behalf of the baddies.[9]

Note the curious reasoning: Our clients become "baddies" when they lose, and our tricks become "dirty" when they fail. Kraft's comment is characteristic in its reference to our alleged "traditional policy" and is accurate in noting that Kissinger's attempt to maintain an American client regime in South Vietnam in explicit violation of the 1973 Paris Agreements did command substantial support until events revealed that it could not succeed.[10]

In a revealing study of public attitudes towards the Vietnam war, Bruce Andrews discusses the well-documented fact that "lower-status groups" tended to be less willing than others to support government policy.[11] One reason, he suggests, is that "with less formal education, political attentiveness, and media involvement, they were saved from the full brunt of Cold War appeals during the 1950s and were, as a result, inadequately socialized into the anticommunist world view." His observation is apt. There are only two avenues of escape from the awesome American propaganda machine. One way is to escape "formal education" and "media involvement," with their commitment to the state propaganda system. The second is to struggle to extract the facts that are scattered in the flood of propaganda, while searching for "exotic" sources not considered fit for the general public—needless to say, a method available to very few.

In discussing the intellectuals, we may invoke a distinction sometimes drawn between the "technocratic and policy-oriented intellectuals" and the "value-oriented intellectuals," in the terminology of the study of the Trilateral Commission cited above.[12] The technocratic and policy-oriented intellectuals at home are the good guys, who make the system work and raise no annoying questions. If they oppose government policy, they do so on "pragmatic" grounds, like the bulk of the "American intellectual elite."

Their occasional technical objections are "hard political analysis" in trast to the "moralism" or "dreamy utopianism" of people who raise o tions of principle to the course of policy.[13] As for the value-orie intellectuals, who "devote themselves to the derogation of leadership challenging of authority, and the unmasking and delegitimation of e lished institutions," they constitute "a challenge to democratic govern which is, potentially at least, as serious as those posed in the past by the tocratic cliques, fascist movements, and communist parties," in the j ment of the trilateral scholars. Much of the current writing on "the ti troubles" in the 1960s is a variation on the same theme, and a fantastic tory" of the period is in the process of creation, to be exposed, perha the "revisionist historians" of a future generation.

A variant of the trilateral argument, not uncommon, is that the "A can commitment to democracy is being undermined by analyses—g ally from the liberal and left part of the political spectrum—which that concern for democracy has played no role in American foreign icy."[14] In fact, a strong case can be made—and often is made, by no from the left—that "it is only when her own concept of democracy, c identified with private, capitalistic enterprise, is threatened by commu [or, we may add, by mild reform, as in Guatemala, for example] tha United States] has felt impelled to demand collective action to defend to intervene outright: "There has been no serious question of her inte ing in the case of the many right-wing coups, from which, of course [anti-Communist] policy generally has benefited."[15] Is it such analys the facts which they accurately describe, that "undermine the Ame commitment to democracy," or, better, reveal how shallow is the co ment? For the statist intelligentsia, it does not matter that such analyse be correct; they are dangerous, because they "challenge the existing tures of authority" and the effectiveness of "those institutions which played the major role in the indoctrination of the young," in the tern ogy of the trilateral theorists, for whom such categories as "truth "honesty" are simply beside the point.[16]

We can distinguish two categories among the "secular priesthood" serve the state. There are, in the first place, the outright propagandist alongside them are the technocratic and policy-oriented intellectual simply dismiss any question of ends and interests served by policy a the work laid out for them, priding themselves on their "pragmatism freedom from contamination by "ideology," a term generally reserv

while the rhetoric to disguise it is the province of the intelligentsia. An Arthur Schlesinger can write, presumably without irony, that under the Carter Administration, "human rights is replacing self-determination as the guiding value in American foreign policy" (see p. 89, above). In such pronouncements we see very clearly the contribution of the technocratic and policy-oriented intellectual to what we properly call "thought control" in the totalitarian states, where obedience is secured by force rather than by density of impact. Ours is surely a more effective system, one that would be used by dictators if they were smarter. It combines highly effective indoctrination with the impression that the society really is "open," so that pronouncements conforming to the state religion are not to be dismissed out of hand as propaganda.

It should be noted that the United States *is* in certain important respects an "open society," not only in that dissident opinion is not crushed by state violence (generally; see, however, note 7), but also in the freedom of inquiry and expression, which is in many respects unusual even in comparison with other industrial democracies such as Great Britain. The United States has no Official Secrets Act, nor the heavily constraining libel laws to be found elsewhere. And in the past few years it has had an important Freedom of Information Act. But this relatively high degree of internal freedom merely highlights the treachery of the intellectuals, who cannot plead that their subordination to the state religion is compelled by force or by constraints on access to information.

Much of the writing on the "national interest" serves to obscure the basic social facts. Consider, for example, the work of Hans Morgenthau, who has written extensively and often perceptively on this topic. In a recent presentation of his views, he states that the national interest underlying a rational foreign policy "is not defined by the whim of a man or the partisanship of party but imposes itself as an objective datum upon all men applying their rational faculties to the conduct of foreign policy." He then cites in illustration such commitments as support for South Korea, containment of China, and upholding of the Monroe Doctrine. He further observes that "the concentrations of private power which have actually governed America since the Civil War have withstood all attempts to control, let alone dissolve them [and] have preserved their hold upon the levers of political decision," (*New Republic,* January 22, 1977). True, no doubt. Under such circumstances, do we expect the "national interest" as actually articulated and pursued to be simply the outcome of the application of rational faculties to objective data, or to be an expression of specific class interests? Obviously the latter, and a serious investigation of the cases Morgenthau cites will demonstrate that the expectation is amply fulfilled. The real interests of Americans were in no way advanced by "containing China" (where was it expanding?) or crushing popular forces in South Korea in the late 1940s and supporting a series of dictatorial regimes since, or ensuring that Latin America remains subordinated to the needs of U.S.-based transnational corporations—the real meaning of our upholding of the Monroe Doctrine in the modern period, or of the (Theodore) Roosevelt Corollary to the Monroe Doctrine which made it the duty of the United States, as a "civilized nation," to exercise its "international police power" in the case of "chronic wrongdoing, or an impotence which results in a general loosening of the ties of civilized society" (cf. Connell-Smith, note 15 above). But it can be argued that the interests of the "concentrations of private power" in the United States that largely dominated the world capitalist system have been advanced by this pursuit of the "national interest." The same holds generally. The idea that foreign policy is derived in the manner of physics, as an objective datum immune to class interest, is hardly credible.

Or, consider a recent analysis by Walter Dean Burnham in the journal of the Trilateral Commission.[20] He notes that the "basic functions" of the state are "the promotion externally and internally of the basic interests of the dominant mode of production and the need to maintain social harmony." The formulation is misleading. These basic functions are not a matter of metaphysical necessity but arise from specific social causes. Furthermore, the "dominant mode of production" does not have interests; rather, individuals or groups who participate in it have interests, often conflicting ones, a distinction that is no mere quibble. And since those who manage this system are also in effective control of the state apparatus, the "basic interests" pursued will tend to be theirs. There are no grounds in history or logic to suppose that these interests will coincide to any significant extent with the interests of those who participate in the dominant mode of production by renting themselves to its owners and managers.

A standard and effective device for obscuring social reality is the argument that the facts are more complex than as represented in the "simplistic theories" of the "value-oriented" critics. Note first that the charge is of course correct: The facts are always more complex than any description we may give. Faced with this contingency of empirical inquiry, we may adopt several courses: (1) We may abandon the effort; (2) we may try to record many facts in enormous detail, a course that reduces in effect to the first, for all the understanding it provides; (3) we may proceed in the manner of rational inquiry in the sciences and elsewhere to try to extract some principles that have explanatory force over a fair range, thus hoping to account for at least the major effects. Pursuing the third—i.e., the rational—approach, we will always be subject to the criticism that the facts are more complex, and if rational, we dismiss the charge as correct but irrelevant. It is instructive that we have no difficulty in adopting a rational stance when considering the behavior of official enemies. The Russian invasion of Afghanistan, for example, surely involves complexities beyond those introduced even in fairly careful analyses of contemporary Soviet international behavior, and surely beyond the standard media accounts. For example, it appears that the major guerrilla groups have been engaged in disruptive operations in Afghanistan since 1973, backed by Pakistan in an effort to destabilize the Afghan regime and bring it to accept Pakistani border claims ("international terrorism," from one point of view; cf. Lawrence Lifschultz, *Far Eastern Economic Review*, January 30, 1981). Nevertheless, such facts as these do not prevent us from focusing on the main point—the Russian invasion—though some commissar might complain that we are ignoring the complexities of history and the difficulties faced by a great power attempting to maintain order with the noblest of intentions.

Another device is the pretense—virtually a reflex reaction—that those who pursue the rational approach are invoking a "conspiracy theory," as they proceed to document the fact that elite groups with an interest in foreign policy (e.g., transnational corporations) attempt to use their power to influence it or direct it, to assume major roles in the state executive, to produce geopolitical analyses and specific programs to guarantee a favorable climate for business operations, etc. With equal logic, one could argue that an analyst of General Motors who concludes that its managers try to maximize profits (instead of selflessly laboring to satisfy the needs of the public) is adopting a conspiracy theory—perhaps business propagandists actually take this stance. Once some analysis is labeled "a conspiracy theory" it can be relegated to the domain of flat-earth enthusiasts and other cranks, and the actual system of power, decision-making, and global planning is safely protected from scrutiny.

A related claim is that critical analysis of the ideological system is a form of paranoia.[21] As noted, it would not be surprising to find in any society a pervasive and systematic bias in the treatment of foreign affairs: Crimes of the state (which can be stopped) are ignored or downplayed, while the spotlight is focused on crimes of official enemies (about which little can be done). In the former category, standards of evidence must match those of physics; in the latter, any fanciful construction will do. In the extreme case, the Soviet press effaces state crimes completely while trumpeting such "facts" as U.S. germ warfare in Korea. Suppose that one documents the expected pattern in the case of the United States. This obviously reveals an extreme form of paranoia. With regard to the first category, it is unfair, ridiculous, to expect the media to be able to discover an eyewitness account of U.S. bombing in northern Laos in *Le Monde* (even when it is brought to their attention), or a Sihanouk press conference calling on the international press to condemn the bombing of Khmer peasants in March 1969 (besides, he didn't specifically say "B-52s" so suppression was legitimate) or a subsequent White Paper of the Sihanouk government on U.S. and U.S.-backed attacks on neutral Cambodia, or Timorese refugees in Lisbon; or to explore the relation between U.S. policies and state terror, starvation and slavery in Latin America, etc. With regard to the second category, the standard line is still more intriguing. Someone who suggests normal standards of adherence to evidence thereby falls into the category of "apologist for atrocities," "defender of the honor of Hanoi," etc. The suggestion that facts matter is easily transmuted into another service for the propagandist. It is not gratifying to the ego merely to march in a parade; therefore those who join in ritual condemnation of an official enemy must show that they are engaged in a courageous struggle against powerful forces that defend it. Since these rarely exist, even on a meager scale, they must be concocted; if nothing else is at hand, those who propose a minimal concern for fact will do. The system that has been constructed enables one to lie freely with regard to the crimes, real or alleged, of an official enemy, while suppressing the systematic involvement of one's own state in atrocities, repression, or aggression on the grounds that the facts are more complex than the emotional and naive critics believe (an exception is tolerated if some evil or misguided individual can be identified as responsible for policy, so that institutional critique is deflected). Given that those who do not accept standard doctrine—e.g., that of the "American intellectual elite" discussed above—have virtually no access to a general audience and that little is required in the way of argument or credible evidence from those of a higher degree of doctrinal purity, the farce plays quite well. It is a system of no small degree of elegance, and effectiveness.

Attempting to pursue a rational course, let us consider American foreign policy since World War II. We are faced at once with some striking features of the world that emerged from the wreckage of the war. Primary among them is the enormous preponderance of American power with respect to the other industrial societies, and *a fortiori*, the rest of the world. During the war, most of the industrial world was destroyed or severely damaged, while industrial production rose dramatically in the United States. Furthermore, long before, the United States had become the leading industrial society, with unparalleled internal resources, natural advantages and scale, and a reasonably high degree of social cohesion. It was natural to expect, under these circumstances, that the United States would use its enormous power in an effort to organize a global system, and it is uncontroversial that this is exactly what happened, though the question "What were the guiding principles?" is indeed controversial. Let us consider these principles.

Where should we look to discover some formulation of them? In a totalitarian society this would pose problems, but the United States really is open in this respect, and there is considerable documentary evidence concerning the vision of the postwar world developed by the very people who were to play the major part in constructing it.

One obvious documentary source is the series of memoranda of the War and Peace Studies Project of the Council on Foreign Relations (CFR) during the war. Participants included top government planners and a fair sample of the "foreign policy elite," with close links to government, major corporations, and private foundations.[22] These memoranda deal with the "requirement[s] of the United States in a world in which it proposes to hold unquestioned power," foremost among them being "the rapid fulfillment of a program of complete re-armament" (1940). In the early years of the war it was assumed that part of the world might be controlled by Germany. Therefore, the major task was to develop "an integrated policy to achieve military and economic supremacy for the United States within the non-German world," including plans "to secure the limitation of any exercise of sovereignty by foreign nations that constitutes a threat to the world area essential for the security and economic prosperity of the United States and the Western Hemisphere." (The concern for the "prosperity of the Western Hemisphere" is adequately revealed by United States policies, say, in Central America and the Caribbean, before and since; this opposition to imperial prerogatives that constrain U.S. capital and access to resources is often adduced by scholarship as evidence that U.S. foreign policy is guided by

"anti-imperialist" commitments). These areas, which are to serve the prosperity of the United States, include the Western Hemisphere, the British
Empire, and the Far East, described as a natural integrated economic unity
in the geopolitical analysis of the planners.

The major threat to United States hegemony in the non-German world
was posed by the aspirations of Britain. The contingencies of the war served
to restrict these, and the American government exploited Britain's travail to
help the process along. Lend-lease aid was kept within strict bounds: enough
to keep Britain in the war but not enough to permit it to maintain its privileged imperial position.[23] There was a mini-war between the United States
and Great Britain within the context of the common struggle against Germany, where, of course, Britain was on the front line—more accurately, the
overwhelming burden of fighting Nazi Germany fell to the Russians,[24] but
let us keep now to the Anglo-American alliance. In this conflict within the
alliance, American interests succeeded in taking over traditional British
markets in Latin America and in partially displacing Britain in the Middle
East, particularly in Saudi Arabia, which was understood to be "a stupendous source of strategic power, and one of the greatest material prizes in
world history," in the words of the State Department.[25] I will return to this
matter, but let us continue to explore the CFR planning documents.

The U.S.-led non-German bloc was entitled the "Grand Area" in the
CFR discussions. Actually, a U.S.-dominated Grand Area was only a second-
best alternative. It was explained in June 1941 that "the Grand Area is not
regarded by the Group as more desirable than a world economy, nor as an
entirely satisfactory substitute." The Grand Area was seen as a nucleus or
model that could be extended, optimally, to a global economy. It was soon
recognized that with the coming defeat of Nazi Germany, at least Western
Europe could be integrated into the Grand Area. Participants in the CFR
discussions recognized that "the British Empire as it existed in the past will
never reappear and . . . the United States may have to take its place." One
stated frankly that the United States "must cultivate a mental view toward
world settlement after this war which will enable us to impose our own
terms, amounting perhaps to a pax-Americana." Another argued that the
concept of the United States security interests must be enlarged to incorporate areas "strategically necessary for world control." It is a pervasive theme
that international trade and investment are closely related to the economic
health of the United States, as is access to the resources of the Grand Area,

which must be so organized as to guarantee the health and structure of the American economy, its internal structure unmodified.

The notion of "access to resources" is marvelously expressed in a State Department memorandum of April 1944 called "Petroleum Policy of the United States," dealing with the primary resource.[26] There must be equal access for American companies everywhere, but no equal access for others, the document explained. The United States dominated Western Hemisphere production,[27] and this position must be maintained while United States holdings are diversified elsewhere. The policy "would involve the preservation of the absolute position presently obtaining, and therefore vigilant protection of existing concessions in United States hands coupled with insistence upon the Open Door principle of equal opportunity for United States companies in new areas." That is a fair characterization of the principle of the "Open Door."[28]

All of this is in accord with the concepts of Grand Area planning, and it also corresponded to the evolving historical process. The United States retained its dominance of Western Hemisphere petroleum resources while the American share of Middle East oil rapidly increased.[29] The British maintained their control of Iranian oil until 1954, when the United States government imposed an international consortium after the CIA-backed coup that restored the Shah, with American companies granted a 40 percent share.[30] Similarly, in the Far East "occupied Japan was not permitted to reconstruct the oil-refining facilities that had been destroyed by Allied bombings, a policy widely attributed in the oil industry of Japan to the fact that the oil bureau of General MacArthur's headquarters was heavily staffed with American personnel on temporary leave from Jersey Standard and Mobil." Later, American-based companies were able to take over a dominant position in controlling Japan's energy resources. "Under the Allied occupation the Japanese government was powerless to block such business links."[31]

Much the same was true elsewhere. For example, the United States succeeded in expelling French interests from Saudi Arabia in 1947 by some legal legerdemain, alleging that French companies were "enemies" as a result of Hitler's occupation of France, so that the 1928 Red Line agreement on sharing oil in the former Ottoman Empire was abrogated (*MNOC*, pp. 50f.). British interests in Saudi Arabia were excluded by a different device—namely, when American companies expressed their fear that "the

British may be able to lead either Ibn Saud or his successors to diddle them out of the concession and the British into it" (Navy Under Secretary William Bullitt), and "told the Roosevelt Administration that direct U.S. Lend Lease assistance for King Saud was the only way to keep their Arabian concession from falling into British hands," the President obligingly issued the following directive to the Lend Lease administrator: "In order to enable you to arrange Lend Lease aid to the Government of Saudi Arabia, I hereby find that the defense of Saudi Arabia is vital to the defense of the United States"—its defense from whom, he did not stipulate, though a cynic might remark that the tacit identification of the United States with the Aramco concession is consistent with the actual usage of the phrase "national interest." Lend Lease had been authorized by Congress for "democratic allies" fighting the Nazis. In other ways as well, the Roosevelt Administration acted to support the American companies against their British rivals, through aid (Saudi Arabia received almost $100 million under Lend Lease, including scarce construction materials) or direct government intervention (*MNOC*, pp. 36f.).

As an aside, recall what happened when Iranians experimented with the curious idea of taking control of their own oil in the early 1950s. After an oil company boycott, a successful CIA-backed coup put an end to that installing the regime of the Shah, which became a powerful United States client state purchasing vast quantities of American arms, conducting counterinsurgency in the Arabian peninsula, and, of course, subjecting the Iranian people to the Shah's pleasant whims.

The coup had other useful consequences. Exxon (i.e., its predecessor corporation) feared that the USSR might gain some share of Iranian oil unless "the problem was solved," in which case it might dump Iranian oil on the world market, depressing prices (*MNOC*, p. 67). But that threat to the free enterprise system was eliminated with the coup.

We should bear in mind that the CIA-backed coup that ended the experiment in Iranian democracy and led to a further displacement of British power was welcomed as a great triumph here. When the agreement was signed between Iran and the new oil consortium organized by the United States government, the *New York Times* commented editorially (August 6, 1954) that this was "good news indeed": "Costly as the dispute over Iranian oil has been to all concerned, the affair may yet be proved worth-while if lessons are learned from it." The crucial lessons are then spelled out as follows:

Underdeveloped countries with rich resources now have an object lesson in the heavy cost that must be paid by one of their number which goes berserk with fanatical nationalism. It is perhaps too much to hope that Iran's experience will prevent the rise of Mossadeghs in other countries, but that experience may at least strengthen the hands of more reasonable and more far-seeing leaders.

Like the Shah. With typical ruling-class cynicism, the *Times* then goes on to say that "the West, too, must study the lessons of Iran" and must draw the conclusion that "partnership, even more in the future than the past, must be the relationship between the industrialized Western nations and some other countries, less industrialized, but rich in raw materials, outside Europe and North America," a statement that must have been most inspiring for the underdeveloped countries that had enjoyed the great privilege of partnership with the West in the past.

The "costs" incurred in this affair, according to the *Times,* do not include the suffering of the people of Iran but rather the propaganda opportunities offered to the Communists, who will denounce the whole affair in their wicked fashion, and the fact that "in some circles in Great Britain the charge will be pushed that American 'imperialism'—in the shape of the American oil firms in the consortium—has once again elbowed Britain from a historic stronghold." The implication is that this charge, or even the concept of American "imperialism," is too obviously absurd to deserve comment, a conclusion based as always on the doctrines of the state religion rather than an analysis of the facts. The exuberance over the "demonstration effect" of the CIA achievement is also typical, though the vulgarity of the *Times* account perhaps goes beyond the ordinary. The theme became familiar with reference to Vietnam in subsequent years.

But let us return to the CFR global planning, which laid out a program for organizing the Grand Area, or if possible, the world, as an integrated economic system that would offer the American economy "the 'elbow room' . . . needed in order to survive without major readjustments"—that is, without any change in the distribution of power, wealth, ownership, and control.

The memoranda, which are explicit enough about Grand Area planning, are careful to distinguish between principle and propaganda. They observed in mid-1941 that "formulation of a statement of war aims for propaganda purposes is very different from formulation of one defining the true national interest." Here is a further recommendation:

> If war aims are stated, which seem to be concerned solely with Anglo-American imperialism, they will offer little to people in the rest of the world, and will be vulnerable to Nazi counter-promises. Such aims would also strengthen the most reactionary elements in the United States and the British Empire. The interests of other peoples should be stressed, not only those of Europe, but also of Asia, Africa and Latin America. This would have a better propaganda effect.

The participants must have been relieved when the Atlantic Charter suitably vague and idealistic in tone, was announced a few months later.

The CFR studies were extended in subsequent years to include analyses of prospects and plans for most parts of the world. The sections on Southeast Asia are interesting in the light of developments there. The analyses that issued from CFR study groups closely resemble the National Security Council memoranda and other material now available in the Pentagon Papers, a remarkable documentary record of the design and execution of imperial planning.[32] The similarity is hardly accidental. The same interests and often the same people are involved. The basic theme is that Southeast Asia must be integrated within the U.S.-dominated global system to ensure that the needs of the American economy are satisfied, and also the specific needs of Japan, which might be tempted again to set its independent course or to flood Western markets unless granted access to Southeast Asian markets and resources, within the overarching framework of the Pax Americana—the Grand Area. These principles were firmly set by the 1950s and guided the course of the American intervention, then outright aggression, when the Vietnamese, like the Iranians, went "berserk with fanatical nationalism," failing to comprehend the sophisticated Grand Area concepts and the benefits of "partnership" with the industrialized West.

The material that I have been reviewing constitutes a primary documentary source for the study of formation of American foreign policy, compiled by those who carried out this policy. We might ask how this material is dealt with in academic scholarship. The answer is simple: It is ignored. The book by Shoup and Minter (see note 22) seems to be the first to examine these records. American scholars justly complain that the Russians refuse to release documentary materials, thus raising all sorts of barriers to the understanding of the evolution of their policies. Another just complaint is that American scholars avoid documentary materials that might yield much insight into the formation of American policy, a fact easily explained in this instance, I believe: The documentary record is no more consistent with the doctrines of the state religion, in this case, than is the historical record itself.

Parenthetically, it might be noted that the Pentagon Papers, which provide a record of high-level policy planning that is unusual in its richness, have suffered the same fate. This record too is ignored—indeed, often misrepresented. There is indeed a spate of scholarly work on United States Vietnam policy, some of which makes extensive use of material in the Pentagon Papers. Typically, however, attention is focused on the 1960s. Then we have a detailed microanalysis of bureaucratic infighting, political pressures, and the like, completely disregarding the general framework, set long before and never challenged by those who were simply applying imperial doctrine as carefully elaborated ten to twenty years earlier. This is a marvelous device for obscuring the social reality by diverting attention from the documentary record concerning the guiding principles of state policy, as clearly revealed in the basic documentation that is characteristically ignored.

Space prevents a detailed review here, but one example may suffice to illustrate. Consider a review of several books on Vietnam by William S. Turley, one of the more critical and independent American academic scholars with a professional involvement in Indochina.[33] He discusses two "prevailing images of American policy-making on Vietnam": the "quagmire hypothesis," which "held that involvement was the result of incremental decisions made without adequate understanding of probable consequences," and "the interpretation that American policy was stalemated by the need of successive administrations, for domestic political reasons, to do what was minimally necessary to avoid losing a war." The book he reviews, by Robert Galluci,[34] finds both of these images too simple and seeks a more complex interpretation through application of a bureaucratic process model. Turley points out that the Pentagon Papers provide important evidence bearing on the questions.

In fact, the Pentagon Papers provide extensive evidence for a different hypothesis, one that goes unmentioned, as it is passed over in silence in the scholarly literature—namely, that American policy in Vietnam was a conscious application of principles of imperial planning that formed part of a consensus established long before the specific period, the 1960s, to which attention is generally restricted. This hypothesis is extensively documented in the Pentagon Papers and elsewhere, but the documentary record is never so much as mentioned in the book under review, the review itself, or academic scholarship generally. The hypothesis in question is simply not fit for discussion in polite company, no matter what the documentation may be. It is not even a competitor, to be rejected.[35]

I do not suggest that in refusing to consider the hypothesis in question or the substantial documentation supporting it, scholars are being dishonest. It is simply that nothing in their training or in the literature generally available to them makes this hypothesis comprehensible. It is a reflection of the success of the educational system in "socialization," the success of what the trilateral analysts call the "institutions which have played the major role in the indoctrination of the young," that certain ideas, however natural and well-supported, do not even come to mind or, if noticed, can be dismissed with derision. People who break away from the consensus have dubious prospects in the media or the academy, in general. The resulting subversion of scholarship is systematic, not individual. Similar phenomena are familiar from the history of organized religion. Anyone who has spent some time in a university knows how it is done. Some young scholars are "hard to get along with" or are "too strident" or "show poor taste in their choice of topics" or "don't use the proper methodology," or in other ways do not meet the professional standards that not infrequently serve to insulate scholarship from uncomfortable challenge (see Chapter 1, note 23 for one of many examples). The ideological disciplines are particularly subject to these tendencies.

Primary documentary sources like the CFR studies and the Pentagon Papers must be investigated with a critical eye and supplemented by much additional evidence if one wants to reach any serious understanding of the evolution of American policy. It might turn out to be the case that the analyses cited above, which are among the few even to concern themselves with the basic documentary record, are inadequate or even seriously in error in the interpretations they provide. What is remarkable and noteworthy, however, is how consistently American scholarship takes a different tack, simply ignoring the documentary record that does not accord with received opinion.

Consider one final example of how the central questions are evaded in academic scholarship. Let us return again to our hypothetical rational observer attempting to discern some of the major factors in foreign policy formation and consider some further facts that should immediately strike him as significant.

Since World War II there has been a continuing process of centralization of decision-making in the state executive, certainly with regard to foreign policy. Secondly, there has been a tendency through much of this period toward domestic economic concentration. Furthermore, these two processes are closely related, because of the enormous corporate influence over the state executive. And finally, there has been a vast increase in overseas investment, marketing, and resource extraction in the post-war period, greatly increasing the stake of the masters of the corporate economy in foreign affairs. To cite one indication, "It has been estimated that earnings from these foreign operations by 1970 contributed between 20 and 25 percent of total U.S. corporate profits after taxes, a very considerable magnitude indeed." [36] The basic facts are uncontroversial. They suggest, perhaps, a certain hypothesis for investigation: Corporations have some influence, perhaps considerable influence, in setting foreign policy. How does academic scholarship deal with this issue?

There is a (rare) discussion of the question by political scientist Dennis M. Ray in the volume on the multinational corporation just cited. [37] He observes that "we know virtually nothing about the role of corporations in American foreign relations." Scholarship has "clarified the influence of Congress, the press, scientists, and non-profit organizations, such as RAND, on the foreign policy process. The influence of corporations on the foreign policy process, however, remains clouded in mystery."

Is this "mystery" somehow inherent in the difficulty of discerning the corporate role, as distinct from the massive impact of scientists and the press on foreign policy? Not at all. As Ray points out, the issue remains clouded in mystery because it is systematically evaded:

My search through the respectable literature on international relations and U.S. foreign policy shows that less than 5 percent of some two hundred books granted even passing attention to the role of corporations in American foreign relations. From this literature, one might gather that American foreign policy is formulated in a social vacuum, where national interests are protected from external threats by the elaborate machinery of governmental policymaking. There is virtually no acknowledgement in standard works within the field of international relations and foreign policy of the existence and influence of corporations.

Note that Ray limits himself to the "respectable literature." He excludes what he calls the literature of "advocacy," which includes two streams:

statements by corporate executives and business school professors, and "radical and often neo-Marxist analyses." In this literature, particularly the latter category, there is much discussion of the role of corporations in foreign policy formation. Furthermore, as Ray turns to the topic itself, he discovers that the conclusions reached seem to be correct. "Few if any interest groups, outside of business, have generalized influence on the broad range of foreign policy," he observes, citing one of the few works in the "respectable literature" that raises the question. Ray believes that scholars will discover these facts if they "begin to examine the question."

In short, if scholars begin to study the question, they will discover the truth of truisms that have been discussed and documented for years outside of the "respectable literature," exactly as one would expect in the light of such basic and fundamental facts about American society as those noted earlier.

It is interesting that Ray never inquires into the causes of this strange lapse in "respectable" scholarship. In fact, the answer does not seem obscure. If we are interested in careful investigation of the inner workings of the Politburo, we do not turn to studies produced at Moscow and Leningrad Universities, and we know exactly why. There is no reason not to apply the same standards of rationality when we find something similar in the United States, though here the mechanisms are entirely different: willing subversion of scholarship rather than obedience to external force.

Moreover, consider Ray's attitude towards those who do study the major and dominant themes, providing the obvious answers that he himself repeats: They are not respectable scholars, in his view, but are engaged in "advocacy"—while the scholarly mainstream, which carefully skirts the major formative influence on foreign policy, does not lose its "respectability" for this curious oversight, and does not seem to him to be engaged in "advocacy."

An anthropologist observing the phenomenon I have been describing would have no hesitation in concluding that we are dealing here with a form of taboo, a deep-seated superstitious avoidance of some terrifying question: in this case, the question of how private economic power functions in American society. Among the secular priesthood of academic scholars, the issue can be mentioned only, if at all, in hushed tones. Those who do raise the question seriously are no longer "respectable." As diplomatic historian Gaddis Smith asserts in a review of recent work by William Appleman

Williams and Gabriel Kolko, they are "essentially pamphleteers" rather than authentic historians.[38]

In a free society we do not imprison those who violate profound cultural taboos or burn them at the stake. But they must be identified as dangerous radicals, not fit to be counted among the priesthood. The reaction is appropriate. To raise the dread question is to open the possibility that the institutions responsible "for the indoctrination of the young" and the other propaganda institutions may be infected by the most dangerous of plagues: insight and understanding. Awareness of the facts might threaten the social order, protected by a carefully spun web of pluralist mysticism, faith in the benevolence of our pure-hearted leadership, and general superstitious belief.

An ideological structure, to be useful for some ruling class, must conceal the exercise of power by this class either by denying the facts or more simply ignoring them—or by representing the special interests of this class as universal interests, so that it is seen as only natural that representatives of this class should determine social policy, in the general interest. As Ray notes, it is not unexpected that foreign policy decision-makers should perceive the world from the same perspective as businessmen: "In this context, we are not dealing simply with phenomena of influence, for national goals may in fact be synonymous with business goals." Extricating the expression "national goals" from its typical mystical usage, the remark approaches tautology.

Outside the ranks of the priesthood the facts are clearly presented in the socially marginal literature of "advocacy" by "pamphleteers" who make extensive and often very insightful use of the relevant documentary sources. Here, it is recognized that the notion of "national goals" is merely a device of mystification, and that the often conflicting goals of various social groups can be conceived in terms other than those set by the masters of the private economy. But the universities, the scholarly professions, the mass media, and society at large are carefully insulated from these dangerous heresies in a highly indoctrinated society, which is commonly described— the ultimate irony—as "pragmatic" and "nonideological." All of this is the more interesting when we realize that the society really is free from ugly forms of totalitarian control and coercion that are prevalent elsewhere.

Carl Landauer, who participated in the short-lived revolutionary government in Bavaria after World War I, remarked that the censorship of the bourgeois press by the revolutionary government marked the "beginning of freedom of public opinion." [39] His point was that the organs of propaganda and opinion, firmly in the hands of ruling groups, destroyed freedom of opinion by their dominance of the means of expression.[40] Clearly one cannot accept the view that state censorship is the answer to the distortion and deceit of intellectual servants of ruling groups. Just as surely, we cannot pretend that there is freedom of opinion in any serious sense when social and cultural taboos shield the formation of policy from public awareness and scrutiny.

It is, in fact, quite true that the business press sometimes tends to be more honest about social reality than academic scholarship. Consider, for example, this reaction to the American failure in Vietnam (and elsewhere) in *Business Week* (April 7, 1975). The editors fear that "the international economic structure, under which U.S. companies have flourished since the end of World War II, is in jeopardy." They go on to explain how,

> fueled initially by the dollars of the Marshall Plan, American business prospered and expanded on overseas orders despite the cold war, the end of colonialism, and the creation of militant and often anticapitalistic new countries. No matter how negative a development, there was always the umbrella of American power to contain it. . . . The rise of the multinational corporation was the economic expression of this political framework.

But "this stable world order for business operations is falling apart" with the defeat of American power in Indochina. Nothing here about our unremitting campaign "to do good" and "advance our moral ideals." They explain further how congressional obstinacy is undermining our efforts to persuade our European allies to support our concept of "a floor price on oil," and the "debilitating impact on international economics" with the "the collapse of U.S. foreign policy around the globe," particularly "if Japan cannot continue to export a third of its products to Southeast Asia." Unless a new "bipartisan foreign policy" (i.e., one-party state) is reestablished, it may be "impossible to maintain a successful international economic framework."

A year later, however, things were looking up, and "it appears that the future of the West again lies in the hands of the U.S. and to a lesser extent, West Germany," American oil policies perhaps being one reason.[41] As the

Business Week editors note, "Trends now at work in the world have greatly strengthened the competitive position of the U.S. economy" with the result that "Washington will have more freedom to maneuver in formulating foreign economic policies than it has had since the early 1960s."[42] In short, the Grand Area is being successfully reconstituted, though the optimism proved a bit premature, in this case.

Occasionally, the light breaks through in statements of public officials as well. Consider for example a Statement by Frank M. Coffin, Deputy Administrator, Agency for International Development (AID), outlining "Objectives of the AID Program":

> Our basic, broadest goal is a long-range political one. It is not development for the sake of sheer development. . . . An important objective is to open up the maximum opportunity for domestic private initiative and enterprise and to insure that foreign private investment, particularly from the United States, is welcomed and well treated. . . . The fostering of a vigorous and expanding private sector in the less developed countries is one of our most important responsibilities. Both domestic private initiative and management and outside investment are important. . . . Politically, a strong and progressive private business community provides a powerful force for stable, responsible Government and a built-in check against Communist dogma.[43]

Another "built-in check" is counterinsurgency, as Coffin goes on to explain, "And we in AID of course have a public safety program which, perhaps to oversimplify, seeks to equip countries to utilize the civilian police in preventive action so that they do not have to place excessive reliance on the military." Oversimplification indeed. Many thousands of people in Latin America and Asia have benefited from this particular element in their "partnership with the West" over the years.[44] Needless to say, all of this is spiced with rhetoric on how our aid program seeks "partnership"—in contrast to those of the Russians and the Chinese, which seek "domination"—and so on. Spectacularly lacking is a comparative analysis of the aid programs to support this claim.

While noting occasional flashes of honesty in the business press, I would not want to imply that businessmen are free from the cant of much academic scholarship. Here is a single example, which could easily be duplicated in years before and since, to the present:

You will point an accusing finger and you will hurl the challenging question: "What about Hayti [sic] and San Domingo, what about Nicaragua, Honduras, and so forth?" It is true we did send military forces to these countries. There did, most regrettably, occur some bloodshed. In the execution of our program we did commit some errors in judgment and in manners. We did, in certain measures, proceed bunglingly and clumsily, as Governments and their agents not infrequently do, especially when, as in the cases under discussion, the task to be undertaken is an unusual and unexpected one, and there are neither traditions which afford guidance nor a trained personnel to attend to the execution. (Incidentally, the very absence of such personnel tends to prove how little the thoughts of our Government and people were on Imperialism.)

But the test is in the answer to the question which in my turn I ask of you: "What was our purpose? Did we go to oppress and exploit, did we go to add these territories to our domain? Or did we go to end an inveterate rule of tyranny, malefactions and turmoil, to set up decent and orderly government and the rule of law, to foster progress, to establish stable conditions and with them the basis for prosperity to the population concerned?"

I think there can be no doubt that it was these latter things we aimed to attain. And having measurably accomplished the task, we did withdraw, or shall withdraw. We left behind, or shall leave behind, a few persons charged with the collection and proper administration of certain revenues, but such arrangements . . . are no more in the nature of exploitation or oppression than the appointment of a person under deed of trust is in the nature of exploitation and oppression.[45]

It would be superfluous to discuss how the United States proceeded to foster progress, prosperity, and an end to tyranny and malefactions in Haiti, San Domingo, Nicaragua, Honduras, and the other parts of Latin America "where we have traditionally been a friend and protector" (see p. 94). The immunity of doctrine to mere fact, in such cases, easily compares with the so-called Communist countries. Such pronouncements closely resemble the blather produced by pundits of the press as the Vietnam war came to an end: The United States involvement was "honorable" though "fraught with mistakes and misjudgments"; "good impulses came to be transmuted into bad policy"; it would be unfair to leave "the impression somehow the United States was responsible for the carnage in Southeast Asia"; our "blundering efforts to do good" turned into a "disastrous mistake"; and so on.[46] Again, it is remarkable how impervious the state religion is to mere factual evidence, extended now over eighty years of imperial aggression, following upon the bloody conquest of the national territory.

I have been discussing one major persistent theme of United States foreign policy, and not a very surprising one—namely, the attempt to create a Grand Area, a global economy, adapted to the needs of those who design United States government policy and the corporate interests that they largely represent. One concomitant of this dominant commitment is the repeated reliance on military force. This is, of course, only the most visible and dramatic device—United States policy towards Chile under Allende or Brazil since the early 1960s illustrates more typical and preferred procedures. But military force is the ultimate weapon to preserve a Grand Area. It is not exactly something new in American history.

James Chace, editor of *Foreign Affairs*, comments on this matter in a recent article. He counts up 159 instances of United States armed intervention abroad prior to 1945. Since World War II, he adds, "We have used military forces in Korea, Indochina, Lebanon, the Dominican Republic and the Congo." He then cites various reasons why we should expect all of this to continue: fears of resource scarcity, concern for the United States sphere of influence in the Caribbean and "regional balances of power" elsewhere, and, finally, the American "concern for human rights and the espousal of liberal, pluralistic democracies." [47]

Recall the cases cited, or other examples of intervention not cited: Iran, Cuba, Guatemala, Chile. In which of these cases was American intervention motivated by concern for human rights and espousal of liberal, pluralistic democracies? It remains a matter of great interest and importance that such utter nonsense can be produced with a straight face and be taken seriously in journalism and academic scholarship.

Chace points out (in part, correctly) that the American people continue to support an activist, interventionist foreign policy. One of the contributing factors is the ideology of American benevolence and international good will, as illustrated in his own remarks. I have cited a number of examples to show how this doctrinal framework governs scholarship, as well as the mass media, journals of current affairs, and the like. Most of these examples illustrate how the facts are simply ignored in the interests of doctrinal purity. But it is interesting to see that even direct and overt self-contradiction poses no particular problem for the secular priesthood, which rarely achieves the sophistication of its theological counterparts. As an illustration, consider another article in which Chace returns to the same themes.[48] Here he discusses the "ironies and ambiguities" of "the American experience," referring to the "moral concern" that is "a typical expression of the American spirit" though "we have found that the pursuit of justice sometimes leads to consequences contrary to those we had intended [and] that, at times, our proclaimed ideals serve to hide—from ourselves even more than from others—motivations of a darker and more complex character." "Experience should have taught us," he concludes, "that we do not always completely understand our own motivations," though he does not discuss the elaborate system of deceit that has been constructed to prevent such understanding. What is remarkable, however, is his discussion of particular cases, for example the *Realpolitik* of the Nixon-Kissinger period. "We were determined to seek stability," Chace asserts, and as an illustration—literally—he offers "our efforts to destabilize a freely elected Marxist government in Chile." Even a direct self-contradiction in successive sentences[49] does not suffice to raise a question about "our own motivations." Rather, the example falls under the category of "irony."

This category serves in the most astonishing ways to disguise reality in the ideological disciplines. Here is a final example, particularly revealing, I think, because of the source. Norman Graebner is an excellent historian, a critic of Cold War idiocies, a "realist" of more or less the variety of George Kennan, to whom the study from which I will quote is dedicated.[50] Graebner accepts the conventional belief that American foreign policy has been guided by the "Wilsonian principles of peace and self-determination." The United States is not "an aggressive, imperialist country" in the twentieth century, as is demonstrated by the many "references to principle" in "its diplomatic language," references notably lacking in the rhetoric of truly aggressive and imperial powers, of course. The "traditional American dilemma" lies in the delusion that, given "the energy or determination of its antagonists," nevertheless "the nation was always assured that it could anticipate the eventual collapse of its enemies and the creation of the illusive world of justice and freedom." He asserts without qualification that "certainly all fundamental American relations with the U.S.S.R. and mainland China after 1950 were anchored to that assumption." It is this "American idealism" that caused so many problems in the postwar period.

Having laid down these basic principles, Graebner proceeds to investigate some particular examples of foreign policy in action. He then makes the following observation: "It was ironic that this nation generally ignored the principles of self-determination in Asia and Africa where it had some chance of success and promoted it behind the Iron and Bamboo curtains where it had no chance of success at all."

Consider the logic. A general principle is proposed: The United States follows the Wilsonian principles of self-determination. Then specific examples are surveyed. We discover that where the principles could be applied, they were not applied; where they could not be applied, in enemy domains, they were advocated (and their advocacy demonstrates that we are not aggressive and imperialistic). Conclusion: It is ironic that the general thesis fails when tested. But the general principle remains in force. In fact, Graebner goes on to lament that "this nation's selfless search for order in world affairs could not sustain the gratitude of a troubled world."

By similar logic a physicist might formulate a general hypothesis, put it to the test, discover that it is refuted in each specific instance, and conclude that it is ironic that the facts are the opposite of what the principle predicts—but the principle nevertheless stands. The example illustrates the difference between ideological disciplines such as academic history and political science, on the one hand, and subjects that are expected to meet rational intellectual standards, on the other.

This example is interesting precisely because the historian in question was an early critic of Cold War doctrine. He argues, on Kennanesque lines, that United States policy was in error. "Error," however, is a socially neutral category. To invoke it is to remain safely within the bounds of the primary dogma: that the United States simply responds to external challenges, and that its policy reflects no special material interests of dominant social groups.

This discussion has so far been fairly abstract. I have not tried to deal with the human consequences of the policy of military intervention against those too weak to strike back, or other measures undertaken to ensure the stability of the Grand Area—policies that it is only reasonable to assume will continue in the future, since there have been no significant institutional changes, and even the critique that developed in some circles during the Indochina war has been fairly well deflected and contained. We may recall how all of this looks from the wrong end of the guns. Eighty years ago a Filipino nationalist wrote that the Filipinos "have already accepted the arbitrament of war, and war is the worst condition conceivable, especially when waged by an Anglo-Saxon race which despises its opponent as an alien or inferior people. Yet the Filipinos accepted it with a full knowledge of its horror and of the sacrifices in life and property which they knew they would be called upon to make." [51] It will be recalled that on that occasion too, our selfless leadership was merely attempting "to fulfill God's purposes in history." Even James Chace concedes that in this case, though there were "moral purposes" alongside of self-interest, "We were hard put to find a moral defense for our behavior. The atrocities committed by American troops there were horrifying, as they resorted to a no-quarter war, taking no prisoners, burning villages and often shooting innocent men, women and children." [52]

One might think that after Vietnam it would be superfluous to go into this matter. Unfortunately, that supposition would be false. When President Carter, in the midst of one of his sermons on human rights, explains that we owe no debt and have no responsibility to Vietnam because "the destruction was mutual," [53] there is not a comment nor a whisper of protest in the American press. And the history of that "tragic error" is now being rewritten to make the people of Indochina the villain of the piece. And when Ford and Kissinger sent their bombers over Cambodia in one final act of violence and murder in that land ravaged by American terror at the time of the *Mayagüez* incident in May 1975, even Senator Kennedy, one of the very few senators to have shown genuine concern over the human consequences of the American war, saw fit to state that "the President's firm and successful action gave an undeniable and needed lift to the nation's spirit, and he deserves our genuine support." [54] The world was put on notice—as if notice were needed—that the world's most violent power had not renounced its commitment to the use of force as a consequence of its defeat in Indochina, at least when the victims are defenseless.

The pattern has continued since. Consider what happened in the demilitarized zone between North and South Korea in August 1976, when two American soldiers were killed by North Korean troops as they attempted to trim a tree under circumstances that remain disputed. For the sake of discussion, let us assume the American account to be entirely accurate: The North Koreans simply murdered them in cold blood. The United States army then cut down the tree, with a considerable show of force, including a flight of B-52s. An important account of this incident was given by William Beecher, former Deputy Assistant Secretary of Defense for Public Affairs, now a diplomatic correspondent. He writes that the original plan was to have the B-52s drop "about 70,000 tons of bombs on a South Korean bombing range only about 10 miles from Panmunjom. . . . But well-placed sources say that at the eleventh hour it was decided that to drop the bombs would be too provocative and might trigger a military response from the truculent North Koreans." [55]

Let us assume that the figure of seventy-thousand tons—more than three Hiroshima equivalents—is mistaken. But why should heavy bombing a few miles from Panmunjom appear "provocative" to the "truculent North Koreans"? Perhaps because they retain some memories of things that happened a quarter-century ago when the United States Air Force so thoroughly devastated their land that there were simply no remaining targets. In keeping with the principle of believing only the American side of the story, let us recall how these events were officially perceived in an Air Force study of "an object lesson in air power to all the Communist world and especially to the Communists in North Korea," a "lesson" delivered a month before the armistice:

On 13 May 1953 twenty USAF F-84 fighter-bombers swooped down in three successive waves over Toksan irrigation dam in North Korea. From an altitude of 300 feet they skip-bombed their loads of high explosives into the hard-packed earthen walls of the dam. The subsequent flash flood scooped clean 27 miles of valley below, and the plunging flood waters wiped out large segments of a main north-south communication and supply route to the front lines. The Toksan strike and similar attacks on the Chasan, Kuwonga, Kusong, and Toksang dams accounted for five of the more than twenty irrigation dams targeted for possible attack—dams up-stream from all the important enemy supply routes and furnishing 75 percent of the controlled water supply for North Korea's rice production. These strikes, largely passed over by the press, the military observers, and news commentators in favor of attention-arresting but less meaningful operations events, constituted one of the most significant air operations of the Korean war. They sent the Communist military leaders and political commissars scurrying to their press and radio centers to blare to the world the most severe, hate-filled harangues to come from the Communist propaganda mill in the three years of warfare.

In striking one target system, the USAF had hit hard at two sensitive links in the enemy's armor—his capability to supply his front-line troops and his capability to produce food for his armies. To the U.N. Command the breaking of the irrigation dams meant disruption of the enemy's lines of communication and supply. But to the Communists the smashing of the dams meant primarily the destruction of their chief sustenance— rice. The Westerner can little conceive the awesome meaning which the loss of this staple food commodity has for the Asian—starvation and slow death. "Rice famine," for centuries the chronic scourge of the Orient, is more feared than the deadliest plague. Hence the show of rage, the flare of violent tempers, and the avowed threats of reprisals when bombs fell on five irrigation dams.[56]

Recall that this is not quoted from Communist black propaganda but from an official United States Air Force study.

The North Koreans, truculent as ever, could not see the beauty of this magnificent air operation, and might find heavy bombing "provocative" today as well, so the original plan was called off.

Only a few years after the USAF succeeded in bringing starvation and slow death to the Asians in Northeast Asia, they were at it again in Southeast Asia. As that war ended, after vast destruction and massacre, the United States insisted on a show of force against defenseless Cambodia during the *Mayagüez* incident. Sihanoukville was bombed, but a planned B-52 attack was called off—wisely, the *New Republic* commented, because of "predictable domestic and world reaction" and possible adverse effects on the *Mayagüez* crewmen—not because it would have constituted another major massacre of Cambodians.[57] A year later United States planes almost carried out heavy bombing in Korea to impress the truculent North Koreans. The American people continue to support an activist foreign policy, so the polls indicate, and the articulate intelligentsia are as usual urging us to forget the "errors" and "miscalculations" of the past and to set forth again on our campaign to instill our moral ideals in an evil and ungrateful world. The institutional structures that lie behind the military episodes and other interventions of the postwar years and the ideological framework of Grand Area planning all remain intact, subjected to little public challenge, effectively removed from popular scrutiny or, in part, even scholarly analysis. It is only reasonable to conclude that the editor of *Foreign Affairs* is quite right when he predicts that military intervention will continue, as will other attempts to enforce "stability" through "destabilization" and to contain and destroy movements that threaten to secede from the Grand Area. It is this threat, whether called "Communist" or something else, that the United States government will bend every effort to contain and destroy, by force if need be, by more delicate means if they suffice, while the intelligentsia divert us with tales about our selfless devotion to principle and moral idealism.

Chapter Three

INDOCHINA AND THE FOURTH ESTATE (1973)

T HE INDOCHINA WAR has cast a long shadow over world affairs, and, by all appearances, will continue to do so. Repeated failures may have "greatly diminished American willingness to become involved in this form of warfare elsewhere," [1] but only in limited respects. The modifications are at most tactical, and the guiding concept of global order remains. In Kissinger's frank formulation of imperial strategy:

> Regional groupings supported by the United States will have to take over major responsibility for their immediate areas, with the United States being concerned more with the overall framework of order than with the management of every regional enterprise.[2]

The vast military and police apparatus of the U.S.-imposed regime in South Vietnam will, it is hoped, be able to play this local role.

Washington is letting it be known that a "strong and stable South Vietnam"—a euphemism for an American satellite—is one of the "anchors" of American strategy: "The U.S. military is counting on South Vietnam as its most reliable partner in the area" and has formulated a new domino theory that postulates the fall of Thailand, perhaps Indonesia and the Philippines, and perhaps even Japan, if South Vietnam "becomes the victim of 'disruptive forces.' " [3]

To be sure, these openly announced goals are in explicit violation of the Paris Agreements, a fact that invariably passes without comment in press reports. The Paris Agreements commit "the United States and all other countries [to] respect the independence, sovereignty, unity and territorial integrity of Vietnam as recognized by the 1954 Geneva Agreements on Vietnam" (Article 1). Pending reunification, which is to "be carried out step by step through peaceful means . . . and without foreign interference," the "military demarcation line" at the 17th parallel is to be regarded as "only provisional and not a political or territorial boundary" (Article 15). But this commitment does not prevent U.S. officials from announcing, quite openly, that the United States will do its best to prevent reunification; and this is regarded as quite natural by the press. In a journal that generally reflects Administration thinking we read, "Very few American authorities . . . are as confident in private as they are in public about South Vietnam's chances of surviving as an independent nation."[4] They are, in short, not as confident as they seem to be about the likelihood that the United States will succeed in its efforts to subvert the agreements into which it entered in Paris. But Washington will surely put forth every effort, exactly as officials publicly proclaim, to improve the chances of South Vietnam's survival as an independent nation in violation of the Paris Agreements, by whatever means are available. All of this may surprise sentimentalists who are still bemused by the idea that the United States government is concerned with "the rule of law" and its "solemn commitments." Even those with a more realistic understanding of modern history might be taken aback at the brazen cynicism of these pronouncements.

One should not assume that it is only the conservative press that accepts as natural Washington's announced intention to treat the Paris Agreements as a scrap of paper. The liberal columnist Joseph Kraft, a dove by the standards of American political discourse, makes the following comment on the breakdown of the cease-fire: "Much of the blame goes to the Communists. Hanoi has never abandoned the objective of unifying all of Vietnam."[5] To translate: Hanoi has never abandoned the objective of living up to the terms of the Paris Agreements, and therefore bears responsibility for the collapse of these agreements. Being a balanced and objective observer, Kraft adds that "just as much of the blame goes to President Thieu." But balance can only go so far. None of the blame is assigned to President Nixon, in his account. Nor does he perceive the Orwellian character of his logic.

The examples just cited are typical of press commentary on the Paris Agreements. At the very moment when the agreements were being signed, Washington was presenting its own version of the text and of the course of events that led to the "settlement." The Washington version of the text, which contradicts it on virtually every major point of substance, in effect grants the United States the right of forceful intervention if its plans for South Vietnam, in explicit violation of the agreements it has signed, are disrupted. Furthermore, the Washington version of the history of negotiations, also plainly at variance with the facts, provides an implicit justification for the use of force in Indochina as well as an effective means for silencing domestic dissent. The press, serving as a faithful instrument of state propaganda, has adopted the Washington version of the substance of the agreements and the course of events that led to them. Thus it is helping to lay the basis in public opinion for renewed support for American aggression in Indochina in violation of the agreements; developments since the cease-fire suggest that this is precisely what will take place. What I would like to do now is to document these characterizations of official statements and the press reaction, which, if correct, have interesting implications with regard to the state of American democracy, quite apart from their import for Indochina and other "regional enterprises" within the "over-all framework of order" controlled by the United States.

The Paris Agreements stipulate that the South Vietnamese people will be free to exercise their right of self-determination without external interference and with full democratic liberties. These are two parallel and equivalent South Vietnamese "parties," the PRG (the Provisional Revolutionary Government, essentially the former NLF) and the GVN (the U.S.-backed Government of Vietnam, what is called "South Vietnam" in U.S. propaganda). These are to achieve national reconciliation and to proceed towards peaceful step-by-step reunification with the North (the DRV), removing the provisional demarcation line separating the two zones at the 17th parallel. The Paris Agreements recapitulate the DRV proposal rejected by the United States in October 1972, as well as the essential provisions of earlier DRV-PRG proposals. Still more significant, the Paris Agreements are drawn, in essence, from the founding program of the National Liberation Front (NLF) in 1960–62, which has not been substantially modified since and has consistently been backed by the DRV.

In July 1962, the NLF issued a "four-point manifesto" calling for an end to hostilities in South Vietnam, the establishment of a coalition government including "representatives of all political parties, cliques, groups, all political tendencies, social strata, members of all religions," which would "organize free general elections" and "promulgate democratic liberties" and "economic policies aimed at safeguarding free enterprise, economic independence." Furthermore:

South Vietnam must carry out a foreign policy of peace and neutrality. It must establish friendly relations with all nations, especially with her neighbors. It must not enter any military bloc or agree to let any country establish military bases on her soil. It must accept aid from all countries [if] free of political conditions. A necessary international agreement must be signed in which the big powers of all blocs pledge to respect the sovereignty, independence, territorial integrity, and neutrality of South Vietnam. South Vietnam, together with Cambodia and Laos, will form a neutral area, all three countries retaining full sovereignty.[6]

The timing was significant. The proposal came shortly after the signing of the Geneva Agreements on Laos, which established a coalition government with a policy of neutralism, prohibiting foreign intervention. "In September 1963 the NLF asked the United Nations for help in establishing a coalition government in South Vietnam similar to the one established in Laos the year before."[7] Other statements of the NLF developed these proposals further, calling also for step-by-step reunification with the North on the principle of equality and non-annexation of one zone by the other, with due concern for the differing characteristics of the two zones. In mid-1964, the NLF "put forth feelers for a proposal for what appeared to be an authentic coalition government" in South Vietnam.[8] However, Pike adds, "Nothing came of these offers." He also explains the reason: No group in South Vietnam, "with the possible exception of the Buddhists, thought themselves equal in size and power to risk entering into a coalition, fearing that if they did the whale would swallow the minnow."[9]

We know from the Pentagon Papers and other sources that Washington was deeply concerned throughout this period that there might be moves towards a political settlement in South Vietnam, compelling the United States to abandon its plans to incorporate South Vietnam within the "over-all framework of order." The politically organized Buddhists were regarded by Ambassador Lodge "as equivalent to card-carrying Communists."[10] General Westmoreland explained that their actions were not "in the interests of the Nation,"[11] putting forth the interesting thesis that only the U.S. military command, not the only two significant political groupings in South Vietnam (the NLF and the Buddhists), understood the true interests of South Vietnam. It was only after the Buddhist political movement was crushed that elections were permitted under conditions that guaranteed U.S. dominance—"moderate measures," as Lodge explained, "to prevent elections

from being used as a vehicle for a Communist takeover of the country." [12]
The U.S. command, recognizing that it had no hope of nourishing its minnow, pursued the next best course to destroy or severely wound the whale,
with consequences that are well known.

What is striking, in the present context, is the close correspondence between the Paris Agreements of 1973 and the earliest proposals of the NLF,
never significantly changed. Having fought a brutal war to prevent the realization of the NLF program of neutrality and political settlement, the
United States has formally capitulated to the forces of revolutionary nationalism, adopting their program virtually in its entirety. On paper, that is.

Much the same is true in Laos. The 1973 Laos agreements recognize the
existence of two parties controlling two zones. They are to reach national
concord under conditions of freedom and mutual respect. In this case, the
agreements grant the Pathet Lao far more than had been demanded in their
earlier proposals. It is recognized that the "neutralists," who had been
driven into a temporary alliance with the left by U.S. subversion in 1958–61,
in reality constitute a segment of the right-wing party. The 1962 Geneva
Agreements granted these "neutralists" the dominant role in a tripartite
government with the rightists and the Pathet Lao. In the case of Laos, then,
Kissinger has succeeded in capitulating to the most extreme demands put
forth by the forces of revolutionary nationalism. Again, on paper.

Washington has offered a very different interpretation of the content of
these agreements. The agreements state that "foreign countries shall not
impose any political tendency or personality on the South Vietnamese people" (Article 9c) and that "the United States will not continue its military
involvement or intervene in the internal affairs of South Vietnam" (Article
4). But the White House announced at once, in its official "summary of
basic elements of the Vietnam agreement," that "the government of the
Republic of (South) Vietnam continues in existence, recognized by the
United States, its constitutional structure and leadership intact and unchanged."

The reason for the parentheses is that this constitutional structure, in an
unamendable article, identifies the GVN as the government of all of Vietnam. Furthermore, this "constitutional structure" outlaws the second of
the two parallel and equivalent parties that are to achieve peaceful reconciliation under conditions of full democratic liberty. The GVN constitution
"opposes communism in every form" and prohibits "every activity designed
to propagandize or carry out communism." Under the system of executive

decrees that passes for a legal structure, the U.S.-imposed regime has interpreted this constitutional provision so broadly that it also prohibits "pro-communist neutralism," including "all plots and actions under the false name of peace and neutrality according to a Communist policy . . ." including any form of expression "aimed at spreading Communist policies, slogans and instructions." True to form, the GVN announced at once, in late January, that any such "illegal" actions would be suppressed by force. Washington, simultaneously, was informing the world of its intention to continue to impose this "political tendency" on the people of South Vietnam, with its constitutional structure intact, thus nullifying not only Articles 4 and 9c but also Article II, which guarantees full freedom of expression, movement, organization, etc. It would have been impossible for Washington to have expressed in a more forthright and plain fashion its intentions with regard to the scrap of paper being signed in Paris.

In his press conference of January 24, Kissinger presented the official interpretation of the agreements and the events leading to them. Particularly interesting was Kissinger's effort to show that the United States had achieved its long-term objectives. His reasoning deserves careful attention. Kissinger distinguished the following issues: "One, is there such a thing as a South Vietnam even temporarily until unification; secondly, who is the legitimate ruler of South Vietnam? This is what the civil war has been all about. Thirdly, what is the demarcation line that separates North Vietnam from South Vietnam." [13] Noting that the January agreements have "specific references to the sovereignty of South Vietnam" and "the right of the South Vietnamese people to self-determination," Kissinger alleged that "we have achieved substantial changes" from the October 9-Point plan announced by Radio Hanoi. This justifies the U.S. refusal to sign in October—and, by implication, subsequent U.S. military tactics, including the Christmas bombings of urban centers in the North.

All of this is blatant deception. The October 9-Point plan explicitly provided for "the South Vietnamese people's right to self-determination" and stated that "the South Vietnamese people shall decide themselves the political future of South Vietnam" through free elections (Point 4). The January agreement introduces no changes, substantial or otherwise, in this regard. Furthermore, the two plans are identical with respect to eventual reunification, "carried out step by step through peaceful means" (Point 5, October; Article 15, January). As for the status of the demarcation line, the Paris Agreements of January merely reiterate the wording of the Geneva Accords of 1954, in accordance with consistent public statements of the DRV and PRG.

Kissinger was attempting to confuse the issue of "sovereignty of South Vietnam" (his issue one) with sovereignty *within* South Vietnam (issue two), bringing in the irrelevant matter of the DMZ (issue three) merely to becloud the matter further. The "enemy" has consistently taken the position with respect to issues one and three that Kissinger falsely claims the United States has now succeeded in introducing into the agreements. The second issue, as Kissinger perceives, is what the war has been "all about": namely, who is to be sovereign within South Vietnam.

Kissinger is pretending that by recognizing the right of the South Vietnamese people to self-determination without external interference (in accordance with the DRV-PRG position), the agreements grant the United States the right to recognize the sovereignty of the GVN as the "sole legitimate government" in the South. The agreements, however, speak only of the "two parties" in the South, which are equivalent in status and must reach agreement as to sovereignty within South Vietnam. The 9-Point plan of October names the two parties as the GVN and the PRG, and these are the two southern parties that signed the 4-Party version of the January agreements. When Kissinger speaks of the "civil war," he presumably intends his audience to understand "the war between North and South Vietnam." Similarly, in his news conference of December 16, 1972, he presented the U.S. government position "that the two parts of Vietnam would live in peace with each other and that neither side would impose its solution on the other by force," and he claimed that this "modest requirement" was rejected by the other side.[14] He slips easily from the notion of self-determination for the South Vietnamese people to the entirely different notion of sovereignty of the GVN as their sole legitimate government. He is attempting to give the impression that the "two parties" that must peacefully resolve their differences are North Vietnam and South Vietnam, whereas the agreements make it plain that these two parties are the GVN and the PRG. To the extent that there is a "civil war," it is between these two parties. Having reached agreement, they are to move towards reunification with the North, peaceably, with no external interference.

As I have already indicated, the identification of the GVN as the "sole legitimate government in South Vietnam" (Nixon's phrase in a speech of January 23) is not only without support in the texts but is in plain violation of their provisions. The original and always primary source of external interference in the internal affairs of South Vietnam has been the United States, and apparently this will continue to be the case. One might dismiss Kissinger's evasions as merely a childish display, were it not for the fact that they may represent official policy. Furthermore, the mass media continue to present Kissinger's conclusions as though they had something to do with the facts, a matter to which I return directly.

Exactly the same charade was enacted in October. On October 26, 1972, Kissinger stated that the Radio Hanoi broadcast of the 9-Point program gave "on the whole a very fair account." [15] He then offered the following paraphrase: "As was pointed out by Radio Hanoi, the existing authorities with respect to both internal and external politics would remain in office." Although there is a studied ambiguity, the natural interpretation of his statement, made still more clear by the context, is that the GVN ("the existing authorities") will remain "in office" as the government of the South, and will deal somehow with the other "party," whose status remains mysterious. But this is not what "was pointed out by Radio Hanoi," which stated, rather, that "the two present administrations in South Vietnam will remain in existence with their respective domestic and external functions," and went on to identify these as the GVN and the PRG. [16]

On the issue that Kissinger now correctly identifies as what the war has been "all about," he was offering a "paraphrase" that was sharply at variance with the broadcast that he conceded was accurate. Having rejected the central principle in the 9-Point program, he then went on to say that "peace is at hand." The reason for the deception was quite obvious at the time. On the eve of the election, Nixon was not willing to reject publicly an agreement that offered return of the POWs and a cease-fire. He preferred to delay any response to the DRV initiative until after the election, when he would have more leverage. The mass media, with characteristic docility, chose to believe that peace was at hand and to overlook the fact that Kissinger was clearly rejecting the central provision of the 9-Point plan. Now apologists lamely argue that Kissinger's statement that "peace is at hand" was a "signal" to the DRV that U.S. intentions were serious. A telephone call would have achieved the same result, without any mysterious "signals," had this been the intention.

In mid-December, Kissinger announced that negotiations had broken down, blaming DRV intransigence and overlooking the fact that the DRV was publicly calling for signing of the 9-Point agreement. Typically, the mass media repeated this nonsense, and depicted poor Kissinger as caught between two irrational adversaries, Hanoi and Saigon.[17] The terror bombing of urban centers in North Vietnam ensued. Though severe damage was caused, the tactic failed. The U.S. Air Force suffered substantial losses, and there were signs of resistance among B-52 pilots. Furthermore, there was an unanticipated and threatening international reaction. Nixon and Kissinger then formally accepted an agreement which is virtually identical to the 9 Points of October. But they continue to misrepresent the central terms of this agreement in exactly the way they misrepresented the October plan, though more blatantly.

Let us now return to the news commentary on the Paris Agreements. The press lauds Kissinger for his brilliant maneuvering, failing to observe that in his genius, he has succeeded in signing the earliest NLF program, in effect. Worse still, the press—in particular, the liberal press—presents the Nixon-Kissinger misrepresentation of the agreements as if it were the text signed in Paris. Thus on the crucial matter of "the South's political status," *Newsweek* asserts that Hanoi has now

> accepted the provision that north and south are divided by a sacrosanct demarcation line, thus tacitly acknowledging the legitimacy of the Saigon regime. . . . Equally vital to the Nixon Administration was specific mention of the "sovereignty" of the Saigon government, and on this point, too, the U.S. had its way. Hanoi finally conceded that, in Kissinger's words, "there is an entity called South Vietnam." In one important sense, the dispute over that question was what the war in Vietnam was all about.

In the same issue, Stewart Alsop proclaims that if the "marvelously elaborate" Nixon-Kissinger settlement "survives more or less intact, we will have won the war." [18]

All of this is plainly false. Recognition of the status of the demarcation line in the terms of Geneva 1954 implies nothing, tacitly or otherwise, with regard to the legitimacy of the Saigon regime. It does imply that "there is an entity called South Vietnam" in the precise sense that has been advocated, with no modification, by the NLF-PRG from the outset. Hanoi has "conceded" nothing by signing an agreement that expresses the position that it has always maintained. There is no specific mention in the agreements of the "sovereignty" of the Saigon government, though Washington pretends otherwise. The war was "all about" the right of the major political force within South Vietnam to participate in governing this "entity," not about its existence. The "enemy," never departing from its insistence on the right of the South Vietnamese people to self-determination without external interference as now provided by the Paris Agreements, has demanded the right to participate in a democratic political process in South Vietnam. The United States, in contrast, has always insisted on imposing the rule of the GVN by force, with a constitutional structure that outlaws the major organized political force in South Vietnam. The Paris Agreements, with their two-party formula, express the unwavering position of the "enemy" in the light of present conditions. It is quite true that the United States "will have won the war" if the Washington misrepresentation, as repeated by *Newsweek*, "survives more or less intact." It is also true that the text of the agreements signed in Paris represents a capitulation to the long-held program of the "enemy."

It is interesting that as the liberal press dutifully proceeds to present state propaganda as fact, the state executive continues to denounce it for its occasional departures from total servility and demands that this "imbalance" be rectified. If there were an honest and independent press, the headlines in January would have read U.S. ANNOUNCES INTENTION TO VIOLATE PARIS AGREEMENTS. An informed press would have observed further that the Paris Agreements incorporate the essential principles of the original enemy program, never modified except in detail. The actual press plays a rather different role in the general system of political indoctrination.

It is a matter of some importance that even those political commentators who have been most outspoken in criticism of the war are reinforcing the illusions that the government is seeking to convey. For example, Tom Wicker writes that

> American policy, which never accepted the Geneva agreement, came to insist, instead, that South Vietnam was a legally constituted nation being subverted and invaded by another power; and that view is implied even in the documents that finally produced the cease-fire.

He adds that "this implication" may have been designed "more nearly to serve Saigon's political needs than to reflect actual American policy in the 1970's."[19] For the reasons already noted, his account of the documents is incorrect. The Paris Agreements merely reiterate the position of the NLF and its North Vietnamese backers with regard to the status of South Vietnam, although the Washington version continues to express the contrary U.S.

view. More important, by promoting such illusions, critical voices in the American press are contributing to the outcome that they most fear: the adoption of Administration rhetoric as policy for the 1970s.

The point deserves emphasis. It might be asked what harm there is in permitting Nixon and Kissinger to conceal their formal capitulation with the rhetoric of "peace with honor." The answer should be obvious. Quite apart from any concern for historical accuracy, consider the likely consequences of success in Administration propaganda efforts. Naturally, the Nixon Administration seeks to convey the impression that its cool courage and unflinching commitment to "peace with honor" compelled the "North Vietnamese" to desist from their "aggression." If the public accepts this view, with the corollary that the GVN remains as the "sole legitimate government of South Vietnam" entitled to use forceful means to control its population, then there will be public support for new forms of American violence if the "sole legitimate government" of South Vietnam begins to collapse, for whatever reason. Nixon and Kissinger may find themselves trapped by their own deceit. If, indeed, their iron will forced the enemy to capitulate, then surely it would be unprincipled to refrain from applying the rod once again if the "legally constituted nation" whose freedom they have won is again "subverted or invaded." One might recall the words of another President, just twelve years ago: "No matter what goes wrong or whose fault it really is, the argument will be that the Communists have stepped up their infiltration and we can't win unless we hit the North." [20]

As an illustration, consider the argument now being offered by the Administration for the saturation bombing of Cambodia. Assistant Secretary of State Marshall Green, testifying before Congress, offered this explanation for the bombing:

> It is related to our desire to see a cease-fire brought about in Cambodia. Our experience in these very difficult negotiations shows that it takes a combination of a clenched fist with one hand and an open hand with the other to bring about negotiations with these characters in Hanoi. [21]

Putting aside the cynicism of these remarks, they have some logic, if, indeed, it was the American "clenched fist" that drove Hanoi and the Pathet Lao to the negotiating table. If, on the contrary, the United States was forced to capitulate because of the failure of its terror tactics, a rather different conclusion follows. There is little doubt, from the record just surveyed, that the latter conclusion is true. One must assume that Green, who is well informed, is aware of this, but no matter: The deluge of propaganda conveyed by the mass media has beaten the American public—if not the resistance forces of Indochina—into submission. Thus Green's nonsensical "explanation" seems plausible to those who have been successfully indoctrinated. By its treachery, the press is once again an accomplice in the destruction of rural Cambodia by U.S. air power.

Perhaps the most striking element in the current program of political indoctrination is the careful orchestration of the POW return—in particular, the publicity given to the reports of torture. Americans, who are well known for their gentlemanly behavior in military affairs, are naturally scandalized at these reports, which, taken at face value,[22] indicate that the North Vietnamese jailers were capable of considerable brutality towards men who came to destroy their homes and murder their families. From press and TV reports, one might be led to believe that the American POWs were captured by the Communists, for the purpose of torturing them, while they were strolling peacefully down Main Street, Iowa. As of this moment the press has not reported the testimony of any POWs who say, I smashed the marketplace of Phu Ly to rubble; I demolished the main hospital of Thanh Hoa; I leveled the city of Vinh; I bombed rural Laos with such intensity that helpless peasants lived in caves deep in the forest without seeing the light of day for years; I destroyed the dikes in Quang Ngai province of South Vietnam; I flew the B-52s that bombed the densely populated Mekong Delta. We know that all of these things happened, and much more. But no one seems to have done it. It was some natural disaster, for which no one bears responsibility, just as there is no human agent responsible for the current devastation of Cambodia by U.S. air power, to judge by editorial comment.

This delicacy is characteristic of press commentary. Craig Whitney, summarizing the "legacy of the war,"[23] speaks of "the punishment inflicted on [the Vietnamese] and their land when the Communists were allowed to operate in it" and of the villagers "driven from their ancestral homes by the fighting." No agent is specified. It just happened. The passive voice is a remarkable rhetorical device. Or consider this report from My Lai, describing the "battered Batangan peninsula," demolished by U.S. bombardment and murderous ground operations: "big guns fire into the peninsula as they have again and again over the eight years that American, South Korean and South Vietnamese forces have been trying to make it safe."[24] "Trying to make it safe"—the phrase captures with perfection the profound moral cowardice of the media, unable to confront the reality of the policies that they have generally supported. The report continues: In 1965, the peninsula "began becoming unsafe for its inhabitants, generally supporters of the Vietcong." Again, there was no human agent who made it "unsafe." The report goes on to quote villagers who accuse the Americans of having killed many people here: "They are in no position to appreciate what the name My Lai means to Americans," the reporter adds philosophically. How could one expect these simple primitive folk to comprehend what a tragedy My Lai was for Americans?

To appreciate more fully the role of the mass media in the current orgy of mass hypocrisy over the POWs, one should recall their treatment of the detailed and extensive reports by veterans concerning the torture of Vietnamese prisoners by U.S. troops and the South Vietnamese to whom they were turned over by U.S. forces, reports that are far more horrendous than anything claimed by the POWs and surely no less credible—the veterans had nothing to gain by making public what they had done and seen. But this was not a fit topic for press or television. Or, consider the virtual media blackout of the American tour in March 1973 by two Frenchmen recently released from Saigon jails, who reported specific cases of torture and assassination in the U.S.-maintained prisons, noting that "all of this is under the control of American advisers who, we are convinced, are aware of everything that happens in the Vietnamese prisons." [25] To have informed the public of the fate of the hundreds of thousands of political prisoners and "detainees," or the U.S. role in domestic repression in South Vietnam, would, clearly, have been inconsistent with the requirements of state propaganda at the moment.

The foreign press is less reserved. The *Far Eastern Economic Review* points out that "the Nixon Administration has had nothing to say about the atrocities which have been going on for many years in these prisons and which still go on, often under the direct supervision of former American police officers." [26] T. J. S. George notes "America's continuing capacity to sustain an air of injured innocence" with regard to the alleged behavior of Hanoi's "ungrateful leaders," who "still exhibit no appreciation of the need for carpet-bombing, fragmentation blasting, blockades and protective reaction strikes on behalf of the Free World":

Interestingly, too, the men who talked of oriental tortures were all able to stand up and speak into microphones, showing scars here and there; none

showed evidence of irreversible malnutrition. Another set of prisoners
was not so lucky. These were the men and women released from South
Vietnam's "tiger cages." Only a handful of them have been seen in public,
and then briefly. They had been held in tiny cages for so long that they
could no longer stand up; they had to shuffle about in crouching positions.
They were all incurably crippled while prolonged malnutrition had
turned them into grotesque parodies of humanity.[27]

The American press has a rather different perspective.

Perhaps the prize for hypocrisy on this matter goes to the *New York Times*
editorial writers. The POW reports, they say, give a

> damning indictment of the Vietnamese Communists, one that cannot be
> erased by the pious denials of the North Vietnamese or their apologists in
> this country. A compelling case can and should be made against the North
> Vietnamese for their clear violations of the Geneva Convention of 1949 to
> which they are signatories. . . . Unfortunately, the record is not unflawed.
> South Vietnam's "tiger cages" for political prisoners at Con Son, the Mylai
> massacre and similar, if lesser, incidents involving American troops, the
> bombing and shelling of civilian areas, torture of prisoners in the field
> and the use of chemical weapons are all violations of the spirit if not the
> letter of international law, for which the highest United States authorities
> cannot escape responsibility, even if the violations were not expressions of
> official policy.[28]

Difficult as it is to believe, the authors of these lines are asserting that
bombing and shelling of civilian areas and the use of chemical weapons
(defoliation) was not official policy. It is unimaginable that they do not
know that this has been official policy since 1965, though perhaps they have
forgotten that it was official policy long before.[29] As to the occasional "flaws
in the record," the *Times* itself has published without editorial comment innumerable examples of explicit violations of the Geneva Conventions by
U.S. troops. To select virtually at random from the miserable record, Malcolm Browne reported that B-52 bomb craters are "surrounded with bodies,
wrecked equipment and dazed and bleeding people. . . . We sent in helicopter gunships, which quickly put them out of their misery," an allied official
stated.[30] The Geneva Conventions require that members of armed forces
who are "placed *hors de combat* by sickness, wounds, detention, or any other
cause, shall in all circumstances be treated humanely." But this action, a

mere detail in the chronicle of atrocities that is a natural consequence of official U.S. policy, merely "flaws the record" while violating the spirit, but not the letter, of the Geneva Conventions.

To the moralists of the *New York Times* editorial board, the Vietnamese are fair game, one must conclude. The editors themselves, having so courageously defended the principles of humanity and self-determination of peoples since the U.S. intervention in Indochina began, are morally entitled to condemn the Vietnamese for their treatment of the pilots who were the instruments of the American policy of massacre and destruction in a foreign land. At precisely the same moral level, the Nazi press might have fulminated—and probably did—over the savage treatment of pilots captured by the European resistance forces.

The POW campaign, nevertheless, is an outstanding achievement of the state propaganda machine. It may well have a significant impact on the public response to American aggression in the future.

It is a fair generalization that the mass media have operated, virtually without exception, within the framework of state propaganda. The war is described as aggression by North Vietnam against the South, with the United States coming to the aid of the beleaguered South Vietnamese—unwisely, the doves maintain, since the exercise in magnanimity was too costly and the means were inappropriate to the just ends sought. Long forgotten, if ever understood, is the plain fact that the United States invaded, occupied, and virtually demolished South Vietnam, expanding the war over all of Indochina, after the failure of its earlier efforts to impose the dictatorship of its choice in the South.

By adopting the framework of government propaganda in the early stages of the U.S. intervention, the press contributed materially to the violence of subsequent years. Any state, democratic or totalitarian, must mobilize public support for dangerous, costly, and vicious policies. By misrepresenting the American intervention as a defense of freedom, the mass media helped mobilize that public support, creating political pressures that would have made it difficult for U.S. policymakers to extricate themselves short of all-out war even if they had so desired. It is astonishing that the simple lesson cannot be learned (assuming, of course, that those responsible have not known it all along), and that the same process may now, once again, be unfolding.

Since the cease-fire was announced, GVN military forces have proceeded to launch military operations throughout South Vietnam, subjecting areas that escape their control to regular and systematic bombardment in an effort to weaken the opposition and to prevent the free movement guaranteed by the Paris Agreements. One of the few reporters still working seriously in South Vietnam, Daniel Southerland, concluded from his extensive investigations that

> the Saigon government has been guilty in by far the greatest number of cases of launching offensive operations into territory held by the other side. Quite a few Saigon troop casualties seem to be attributable to Saigon attempts to build outposts in zones which have been recognized for years as NLF base areas. The Thieu government also seems to feel that it has the right, despite the cease-fire, to take back territory which it lost during last year's big Communist offensives.[31]

Other reports from South Vietnam confirm this assessment.[32] Southerland had earlier reported from Long Khanh Province that a few days after the cease-fire, "government forces did not hesitate to use the heaviest weapons at their disposal, including bombs, artillery shells, and helicopter rockets" in retaking twelve hamlets that Communist troops had "penetrated"; "the brutal manner in which the government forces blasted their way back into the hamlets has hardly won friends."[33] A Western cameraman who spent twenty-four hours in a "Vietcong-controlled zone" reported that "a South Vietnamese helicopter gunship sprayed a village in a raid lasting more than a half an hour" and that villagers predicted, to within five minutes, the onset of the regular evening artillery bombardment.[34] A few weeks later, Southerland reported from Trung Lap village that the government was forcibly preventing people from returning to the hamlets from which they had been driven by U.S. Army forces several years before, burning down houses in their old hamlets and confiscating identification papers in an effort to discourage resettlement and "as a means of keeping a hold on villagers." In the way of further "discouragement," those who nevertheless return are "constantly being harassed by government artillery fire." "Each day they picked up shell casings and fragments from the napalm cannisters and helicopter rockets which continue to shatter the countryside here." Villagers complained that "the soldiers beat us up if we go to our fields." Police and army officers stated that they knew nothing of the peace agreements and had orders not to let villagers "go over to the other side." "When people ask us about the peace agreement, we tell them that this is nothing more than a cease-fire in place, and the people are supposed to stay in place."[35]

The most significant feature of the immediate post-cease-fire period is that the GVN is living up to its word, systematically calling upon its military and police forces to violate the agreements, employing the ample means of violence provided to it by the United States.

All of this recalls the behavior of the Diem regime in the mid-1950s. The 1954 Geneva Accords, which Diem publicly renounced by January 1955, guaranteed democratic liberties and prohibited reprisals or discrimination (Article 14c). Diem instituted "pacification" programs which the correspondent for the London *Times* and *Economist*, David Hotham, described in these terms: "They consist of killing, or arresting without either evidence or trial, large numbers of persons suspected of being Viet-Minh or 'rebels.' " [36] The Diem army conducted "massive expeditions" to peaceful Communist regions, arresting tens of thousands and killing "hundreds, perhaps thousands of peasants," destroying "whole villages . . . by artillery" in operations that were "kept secret from the American public." [37] Diem's forces were trained, equipped, and advised by the United States. His secret police "was largely the brainchild of a highly respected, senior U.S. Foreign Service professional," General Lansdale reported secretly in 1961, adding: "I cannot truly sympathize with Americans who help promote a fascistic state and then get angry when it doesn't act like a democracy." [38] These methods were temporarily successful in crushing the Viet Minh and others in the South, in direct and immediate violation of the Geneva Accords, although as the U.S. Military Assistance Advisory Group (USMAAG) warned in July 1957, "The Viet Cong guerrillas and propagandists, however, are still waging a grim battle for survival" and still attempting to form groups "seeking to spread the theory of 'Peace and Co-existence,' " [39] along with other similar crimes against the state. As in the 1950s, the U.S. commitment to the Thieu regime signifies an intention to violate the central provisions of the agreements that had just been signed.

In the past, "bombing halts" were in fact bombing redistributions, as planes were simply shifted elsewhere. The January 1973 "cease-fire" is no exception. Bombing in February reached seventy thousand tons. All American B-52s in the region were assigned the task of saving the collapsing U.S.-backed Cambodian regime from guerilla forces, often described as "North Vietnamese," although it is now conceded that "hardly any North Vietnamese or Vietcong forces are still fighting against the Cambodian army." [40] International relief officials in Phnom Penh estimate that "no fewer than 3000 civilians have been killed in [the Phnom Penh] area" in the last three weeks of March.[41] This was prior to the intensified bombing which reached the level of 3,600 tons a day on April 2–3.[42] B-52 carpet bombing is reported on the outskirts of Kompong Thom and within ten miles of Phnom Penh.[43] Its general character is conveyed by the following remark by a U.S. intelligence officer after refugee interrogations on "the 30th consecutive day of intensified American bombing in Cambodia": "Bankrom has been completely leveled. There have been many dead, many wounded and many secondary explosions. We judge the bombing results quite satisfactory."[44]

The Pentagon has announced its plan to expend billions of dollars in an effort to preserve the military-police apparatus that constitutes its sole hope for victory—that is, for successful violation of the agreements in Vietnam. It is admitted that 7,200 "civilians" are now employed by the Pentagon in South Vietnam, the majority of them as technicians with the GVN armed forces, under the supervision of Major-General John Murray. "Contract civilians will handle maintenance, logistics, and training jobs formerly performed by the U.S. military . . . many are retired military men."[45] Perhaps American "civilians" will be at the controls as the GVN air force undertakes the systematic bombing of South Vietnam and probably Cambodia, as suggested by Pentagon spokesman Jerry Friedheim.[46] Recall that according to the Paris Agreements, "The United States will not continue its military involvement or intervene in the internal affairs of South Vietnam," and, "Within 60 days of the signing of this agreement, there will be a total withdrawal from South Vietnam of troops, military personnel, including technical military personnel and military personnel associated with the pacification program, armaments, munitions and war material of the United States and those of . . . the other foreign countries allied with the United States and the Republic of Vietnam [GVN]. . . . Advisers from the above-mentioned countries to all paramilitary organizations and the police force will also be withdrawn within the same period of time" (Articles 4, 5, 3a). Henry Kissinger, in his January 24 conference presenting the Washington version of the agreements, made it clear that the United States maintains the right to provide "civilian technicians serving in certain of the military branches."

The new "aid" program calls for an expansion of the police surveillance system and the prisons, which will continue to produce the "grotesque sculptures of scarred flesh and gnarled limbs" described by a *Time* reporter as some political prisoners were released.[47] More generally, the plans to incorporate South Vietnam within the global economy dominated by the

United States, put in abeyance at the time of the 1972 offensive, will undoubtedly be resurrected, to the extent possible.[48] Leaving no stone unturned, the Saigon regime is not only seeking foreign investment but also is offering tourist trips to South Vietnam featuring bars, nightclubs, massage parlors, dance halls, and casino centers, and also trips to "the 'preserved' remains of Quang Tri, An Loc, and Kontum. Bus tours taking tourists to these shattered cities will cheerfully blast out recorded commentaries on the said piles of rubble. And an extended tour is even being planned to the bomb-scarred demilitarized zone."[49] Thus the American efforts to "modernize" South Vietnam, which have so intrigued academic ideologues in recent years, may have a considerable economic pay-off—if only the enemy will observe the terms of the ceasefire as these are defined in Washington.

President Nixon warns "that based on my actions over the past four years, that the North Vietnamese should not lightly disregard such expressions of concern, when they are made, with regard to a violation."[50] Commenting on this warning to cease "infiltration," James Reston observes that "Hanoi is obviously cheating on the truce agreement and cheating big," challenging our reliance on its "good faith."[51] He cites no other violations of the agreements; no such denunciations were heard when the United States and the GVN announced their intention to violate the agreements that they were about to sign, or when the Saigon regime, in accordance with its official pronouncements, then proceeded to impose its control over the population by a systematic program of force and violence, with full support from Washington. Reston's quite typical reaction is understandable, on one fundamental assumption: that the Washington version of the Paris Agreements is the operative version, while the text itself is to be disregarded as a meaningless exercise in deception. Judging by press commentary and popular reactions, it appears that Washington has succeeded in imposing its interpretation of the agreements on the public and the mass media, in one of the most effective exercises in political indoctrination in recent memory. This was done in the American way: not by suppressing all information—the text, after all, was available—but by overwhelming the facts with a flood of lies, relying on the traditional willingness of the mass media to report government propaganda as fact. Exactly the same means were employed to establish the mythology of U.S. intervention to defend South Vietnam from aggression at the time when an American expeditionary force was invading South Vietnam, not to speak of innumerable other episodes of the Cold War era. In short, the traditional free market in ideas:

All information is in principle available, and each agent in our pluralistic society—the state, the mass media, the corner druggist—is permitted to say what he pleases without censorship. If the concentration of power leads to a predictable result, this is part of the price that we, and the victims of American power, must pay for freedom.

An American reporter held for several days in NLF-controlled territory made the interesting observation that cadres

> had obviously made a great effort to familiarize everyone in their area with the terms of the [Paris] agreement. This was in sharp contrast to areas under Saigon government control where the specific provisions of the agreement go unpublicized and where local government officials sometimes seem to have only the vaguest idea of what is in the agreement.[52]

Stanley Karnow reported from Saigon that:

> Significantly, the North Vietnamese have distributed millions of copies of the Paris agreement, and have broadcast its contents in detail. Only a few Saigon newspapers have been authorized to publish excerpts from the document.[53]

Saigon, of course, resorts to outright censorship rather than the American free market model, which achieves virtually the same effect in a more stable society. It is quite natural that the PRG and DRV should seek to publicize the agreements while the GVN and United States attempt to suppress them, by the appropriate means. This is an entirely predictable consequence of the fact that the agreements constitute a capitulation by the U.S.-GVN to the position of the Vietnamese enemy. Given the suppression of the actual terms of the agreements, it is quite possible for U.S. officials to warn of renewed U.S. military operations, including bombing of "military targets in the Hanoi-Haiphong area," all "aimed at forcing greater compliance with the cease-fire"[54] as this is defined in Washington's Operation Brain Wash. The result, very likely, will be a third phase of the Indochina war, with considerable public support for renewed American aggression, at least until the costs mount too high.

Chapter Four

THE REMAKING OF HISTORY (1975)

AMERICAN IMPERIALISM has suffered a stunning defeat in Indochina. But the same forces are engaged in another war against a much less resilient enemy, the American people. Here, the prospects for success are much greater. The battleground is ideological, not military. At stake are the lessons to be drawn from the American war in Indochina; the outcome will determine the course and character of new imperial ventures.

As the American-imposed regime in Saigon finally collapsed, Japan's leading newspaper, *Asahi Shimbun,* made the following editorial comment:

> The war in Vietnam has been in every way a war of national emancipation. The age in which any great power can suppress indefinitely the rise of nationalism has come to an end.

The comment on the war in Vietnam is fairly accurate. The projection for the future, far too optimistic.

The question is a critical one. The great powers surely do not take the American failure in Vietnam as an indication that they can no longer use force to "suppress the rise of nationalism." In fact, during the period of its Vietnam debacle, the United States achieved some notable successes elsewhere, for example in Indonesia, Brazil, Chile, and the Dominican Republic. And the lessons of Vietnam surely do not teach our partners in détente that they must relax their brutal grip on their imperial domains.

Apologists for state violence understand very well that the general public has no real stake in imperial conquest and domination. The public costs of empire may run high, whatever the gains to dominant social and economic groups. Therefore the public must be aroused by jingoist appeals, or at least kept disciplined and submissive, if American force is to be readily available for global management.

Here lies the task for the intelligentsia. If it is determined that we must, say, invade the Persian Gulf for the benefit of mankind, then there must be no emotional or moral objections from the unsophisticated masses, and surely no vulgar display of protest. The ideologists must guarantee that no "wrong lessons" are learned from the experience of the Indochina war and the resistance to it.

During the Vietnam war a vast gap opened between the nation's ideologists and a substantial body of public opinion. This gap must be closed if the world system is to be managed properly in coming years. Thus we are enjoined to "avoid recriminations," and serious efforts will be made to restrict attention to questions that have no significance or long-term implications. It will be necessary to pursue the propaganda battle with vigor and enterprise to reestablish the basic principle that the use of force by the United States is legitimate, if only it can succeed.

If America's Vietnam "intervention" is understood, as it properly must be, as a major crime against peace, then an ideological barrier will be erected against the future use of U.S. force for global management. Hence those who are committed to the founding principles of American imperialism must ensure that such questions are never raised. They may concede the stupidity of American policy, and even its savagery, but not the illegitimacy inherent in the entire enterprise, the fact that this was a war of aggression waged by the United States, first against South Vietnam, and then the rest of Indochina. These issues must be excluded from current and future debate over the "lessons of the debacle," because they go directly to the crucial matter of the resort to force and violence to guarantee a certain vision of global order.

Pursuit of the forbidden questions leads to examination of the origins and causes of the American war. Elaborate documentation is now available, and the conclusions indicated seem to me fairly clear. It was feared—under the plausible assumptions of the more rational versions of the "domino theory"—that Communist social and economic success in Indochina might cause "the rot to spread" to the rest of mainland Southeast Asia and perhaps beyond, to Indonesia and South Asia as well. In internal policy documents, the war planners wasted little time on the lurid variants of the domino theory served up to terrorize the public. What concerned them primarily was the demonstration effect, what was sometimes characterized as "ideological successes."

An egalitarian, modernizing revolutionary movement in one area might serve as a model elsewhere. The long-term effects, it was feared, might go so far as an accommodation between Japan, the major industrial power of the East, and Asian countries that had extricated themselves from the U.S.-dominated global system. The end effect would be as if the United States had lost the Pacific war, which had been fought, in part, to prevent Japan from creating a "new order" from which the United States would be effectively excluded. Certainly the issues are more complex; I have examined them elsewhere in more detail.[1] But this, I think, is the heart of the matter.

It is possible to condemn American imperialism and yet remain within the framework of official ideology. This can be achieved by explaining imperialism in terms of some abstract "will to power and dominion," again, a neutral category that does not relate to the actual structure of our social and economic system. Thus, an opponent of the Vietnam war can write that "American involvement in Vietnam represented, more than anything else, the triumph of an expansionist and imperial interest"; "America's interventionist and counterrevolutionary policy is the expected response of an imperial power with a vital interest in maintaining an order that, apart from the material benefits this order confers, has become synonymous with the nation's vision of its role in history." But his criticism is not labeled "irresponsible" by mainstream scholarship and commentary, for he adds that "in the manner of all imperial visions, the vision of a preponderant America was solidly rooted in the will to exercise dominion over others, however benign the intent of those who entertained the vision." The criticism is responsible because it presupposes benign intent and does not explore the nature of this "dominion," which may therefore be understood as some socially neutral trait.[2] A threat to dominant ideology arises only when this "will to exercise dominion" is analyzed in terms of its specific social and economic components and is related to the actual structure of power and control over institutions in American society.[3] One who raises these further questions must be excluded from polite discourse, as a "radical" or "Marxist" or "economic determinist" or "conspiracy theorist," not a sober commentator on serious issues.

In short, there are ideologically permissible forms of opposition to imperial aggression. One may criticize the intellectual failures of planners, their moral failures, and even the generalized and abstract "will to exercise dominion" to which they have regrettably, but so understandably succumbed. But the principle that the United States may exercise force to guarantee a certain global order that will be "open" to the penetration and control of transnational corporations—that is beyond the bounds of polite discourse.

Accordingly, the American intelligentsia now face several major tasks. They must rewrite the history of the war to disguise the fact that it was, in essence, an American war against South Vietnam, a war of annihilation that spilled over to the rest of Indochina. And they must obscure the fact that this aggression was constrained and hampered by a mass movement of protest and resistance, which engaged in effective direct action outside the bounds of "propriety," long before established political spokesman proclaimed themselves to be its leaders. In sum, they must ensure that all issues of principle are excluded from debate, so that no significant lessons will be drawn from the war.

What conclusions then, are to be drawn from the horrendous experience of Vietnam as the war draws to an end? There are those who regard the question as premature. The editors of the *New York Times* tell us that:

> Clio, the goddess of history, is cool and slow and elusive in her ways. . . . Only later, much later, can history begin to make an assessment of the mixture of good and evil, of wisdom and folly, of ideals and illusions in the long Vietnam story.

We must not "try to pre-empt history's role." Rather, "this is a time for humility and for silence and for prayer" (April 5, 1975).

There is at least one lesson that the Vietnam war should have taught even the most obtuse: It is a good idea to watch the performance of the free press with a cautious and skeptical eye. The editorial just cited is a case in point. The editors call for reason and restraint. Who can object? But let us look a little further. They go on:

> There are those Americans who believe that the war to preserve a non-Communist, independent South Vietnam could have been waged differently. There are other Americans who believe that a viable, non-Communist South Vietnam was always a myth and that its present military defeats confirm the validity of their political analysis. A decade of fierce polemics has failed to resolve this ongoing quarrel.

We must be silent and pray as we await the verdict of history on this "complex disagreement."

The *New York Times* editors, in their humility, do not presume to deliver Clio's verdict. But they are careful to define the issues properly. The hawks allege that we could have won, while the doves reply that victory was always beyond our grasp. As for the merits of these opposing views, which mark the limits of responsible thinking, we must await the judgment of history.

There is, to be sure, a third logically possible position: Regardless of Clio's final judgment on the controversy between hawks and the doves, the United States simply had no legal or moral right to intervene in the internal affairs of Vietnam in the first place. It had no right to support the French effort to reconquer Indochina, or to attempt—successfully or not—to establish "a viable, non-Communist South Vietnam" in violation of the 1954 Geneva Accords, or to use force and violence to "preserve" the regime it had imposed.

The only judgment that Clio is permitted to hand down is a judgment of tactics: Could we have won? Other questions might be imagined. Should we have won? Did we have the right to try? Were we engaged in criminal aggression? But these questions are excluded from the debate, as the *New York Times* sets the ground rules.

There is method in the call for humility, silence, and prayer. Its manifest purpose is to restrict such controversy as may persist to questions of tactics, so that the basic principle of official ideology will stand: Alone among the states of the world, the United States has the authority to impose its rule by force. Correspondingly, the authentic peace movement, which challenged this basic doctrine, must be excluded from all future debate. Its position does not even enter into the "complex disagreement" that so troubles the editors of the *New York Times*.

It is interesting that not a single letter was published challenging the remarkable editorial stand of the *Times* in these terms. I say "published." At least one was sent; probably many more. The *Times* saw fit to publish quite a range of opinion in response to the editorial, including advocacy of nuclear bombardment (May 4, 1975). But there must, after all, be some limits in a civilized journal.

The *Times* is not alone in trying to restrict discussion to the narrow and trivial issues formulated in its editorial. The *Christian Science Monitor* gives this assessment:

Many voices, including this newspaper, regard the communist victory as a tragedy, believing the U.S. involvement in Vietnam to have been honorable, although the conduct of the war in both its political and military phases was fraught with mistakes and misjudgments. Others will argue, with equal cogency, that America should long ago have realized its mistakes and moved rapidly to extricate itself and permit the South Vietnamese to work things out for themselves. But surely there can be a unifying consensus. . . . (April 22)

Note that the opposing view is assumed to share the *Monitor's* basic premises, while differing on a question of timing. In fact, this is the standard position put forth in the national media, with a few honorable exceptions. Criticism of state policy is always welcome, but it must remain within civilized bounds. An Arthur Schlesinger may express his skepticism with regard to Joseph Alsop's prediction that the American war will succeed, for he goes on to stress that "we all pray that Mr. Alsop will be right." It is obvious, without discussion, than any right-thinking person must pray for the victory of American arms. As Schlesinger explained in 1967, American policy may yet succeed, in which event "we may all be saluting the wisdom and statesmanship of the American government" in conducting a war that was turning Vietnam into "a land of ruin and wreck." [4] But he thought success to be unlikely. Had he gone on to urge that the United States abandon its failed enterprise, the *Monitor* would concede, in retrospect, that this extreme proposal had cogency equal to its own.

The *Washington Post* has perhaps been the most consistent critic of the war among the national media. Consider, then, its editorial response to the termination of the war. In an April 30 editorial entitled "Deliverance," the *Post* insists that we can "afford the luxury of a debate" over the meaning of this "particular agony." Americans should develop "a larger judgment of the war as a whole," but it must be a balanced judgment, including both the positive and negative elements:

For if much of the actual conduct of Vietnam policy over the years was wrong and misguided—even tragic—it cannot be denied that some part of the purpose of that policy was right and defensible. Specifically, it was right to hope that the people of South Vietnam would be able to decide on their own form of government and social order. The American public is entitled, indeed obligated, to explore how good impulses came to be transmuted into bad policy, but we cannot afford to cast out all remembrance of that earlier impulse. For the fundamental "lesson" of Vietnam surely is not that we as a people are intrinsically bad, but rather that we are capable of error—and on a gigantic scale. That is the spirit in which the post-mortems on Vietnam ought now to go forward. Not just the absence of re-crimination, but also the presence of insight and honesty is required to bind up the nation's wounds.

Note again the crucial words "wrong," "misguided," "tragic," "error." That is as far as "insight and honesty" can carry us in reaching our judgment.

The *Post* encourages us to recall that "some part of the purpose" of our policy in Vietnam was "right and defensible," namely, our early effort to help the people of South Vietnam "to decide on their own form of govern-ment and social order." Surely we must agree that it is right and defensible to help people to achieve this end. But exactly when was this "early im-pulse" revealed in action? Let us try to date it more precisely, recalling on the way some of the crucial facts about the war.

Was it in the pre-1954 period that we were trying to help the people of South Vietnam in this way? That can hardly be what the *Post* editors have in mind. At that time, the United States was backing the French in their effort to reconquer Indochina.[5] As Truman's Secretary of State, Dean Acheson, noted, success in this effort "depends, in the end, on overcoming opposition of indigenous population." The Vietnamese resistance forces were led by Ho Chi Minh, whose appeals for American assistance had been rebuffed. No one had the slightest doubt that he had immense popular support as the leader of Vietnamese national forces. But, Acheson explained, "Question whether Ho is as much nationalist as Commie is irrelevant." He is an "out-right Commie." We must therefore help the French who are determined, in Acheson's phrase, "to protect IC [Indochina] from further COMMIE en-croachments." Nothing here about helping the people of South Vietnam to determine their own fate.

Perhaps it was after the Geneva Accords that our "early impulse" flour-ished. Hardly a plausible contention. The ink was barely dry on the agree-ments when the National Security Council adopted a general program of subversion to undermine the political settlement, explicitly reserving the right (subject to congressional approval) to use military force "to defeat local Communist subversion or rebellion not constituting armed attack"— that is, in direct violation of the "supreme law of the land." Such force might be used "either locally or against the external source of such subversion or rebellion (including Communist China if determined to be the source)." The U.S.-backed Diem regime launched a violent and bloody repression, in defiance of the accords that we had pledged to uphold, in an effort to destroy the southern forces that had participated in defeating French colonialism. This slaughter appeared to be fairly successful, but by 1959 the former Viet Minh forces, abandoning their hope that the Geneva Accords would be implemented, returned to armed struggle, evoking the predictable wail of protest in Washington. Surely, then, this was not the period when the United States showed its deep concern for the right of the South Vietnamese people to self-determination.

Perhaps the *Post* is referring to the early 1960s, when U.S. officials estimated that about half the population of South Vietnam supported the National Liberation Front (NLF) and, in the words of the Pentagon Papers historian, "Only the Viet Cong had any real support and influence on a broad base in the countryside," where 80 percent of the population lived. President Kennedy dispatched U.S. forces to suppress the "subversion or rebellion" that was bringing about the collapse of the Diem regime, which was described in the Pentagon Papers as "essentially the creation of the United States." By 1962, U.S. pilots were flying 30 percent of the combat missions, attacking "Viet Cong" guerrillas and the population that supported them. The local forces organized, trained, advised, and supplied by the United States undertook to remove more than one-third of the population by force to "strategic hamlets," where, in the phrase of the Administration's leading dove, Roger Hilsman, they would have a "free choice" between the Government and the Viet Cong. This magnanimous effort failed, Hilsman explains, because of inefficient police work. It was never possible to eradicate the Viet Cong political agents from the hamlets where the population was concentrated. How could a person exercise a "free choice" between the Government and the Viet Cong when the Viet Cong agents—his brothers or cousins—had not been eliminated?[6]

Plainly, we may dismiss the possibility that this was the period in question.

After the coup that overthrew Diem in November 1963, South Vietnam was finally on its way to democracy, according to official propaganda. But this period, unfortunately is not a likely candidate for the *Post*'s award for good behavior.[7] Through 1964 the NLF was offering a settlement on the Laotian model, with a coalition government and a neutralist program.

Meanwhile the United States was maneuvering desperately to avoid what internal documents refer to as "premature negotiations." The reason, as explained by U.S. government scholar Douglas Pike, was that the non-Communists in South Vietnam, with the possible exception of the Buddhists, could not risk entering a coalition, "fearing that if they did the whale would swallow the minnow." As for the "Buddhists" (i.e., the politically organized Buddhist groups), General Westmoreland explained in September of that year they were not acting "in the interests of the Nation." As Ambassador Henry Cabot Lodge later saw it, according to the Pentagon historian, the Buddhists were "equivalent to card-carrying Communists." The United States' position was that the two substantial political forces in the south, the southern whale and the Buddhists, must be prevented from deciding on their own form of government and social order. Only the United States understood "the interests of the Nation." Thus the United States tried to nourish its minnow, which at that point was General Khanh and the Armed Forces Council. As Ambassador Lodge explained, the generals are "all we have got." "The armed forces," Ambassador Maxwell Taylor elaborated, "were the only component of Vietnamese society which could serve as a stabilizing force."

By January 1965, even the minnow was slipping from the American grasp. According to Ambassador Taylor's memoirs,[8] "The U.S. government had lost confidence in Khanh" by late January 1965. Khanh, he writes, "was a great disappointment." He might have been "the George Washington of his country," but he lacked "character and integrity," and was therefore told to get lost a few weeks later. Khanh's lack of character and integrity was clearly revealed that fateful January. He was moving then towards "a dangerous Khanh-Buddhist alliance which might eventually lead to an unfriendly government with which we could not work," Taylor explained.

Actually there was more to it than that. Khanh apparently was also close to a political settlement with the NLF. Speaking in Paris on "South Vietnam Day" (January 26, 1975), General Khanh stated, as he had before, that "foreign interference" had aborted his "hopes for national reconciliation and concord between the belligerent parties in South Vietnam" ten years earlier. In support of this contention, he released the text of a letter sent to him on January 28, 1965, by Huynh Tan Phat, then vice-president of the Central Committee of the NLF, in reply to an earlier letter of Khanh's. Phat affirmed his support for Khanh's express demand that "the U.S. must let South Vietnam settle the problems of South Vietnam" and his stand "against foreign intervention in South Vietnam's domestic affairs." He expressed the willingness of the NLF to join Khanh in "combat for national sovereignty and independence, and against foreign intervention." These negotiations would have led to unity against the United States and an end to the war, Khanh stated. But within a month of this interchange, "I was forced to leave my country, as a result of foreign pressure."

In late January, according to the Pentagon Papers, General Westmoreland "obtained his first authority to use U.S. forces for combat within South Vietnam," including "authority to use U.S. jet aircraft in a strike role in emergencies" (three years after U.S. pilots began to participate in the bombing of South Vietnam). The timing was not accidental. To avert a political settlement among South Vietnamese, the United States undertook the regular, systematic bombing of South Vietnam in February (at more than triple the level of the more publicized bombing of the North), and not long after, an American expeditionary force invaded South Vietnam.

In short, the period from the Diem coup to the outright U.S. invasion of early 1965 can hardly be described as a time when the United States acted on its early impulse to help the people of South Vietnam to decide their own future.

What about the period after February 1965? Here, the question is merely obscene.

In January 1973, Nixon and Kissinger were compelled to accept the peace proposals that they had sought to modify the preceding November, after the presidential elections. Perhaps this marks the beginning of the period to which the *Post* editors are referring. Again, the facts demonstrate clearly that this cannot be the period in question. See Chapter 3.

It must be, then, that the last days of the war mark the period when the United States sought to contribute to self-determination in South Vietnam. In fact, the editors of the *Post* tell us that "the last stage of an era-long American involvement in Vietnam was distinctive . . . because during that brief stage the United States acted with notable responsibility and care," removing Americans and thousands of Vietnamese. "The United States also, in the last days, made what seems to us an entirely genuine and selfless attempt to facilitate a political solution that would spare the Vietnamese further suffering."

Very touching. Granting, for the sake of discussion, the sincerity of this genuine and selfless attempt, this certainly proves that our involvement in Vietnam was a mixture of good and evil, and that "some part of the purpose of [U.S.] policy was right and defensible," specifically, our "early impulse" to help the people of South Vietnam "to decide on their own form of government and social order." Let the debate go forward, then, without recriminations and with insight and honesty, as we proceed to bind up the nation's wounds, recognizing that we are capable of tragic error, but insisting on our "good impulses" which "came to be transmuted into bad policy" by some incomprehensible irony of history.

The U.S. government was (partially) defeated in Vietnam, but only bruised at home. Its intellectual elite is therefore free to interpret recent history without any need for self-examination.

In the current flood of essays on "the lessons of Vietnam," one finds very little honest self-appraisal. James Reston explains "the truth" about the recent disaster in the following terms:

> The truth is that the United States Government, in addition to its own mistakes, was deceived by both the North Vietnamese, who broke the Paris agreements, and by the South Vietnamese, who broke the Paris agreements, and then gave up most of their country without advance notice. (*New York Times*, April 4, 1975)

The United States commits mistakes, but the Vietnamese—North and South—are guilty of crimes, breaking agreements that they had undertaken to uphold. The facts are a little different. As the Paris Agreements were signed, the White House announced that it would reject every major principle expressed in the scrap of paper the the United States was forced to sign in Paris.[9]

The United States proceeded to support the Thieu regime in its announced efforts to violate the agreements by massive repression within its domains and military action to conquer the remainder of South Vietnam. In the summer of 1974, U.S. officials expressed their great pleasure at the success of these efforts, noting that the Thieu regime had succeeded in conquering some 15 percent of the territory administered by the PRG, making effective use of the enormous advantage in firepower it enjoyed thanks to the bounty of the United States. They looked forward with enthusiasm to still further successes.[10]

But none of this counts as an American violation of the Paris Agreements. It is only the evil Vietnamese, North and South, who are guilty of such crimes. This is a matter of doctrine. Facts are irrelevant.

Furthermore, "our Vietnamese" not only broke the Paris Agreements, but also gave up most of their country without giving us advance notice. Reston complains that "the Thieu Government didn't even give Mr. Ford a chance to be fair at the end. It just ordered the retreat, called in the television cameras, and blamed America for the human wreckage of its own failures." How ungrateful and unworthy are these Vietnamese Ford in his innocence, was again deceived; he "was almost unfair to his own country. For he left the impression that somehow the United States was responsible for the carnage in Southeast Asia." That we should be so falsely accused . . .

After many years, one expects nothing different from this worthy pundit. Let us turn, then, to the *Times*'s most outspoken dove, Anthony Lewis, a serious and effective critic of the war in the 1970s. Summing up the history of the war, he concludes:

> The early American decisions on Indochina can be regarded as blundering efforts to do good. But by 1969 it was clear to most of the world—and most Americans—that the intervention had been a disastrous mistake.

Congress and most of the American people "know now that intervention in Southeast Asia was a mistake from the beginning," "that the idea of building a nation on the American model in South Vietnam was a delusion," "that it did not work and that no amount of arms or dollars or blood could ever make it work." Only Ford and Kissinger have failed to learn "the lessons of folly." The lesson of Vietnam is that "deceit does not pay; it may have worked in some other century or some other country, but in the United States at the end of the twentieth century it cannot." Thus "a crucial element at the end was the same one that caused disaster all along: deception by American officials—deception of others and ourselves." This should "afford insight into what went wrong in general." He quotes with approval the judgment of the London *Sunday Times:* "The massive lies involved in the Asian policy have done as much to damage American society and America's reputation as the failure of the policy itself." [11]

The lesson, then, is that we should avoid mistakes and lies, and keep to policies that succeed and are honestly portrayed. If only our early efforts to do good had not been so "blundering," they would have been legitimate. This includes, one must assume, such efforts to do good as our support for the Diemist repression after 1954, or the combat operations of the early 1960s by U.S. forces and the troops they trained and controlled, or the strategic hamlet program, or the bombing of more than a hundred thousand montagnards into "safe areas" in 1962, and on, and on. Recall Bernard Fall's estimate that by April 1965, before the first North Vietnamese battalion was detected in the South, more than 160,000 "Viet Cong" had fallen "under the crushing weight of American armor, napalm, jet bombers and, finally, vomiting gases." [12] But all of these were "blundering efforts to do good," though *by 1969* we should have seen that the "intervention" was a "disastrous mistake."

Finally, consider the thoughts of TRB (Richard Strout), the regular commentator of the *New Republic* (April 25). He writes from Paris, where he has been visiting monuments that record Hitler's crimes. The emotional impact is overwhelming: "I hated the maniac Hitler crew; I could never forgive the Germans." But, he continues, "other nations have lost their senses too; was this not the land of the guillotine? And then, of course, I thought of Vietnam."

At last, someone is willing to contemplate the *criminal* nature of the American war. But not for long. The next sentence reads: "It was not wickedness; it was stupidity." It was "one of the greatest blunders of our history." There is a message: "Watching the long tragedy in living color has been a chastening experience but the act of bravery is to face up to it." If we can do so, perhaps there will be "the dawn of a new maturity—a coming of age."

Our "bravery," however, can go only so far. Our "new maturity" cannot tolerate the questioning of our fundamental decency.

Since TRB recalls "the maniac Hitler crew," perhaps we may go on to recall the self-judgment of the Nazi criminals whom he so passionately detests. We might recall the words of Heinrich Himmler, speaking of the massacre of the Jews:

> To have gone through this and—except for instances of human weakness—to have remained decent, that has made us tough. This is an unwritten, never to be written, glorious page of our history. [13]

By Himmler's standards, the toughness of the American government must be exalted indeed. We have gone through this, and yet remained decent. Blundering perhaps, but fundamentally decent. And if anyone doubts our toughness, let them ask the Cambodians.

We did, of course, have our instances of human weakness. By our standards, My Lai was such an instance; the criminals were dealt with properly in a demonstration of our system of justice. It is true that we did not apply exactly the same standards that were brought to bear in the case of General Yamashita, hanged for crimes committed by troops over whom he had no control in the last months of the Philippine campaign. But at least Lieutenant Calley spent some time under house arrest. The long arm of justice, however, does not reach as far as those responsible, say, for Operation SPEEDY EXPRESS in the Delta province of Kien Hoa in early 1969, which succeeded in massacring eleven thousand of those South Vietnamese whose right to self-determination we were so vigorously defending, capturing 750 weapons and destroying the political and social structure established by the NLF. This operation was more than merely decent: "The performance of this division has been magnificent," General Abrams rhapsodized, in promoting its commander.[14] We can be sure that the custodians of history will place these glorious pages in our history in the proper light.

Our own respectable doves share some fundamental assumptions with the hawks. The U.S. government is honorable. It may make mistakes, but it does not commit crimes. It is continually deceived and often foolish (we are so "naive and idealistic" in our dealings with our allies and dependencies, Chester Cooper remarks), but it is never wicked. Crucially, it does not act on the basis of the perceived self-interest of dominant social groups, as other states do. "One of the difficulties of explaining [American] policy," Ambassador Charles Bohlen explained at Columbia University in 1969, is that "our policy is not rooted in any national material interest of the United States, as most foreign policies of other countries in the past have been."[15] Only those who are "radical" or "irresponsible" or "emotional"—and thus quite beyond the pale—will insist on applying to the United States the intellectual and moral standards that are taken for granted when we analyze and evaluate the behavior of officially designated enemies or, for that matter, any other power.

It is a highly important fact that the majority of the American people strayed beyond the bounds of legitimate criticism, regarding the war as immoral, not merely a tactical error. The intellectuals, however, generally remained more submissive to official ideology, consistent with their social role. This is evident from commentary in the press and academic scholarship. The polls revealed a negative correlation between educational level and opposition to the war—specifically, principled opposition, that is, advocacy of withdrawal of American forces. The correlation has been obscured by the fact that visible and articulate opposition to the war, not surprisingly, disproportionately involved more privileged social strata. The greater subservience of the intelligentsia to state ideology is also demonstrated in a recent study of the "American intellectual elite"[16]—if one is willing to tolerate this absurd concept for the sake of discussion. The study reveals, as should have been anticipated, that these more subtle thinkers generally opposed the war on "pragmatic" grounds. Translating to more honest terms, the intellectual elite generally felt that we couldn't get away with it (at least after the Tet offensive), or that the cost was too high (for some, the cost to the victims).

The essential features of U.S. policy in Indochina were clearly illustrated in the final incident of the American war, the *Mayagüez* incident. On May 12, 1975, the U.S. merchant ship *Mayagüez* was intercepted by Cambodian patrol boats within three miles of a Cambodian island, according to Cambodia—within seven miles, according to the ship's captain. Shortly after midnight (U.S. Eastern Daylight Time) on May 14, U.S. planes sank three Cambodian gunboats. That afternoon, the secretary-general of the United Nations requested the parties to refrain from acts of force. At 7:07 P.M., Cambodian radio announced that the ship would be released. A few minutes later, Marines attacked Tang Island and boarded the deserted ship nearby. At 10:45 P.M., a boat approached the U.S. destroyer *Wilson* with the crew of the *Mayagüez* aboard. Shortly after, U.S. planes attacked the mainland. A second strike against civilian targets took place forty-three minutes after the captain of the *Wilson* reported to the White House that the crew of the *Mayagüez* was safe. U.S. Marines were withdrawn after heavy fighting. The Pentagon announced that its largest bomb, fifteen thousand pounds, had been used. The operation cost the lives of forty-one Americans, according to the Pentagon (fifty wounded), along with an unknown number of Cambodians.

A few days later, in an incident barely noted in the press, the U.S. Coast Guard boarded the Polish trawler *Kalmar* and forced it to shore in San Francisco. The ship was allegedly fishing two miles within the twelve-mile limit established by the United States. The crew was confined to the ship under armed guard as a court pondered the penalty, which might include sale of the ship and its cargo. There have been many similar incidents. In one week of January 1975, Ecuador reportedly seized seven American tuna boats, some up to one hundred miles at sea, imposing heavy fines.

President Ford stated in a May 19 interview that the United States was aware that Cambodian gunboats had intercepted a Panamanian and a South Korean ship a few days before the *Mayagüez* incident, then releasing the ships and crews unharmed. Kissinger alleged that the United States had informed insurance companies that Cambodia was defending its coastal waters, but the president of the American Institute of Marine Underwriters was unable to verify any such "forewarning."

Evidently, the *Kalmar* and *Mayagüez* incidents are not comparable. Cambodia had just emerged from a brutal war, for which the United States bears direct responsibility. For twenty years, Cambodia had been the victim of U.S. subversion, harassment, devastating air attacks, and direct invasion. Cambodia announced that hostile U.S. actions were still continuing, including espionage flights and "subversive, sabotage and destructive activities" and penetration of coastal waters by U.S. spy ships "engaged in espionage activities there almost daily." Thai and Cambodian nationals had been landed, Cambodia alleged, to contact espionage agents, and had confessed that they were in the employ of the CIA. Whether these charges were true or not, there can be no doubt that Cambodia had ample reason, based on history and perhaps current actions, to be wary of U.S. subversion and intervention. In contrast, Poland poses no threat to the security or territorial integrity of the United States.

According to Kissinger, the United States decided to use military force to avoid "a humiliating discussion," failing to add that the supreme law of the land obliges the United States to limit itself to "humiliating discussion" and other peaceful means if it perceives a threat to peace and security. Aware of its legal obligations, the United States informed the United Nations Security Council that it was exercising the inherent right of self-defense against armed attack, though evidently it is ludicrous to describe the Cambodian action as an "armed attack" against the United States in the sense of international law.

Despite official denials, the American military actions were clearly punitive in intent. The *Washington Post* reported (May 17) that U.S. sources privately conceded "that they were gratified to see the Khmer Rouge government hit hard." Cambodia had to be punished for its insolence in withstanding the armed might of the United States. The domestic response indicated that the illegal resort to violence will continue to enjoy liberal support, if only it can succeed (assuming that we regard the loss of forty-one marines to save thirty-nine crewmen who were about to be released as "success"). Senator Kennedy stated that "the President's firm and successful action gave an undeniable and needed lift to the nation's spirit, and he deserves our genuine support." [17] That everyone's spirits were lifted by still another blow at Cambodia may be doubted. Still, this reaction, from the senator who had been most closely concerned with the human impact of the American war, is important and revealing. Senator Mansfield explained that Ford's political triumph weakens antimilitarist forces in Congress. Supporting his conclusion, on May 20 the House voted overwhelmingly against reducing American troop commitments overseas. House Majority leader Thomas P. O'Neill reversed his earlier support for troop reductions.

There were a few honorable voices of protest. Anthony Lewis observed that "for all the bluster and righteous talk of principle, it is impossible to imagine the United States behaving that way toward anyone other than a weak, ruined country of little yellow people who have frustrated us."

On the liberal wing of the mainstream, John Osborne chided Lewis in the *New Republic* (June 7) for his failure to see "some good and gain" in the *Mayagüez* incident. Osborne himself felt that the President acted "properly, legally, courageously, and as necessity required." There were, to be sure, some "flaws." One of these flaws, "disturbing, avoidable, and to be deplored," was the tentative plan to use B-52s. But our honor was saved, according to Osborne, when the plan was rejected "partly because of predictable domestic and world reaction and partly because heavy bombing would almost certainly have worsened rather than bettered the lot of the *Mayagüez* crewmen."

Another possible consideration comes to mind: Bombing of defenseless Cambodia with B-52s, once again, would have constituted another major massacre of the Cambodian people. But no such thoughts trouble the mind or conscience of this austere tribune of the people, who sternly rebuked those "journalistic thumb-suckers" who raised questions in the wrong "manner and tone" in "a disgrace to journalism."

Top Administration officials informed the press that it was Henry Kissinger who "advocated bombing the Cambodian mainland with B-52s during the recent crisis over the captured ship *Mayagüez*." [18] Thankfully, he was overruled by others more humane, who felt that carrier-based bombers would be punishment enough.

The incident reveals the basic elements in U.S. policy towards Indochina: lawlessness, savagery, and stupidity—but not complete stupidity, as one can see from the success in arousing jingoist sentiments at home. The crucial matter is lawlessness, in the specific sense of violating the principle that force may not be used for any purpose except for genuine self-defense against armed attack. The significance of this matter is obvious if only from the fact that it is so generally excluded from discussion of the "lessons of Vietnam" in the mass media, the journals of opinion, and—we may safely predict—academic scholarship.

Within the ideological institutions—the mass media, the schools, and the universities—there is every reason to expect that the task of excluding these issues will be carried out with a fair measure of success. Whether these efforts will succeed in restoring the conformism and submissiveness of earlier years remains to be seen.

The *Post* editorial was certainly correct in denying that "we as a people are intrinsically bad." In fact, "we as a people" recognized that the war was something more than a mistake. In 1965, teach-ins, demonstrations, town forums, extensive lobbying, and other forms of protest reached substantial proportions, and by 1967 there were enormous mass demonstrations, large-scale draft resistance, and other forms of nonviolent civil disobedience. Not long after, the American political leadership came to understand why imperial powers have generally relied on mercenaries to fight brutal colonial wars, as the conscript army, much to its credit, began to disintegrate in the field. By 1971, to judge by the polls, two-thirds of the population regarded the war as immoral and called for the withdrawal of American troops. Thus "we as a people" were, by then, neither doves nor hawks in the sense of responsible editorial opinion and the overwhelming majority of the political commentators.

It has become a matter of critical importance to reverse the ideological defeats of the past decade and to reestablish the doctrine that the United States is entitled to use force and violence to impose order as it sees fit. Some propagandists are willing to put the matter quite crudely. Thus Kissinger, in his academic days, wrote of the great risks if there is "no penalty for intransigence." But there are more subtle and effective means. The best, no doubt, is to reconstruct somehow the shattered image of the United States as a public benefactor. Hence the emphasis on our naiveté, our blunders, our early impulses to do good, our moralism and lack of concern for the material interests that dominate the policy of other powers.

Where this doctrine is not blandly asserted in foreign policy debate, it is insinuated. Consider, as a crucial case in point, the current debate over the use of military force to ensure American control over the world's major energy resources in the Middle East, and thus to maintain our capacity to control and organize the "free world." For the moment, the debate over such intervention is the pastime of intellectuals.

But the situation is unstable. No one can predict what the future may bring. Within the narrow spectrum of responsible opinion there is room for disagreement over the tactical question of how American hegemony is to be established, in the Middle East or elsewhere. Some feel that force is necessary to guarantee "American interests."[19] Others conclude that economic power and normal business procedures will suffice. No serious question may be raised, however, concerning our right to intervene, or the benevolent purposes that will guide such moves, if we are forced to counteract "the aggression of the oil-producing countries against the economies of the developing and developed worlds."[20]

It comes as no surprise, then, to discover that in the current debate over U.S. intervention in the Arabian peninsula it is generally accepted on all sides that after having successfully established its rule, the United States will guarantee a fair and equitable distribution of Middle East oil. The proposition that the United States will or might act in this way is rarely questioned. But consider now the basis for this tacit assumption. Is it an induction from the historical record? That is, can we found this belief on American conduct in the past with regard to its agricultural resources or raw materials or the products of its industrial plant? When the United States dominated world trade in oil, did it use its power to guarantee that its European allies, for example, would benefit from the low production cost of Middle Eastern petroleum? These questions are hardly worth discussing.

Of course, it might be argued that the leopard will, for some reason, change its spots. But then, we might speculate that the Arab oil producers are no less likely to use their control over petroleum to ensure a fair and equitable distribution. The Arab oil producers, for example, expend a far greater proportion of their GNP for foreign aid than the United States or other industrial powers have ever done, and a far larger proportion of their aid goes to poorer countries.[21] Thus, if history is a guide, perhaps we should encourage Saudi Arabia and Kuwait to conquer Texas, rather than debating the merits of an American invasion of the Middle East. In fact, the whole discussion suggests a dangerous case of advanced cretinism. What is remarkable about the recent debate is that it proceeds at all, given the absurdity of the hidden premise.

Nothing could indicate more clearly how wedded the intelligentsia remain to the doctrine of American benevolence, and the corollary principle that the United States is entitled to resort to force and violence to maintain "global order"—if only we can succeed, and, as the more sensitive will add, if only we are not too brutal about it.

The entire American record in Indochina can be captured in the three words "lawlessness," "savagery," and "stupidity"—in that order. From the outset, it was understood, and explicitly affirmed, at the highest level of policymaking, that the U.S. "intervention" in South Vietnam and elsewhere was to be pursued in defiance of any legal barrier to the use of force in international affairs. Given the indigenous strength and courage of the South Vietnamese resistance, the United States was compelled to undertake a war of annihilation to destroy the society in which it gained its support—the society "controlled by the Viet Cong," in the terminology of the propagandists. The United States partially succeeded in this aim, but was never able to construct a viable client regime out of the wreckage. When Washington was no longer able to call out the B-52s, the whole rotten structure collapsed from within. In the end, the interests of American ruling groups were damaged, in Southeast Asia, in the United States itself, and throughout the world. Lawlessness led to savagery in the face of resistance to aggression. And in retrospect, the failure of the project may be attributed, in part, to stupidity.

Intellectual apologists for state violence, including those who describe themselves as doves, will naturally focus on the stupidity, alleging that the war was a tragic error, a case of worthy impulse transmuted into bad policy, perhaps because of the personal failings of a generation of political leaders and incompetent advisers. Stupidity is a politically neutral category. If American policy was stupid, as in retrospect all can see it was, then the remedy is to find smarter policymakers; presumably, the critics.

Some opponents of the war were appalled by the savagery of the American attack. Even such a prominent hawk as Bernard Fall turned against the war in the belief that Vietnam was unlikely to survive as a cultural and historic entity under the American model of counterrevolutionary violence. It is true that the Nazi-like barbarity of U.S. war policy was the most salient and unforgettable feature of the war, in South Vietnam and elsewhere in Indochina. But savagery too is a politically neutral category. If the American leadership was sadistic, as it surely was, the remedy—it will be argued—is to find people who will pursue the same policies in a more humane fashion.

The more critical matter is the lawlessness, specifically the resort to force to maintain a "stable world order" primarily in the interests of those who claim the right to manage the global economy.

Suppose that the system of thought control reestablishes the doctrine that the United States remains exempt from the principles we correctly but hypocritically invoke in condemning the resort to force and terror on the part of others. Then the basis is laid for the next stage of imperial violence and aggression. As long as these doctrines hold sway, there is every reason to expect a reenactment of the tragedy of Vietnam.

Chapter Five

ON THE AGGRESSION OF SOUTH VIETNAMESE PEASANTS AGAINST THE UNITED STATES (1979)

LTHOUGH A LONGTIME DEFENDER of the U.S. interven-
tion in Vietnam, Guenter Lewy pretends here to be above the battle,
bringing "light, rather that heat" to an experience "more complex
than ideologues on either side" would allow (v,vii). He also believes that his
portrayal of the war is "novel and occasionally startling in both fact and significance" (v). This work rests, however, on a foundation of unexamined
chauvinist premises capable of rationalizing virtually any form of aggression and violence, and its scholarly facade crumbles at almost random
scrutiny. The novelty of Lewy's book is the combining in a single volume of
a review of factual materials that others have presented in condemnation of
the war with the standard conclusions of state propaganda. To achieve this
marriage, Lewy is compelled to misuse and misrepresent documentary material, ignore critical evidence, and descend to a quite "startling" moral
level.

Lewy had access to substantial new documentation from U.S. government sources. What he has culled from it is by and large insignificant, although occasionally he provides some new evidence of interest. To cite one
case, Lewy reports a military analysis of "air operations in the populated
Delta area" in January 1963 involving "indiscriminate killing" which
"took a heavy toll of essentially innocent men, women and children" (96).
Elsewhere he notes that "during the year 1962 American planes flew 2,048
attack sorties" (24) and that villages in "open zones" were "subjected to
random bombardment by artillery and aircraft so as to *drive the inhabitants*

Review of Guenter Lewy, *America in Vietnam* (Oxford: Oxford University Press, 1978).

into the safety of the strategic hamlets" (our emphasis; 25). A serious historian would ask how this early and extensive U.S. participation in an assault
on the rural population of South Vietnam bears on the question of the legitimacy of the U.S. presence and the locus of aggression. But Lewy never
raises these issues. His only comment is that the "indiscriminate killing"
was "counterproductive."

Lewy's concept of "innocence" deserves careful attention. He comments
on the "difficult question" of determining who should be considered "innocent" as villages were destroyed by napalm and "the lavish use of American
firepower" (55). He recognizes that "in large measure the war was a revolution which started in the hamlets and that therefore the Viet Cong were already among the people when we went to the hills" (86, citing Francis
West). It was necessary to remove the fish from the water. Therefore, "until
late 1968 the prevalent but uncodified policy was that of compulsory reloca-
tions and displacement by military pressure through combat operations,
crop destruction and the creation of specified strike zones" (65). This too
was "counterproductive" since, as U.S. advisors discovered, "Putting the
people behind barbed wire against their will is not the first step towards
earning their loyalty and support" (181). Other studies found that "our un-
observed fire alienates the local peasants in most cases, thus harming our efforts to break down their loyalty to and support for the Viet Cong" (100).
Operation CEDAR FALLS removed thousands of people "presumed to be either members of VC families or VC laborers" then demolishing their villages and destroying the land with Rome Plows (64). In Operation MALHEUR
thousands of villagers were evacuated and their houses burned and "the extensive use of artillery and air strikes with high explosives and napalm . . .
resulted in large-scale destruction and the deaths of villagers and many refugees" in an area where "many villagers belonged to VC associations and
voluntarily helped the VC," leaving a "picture of desolation" typical of the
region (70).

After page upon page of such descriptions, the rational reader would conclude that the United States was guilty not only of aggression but also of unspeakable barbarism. Lewy, however, does not draw such conclusions. The
reason is that the villagers were not "innocent"—they were supporting the
South Vietnamese revolutionary forces that were resisting the United States
and the client regime it had installed, what Lewy calls their "legitimate
government" (93). Legitimacy does not derive from the consent of the governed, but rather from the will of a foreign power.[1] As Lewy concedes, the

"legitimate government" was the fiefdom of a "privileged elite" supported mainly by "the military officer corps" and unable to win the loyalty of the people, while the South Vietnamese enemy had a "strong political apparatus" and "gradually and skillfully [drew villagers] into the NLF village organization" by such means as "redistributing wealth and status" while "the government relied for its survival on force alone" (94–95, 58, 19, 176). In fact, Lewy ignores substantial evidence bearing on this crucial matter from U.S. government sources,[2] but even without it, the real situation is sufficiently evident from his own brief remarks.

For Lewy, then, an "innocent villager" is one who accepts the rule of foreign force and its local client. If a villager is not "innocent," he may legitimately be blasted by U.S. bombs, his villages may be burned to the ground, and he may be forcefully moved behind barbed wire, where he is granted what Lewy calls "security" and "protection" by his "legitimate government." By revealing with such utter clarity the levels of moral degradation to which it is necessary to sink to justify the U.S. war, Lewy has unwittingly provided one of the most devastating critiques yet to appear in print.

Recall that Lewy is not writing just military history but a moral tract. He writes that "the reasoned conclusion of this study" is "that the sense of guilt created by the Vietnam war in the minds of many Americans is not warranted" (vi). Lewy is concerned over "the impairment of national pride and self-confidence that has beset this country since the fall of Vietnam" (vii), based on the belief that it is immoral to destroy a rural society and to drive its people to fortified encampments where they are "protected" from the local groups they willingly support. This error can be rectified once we recognize that the millions of people treated in this manner by the United States were not "innocent." The only problem raised by "the damage done to Vietnamese society by allied military operations" is that it was a "handicap to pacification" (95).

While the South Vietnamese who tried to resist the U.S. attack were not "innocent," the U.S. government was. If, however, one does not postulate with Lewy that South Vietnam was imperial property, but that the South Vietnamese had a right to determine their own fate, then the U.S. presence was illegitimate from the start and we are dealing with unprovoked external aggression. This fundamental issue Lewy never addresses directly. It is intriguing to watch the maneuvers. He begins by dismissing pacifists who repudiate resort to military force, then turning to the narrower question of whether U.S. military force was properly used, always overlooking the fact that a non-pacifist may accept the resort to force in self-defense against "armed attack" in accordance with international and domestic law, while rejecting aggression.

Lewy concedes the popularity of the Viet Minh after the 1954 Geneva Accords, but stresses that the United States did not sign the final declaration calling for unifying elections and was therefore not bound by it. How this refusal to accept the terms of a political settlement gave the United States the right to impose its will on the people of South Vietnam Lewy never explains. He passes in silence over the actual U.S. government response to the 1954 accords, specifically, the recommendation of the National Security Council to use force in explicit violation of law to defeat "local Communist subversion or rebellion not constituting armed attack," a recommendation that was implemented by installing a regime that launched a reign of terror, then joining it in expanding violence (as noted above) when its terrorism evoked a response that it could not contain. Essentially, then, Lewy merely *assumes* imperial prerogatives, noting that "American leaders did consider it vital not to lose Vietnam to a Communist-led insurgency directed and supported by North Vietnam" (418). We will see directly how he distorts the uncontested facts about the relative timing.

"By May 1955," Lewy tells us, France "was out of Vietnam and the U.S. had assumed responsibility for large-scale economic and military aid" (11). It took over what Lewy implies was the equally legitimate "responsibility" of the French. The subsequent war, Lewy explains, was "not of an international character" and the United States was "not an occupying power but a cobelligerent, there with the approval of the GVN" (227–28), namely, the government it installed and defended from its population by violence. Lewy adopts the imperial premise as easily as a Soviet Lewy would swallow a parallel argument on the Soviet right to define the "legitimate" government of Czechoslovakia or Afghanistan.

On matters of international law, Lewy always searches for the interpretation that will rationalize anything that the United States did. He cites a RAND Corporation study of the crop destruction program which indicated that it was seriously damaging the civilian population, causing intense hatred of the United States and Saigon, and not even serving to deprive the insurgents of food. The program violated the army's own code and was therefore "disguised as a South Vietnamese activity." Lewy defends it on the ground that the military *thought* and *claimed* that it was useful. It contributed to "the overall resource-denial program" and forced civilians into refugee camps so that "as a result, the VC suffered manpower shortages for support purposes." Furthermore, Lauterpacht "even grants the right of general devastation in order to deprive guerillas of their sustenance" (259–62). Thus Lewy disposes of international law on two levels. First, he assumes the right of the United States to impose its will by force on the people of South Vietnam, an act regarded as aggression when performed by hostile states; and having accorded this unique right to the United States, he concludes that military necessity may justify annihilation. Thus, "If guerillas live and operate among the people like fish in the water, then, legally, the entire school of fish may become a legitimate military target," in which case moral blame falls on the guerrillas "who have enlarged the potential area of civilian death and damage" (306). If the guerrillas continue to live in their villages, they are morally culpable and they and their families may be incinerated.

On Lewy principles, devastation and killing may be prodigious in relation to any military gains, but this is at most "counterproductive" or "obtuseness and mistakes" (262) if there are claimed military benefits. Only admittedly pointless killing would be criminal, something that no state ever admits. Lewy quotes critics of the U.S. war who wrote that the United States was committing war crimes "in the layman's sense of this term" (224),[3] failing to understand the reason for the qualification: namely, that every state has its Guenter Lewys who will stretch an elastic legal code to accommodate whatever atrocities "military necessity" and available military technology find convenient. On his principles, it would take very little effort to justify gas chambers—for example, as part of a "manpower resource-denial program" if an entire rural population is "guilty" and "general devastation" is therefore justified in any case. Even an internal minority could be handled in this manner with little adjustment to the principles involved if, for example, social theorists and the state sincerely believed that this "race" was a cancerous evil, contaminating healthy genes and plotting subversion. The efficient surgical excision of such a group by "general devastation" or other modes of disposal would be, in Lewyesque terms, a "socio-military necessity," that should be evaluated in terms of efficiency in pursuing the state objective. It might conceivably be counterproductive.

In discussing the treatment of prisoners, Lewy shows his reasonableness by acknowledging "several cases" of U.S. maltreatment and torture. These are treated with antiseptic brevity, and Lewy takes pains to put them into a context of the "frustration resulting from fighting an often unseen enemy,

the resentments created by casualties," etc. In dealing with Communist in-
humaneness, however, he gives a plenitude of detail, with an unconcealed
moral indignation totally absent from his grudging admission of U.S.-
Saigon torture, and factors that might "explain" such acts by the enemy are
treated with sarcasm ("Hanoi assures the world that despite the terrible
crimes the U.S. pilots had committed . . ."[334]). He even matter-of-factly
"explains" Saigon torture: The police were not highly professional, prison
guards were underpaid, and "South Vietnamese" have a low regard for
human life. Lewy makes no explicit comparison of numbers and modes of
tortures, concentrating instead on the details of North Vietnamese treatment of U.S. pilots, avoiding the massive evidence that Saigon-U.S. torture
and killing of prisoners was systematic and large-scale. Another method-
ological dichotomy: He suggests that the damage to tiger-cage victims was
simulated as part of a propaganda conspiracy among highly organized and
politicized prisoners; whereas the "debriefed" testimony of the U.S. pilots is
accepted at face value and without question. Lewy does not report the com-
parisons offered by journalists, for example, in the *Far Eastern Economic
Review* (March 26, 1973), where it was noted that U.S. POWs "who talked of
oriental tortures were all able to stand up and speak into microphones,
showing scars here and there" whereas those released from U.S.-run jails in
Saigon "were all incurably crippled while prolonged malnutrition had
turned them into grotesque parodies of humanity." Lewy also makes a
sharp distinction between the nasty ARVN and the constraining U.S. forces:
"The success achieved by American intervention against the abuse and torture of VC suspects is difficult to assess . . . [but] on the whole, American influence helped somewhat to mitigate the cruelties to be encountered in any
civil war" (288). This is based on no evidence, merely self-serving statements of U.S. officials. It also flies in the face of such facts as U.S. sponsorship of the Phoenix program, U.S. supply and training functions, funding of
prisons and interrogation equipment and centers, and the replication of
similar operations in Brazil, Chile, Uruguay, the Philippines, etc.[4]

While Lewy carefully avoids the question of U.S. aggression, he insists
that "the notion of 'foreign aggression' [is] in itself perfectly justified and
supported by the facts" (41), namely, North Vietnamese aggression. And although an imperial U.S. right to dominate is an implicit premise fundamental to his case, Lewy gives a great deal of attention to an alleged North
Vietnamese aggression in trying to legitimize U.S. intervention. Let us see
how he proceeds to establish his claim.

Evidently, the question does not arise in the pre-1954 period. After Geneva, Lewy notes, "The Viet Minh, defending the interests of the peasants and basking in the glory of having defeated the French, not only were popular and in effective control of large parts of the south, but they also had a highly efficient organization ready to take advantage of the democratic liberties proclaimed in the final declaration of the Geneva conference" (14). For this reason, it was "justifiable" for the U.S.-imposed regime temporarily to institute "dictatorial measures"; obviously, democratic procedures are unfeasible if the wrong people will win. Lewy then alleges that Communist terror "predictably goaded the Diem regime into stepping up its clumsily pursued and often brutal antiterrorist campaign" (16). As the basis for this conclusion, he cites Jeffrey Race, who in fact provided substantial documentary evidence to the contrary, concluding that the Communist party held "that, except in limited circumstances, violence would not be used, even in self-defense, against the increasing repressiveness of the government," even though U.S.-backed terrorism was decimating "the southern organization." When self-defense was finally authorized, Race continues, government forces collapsed, and even though "the government terrorized far more than did the revolutionary movement," "by early 1965 revolutionary forces had gained victory in virtually all the rural areas of Long An" (the province near Saigon that he was studying).[5]

How does Lewy succeed in turning Race's conclusion into its opposite? By avoiding the main thrust of his documentation and argument and citing only his conclusion that the 1959 decision to initiate armed activity (in response to years of terrorism by the U.S. client regime) was taken in Hanoi, a question that is totally irrelevant to the interaction between U.S. Diem terror and the use of force by the former Viet Minh. This is a typical example of how Lewy uses documentary evidence. He also cites Joseph Buttinger, failing to mention his conclusion that "future historians may very likely regard the claims that in South Vietnam the United States was defending a free country against foreign aggression among the great political lies of this century."[6] Lewy also cites U.S. government specialist Douglas Pike, failing to report his conclusion that the NLF "maintained that its contest with the GVN and the United States should be fought out at the political level and that the use of massed military might was in itself illegitimate" until forced by the United States and its client regime "to use counter-force to survive."[7]

While Lewy's government sources consistently regarded the NLF as the only "truly mass-based political party in South Vietnam" (Pike), Lewy con-

cludes that it was "impotent" as "revealed" by North Vietnamese dominance of the postwar system (18). He fails to note that this result followed
years of U.S. violence that had virtually destroyed the NLF and the peasant
society in which "the fish were swimming," and the bombing of the North
that had drawn northern regulars into the war, exactly as planners had anticipated.

In a further effort to establish his thesis of North Vietnamese aggression
in the face of the obvious facts, Lewy refers to a captured document reporting the party meeting in Hanoi in December 1963. He fails to convey the
contents of this internal party document, which defines the war as "a struggle of the South Vietnamese people," etc. Its major recommendation is that
"the revolutionary people in SVN must promote a spirit of self-reliance,"
struggling against "an enemy who is weak politically and morally but
strong militarily and materially." The South Vietnamese people must "settle their own problems" since "revolution is a creative achievement of the
masses." The role of the North is to build socialism and "to increase aid to
the South," which must conduct its own struggle in a spirit of self-reliance.

It is astonishing to see this document offered as evidence for North Vietnamese aggression at a time when U.S. military forces were already devastating South Vietnam. We might add that detailed quotes from this
document and analysis of it have long been in print in discussion of earlier
efforts by propagandists to misrepresent it in Lewy's manner.[8]

The evidence is overwhelming that when the United States expanded its
aggression to a full-scale invasion in early 1965 it had no evidence of a
North Vietnamese troop presence, and thus obviously could not plead "collective self-defense," ludicrous as the claim is in any event. As late as July
1965, the Pentagon was still concerned over the "probability" that North
Vietnamese units might be in or near the South, five months after the initiation of intensive bombing of North Vietnam.[9] Lewy tries to counter such
facts (which he nowhere cites) by appealing to a May 1968 State Department study which claimed that elements of the North Vietnamese 325th
Division arrived in the South in December 1964–March 1965, the earliest
having left in October 1964 (after the August bombing of North Vietnam).
A historian, of course, would seek to determine the credibility of this study,
introduced into the *Congressional Record* in an effort to gain some support
for the war. Lewy does not; what emanates from the U.S. government is
sacrosanct. But let us take it at face value. Lewy fails to point out that this
document states that "at least until 1959, [the 325th Division was] report-

edly composed entirely of South Vietnamese" (its later composition is not mentioned). Thus a historian would conclude that quite possibly South Vietnam was invaded by South Vietnamese in early 1965 (three years after U.S. air attacks against South Vietnam began, ten years after the onset of U.S.-backed terrorism in the South, several months after the first bombing of the North after the faked Tonkin Gulf incident of August 1964). Furthermore, simple logic shows that the question is irrelevant to the issue of justification for the accelerated U.S. invasion in 1965, since its motives must be assessed on the basis of evidence then available, not what was concocted years later to provide retrospective justification for U.S. aggression when domestic support was waning.

But for Lewy, logic is as irrelevant as fact. Thus he is able to write that "the commitment of American troops was defensive in the sense of seeking to forestall a South Vietnamese defeat" in April 1965 (43), before there was any evidence of the presence of North Vietnamese regular units, where his term "South Vietnamese" refers to the U.S. implantation that lacked popular support and was being overthrown by an indigenous rebellion despite massive application of U.S. force.

Lewy's commitment to a higher truth is shown in his handling of materials long exposed as propaganda fabrications, but convenient to his case. For example, he cites figures of fifty thousand executed during the North Vietnamese land reform and estimates by Hoang Van Chi of one-half million executed. His source is Bernard Fall, who used Chi as his source. In a footnote, Lewy writes that "attempts by the Hanoi sympathizer D. Gareth Porter to deny the scope of this terror remain unconvincing." This ends the discussion. In fact, Porter demonstrated that Chi (who was employed and subsidized by Saigon and U.S. intelligence) grossly falsified documents and based his estimate of deaths on one village where one person was allegedly executed, extrapolating from this sample to the whole of North Vietnam. The former head of the Central Psychological War Service for the Saigon army at the time later informed the press that the land reform atrocities were "100% fabricated" by Saigon authorities, with the assistance of U.S. and British intelligence. In a subsequent and more detailed study, Edwin Moise notes further that Chi made no mention of atrocities in 1955: "It was only in later years that his memories began to alter," namely, after the Hanoi regime began producing evidence on "errors and failures" in the land reform which Chi then proceeded to falsify, adding his "extrapolation." [10] Lewy cites none of this material. To a true believer in the state religion, it simply doesn't matter. Chi's evidence, now totally discredited from the standpoint of scholarship, is unchallengeable in propaganda tracts since it supports what the U.S. government would like people to believe.

Similarly in the case of the Hue massacre, Lewy simply accepts government statements as fact, never so much as mentioning the evidence that has been presented challenging them or the assessments by independent observers such as the British journalist Philip Jones Griffiths, who wrote that most of the victims "were killed by the most hysterical use of American firepower ever seen" and then designated "as the victims of a Communist massacre." [11] Again, evidence and argument are simply irrelevant. The government has spoken. What more is there to say? Anyone who questions the claims that Lewy accepts on purely doctrinal grounds is dismissed as a "Hanoi sympathizer," whatever his views may be about Communism or "Hanoi." It must be understood that Lewy uses this term throughout in a technical sense, applying it to anyone who does not meet his standards of servility to the state.

Lewy, in fact, goes beyond the propaganda fabrications of state officials in his desire to put a good face on U.S. actions in Vietnam. Thus, in regard to the Phoenix program, William Colby and other officials have acknowledged that mistakes were made in identifying "Vietcong infrastructure," and that, regrettably, many innocent people may have been killed. Other analysts and observers have gone further, claiming that the Phoenix program of selective murder was quickly transformed into a system of indiscriminate killing, given the combination of ignorance, total corruption, a bounty and quota system, and the fact that, as one U.S. adviser noted, Saigon authorities "will meet every quota that's established for them." [12] Lewy, however, uses the officially acknowledged fact that most of the Phoenix murders were not originally "targeted" to show that Phoenix was more benign than its critics suggest, as it "undermines the charge that the Phoenix program was a program of planned assassinations" (281). It never occurs to Lewy that a planned assassination program run amok would kill well beyond "targets," and his implication that there is something healthy about large numbers of *unplanned* assassinations is remarkable even for Lewy. Thus, while even a Colby may admit that the killing of untargeted victims suggests something improper, a Lewy turns this into further apologetics. He concedes that the program had "weaknesses" and claims that it was of limited effectiveness for U.S. purposes, but this spokesman for Western humanism never suggests that the massacre of large numbers of ordinary civilians is troublesome in itself. The Lewy defense of indiscriminate killing calls to mind Congressman William Goodling's justification for U.S. bombing in Cambodia: "Our bombs don't single out certain segments or certain peoples in Cambodia. Our bombs hit them all. And whether you thought it was right or I thought it was right, the military at that particular time thought it was right." [13] Here are a politician and a propagandist on the same wavelength.

Lewy's scholarly integrity is also revealed by his handling of independent studies of military operations that he examines. This is particularly important, since he relies so heavily on military documents, a valuable but biased source. For example, in dealing with the U.S. command's version of SPEEDY EXPRESS a historian would make careful use of the published study of this operation by Alex Shimkin and Kevin Buckley, and also of Buckley's notes, at least those parts that have been in print since 1975.[14] They found that the "awesome firepower" of the U.S. 9th Infantry division caused a "staggering number" of civilian deaths in a peaceful province that had largely been under local NLF control. Most of the killings were the result of "a relentless night and day barrage of rockets, shells, bombs and bullets from planes, artillery and helicopters," including night attacks. In one village every house was destroyed. A neighboring village was the target center for B-52 raids according to a MACV location plot. Even in deep bunkers, children were killed by concussion—but then, they were not "innocent," since their parents supported the South Vietnamese enemy.[15]

Describing the "spectacular" results of SPEEDY EXPRESS. Lewy makes no use of the Shimkin-Buckley study, remarking only that "the assertion of Kevin P. Buckley of *Newsweek* that perhaps close to half of the more than 10,000 killed . . . were noncombatants remains unsubstantiated" (143). The assertion was not Buckley's; he cited a U.S. pacification official. But it is true that it remains "unsubstantiated," as does the official figure of 10,883 that Lewy cites, which is of course an ugly joke down to the last digit. The U.S. command had no idea how many people were killed by bombs, napalm, and antipersonnel weapons. An honest study would at least have mentioned some of the horrifying material collected by Shimkin and Buckley and would have considered the significance of this murderous U.S. assault on a peaceful region under local NLF control. Lewy, however, keeps to official sources, merely expressing some skepticism as to whether what he calls "the amazing results of Operation SPEEDY EXPRESS" should "be accepted at face value."

Lewy's blind faith in his leaders is revealed no less strikingly in his discussion of the bombing of North Vietnam. According to U.S. government documents, the bombing was aimed at military targets and damage to civilians was minimal. Western diplomats, non-Communist journalists, and numerous other visitors have reported that large areas of North Vietnam were totally devastated. The city of Vinh was leveled in 1965 and was so heavily bombed later that not even the foundations of buildings remain. Much of the country is a moonscape, where there is no visible sign of life.[16] But according to Lewy, none of this happened. How can one dare to confront government pronouncements with mere fact? And where something may have happened, he is quick with the predicted defense. The city of Thanh Hoa was bombed, but then there was an important bridge several miles away. As Lewy could easily have discovered, the Thanh Hoa hospital, destroyed by bombing, is miles from the bridge, and the area between was largely spared; the bombing of the bridge was highly concentrated, so that everything nearby was reduced to rubble, including a former village. But of course this fact, even if it were acknowledged, falls under "military necessity." The result is a form of apologetics for massacre and destruction, often mere denial of plain fact, for which no comparison comes to mind apart from the worst excesses of Nazi and Stalinist "scholarship."

Wherever one opens this tract one finds comments that would simply be regarded as comical if discovered in enemy propaganda. Thus Lewy writes that "with regard to the years 1965–67 it is possible to maintain that the North Vietnamese merely matched the massive American buildup" (41). That is, the estimated fifty thousand North Vietnamese "merely matched" the half-million-man U.S. expeditionary force backed by enormous air and naval forces. Had Lewy written that the North Vietnamese "merely matched" the buildup of Korean and Thai mercenaries it would have been almost accurate. Of course, one can discern Lewy's meaning when the clouds of propaganda are dispelled. He points out elsewhere (56) that the "enemy" was perhaps more than matching the U.S. military buildup in late 1965. A few computations reveal, as other sources have reported, that this "enemy buildup" was overwhelmingly local recruitment by the South Vietnamese revolutionaries in direct response to the full-scale U.S. invasion. To Lewy, however, the South Vietnamese are aggressors in their own villages, while the U.S. is defending the "security" of the population by blasting them out of their homes and driving them to concentration camps where they can be "protected."

Space prevents a more thorough analysis. It is easy to demonstrate, as these few examples illustrate, that this work is a parody of scholarship. Intellectually worthless and morally grotesque, it is, nevertheless, important—not for its substance, but for what it reveals about Western culture. Imagine that the Russian government were to release documents concerning the invasion of Hungary and that some Soviet "historian" were to use them, dismissing out of hand the question of the legitimacy of the Russian intervention, seriously distorting the documentation he cites, accepting the most ludicrous propaganda fabrications, omitting crucial evidence and historical context, and offering the moral premise that it is legitimate to massacre Hungarians who are not "innocent" because they cooperate with Hungarian "terrorists." Perhaps such a study would be published by some Russian research center as a specimen of Soviet propaganda. It is inconceivable, however, that it would be published by the Oxford University Press as an authoritative account of the Soviet intervention or described by U.S. reviewers as "sophisticated and profound" (*Foreign Affairs*).

Thus the reaction to this squalid tract is of interest, though its content is virtually without value apart from some footnotes to military history. Needless to say, this is not the judgment that will be presented by the Western media, though it is difficult to believe that such a clumsy piece of propaganda will enter the scholarly record.

Chapter Six

KISSINGER, *THE WHITE HOUSE YEARS* (1980)

IN A STUDY of Kissinger's foreign policy written before his memoirs appeared, Seyom Brown describes Kissinger as "the arch practitioner of the razzle-dazzle, 'can do' American pragmatism," his performance "a brilliantly executed series of improvisations," perhaps "more shuttle than substance."[1] The fifteen-hundred-page memoirs, covering Nixon's first term, confirm that assessment. Many pages are devoted to what Kissinger calls "philosophy" ("The statesman's responsibility is to struggle against transitoriness and not to insist that he be paid in the coin of eternity," "to strive, to create, and to resist the decay that besets all human institutions") and to the lessons of history ("There can be no peace without equilibrium and no justice without restraint"; 55). The discussion throughout is as vapid as these examples suggest. Our goal is "peace and justice" (70), "a global equilibrium" (192), "to find a trajectory toward a world where no one had ever been" (809). The statesman must struggle "to rescue some permanence from the tenuousness of human foresight" (747). The text is sprinkled with such words as "paradoxical" and "ironic." It would be a mistake to think that behind this lies some subtle "conceptual framework" or global design. Rather, Kissinger's memoirs give the impression of a middle-level manager who has learned to conceal vacuity with pretentious verbiage.

"Equilibrium was the name of the game," Kissinger explains (764). But what is "equilibrium"? "Equilibrium" is secured by thwarting "Moscow's geopolitical ambitions" (764); "we would not ignore, as our predecessors had done, the role of the Soviet Union in making the war in Vietnam possible" by "massive supplies to North Vietnam" (133, 121)—a reasonable

Review of Henry Kissinger, *The White House Years* (Boston: Little, Brown & Co., 1979).

stance, on the assumption that the United States owns the world. Still another threat to "equilibrium" was "Soviet aggressiveness in the Middle East" (801), as when antiaircraft systems and military personnel were sent to Egypt after Israeli bombing deep inside Egypt using U.S.-supplied Phantom jets. Other illustrations include "proxy wars by India and Syria" (1255), Hanoi's refusal to make peace on Kissinger's terms, Allende's electoral victory in Chile, all "facets of a global Communist challenge" (594). In the face of this global Soviet challenge, Washington must "strengthen security in an international system less dependent for stability on permanent American intervention" (765). The United States must continue to be "the bulwark of free peoples everywhere" (1014)—as in Guatemala, the Philippines, Chile, Iran, Indochina, the Dominican Republic, etc.

From many such passages, the meaning of "equilibrium" (or "stability") emerges clearly: It increases or declines as U.S. dominance of the global system increases or declines. Any decline is part of a global challenge orchestrated by Moscow (or earlier, Peking; in 1969, Kissinger "still considered the People's Republic of China the more aggressive of the Communist powers"; 173). The problem we face is that the USSR is intent on "waging a permanent war for men's minds," "mocking the traditional standard of international law that condemns interference in a country's domestic affairs" by sponsoring "upheavals, revolutions, subversion" with no concern for "Western concepts of goodwill." They understand only "self-interest," so that there is no point in "appeals to a sense of moral community" (117–25). They are so different from us, in these respects.

The world, unfortunately, sometimes fails to understand. Thus as "American self-doubt" became "contagious" in the 1960s, "European intellectuals began to argue that the Cold War was caused by American as well as by Soviet policies" (57), while "a vocal and at times violent minority" in the United States challenged "the hitherto almost unanimous conviction that the Cold War had caused by Soviet intransigence" alone (65). Critics sometimes even "alleged that our [weapons] programs triggered Soviet responses rather than the other way around" (199). We should learn, however, from the Cuban missile crisis, where Kennedy established "a psychological balance" so that some progress was possible (126); elsewhere, Kissinger notes that "Khrushchev's humiliation in Cuba was one cause of his overthrow two years later" and that "the Soviet Union, reacting in part to its humiliation in the Cuban missile crisis of 1962, had undertaken a massive effort to augment its military strength across the board" (196–97). "Psychological balance" equals "humiliation of the Soviet Union." Only the most deluded could believe that U.S. initiatives contribute to international tension.

Our "malaise" is so deep that it requires not "expertise" but "philosophy," particularly because of the "ominous change" in the nature of power. "The capacity to destroy proved difficult to translate into a plausible threat even against countries with no capacity for retaliation"; power has "turned abstract, intangible, elusive" (66–67), as the peasants of Indochina can testify.

One should not try to assess such pronouncements, which abound, as if they represented some effort at analysis of contemporary history. Kissinger's conception of the U.S. role in the world is encapsulated in his criticism of pre-Kissinger policy as "oscillat[ing] . . . between optimistic exuberance and frustration with the ambiguities of an imperfect world" (57); the invariant commitment of the United States, by definition, is to overcome these imperfections. These are simply the effusions of someone with no understanding of history and no interest in it. As in his academic writings, Kissinger reveals himself to be an unquestioning advocate of the use of American power to establish global dominance, a person who can be assigned the management of this power by others who are concerned with the real motives for its exercise, a question that is outside Kissinger's purview.[2]

Kissinger claims that prior to his involvement in policy formation, there was no geopolitical tradition in the United States, where "by 'geopolitical' I mean an approach that pays attention to the requirements of equilibrium" (914). This geopolitical concern for equilibrium, as history shows, usually suggests "siding with the weaker to deter the stronger" (915)—which does not imply that the USSR should side with Vietnam or Cuba to deter the United States. It is, of course, sheer nonsense to claim that Kissinger introduced the concept of "geopolitics" to American foreign policy.[3] Others, who are concerned with fact, understand the concept in more rational terms. For example, *Business Week* (January 28, 1980) called for a "revival of geopolitics," noting that thirty years ago "Washington planned protection of vital raw materials through intensive intelligence and military contingency operations," just as an earlier (and realistic) analysis (April 7, 1975) explained how "fueled initially by the dollars of the Marshall Plan, American business prospered and expanded on overseas orders. . . . No matter how negative a development, there was always the umbrella of American power to contain it. . . . The rise of the multinational corporation was the economic expression of this political framework," though "this stable world order for business operations is falling apart" in the mid-1970s. But there are no such lapses in Kissinger's orations. The Marshall Plan, for example, merely "expressed our idealism" (61), just as "American moral leadership" did throughout the postwar period (380).

Kissinger admires Bismarck's maxim that "courage and success do not stand in a causal relationship; they are identical" (905). Courage, as he has explained in his academic writings and illustrates throughout these memoirs, and more significantly in his actions, is the willingness to smash opponents incapable of retaliation and to "face up to the risks of Armageddon," [4] for example, in "go[ing] to the brink over Pakistan" (1293). He explains how "we might inculcate habits of moderation" in the Soviet leadership (1204); this, immediately following his prideful account of the bombing of Hanoi and Haiphong, the mining of Haiphong harbor, and the use of B-52s in the South ("bombing and mining had greatly improved Hanoi's manners" [1303], demonstrating that "only the fear of resumed military operations would keep Hanoi on course"; 1431). The bombing of Hanoi and Haiphong was initiated in the full expectation that the Russians would cancel the planned summit, a fact that does not deter Kissinger from castigating the media for their similar assessment (1200, 1191). It is not difficult to manifest "courage" of this sort when the enemy is too weak to strike back and one trusts that others with real power will not be insane enough to respond with similar "courage."

While Kissinger has nothing rational to say about the goals or framework of policy, he treats the reader to extensive detail on such world-shaking topics as the theory of negotiations, the styles of various political leaders, their ranking on the humor quotient, and so on. Throughout, he describes his masterful handling of negotiations and his victories in single-handed combat over his tormentors, from "Ducky" (Le Duc Tho) to university presidents and academic colleagues, who repeatedly reveal their silliness in his rendition of their interventions. The reader's awe at Kissinger's brilliance is perhaps tempered slightly by his account of a Russian report of Brezhnev's comparable achievements, which recalls "Dean Acheson's famous dictum that no one ever lost a debate in a memorandum of conversation dictated by oneself" (1208).

Only in conversation with "the Colossus of de Gaulle" does Kissinger falter, and in an interesting manner. Kissinger attempts to explain to de Gaulle that the United States must continue to pound Indochina because "a sudden withdrawal might give us a credibility problem." "Where?" de Gaulle asks. "The Middle East," Kissinger suggests. " 'How very odd,' said the General from a foot above me. 'It is precisely in the Middle East that I thought your enemies had the credibility problem' " (110). One wonders whether de Gaulle left it at that, or proceeded further to demolish Kissinger's rationale for destroying Indochina. In any event, Kissinger records no response, and in fact nowhere explains how American "credibility" was secured by his murderous conduct of the war.

Kissinger has been accused of treating the war in Cambodia, obviously enflamed by his initiatives despite pathetic attempts at self-justification, as a "sideshow." [5] His memoirs reveal that the characterization is correct: The war was extended to Cambodia to help achieve U.S. aims in South Vietnam; "Cambodia was *not* a moral issue" (his emphasis; 515). But the criticism is too limited. Vietnam too was a "sideshow." For Kissinger, the war was fought to establish "credibility," and for his predecessors, "to show that the 'war of liberation' . . . is costly, dangerous and doomed to failure" (General Maxwell Taylor, February 1966)[6] and to prevent a "domino effect," namely, the danger that social and economic successes in Indochina might cause "the rot to spread" throughout the U.S.-dominated system.[7]

Kissinger, however, deals with none of these topics, limiting himself to standard patriotic speeches: "Our predecessors had entered in innocence, convinced that the cruel civil war represented the cutting edge of some global design"; "our entry into the war had been the product . . . of a naive idealism that wanted to set right all the world's ills and believed American goodwill supplied its own efficacy" (226, 230). In fact, in the 1940s analysts clearly understood that in aiding France they were combating the nationalist movement of Vietnam, and despite later pretense, the clearer-headed (e.g., field operations coordinator of the U.S. Operations Mission John Paul Vann) always understood that this was true in South Vietnam,[8] at least until U.S. might had succeeded in demolishing the society. Idealism and good will played as much of a role as they did when Russia invaded Hungary or Afghanistan. Kissinger's account, which would embarrass a moderately well-informed high school student, cannot even maintain consistency. Thus we read that the Vietnamese have "little sense of nationhood" though "they have fought for centuries . . . to determine their national destiny" (231, 274).

What is perhaps more interesting is Kissinger's complete failure to comprehend the dynamics of the Cold War. He says (and probably believes) that "we became involved because we considered the warfare in Indochina the manifestation of a coordinated global Communist strategy" (64). He also reports, correctly this time, that when the USSR invaded Czechoslovakia, "they did so amid a smokescreen of accusations against the United States, West Germany, and NATO for 'interfering' " (116). Much the same is true when the USSR now invades Afghanistan, just as the United States was defending freedom from a global Communist conspiracy when it overthrew the government of Guatemala or invaded the Dominican Republic. But the real function of the Cold War is far beyond Kissinger's comprehension or concern.[9]

In his efforts to achieve "equilibrium," Kissinger was beset by enemies on every hand: not only Russia and its various "proxies," but also the bureaucracy, Congress, the media, his academic colleagues, arms-control specialists, the young (who, contrary to appearances, were not really protesting the war, but were "stimulated by a sense of guilt encouraged by modern psychiatry and the radical chic rhetoric of upper middle-class suburbia," overcome with "the metaphysical despair of those who saw before them a life of affluence in a spiritual desert"; 297, 299), the American public, and finally, the world. During the 1972 Christmas bombings, a noble effort to achieve peace, "Not one NATO ally supported us or even hinted at understanding our point of view" (1453); "world opinion had been oblivious to Hanoi's transgressions" and believed Hanoi "to be the victim of American 'oppression' when it had started every war in Indochina since 1954" (1425). Fifteen hundred pages do not suffice to provide evidence for this repeated and essential claim. Again, it would be pointless, in this context, to enter into a detailed discussion of the actual facts—say, the U.S. subversion of the 1954 Geneva Accords (Kissinger is outraged over Hanoi's "flagrant violation of the Geneva Accords" eighteen years later; 1115), the massive U.S.-backed assault against the anti-French resistance in the late 1950s, the U.S. bombing of the South in the early 1960s, the full-scale invasion of the South before there was evidence of the presence of any regular North Vietnamese forces, the successful overthrow of the government of Laos in 1958 after a Pathet Lao electoral victory, etc., etc. Facts are plainly irrelevant to this style of discourse, and Kissinger never asks why the world was so oblivious of his version of them: why the world believed that our "war to resist aggression had turned into a symbol of fundamental American evil" (56), unaccountably.

The most terrible enemies were the Vietnamese—North and South. The "diplomatic style" of Hanoi was "maddening," with its "almost morbid suspicion and ferocious self-righteousness . . . compounded by a legacy of Cartesian logic," contrasting with the American style, based on "the American belief in the efficacy of goodwill and the importance of compromise" and "an ethic of tolerance" (259). Our client Thieu and his associates were "egregious," "despicable," "outrageous" (1326, 1358), generating in Kissinger "that impotent rage by which the Vietnamese have always tormented physically stronger opponents" (1327). Their methods were "obnoxiously Vietnamese," specifically, Thieu's "egregious, almost maniacal, tactics and his total insensitivity to our necessities" (1467). Thieu applied "to us the elusive tactics Vietnamese reserve for foreigners" in an effort "to grind us down" (1322), just as Hanoi "sought to grind us down" (1329). In the real world context, remote from Kissinger's story, it was the Americans who were "grinding the enemy down by sheer weight and mass" (pacification chief Robert Komer[10]); Kissinger, of course, saw none of this—from his visits to Vietnam he recalls only "idealistic Americans working under impossible conditions to bring government and health and development to a terrified and bewildered people" (230). Americans, in their naiveté and idealism, were "ever unequal to the complexities of Vietnamese psychology" (1375). "Whether in making war or peace, Vietnam seemed destined to break American hearts" (1445). Even the Vietnamese language, "with its finely shaded meanings quite beyond our grasp," was an enemy (1325). By the end, Kissinger is virtually frothing at the mouth over the "arrogance" and "insolence" (his favorite word) of Vietnamese on all sides. The basic colonialist, indeed racist attitudes can no longer be concealed, as his frenzy mounts.

A man of deep sensitivity, Kissinger is appalled by the lack of compassion revealed by his domestic enemies (who were numerous: "all the press, the media and intellectuals have a vested interest in our defeat"; 1390)—though there were occasions on which some of the press were "compassionate" (293, 1011). The doves, he writes, "have proved to be a specially vicious kind of bird"; there was "no civility or grace from the antiwar leaders" (295). The "most poignant fate" was visited on Robert McNamara, demoted to head of the World Bank (295). Walt Rostow was "mercilessly persecuted," "not reappointed to his professorship at the Massachusetts Institute of Technology" (295) (he received a full professorship at the University of Texas). The example is typical of Kissinger's difficulties with the real world. True, Rostow was not reappointed—by a political science department no less hawkish than he. In fact, a group of antiwar students and faculty did initiate an inquiry to determine whether an issue of academic freedom arose, announcing their intention to protest if this were the case, on the grounds that war criminals should not be denied appointment on political grounds.[11] But it quickly became obvious that Rostow's wartime record could hardly have been a factor in his rejection by his colleagues, who were not quite "antiwar leaders." Not even the most trivial example escapes Kissinger's mania for falsification.

Others too deserve "compassion," specifically, the Shah, "a pillar of stability in a turbulent and vital region." He was a "dedicated reformer" who was "undermined by his successes" while "wrestling perhaps with forces beyond any man's control" (as contrasted, say, with the leadership in Indochina after the great peacemaker had completed his work). The Shah "understood that the dangers to Iranian independence had historically come from the north," not from England and the United States. "He had been restored to the throne in 1953 by American influence [sic] when a leftist government had come close to toppling him" (the Mossadegh government was "leftist," by definition, by virtue of the decline in "equilibrium" caused by its moves towards independence). He then pursued his "noble aspirations," though, to be sure, some of the methods were "unworthy of the enlightened goals." If the Shah was "authoritarian," this was "in keeping with the traditions, perhaps even the necessities, of his society." The "most implacable opposition" to him, as we see from the events of 1978, was narrowly based: landowners, mullahs, and "radicals." "Nor can it be said that the Shah's arms purchases diverted resources from economic development"; the United States simply tried "to match the influx of Soviet arms into neighboring countries" (1258f.).

As always, Kissinger wisely refrains from offering any evidence for his pronouncements, which, in this case, pass beyond his usual ignorance or deception. The factual record shows that the Shah's enlightened policies were a disaster for a large part of the rural population and the urban poor, and that vast resources were squandered with the help of the huge Nixon-Kissinger program of recycling petrodollars by pouring arms into the hands of the "guardian of the Gulf," with consequences that are well known.[12] There is barely a phrase in Kissinger's account that rises above absurdity.

Kissinger describes how he visited Teheran after leaving Moscow, comparing the grim atmosphere there with Teheran, where he "felt almost a physical sense of relief" because "the warm goodwill was tangible" and the visit "humanly engaging," not dampened by the misery of poor peasants driven to urban slums or by "a history of torture which is beyond belief" in a country with perhaps the worst human rights record in the world, according to Amnesty International at about the same time. His conclusion is that we should now show compassion—to the Shah, not his victims. "The least we owe him is not retrospectively to vilify the actions that eight American Presidents—including the present incumbent—gratefully welcomed," such as murder, torture, and vast robbery and corruption. We will "impress no one by condemning him now"—at least no one who counts, excluding, for example, Iranians or others in the Third World. As for the possibility of examining our own record in applying "influence" to place this tyrant on his throne, establishing and training his dreaded secret police, providing the means for massive repression to the very end of his bloody rule, creating an economy that squandered vast wealth while perpetuating, sometimes intensifying, misery and impoverishment—that question, needless to say, does not arise.

It also goes without saying that no compassion is recommended for the beneficiaries of Kissinger's efforts to maintain "equilibrium" and "credibility" in Indochina, Chile, Bangladesh, or elsewhere.

Kissinger's noble endeavors to achieve peace and justice are framed by the Indochina war. The first challenge he faced was the "unprovoked offensive" launched by Hanoi in February 1969 with "extraordinary cynicism," violating the "understanding" reached the previous November when the United States ceased the bombing of the North (but not the South, or Laos, where the bombing was in fact intensified). Hanoi did not stop to test the "professions of intent" of the new Administration, but moved at once "to step up the killing of Americans" (239–42). The story ends when Kissinger finally compelled Hanoi by massive force to accept peace on his terms, after which he would have left office, had his great achievement not been undermined by Watergate and renewed North Vietnamese aggression. It was the "unprovoked offensive" of February that justified the "secret bombing" of Cambodia from March 1969, "after prayerful consideration" (253); then, as at the time of the April 1970 invasion, "The precipitating issue was the Communist sanctuaries from which the North Vietnamese had tormented our forces" (459), who, obviously, had every right to be in South Vietnam to "defend" the population, as they had been doing since U.S. forces began to engage in bombing of villages, defoliation, and forced population removal in the early 1960s.

A look at the facts reveals, as usual, a rather different story. Let us begin with the events of 1968–69. According to the Kissinger version, after the November bombing halt (redistribution, to be more exact), General Abrams undertook new tactics: He "concentrated on protecting the population" (236). Turning to the real world, Averell Harriman, who was U.S. negotiator in Paris, testified before Congress that in October–November 1968, Hanoi's withdrawal of 90 percent of its forces from the northern two provinces (Kissinger asks in early 1969: "Why did NVA [North Vietnamese army] units leave South Vietnam last summer and fall?"; 238) permitted General Abrams to move forces to the region near Saigon "to strengthen our position there." [13] The American command shifted to Abrams's new concept of "total war," with more aggressive tactics aimed at the VC "infrastructure" and main forces. By February, the rate of American-initiated contacts had increased 100 percent, U.S. military officers reported with much gratification, thereby confirming Harriman's opinion that the February offensive was a response to U.S. actions. "Allied officials concede that the current enemy offensive may in part be a reaction to this added pressure," along with the "accelerated pacification campaign." [14]

What of the "accelerated pacification campaign"? After the "bombing halt," the U.S. command launched several of the fiercest campaigns of the war against the population of the South, for example, the six-month-long Operation SPEEDY EXPRESS in the Mekong Delta province of Kien Hoa (December 1, 1968), where there appear to have been no North Vietnamese troops, and where the "infrastructure" of the indigenous NLF, which largely controlled the province, was decimated at a cost of thousands of civilian casualties by "a relentless night and day barrage of rockets, shells, bombs and bullets from planes, artillery and helicopters," along with B-52 attacks (some targeted directly on villages), defoliation, and ground sweeps that rounded up the population and sent them to prison camps (Kevin Buckley, head of the Saigon bureau of *Newsweek*).[15] Or Operation BOLD MARINER, launched in January 1969, which drove some twelve thousand peasants (including, apparently, the remnants of the My Lai massacre) from the caves and bunkers in which they had endeavored to survive constant U.S. bombardment, after which the land was leveled with artillery barrages and Rome Plows to ensure that nothing would grow in an area where the dikes had long been destroyed by U.S. bombing. Reporting from the Mekong Delta—far from the "unprovoked offensive"—Peter Arnett reported that the "conflagration . . . is tearing the social fabric apart"; in "free-fire zones, the Americans could bring to bear at any time the enormous firepower available from helicopter gunships, bombers and artillery . . . fighter-bombers and artillery pound the enemy positions into the gray porridge that the green delta land becomes when pulverized by high explosives." [16] There were massive casualties, including the civilians who were being "protected" by the new tactics. Not a word about any of this appears in Kissinger's account of the "unprovoked offensive" launched with such "extraordinary cynicism" by Hanoi, justifying the "secret bombing" of Cambodia.

Kissinger's selective account is natural, on the assumption that the South Vietnamese were fair game. The assumption appears to be common to Kissinger and many of his critics. For example, in a critical review of Kissinger's memoirs in the *New York Times* (November 11, 1979), Barbara Tuchman dismisses his anger over the "unprovoked offensive" on the following grounds: "Is an offensive supposed to be bloodless? Is there something peculiarly shocking about killing enemy soldiers in war?" Kissinger "seems inappropriately indignant," she feels, saying nothing about the savage intensified U.S. attacks in the South (regularly, against South Vietnamese civilians) that preceded the "unprovoked offensive."

What about the sanctuaries along the border from which the "North Vietnamese" were "tormenting our forces"? Sihanouk once referred to "the cynicism of the United States executive" in describing "our resistance" as " 'foreign intervention' on our own soil." "Where then should our liberation armies go?" he asked. "To the United States?" "Have the United States aggressors, through some operation of the Holy Ghost, become pure-blooded Indochinese?" [17] The U.S. forces, of course, had sanctuaries extending from Guam to Thailand from which they battered all of Indochina. In fact, forces trained and organized by the United States had been attacking Cambodia from sanctuaries in South Vietnam and Thailand from the late 1950s (not to speak of an abortive CIA-backed coup in Phnom Penh in 1958), and increasingly from 1964, causing many civilian casualties. U.S. military personnel and aircraft were often directly involved. The enormous U.S. military operations in South Vietnam in early 1967, aimed primarily at driving out the population, no doubt also drove many into Cambodia, where they became "North Vietnamese," the technical term for Vietnamese who did not follow American orders. It is interesting that as late as May 1967, after these operations, the Pentagon expressed concern that Cambodia was "becoming more and more important as a supply base—now of food and medicines, perhaps ammunition later." [18] The North Vietnamese forces in the South were drawn into the war—exactly as U.S. planners had anticipated—when the United States attacked the North in August 1964 and systematically from February 1965, simultaneously initiating far heavier systematic bombing of the South and a full-scale invasion. But according to Kissinger, North Vietnam had ruthlessly invaded Cambodia in setting up "sanctuaries" along the borders, and many of his critics agree; Tuchman, for example, states that "the North Vietnamese were unquestionably the first to violate the neutrality of Cambodia—as the Germans were of Belgium in 1914."

If one accepts Kissinger's unargued premises about the right of the United States to attack South Vietnam and to organize its clients to attack Cambodia, as many of his critics evidently do, then one might conceivably make a case for the "secret bombings" of sanctuaries from which American forces were being "tormented." It is the premises, however, that are cynical beyond description.

I have placed the phrase "secret bombings" in quotes for a reason. Kissinger asserts repeatedly that Cambodia never "claimed that there were Cambodian or civilian casualties" (249), that the border regions attacked were "unpopulated" (247), and that Sihanouk never objected to American bombing of Cambodia (250, and elsewhere). In fact, on March 26, a week after the "secret bombings" began, the Cambodian government condemned the bombing and strafing of "the Cambodian population living in the border regions . . . almost daily by U.S. aircraft," with increasing numbers of people killed and material destroyed, alleging that these attacks were directed against "peaceful Cambodian farmers" and demanding that "these criminal attacks must immediately and definitively stop." At a March 28 press conference, Sihanouk emphatically denied reports that he "would not oppose U.S. bombings of communist targets within my frontiers," adding that "unarmed and innocent people have been victims of U.S. bombs," including "the latest bombing, the victims of which were Khmer peasants, women and children in particular." He appealed to the press "to publicize abroad this very clear stand of Cambodia—that is, I will in any case oppose all bombings on Cambodian territory under whatever pretext." The appeal was in vain. The bombings were "secret" in the sense that the media kept them secret; Sihanouk's statements have yet to appear in mainstream books or journals in the United States.[19]

On January 3, 1970, Sihanouk's government—recognized by the United States—issued an official White Paper giving specific details of U.S. and U.S.-client attacks on Cambodia up to May 1969, including 5,149 air attacks, with dates, places, casualties, photographs, etc. There was no mention in the U.S. press, to my knowledge, though the facts were readily available.[20] The belief that these areas were virtually "unpopulated," always untenable, was exploded by the reports of U.S. correspondents who entered Cambodia with the attacking U.S.-GVN forces in April.[21] U.S. correspondent T. D. Allman reported in the *Far Eastern Economic Review* in February 1970 that in a border area that Nixon and Kissinger describe as one of the most dangerous sanctuaries, he could find no Vietnamese, though "United States aircraft violate Cambodian air space and bomb and strafe Cambodian territory" regularly, causing many casualties.[22] There are many similar eyewitness reports, all studiously ignored in this "history," and also by many of Kissinger's critics.

These "oversights" are typical. Writing of Laos, also allegedly subverted and ruthlessly invaded by Hanoi with no provocation, Kissinger observes that "early in 1970 Laos briefly became the focal point of our Indochina concerns" because "a North Vietnamese offensive was threatening to over-run northern Laos" (451). He reviews the "history," which he says "is of some importance." A few things are missing, however, from the successful American effort to undermine a political settlement in the 1950s to the massive U.S. bombing in the late 1960s directed against the civilian population of northern Laos and intensified under Kissinger—in yet another falsehood, he states that U.S. actions were accurately reported by the media, which in fact suppressed eyewitness reports of the bombing by Jacques Decornoy of *Le Monde*. Kissinger also forgets to mention that the "North Vietnamese offensive" restored the territorial division that had existed from 1964 to August 1969, when the CIA mercenary army swept through the area after the terror bombing of the civilian society that also escapes notice.

Kissinger's further claim that "the number of North Vietnamese troops stationed in Laos had risen to 67,000" by 1970 (450) repeats a claim in a Nixon speech of March 6, 1970, that was a joke among the press corps in Vientiane (where I happened to be at the time). The standard U.S. estimate for some time had been fifty thousand troops; Nixon's revised estimate was an attempt to substantiate charges about a "North Vietnamese invasion." But he had neglected to inform U.S. intelligence of this new influx of troops, so that the American military attaché in Vientiane was still repeating the fifty-thousand figure. As the head of the *Time-Life* bureau in Indochina, H. D. S. Greenway, wrote, "The President's estimate of North Vietnamese troop strength in Laos was at least 17,000 higher than the highest reliable estimate in Vientiane, including the estimates of the Americans themselves." [23]

The fifty-thousand figure also merits comment. It does not distinguish forces in northern Laos (where the "invasion" took place) from those in the South, an extension of the Vietnam war. It does not distinguish combat troops from support and communication units, which military observers in Vientiane estimated at about three-fourths of the North Vietnamese force, not surprising since all supplies, including food, had to be brought through a heavily bombed area. It also might be recalled that U.S. planes bombing North Vietnam from Thai sanctuaries had been guided from American outposts in northern Laos, quite apart from the earlier history of subversion that Kissinger ignores. Arthur Dommen, an intensely anti-Communist American specialist on Laos, estimated that only one combat regiment of North Vietnamese troops was available in northern Laos in 1968. There is a mass of relevant evidence on the topic,[24] but what is striking is that in reviewing the "important" history, Kissinger mentions literally none of it, just as he excises the entire American role.

Let us turn next to Kissinger's "peace." According to his version, the massive bombing of North Vietnam in 1972 drove Hanoi to accept in October a peace plan even more favorable to the United States than "the terms we ourselves had put forward for two years" (1392). But after the November presidential election, Hanoi refused to negotiate, with typical insolence, so the United States had to carry out the Christmas bombings to compel them to accept U.S. terms in January. As always, Kissinger wisely avoids the available documentation, such as the texts of the October and January agreements or his public analyses of them at the time. But even from the scattered and self-serving excerpts he selects, it is obvious that his story can hardly be taken seriously.

Space prevents a detailed analysis, but the basic facts are easily documented. The U.S. position had been that the GVN (Government of Vietnam, which, as Kissinger remarks, had been "put into office by a coup organized by our predecessors"; 1013), must remain as the government in the South, after which "free elections" might be held under its auspices; engagingly, Kissinger observes that "whoever controlled the government would win" (1031; see also 1311). The 1962 program of the National Liberation Front of South Vietnam (NLF) demanded a share (which would no doubt have become the dominant share) in the governance of South Vietnam, which was to form a neutral zone with Laos and Cambodia, following "an independent, sovereign foreign policy" and proceeding towards "step-by-step reunification" as agreed in the 1954 Geneva Accords. Naturally, the United States rejected any such idea, since it knew that its clients could not survive political competition in the South.[25] The central provision of the October 1972 agreement was that there are two administrations in the South, the GVN and the PRG (the former NLF), which are to proceed to a political settlement in the South, then to reunification with the North. In agreeing to this formula, the United States abandoned its long-term program of imposing the rule of the GVN on South Vietnam.

Since the United States was obviously delaying, Hanoi announced the terms of the agreement on October 26. Kissinger then appeared on television to announce that "peace is at hand." A careful reading of his statement, however, reveals that he was rejecting the central element of the agreement: that the PRG is parallel and equivalent to the GVN in the South. Obviously, peace was not "at hand." Kissinger then attempted to modify the agreements in various ways, leading to the Christmas bombings, after which the United States signed a treaty in Paris which differed in only the most insignificant respects from the October agreements—which Hanoi had been urging the United States to sign throughout the period when Kissinger claims that in their insolence, they were refusing to negotiate.

This, however, is only half the story. Exactly as in October, though more explicitly, Nixon and Kissinger announced at once that they would disregard the agreement that they signed in Paris in January. The treaty itself was based on the principle that the GVN and PRG were parallel and equivalent parties and that "foreign countries shall not impose any political tendency or personality on the South Vietnamese people." But the White House summary stated that "the government of the Republic of (South) Vietnam continues in existence, recognized by the United States, its constitutional structure and leadership intact and unchanged." Nixon announced that the United States would continue to recognize and support the GVN as "the sole legitimate government of South Vietnam." Its constitutional structure, in an unamendable article, identified this government as representing all of Vietnam and stated that "every activity designed to propagan-

dize or carry out communism is prohibited"—so much for the guaranteed
open political competition of the treaty. To dispel any doubt, the Thieu
regime announced at once that it would repress by force any support shown
for the second of the two parties in the South. Furthermore, it did so; and, as
all serious observers agree, in essence, the GVN went on the offensive in
1973 (with full U.S. backing), while the "enemy" responded in 1974.[26]

In short, the text of the agreements of October and January represented
a major concession by Kissinger, whereas the interpretation of the text provided by Kissinger and Nixon maintained their long-standing commitment
to impose the rule of the U.S. client regime in the South in defiance of the
scrap of paper signed in Paris, leading to renewed warfare largely initiated
by the U.S.-GVN and ultimately retaliation from the Communist enemy
and the overthrow of the U.S.-imposed regime. A very different story from
the one that Kissinger relates, but a story with the virtue of accuracy, and
one quite obvious at the time to anyone whose eyes were open, crucially not
the American press.[27]

Kissinger was aided in his deceit by the fact that the media largely accepted his version of the agreements, which rejected their basic principles,
as if it were the text itself. Thus the basis was laid for great indignation
when there was a military response to GVN land-grabbing operations,
which U.S. officials were proudly announcing through early 1974. From the
actual history, the Christmas bombings emerge as simply another chapter in
a long history of murderous cynicism.

The truth can even be disentangled from Kissinger's obfuscation. Thus,
Kissinger reports a letter from Nixon on October 19, 1972, stating that "the
GVN must survive as a free country" (sic), backing Kissinger's message to
Thieu that "the government we have recognized [the GVN] is the government of the Republic of South Vietnam and its President" (sic; 1369, 1353).
The reason for Kissinger's rejection of the treaty he signed was the familiar
one; as Ambassador Bunker told Nixon and Kissinger on August 31, 1972,
the GVN "fear that they are not yet well enough organized to compete politically with such a tough disciplined organization" (1324). Kissinger notes
that he thought at the end "that Saigon [the GVN], generously armed and
supported by the United States, would be able to deal with moderate violations of the agreements" (1359), though Watergate foiled this plan; nothing
is said about the U.S.-GVN violations which demolished the treaty in 1973,
in accordance with Washington's clear rejection of its terms. On January 6,
1973, Nixon stated that "he would settle for the October terms" (1462), de-

stroying Kissinger's rationale for the Christmas bombings, as does the text of the January treaty itself. Kissinger concludes by noting that on January 21, Thieu requested "some unilateral statements by the United States that we recognized Saigon as the legal government of South Vietnam," which "was consistent with our interpretation of the agreement" (1470) though flatly inconsistent with its text, a fact that he considers too insignificant to deserve mention. And so on.

As usual, Kissinger has succeeded in establishing his version of history among his sympathetic Western audience. Thus, the British military historian Michael Howard, reviewing the memoirs in the *Times Literary Supplement* (December 21, 1979), writes that "those who opposed the [Christmas] bombing of Hanoi have not convincingly shown how else the North Vietnamese could be brought to negotiate."

Occasionally, Kissinger lets drop hints that at some level of awareness he understood the true nature of the American war. The problem we faced was that our enemy was "fighting on familiar terrain," fighting a political war against our military war (232). The basic problem we faced was "psychological": "How does one convince a people that one is prepared to stay indefinitely 10,000 miles away against opponents who are fighting in their own country?" where "the Viet Cong infrastructure undermined the South Vietnamese government in the populated countryside," while the North Vietnamese "tempted our forces to lunge into politically insignificant areas" (232–33). By 1969, after seven years of American attacks against the rural population and four years of all-out war, the U.S. embassy in Saigon "estimated that a Communist infrastructure still existed in 80 percent of the hamlets" (236)—though by then, much of the population had been "urbanized" by American military force. Kissinger asks an interagency committee, "How do we know what the infrastructure is that we've destroyed?" (434)—that is, does the social organization of our South Vietnamese enemy still survive, despite our attack? Another problem was that the army we organized in the South (ARVN) "would rapidly suffer desertions and loss of morale" if moved out of its home region, while the "North Vietnamese" could "hide in the population" (989–90); "attrition is next to impossible to apply in a guerrilla war against an enemy who does not *have* to fight because he can melt into the population" (34; his emphasis). Worse still, ARVN "only rarely" had "conducted major offensive operations against a determined enemy," confining itself to "usually unopposed sweeps of the countryside in support of pacification" (992, 1002), i.e., attacks on the civilian population of the South. "The North Vietnamese hiding in the population and able to choose their moment for attack wore us down" (1005), referring to the pre-1968 period, when, as all agree (even Kissinger), the "enemy" was overwhelmingly South Vietnamese. Even though U.S. force had succeeded in "improving the military position of our ally," "Thieu and his government were simply not ready for a negotiated peace" (1046, 1323). From a scattering of statements of this sort, the truth emerges, despite Kissinger's heroic efforts to conceal it.

Throughout, Kissinger's memoirs keep to a comparable intellectual and moral level. Thus, he explains the "tilt to Pakistan" at the time of the atrocities in East Pakistan (which, it appears from his account, the United States never criticized, even in private) on the grounds that it was necessary to maintain the secrecy of the impending trip to China from Pakistan; the trip might otherwise have been delayed by several months (854). Putting aside the hypocrisy of this argument, why was it necessary to maintain secrecy? As he makes clear, China did not approve—indeed, it was much annoyed (740, 742). The only explanation for the secrecy is that the crucial "razzle-dazzle" would have been imperiled without it, so that much of the fun would have been lost. So much for the massacres in East Pakistan (Bangladesh).

Kissinger defends his efforts to subvert Chilean democracy on the grounds that the "anti-Allende vote" in 1970 was 62.7 percent (653). He notes, however, that the Christian Democratic vote (approximately equal to Allende's) went to a left-wing candidate "whose program differed from Allende's largely on procedural points and in his sincere dedication to the democratic process" (665). Thus the vote for Allende's program was actually two-thirds. As for Allende, "by definition his would be the last democratic election" (655), a pronouncement in blissful disregard of the fact that democratic elections continued under Allende, though never under the brutal regime that overthrew him in a U.S.-backed coup. A further proof that Allende was a committed totalitarian is that "various measures taken by Allende's government were declared to be unconstitutional and outside the law by the Chilean Supreme Court" (683)—so we conclude that F.D.R. too was a totalitarian. It is unnecessary to discuss Kissinger's account further; it is effectively demolished, with the documentation that Kissinger scrupulously avoids, by Armando Uribe in *Le Monde diplomatique* (December 1979). To cite only one example, Kissinger claims that on receiving a message of congratulation from Nixon, "Allende gave no evidence of a conciliatory approach. The tenor of his administration was set" (680), so that one obviously cannot blame the United States for the deterioration of relations. Kissinger does not quote Allende's response. Uribe does, citing long passages from the official document in which Allende expressed the desire of his government "to maintain good relations with the United States" on the basis of mutual recognition of the "dignity" and "national interests" of the other party, among other reasonable and conciliatory remarks. Again, one can see why Kissinger is so careful to avoid documentation.

Not always, however. Thus Kissinger's claims concerning North Vietnamese sanctuaries are "confirmed" by a propaganda document issued by the Pol Pot government in late 1978 which was a bitter attack on Vietnam in the midst of a war in which the Pol Pot regime was facing annihilation. To this historian, the document provides credible evidence "confirming" American charges against Vietnam. Kissinger does not even refer to the document, absurd as that would be, but rather to press reports concerning it (241, 506).

Occasionally, Kissinger makes the mistake of actually citing a source that is easily checked. Thus he claims that William Shawcross "excused the Khmer Rouge atrocities" and that Richard Dudman "alleged that there was insufficient evidence the atrocities ever took place" (1485). Turning to his sources, we discover that Shawcross bitterly denounced the atrocities, concluding that the Khmer Rouge had turned Cambodia into a "hell on earth." Shawcross reports correctly that the ferocious American bombings of 1973 decimated the peasant army and cites official records which show that heavily populated areas were being intensively bombed by B-52s. State Department studies and other sources confirm that Khmer Rouge policies became far harsher in 1973. A former Foreign Service officer in Phnom Penh, now an academic specialist on Cambodia, testified before Congress that "the leadership hardened its ideology" in 1973–74 and that the incredible bombing of 1973 "may have driven thousands of people out of their minds"; "to a large extent, I think, American actions are to blame" for postwar atrocities (David Chandler).[28] Try as he may, Kissinger cannot alter the facts with false accusations leveled against people who have exposed his machinations, any more than he can provide an answer to Lon Nol's ambassador to Washington, who said, as the war ended: "Let's face it, you took advantage of us, of our inexperience. As you are much cleverer than we are, you could induce us into this fighting . . . If the United States had respected our neutrality then the fighting, the killing and things might not have happened."[29]

Kissinger's allegations concerning Dudman are no less scandalous. Dudman never questioned that ample evidence of atrocities existed. Rather, he raised questions about reliance on Vietnamese sources in the midst of a war and about the way evidence was used to determine the *scale* of the deaths and killings, questions that would be recognized as pertinent by any serious person, though it is hardly surprising that they lie far beyond Kissinger's comprehension.

Kissinger's sections on the Middle East—presented with characteristic self-adulation—review the early stages of his blunders, which were a major factor in setting the stage for the October 1973 war, specifically, his rejection of Sadat's repeated overtures in 1971–72 and his blind insistence on interpreting the Arab-Israel conflict as part of a global Russian challenge. As always, he makes no mention of the U.S. role in stimulating conflict—for example, the vast flow of armaments to Israel (including Phantom jets, which began to arrive in September 1969), which enabled it to undertake the "deep penetration" raids in Egypt that precipitated the entry of Russian antiaircraft systems and military personnel, and to bomb the Suez zone so intensively that a million and a half people were driven out, according to former Israeli Chief-of-Staff Mordechai Gur. The Israeli ambassador to Washington, Yitzhak Rabin, reports his understanding that the Nixon Administration favored the Israeli "deep penetration" raids and even further escalation, so as to undermine Nasser.[30] We learn nothing about any of this from Kissinger.

Similarly, in the Jordan crisis of 1970, Kissinger sees a Russian hand—they were "not helping to rein in their clients" (609). William Quandt, who was deputy to Harold Saunders (Kissinger's senior staff assistant on the Middle East) from 1972 to 1974, comments on the basic "flaw" in Nixon's and Kissinger's view of the crisis, namely, their emphasis on its "global U.S.-Soviet dimension," whereas in fact "the Soviet adopted a cautious policy" and "warned against all outside intervention in Jordan," calling for a ceasefire.[31] Kissinger describes the same facts quite differently, interpreting the Russian position as "Soviet premonitions, following our strategy of creating maximum fear of a possible American move" (627).

Kissinger makes clear that "there was no White House support at all" for State Department efforts to secure a settlement in 1971 (1279), well after Sadat's offers to make peace on the pre-June 1967 borders, in essential accord with the State Department's "Rogers Plan." Kissinger's aim "was to produce a stalemate until Moscow urged compromise or until, even better, some moderate Arab regime decided that the route to progress was through Washington" (1279)—as Sadat surely had, though Kissinger did not understand this. Even after Sadat's "massive purge of pro-Soviet elements in his government" (1283), the light did not dawn. "Until some Arab state showed a willingness to separate from the Soviets, or the Soviets were prepared to dissociate from the maximum Arab program, we had no reason to modify our policy" of stalemate (1291)—a statement that is remarkable not only for its colossal ignorance (Saudi Arabia, for example, was not willing "to separate from the Soviets"?) but also for its obtuseness in refusing to move towards peace out of absurd "geopolitical" fantasies.

Quandt's plausible conclusion is that Sadat "had risked his relations with the Soviet Union by moving against its supporters and by helping to crush a communist coup in Sudan in July. Not only had he failed to win the Americans to his side, but the Americans were considering new arms agreements with Israel. Frustrated and humiliated, Sadat decided to abandon the interim-settlement idea. The result was a two-year diplomatic stalemate," ended after the October 1973 war.

The quite surprising early successes of Egyptian and Syrian military forces in October 1973, which led even a reluctant Saudi Arabia to join in a petroleum boycott, succeeded in penetrating the clouds. If there is one thing that Kissinger does indeed understand, it is the mailed fist. Recognizing that Egypt was not a basket case, as he had previously assumed, and that the oil-producing states could not be dismissed entirely as an independent force in world affairs (as oil company executives had been privately warning for some time),[32] Kissinger changed tactics, accepting Sadat's long-standing offers to convert Egypt into a client state of the United States. He then turned to the policies that will not doubt be described with equal accuracy and perception in the second volume of his memoirs, seeking to incorporate Egypt within the U.S.-dominated system while removing it from the Middle East conflict by "step-by-step diplomacy" so that Israel could maintain its control over the occupied territories and its dominant political-military position in the region as an American surrogate, within the Iran-Israel-Saudi Arabia alliance that was at the time regarded as the basis for U.S. domination of the region.[33] But this carries us beyond our story here; volume one of the memoirs terminates before these events took place.

Kissinger notes that in September 1971, the USSR indicated its willingness "to withdraw its combat forces from Egypt in case of a final settlement" along the lines of Sadat's rebuffed offer, but "we had no incentive to proceed jointly with Moscow" because "there was no sign of the Soviet Union's willingness to press its clients toward flexibility" (838, 1288), where "flexibility," not defined, amounted to acceptance of Israeli control of territories occupied in 1967. The real story is that he assumed that "equilibrium," in his special sense of the term, would be served by maintaining the Israeli dominance that he regarded as unchallengeable—until forced to revise his assumptions after the October war to which he contributed so effectively.

Kissinger's memoirs abound in examples of the sort I have discussed. They reveal the enormous dangers posed to peace, minimal justice or humanity, even survival, by a combination of limited understanding, tremendous military force, and willingness to show "courage" by "going to the brink." The one great talent that Kissinger manifests here, as throughout his career, is a capacity to befuddle the media and public opinion. Academic scholarship also takes his preposterous statements about international affairs and his "geopolitical" inanities quite seriously, even in critical commentary. As for the media, to take a perhaps extreme example, the book review editor of the *Boston Globe*, who finds Kissinger "perceptive" and "humane" in his memoirs, writes that "either we accept, or try to accept, what he is saying, given his massive ego, or wait for 20 or more years before making a judgment." [34] No other reaction is imaginable.

In fact, a rather different assessment is suggested by one of the more profound thoughts that graced Kissinger's academic writings—his explanation that "the deepest problem of the contemporary international order" may derive from the failure on the part of people outside the West, who have not undergone the Newtonian revolution, to understand that "the real world is external to the observer." [35] Reading these memoirs, one might conclude that Kissinger is really a man of the sixteenth century, in his weird sense.

A review of Kissinger's version of history should not be confused with an account of his actions while in a position of political power from 1969 to 1975. This is not the place to undertake the latter task. An account of his tenure in office would focus on other topics, such as the recognition by Nixon and Kissinger of the fact that the period of undisputed U.S. global hegemony was at an end, and that it would henceforth be necessary to come to terms with certain facts of the international order. Their moves towards "détente" amounted to an acceptance of long-standing Soviet efforts to construct a world system of bipolar management, in which each of the superpowers would control its own domains without essential interference, though with some skirmishing in disputed territory and the right to exploit targets of opportunity. They also responded to Chinese efforts to join this global system, and sought, as any rational advocates of U.S. power would, to play the USSR and China against one another to the extent possible. Furthermore, after a brief experiment with neomercantilist policies in 1971, Nixon and Kissinger recognized that it would be necessary to adopt what was later called a "trilateralist" position with regard to the First World of industrial capitalism, with Europe and Japan brought into a collective management in which, however, the board of directors would remain in Washington. After his disastrous management of Middle Eastern affairs leading to the October war, Kissinger moved towards a position of rational imperialism in this region too, as noted above. Throughout the world, Nixon and Kissinger attempted to develop a system of surrogate states (e.g., Iran) which would manage the affairs of their own region in the U.S. interest, a position that proved only marginally successful, though it accorded with the realities of diminishing U.S. power relative to other rising power centers. The USSR faces similar dilemmas, contrary to much contemporary fantasy. As for Indochina, while Kissinger did not succeed in maintaining a U.S. client state in South Vietnam, he was successful in the larger objective of creating sufficient carnage so that the threatening prospect of postwar recovery and successful development was averted, a policy pursued by his successors by other means.

If we accept the assumptions of U.S. policymakers, these are not inconsiderable achievements. That Kissinger was able to realize them, despite his obviously limited grasp of world affairs and his fantastic interpretations of contemporary history, is a reflection of the enormous power of the United States, which, while not on the scale of earlier years relative to its rivals (including its allies), is still immense. With such reserves of power at one's command, it is difficult to fail to achieve many of the objectives of U.S. foreign policy. What made Kissinger particularly useful as a manager of state policy, however, was not his intermittent grasp of the realities of power but rather his remarkable capacity to mislead and confuse the public, particularly, the articulate intelligentsia. This is an art that he mastered with near genius, as the reception of these generally ridiculous memoirs once again illustrates.

Chapter Seven

TOWARDS A NEW COLD WAR (1980)

THESE ESSAYS have so far focused on relations between intellectuals and the state at one particular historical moment, in the aftermath of the Vietnam war. The consequences of the war for the international system were not negligible, but it led to no structural or institutional changes in Western societies. It is therefore to be expected that the programs of counterrevolutionary intervention rooted in these institutional structures will persist as they have through the "post-colonial era," taking new forms in the context of conflicts over scarce resources and the conditions of exploitation. But such programs require a docile and obedient population. It has therefore been imperative to overcome what is now called the "Vietnam syndrome," that is, the reluctance on the part of large sectors of the population of the West to tolerate the programs of aggression, subversion, massacre, and brutal exploitation that constitute the actual historical experience of much of the Third World, faced with "Western humanism." In part as a consequence of the Indochina wars, dangerous feelings of sympathy for oppressed and suffering people developed in Western society. These had to be reversed and the image of Western benevolence restored, a difficult task, but one that was forthrightly addressed and carried out with great skill by the Western propaganda system.

It is unrealistic to suppose that the propaganda campaign was planned or centrally orchestrated. Rather, it was conducted on the basis of perceived self-interest, with the willing cooperation of the secular priesthood in conformity with traditional and quite intelligible tendencies towards service to the state. Opportunities were seized and exploited as they arose. Nixon's petty criminality provided an occasion to personify the evil that could not be denied and to expunge it from the body politic, its institutional structures protected from scrutiny; his serious crimes—the merciless bombing of Laos and Cambodia and the murderous "pacification" campaigns in South Vietnam, the domestic terrorism of the national political police that was exposed during exactly the Watergate period, vastly exceeding in scale and significance anything charged against Nixon—were no part of the Watergate farce. Now cleansed and purified, the U.S. government embarked on a noble campaign to defend human rights everywhere—at least, everywhere east of the Elbe—to the applause of its allies, eager to reap what benefit they might from the exercise. Meanwhile, the docile intellectuals of the Western world assumed the task of presenting in the most lurid light the suffering, brutality, and terror to be found throughout the shattered societies of Indochina, often effacing the Western role and responsibility. As for the bitter consequences of Western actions elsewhere, these are noted at most on an episodic basis, rarely subjected to systematic analysis or traced to their causes. Whenever the flimsiest opportunity arises, the West is portrayed as a victim, not an active agent in world affairs, suffering the blows of its tormentors everywhere, but now increasingly aroused to defend its legitimate interests and the values it proclaims.

These and other noteworthy propaganda successes have helped set the stage for a renewed commitment to militarization as a mechanism for imposing order on a domestic and international society that is regarded as dangerously "out of control." By the latter stages of the Carter Administration, the predictable and predicted moves were already evident. In late 1978— long before the Russian invasion of Afghanistan or the taking of the hostages in Iran—President Carter stated that "our goal . . . is to increase the real level of defense expenditures."[1] Later, he proudly announced that whereas "defense spending dropped by one third in those eight years before I became President," since he assumed office "outlays for defense spending [have] been increased every year."[2] In November 1978, the *New York Times* reported that "Administration sources said that the Defense Department was especially gratified because Carter has decided to cut about $15 billion out of the normal growth of a range of social and domestic programs" while raising military spending by some $12 billion. "Officials indicated that the 'guns and butter' argument waged within the Administration has now, in fact, been settled by Carter in favor of the Defense Department."[3] Meanwhile, in direct violation of campaign promises, the Carter Administration stepped up arms sales,[4] while also accelerating the development of new strategic weapons and pressuring its allies to install nuclear missiles (with, it is reported, a flight time of five minutes to Moscow) in Western Europe.

It goes without saying that Western initiatives are only one element in this race towards disaster, which have led many commentators to speak ominously of the mood of 1914 and 1939. But they nevertheless constitute one significant component. What deserves specific mention in this context is the contribution to this dangerous state of affairs that has been made by the remarkably effective campaign to reconstruct the ideological system that was battered by the Indochina wars.

The taking of the American hostages in Iran was also exploited, not without cynicism, as a target of opportunity in the process of overcoming the "Vietnam syndrome." Shortly after the crisis erupted, the *New York Times* ran a front-page story by Hedrick Smith headlined "Iran Is Helping the U.S. to Shed Fear of Intervening Abroad."[5] Smith reported "an important shift of attitudes" in Washington "that, many believe, will have a significant long-term impact on the willingness of the United States to project its power in the third world and to develop greater military capacities for protecting its interests there." "We are moving away from our post-Vietnam reticence," one policymaker said. Democratic National Chairman John White stated that "we may have reached a turning point in our attitude toward ourselves, and that is a feeling that we have a right to protect legitimate American interests anywhere in the world." Senator Frank Church indicated support for military intervention in the Middle East "if our interests were threatened." The "lesson of Vietnam," Smith reports, is that we must be "more-selective" in the use of military power with a more careful calculation of the costs to us, as we consider intervention "in such troubled regions of potential American influence as the Middle East and the Caribbean." Consider what must be intended if our influence in these regions is regarded as only "potential."

Such reactions are a very natural culmination of the process of reconstruction of imperial ideology that has been progressing step by step for the past years. It is hardly surprising that in Kuwait and other Middle Eastern states bitter resentment is expressed over the concept of "legitimate American interests" that may be "protected" by U.S. armed force, a fact little noted or appreciated here since it is assumed that the resources of the world are ours by right. On similar assumptions, the respected political commentator Walter Laqueur suggested that Middle East oil "could be internationalized, not on behalf of a few oil companies but for the benefit of the rest of mankind," though his concern for the benefit of the rest of mankind did not extend to the natural conclusion that the industrial and agricultural resources of the West should also be internationalized and made generally available.[6]

In January 1978, Secretary of Defense Harold Brown ordered the Pentagon to plan for a rapid deployment force of 100,000 men backed by air and naval units for possible intervention in the Persian Gulf region or elsewhere, renewing plans that had been blocked by a Congress hobbled by "post-Vietnam reticence"—for example, by the conservative Senator Richard Russell, who warned that "if it is easy for us to go anywhere and do anything, we will always be going somewhere and doing something," with consequences that were dramatically evident at the time. The lesson of the hostage crisis in Iran is supposed to be that we should overcome our "reticence," develop more destructive strategic weapons, deploy forces prepared for rapid intervention throughout the world, "unleash" the CIA, and otherwise demonstrate our pugnacity.

That such lessons should be drawn from the taking of the hostages in Iran is quite revealing. It is obvious on a moment's thought that a rapid deployment force, now estimated at 200,000 men,[7] would be no more effective than the MX missile system in rescuing the hostages or preventing the takeover of the embassy (or deterring the USSR in Afghanistan); and that it was precisely the policies of military intervention and subversion that led to the Iranian debacle, while subjecting Iranians to a quarter-century of torture, murder, and suffering—"progressive methods of development," as U.S. ideologists describe what was taking place when the U.S.-trained secret police were gouging out eyes of children and much of the rural population was being driven to miserable urban slums while the agricultural system collapsed and Iran practically sank into the sea under the weight of American armaments. The hostage crisis served as a useful opportunity to advance policies that derive from other interests and concerns.

As the decade of the 1970s came to an inauspicious end, NATO, under U.S. pressure, agreed to deploy in Western Europe new advanced missiles targeted against the Soviet Union, the USSR invaded Afghanistan, and the Carter Doctrine was proclaimed, calling for still further increases in the military budget, including not only intervention forces but also preparations for a peacetime draft and the MX missile system, vast in scale and cost and a major contribution to an escalating arms race. War clouds are gathering. We are entering the period of what some are calling "the New Cold War."

If there is indeed a renewal of superpower confrontation, it is likely to resemble the Old Cold War in certain respects but to be crucially different in others. Consider first some likely similarities. The Cold War is generally described as a "zero-sum game" in which the gains of one antagonist equal the losses of the other. But this is a highly questionable interpretation. It would be more realistic to regard the Cold War system as a macabre dance of death in which the rulers of the superpowers mobilize their own populations to support harsh and brutal measures directed against victims within what they take to be their respective domains, where they are "protecting their legitimate interests." Appeal to the alleged threat of the powerful global enemy has proven to be a useful device for this purpose. In this respect, the Cold War has proven highly functional for the superpowers, which is one reason why it persists despite the prospect of mutual incineration if the system misbehaves, as sooner or later it very likely will. When the United States moves to overthrow the government of Iran or Guatemala or Chile, or to invade Cuba or Indochina or the Dominican Republic, or to bolster murderous dictatorships in Latin America or Asia, it does so in a noble effort to defend free peoples from the imminent Russian (or earlier, Chinese) threat. Similarly, when the USSR sends its tanks to East Berlin, Hungary, Czechoslovakia, or Afghanistan, it is acting from the purest of motives, defending socialism and freedom against the machinations of U.S. imperialism and its cohorts. The rhetoric employed on both sides is similar,[8] and is generally parroted by the intelligentsia in each camp. It has proven effective in organizing popular support, as even a totalitarian state must do. In this respect, the New Cold War promises to be no different, and can be understood in part as a natural outcome of the effort to overcome the "Vietnam syndrome."

Another typical gambit is the pretense that only a show of force will deter the superpower antagonist from its relentless marauding and subversion. The actual dynamics of the Cold War system suggest a rather different conclusion. Typically, acts of subversion, violence, and aggression, or development and deployment of new weapons systems, have had the predictable effect of reinforcing those elements of the antagonist state that are committed, for their own reasons, to similar practices, a recurrent pattern throughout the Cold War period. Examples that are cited in support of the standard thesis regularly collapse on examination, e.g., Angola, where the U.S.-

backed South African intervention is generally disregarded in Western propaganda on the Cuban menace, and a more accurate assessment would take note of "the manner in which Kissinger tried to foment and sustain a civil war in Angola simply to convince the Russians that the American tiger could still bite." [9] It does not, of course, follow that a willingness to seek accommodation would mechanically lead to a relaxation of tensions and a reduction of international violence, but its role as a possible factor should not be discounted.

One persistent element of the Cold War system is the portrayal of the superpower antagonist in the most menacing terms. In Soviet propaganda, the United States is led by warmongers deterred from their limitless drive for expansion only by Russian power. In the West, it is now an article of faith that the Soviet Union is outspending its rivals in a race towards military domination of the planet. There is some basis of truth in these competing claims, as is usually the case even in the most vulgar propaganda exercises, but it is revealing to disentangle the element of truth from the web of distortion. The claim that the USSR is unrivaled in its commitment of resources to military production is based largely on CIA analyses which estimate the dollar equivalent of the USSR military effort; thus the question asked is what it would cost the United States, in dollars, to duplicate the military force deployed by the USSR. As a number of commentators have observed,[10] these calculations have a built-in bias. The Soviet military force is labor-intensive, in contrast to the military system of the West with its superior technological level and higher cost of labor relative to capital. It would be highly inefficient, and extremely costly, for the United States to duplicate a technologically less advanced Soviet military machine that relies heavily on manpower. Hence calculations of dollar equivalents considerably exaggerate Russian power. For the United States to duplicate the Russian agricultural system, with its intensive use of human labor power and low level of technology, would also be extremely expensive. But we do not therefore conclude that the Russians are outmatching us in the field of agricultural production. For similar reasons, calculations of dollar equivalents give a highly misleading picture of relative military strength.

Suppose that we were to reverse the process and estimate a ruble-equivalent of the American military force. This would be a meaningless exercise. It is probable that the Soviet Union simply lacks the technological capacity to duplicate the American military machine, so the ruble-equivalent would be infinite. These observations simply point up the absurdity of the calculations that are used to frighten the populations of the West so that they will be induced to support the militarization of their own societies. The absurdity is heightened when we note that NATO, by any calculation, outspends the Warsaw Pact,[11] and when we bring into consideration such factors as the Sino-Soviet conflict and the strained relations between the Soviet Union and its Warsaw Pact allies. Holzman notes that the American Joint Chiefs-of-Staff consistently conclude that the United States fields the world's most powerful military force, despite the insistent claims that the Russians are outspending us in their drive for world domination. The paradox is resolved when the analyses of relative military strength are dissected. No doubt an an analysis of Soviet propaganda would reveal comparable duplicity.

The fact is that both of the superpowers—and many lesser powers as well—are ruining their economies and threatening world peace, indeed human survival, by a mindless commitment to military production for themselves and for export. Many factors contribute to the emphasis on military production, quite apart from the drive for global dominance. There has always been a temptation to resort to chauvinist appeals and militarization to deal with social and economic crises that appear unmanageable. The domestic power of the military-bureaucratic elite that rules the Soviet Union is enhanced by the diversion of resources to military production. In the 1950s, liberal economists in the United States denounced the Eisenhower Administration for insufficient military spending, testifying before Congress that it was frittering away American affluence in "indulgences, luxuries, and frivolities" while the United States faced "the possibility of annihilation or humiliation" (Walter Heller), and calling for "accelerating and enlarging our defense effort" rather than diverting military resources to consumer goods for people who already have a "frivolous standard of living" (James Tobin).[12] When the Kennedy Administration came to power, it followed their advice, using a faked "missile gap" as a propaganda device and relying on massive military expenditures as a mechanism for economic growth, thus setting off the arms race of the 1960s, accelerated by the needless humiliation of Khrushchev at the time of the Cuban missile crisis.[13] Without the benefit of Keynes, the fascist states of the 1930s also proved that the "new economics" works, as economies were stimulated by programs of rearmament. In principle, other methods are available, but a look at the class character of the major industrial powers helps to explain why governments have so commonly turned to production of waste (primarily,

armaments) and bribes for the wealthy in their efforts to stimulate a slug-
gish economy (see Introduction). Unfortunately, a great many factors—the
drive for domestic and global power, the need to mobilize popular support
for costly government programs, the concern to recycle petrodollars by exploiting the comparative advantage of the industrial powers in advanced
technology (the arms trade), the requirement that state-induced production
must not harm but rather must enhance the interests and power of the private empires that control the economy and largely staff the state executive
in the state capitalist democracies—all converge on military production.
Unless effective mass popular movements develop committed to different
aims, the likely consequences are rather gloomy. In these respects too, the
New Cold War is likely to resemble its earlier phase, though the risks are
now considerably more grave.

Focus on Middle East oil production is still another respect in which the
New Cold War is likely to resemble its earlier phase. Speaking to congressional leaders who were reluctant to return to military confrontation in February 1947, Secretary of State George Marshall warned them that "if
Greece should dissolve into civil war" and Turkey should fall, then "Soviet
domination might thus extend over the entire Middle East and Asia," an
early version of the "domino theory." A more realistic concern, as already
discussed (cf. Chapter 2), was the question of how domination over the stupendous natural resources of the Middle East would be shared among the
industrial capitalist states, with the United States gradually taking over positions that had long been held by Britain and France. According to James
Forrestal, Marshall's first response to Britain's announcement that it was no
longer capable of controlling Greece was that this was "tantamount to
British abdication from the Middle East with obvious implications as to
their successor," [14] though the collapse of Britain's imperial position may
well have been proceeding more rapidly than was anticipated in Grand Area
planning at that point.

Joyce and Gabriel Kolko point out that the U.S. "dilemma . . . involved
Western European capitalist nations rather than Russia" at that stage of
planning, leading to the enunciation of the Truman Doctrine, with the
Middle East one among a number of factors.[15] Nevertheless, the "Russian
threat" was invoked, with adroitness and cynicism, in the style that became
typical of subsequent Cold War interventionism, which, no doubt, learned a
valuable lesson from this success. Dean Acheson, in his memoirs, takes

credit for converting congressional leaders to the new doctrine in February 1947 with this rhetoric:[16]

In the past eighteen months, I said, Soviet pressure on the Straits, on Iran, and on northern Greece had brought the Balkans to the point where a highly possible Soviet breakthrough might open three continents to Soviet penetration. Like apples in a barrel infected by one rotten one, the corruption of Greece would infect Iran and all to the east. It would also carry infection to Africa through Asia Minor and Egypt, and to Europe through Italy and France, already threatened by the strongest domestic Communist parties in Western Europe.

Acheson surely knew that the Soviet Union had already been rebuffed in its efforts to modify the Straits regime in its favor and gain a share in the exploitation of Iranian oil, and presumably was also aware that Stalin was urging restraint on the Greek guerrillas (recognizing that Greece was in the American sphere of influence) and instructing the Communist parties of the West to join in the reconstruction of capitalism. But the Russian threat served as a powerful device to mobilize support for intervention.

It is interesting that Acheson takes great pride in this exercise in deception. Acheson's concern over the dangers of democratic politics in the West is no less noteworthy. The New Cold War displays similar features once again, as is hardly necessary to document.

According to the "New Cold Warriors," the search for military bases in the Middle East and the general program of militarization of American society are "defensive measures" taken to protect potential victims of Russian aggression.[17] Senator Church is more honest when he speaks of protecting "our interests," a fact that is well understood by those we are preparing to "protect." When the Islamic states met in Islamabad to condemn the Russian invasion of Afghanistan, they did not fail to warn against U.S. intervention as well, a fact that was hardly highlighted in the U.S. press. A business-oriented review of economic and political news from the Middle East notes that the meeting "adopted a Saudi-inspired resolution to protect Iran from the effects of an American boycott," and reports that the Gulf countries "are more worried about the potential reaction of the U.S. to the crisis than they are about Soviet intervention itself." The Middle East is heading towards war, one official stated, "but towards a war which would mean the sharing by the superpowers of its oil and mineral wealth."[18] Subsequent indications confirm that these fears remain dominant.

When these facts are noted in the U.S. press, the phenomenon is often attributed to the mysterious process of "Finlandization," whereby states accommodate to Russian power because they recognize the weakness of the United States. Thus their expressed opposition to U.S. military intervention is neatly converted into an appeal that American military power be enhanced so that our "defensive umbrella" can be extended to states that would willingly take shelter under it if only they could place their trust in U.S. force.[19] This fanciful interpretation is easy enough to explain, given the commitments of its authors to U.S. interventionism and, in many instances, Israeli power. A more serious look at the facts shows quite clearly that the primary concern of the states in question is Israeli military power, which they regard as the primary threat as long as Israel continues with U.S. support to occupy territories conquered in 1967. Furthermore, they have repeatedly stated that they feel no less threatened by the U.S. intent to "defend its legitimate interests" than by the potential Russian menace.

The doctrine of the "New Cold Warriors" holds that one of the greatest threats to world peace now lies in western Pakistan, where the Russians are preparing to march towards the Gulf in order to take control of the Middle East oil that belongs to us as a natural right. We must therefore dispatch military forces to the region and arm General Zia, one of the most unpopular rulers in Pakistan's history. A Russian agent in the State Department, at least one who happened to have the strange desire to be incinerated along with the rest of us, could offer no better advice. General Zia's arms will not deter a Russian army any more than a few thousand U.S. marines in the Gulf, nor is there any indication that the Soviet Union would be insane enough to invade Pakistan; the invasion of Afghanistan, while brutal and reprehensible, was characteristic of Soviet military actions in that it aimed to maintain a position of power already attained, now under internal attack.

But arms for General Zia will be used—for internal repression, a fact of which many Pakistanis are gloomily aware, so we learn (as if we had to learn it) from reports from Pakistan in the foreign press. The Baluch of western Pakistan seem rather ambivalent about the threat of Russian aggression or even the invasion of Afghanistan. One reason is that they are aware of recent history, even if most Americans are not. They recall, for example, that in the mid-1970s, U.S. helicopter gunships supplied via the Shah were used by the Pakistani army to murder them and destroy their villages.

They do not exactly welcome the American "aid" now being offered. The *Manchester Guardian* observes editorially: "More American helicopter gunships blasting Baluchis; the finest Russian propaganda in the world. . . . The West will be in appalling dilemma, reviled in Baluchistan, the Frontier and Sind as the succourer of the oppressor," [20] and reviled as well by other Pakistanis, who may turn to the Russians for support against their tormentor, "defending" them with U.S. aid. A report from Rawalpindi quotes a Baluch chief who says: "If the West props up Zia and the Russians move south, there will be no civil resistance as I see it. Some might even be prepared to aid them." And a Pakistani politician adds: "This aid America is talking about is not aid to the people. It is aid to the army junta. They will perhaps use it on the wrong people—on the Pakistanis and particularly the Baluchis." [21] A realistic judgment.

U.S. planners are presumably not unaware of the possible dynamics: arms for General Zia, internal repression, expansion of Russian influence as the victims turn to the USSR for support, a new Afghanistan, nuclear holocaust. But the dangers are regarded as insignificant in comparison with the importance of overcoming "post-Vietnam reticence" and eliminating the annoying domestic barriers to military intervention and other harsh measures to protect "our interests"—that is, the interests of those whose power in the private economy gives them a dominant influence over policy formation, and who believe that they stand to gain (though "we" may not) by maintaining a world system in which they are free to exploit human and material resources. A serious inquiry into U.S. foreign policy will show that these are the central factors that govern it, however they may be obscured by ideological obfuscation.

A look at some of the American successes during the Old Cold War reveals that those we intend to "protect" have good reason for fear. The first major U.S. intervention in defense of freedom was in Greece, when Britain, which invaded and conquered Greece after the Nazis had withdrawn, could no longer maintain its position there in 1946–47 after its success in undermining the anti-Nazi resistance and restoring royalist elements and Nazi collaborators to state power, setting off a wave of violence and persecution that finally evoked armed resistance. Displacing the British, the American military mission (AMAG: American Mission for Aid to Greece) lent its fervent and uncompromising support to state violence, which included the imprisonment without trial of tens of thousands of people in concentration camps where they were subjected to "reindoctrination" if they "were found to have affiliations which cast grave doubt upon their loyalty to the state," in the words of the AMAG chief. (It was only many years later, when the atrocity could be charged to an official enemy, that Westerners became exercised over "reeducation camps"; similarly, British and American reeducation camps for hundreds of thousands of German and Italian POWs up to three years after the war's end, where the victims were not only indoctrinated but also subjected to forced labor and severe mistreatment, are described in the West—if noted at all—as an amazing example of Western humanism, as contrasted with the atrocious behavior of the Vietnamese.)[22] Many thousands were executed and tens of thousands exiled, with the full support of the United States. U.S. chargé Karl Rankin warned in May 1948 that "there must . . . be no leniency toward the confirmed agents of an alien and subversive influence." Execution of political prisoners was legitimate, he argued, because even though when arrested they may not have been "hardened Communists, it is unlikely that they have been able to resist the influence of Communist indoctrination organizations existing within most prisons." Secretary of State George Marshall approved of the "administration of [Greek] justice." Meanwhile, U.S. intelligence engaged in extensive surveillance of Greek citizens and assisted the government in carrying out mass deportations of alleged subversives to concentration camps and reeducation centers, while forwarding to the FBI the names of U.S. citizens who wrote letters protesting executions; the FBI reciprocated by sending reports to the U.S. embassy on alleged Communist ties of Greek-American organizations.

The British protested some of these actions, but were rebuffed. When a British official objected that it was "unwise" to round up fourteen thousand people and exile them without trial to island concentration camps, American Ambassador Lincoln Mac Veagh responded that the Greek government "had to throw their net very wide to catch the right people," whom he estimated at about "a dozen key men." This was the first major action undertaken after the United States took control under the aegis of the Truman Doctrine.

When the war was approaching its final stages, the United States insisted on the policy of systematic removal of population by force and backed renewed programs of mass arrest and executions, moderating these commitments only in the very last months of the war. Continued "screening and re-education" were recommended by the U.S. mission for the postwar period, while the State Department fought to block any substantive U.N. recommendations on amnesty, leniency, or an end to political executions.

Throughout, a prime concern of Washington and the U.S. mission in Greece was the unfavorable publicity resulting from the terror it advocated and organized. Measures were taken to control the flow of news. The State Department succeeded in preventing the *New York Times* from publishing stories on U.S. embassy support for repressive programs, and in convincing the United Press to appoint a "double-breasted Americano" as UP representative in Greece in place of a *Christian Science Monitor* correspondent whom the department considered a leftist. The U.S. government also succeeded in aborting an investigation of the assassination of U.S. correspondent George Polk when evidence began to mount that it was a right-wing assassination rather than the responsibility of the Greek left as had been claimed; the Pentagon withdrew the Air Force colonel who had been designated to investigate the murder by the Overseas Writers Association after he became convinced that the "extreme right" had committed the murder.

Meanwhile, the United States engaged in extensive psychological warfare operations, of which the ugliest example was fabrication of lies concerning the alleged "abduction" of children by the guerrillas (secretly, government officials conceded the fabrication); the Greek government was itself forcibly evacuating children from rebel-held territory. These allegations (whether there was some substance to them or not is, evidently, a question separate from the conscious fabrication) remained a staple of subsequent propaganda.

The long-term legacy of U.S. support for state terror in Greece was profound, culminating in the fascist coup of 1967, which was also welcomed and backed by the United States, sometimes with rhapsodic commentary on the opportunities it afforded for American business interests.[23]

The Greek experience reveals clearly the true meaning of President Truman's call "to support free peoples who are resisting attempted subjugation by armed minorities or by outside pressures."

Another success was the overthrow of the reformist Arbenz government in Guatemala in 1954, with consequences that are generally ignored in the United States. Some of these are graphically portrayed, for example, in a report from Guatemala by British journalist Anthony Wild.[24] "Migrant labor," he writes,

> is at the core of Guatemala's economic system. Four million rural poor, most of them Indians descended from the Maya, scratch a bare existence from growing maize on plots that are shrinking by inheritance with each

generation; with no jobs in their home villages, an estimated 1.5 million workers migrate for up to three months of the year, often taking wives and children with them. . . . The appalling living and working conditions in which [the great *haciendas*] keep them are the foundation on which the fabulous fortunes of Guatemala's elite are built.

The migrants work ten to twelve hours a day in broiling sun, then returning to their galleys, which are "hotbeds of disease" where "women shiver with malaria on a mattress of corrugated cardboard" and "the eyes of a little girl of six are half closed up with matter, for lack of washing." Drinking water, fetched from a stream half a mile away, "is white with pollution." Others "are poisoned by insecticides sprayed indiscriminately and excessively from light planes" or "die in horrific road accidents as badly maintained lorries, bringing them from their villages packed in like cattle to the slaughter, plunge off mountain roads." The laborers and their families "live little better than factory chickens or slaves on the Atlantic passage." In the galleys, "people sleep on long wooden platforms, stacked one on top of another like shelves, five layers deep in the centre and three by the walls . . . each shed sleeps an unbelievable 700 people in a space 10 yards wide by 30 yards long and 25 feet high." "The migrants are recruited in squads of 20 to 30 people from the same village. Often, the recruiter will pocket the migrant's entire wages, owed to him because of loans at 100 per cent interest, contracted in the summer months to buy food on the market when the peasants' own granaries are running out of maize." "Nearly two-thirds of the land of the big estates is kept vacant," Wild adds, "held as a status symbol or a hedge against inflation. . . . Trade union leaders are being murdered in an attempt to intimidate the workers," preventing the growth of peasant unions that might mitigate these horrors. Meanwhile right-wing death squads, closely linked to the government, kill tens of thousands with impunity.[25]

The London Anti-Slavery Society reports that 80 percent of the total labor force is comprised of seasonal migrant workers, who have been reduced by the Labor Code "to a position of virtual servitude at the hands of landowners and their labour contractors." It too gives details of massive atrocities committed by the government.[26]

Wild notes that the last government to propose "a moderate land reform which transferred . . . vacant land to landless and near-landless," thus offering them freedom from dependence on such labor, "was toppled in 1954 by the U.S.-backed invasion of Colonel Castillo Armas." This invasion was justified under the doctrine that the United States had the right to intervene to "save" the free people of Guatemala from international Communism, the natural corollary to the Truman Doctrine and the predecessor of the Khrushchev, Johnson, and Brezhnev doctrines, which were quite similar in tone, even rhetoric, as noted earlier.

The horrors of Guatemala are the direct and natural result of U.S. military intervention within the ideological framework of the Old Cold War, in 1954 and in subsequent years. Hundreds of thousands have died as a result of this intervention—tens of thousands by assassination, often with torture and mutilation; many more from malnutrition and disease—while millions live in conditions of virtual slavery. The National Council of the Jesuit Order in Guatemala recently issued a statement reporting that "in Guatemala, it is only necessary to open one's eyes to realize that here we are ruled by a system of anti-Christian power which destroys life and persecutes those who fight for life. . . . This anguishing situation is being maintained with a repression among the most severe in Guatemala's recent history. A regime of unjust force is trying to prevent the working people from reclaiming their just rights." They reported over three thousand killings in the first ten months of 1979 by death squads that operate "with total impunity. It is axiomatic that in Guatemala there are no political prisoners, only the dead and disappeared."[27] The story can be repeated throughout much of the Free World.

In the democratic socialist journal *Dissent* (Fall 1980), Henry Pachter condemns the comment by H. Brand in the same journal (Spring 1980) that "American hegemony is generally in no way preferable to the Russian kind." That "embarrassing sentence," Pachter writes, treats foreign policy as a "beauty contest." "Is there no difference," he asks rhetorically, "between the violent subjection of one country by another and *the hegemony* of a big country trading with its smaller neighbors?" Perhaps the peasants of Guatemala might have something to say in response, if anyone were to ask; as might many others, who, for some reason, see U.S. intervention as going beyond trade.

To turn finally to another continent, consider Zaire, a potentially rich country subjected to repeated Western intervention in the framework of the Cold War system. The *London Financial Times* informs us[28] that the West feels that it must support President Mobutu because "there is no alternative"; he is the "bulwark against the spread of Soviet influence in Central and Southern Africa," and his country is rich in resources that the industrial powers crave. No matter, then, that the incredible corruption and terror of his rule have had a "devastating impact" on the lives of the country's 26 million people, as, for example, the cost of essential food items has gone up 540 percent in the past four years, while in 1979 real wages and salaries were 60 percent below their 1970 level, and much of the population starves, surviving at best in hopelessness and degradation.

To gain a further grasp of some of the realities that are obscured in Free World propaganda, one may turn to another recent study of the London Anti-Slavery Society. This received little notice in the United States. I found it discussed only in a Reuters report in the *Christian Science Monitor,* which appeared not in the news section but in the "living" section, which is reserved for "human interest stories" (December 19, 1979). The report alleges that almost 200 million children live under conditions of slavery, "often in dismal poverty." "Children have been maimed in India to become more effective beggars, sold to work under appalling conditions in factories in Thailand, and turned into Latin American chattel slaves at the age of three." "Latin America is singled out in the book as the continent where child labor will probably be harder to eradicate than anywhere else in the world. In countries with large Indian populations like Bolivia, girls as young as three are 'adopted' by white families, the book says. Traditionally they are sexually available to the sons of the family, not allowed to marry, and the children they conceive become virtual chattel slaves in turn." [29]

It would be an error to say that the harsh conditions of child labor evoke no concern in the humanitarian West. Thus, many articles have been written expressing shock and horror over the fact that in Cambodia under the Khmer Rouge, children were put to work in collectives. The vast and systematic enslavement of children throughout the Free World, however, deserves no comment. Nor is there any effort to determine why the situation appears to be most grim in the regions that have been exposed for so long to Western benevolence. Quite generally, starvation, massacre, slavery, and other atrocities within the Free World are either ignored or occasionally noted as curiosities perhaps attributable to some act of God or to the failure of the natives to absorb the message of "Western humanism," surely not to conscious human acts taken by the leaders of the Free World in accordance with institutional demands that reflect the structure of power in the state capitalist democracies.

The British economist Joan Robinson once described the American crusade against Communism as a "crusade against development." It would be accurate to regard it as a crusade against independent development outside of the structure of the global system of exploitation organized under the umbrella of U.S. power after World War II. There is no dearth of documentary evidence on the planning behind this crusade; for example, the Grand Area planning discussed in Chapter 2, which, as noted there, remains under a taboo in American scholarship, discussed only far from the mainstream, despite—or perhaps because of—the fact that it provides a valuable insight into the reality that lies behind conventional rhetoric. This reality is remote from conventional ideology, but is lived every day by hundreds of millions of people whose torment is of little concern to Western moralists—unless, of course, they are aroused by "Communist agitators" and subjected to "alien influences." This reality is not a collection of strange coincidences or an indication of the limits of American power to do good, as is constantly proclaimed, but is in significant and deplorable measure a direct and predictable consequence of policy decisions based on the principles expressed in the cool and antiseptic rhetoric of the planners. Until we come to appreciate these facts, we will understand very little about the contemporary world.

I have been discussing some features of the Old Cold War that one may expect, I believe, to persist if it is successfully resurrected. But there will also be differences. The world is not what it was a generation ago. It is doubtful that the United States, no longer in a position of overwhelming dominance, can devote its resources to the production of waste while maintaining its position in international trade—of course, apart from sales of military equipment, which continue to increase, not solely from the United States. Efforts to pressure U.S. allies to "bear their share of the burden" of military expenditures are not likely to prove too successful. Europe and Japan have shown little enthusiasm for the new crusade. East-West trade in Europe is now quite substantial, as traditional relationships are being reestablished, and it is unlikely that the European powers will be willing to sacrifice it. American allies may choose to take their own independent initiatives, not only towards the USSR but also towards the Middle East and other resource-rich areas, realizing long-term fears of American planners. It is worth recalling Henry Kissinger's warning, in explaining the thinking behind the "Year of Europe" in 1973, about "the prospect of a closed trading system embracing the European Community and a growing number of other nations in Europe, the Mediterranean, and Africa" from which the United States might be excluded. The proper organization of the world system, he explained, should be based on the recognition that "the United States has global interests and responsibilities," while our allies have "regional interests"; the United States must be "concerned more with the overall framework of order than with the management of every regional enterprise," these being accorded to our allies, as he elaborated elsewhere.[30] But this version of "trilateralism" is unlikely to survive for long.

The Trilateral Commission, which was formed in 1973 to come to terms with the problems of fragmentation within the First World of industrial capitalism, was quite correct in describing the international system that arose from World War II in these terms: "For a quarter century the United States was the hegemonic power in a system of world order"[31]—correct, at least, if we interpret the phrase "world order" with appropriate irony. It is true that in the system that arose from the ashes of World War II, the United States was in a position of quite considerable power, sufficient to materially influence historical developments though not to control them completely in its interests. It is hardly surprising, then, that it attempted to organize a global system, or at least a Grand Area, in the interests of those who held domestic power. The USSR created its own power bloc in Eastern Europe and to some degree China. This was the basic structure of the Old Cold War, but the world is now radically different. China is an American ally and a bitter enemy of the USSR, a major shift in the balance of world power in favor of the United States. And the capitalist world is drifting towards a kind of trilateralism which may eventuate in three partially closed trading blocs—a dollar block, a yen bloc, a European Currency Union bloc—as a recent OECD study suggests, with international consequences that are uncertain, and in many ways ominous. Those who recall the mood of 1914 and 1939 do so with some reason.

There is no doubt that U.S. power has waned as the bipolar system of the postwar years has gradually evolved to something more complex. The same is true of Soviet power. A recent study of the Center for Defense Information in Washington, tracing Russian influence on a country-by-country basis since World War II, concludes quite reasonably that it reached a peak in the late 1950s and has since declined to the point where by 1979, "the Soviets were influencing only 6% of the world's population and 5% of the world's GNP, exclusive of the Soviet Union."[32] For reasons already discussed, Cold War ideologists in both camps like to pretend that their adversary is marching from strength to strength, but the facts hardly support these conclusions. Though their capacity to destroy grows steadily, neither the United States nor the Soviet Union now has the power it once was able to wield in world affairs, and this process is not likely to be reversed.

Europe and Japan pose a greater potential threat to U.S. world power than the Soviet Union, if they move towards a more independent role. And a U.S.-sponsored New Cold War may press them in that direction, raising the possibility of new and unanticipated crises and alignments. In the shorter term, one may expect the superpowers to create new and more awesome forces of destruction and to try to subjugate those who stand in the way of their global ambitions, marching towards nuclear catastrophe.

The recent steps towards Armageddon have evoked little articulate protest in the United States, though there is a substantial ground swell of popular concern. This testifies again to the great success of the campaign to overcome the "Vietnam syndrome" (see, however, pp. 46, 55f.). A few recent examples will illustrate the astonishing achievements of the efforts to restore what Hans Morgenthau once called "our conformist subservience to those in power"—though as noted in these essays, the distance that had to be traveled was far less than is often supposed. First, some additional words of background.

The war against the world's poor and oppressed reached its peak under the liberal democratic administrations of the 1960s, with the considerable amplification of the doctrine and practice of counterinsurgency and counterrevolutionary subversion and violence. A plague of neofascist states spread through Latin America and elsewhere as well. Brazil, because of its size and power, was a particularly significant example. The U.S.-backed military coup of 1964 placed in power a repressive and murderous regime that carried out an "economic miracle" while keeping the great mass of the population in conditions of grinding poverty and actually lowering the already miserable standard of living for many of them. It also had a noticeable "domino effect," contributing to the spread of U.S.-backed military dictatorships committed to repression and violence. As always, U.S. support for the Brazilian coup was justified on the grounds that "the nation needed it in order to free itself of a corrupt government which was about to sell us out to international communism" (General Andrew O'Meara, Commander of the U.S. Southern Command, testifying before Congress in 1965). President Kennedy's ambassador to Brazil, Lincoln Gordon, described the Brazilian "revolution" as the "the single most decisive victory for freedom in the mid-twentieth century."[33] Similarly, the Indonesian coup a year later was welcomed in liberal circles as a vindication of the U.S. policy of standing firm in Indochina, while the resulting massacre of hundreds of thousands of landless peasants, if noted at all, was dismissed as an unfortunate reaction to Communist plotting. The revolution in Cuba, in contrast, was understood to pose such threats to human rights and civilized values that the leader of the Free World subjected Cuba to invasion, subversion, embargo, terrorism, poisoning of crops and livestock—and now, after this record, stands in judgment over Cuba for its violation of human rights.

The situation in Latin America has not gone unnoticed in establishment media. Richard Fagen writes in *Foreign Affairs* (Winter 1979) that the Linowitz Commission was accurate in describing the "plague of repression" that had settled over Latin America by 1976: "At no time in the recent history of the hemisphere had the incidence of military rule been so high, the gross violations of political and human rights so widespread, and the use of officially sponsored assassination, torture and brutality so systematic." But in journalistic or scholarly discussion these facts are rarely related to U.S. initiatives; rather, these developments show that it is not within the power of the United States to eliminate inequality and poverty, as it has been striving so desperately to do for so many years in Brazil, Paraguay, Nicaragua, Guatemala, and elsewhere within the domains of its influence and control.

Actually, it is interesting to inquire into the relation between human rights violations and U.S. aid and support. There does, in fact, appear to be a correlation, which has been noted in several studies, one of them by Edward S. Herman and myself (see our *Political Economy of Human Rights,* vol. 1). We found, as did Michael Klare in an independent study, that the deterioration of the human rights climate in some Free World dependency tends to correlate rather closely with an increase in U.S. aid and support. Of course, one must be cautious with statistical correlations; the correlation in question should not be interpreted as implying that the U.S. government is rewarding some ruling group for the the increase in torture, death squads, destruction of unions, elimination of democratic institutions, decline of living standards for much of the population, etc. These are not a positive priority for U.S. policy; rather, they are irrelevant to it. The correlation between abuse of human rights and U.S. support derives from deeper factors. The deterioration in human rights and the increase in U.S. aid and support each correlate, independently, with a third and crucial factor: namely, improvement of the investment climate, as measured by privileges granted foreign capital. The climate for business operations improves as unions and other popular organizations are destroyed, dissidents are tortured or eliminated, real wages are depressed, and the society as a whole is placed in the hands of a collection of thugs who are willing to sell out to the foreigner for a share of the loot—often too large a share, as business regularly complains. And as the climate for business operations improves, the society is welcomed into the Free World and offered the specific kind of "aid" that will further these favorable developments. If the consequences are, for example, that crops are produced for export by wealthy landowners or transnational agribusiness while the population starves, that is simply the price that must be paid for the survival of free institutions.

The correlation just cited, and the obvious explanation for it, reveal that there may well be a relation between U.S. foreign policy and human rights, though not precisely the one that is widely heralded throughout the international propaganda system. No less striking than the correlation is the general avoidance of all of these matters in respectable scholarship. In this context, it is possible for an American President to stand up and proclaim that concern for human rights is "the Soul of our foreign policy," and to be listened to with respect—even critics limit themselves to noting "contradictions," "inconsistencies," and "deviations," thus reinforcing the basic principle of the propaganda system, that the United States is committed to a program of freedom and human rights (as is the West in general), one of the great lies of modern history, and one of the most effective.

The spread of neo-fascist torture-and-corruption states in the Third World under U.S. sponsorship has in part been a response to "the lessons of Vietnam." General Maxwell Taylor, who has been described as the *éminence grise* of the Kennedy Administration, explained that "the outstanding lesson [of the Indochina conflict] is that we should never let another Vietnam-type situation arise again. We were too late in recognizing the extent of the subversive threat. . . . We have learned the need for a strong police force and a strong police intelligence organization to assist in identifying early the symptoms of an incipient subversive situation."[34] This was in December 1965, after the Brazilian and Indonesian coups, after the invasion of the Dominican Republic, events that revealed how well the lessons of Vietnam had been absorbed by ruling groups that have a historical memory, a capacity to learn, and a high level of class consciousness, and that benefit by the absence of any substantial domestic critique. True, the "Vietnam syndrome" and the "crisis of democracy" impeded their programs for a time, but it is hoped that these maladies of our social order have now been overcome.

The refusal of Western ideologists to consider the systematic character of the impact of the West, specifically the United States, is particularly striking in discussion of the Caribbean and Central America, traditionally the region in which the United States has resorted to direct aggression and other forms of intervention. Typically, the problems of this region are described as though the United States were simply a passive onlooker, helpless to alleviate them despite its endless good will. For example, the *New York Times Magazine* devoted its lead story on May 25, 1980, to a discussion of "Radical Winds of the Caribbean" by Tad Szulc, a highly regarded investigative reporter who is known for his independence of mind and crusading journalism in the area of foreign affairs. It is illuminating to watch how he proceeds.

Szulc begins by noting that "when most people in the United States think of trouble in the Caribbean, they think of Fidel Castro's Cuba . . . it has been the Castro regime that brought us the Bay of Pigs, the missile crisis, the Soviet military presence in the Caribbean and, most recently, the flood of refugees into Florida." Szulc is, of course, correct in saying that Castro is generally regarded by the well-indoctrinated American public as *the* source of trouble in the Caribbean, though he goes somewhat beyond the propaganda norm in writing that Castro "brought us the Bay of Pigs"—one can perhaps imagine some party hack writing in *Pravda* that "Dubcek brought us the tanks in Prague." The other examples are hardly less interesting. The number of people fleeing to the United States from intolerable conditions to the south is in the millions annually; immigration officials estimate that about 1 million escape detection. Since 1972, there has been a flood of "boat people" from Haiti, traveling eight-hundred miles through shark-infested waters in leaky tubs to be interned by immigration officials and sent back to the Duvalier dictatorship (a few dozen received asylum between 1972 and 1978). A still more horrifying example is the denial of asylum to refugees from El Salvador, whom the U.S. government regularly compels to return to face torture, mutilation, and murder by the gangsters armed and trained by the United States. One can easily imagine the consequences if the United States were to open its doors and welcome refugees from virtually any country of the region. One estimate is that 20 percent of the Caribbean population has come to the United States since World War II.[35] But it is only the refugees from Castro's Cuba whose plight reveals the horrors of their native land, which had the misfortune to be forced out of the Free World.

Szulc then proceeds to explain that the common view is in error: "The roots of the Caribbean problems are not entirely Cuban." Rather, it is the "Soviet offensive" in the region that is to blame, alongside of "Cuban adventurism." As an illustration, he observes that the Soviet Union has rejected "the notion that the Caribbean is an American *mare nostrum*," a clear sign that they are intent on trouble-making. There are, of course, some more general problems in the region: "the pressing need to free the population from grinding poverty and endemic unemployment," one cause for the flight of the population. In Grenada, for example, about two-thirds of the population live abroad, including "the brightest and best-educated young people"; it was Soviet and Cuban "adventurism" in Grenada that directly inspired Szulc's article. These problems are long-standing: "The seeds of the present turmoil in the Caribbean were sown in the days of colonial greed and mismanagement"; England, Spain, France, and the Netherlands are mentioned. "The unanswered question is the extent to which Cuba and the Soviet Union proposes [sic] to exploit the turbulent situation." Nowhere in this extensive discussion is there any indication that the United States has played any role in bringing about the "trouble in the Caribbean," apart from its "indifference" to the social and economic problems that have been brewing.

Scholarship is hardly different. Consider, for example, the contributions of two outstanding specialists on foreign policy to a *Foreign Affairs* symposium on "America and the World 1979."[36] Robert Scalapino writes that "American policies toward Indochina during 1979 were dominated by two considerations: a deep compassion for the tremendous human suffering throughout the region, and a strong distaste for Hanoi's policies and alignments." The latter is no doubt true, though it might have been useful to comment on the U.S. role in driving Hanoi into a close alliance with the Soviet Union that it surely did not prefer. What about the "deep compassion," surely merited, given the U.S. role in causing the tremendous suffering throughout the region by devastating the societies and the land. In Laos, where the agricultural system was destroyed by a relentless bombing campaign against an entirely defenseless peasant population, hundreds of thousands face starvation while the United States shows its deep compassion by withholding more than a tiny trickle of aid. A year earlier, a ludicrously small U.S. contribution was dispatched with great fanfare, but it turned out that this amount was quietly deducted from the regular U.S. contribution to a U.N. aid program for Laos, demonstrating that there are no limits to the hypocrisy of the "human rights" crusaders.[37] It is superfluous to review the destruction of Vietnam for which U.S. terror is responsible. Expressing its "deep compassion for the tremendous human suffering" that has resulted in Vietnam, the United States, in 1979, successfully pressured the World Bank to withdraw its only development loan to Vietnam and then compelled the International Monetary Fund to do likewise.[38] According to the *Far Eastern Economic Review,* the letter written by World Bank President Robert McNamara announcing the Vietnam loan moratorium was drafted by Fred Bergsten, Assistant Secretary of the U.S. Treasury Department in the Human Rights Administration. The *Review* was informed by an unidentified source in the IMF that "since 1977, the U.S. has constantly refused to make any accommodation with Vietnam, forcing it further and further into the Soviet camp"—and, correspondingly, entitling American scholars to deplore Hanoi's "alignments." (See pp. 26f., 75.)

Robert Tucker, one of the better-known academic doves and a leading commentator on international affairs, writes in the same issue that "the American role in Southeast Asia has been transformed in the course of a decade from that of imperial guarantor of the area to one of tacitly supporting Chinese policy and of performing humanitarian missions." Putting aside discussion of the interesting notion of "imperial guarantor" or the intriguing idea that the United States simply follows the Chinese lead, having withdrawn from world affairs under the impact of the "Vietnam syndrome," what of the "humanitarian missions" performed by the United States in Southeast Asia in the late 1970s? Among them is the consistent U.S. support for the brutal Marcos dictatorship in the Philippines. A still more notable example is the U.S. support for the Indonesian invasion of East Timor, including diplomatic support to prevent effective international action (U.N. Ambassador Daniel P. Moynihan, widely praised for his courage in denouncing Idi Amin as a "racist murderer" and for other comparable acts of heroism, specifically takes credit, in his memoirs, for preventing any U.N. action that might have restrained the Indonesian aggressors, an admission that elicited no comment from reviewers or other admirers), a continuing flow of arms accelerating under the Human Rights Administration, extensive lying to Congress, and an extremely effective cover-up by the press in one of the more dramatic examples of media servility in recent years.[39] It is quite true that U.S. allies, specifically Japan, have tried their best to contribute to the slaughter in similar ways, but primary credit falls to the U.S. government. The result has been the massacre of tens if not hundreds of thousands of people and a level of suffering among the remnants that was comparable to that in Cambodia in the same years. Surely a "humanitarian mission" of the highest order.

It is remarkable that knowledgeable American specialists can produce such drivel, but even more significant that it elicits no response. We would be appalled to read comparable remarks on the Russian role in the world produced by Soviet apologists, but it is regarded as entirely reasonable for American intellectuals, who are subject to no threats of state violence, to engage in a comparable display of obedience to the state propaganda system.

The humanitarian missions to which the U.S. government is devoting its energies out of its deep compassion for the suffering people of Southeast Asia deserve more attention than I can devote to them here. The zealous efforts of the industrial democracies to help implement Indonesian atrocities in East Timor are merely a by-product of their relations to Indonesia, which has thrown itself open to their plunder since the military coup of 1965. The United States, Japan, France, and their allies have no positive interest in the massacre of the population of East Timor, contrary to what is suggested by consideration of their actions. It is merely that the fate of the Timorese is of null import given the higher importance of exploiting the wealth of Indonesia. The case of Indochina is more complex. The United States did win a significant victory in Indochina, a fact that is crucial to the understanding of postwar events. True, it did not achieve the goal of retaining Indochina within the American system, so that its people could enjoy the happy life of the peasants, urban slum-dwellers, torture victims, and child slave laborers of Thailand, Indonesia, the Philippines, and Latin America. But that was always a secondary goal. The primary goal was to ensure that "the rot would not spread," in the terminology favored by the planners. In South Vietnam itself, the United States did win the war. The battering of the peasant society, particularly the murderous post-Tet accelerated pacification campaigns, virtually destroyed the indigenous resistance by eliminating its social base, setting the stage for the northern domination now deplored by Western hypocrites—exactly as had been predicted many years before.[40] In Cambodia, the horrendous bombing campaign of 1973, which was directed primarily against the peasant society, was a significant factor in brutalizing the Khmer Rouge victors, a conclusion supported by U.S. government studies and other sources.[41] In Laos, the prospects for peaceful development in one of the world's poorest countries were destroyed by American subversion and military attack. North Vietnam, while not conquered, was left in ruins.

The terrible prospect of successful economic development has been overcome for a long time, perhaps permanently. No one knows when, or if, the land and people poisoned by chemical warfare and bombed to ruin will be restored to a viable social order. The postwar policy of refusing reparations, aid, or normal relations with Vietnam and blocking assistance from other sources where possible is perfectly rational, as a further contribution to ensuring maximal suffering. It also succeeded in driving Vietnam into alliance with the Soviet Union as the only alternative remaining, again a consequence eagerly exploited by the Western propaganda system. By systematically creating conditions under which existence is reduced to virtually the zero grade, Western power has attained its primary ends throughout Indochina. The West has once again taught the lesson that European civilization has offered to the world for centuries: those who try to resist the technologically advanced but morally primitive Western societies will pay a bitter price.

It is in this context that we can fully appreciate the pronouncements of Western commentators.

A curious, and perhaps unique feature of Western propaganda systems is that those who serve them not only are not subjected to criticism but are in fact lauded for their amazing courage in marching to the beat of the patriotic drums. For example, Peter Kovler writes that there were "heroic exceptions" to the alleged attempts by American intellectuals to "defend Indochinese governments against the 'unverified' charges of killing and genocide that were made by 'hysterical' refugees." [42] These attempts, incidentally, are a typical fabrication of the propaganda system, which has endeavored to create the appearance of a great debate over atrocities in Indochina, undeterred by the fact that American intellectuals were virtually uniform in vigorous denunciation of the official enemy, sometimes on the flimsiest evidence, in conformity with the needs of state propaganda. Criticism of refugee reports is virtually nonexistent, and the rare attempts to inquire into the credibility of those who transmitted the reports, as any rational person would do (e.g., in the case of germ warfare charges against the United States in Korea), or otherwise to determine the facts were castigated as an intolerable deviation from doctrinal purity, even though they were regularly coupled with condemnation of reasonably well-documented atrocities. At the same time the intellectual community refused even to hear about, let alone investigate or try to stop, the numerous atrocities for which the United States was responsible in the same period—in Timor, to cite just one obvious example, where in contrast to Cambodia, atrocities could have been brought to a halt by political action here.

But more interesting is the reference to the "heroic exceptions" to this fabricated pattern. Kovler's first example is Leo Cherne, director of the International Rescue Committee, "who, between 1975 and 1977, tried to get the United States Government to pay attention to the plight of some exotic individuals called 'boat people.' " Leo Cherne is, in fact, one of the more extraordinary apologists for violence and massacre in recent years, as, for example, in his supremely cynical description of the victims of U.S. bombings in South Vietnam cited above, Chapter 2, note 1. But let us forget his past contributions, and consider his "heroism" in calling attention to the plight of the "boat people" from 1975 to 1977. A minor problem is that there were very few "boat people" during that period, at least "boat people" who count: There were 100,000 or more boat people who fled the Philippines and many thousands who attempted to escape from Haiti, not to speak of the refugees who fled U.S.-backed terror in Timor and in fact many millions of others throughout the world. But let us forget this, too, and consider the idea that it requires "heroism" to denounce atrocities attributed to an official enemy, to the overwhelming applause of articulate opinion. This concept is perhaps novel in the history of modern propaganda.

For the student of contemporary propaganda, it is particularly instructive to observe how the torment of Cambodia has been exploited by cynical Western humanitarians, desperately eager to overcome the "Vietnam syndrome." In an article on the Russian invasion of Afghanistan, Ben Bradlee quotes Theodore Eliot, dean of the prestigious Fletcher School of Law and Diplomacy at Tufts University, on the possibility of Russian genocide in Afghanistan: "Genocide? If they did it in Cambodia, why not in Afghanistan?" [43] With equal logic, one might have commented in 1965 on the likelihood of U.S. genocide in Vietnam: "Genocide? If they did it in Nazi Germany, why not in Vietnam?" Or consider the following, observation by Dennis Bloodworth, a well-known Asia correspondent, in an article on Pol Pot.[44] Pol Pot's Cambodia serves as "a grotesque caricature which warned the world against theorising left-wing iconoclasts eager to smash the existing order." Remember Pol Pot's cadres and his peasant army when you hear someone proposing radical social change in the advanced industrial West. In a society less thoroughly indoctrinated than ours, such commentary would merely be greeted with ridicule. In the Western democracies, however, it is

taken quite seriously, again, a revealing indication of the awesome effectiveness of Western propaganda systems.

The vast effort to overcome the "Vietnam syndrome" has not limited itself to whitewashing the West for its recent humanitarian endeavors, but
has gone beyond, to submerge the entire history of imperialist savagery, and
with no little success. A British intellectual can write, without shame, of "a
growing indifference in Africa and Asia to a tradition of Western humanism—which had been imposed, first by European colonial powers as they
spread their influence throughout the world, and more recently, by the
United States in the name of the 'American century.' "[45] Such comments
suggest some interesting research projects: For example, one might conduct
a survey among the aboriginal population of Tasmania to determine how
well they have absorbed the lessons of Western humanism. Somehow,
where they managed to survive, the natives often fail to grasp the humanist
message, even the more anglicized among them; for example, Jawaharlal
Nehru, who observed that the ideology of British rule in India "was that of
the herrenvolk and the Master Race," an idea that is "inherent in imperialism" and "was proclaimed in unambiguous language by those in authority"
and put into practice as "Indians as individuals were subjected to insult, humiliation, and contemptuous treatment,"[46] not to mention somewhat more
severe practices. As for the humanism of the American century in the Third
World, no comment is required.

In an intellectual climate of the sort illustrated in these examples, which
are typical of a substantial segment of articulate opinion, the managers of
the national security state may proceed—so they believe—to reconstruct
the Cold War framework for interventionism without too much fear of domestic protest. On the contrary, liberal journals will publish discussions of
the "real reason" for the problems of the Middle East: "the profound reluctance of Western powers to do what is required in order to protect their own
interests: namely, to make their strength visible and respected," using "political and military means" to "destroy . . . [the] . . . OPEC monopoly."[47]
(Typically, this call for overcoming "Western deference in the Middle East"
and using military force to "defend Western interests" against the disrep-
utable locals is subheaded: "If the U.S. is not willing to counter the Russians,
who is?"—Kedourie also does not enlighten the reader as to whether the
Continental powers should invade Britain to "defend their interests" by
taking over its petroleum resources, which fetch higher prices on the world
market than those of the "sheiks" who are bent on destroying Western civi-

lization.) In short, sophisticated, hardheaded realism: If they talk out of turn or don't behave, smash them in the face. The rhetoric may take its honored place in the annals of imperialism, serving as a further testimonial to the distinguished record that has been compiled by cultivated opinion in advanced civilizations.

In an important study discussed in Chapter 1, the Trilateral Commission warned of the danger posed to democracy by the involvement of large parts of the population in the political arena during the terrible sixties, and by the work of "value-oriented intellectuals" who "challenge the existing structures of authority," undermining the effectiveness of "those institutions which have played the major role in the indoctrination of the young," such as the universities. The critique of the system of indoctrination by students and some others terrorized many intellectuals no less than the involvement of the formerly apathetic population in the democratic process, a fact illustrated in some of the paranoid fantasies later published in full seriousness: e.g., the description by G. Rees of how during this terrible period, the thesis that the universities must be destroyed "rang across every campus in the United States, and libraries were burned, and universities wrecked."[48] Others write of "the degenerating state of affairs" in the universities in 1968, "when it was impossible to imagine anything more slimy, sickly and stifling than the moral climate in that university" (Rochester University, in this specific case), though by 1975 "the Blacks were starting to become citizens" instead of "a curse" as they were in 1968, "the pus was being squeezed out of the universities," and, in general, the nation's "moral fibre" was being restored.[49] Again, the rhetoric is revealing, as are the hysteria and fabrication, and the ideals and attitudes that are implicit in such commentary.

How completely the population has succumbed to the campaign of indocrination during the 1970s is an open question. It has often been the case in the past that the articulate intelligentsia have tended to be both the committed partisans of the propaganda system and its most submissive victims, and there are indications that this may once again be true. It did not take long for the impressive intellectual edifice of conformism and subservience erected by the mainstream intelligentsia to collapse during the 1960s, and while it is partly true that the pus has been squeezed out of the universities—at least the elite universities that train the managers and leadership class—there is nevertheless, as there has been throughout the allegedly silent seventies, considerable ferment at the grass-roots level. The rivalries within the international system, the increasingly severe economic crisis, and the objective crisis over resources and destruction of the environment pose nontrivial problems for established power, and create opportunities for those who are committed to a different vision of the future than the one put forth by its spokesmen. The drive towards intervention, militarization, increased authoritarianism, submissiveness to the doctrinal system, and possibly eventual nuclear destruction is the result of human decisions taken within human institutions that do not derive from natural law and can be changed by people who devote themselves to the search for justice and freedom.

Chapter Eight

RESURGENT AMERICA (1981)

E VERY SO OFTEN an article appears in the prestigious journal *Foreign Affairs* of the Council on Foreign Relations which merits particular attention for the insight it provides not only into evolving policy but also into the mentality of the planners and their advisers. A well-known example is Samuel Huntington's paper "The Bases of Accommodation" (July 1968), a brutally explicit characterization of the program, already well advanced, to undercut the rural revolution in Vietnam by destroying its social base through "forced-draft urbanization and modernization" which would "produce a massive migration from countryside to city" by the "direct application of mechanical and conventional power," that is, by mass murder and physical destruction of a defenseless rural society. The lead article by Robert W. Tucker in the issue of Winter 1980/81 deserves close attention as another example of this genre. In its intellectual style as well as its specific content; Tucker's article, entitled "The Purposes of American Power," gives a valuable picture of the thinking that animates advisers and planners in significant sectors of the "foreign policy establishment," and of the range of policy options that are under active consideration.

Tucker is no fanatic ideologue of the Heritage Foundation type. He is a leading scholar of international affairs, and while he describes himself as "of the Right," he was something of an academic dove on Vietnam. He is the author of a study of the so-called radical critique of U.S. foreign policy which, while deeply flawed by factual and logical error, is nevertheless noteworthy in that it at least attempted to understand the nature of this critique and to consider its content, something of a rarity in the academic world, which has generally preferred silence or caricature.[1] Tucker is reported to

have been close to Reagan's foreign policy advisers, but the choices and policies he outlines, and the attitudes he reveals, are "above party," and should,
I think, be taken very seriously by people who hope to understand the future
that is being planned.

Tucker begins by suggesting that we are now facing the third major turning point in U.S. foreign policy since World War II: "On this, at least, there
is widespread agreement." The first such turning point was the initiation of
the "containment policy" in 1947. Tucker's manner of presentation suggests that he perhaps conceives of his statement as a counterpart to the famous "Mr. X" article by George Kennan entitled "The Sources of Soviet
Conduct," which appeared in the same journal in July 1947, and which, in
the words of a recent study, introduced the term "containment," which
"quickly became a capsule characterization of postwar American policy toward the Soviet Union." [2]

The second turning point was the acceptance of détente in the early
1970s, terminating the commitment to containment in the earlier sense.
And the third, which is his topic here, is the current reversal of détente and
the turn towards a more activist role, which may take one of two forms:
"Our alternatives today are either a policy of a resurgent America intent
once again on containing wherever possible the expansion of Soviet influence—as well as the expansion of communism generally—or a policy of
moderate containment that may prove inadequate to sustain the power and
discipline even to protect interests on which our essential security depends."
Tucker clearly takes the "resurgent America" option to be preferable if feasible: If moderate containment "is less demanding, it is also considerably
less appealing in the promise it holds out: not of a world moving progres-
sively under American leadership toward the eventual triumph of liberal-
capitalist values, but of a world in which America would have to abandon
expectations that only yesterday she confidently held." But the costs of the
more appealing option may be too high, he fears, and the "prevailing public
mood" appears to him to be supportive of at most a more modest policy. It
may be, then, that "the policy of a resurgent America," however appealing,
will be beyond our realization.

What is interesting, however, is not Tucker's personal assessment of costs
and public commitment, but the premises shared by both of the options he
lays forth. Let us therefore explore these, returning to the differences in
practice between the preferable turn towards a resurgent America and the
more limited scope of the less appealing moderate alternative.

The postwar policy of containment, announced, as Tucker writes, "in the sweeping language of the Truman Doctrine," in fact provided the framework for the interventionist programs of the following years; aggression or subversion in the Third World was invariably justified as "defensive action" undertaken to "contain" Soviet or Chinese expansionism, just as the "Western imperialist threat" is regularly invoked by Soviet propaganda when the tanks are sent to Berlin, Budapest, Prague, or Kabul. Tucker often adopts the conventional rhetoric of scholarship in this regard, with much talk about the grave dangers posed to us by Soviet power and the problem of inducing Moscow "to accept an American-inspired definition of moderate behavior," an unlikely prospect, he believes. But he knows very well, as we shall see, that the real problem lies elsewhere: not a Soviet threat to our security in the literal sense of this term, but the threat to our interests (as conceived by those who own and manage American society) posed by moves towards independence, primarily in the Third World.

A major factor behind the turn towards détente and "the logic of retrenchment" was, of course, the enormous and unanticipated cost of the Indochina war. Tucker presents what he calls the "liberal and moderate critique" of the U.S. war, namely, that "Vietnam was above all the product of intellectual error." Any critical analysis that goes beyond this framework is "immoderate" and is therefore to be dismissed, in accordance with the canons of scholarly decorum. In this assessment, Tucker falls well within the mainstream of intellectual opinion during the war and since.

In 1973 there arose "the first serious test, and failure, of the promise of détente," namely, the 1973 Arab-Israeli war, which showed that the Soviet Union would not "subordinate high policy to such benefits as an improved economic relationship might bring." It is axiomatic that the war reflected "Soviet high policy," a doctrine of faith that is difficult to square with the facts, to which I will briefly return, but that is so useful that it is simply assumed. These events illustrate a more pervasive "failure of the promise of détente," namely, "Soviet insistence upon being treated as an equal of America." The U.S. interpretation of détente was, of course, quite different: that the USSR should be satisfied with its role as a junior partner in global management.

Immediately following the 1973 war, "the failure in 1973–74 to respond to the Arab oil embargo raised from the outset the issue of right of access to the oil supplies of the Persian Gulf." While Tucker concedes that "the Soviets have been—at least, until recently—quite cautious and tentative in tak-

ing such advantage as they might have from the decline of the Western position in the Gulf," nevertheless we must bear in mind that at some time in
the future they may choose "to inhibit and, it may be, to openly challenge
the attempted reassertion of Western power in this vital region."

The "failure to respond" to which Tucker refers is presumably to be understood as the failure to resort to the threat of military force, as he had at
once advocated,[3] to guarantee the "right of access" to the energy reserves of
the Gulf region. Another axiom, too obvious to require explicit mention, is
that the United States, and the global bloc that it dominates, has this "right
of access," whereas, in contrast, hundreds of millions of starving people of
the Third World do not have a comparable right of access to the agricultural
resources of the United States, though their need is vastly greater than the
needs of the industrial capitalist societies for Middle East oil. But again, it
would be "immoderate and illiberal" to pursue the implications of this disparity of fundamental rights, so let us put the question aside.

This challenge to our basic rights is the crucial element that necessitates
the current reversal of foreign policy towards the reassertion of Western
(primarily American) power. It is, very simply, a matter of "need," and thus
is a feature common to the more appealing concept of a resurgent America
or the second-best alternative of moderate containment. It is unreasonable
to expect that the "power vacuum" in the Gulf can persist. It will "eventually be filled, whether by the one or the other superpower or by both"; "the
competition for control of the area is about as certain as anything can be in
politics." Putting aside sentimentality and assuming "the persistence of a
more traditional world, we have little alternative but to respond to a conventional security threat in the way that states have regularly responded to
such threats"; "we have no choice when faced by threats that, if permitted
to go unmet, could result in sacrificing interests on which the nation's economic well-being and the integrity of its basic institutions depend."
Though Tucker makes the required genuflections to the specter of Soviet
military power ("An imbalance of military power, present or prospective,
must be met by countervailing military power," etc.), he is sufficiently at
home in the real world to recognize that "more likely, a threat to access will
arise primarily from developments indigenous to the Gulf." There is, he
concludes, "no reliable substitute for Western power in the Gulf," where
"power" means military power: "A viable strategy in the Persian Gulf, then,
must have as its goal the creation of a conventional force structure that can

effectively deal with the contingencies that may arise short of a determined Russian assault."

With the doctrine that we are entitled to use force to control the Gulf against an indigenous threat or to overcome a "prospective" imbalance of military power—in effect, a preemptive strike—and that this right resides in the potential threat to our economic privilege and the integrity of our basic institutions, we reach the outer limits of great-power cynicism. One who is so inclined will have little difficulty in extracting similar pronouncements from the Nazi archives. Note again, in this connection, that while Tucker recognizes the propaganda value of the "Soviet threat"—a Cold War staple—he retains his grasp of reality: The real threat to our "right of access" is indigenous. Small wonder, then, that even ruling elites closely bound to the United States in the Gulf have warned against the reassertion of U.S. military power. As Tucker observes, "Whereas Western Europe on balance welcomed the American 'intervention,' the states of the Persian Gulf are still very far from doing so."

Recall again the basic doctrine: The "threat" that we must overcome with military force is not the threat of Soviet aggression, but rather the indigenous threat that may block our "right of access" to the resources of others, endangering our "economic well-being and the integrity of [the nation's] basic institutions," specifically, the "internal order" of the states of the region (see below). Tucker is, of course, quite correct in stating with such bluntness the operative principles that govern the behavior of a "great power," to an audience that presumably may be spared the usual fraudulent pretense about "Wilsonian principles of freedom and self determination," "human rights," or other variants of the standard rhetoric that defaces mainstream scholarship. It is, in fact, a great merit of his article to dispense with this conventional apparatus of deception.

Tucker states correctly that "it is the Gulf that forms the indispensable key to the defense of the American global position." In fact, there is no doubt that U.S. global dominance in the postwar period has been closely linked to control over the major energy reserves of the world, which must remain under U.S. control if this "global position" is to be maintained. The "first priority," then, for a resurgent America "is the restoration of American power generally and, above all, in the Persian Gulf." Tucker reiterates, with appropriate forcefulness, what I have called elsewhere "Axiom One of international affairs." [4]

So far, Tucker has been discussing what he calls "the realm of necessity." After some philosophical asides, he then turns to the second major area where U.S. military intervention is in order, namely, Central America. In this connection, he poses "the difficult, perhaps even insoluble distinction between need and want," a profound problem to which we may turn our minds when, at last, the bombs begin to fall. The point is that whereas in the Persian Gulf region, restoration of U.S. dominance is a matter of "need," in Central America it is simply a matter of "want." No threat to our economic well-being or to the integrity of our basic institutions would result from re- luctance to resort to violence in Central America, the reticence that Tucker found so "demeaning" in the case of the Persian Gulf (see note 3).

Nevertheless, we have the right to use force to control the fate of the peo- ple of this region. This right is based on two fundamental principles. First, it derives from history:

> Central America bears geographical proximity to the United States, and historically it has long been regarded as falling within our sphere of in- fluence. As such, we have long exercised the role great powers have tradi- tionally exercised over small states which fall within their respective spheres of influence. We have regularly played a determining role in making and in unmaking governments, and we have defined what we have considered to be the acceptable behavior of governments

—the behavior of Trujillo, Somoza, the murderous cliques that have ruled Guatemala and El Salvador, Duvalier, and so on. In addition to the right of intervention that derives from our historic practice in imposing acceptable behavior, there is a second factor: "In Central America our pride is engaged. . . . If we do not apply a policy of a resurgent America to prevent the coming to power of radical regimes in Central America, we have even less reason to do so in other areas. . . ."

In summary, "reasons of pride and historic tradition" afford us the right to resort to force in this region. An additional factor is that "it is here, if any- where, that we enjoy clear military superiority"; we can murder and destroy at relatively little cost, Tucker appears to believe, so that the pragmatic con- siderations that inform the "liberal and moderate critique" of foreign pol- icy pose no impediment.

With these remarks, we go well beyond the normal bounds of great- power cynicism. An assiduous search would be required to find historical analogues to the doctrine that "want," as opposed to "need," justifies the resort to force and violence to ensure "acceptable behavior" in our domains, or that reasons of pride and a history of massacre, torture, violence, and oppression provide sufficient grounds for perpetuation of the policies of the past. But let us again put aside "immoderate and illiberal" considerations such as these and return to the analysis. Tucker draws the obvious conclusions from the doctrines that he has laid forth: "Radical movements or radical regimes must be defeated. . . . Right-wing governments will have to be given steady outside support, even, if necessary, by sending in American forces."

"It can be done," Tucker assures us. And clearly no question can be raised about our right to do it, for reasons already explained. But another question does arise: "Why should we do it?" Here the policies of moderate containment and resurgent America diverge; we must contemplate the deep philosophical distinction between need and want and consider the calculus of costs. There are a number of problems, and they are worth considering, Tucker urges, when it is only our wants rather than our needs that are at stake. One problem is that the clients we will place or maintain in power will be unable to "enlist the support of centrist elements," because "these elements no longer exist in Central American states"—ever a realist, Tucker recognizes that the standard pretense of the State Department and the media is merely fraud, designed to pacify the domestic population; for example, the pretense that in El Salvador, the United States is supporting "centrist elements" against the lunatics of left and right.

There are other respects in which "a return to a policy of the past" may not be as easy as we might hope, despite the relative scale of U.S. military power as compared with the forces that can be organized by peasants in Guatemala or El Salvador:

> We have now passed the period of overthrowing an Arbenz in Guatemala, when disposing of governments to which we took offense was quite an easy undertaking. Today we must expect to deal with a far more determined and effective opposition. The price promises to be markedly greater, and it will have to be paid not only in the actions we take but in the reaction of others—particularly, though not only, in Latin America— to our actions.

Tucker does not elaborate (and of course, the "price" to be paid is not intended to cover the irrelevant matter of the cost to the victims), but his observation is correct. Mexico, no longer a power to be dismissed, is not likely to be pleased at the prospect of a resurgent America on both its northern and southern borders, eyeing its oil and other resources. And Europe too may be willing to exploit the opportunity to restore a position in Latin America from which it was gently removed during and after World War II, perhaps by taking the side of insurgents that it believes may represent the tide of history, employing the appropriate rhetoric of liberation and social justice.[5] Still, Tucker believes that "there is no persuasive reason for believing" that "a return to a policy of the past" will not "work in Central America," despite the new hazards that arise. Presumably, he maintains the interesting doctrine that he had expressed earlier (see note 3) with regard to the Middle East: "Given the American force structure and the experience we possess, however, why is it unreasonable to insist that the burden of proof rests upon those who insist we lack the military capability to intervene successfully?" Evidently, no other question might arise.

Tucker does not present a clear answer to the dilemma, but since our interest here is in exploring the assumptions of policy rather than the calculation of costs, we may put it aside. The sole policy issue, in Tucker's view, is "between those who define our sphere of influence to include the internal order of states, and those who do not," a question that does not arise with respect to the Persian Gulf, where "we are necessarily concerned with internal order because this issue cannot be separated from a vital interest in access to oil supplies," but that does arise when it is only our pride and the perpetuation of historical patterns of behavior that are at issue.

The policy of resurgent America "presupposes a position of clear military superiority; it cannot be prudently undertaken from a position of parity or even from a position of slight advantage." Furthermore, "It will not do, then, to charge that a resurgent America will be an interventionist America. Any policy of containment must accept the risk of intervention, and in circumstances that we may find in many ways undesirable." But we must courageously face these risks. Note again the characteristic way in which the concept of "containment," formulated for propaganda purposes as applicable to the superpower enemy, is applied in practice to the "containment" of indigenous threats to our privilege in the Middle East, and indigenous threats to our pride in Central America. The "containment" rhetoric should not obscure the fact that "it is the Third World that we are talking about." Much the same was true in the period of the Old Cold War.

Among the "risks" that we must face is the risk of an aroused public opinion. Tucker observes that "success is the great solvent of serious public dis-affection over foreign policy, and particularly over military intervention. . . . Unless future interventions can find a justification in security interests that the public finds compelling they will have to enjoy relatively quick and cheap success." This is the real lesson of Vietnam, Tucker points out. The lesson had been drawn long before by astute political scientists—for example, by Ithiel Pool, then chairman of the Department of Political Science at MIT, who explained in 1969 that "our worst mistake in Vietnam clearly was to initiate the bombing of the north," for the following reasons:[6]

> Before that started, it was my view that the United States as a democracy could not stand the moral protest that would arise if we rained death from the skies upon an area where there was no war. After the bombing started, I decided I had been in error. For a while there seemed to be no outcry of protest, but time brought it on. Now I would return to my original view with an important modification, namely, time. Public reactions do not come immediately. Many actions that public opinion would otherwise make impossible are possible if they are short-term. I believe we can fairly say that unless it is severely provoked or unless the war succeeds fast, a democracy cannot choose war as an instrument of policy.

Or, he might have added, unless the loyal intelligentsia succeed in portray-ing an attack on some peasant society as defense against "internal aggres-sion"; Robert McNamara was one of those who observed, not inaccurately, that the "hue and cry" over bombing related primarily to the North in 1965, though by then the United States Air Force had been mercilessly pounding South Vietnam for three years.[7] Or, still better, unless the media simply maintain silence about our raining "death from the skies upon an area where there was no war," as in northern Laos or Cambodia, so that in later years this can be referred to as "a secret bombing."

Tucker believes that "the Soviet Union would not only accept but proba-bly endorse" the policy of resort to force in Central America on the basis of our "want," "since it would be seen to help legitimize much of its own be-havior." Again, I think he is correct. Given the real functional significance of the Cold War, already discussed (see Introduction, p. 3; Chapter 7, p. 205), it is not implausible to conjecture that each of the major actors in the world arena will secretly welcome a display of brutality by the official enemy.

While generally realistic, Tucker predictably succumbs to illusion on one topic, namely, Israel. We have already seen an example: his assumption that the Arab-Israeli war of 1973 was a reflection of Soviet "high policy." In fact, it was a direct consequence of the refusal by the United States and Israel even to consider Sadat's offers of a negotiated peace settlement, as already noted (see pp. 197–8).[8]

Similarly, it is hardly reasonable to appeal to the alleged "notorious fact that there is no consensus among Arab states on what a 'satisfactory' solution [to the Palestinian issue] would consist of and that such a consensus is not likely to emerge." This is one of several conventional theses advanced in an effort to show that it is not really of crucial importance to settle the Palestinian problem. The misrepresentation, in this case, is highlighted by the fact that Tucker's article appeared just as the Islamic Summit expressed such a consensus, in more forceful terms than before. In the past, most of the Arab states have expressed some form of support for the two-state settlement that now reflects the general international consensus outside of the United States and Israel. Another standard argument, also untenable, is that the Iran-Iraq war shows that it is not the Palestinian issue that keeps the Middle East in turmoil; the logic apparently is that the Palestinian issue is demonstrated not to be a source of turmoil and conflict if there are other problems in the region as well. The general obfuscation in this connection may be explicable in part by a factor that Tucker does not mention: the perceived role of Israel as a local gendarme within the global system organized by a resurgent America. But the relevant factors are, I believe, considerably more complex.[9]

While as noted, Tucker spares us the usual nonsense about "Wilsonian ideals" and "human rights," he does adhere to the general conventions of responsible scholarship by carefully avoiding any reference to the actual factors that determine the formation of global policy, wandering off into vacuous but unthreatening musings, some already cited, about the fear that "the American example and American influence would become irrelevant" in a world "in which America's political and economic frontiers would become coterminous with her territorial frontiers." As in his earlier writings, and in mainstream scholarship generally, he draws back from the obvious question: which specific aspects of the American example and American influence concern those who formulate policy? Is the concern over Cuba, Nicaragua, Guatemala under Arbenz, or Allende's Chile motivated by the lingering fear that the new societies might lose interest in American baseball or current best-sellers? We need not tarry over the possibility that it is the actual or potential failure to develop democratic political institutions that arouses the concern of planners. These questions would be raised at once, and given the obvious answers, by anyone committed to discovering and presenting the truth about the formulation of "high policy," so it comes as no surprise to find, once again, that they do not surface in responsible scholarship.

The principles that Tucker expounds reflect a substantial consensus among foreign policy elites, as he correctly observes, though they may differ on the tactical question of where and how we should pursue our rights, needs, and wants. The underlying concerns were voiced in the early 1970s, when the partial failure of U.S. policies in Indochina was becoming evident, and they were reiterated more strongly as the U.S.-imposed regimes collapsed. The business press, for example, warned that "it is impossible to maintain a successful international economic framework" in which U.S.-based multinationals can prosper when the "retreat from power has gotten out of hand," as was happening under the Nixon doctrine.[10] Détente and tri-lateralism are acceptable, in recognition of the undoubted fact that the United States is no longer "the hegemonic power in a system of world order" as it was until 1970,[11] but this retreat from power cannot reach the point where U.S. dominance of the global system is seriously threatened, either by a Soviet Union aspiring to equality, or by our allies, or by relatively independent Third World nations and blocs. This is the message expressed in an unusually clear and blunt manner in Tucker's call for a more activist foreign policy, and if feasible, the more appealing policy of a resurgent America.[12]

Calls for a resurgent America are widely voiced elsewhere. In the *New Republic*, J. B. Kelly writes that "through their vacillation and willful self-delusion over the past decade, the Western nations have left themselves no alternative but to project their military power into the Gulf region."[13] This may lead to "an upsurge of Moslem fanaticism against the West," Kelly observes, but "whether it will amount to more than a ritual outpouring of scurrility and the customary carnival of ruffianism is hard to say." Reviewing a book by the same thoughtful scholar, D. C. Watt expresses his concern that Kelly's views may be rejected by "the liberal orthodoxy, secretly floated by the flood of Arab money into the Western institutions of higher learning."[14] It is continually necessary to remind oneself that fantasy of this nature is taken quite seriously by many Western intellectuals.

The editors of the *New Republic* go on to deplore Carter's "failure to defend the capitalist democratic idea" in his "moralistic excesses," allowing Nicaragua and Iran to go down the drain and withholding aid from the "moderate military-Christian Democratic junta" that had presided over the massacre of ten thousand people in El Salvador, unable to investigate or bring to trial a single officer of the military and police forces responsible for the overwhelming mass of the terror. If we are "forced to choose between an Anastasio Somoza and a Cuban-backed Sandinista movement the U.S. cannot do anything in its own interest but back Somoza," the editors add.[15] The editors understand very well what this advice implies, at least if they read the pages of their own journal; see, for example, Chapter 2, note 44. One could hardly expect the editors of this liberal journal to be concerned over a description by the reporter for the *Wall Street Journal* of "a degree of poverty and desperation that is startling, even by Latin American standards."[16] But the lives of the people of Nicaragua naturally count for very little when weighed in the balance against "U.S. interests."

With regard to El Salvador, the editors conclude that if military aid to the junta does not suffice "to hold the center in place," then we will have to intervene with military force, because "one Nicaragua and one Cuba are enough in the region." Since this is a liberal journal, the editors add the familiar mumbo-jumbo: "Should this come to pass, the U.S.—at the least— should insist that repression and alienation of the population be kept to a minimum, and exact a promise of immediate reform."[17] The editors explain that these moves are justified, since we are better than they are, as shown, for example, by the fact that "it is better in Thailand than in Vietnam and Cambodia"—which proves, perhaps, that millions of tons of bombs and napalm are even more harmful than American aid, a possibly relevant factor that the editors neglect to mention. In the same vein, in one of their ritual condemnations of the United Nations, the editors denounce the organization because it "cannot protect Afghanistan or Vietnam,"[18] failing to cite their earlier condemnation of the U.N. for its inability to "protect Vietnam" while it was under savage U.S. attack.

Similar conclusions are expressed by Maurice Duverger, who explains in *Le Monde* that if Reagan "had to choose between Pinochet and Castro, he could do nothing else but plump for the former."[19] This recalls John F. Kennedy's famous remark, reported by Arthur Schlesinger, that while we would of course always prefer a decent democratic regime, if compelled to choose between a Trujillo and a Castro (the latter category including in practice Arbenz, Allende, Bosch, Goulart etc.), we must back the former.

Shifting to the conservative side of the spectrum, we read in an editorial of the *Wall Street Journal* that "the suffering in El Salvador is a bloody metaphor indeed, for what happens when the United States tries to shirk its worldwide responsibility to provide an alternative to Marxist revolution." The complaint is coupled with dismay that perhaps "Americans have grown too fat and lazy to reassume the responsibilities of containment." [20] Meanwhile in *Commentary* (January 1981), the new U.N. ambassador, Jeane Kirkpatrick, derides the ridiculous idea that "forceful intervention in the affairs of another nation is impractical and immoral."

It would be an interesting experiment to take these various pronouncements about our rights, needs, wants, justifications, and proper goals, including the rhetoric in which they are couched, and to translate them into a Russian equivalent, then asking what the reaction would be in the United States or the West generally to the discovery of such documents in the major Soviet journals. One can easily understand why even in the parts of Latin America that tend to be most pro-U.S., considerably more of the general public (and an even larger percentage of the educated elites) regard the United States as an economic and military threat than perceive the Soviet Union in this light.[21]

Political, intellectual, and business "elites" are intent on learning the lessons of the Vietnam war, and the same should be true for people who are appalled by their commitment to murder and oppression in the service of their needs and wants. The spontaneous and largely leaderless mass peace movement in the United States, which so frightened those in power, had its impact, but it was far too slow to develop. The time to stop the Vietnam war was in 1960–61, when plans were being laid for the direct U.S. attack on South Vietnam that began shortly after, as it became clear that the regime installed by the United States would be unable to control the population with the resources of violence and repression that had been provided. Correspondingly, the time to stop the coming Central American war is now. And the opportunity is there. While the propaganda system is continually announcing the shift to the right and conservative takeover, the fact is that popular opposition to U.S. aggression is far higher now than it was at a comparable stage of the Vietnam intervention.

In El Salvador the regular armed forces of the U.S.-backed military regime are conducting a large-scale massacre of the peasant population, in cooperation with their paramilitary allies. Journalists and international observers are excluded from the areas where the massacre is taking place, but a congressional delegation and at least one reporter have visited the Honduran border areas where tens of thousands of peasants, mostly women and children, have fled from government terror. Representative Gerry Studds of Massachusetts, spokesperson for the congressional delegation, reported that the refugees they found subsisting in desperate poverty said "without exception" that they were "all fleeing the army that we are supporting"; "every person had a tale of atrocity by government forces, the same ones we are again outfitting with weapons." Despite repeated questions, members of the delegation were unable to find a single refugee who reported having been "attacked or harassed by the guerrilla forces." [22] In a lengthy report from the border areas, Édouard Bailby gives extensive details of gruesome atrocities, concluding that the eyewitness reports he gathered "leave no room for doubt concerning the genocide in which the Salvadorean National Guard and the extreme right-wing commandos of ORDEN are engaged." [23] While the term "genocide" is an exaggeration, the testimony now available from these and other sources is similar in character to the reports that led to widespread accusations of genocide or "autogenocide" leveled against the Khmer Rouge in Cambodia from mid-1975. The response in the United States is rather different, however. The reason is simple, and familiar. In Cambodia, the atrocities could be charged to an official enemy, and there was little if anything that could be done to stop them. In El Salvador, in contrast, the atrocities are the direct responsibility of the United States, and can very easily be stopped, the crucial point, which far outweighs the question of relative scale of massacre on any moral balance. Hence the predictable and typical behavior of the media in the two cases. [24] The same factors explain the difference in the international response to the flight of sixty thousand refugees from government terror in El Salvador, many to miserable encampments along the border where the U.N. refugee commission operates on a pittance, as compared to the reaction to the flight of some seventy thousand boat people from Vietnam by November 1978, escaping misery and oppression in a land that had been ravaged by American power. [25]

The military regime that has been massacring the population in El Salvador may not hold, even with substantial U.S. support and continued U.S. leadership of an international assault on the peasant population (83 percent of the government's arms came from Israel at last report; [26] military advisers have reportedly been provided by Argentina; [27] brutal attacks on the peasant population have been coordinated with the military forces of Honduras; [28] etc.). Tucker is right to think that a Central American war will not be as easy as the overthrow of the democratic regime of Guatemala in 1954, setting the stage for the "acceptable behavior" of the U.S. clients then installed and since maintained in power (see Introduction and Chapter 7). And a Central American war may well be the consequence of direct U.S. intervention. U.S. military intervention in the Middle East may trigger internal and international reactions that will lead to great-power conflicts and possibly nuclear war, quite apart from the effects for the local victims.

Tucker draws back from directly advocating the more "appealing" program of resurgent America on grounds of an estimate of costs, including the costs of an aroused public opinion, a factor that can be influenced, as in the past. His outline of this program, and the many others like it, should not be dismissed as outlandish or absurd, but rather taken as a warning to be heeded before it is too late.

Chapter Nine

ISRAEL AND THE PALESTINIANS (1975)

O NE LAND—TWO NATIONS: That is the essence of the problem of Israel and the Palestinians. To be sure, the problem has always had regional and international dimensions. Given the strategic and economic importance of the region, great-power intervention has always been a decisive factor in determining the course of events. If the local problem of two claimants to the same territory is not amicably resolved, then a settlement will be imposed by external force, with no regard for the needs and interests of Israeli Jews or Palestinian Arabs. It is not out of the question that the present course will lead to the national destruction of both groups.

Proponents of each of the national movements are quick to dismiss the competing claims. I will not review the familiar debate. It is a simple and pointless exercise to construct an argument to demonstrate the legitimacy of the claims of either side and the insignificance of the demands of its opponent. Each argument is convincing in its own terms. Each claim is, in a sense, absolute: a plea for national survival. Those who urge the demands of one or the other partner in this deadly dance, deaf to conflicting pleas, merely help pave the way to an eventual catastrophe. Such behavior is pathetic on the part of direct participants; disgraceful, on the part of those partisans from afar who will not have to pay the costs of their fanaticism. One may recall Chaim Weizmann's rebuke to American Zionists for urging "other people to the barricades to face tanks and guns"—"the speeches are made in New York," Weizmann added, "while the proposed resistance is to be made in Tel Aviv and Jerusalem." [1] The same might be said—and probably has been—by Palestinians with regard to those who urge them on towards self-destruction.

Like it or not, there is little doubt that participants in the local conflict will continue to identify themselves as Jews and Arabs and to demand self-government and national institutions. On this assumption, which surely seems realistic, any thought of a unitary democratic secular state in Mandatory Palestine is an exercise in futility. It is curious that this goal is advocated in some form by the most extreme antagonists: the Palestine Liberation Organization (PLO) and expansionist elements within Israel. But the documents of the former indicate that what they have in mind is an Arab state that will grant civil rights to Jews, and the pronouncements of the advocates of a Greater Israel leave little doubt that their thoughts run along parallel lines, interchanging "Jew" and "Arab." These are, in fact, charitable interpretations, in both cases.[2]

THE CURRENT SITUATION

As I write (November 1974), prospects are gloomy. The conference of Arab states at Rabat has designated the PLO as the sole legitimate representative of the Palestinians. The United Nations has in effect endorsed this position. The government of Israel refuses adamantly to deal with the PLO. As long as this impasse persists, the probability of war is appreciable. As critics of Israeli government policy have been warning, Israel has now backed itself into a corner, facing almost complete diplomatic isolation, committed to policies that can only be implemented at the grave risk of war, hence the risk of eventual destruction of a state that can lose only once and that can never finally defeat its adversaries.[3]

What is the likelihood of a change in the Israeli attitude towards the Palestinians and their organizations? The official Israeli government position, as presented in a "Decision of the Government of Israel," July 21, 1974, is the following:

> The Government will work towards negotiations for a peace agreement with Jordan. The peace will be founded on the existence of two independent States only—Israel, with united Jerusalem as its capital, and a Jordanian-Palestinian Arab State, east of Israel, within borders to be determined in negotiations between Israel and Jordan. In this State, the independent identity of the Jordanian and Palestinian Arabs can find expression in peace and goodneighbourliness with Israel.[4]

This position was reaffirmed by Foreign Minister Yigal Allon in October 1974 before the U.N. There is, he affirmed, a problem of "Palestinian identity," but it "can and should be solved in the context of the settlement of the dispute" between Israel and Jordan, which is "already the national home of the Palestinians." The PLO, Prime Minister Yitzhak Rabin asserts, is not the legitimate representative of the Palestinians, "since nobody has elected them." [5] The government and American Zionists generally insist that the PLO cannot claim to speak for the Palestinians in the "administered territories" of the West Bank ("Judea and Samaria," in Israeli parlance) and the Gaza Strip. At the same time, Israel refuses to permit independent political organization or free political expression in the occupied territories, and the repression of the past years has been sharply intensified under the present Rabin government. The reason for the repression is simple: Any relaxation leads to the expression of pro-PLO sentiments. [6] The contradiction is complete, and the impasse, total.

These policies have wide support within Israel. Thus, a leading dove, Arie Eliav, publicly opposes a Palestinian state "in the administered areas separate from the state of Jordan," and advocates instead some kind of partition of the West Bank and Gaza Strip between Israel and Jordan, optimally with "Israeli supervision or joint supervision by the two states" over these territories. [7]

Meanwhile, Israeli settlement in the occupied territories continues, again with substantial popular support. In a recent poll, 71 percent approved of settlement in "Judea and Samaria" if initiated by the government, with less than 14 percent opposed. [8] Every move in this direction is a step towards war.

Only marginal political groups in Israel have been calling for withdrawal from the occupied territories, which now plainly entails recognition of the PLO. State policy, particularly since 1970, has been moving towards integration of the territories. A program of virtual annexation was presented by the governing Labor party in its August 1973 electoral program. After the October war, the program was modified, but these plans will be reinstituted if the only alternative is to deal with the Palestinians.

Of course, these policies can be pursued only with U.S. backing. As of mid-1970, American policy was expressed in the Rogers Plan, which called for Israeli withdrawal in the context of a peace settlement. This proposal was abandoned by the United States as Henry Kissinger took over control of American policy towards the Middle East in 1970, [9] instituting what should no doubt be called the "Kissinger Plan": tacit support for *de facto* Israeli annexation of the territories. Given the widely held belief that Israel's military and technological predominance was unchallengeable in the foreseeable future, the Kissinger Plan made a certain amount of sense, putting aside its characteristic cynicism and the equally characteristic blindness to longer-term historical tendencies, even though it did maximize the risk of war. The assumptions, however, were proven false by the October 1973 war. With the collapse of Kissinger's policies in October,[10] the United States began a slow return towards something like the abandoned Rogers Plan, but this process depends on developments within the Arab world that are presently quite difficult to assess.

The program of *de facto* annexation raised with particular urgency what is called in Israel the "demographic problem," that is, the problem posed by the existence of Arabs in a Jewish state. There are only two ways for a Jewish state to become a functioning democracy: by restricting the "Jewishness" of the state to mere symbolism, or by guaranteeing that all citizens are Jews. The prospects for the former seem slight, a matter to which I will return. Those who believe otherwise might well embrace the official PLO slogan of democratic secularism. The alternative policy, namely, guaranteeing that citizens are Jews, can be achieved only by a program of expulsion. Then, indeed, Israel will be Jewish in the way that England is English, in accordance with a traditional Zionist slogan. Under the U.S.-Israeli program of *de facto* annexation, the demographic problem could no longer be swept under the rug, since the "Jewish state" would soon have a population of Arabs approaching 50 percent. The Gaza Strip alone would double the Arab population of Israel, and Israeli officials have repeatedly insisted that this region will remain part of Israel under any peace settlement, a position that provokes little dispute within the political mainstream. As for the future borders of the Jewish state, it is also agreed with near unanimity in Israel that the Golan Heights will be retained under any settlement, and Rabin has stated that Jewish settlement in the Jordan Valley is based "on the premise that the settlements being established will remain included within our rule."[11] In the region west of Gaza, "new settlement outposts [are] planned for settling the Rafah approaches between Yamit and Beersheva,"[12] and it is generally agreed that the border with Egypt must be removed from the Gaza Strip.[13] Hence the "demographic problem" is severe.

Various solutions to the dilemma have been proposed. The current (1974) premier, Yitzhak Rabin of the Labor party, has occasionally been quoted in the press on this issue:

I would like to create in the course of the next 10 to 20 years conditions which would attract natural and voluntary migration of the refugees from the Gaza Strip and the West Bank to East Jordan. To achieve this we have to come to agreement with King Hussein and not with Yasser Arafat.[14]

Elsewhere, Rabin has explained his current views as follows:

We must solve the problem in a form that will permit the Palestinians, if such is their wish, to have a voice—but only in the framework of a Jordanian-Palestinian state. I do not believe that there is a place for a third state between Israel and Jordan. *There is a need for a place to which it will be possible to transfer the quarter-million refugees who live in crowded conditions in the Gaza Strip.* This place cannot be other than Jordan, the one state in which Palestinians were absorbed in the society, to such a degree that they constitute half the government officials in Jordan.[15]

Rabin had expressed similar ideas before he became prime minister. In a symposium of Israeli ex-chiefs of staff, he proposed "to make such conditions that during the next ten years, there would be a natural shifting of population to the East Bank" of the Jordan. There should be "a minimum of refugees in the West Bank" and "the problem of the refugees of the Gaza Strip should not be solved in Gaza or in El-Arish, but mainly in the East Bank."[16]

Rabin is regarded as a dove. When his government was formed, Moshe Dayan was appalled, saying that "not in my worst dreams" could he have imagined such a cabinet.[17] Actually, Dayan's view of the matter is not very different. He urges that Israel should not annex the occupied territories but should nevertheless encourage Jewish settlement freely in them and maintain military control over them. In his view, "Judea and Samaria" are part of the Jewish homeland and Israel should insist on the right of permanent Jewish settlement everywhere on the West Bank and the right to maintain military bases as required throughout this region.[18] In the same Knesset speech in which he outlined this program, Dayan went on to say that as for the refugees, "the Arab states now have land and water and also funds and Arab nationhood, and with all of this they can solve the refugee problem in their lands." With minor variations, this is in fact the standard position, and is commonly expressed in the United States as well. Though American

Zionists are naturally displeased with the analogy, the fact remains that this position is analogous to that of extremist Arab nationalists who urge that European Jews should be resettled in Europe, where there are many European states and ample resources.

The long-range hope that somehow the Arabs will move away is no doubt one factor in the refusal by the government or much of the left-liberal opposition to contemplate a Palestinian state. A West Bank ministate could not absorb the Arabs of Gaza along with refugees elsewhere. A Jordan-Palestine of the Rabin-Eliav variety might well absorb the Palestinians of most of the West Bank and elsewhere, under the guise of settlement in their former homeland of Palestine, leaving the occupied territories effectively under Israeli control.

It appears that the Golda Meir government actually made concrete proposals to Jordan in secret meetings, offering to permit Jordanian officials to conduct civil administration in parts of the West Bank under Israeli military occupation. The West Bank Palestinians would have become Jordanian citizens, though the area would have remained under Israeli military control, and, presumably, Jewish settlement could also proceed. Hussein's rule could only be imposed by force, as is generally recognized. Commenting on these secret proposals, Reserve-General Mattityahu Peled remarks that "even the worst of the European imperialist powers never reached such a degree of cynicism," namely, to abandon any responsibility for subject populations while maintaining military control over them—and in this case, we may add, guaranteeing the right of settlement by civilians of the dominant military power who claim "historic rights" to the territory in question.[19] Peled's comments are overly harsh; European imperialism is guilty of far worse. But his dismay over these plans is understandable. He adds, realistically, that Egypt will not accept such an outcome, so that this policy, apart from its moral premises, increases the likelihood of future war.

The idea of inducing Palestinian Arabs to leave has often been expressed, in one or another form, in internal Zionist discussion over the years; it is, indeed, implicit in the concept of a democratic Jewish state. One of the founders of the socialist movement in the Palestinian *Yisbuv,* Berl Katznelson—who elsewhere advocated binationalism[20] and warned that Jews would betray the Zionist ideal if they sought a Jewish state in which they would be the Poles and Arabs would be the Jews—had this to say on one occasion:

The matter of transfer of population raises a dispute among us: permitted or forbidden. My conscience is completely silent on this matter: a distant neighbor is better than a nearby enemy. They will not lose by their transfer and we will surely not. In the final analysis, this is a political resettlement reform for the benefit of the two sides. For a long time I have thought that this is the best solution, and in the days of the riots I was confirmed in my recognition that this result must come about some day. However, it did not occur to me that the transfer "outside of the Land of Israel" means to the neighborhood of Shechem [on the West Bank]. I believed, and I still believe that they must ultimately move to Syria and Iraq.[21]

Similar thoughts were harbored privately by other socialist Zionists. Joseph Weitz, who was director of the Jewish National Fund Land and Afforestation Division and one of those responsible for the "outpost settlements" that helped determine the partition boundaries,[22] wrote recently in *Davar* that in his diaries of 1940 he had recognized that "there is no room in this country for both peoples" so that the only solution is complete "transfer" of all Arabs at least from west of the Jordan.[23] American Zionists also view this prospect with equanimity, while insisting that the historical injustice resulting from the population transfer undertaken by imperial Rome two thousand years ago must be rectified. Thus, democratic socialist Michael Walzer observes with reference to Israel that "nation building in new states is sure to be rough on groups marginal to the nation," and sometimes "the roughness can only be smoothed . . . by helping people to leave who have to leave,"[24] even if these groups "marginal to the nation" have been deeply rooted in the country for hundreds of years, and constituted the overwhelming majority not many years ago. Walzer's point must surely be conceded, though he does not formulate it with sufficient clarity. If Israel is to be both a democratic state and a Jewish state, then non-Jews must be expelled, unless there is an evolution towards democratic secularism for which, at the moment, there are no indications and no substantial support.

Similar concepts are implicit, occasionally, even in the writings of Israeli civil libertarians. In an eloquent condemnation of the new tendency in Israel to dismiss "the humanist philosophy of the Gentiles" in favor of an allegedly "Jewish" commitment to the superior rights of the nation, Knesset member Shulamit Aloni protested against those who settled illegally in "Judea and Samaria," pretending that they will grant equal rights to a million Arabs in Greater Israel. She argues that equal rights cannot be granted "in the framework of a binational state," offering recent events in Cyprus as a proof:

> The failure in Cyprus is not that of the United Nations. It is a failure of the binational state idea. We should remember that the proportion of Turks in Cyprus compared to the Greeks is smaller than that of the Arabs in the Land of Israel compared to the Jews.[25]

Accepting, for the sake of argument, Aloni's interpretation of the facts,[26] consider the implications of these remarks. Note first that Cyprus could hardly be called a binational state. Rather, it resembled Israel today more than a hypothetical binational state, with a Turkish minority of about the same proportions as the Arabs of pre-1967 Israel. If this idea has failed, as Aloni argues, and the only alternative is the *de facto* partition and "population exchange" that took place in Cyprus after the Greek officers' coup and the Turkish invasion, then it would seem to follow that the Arabs of Israel should be expelled (or "exchanged") after the establishment of an Arab state "East of Israel," including "parts of Judea and Samaria," as Aloni proposes. While she nowhere advocates such "population transfer," it would appear to be implicit in her analysis.

Others are more explicit. Hagi Eshed, writing in the Labor party journal *Davar*, describes the establishment of a Palestinian state organized by the PLO as such a grave danger that "we cannot disqualify in advance nor reject outright any means or feasible solutions aimed at preventing this danger." He adds:

> In this context the idea of a population transfer has emerged, an idea that had not been totally rejected by Berl Katznelson nor even the British Labor Party.... Perhaps we cannot avoid raising anew the feasibility of transferring part of the refugees and even the permanent settlers of Judea, Samaria and Gaza to Jordan. Such a possibility will certainly arise if Jordan joins a war against Israel. It may be one of the possible outcomes of the renewal of war.[27]

Israel will, very likely, now attempt to create a Quisling leadership on the West Bank and to hold on to what territories it can, in the hope that sooner or later the occupation will be accepted, or, at worst, the failure of other methods for recovering the occupied territories will impel the Arab states to accept the Israeli-Jordanian solution. At the Rabat conference, Hussein "complained that the United States plan called for the reestablishment of Jordanian administration in certain parts of the West Bank with the area remaining under Israeli military control" [28]—the Israeli plan mentioned earlier. While the Rabat conference has undercut such plans for the moment, the longer-term possibility cannot be completely discounted. Again it must be stressed that even if successfully implemented, such a program could only delay the next major war, and would maintain the situation of economic crisis in an Israel that is forced to devote enormous resources to military preparation against adversaries of limitless wealth.

These are the likely prospects as long as U.S. support for Israeli annexation continues. This support will probably continue, if the Arab oil producers do not pressure the United States to compel Israel to withdraw to its pre-June 1967 borders. Whether they will do so depends on nationalist forces within the Arab world: the threat of "Qaddafist" coups by nationalist officers, popular unrest, and other obscure factors. The situation is complex, since Saudi Arabia, always the central concern of U.S. policy in the region, has an indirect stake in Israeli power, which stands as a barrier to radical Arab nationalism and Russian influence. There are strange alliances in the Middle East. Saudi Arabia has no love for Iran, but is happy to have Iranian forces engaged in counterinsurgency on its borders in Dhofar. A tacit alliance between Israel, Iran, and Saudi Arabia—overt, between Israel and Iran—with Turkey in the background, is a real possibility, in the framework of a Pax Americana.

Despite this possibility, pressure on the United States is likely, and despite much saber-rattling in the American press, it will probably be effective. At this point, Israel would have two options: to yield, or to go to war in the hope of achieving a quick victory and perhaps provoking a superpower confrontation that would again cement the Israeli-American alliance. The latter option might be chosen, despite the enormous risks, if Israel senses that there is some support for it in the United States. A respectful hearing is given in Israel to American political analysts who strongly imply that Israel will receive American backing if it takes a hard line. While such urgings are the height of irresponsibility, they may have their effect.

Suppose that the United States does impose a settlement by force, compelling Israel to return to the pre-1967 borders with the safeguards, such as they are, outlined in the U.N. resolutions and the Rogers Plan. If Israel ac-

cepts this outcome, a Palestinian entity of some sort will be established, organized by the PLO. The result will probably be a kind of "Latin American-
ization" of the region, with a network of hostile states, dependent on the
United States, and highly susceptible to reactionary forces within under
conditions of tension and resentment.

For Israel, this arrangement is surely far less dangerous than the annexationist programs advocated by both major political groupings and supported
virtually without question by American Zionists. Though these groups base
their public opposition to a Palestinian entity on grounds of security, this argument can hardly be taken seriously. The problems for Israel lie elsewhere.
For one thing, it would be necessary to abandon the hope for integration of
substantial parts of the occupied territories within Israel, with the concomitant program of "population transfer" discussed earlier. Furthermore, Israel would suffer a severe loss of élan and the situation might revert to the
depressed conditions of 1966. A further consequence might well be an increase in emigration, as in 1966, and redirection of the Russian Jewish emigration, if it continues, towards the West,[29] which is not likely to be
delighted with the prospect. All of this stirs ugly memories from the 1930s
and the war years, when the United States was pleased to have Jewish refugees from Nazism go to Palestine, but was unwilling to absorb them here,
even preventing refugees from landing in the United States, in one notorious case, though they had postdated U.S. visas.

A TWO-STATE SOLUTION

Two states west of the Jordan, one Jewish, one Palestinian: That would be a
possible outcome of the conflict of claims to the same territory. The original
General Assembly resolution of 1947 was based on this principle, but much
has changed since, including the potential boundaries of the two states. The
Palestinian state would be a pale reflection of what was contemplated at
Lake Success. It is possible to build a case, as is commonly done in the United
States, that these changes result solely from Arab intransigence, but the essential facts are in reality considerably more complex. Putting interpretation of the history aside, it is possible to imagine a stable two-state
settlement west of the Jordan, essentially with the pre-1967 borders.

Such an arrangement would very likely satisfy the Arab oil producers,
since the threat of radical Palestinian nationalism would be contained. It is
unlikely that Syria or Egypt would raise problems once their territories are

recovered. The arrangement would also satisfy the primary concerns of U.S. foreign policy: to ensure that other industrial societies do not gain independent access to the vast energy resources of the Middle East. The Soviet Union understands very well that the United States will not tolerate a challenge to its domination of the region. And the other potential rivals of the United States are in no position to undertake a challenge to American hegemony.

For Israel, it would be preferable for a settlement of this sort to be achieved through negotiations, but that is impossible as long as Israel refuses to deal with the PLO and regards its primary negotiating partner as the United States, and as long as the PLO takes its minimal negotiating position to be the elimination of Israel. A solution imposed by imperial force is hardly to be welcomed, but it is not easy to conjure up a preferable and feasible alternative. It appears that some segments of the Israeli left privately hope for such an outcome, as the least intolerable, under present circumstances.

A Palestinian state will be subordinated to Israel and Jordan, which will be allied to ensure that it has limited scope for development or independence. It can expect little assistance from the wealthy Arab states. The PLO should be no less able than other national movements to produce a group of leaders who can adapt themselves to this situation. The West Bank and Gaza Strip might continue to provide Israel with a reservoir of cheap labor, as has been the case since 1967. It is likely that a Palestinian state will be a mirror-image of Israel: an Arab state, based on discriminatory principles much like those of its counterpart, possibly exaggerated in a state founded on despair and subservience to its neighbors. Both states, one must expect, will be based on the principle of denial of rights to citizens of the wrong category. One can expect nothing else of a Jewish state or an Arab state, just as we would know what to expect of a white state or a Catholic state. The seeds of conflict will remain. This kind of Balkanization might well satisfy American imperial interests as well as the interests of the Arab states, which will be happy to have an end to Palestinian revolutionary rhetoric. The most important long-term consequence of the Rabat decision, from the point of view of the Arab states, may be that Palestinian energy will be directed towards a little region contained within a Jordanian-Israeli alliance, posing no further threat to ruling circles elsewhere. The outcome will be a painful one for Jews and Palestinians, but, as noted at the outset, it has always been likely that if they are unable to settle their local conflict, external force will sooner or later be applied to resolve it for them in a way that has little relation to their needs and interests.

MYTHS AND REALITY

Conceivably, if tensions reduce in the region, the Jewish and Palestinian states might begin to dismantle discriminatory structures. Moves in this direction would require changes in popular attitudes and aspirations, not to speak of institutional structures, that would be virtually revolutionary. This may seem a harsh and unfair judgment, but I think that recent history tends to support it. The PLO exercises sovereignty nowhere. Thus one can only speculate about the meaning of its programs and their likely realization. But the State of Israel has existed for more than twenty-five years. From its experience, we can learn a good deal about the problems of a multinational society committed in theory to democracy. At least this is so, if we are willing to attend to the facts.

One fact is that for Israeli Jews, standards of freedom and democratic rights are easily on a par with those realized elsewhere. At the same time, Israel is a Jewish state with non-Jewish residents, some of them citizens, others stateless. Israel regards itself and is generally described as a Western-style democracy, but this characterization is misleading. In fact, the state is based on a fundamental and so far irresoluble contradiction. There is a commitment to democracy, but it is unrealizable, because the "Jewishness" of the Jewish state is no mere matter of symbolism but is built into the institutional structure and ideology in a fundamental manner and is subject to little internal challenge or debate. Only confusion can result from failure to perceive that Israel is not based on the model (however imperfectly realized) of the Western democracies.

Illusions about this question are most striking in the writings of left-liberal American Zionists. Michael Walzer, a Harvard University historian and political scientist, is one of the few to have tried to deal with the issue. He writes that a democratic secular state "already exists in substance" in the former Palestine, namely, the State of Israel. Hence there is no merit in the propaganda of the Palestinian organizations that demand the establishment of a democratic secular state. True, the "power of Orthodox Jews" is greater than it should be. But apart from this, Walzer perceives no departure from democratic principle in the State of Israel.[30] No problems of principle arise, in his view, as a result of the fact that the state is a Jewish state.

Walzer's efforts to evade the obvious give a certain insight into the intellectual level of left-liberal American Zionism. Evidently, if Israel is a Jewish state with non-Jewish citizens, then the respects in which the state is "Jewish" will be respects in which non-Jews are denied equal rights. Evidently, democratic principle is violated when a state discriminates between two categories of citizens, the severity of the violation depending on the nature of the discrimination (insignificant, in this case, if the "Jewishness" of the state is a matter of symbolism, and correspondingly important if it is not). Walzer claims to find these truisms "unintelligible." He counters with the following analogy. Suppose that Indonesia discriminates against Chinese. Then, he asks, would it be proper to say that Indonesia "is Indonesian in that respect, and therefore undemocratic"? Obviously, he continues, this would be an absurd conclusion; we would say that Indonesia is undemocratic in these respects, but not by virtue of its being an "Indonesian state." Therefore, Walzer concludes, my observations on the discriminatory character of a Jewish state must reflect an opposition to "the nationhood of the Jews (but of no one else)." [31]

Walzer's reasoning is remarkable. Evidently, the appropriate analogy would pair Israel-Indonesia, Jewish-Malayan, Arab-Chinese. Correcting for Walzer's gross error in reasoning, suppose that Indonesia were to define itself as a "Malayan state," and were then to subject non-Malayans to repression or otherwise discriminate between Malayans and Chinese to the advantage of the former. Would we then say that *Indonesia is Malayan in these respects and therefore undemocratic,* by virtue of its being a "Malayan state" (the italicized phrase being the corrected version of Walzer's analogy)? The answer is obviously: Yes, we would, and we would sharply criticize the notion of a "Malayan state" with non-Malayan citizens as violating fundamental principles of democracy. These points are so elementary that it is quite remarkable that it is necessary to spell them out in such detail. These truisms are intolerable to left-liberal American Zionists such as Walzer, who therefore seek to create a complex web of error and falsification in an effort to obscure the plain facts and crucial principles.

To take another case, consider the discussion of Israeli democracy by Carl Cohen, a philosopher who has dealt extensively with problems of democracy. He arrives at conclusions quite similar to Walzer's.[32] He sees the Israeli record as "remarkably good," despite the trying circumstances. In his view, in Israel all citizens are full participants with equal rights regardless of national affiliation:

Ugly terrorism, in the very bosom of daily life, has not resulted in the deprivation of rights to non-Jewish minorities. Indeed the continuing participation of Arab and other minorities in the life of the Israeli community—in local and national government, in economic and cultural activities—is a tribute not only to the self-control of the Israeli Jews but to the evident loyalty of Israelis of all religions and backgrounds. That loyalty has rendered suppression unthinkable.

There have been certain abuses of due process, Cohen notes, and instances of discrimination "in some social circles, in some fields of employment, in some housing developments." And "handling of suspected or known terrorists, infiltrators" has sometimes not been above reproach. But the "pluralistic ideal" is remarkably close to achievement. As for the Israeli Arabs, the largest ethnic minority, "Full civil rights—personal, political and economic—are theirs. . . . With respect to *rights*, in theory and in practice, the Arab minority is well protected." The ideal of democracy, with equal rights for all, "is an ideal seriously pursued, and it is, in fact, realized to a degree of which we Americans, who befriend and support Israel, may be proud."

Such observations can easily be multiplied. Like many other commentators, Walzer and Cohen never ask how it is possible for a state founded on the principle of Jewish dominance to be a democracy with equal rights for all regardless of national affiliation. They merely avoid the contradiction, following the traditional pattern of self-deception of those Zionists who spoke of a state that would be as Jewish as England is English. That sounds fair enough, until we realize that citizens of England and their offspring are English, whereas citizens of the Jewish state (or children born there) are not Jewish, unless the Orthodox rabbinate so determines.

Israeli liberals also tend to ignore the dilemma. The dean of the Tel Aviv University Law School, Amnon Rubinstein,[33] describing the program of his new political grouping *Shinui* (Change), states that: "We want to bridge the gap between the two communities in Israel—the Ashkenazim [European Jews] and the Eastern Jews."[34] There is, however, a third community in Israel: non-Jews, approximately 15 percent of the population apart from the occupied territories. It is striking, and characteristic, that their status is simply ignored.

Walzer and Cohen present no serious supporting evidence; thus it is impossible to know how they arrive at their conclusions. To test these conclusions, it would be necessary to consider factual analyses or to hear what the

Arabs have to say—their testimony on the matter of Arab rights is likely to be more illuminating than the unsupported opinions of American Zionists. Neither course is very easy to pursue. As one liberal American Zionist points out in a study of Israeli society, "Unhappily, social scientists have devoted little attention to the Arabs in Israel." He goes on to point out, correctly, that this is a symptom of a more general problem, that there is really no place for Arabs in the Jewish state: "The very powerful ethic of equal opportunity and full political equality must compete against the equally powerful ethic of a Jewish State."[35] And the fact is that the latter wins, hands down. Critical Zionist analysts of Israeli society who are not social scientists also tend to ignore the Arab minority. It is, again, characteristic that a highly regarded study entitled *The Israelis* should have nothing to say about those Israelis who belong to the one-seventh of the population that is not Jewish.[36] There are a few studies of the Israeli Arabs by Zionist scholars, but they are of little value, and largely ignore the serious issues that dominate the reports and studies produced by Israeli Arabs themselves.

As for writings by Arabs in Israel or expressions of popular opinion, these too are scanty. Contrary to the claims of American Zionists, these voices have been effectively stilled. Arab intellectuals have been heavily censored, repressed, subjected to "administrative detention" or house arrest, or compelled to leave the country. It is remarkable that American civil libertarians have defended these practices, or denied the facts.[37] The most extensive discussion to date of the status of Arabs in Israel is in the work of Sabri Jiryis, an Israeli Arab lawyer who was confined under detention and house arrest for over a year without charge and now lives in Beirut. The picture he presents differs radically from the commentaries by left-liberal American Zionists. He gives a detailed analysis of the suppression of civil rights of Arabs, their dispossession through expropriation in the 1950s, the blocking of efforts at independent political expression, the tight controls exercised over the Israeli Arab intelligentsia, the continued application of the British Mandatory laws,[38] and so on. Jiryis relies primarily on Israeli sources, including court records. As far as I can determine, his account is quite accurate. Similarly, Fouzi el-Asmar, the "terrorist commander" of Dershowitz's inflamed imagination, now residing in the United States, has given a detailed account of the means used to expropriate Arabs, again relying on Israeli sources.[39] But one would have some difficulty in locating his work or the sources on which it is based, or in fact any serious treatment of the issue, in the extensive English language literature on this subject.[40]

Reports by Israeli Arab intellectuals who are sympathetic to Israel are not entirely lacking. After a visit to Arab villages and towns in 1966, Elias Tuma, an Arab citizen of Israel until 1969, wrote that the Arabs live "in a state of disorganization, distrust, and despair," particularly the younger generation. Arabs have given up farming and taken up wage-labor in Jewish enterprises, not from choice, but because of government land policies. "The grievances I heard against the land policy had no end." The general feeling was "that the government was pursuing policies that would ultimately lead to their destruction as farmers." Charges included expropriation, refusal to grant building permits on land reserved for future Jewish settlement, state-imposed price differentials for agricultural products that support Jewish production while barely covering production costs for Arabs, and so on. "The people are convinced that the government had bad intentions toward their land and was doing all it could to expropriate them by what might seem like legal procedures." Most of Tuma's information comes from discussions with workers and the self-employed. "Teachers, social workers, and white-collar employees refrained from talking unless I managed to see each one separately." They sympathized with the complaints, but were afraid to talk for fear that the numerous government informers would report what they say to the military authorities. "Those who held salaried jobs thought it wiser to be silent if they wanted to keep their jobs."

Jewish friends, Tuma reports, have little reaction to these facts. He quotes one "high-ranking official": "This is the way things are. We are in a democracy, and the minority must obey the majority. They are living better than do the Arabs under Nasser. If they do not like us, let them get out." Since assimilation is ruled out—intermarriage is illegal, and reportedly Arabs are not even permitted to take Jewish names—Tuma expects either demoralization of the Arab community or, conceivably, a violent insurrection. I stress again that these are the views of an Arab intellectual who is by no means hostile towards Israel.[41]

Jerusalem is often put forth as the prime example of how Arabs thrive under Israeli rule. The few reports available in the West raise numerous questions about this success, even apart from the recent rioting in East Jerusalem in support of the PLO. Government programs make explicit the goal of preserving the "Jewish character" of Jerusalem through segregated housing development, overwhelmingly for Jews. In the latest elections (December 1973), most Arabs refused to participate. Reporting from Jerusalem, Henry Kamm observed that "many here feel that Arabs who vote are either

municipal employees protecting their jobs or merchants requiring licenses
or permits, or poor people responding to political bribes." Others reacted on
the principle that the election "is not ours. It's against our will." The election was denounced in the Jerusalem Arab press, but editorials taking this
position were blocked by Israeli censorship.[42]

Another American reporter observes that "there is little social interaction" and "feelings of resentment can be heard." One Arab commented:
"The problem is that Jews do not treat us as equals. I cannot go and stay
overnight in the new part of Jerusalem, for instance," because of the official
segregation. An Arab shopkeeper added:

> The Jews are still my friends and they are good to me. But the main thing
> is to have equality. I can't sell my business to an Arab—only to a Jew. An
> Arab can't go into the new town and buy a business there but a Jewish
> merchant can buy here. There should be equality and we should be
> friends. Then if old Jerusalem is under Israel that's fine.[43]

Unfortunately, there is to be no equality. Opposition within Israel to the discriminatory structures that guarantee Jewish dominance is minimal. There
is no tendency in this direction, so far as I can discern.

Recall again Cohen's report of the intense loyalty of Israeli Arabs to the
state, which "has rendered suppression unthinkable," and which results
from the fact that "full civil rights . . . are theirs."

There are a few relevant studies in Israeli sources. In one analysis, based
on actual research, not mere impression or faith, Ian Lustick argues that
"the widening socio-economic gaps between Arabs and Jews" result from
the "separation of Arabs from the institutions of power in Israeli society";
since the roots of the problem "lie in the parochial character of Israel's most
basic institutions and the differential consequences of their operation for
the Jewish and Arab sectors," the problem will not be resolved and may only
be aggravated by a peace settlement. In his factual analysis of the issues, he
describes "the anger which flows from these perceptions" of the lack of
"the full rights that should accrue to [Arabs] as law-abiding Israeli citizens."
These rights are defined "in terms of land expropriated for use by Jewish
settlements, electricity, roads, and water supplied free to Jews and at enormous expense to Arabs, the failure of the government to establish industry
in the Arab sector, and the inability of Arab university graduates to secure
employment outside of the teaching profession."[44]

While Cohen's description is far closer to the norm, such facts as are available indicate that Lustick's is far closer to the truth. It is because they comprehend very well the fundamental discriminatory institutions and practices of the Jewish state, Lustick argues plausibly, that Arabs have flocked to the Communist party (Rakah)—a phenomenon that would be difficult to explain if Cohen's account had any relation to the facts.[45]

Lustick's study is particularly valuable in that it exhibits some of the means by which Jewish dominance is maintained. He studied one device that has proven very effective, namely, reliance on the Jewish Agency for agricultural development. This quasi-governmental body supplies electricity, paves roads, and "assumes responsibility for the supply of all basic services and housing as well as the capital base for whatever industry or agricultural development is to take place." More than $1.2 billion has been spent by the Jewish Agency on the development of Jewish agricultural settlements since 1948. Through this device, a "tremendous gap in capital inflow" exists between the Arab and Jewish sectors, which "helps explain not only the gap in living standards between Jews and Arabs . . . but also the gap in means of production." While all Jewish villages have electricity, only about half of the Arab villages do. Economic development in the Arab sector is so low that "nearly 90% of Arab village working men must travel each day to and from Jewish towns and cities in order to find employment." Furthermore, "Arabs are concentrated in low paying, low skilled jobs, whereas Jews occupy the higher status and higher paid administrative and white collar positions," and it seems that "these developmental gaps, in terms of job distribution, are widening rather than closing." What is important, in the present connection, is "the role which Israel's major political, economic, and governmental institutions play in maintaining this fundamental inequality"—exactly as a rational observer would expect in a Jewish state with non-Jewish citizens. No doubt this lies behind the anger of Israeli Arabs described by objective Zionist observers, and the demoralization reported by Arab intellectuals.

Official statistics naturally require interpretation, but *prima facie*, they appear to reflect the policy of fostering inequality. Thus in 1973, of 1,815 dunams of cultivated area under irrigation, 1,753 were "Jewish farms" and 62 "non-Jewish farms." The Arab population doubled from 1960 to 1972, but cultivated area of "non-Jewish farms" dropped by about 12 percent from the near-peak year 1960–61 to 1972–73, as Arab farmers moved—hardly by choice, it appears—to other occupations, primarily construction labor.[46]

The grievances against the land policies noted by Tuma and others are easy to understand. In the first decade after the establishment of the state, about 1 million dunams of land were expropriated for Jewish use, through a complicated series of legal and extralegal maneuvers.[47] The process continued in the 1960s under such programs as the "Judaization of the Galilee," the most notorious example being the expropriation of lands of Arab villages for establishment of the all-Jewish city of Karmiel; the land was originally set aside for a military reservation, and local Arabs, who sensed what was coming, were officially assured at that time that there was "no basis" for their fears that this was a preliminary step towards confiscation.[48] After the 1967 war, similar operations were conducted in the occupied territories. They continue now. According to a document submitted to the government by the Mapam party, written largely by members of kibbutzim in the western Negev, in the region southwest of the Gaza Strip about 30,000 dunams were expropriated in 1969 from "Bedouins" (who, incidentally, describe themselves as farmers), and another 120,000 in January 1972, with 6,000 Bedouins evacuated. So far, there has been no new land or housing provided for those evacuated, and the document reports a plan to extend the program to an area of a million to a million and a half dunams entailing the deportation of about 20,000 farmers from all the agricultural land.[49] Again, the alleged grounds are "security." [50]

In the absence of comprehensive studies utilizing official documents and interviews with those directly involved, only parts of the story can be pieced together from reports that have appeared randomly and accidentally, as in the case just mentioned, where neighboring kibbutzim protested. The legal basis for the various programs is often obscure. The example that Lustick discusses—namely, reliance on a quasi-governmental body that carries out development and settlement programs only for Jews—is perhaps typical.

An interesting case is the system of land laws of the state. Prior to the establishment of the State of Israel, land was purchased on behalf of the Jewish people by the Keren Kayemeth Leyisrael (Jewish National Fund; henceforth, JNF). The JNF was established "for the purpose of settling Jews on such lands" as were acquired, "to make any donations . . . likely to promote the interests of Jews," "to make advances to any Jews in the prescribed region," to use charitable funds in ways which "shall in the opinion of the Association be directly or indirectly beneficial to persons of Jewish religion, race or origin." [51] The JNF is now "a public institution recognized by the

Government of Israel and the World Zionist organization as the exclusive instrument for the development of Israel lands." [52] Its earlier principles remain in force, under this new official status. The JNF is "a Company under Jewish control . . . engaged . . . in the settlement of Jews" and promoting such settlement. Lands owned by the JNF are exclusively for Jewish use, in perpetuity. These lands "shall not be transferred either by sale or in any other manner." [53] Furthermore, non-Jewish labor cannot be employed on these lands.

Prior to 1948, the JNF was a private self-help organization of a national group. It is now an official agency of the state. Its exclusivist principles have simply been absorbed as one element of the official policy of Jewish dominance in a Jewish state.

Under a covenant signed between the State of Israel and the JNF in 1961, the JNF undertook to establish a Land Development Administration and to appoint its director, "who shall be subordinate" to the JNF. This Development Administration is responsible for the "scheme for the development and afforestation of Israel lands," and "shall engage in operations of reclamation, development, and afforestation of Israel lands as the agent of the registered owners." Furthermore, "The Board for Land Reclamation and Development attached to the Keren Kayemeth Leisrael [JNF] shall lay down the development policy in accordance with the agricultural development scheme of the Minister of Agriculture," and "shall supervise the activities of the Development Administration and the manner in which it carries this Covenant into effect." This board is headed by the chairman of the board of directors of the JNF or "a person appointed in that behalf" by the JNF. The JNF itself "shall continue to operate, as an independent agency of the World Zionist Organization, among the Jewish public in Israel and the Diaspora . . . ," while continuing to function as the exclusive instrument for the development of Israel lands, with no change in the discriminatory principles cited earlier, which are natural enough in an agency of the World Zionist Organization.

The phrase "Israel lands" refers to state-owned lands. Official figures give these as over 75 percent of the land area within the pre-June 1967 borders, with another 14 percent owned by the JNF. The law permits state land to be transferred to the JNF; otherwise, it is inalienable, with minor exceptions. For over 90 percent of the land of the Israeli state (pre-June 1967), the Development Authority is under the control of a company that represents not the citizens of Israel but the Jewish people, in Israel and the Diaspora, and that is committed to the principle that it shall use charitable donations in such ways as are "beneficial to persons of Jewish religion, race or origin."

Given its status as "the exclusive instrument for the development of Israel lands," it is important to determine how the JNF interprets the state's land laws in its official publications. In the 1973 *Report,* we read:

> Following an agreement between the Government of Israel and Keren Kayemeth Leisrael [JNF], the Knesset in 1960 enacted the *Basic Law: Israel Lands* which gives legal effect to the ancient tradition of ownership of the land in perpetuity by the Jewish people—the principle on which the Keren Kayemeth Leisrael was founded. The same law extended that principle to the bulk of Israel's State domains.[54]

These laws "extended the Keren Kayemeth principles of inalienability of the soil and its use in terms of hereditary leaseholdship to all public holdings in Israel, i.e., to 92% of the State's surface prior to June, 1967."[55]

There appears to be no explicit basis in law for the conclusion in the official JNF *Report* that the JNF principle of ownership of land by the Jewish people was extended to state lands by the 1960 law. Nevertheless, one will not, of course, lightly disregard the interpretation of the law by the authority that has exclusive responsibility for land development. We see here another example of the tendency noted earlier to shift, virtually unconsciously, from the notion "Israeli" to the notion "Jewish"—again, as one would expect in a Jewish state. This tendency not only appears in commentary and discussion and in the interpretation of the law by responsible agencies, but also in judgments by the courts on the question of who is a Jew—a critical question, in a Jewish state. In the case of Dr. George Tamarin, a lecturer at Tel Aviv University who requested alteration of his nationality identification from "Jew" to "Israeli," the High Court ruled that "there is no Israeli nation apart from the Jewish people, and the Jewish people consists not only of the people residing in Israel but also of the Jews in the Diaspora." Thus the Court rejected the appellant's contention that Israel was something other than the Jewish people, holding that "no man can create a new nation with his own breath and say I belong to it."[56]

If, indeed, the principle on which the JNF was founded is now interpreted by the Development Authority as applying to all state lands as well as JNF lands, it follows that non-Jewish citizens are effectively excluded from nine-tenths of the land area of the country (pre-1967). To determine whether the JNF interpretation of the law applies in practice, one would have to examine the record of leasehold contracts given by the Land Authority since 1961. I do not know whether this is possible; secondary sources give little information. Orni's JNF monograph[57] states that "the leasehold contracts issued by the Land Authority in general follow in their wording those used by the Jewish National Fund in the decades preceding the Agreement." In that period, the contracts certainly excluded non-Jews. Non-Jews could not lease JNF lands, and furthermore, the JNF lease reads, "The lessee undertakes to execute all works connected with the cultivation of the holding only with Jewish labour."[58] Orni gives several examples of leasehold contracts: for moshavim, kibbutzim, moshavim shittufiyim, and "a registered Company functioning as lessee." The first three categories are solely Jewish. The latter need not be, but it would be interesting to determine whether (and if so, when and where) Arab companies have been able to lease state lands. Surveying the array of laws, principles, and institutions, it would seem reasonable to speculate that since 1961, it has been general policy to settle Jews on state lands (and surely, on JNF lands), perhaps apart from cases where expropriated Arabs were transferred to state lands. But in all of the abundant literature on Israeli society, I can find no information whatsoever about this crucial subject.

Orni's interpretation of the impact of the laws in his quasi-official monograph is rather similar to that of the JNF *Report*. He writes that "in 1960, the State of Israel adopted the JNF guidelines for all publicly-owned lands, i.e., for over 90% of the State's area at that date"; by these laws "over 90% of the country's surface had by then become public property to which the JNF's agrarian principles could be applied." Discussing the work of Dr. Abraham Granott, who headed the JNF, Orni explains that he "from 1948 onward worked systematically for the incorporation of JNF principles into Israel's legislation and their extension so as to cover all public property. . . . Thanks to Dr. Granott's persistent efforts, the final and decisive stage was reached with the signing of the 1960 Agreement between the Government and the JNF and the simultaneous adoption by the Knesset of the Land Laws." He notes that the "most important" of the founding principles of the JNF was the "demand that the land purchased should forever remain the property of the Jewish people." One may tentatively conclude from these and other comments that the law is being interpreted by those responsible for land development as generally restricting it to Jewish use. The matter seems similar to the earlier system of expropriation described by Jiryis. There was no particular law that stated that lands could be taken from Arabs for exclusive use by Jews, but there was a network of conditions, interpretations, bureaucratic structures for making determinations, etc., that had just this effect. Similarly, there is no law that states that Jewish farms receive priority for electrification, etc., but resort to quasi-governmental institutions achieves this result, as noted earlier.

Again, it is important to stress, first, that in the absence of any comprehensive study, judgments can only be tentative; and second, that as Fein points out in the comments cited above (see note 35), the absence of such studies in part reflects the nature of the problem. Still, it is fair to conclude tentatively that the system of land laws operates much in the manner of the other programs discussed, namely, as a complex device for guaranteeing Jewish dominance. Hence the grievances among dispossessed Arab peasants.

Examples of application of the laws and discriminatory practices are occasionally reported. In one recent incident, a Druze mason, a twenty-year veteran of the Israeli Border Patrol, was not allowed to open a business in the all-Jewish town of Karmiel (see above, p. 264). In 1971, the Agricultural Ministry brought legal action against Jewish settlements that had leased land to non-members, mostly Arabs, "in violation of the law which prohibits the lease of national land." The practice was stopped. The incident was regarded as particularly serious because "in certain cases it was even revealed that the [Jewish] settlers leased lands to Arabs who had lived there prior to the war of independence [1948] and a situation began to develop in which Arabs were returning in an indirect way to their lands." [59] The experience of several Arab villages is reported by David Caploe. [60] Lands were taken from villages "for security reasons" and later turned over to the JNF. Villagers who refuse to sell land to the JNF are harassed until they find it difficult to refuse. In one case, villagers report that a neighboring Mapam kibbutz erected barbed-wire fences to separate the village from its grazing lands so as to contribute to the JNF pressures on the villagers. Compensation, they allege, is far below land values. Caploe's figures indicate that the villages in question were deprived of much of their land by such measures, and that as a result most villagers must seek wage labor elsewhere. Comprehensive documentation is lacking, but the sporadic reports available give ample basis for understanding the grievances of the Arab citizens of Israel.

Two facts are particularly worthy of notice with regard to the system of discrimination that has just been briefly reviewed. The first is that one has no inkling of any of this in the encomiums to Israeli democracy that appear regularly in left-liberal publications in the United States. The second is that this system of principles is presented to "progressive opinion" in the West with considerable pride. Thus, Orni's JNF monograph is directed to "alert opinion in the free world, with collegiate youth in the forefront," which "is in a turmoil of soul-searching" and critical examination of "social, economic and political relationships." "What is hoped . . . is that people abroad who wish to form an opinion on Israel—be it on the political, social or cultural plane—will see need to include in their study also the subject of its achievements in the agrarian sphere"—in particular, the achievements under settlement and development programs conducted by quasi-governmental agencies that use charitable contributions for the benefit of "persons of Jewish religion, race or origin" and based on the "ancient tradition of ownership of the land in perpetuity by the Jewish people."

The achievements in the agrarian sphere, Orni explains, are based ultimately on Biblical precept, with its "deeply-rooted sense of social justice and a consciousness of the duty to protect the community's poorer and weaker strata." Orni notes, with some justice, that "to a surprising degree, it is possible to deduce the form and spirit of a government or a society . . . from the laws, customs and arrangements it applies to immovable property." Looking at those laws, customs, and arrangements, we discover that they embody a remarkable and perhaps unconscious system of severe discrimination. Orni reports that the London Zionist Conference of 1920 established that "the guiding principle of Zionist land policy is to transfer into the common possession of the Jewish people those areas in which Jewish settlement is to take place," with the JNF as "the instrument of Jewish land policy" which will act to "transfer the land into Jewish possession" and "make Jewish labor secure." But he never asks what all of this implies, as this "guiding principle" is worked into the "laws, customs and arrangements" of a state that assigns responsibility for development of over 90 percent of its land to a company that represents not the citizens of the state but rather the Jewish majority and the Jewish people in the Diaspora.

Orni's point is that the system governing immovable property in effect socializes such property, a testimony to the egalitarian and just character of the Israeli state. The conclusion may be legitimate, insofar as we restrict attention to the Jewish majority. But there is a typical oversight: There are non-Jews in the Jewish state. Correcting for the oversight, we reach rather different conclusions.

State ownership in itself guarantees no human rights. Thus King Leopold of Belgium made the state owner of 90 percent of the Congo territory, so that "native rights in nine-tenths of the Congo territory being thus declared non-existent, it followed that the native population had no proprietary right in the plants and trees growing upon that territory." [61] More generally, white settlement was established in Africa by

> the adopting by a white ruling race of legal measures designed expressly to compel the individual natives to whom they apply to quit land, which they occupy and by which they can live, in order to work in white service for the private gain of the white man. [62]

To be sure, Israel is not white Africa. Far from it. [63] But the principle of exclusive rights for the settlers who displaced the native population, with its predictable consequences, is deeply embedded in the institutional structures of the state, almost to the point of lack of awareness. This is a serious matter. The actual record, and the failure to comprehend it, indicate that far-reaching and quite radical changes will be necessary if the system of discrimination is to be dismantled.

In his study, Orni points out that the 1948 war "brought in its wake a revolutionary reversal in land ownership" [64] and that "the situation created by the Six Day War [June 1967] made land redemption through purchase again a vital task." It is quite true that after 1948, substantial territories were expropriated from Arabs, including those who remained in Israel. JNF holdings increased from 936,000 dunams in May 1948 to almost 3,400,000 in 1950. [65] And after the 1967 war, the JNF began to work in the occupied territories as well. Orni alleges that "today, as in the past, transfers are entirely voluntary." [66] That is far from true. In the occupied territories, the villagers of Aqraba were forced to evacuate their fields after defoliation by the Israeli Air Force; the lands were then "transferred" to Jewish settlement. The Bedouin farmers of Pithat Rafiah were expelled, their wells closed, and their lands fenced in and then converted to Jewish use, their homes, mosques, cemeteries bulldozed. Reports from within Israel, some cited earlier, indicate that all sorts of pressures have been applied to coerce (or, if one prefers cynicism, "induce") Arabs to sell land, and that in many cases, lands were simply expropriated by the state and then turned over to Jewish settlement.

As for the "voluntary transfers" in the pre-state years, it may be true that the absentee landlords and feudal proprietors were willing to sell their land, but there is no lack of evidence that peasants were forcibly displaced. This was always understood by the Zionist leadership. Arthur Ruppin, who was in charge of land purchase and who played a major role in founding the binationalist Brith Shalom, wrote in 1930 that it was illusory to believe that Jewish settlement could be carried out without damaging Arab interests, if only because "there is hardly any land which is worth cultivating which is not already being cultivated, [so that] it is found that wherever we purchase land and settle it, by necessity its present cultivators are turned away, whether they are owners or tenants . . . The advice we tend to give the Arabs—to work their land more intensively, in order to manage with a smaller allotment of land—may appear to the Arabs as a joke at the expense of the poor" since the peasants have neither the requisite capital nor agricultural knowledge.[67] Ruppin wrote that until that time, most purchases had been of sparsely settled land, though this would no longer be possible. That is not the whole story, however. According to a Zionist pacifist who was one of the early settlers of Nahallal:

When the land of Nahallal was purchased there was an Arab village on the hill, Mahllul. The Jewish National Fund left the Arabs some of the land so that they could subsist under the stipulation that if within six years they could refund the Jewish National Fund they could hold the land. They could not raise the money and were forcefully removed from the land.[68]

Thousands of tenants were evicted in the land purchases of the early 1920s,[69] and in fact, years before, Zionist commentators had objected to the forcible displacement of local inhabitants.

Perhaps this is enough to underscore the obvious: The Zionist movement, from the start, could not help but injure and impinge on the rights of the people who lived in the country. Furthermore, the belief that a Jewish state with non-Jewish citizens can be a democracy guaranteeing equal rights to all is not tenable, and the practice of a quarter-century simply demonstrates that what was to be expected did in fact occur.

In the light of the factual record, the reports and analyses by American

Zionist intellectuals make depressing reading. One can perhaps offer a rationale for the historical development on grounds of conflict of rights and greater need, and in terms of the perceived need to create a Jewish proletariat rather than a Jewish planter-aristocracy ruling the native Arab population. The problems that arose were not trivial, and if we grant the right of Jewish settlement, the policies of the JNF and the *Yishuv* in general until the establishment of the state can perhaps be justified as the least unjust option under unfortunate circumstances—though it is worthy of note that the system of discrimination against Arab labor and boycott of Arab produce was criticized from the left at the time, within the Palestinian *Yishuv*.[70] Since the establishment of the state, no such justification is possible. It is presumably for this reason that the facts are simply ignored or denied. Thus we read that Israel is already a democratic secular state with full equality of rights for all, or that "major victories" have been won on matters of civil liberties which "still leave the Arabs cut off from whatever sense of Jewishness is fostered by the Israeli state," but nothing more; thus their situation is no different from that of minorities throughout the world, for example, Arab citizens of France who may have little interest in Bastille Day.[71] As so often in the past, many left-liberal intellectuals are quick to deny injustice and repression in states that claim their loyalty. Until these illusions are recognized and dispelled, there can be no serious discussion of the dangerous and explosive problems of the Middle East.

Israeli Jews also suffer from the commitment to Jewish dominance. The severe religious controls over personal life, deplored by liberal American Zionists as well as Israeli civil libertarians, are in part a result of the need to enforce a second-class status for non-Jews, and are therefore likely to persist irrespective of the problems of coalition politics. Some basis must be established to distinguish the privileged majority from the remainder of the population. Thus, even if the majority of Jews have little interest in Judaism as a religion, it is natural that the rabbinate is given a major role in the affairs of state and that theocratic patterns that are foreign to traditional Judaism develop. It will not be an easy matter for the Jewish majority in a Jewish state to free itself from religious intrusion into personal life.

A further concomitant of life in a society based on discrimination is the rise of all kinds of racial mythology. In the long run, this will prove damaging to a society that survives by virtue of its technical rationality, just as it is harmful to cultural and intellectual life, and, of course, to the oppressed minority. Such mysticism has been on the rise since 1967. The issue of "historic rights" is a case in point (see note 5). The first official commitment to the principle that the "historic right of the Jewish people to the land of Israel is beyond question" was in 1972, in a parliamentary motion responding to Hussein's plan for a Jordanian federation.[72] Although Israel will surely not impress many people by founding its case on Biblical authority, it is remarkable that a belief to the contrary is often expressed. Thus, in a mass circulation daily, Michael Deshe explains that the root problem in the Arab-Jewish conflict is that the Arabs have made a "terrible error," and "if only we can succeed in convincing our enemy-neighbors that their point of view is based on a false premise, lacking foundation," then perhaps a settlement is in sight. Their error is their failure to understand that "the original people of this land, its legal owners," have now returned to it, and that "no temporary inhabitant, even if he lives here for 1000 years," can claim superseding rights. Just as the Arab conquerors in Spain were finally driven out by its native inhabitants, so the land of Israel, which "was never an Arab land," must return to "the legal owners of the land." The Arabs must be persuaded to understand this "historical and legal fact." Even in 1967, the territories they lost were "Jewish territories," which "had been conquered in Arab hands for generations." The Arabs have "no national rights in this land," but its "true and legal owner, the Jewish people," should nevertheless graciously arrive at some compromise with the temporary Arab residents. We must explain these facts to the Arabs, thus laying the basis for a peaceful settlement, he argues, with apparent seriousness.[73]

The Ministry of Education and Culture is not far behind on the matter of "historic rights." A new textbook distinguishes between "the State of Israel," which has defined geographical borders, and "the historic land of Israel, to which the [Jewish] people was bound in all generations by prayer, customs, attempts to immigrate, and the struggles of the Messianic movements." The latter concept, which is "a significant concept from the geo-historical point of view," refers to a region that extended to parts of Syria, most of Transjordan, and parts of what is now Iraq, during the period of the First Temple, so the new texts explain. In the same report, the minister of education explains that

it is important that the youth should know that when we returned to this country we did not find here any other nation, and certainly no nation that lived here for hundreds of years. Such Arab inhabitants as we found here arrived only some tens of years before us, in the thirties and the forties of

the nineteenth century, as refugees from the oppression of Muhammad
Ali in Egypt.

This new page of history is designed to contribute to

the effort to reestablish Zionism, both with regard to the moral and humane character of the return to Zion, and also in the matter of the foundation of our rights to the Land of Israel. It is important that the young
Israeli will be ready to debate with an educated young Arab or with the
New Left that calls him an imperialist mercenary.[74]

Even among critics of chauvinist tendencies one finds such arguments in
an extraordinary muddle. Thus Arie Eliav (*op. cit.*) asserts that there can be
no doubt as to the "historic right of the Jewish people to the Land of the
Twelve Tribes," though "part of those historic rights" should be waived, in
the interest of peace. In successive paragraphs, he writes that Jews are almost unique among the nations of the world in that they "are the direct descendants of their forefathers in the land of Israel, and that their genealogy
was never severed, from the time of the destruction of the Temple to this
very day"—yet "on returning to our country we brought with us pigments
from all the countries of the Diaspora: the mahogany black of the Cochin
Jews, the burnished copper of the Jews of Yemen, and the white skin of the
Jews of Ashkenaz (Germany) and the north." As for the Palestinians, "It is
very likely that these Arabs were the descendants of ancient settlers: Jews,
Samaritans," etc., but Israeli Jews should nevertheless not deny the national
rights of the Palestinians merely because the Palestinians "came here as
conquerors." (See note 5.)

    While some Israelis may be able to convince themselves of the force of
these arguments about "historic rights" and racial origins, the belief that
others will find them compelling indicates a severe case of irrationality. Israel can ill afford to sink into a system of mystical beliefs. In its present precarious position, a loss of the capacity for clear-headed and objective
analysis can be extremely dangerous. But since 1967, there has been a dangerous drift in this direction. One example is the "vision of our own om-
nipotence and of total Arab ineptitude"[75] that was surely a factor leading to
the "earthquake" of October 1973. I think it is not surprising that these
striking changes in the mentality of the Israeli public should have come
about during a period when a policy of creeping annexation raised to the

fore the problem of how a Jewish state, with a commitment to democracy and equality of rights, would deal with a substantial population that cannot be granted these rights, consistent with the founding principle of the state.[76]

SOME POSSIBLE ALTERNATIVES

It is difficult to see how Israel and the Palestinians can extricate themselves from the dynamics outlined earlier, leading either to war, or to continued Israeli domination of most of the occupied territories with war always threatening, or to a two-state solution west of the Jordan imposed by imperial force. But that is not to say that the Israeli or Palestinian left, or those who sympathize with their aspirations, should adopt any such program. The prospects for libertarian socialism in the United States, at the moment, are perhaps no greater than the apparent prospects for capitalist democracy in the eighteenth century. But that is plainly no reason to abandon hope. Correspondingly, in the Middle East there have always been, and remain, alternatives that are much to be preferred to the system that is evolving. In the face of current tendencies, the left may still try to work towards a very different resolution of the complex problems of Israel and Palestine.

Of course, the initiative lies elsewhere. In situations of national conflict, the initiative lies generally in the hands of chauvinistic and violent elements whose task is to embitter relations among people who must someday live in harmony if they are to survive in any decent manner at all, with such tactics as shooting up apartments with submachine guns or bombarding refugee camps with planes and gunboats. The goal may be to vanquish the enemy by force, but neither party will achieve that end, though either may succeed in creating a situation in which both national groups will be demolished, each firm in its own rectitude, marching towards destruction to the applause of blind and fanatic partisans a safe distance removed.

One possibility that might be imagined if a two-state settlement is reached is the dismantling of the discriminatory structure of the Jewish and (it is safe to assume) Palestinian states. For reasons discussed above, such moves will require radical changes within Israel and, presumably, the new Palestinian state as well. But it is possible to work for such changes. A second possibility, which might be pursued along with the first, is to move towards integration of the two states, first through some federal structure (perhaps sooner or later including Jordan as well), and later, with the growth of trust and mutual interest, towards a binational arrangement of the sort that was advocated by much of the Zionist movement prior to the Second World War, based on the principle that "whatever the number of the two peoples may be, no people shall dominate the other or be subject to the government of the other." [77]

It is useful to recall, in this connection, that in the period before the Second World War, Zionist leaders, particularly those associated with the labor movement that dominated the Palestinian *Yishuv*, forcefully opposed the idea of a Jewish state, "which would eventually mean Jewish domination of Arabs in Palestine," on grounds that "the rule of one national group over the other" is illegitimate and that the Arabs of Palestine "have the right not to be at the mercy of the Jews." [78] It has been argued that opposition to a Jewish state within the Zionist movement was merely a cynical tactic. [79] Thus, some Arab initiatives towards binationalism were in fact rebuffed by Zionist leaders who, a few years earlier, had advocated similar positions themselves in a period of complete Arab rejection of such attempts. Some Zionist leaders have argued quite explicitly that official denial of the goal of a Jewish state was merely a tactic, a matter of waiting for the "propitious moment." In his autobiography, Nahum Goldmann condemns the chauvinist spokesman Ze'ev Jabotinsky for expressing "his political ideas at the wrong moment":

> The rightness of a political idea is never absolute; it always has a lot to do with the propitious moment. When Jabotinsky demanded, at the exciting Seventeenth Zionist Congress in 1931, that the official Zionist program include the establishment of a Jewish state, this demand, which was rejected by the vast majority, was at that time politically absurd. If the congress had accepted this plank, continued resettlement and the peaceful conquest of Palestine would have been impossible. All of us who voted against it desired a Jewish state just as fervently as Jabotinsky did, but we knew that the time was not ripe. Not until the time seemed to have come, at the Biltmore Conference during the Second World War, did we proclaim the establishment of the Jewish state as a political demand. [80]

If Goldmann is correct, then it was pure hypocrisy for Ben-Gurion, Katznelson, and other labor Zionist leaders to expound on the injustice of the concept of a Jewish state, to "declare before world opinion, before the workers' movement, and before the Arab world, that we shall not agree, either now or in the future, to the rule of one national group over the other"; [81] or for

Chaim Weizmann to state, in his opening speech at the 1931 congress, that "we, on our part, contemplate no political domination" but rather "would welcome an agreement between the two kindred races on the basis of political parity."[82]

I doubt the accuracy of Goldmann's interpretation, many years after the event and after a Jewish state had in fact been established. Views such as those just cited were commonly expressed in internal memoranda and discussions, and in a context that suggests that the commitment to non-domination was undertaken with extreme seriousness. It should be recalled that this was a period of intense class struggle as well as national conflict in Palestine, a period when a labor leader like Ben-Gurion could not only oppose Jabotinsky's call for a Jewish state, but also his advocacy of fascist-style organization and strike-breaking, and could in fact write an article entitled "Jabotinsky in the Footsteps of Hitler." Socialist and humanist forces within the Zionist movement, particularly in the *Yishuv*, were very powerful. Given the historical circumstances and the social context, one must, I think, reject Goldmann's cynical assessment and accept rather the conclusion of Susan Lee Hattis in her recent study[83] that "there is no doubt that during this phase [1931] MAPAI was advocating a bi-national state in Palestine," as were workers' groups to its left, and also liberal currents within the World Zionist Organization. Katznelson defined the general concept, rather vaguely to be sure, in the following way at the time:

What then constitutes a bi-national state? It is a state whose two nationalities enjoy an equal measure of freedom, independence, participation in government, and rights of representation. Neither nationality encroaches upon the other. The term "bi-nationalism" as a whole is of import only if it is expressed in political-judicial norms securing the principle of the political parity of the nationalities. This it is that converts the state into a State of nationalities, differing fundamentally from the national State. . . . What it signifies is that a bi-national political order does not recognize the population at large but takes cognizance of its two national segments to both of which the right to share in shaping the country's regime is secured in equal measure and both of which are equally entitled to guide its destinies.[84]

This is not to deny that socialist Zionists would have preferred a situation in which there were no Arabs to concern themselves about. But they also recognized that in the real world the Arabs did exist and lived on the land, and constituted a large majority of the population. Similarly nonsocialist groups such as Brith Shalom observed that binationalism "is not the ideal but the reality, and if this reality is not grasped Zionism will fail"[85]—at least, Zionism as understood generally by left and liberal Zionists.

A great deal happened in subsequent years to undermine these convictions and reverse the direction of the Zionist movement. The bitter conflict in Palestine between 1936 and 1939 was one such factor, but dominating everything was the rise of Nazism and the growing awareness that it implied the physical destruction of European Jewry. Particularly after the British White Paper of 1939, limiting Jewish immigration to Palestine, other and more urgent demands displaced the ideals of left and liberal Zionism, and in 1942 the demand for a Jewish state was adopted as official policy. To use Goldmann's phrase, "the time was not ripe" for advocacy of binationalism, or so it might be argued. But history moves on, and it may be that the time is now ripe to resurrect the basic principles of the Zionism of a different era. The general principle that neither of the two national groups should dominate or be subservient to the other was a valid one when it was enunciated, and it might once again be adopted by the left, within Israel and among the Palestinians. It can, of course, only serve now as a general principle under which left-wing movements might conceivably unite. As an editorial statement in an Israeli journal puts it, "binationalism could . . . be a banner or a long-range program on which Jews and Arabs could unite and which could make them readier to yield the short-range concessions that more immediate agreements will demand."[86]

If each of the national movements presents to the other a face of stony intransigence, short-term accommodation is excluded. Within the framework of a broader long-term program that might satisfy the just demands of both groups for national institutions, equal rights, social justice, and access in principle to all of the territory of the former Palestine, short-term accommodation might well be facilitated. While it is natural to suppose that one's ends can only be attained through the use of force and armed struggle, the conclusion is not necessarily correct. I think, in fact, that it is far from correct, and that it is, furthermore, suicidal as a guide to policy, both for Israeli Jews and Palestinians.

Assuming that two states will be established—under present circumstances, probably by imperial force—moves towards internal democratization and towards federal arrangements might well be contemplated. Such programs are not without support within Israel. The president of the Council of the Sephardic Community in Israel, Elie Eliachar, has sharply criticized the refusal of the Europe-oriented Israeli leadership to recognize Palestinian nationalism, to seek good relations with the local Arab population, or to bring authentic voices of the Oriental Jewish community into the "establishment" for fear of "levantinization" and "Arabization" of the society. He expresses his hope that if these policies change, there will eventually be "some form of federal arrangement" between Israel and a "future Palestinian entity," with Jerusalem as the shared capital.[87] Other proposals along similar lines have also occasionally appeared. In the 1967–73 period, Israel had a real opportunity to move in this direction. Such moves might have made a good deal of sense had they been based on the traditional Zionist principle of equality and non-domination. The barrier was never security; on the contrary, such programs would have substantially reduced the security risk by offering an acceptable long-term political solution to the Palestinians.[88] Again, it must be stressed that security for Israel lies in political accommodation and creation of bonds of unity and solidarity with the Palestinian population, not in military dominance, which will at best only delay an eventual catastrophe, given the historical, political, and economic realities. The problem was not security but rather the commitment to Jewish—in fact, European Jewish—dominance in the Jewish state. While the opportunities of the 1967–73 period have now been lost, nevertheless, under the changed circumstances, certain possibilities still exist.

Either of the possibilities mentioned—democratization or moves towards further integration—require substantial, if not revolutionary, changes in popular attitudes and aspirations. It seems to me reasonable to suppose that such changes could only come about as part of a broader movement of the left seeking social justice and, ultimately, radical reform or social revolution. Within such a context, the common needs of Jews and Palestinians could find expression, even granting the stability of national ties. I emphasize again that within the framework of a long-term program of reconciliation, it is possible to imagine short-term steps that would otherwise be difficult to initiate. It is unrealistic to dismiss long-range proposals as "utopian." They may provide the only basis for the simpler and more immediate steps that will reduce tension and permit the growth of mutual trust and the expression of common interests that cross national lines—specifically, class interests—and thus lay the groundwork for an eventual just and peaceful settlement.

By their very nature, programs of democratization, federation, or socialist binationalism cannot be advanced by armed struggle, military force, or
outside intervention. They must arise from forces within each of the national movements that are now engaged in a bitter and suicidal struggle,
forces that will never be able to crystallize or progress under conditions of
conflict. Even taking at face value the PLO program, one must surely conclude that the commitment in principle to armed struggle aimed at the destruction of Israeli social and political institutions is a hopelessly irrational
strategy, which can only make the stated goals even more difficult of attain-
ment than they presently are, quite apart from the question of whether
these are the proper goals. And the more recent tactic of directing murderous attacks precisely against the poor Oriental segment of the Israeli community can only be described as insane, quite apart from its moral level,
given the professed goals. Authentic libertarian movements, if they develop, will follow a very different course.

With the collapse of pre-October 1973 exuberance, it is to be expected
that the Israeli government will also put forth some version of a federal solution as the only means for maintaining control of the occupied territories
in coordination with an imposed Quisling leadership. According to a recent
report, Israeli Defense Minister Shimon Peres announced in a talk in Tel
Aviv "that he favors a federation between Israel and the Arabs of the west
bank, excluding the PLO." [89] Such proposals are meaningless at best, deeply
cynical at worst. The condition that the PLO must be excluded means that
the State of Israel will determine what is "acceptable political expression"
within the West Bank, which will therefore remain nothing but a colony of
a Greater Israel. Peres's proposal fails on three counts: (1) It does not arise
from each of the two communities that are to enter into federation, but is to
be imposed on one by the other; (2) it is not based on the principle of equality and non-domination; (3) it is too late. That is, a proposal of this sort, despite its fundamental defects of principle, might have had some meaning
prior to October 1973, when it could have been interpreted as a gesture by Israel, perhaps ultimately meaningful, towards political accommodation.
Now, its meaning is all too plain. The fact that the proposal is made at all signifies a belated recognition that the policy of reliance on force was a grave
error. Unfortunately, the error cannot be rectified by the means proposed.

Let us suppose, as a point of departure, that a two-state solution is imposed by the great powers in cis-Jordan. Add further the reasonable supposition that the Palestinian state will mimic the Jewish state in its

discriminatory institutions and in the ties of the dominant majority to an external "nation." Libertarian socialist elements within the two states, should they exist and survive an imperial settlement, ought then to turn their attention to combating discriminatory institutions and practices as well as the structures of exploitation and oppression within each state. Right-wing elements will have their own reasons for maintaining tensions and hostility, if only to suppress class struggle. Correspondingly, socialist movements will seek to reduce inter-state tension and will search for allies across national and state lines. They should, I believe, place on the agenda, within each society, a program for federalism worked out by cooperating forces within the two states and coupled with a program for social change. The inevitable tendency towards discrimination against the national minority might be alleviated somewhat within a federal structure. Furthermore, the very existence of such a joint program, even if its realization is only a future possibility, should facilitate moves towards relaxing hostilities.

A federal system would involve a sharing of political power between a centralized authority and two regions. It is then possible to envision further steps, natural for libertarian socialists at least, towards distribution of political power among municipalities or cantons with a varied mixture of Jews and Arabs. Socialists will work for democratization of the economy through workers' councils, with higher economic integration of production and regional units through federation. Two parliaments might be established— one Jewish, one Arab—each with veto power over decisions affecting international relations or state policy. National institutions might exist side by side for the organization of cultural and social life. Options should also exist for individuals who choose to identify themselves not as Jews or as Arabs but in different terms. Thus, there should be a possibility to live one's life simply as an individual. Workers' organizations will develop joint interests, along class rather than national lines, and might in the course of time discover that their fundamental interests will be realized only through common programs to create a socialist society that might well preserve parallel national institutions, either throughout the common territory or through a cantonal federal arrangement. Immigration should give priority to Jews and Palestinians. Depending on events elsewhere, there might be moves towards a broader Middle East federation, or closer relations with socialist movements in Europe and elsewhere.

In earlier periods, some detailed programs were developed for a binational state.[90] In many parts of the world, socialist movements must seek a way to combine a commitment to an end to domination and exploitation with a recognition of national and ethnic bonds within complex multinational societies. In the advanced industrial societies as well, ethnic and racial conflicts stand in the way of movements working for social justice, and are often manipulated and exacerbated for the purpose of preserving privilege and oppression. Ultimately, socialist movements must be internationalist in their orientation, but "internationalism" does not imply opposition in principle to national ties or to other forms of voluntary association among individuals.

Developments within the industrial societies will naturally set certain bounds on what can be achieved elsewhere. Socialist internationalism is the only force that can prevent imperialist intervention in the long run, or that can come to terms with the critical problems of the global economy, so it seems to me. There are certain steps that can be taken by the left in particular regions such as the Middle East, with the support of sympathetic groups outside. Such steps might, perhaps, lead towards a more peaceful and just resolution of local conflicts, and even contribute to the growth of an international movement that may be able to face and overcome the much more far-reaching problems that arise in a world of authoritarian states and oppressive institutions and practices.

AFTERWORD (1981)

THE PRECEDING ARTICLE was written in November 1974 (apart from updated footnotes). At the time, it was accurate to place the Israeli refusal to move towards a political settlement on a par with that of the PLO, as indicated. A year later, and since, it would be more accurate to compare the position of the State of Israel with that of the rejection front within the PLO. Other segments of the PLO, which claim to represent an overwhelming majority, have modulated the earlier positions described, but these moves have been met with official disdain on Israel's part. The Rabin government, like its predecessors, continued to insist that Israel would retain the Gaza Strip, most of the Golan Heights, a vastly expanded Jerusalem, areas of Jewish settlement in the Jordan Valley, parts of northeastern Sinai, Sharm el-Sheikh (Israeli "Ophira") and an access to it, while what is left of the West Bank may be turned over to Jordan under an arrangement that grants Israeli military control, or with some form of home rule instituted under the occupation.[1] These pronouncements on future borders by government officials were entirely consistent with the development program that was being executed. Prime Minister Golda Meir once tersely formulated the basic premise of state policy as follows: "The frontier is where Jews live, not where there is a line on the map."[2] The principle of "building facts," deeply engrained in the consciousness of the present generation of leaders of the Labor party, remained state policy under their rule, and was considerably extended in application under the subsequent Likud government.

Meanwhile, Arab attitudes were slowly changing. A two-state settlement was endorsed, without enthusiasm, by "notables" in the West Bank[3] and by spokesmen for the PLO. In an interview in Beirut aired over the National Public Radio network in the United States on May 26, 1975, the official spokesman of the PLO, Shafiq el-Hout, stated that "one cannot deny the fact that we might have to pass through a stage where [there will exist] two

Palestine states—an Israeli state and a Palestinian state—living together converting their contradictions and trying to convert their means of fighting into peaceful ones," leading ultimately, he hopes, to a unitary democratic state achieved through peaceful means—"and you can underline, although we are speaking on the radio, the word 'peaceful,' yes."[4] A similar position was endorsed in still more explicit terms by Sabri Jiryis of the Palestinian National Council[5] and, earlier, by Said Hammami of the London bureau of the PLO.[6]

These spokesmen are unclear as to the borders they have in mind, and Israelis have objected to their insistence that the establishment of Israel was "a grave political error" that should be rectified by peaceful means.[7] Furthermore, these statements fall short of the specific commitments that many Israeli commentators regard as imperative even in advance of any indication of Israeli willingness to accept the fact of Palestinian nationalism—which in the real world means the PLO. But it seems to me fair to say that by 1975 the PLO had given as clear an indication of its willingness to accept a two-state solution as one might reasonably have expected under prevailing conditions.

Within Israel, there has been no comparable willingness to accept or even to consider a two-state settlement: On the contrary, the Labor government never departed from its official decision of July 21, 1974, cited above (p. 231), insisting that Israel would have no dealings with representatives of the PLO and would discuss no *political* issue with any Palestinians, no matter what their political views.[8] To date, the Labor party has not deviated from this position, and the "autonomy" proposals of the Begin government, particularly when interpreted in the light of their settlement policies, amount to a total rejection of any meaningful form of autonomy for the population of the occupied territories.

Israeli analysts understood very well the likelihood of convergence between the superpowers on a two-state settlement, though they underestimated the determination of the United States to ensure that no other power—the USSR, or the Western European states—enter into Middle East diplomacy (cf. Chapters 11, 12). The liberal journal *Ha'aretz*, in an editorial comment on secret meetings between Soviet envoys and Prime Minister Rabin in Israel, had this to say:

> Within this context, it is important for Israel to remember that the difference between Washington's and Moscow's attitudes concerning an overall

agreement is small . . . although from Israel's viewpoint, the two super-powers' attitudes are exceedingly remote from hers in this matter. Regarding Israel's security, there never existed a difference. The two powers accept Israel's right to exist securely within agreed borders. They are both prepared to guarantee this. . . . Concerning the central issue of borders, Israel will need to conduct a political battle at Geneva, not just against the Arab countries and the Soviet Union but also against the United States.[9]

The comment is basically accurate, though the Geneva meetings were aborted as a result of U.S. diplomacy, which insisted upon a unilateral U.S. role in mediating the conflict. It is, however, true that the United States has no sustained interest in guaranteeing the Israeli occupation, and sooner or later is likely to join the international consensus in favor of a two-state settlement, particularly if there is pressure from the oil-producing states of a meaningful kind and if the American people prove to be unwilling to foot the bill, which is not small.

The U.S.-Israeli opposition to a two-state settlement has persisted so far, however. Thus, the United States vetoed a Security Council resolution of January 26, 1976, supported by the Arab states and the PLO, calling for a two-state settlement on the pre-June 1967 borders with "appropriate arrangements . . . to guarantee . . . the sovereignty, territorial integrity and political independence of all states in the area and their right to live in peace within secure and recognized borders"—in effect, a modification of U.N. Resolution 242 to allow for a Palestinian state. Israel and the United States were alone in opposing an Egyptian resolution of December 1976 in the U.N. General Assembly calling for convening the Geneva conference on the Middle East by March 1977, even though "so cautious and moderate were the terms of the resolution that the Israeli Government is understood to have given serious consideration to supporting it."[10] The Israeli objection was based primarily on the fact that this resolution specified that "all the parties" to the conflict, including the PLO, should participate in preparations for the conference.[11] In opposing the earlier Security Council resolution, Prime Minister Rabin made explicit his position that "it is imperative that the whole solution of the Palestinian issue should be tied to Jordan" and that Israel "should vehemently oppose any tendency to establish a third state in the area between it and Jordan." He emphasized that "any Israeli agreement for political negotiations with a Palestinian faction necessarily lays the groundwork for such a possibility,"[12] and therefore must be rejected.

Note the reference to *any* Palestinian faction. In an interview in *Newsweek* Rabin again emphasized the Israeli refusal to negotiate with the PLO or to enter into "political negotiations with Palestinians," PLO or not: The Palestinian problem is solely a refugee problem, he emphasized.[13] The Israeli cabinet rejected a proposal that Israel should "announce publicly its willingness to negotiate with any Palestinian group that would recognize Israel, renounce the use of terrorism against this country and accept the principles of the Security Council's Resolutions 242 and 338"[14]—what later became known as the "Yariv formula," discussed but never accepted. Rabin—and, needless to say, his successor—never departed from what the Labor party journal referred to as his "Three No's," including "total opposition to negotiation with the PLO even if the latter recognizes the State of Israel and its right to exist and stops terror acts altogether."[15] The same remains true of the two major political groupings in Israel today.

The Palestinian National Council, the governing body of the PLO, issued a declaration on March 20, 1977, calling for the establishment of "an independent national state" in Palestine—rather than a secular democratic state of Palestine—and authorizing Palestinian attendance at an Arab-Israeli peace conference. Commenting, the *New York Times* (March 21, 1977) noted that "the acceptance by the P.L.O. of the concept of a small Palestinian state, although the idea is still rejected by Israel, is considered to be a vital step in Palestinian movement toward peaceful coexistence with Israel," while citing Prime Minister Rabin's response: "that the only place the Israelis could meet the Palestinian guerrillas was on the field of battle." The Palestinian National Council declaration was not very surprising, given statements of the sort cited above and others, e.g., that of Farouk Kaddoumi, chief of the PLO Political Department, who insisted "on the creation of an independent Palestinian state in the West Bank and Gaza as soon as these two territories are liberated from Israel."[16]

Subsequently, the PLO went still further, leaking a "peace plan" published in Beirut, which, among other things, stated, with regard to the Palestine National Charter, that it would not serve as the basis for relations among states any more than the founding principles of the World Zionist Organization do, and adding:

> It is to be assumed that a commitment would be made that, after the Palestinians secured the primary rights they are demanding, the means of achieving the aims of the charter would become subject to change—such

a change in the nature of the struggle that these aims would be achieved by peaceful means. If a State came into being, the body representing the Palestinian people would issue a constitution for this State, taking into account existing realities and agreements.[17]

There remain various ambiguities and unclarities in these and similar proposals and declarations, and the PLO retains a commitment to armed struggle—exactly as Israel does; see Rabin's statement just quoted, which remains the position of Likud and the Labor party—as long as the right of the Palestinians to national self-determination in a West Bank-Gaza Strip state is not realized. The Palestinians have claimed that they are fully supported by the Arab states in their advocacy of a separate state. Henry Tanner reported in the *New York Times*, citing Palestinian sources, that "the principle of a West Bank state has been accepted now, although reluctantly, by all the major groups in the Palestine Liberation Organization," including the group "that carries out Syrian policy," and by the Arab states, "even Libya and Iraq," so that "there is a virtual consensus among the Arabs on this point." [18] The U.N. record partially reviewed above supports this conclusion.

While the PLO has been moving towards support for a two-state settlement, and the Arab states as well, Israel continues to oppose any such concept adamantly, still with U.S. support, which remains crucial, not only because of predominant U.S. power in the region but also because the United States is directly funding the occupation and the settlement of the occupied territories and their continued integration into Israel. When Secretary of State Cyrus Vance toured the Middle East in 1977, the mayors of major West Bank towns sent him a letter calling for an independent state alongside of Israel and stating that the Arab Palestinian people had chosen as "its sole legal representative, irrespective of the place . . . the PLO under the leadership of Mr. Yasser Arafat," an act of considerable courage given the nature of the occupation. At the same time, the Israeli Knesset approved a resolution by a vote of 92 to 4 that rejected the PLO as "a discussion partner for the State of Israel in any Middle East peace negotiations," [19] thus rejecting in the clearest terms the right of self-determination. I have already pointed out that this position was—and remains—quite independent of any stand that the PLO might take with regard to Israel, U.N. resolutions, reliance on force, or whatever, and extends as well to any organized Palestinian group, as the Labor cabinet made explicit in preparing for the U.N. Security Council debate of January 1976 (see above).

In January 1981, Dr. Issam Sartawi of the PLO sent a letter of congratulations on the occasion of the fifth anniversary of the Israel Council for Israeli-Palestinian Peace, citing Yasser Arafat's approval of "the ongoing peace talks with Sheli [a small peace party with two seats in the Israeli Knesset] as quoted in *Al-Hawadess,* 19 December 1980," and adding that "sooner than all our combined enemies think, peace shall and must reign between the Palestinian and Israeli states and their peoples." The French Press Agency communiqué from Beirut stated on January 13 that "it is reasonable to surmise that Mr. Sartawi has sent the letter on the directive of Mr. Arafat himself." [20] Commenting, (Res.) General Mattityahu Peled of the Israel Council adds that in the *Al-Hawadess* interview that Sartawi cites, Arafat

> stated that those very talks were being conducted pursuant to the [Palestinian National Council] resolution of 1977 and that he was bound by that resolution to maintain those contacts with the various Israeli political parties mentioned in the interview. Furthermore, he stated that "anyone who is prepared to join these talks is welcome to do so." No clearer invitation to other Israel parties to join the talks can be offered, considering the open hostility toward the PLO by the Israeli government and of its major opposition, the Labor party.

Peled also condemned the decision of the Socialist International in its November 1980 Madrid Congress to support the Israeli Labor party, pointing out that

> the political chapter of the new platform of the Labor party, which calls for "active defence against the PLO both in the security and ideological-political arena," and for the imposition of Israeli sovereignty over approximately fifty percent of the West Bank and the Gaza Strip and the whole of the Golan Heights as a minimal condition for making peace with Jordan and Syria, can best be described as a program for war and not a contribution to peace. For in practical terms what the new Labor platform means is simply that peace has become conditional upon the Arab consent to the elimination of all national aspirations of the Palestinian people and to the territorial expansion beyond the June 4, 1967, borders. This far exceeds what can be called "minor rectifications."

Peled points out further that the Socialist International rejected an alternative resolution, "vehemently opposed by the Israeli Labor delegation and actively supported by the PLO observer," which called for basing peace in the Middle East "on the security of Israel as well as all the other States in the region, and on a definitive solution to the Palestinian problem, founded on the recognition of the Palestinian people's legitimate rights. . . . The problem, however, continues to be the establishment of direct and positive relations between the Israelis and Palestinians, between a State whose sovereignty and integrity must be respected and the PLO, an organization representing the Palestinian people and widely recognized as such on an international level." [21] The cynical (or, Peled suggests, perhaps ignorant) decision of the Socialist International to opt for military confrontation, Israeli expansionism, oppression of the Palestinians and denial of their elementary rights, rejecting the framework for a peaceful settlement based on mutual recognition, brings the International into close alignment with the mainstream of liberal opinion in the United States, in opposition to the general international consensus in favor of a two-state settlement.

A few weeks after Sartawi's letter appeared, the third Islamic Conference summit meeting in At-Taif, Saudi Arabia, took the strongest position it had yet adopted in favor of the PLO.[22] It called for "Israel's total and unconditional withdrawal from all the occupied Palestinian and Arab territories and the restoration of the inalienable rights of the Palestinian people, including their right to return, to self-determination and to the establishment of their independent state on the land of Palestine under the leadership of the PLO," while recognizing "the question of Palestine as the core of the problem of the Middle East and number one issue of the Islamic nation." It also called for "the liberation of Arab Jerusalem to make it the capital of the Palestinian state" and called for a "holy jihad" to achieve these aims, noting that "jihad has an Islamic meaning which is not open to interpretation or misunderstanding." [23] The Saudi Arabians explained further the aim of the jihad: "The struggle being launched is only aimed at liberating 'the territories occupied since 1967' (the territorial integrity of Israel proper is thus not in question); the Arab-Muslim community is determined to 'explore peaceful paths other than the Camp David path for restoring the Palestinians' legitimate rights to self-determination and an independent state in Palestine.' " [24] King Hussein of Jordan "reaffirmed that he is not one of the parties involved in the Palestinian conflict, hence dashing the hopes—

whether real or not—being cherished in Jerusalem and Washington. The Hashemite king named the PLO—to applause from his fellows—as the 'sole' interlocutor capable of 'building an independent state in Palestine,' and Mr. Yasir Arafat, leader of the fedayeen organization, treated here as a head of state, was one of the first to embrace him." [25] Israel's response was that the resolutions "reflect the same blind hatred, the same recalcitrant and dark fanaticism, the same obtuseness and disregard for the truth, the same adamancy not to recognize the existence of a Jewish people possessing national rights in this land and in this region" as that of the Jerusalem Mufti Haj Amin Al-Husseini in the 1930s and 1940s. [26]

The PLO has surely not abandoned its hopes that a two-state settlement will only be the first stage in an evolution leading to something else—according to its official claims, a "secular democratic state." It is difficult to see why one should object to that stance, if it is agreed that any further developments are to take place by peaceful means. The PLO is now in a position that is reminiscent, in many ways, of that of the Zionist organization in the 1930s and 1940s. It is perhaps useful to recall that when the Zionist movement authorized its leadership to negotiate for partition in 1937, it reiterated its claim to all of Palestine (as the government of Israel still does, by an official 1972 declaration of the Knesset), and Ben-Gurion even declared in a speech of 1937 that

> the acceptance of partition does not commit us to renounce Trans-Jordan; one does not demand from anybody to give up his vision. We shall accept a state in the boundaries fixed today, but the boundaries of Zionist aspirations are the concern of the Jewish people and no external factor will be able to limit them. [27]

Yasser Arafat has spoken in similar terms. The leaders of the Likud government went much further. In June 1948, after the state was established, the Herut movement, headed by Menahem Begin, established its "Principles" which declared that "the Hebrew homeland, on both banks of the Jordan River, is an historical and geographical whole," that "the partition of the homeland is an illegal act and does not bind the Jewish people," and that "the task of this generation is to reunite the divided parts of the homeland and establish on them Jewish sovereignty," establishing a "new society" on both banks of the Jordan which will have "the Jewish Torah . . . [as] . . . the constitution of this state." [28] Begin himself wrote:

The partition of the Homeland is illegal. It will never be recognized. The signature of institutions and individuals of the partition agreement is invalid. It will not bind the Jewish people. Jerusalem was and will forever be our capital. Eretz Israel will be restored to the people of Israel. All of it. And forever.[29]

One can imagine how a committed anti-Semite might have exploited such declarations. As an aid to the imagination, it suffices to see how American "supporters of Israel" exploit much less extreme statements, real or alleged, by some Palestinians today.

Partisans of one or the other side commonly deny the right of national self-determination to their opponent, arguing that Jews can be absorbed as a religious group in an Arab state or can migrate elsewhere, the "Arab Jews" to the Arab states from whence they came and the European Jews to Europe and the United States, which are wealthy enough to absorb them easily; and at a parallel moral level, that Palestinians can live as a minority in a Jewish state or can be absorbed elsewhere in the Arab world. These are, respectively, the positions of the Rejection Front of the PLO and the State of Israel, including both major political groupings. Israeli intransigence on this issue ensures that conflict will persist, with endless misery and suffering and with the threat of a major war never far removed. This position will not be modified as long as the United States supports it, both diplomatically and with enormous military and economic aid.

The state of opinion in the United States will be a significant factor in determining the course of events. After a tour in the United States, Mattityahu Peled, an Israeli Arabist who served on the General Staff during the 1967 war and was subsequently one of the founders of the Israel Council for Israeli-Palestinian Peace, described the "state of near hysteria" among the American Jewish community and their "blindly chauvinistic and narrowminded" support for the most reactionary policies within Israel, which poses "the danger of prodding Israel once more toward a posture of calloused intransigence." He concluded that "the established Jewish leadership in America does not really support Israel as a free democratic nation, but is completely mobilized in the service of a certain particular school of political thinking in Israel," namely, the most intransigent and expansionist elements.[30] He might have added that the same has been true of major currents of American opinion, including its left-liberal component, with few exceptions. The massive Israeli military victory in 1967 touched off a wave of enthusiastic support for Israeli expansionism among the intelligentsia. The sources for this remarkable phenomenon, in my opinion, lie more in domestic American problems than in the politics of the Middle East,[31] but whether this analysis is correct or not, the phenomenon itself is plain enough. Among these groups, and not only the American Jewish community, "the idea that Arab hostility is immutable is raised to the level of a dogma of faith rather than considered as a political reality susceptible of change, and the occupied territories are regarded as a strategic asset to Israel though events prove that they are fast becoming an unbearable liability" (Peled). The behavior of these groups, with their substantial influence in the media and journals of opinion, contributed to the outbreak of the 1973 war, which was a near disaster for Israel while apparently bringing the world close to nuclear war (see Chapter 12). If they maintain their grip on major sectors of American opinion, they will help pave the way towards further catastrophe, along with their relatively insignificant partners, those tiny segments of the American left that urge the Palestinians on to suicide while denying Jewish national rights.

Given the overwhelming American support for the Israeli conquests of 1967, there has never been a realistic possibility that Israel would accept a peaceful settlement, which would necessarily involve relinquishing control of the conquered territories. By early 1971, certainly, the Israeli government recognized that such a settlement could be attained, but explicitly rejected it (see Chapter 12). As noted earlier, Israel moved at once to prevent any meaningful political organization in the occupied territories, even in opposition to the PLO (cf. note 88 of the main chapter, above). Typically, moderate Palestinian intellectuals have been prime targets of repression, for example, Dr. Hanna Nasr, President of Bir Zeit College on the West Bank, who was summarily expelled without credible charge. Writing in the Labor party journal *Davar* (May 16, 1980), Dani Rubinstein observes that "the history of deporting Arab personalities from the West Bank is strange." At first, such supporters of Jordanian rule as the mayors of East Jerusalem and Ramallah were expelled, those called "traditional" or "moderate" in Israeli terminology. Then leaders who were regarded as PLO supporters and Communists were expelled, and more recently, elected officials on the West Bank regarded as moderates. He concludes that Israel is simply attempting to eliminate all possible negotiating partners, whether "moderate traditionalists," or PLO supporters (who reflect popular opinion in the occupied territories), or Communists. Arab leadership in the West Bank "in fact cannot exist" under the occupation. There is nothing strange about this; it is a natural consequence of the determination, from shortly after the 1967 conquest, to maintain control of the occupied territories, a decision that was inevitable in the light of U.S. support for it, despite some vacillation and internal conflict within the U.S. government to which we return in Chapter 12.

The Labor government moved at once to consolidate the occupation,[32] while also rejecting Sadat's 1971 peace offer. The Begin government accelerated the process with more extensive expropriation of Arab lands for Jewish settlement, while at the same time incurring the wrath of the Labor party by agreeing to evacuate the Sinai within the Camp David framework, dismantling settlements established there by the Labor government. The main thrust of Israeli policy in the occupied territories is to integrate them within Israel, undermining Arab agriculture and independent economic, social, and political development in general and converting the work force into a source of cheap labor that will serve as an underclass for Israel with much the same functions as the "guest workers" in Europe. Shai Feldman of the Center for Strategic Studies of Tel Aviv University comments quite accurately in *Foreign Affairs* (Spring 1981) that "at present, important sectors of Israel's economy cannot function without manpower provided by the West Bank and the Gaza Strip," particularly "Israel's tourism, construction, and, to a somewhat lesser degree, agriculture." Similar developments proceed in a natural way with regard to the Arab population within the Green Line (pre-June 1967 boundaries). The settlement and development policy in the occupied territories is designed to isolate areas of Arab population concentration and to enable Israel to exploit for its own purposes the water resources of the West Bank, a crucial matter for a state that exploits its own limited water resources to something approaching 100 percent efficiency. The end result of these programs is to integrate the occupied territories so completely within Israel that they become in effect part of the state, subordinated to the needs of Israel and its Jewish population, thus eliminating any meaningful expression of Palestinian national rights and "marginalizing" the indigenous population.

To attain these ends in the face of increasing popular resistance, it has been necessary to intensify the harshness of the occupation. The population of the Gaza Strip had been effectively "pacified" by 1971, with considerable brutality,[33] and with the expulsion or flight of most of the population of the Golan Heights in 1967, that region poses few indigenous problems for Israeli control. The West Bank has been a more difficult nut to crack. Occasional reports in the U.S. press of the more sensational incidents (e.g., the terrorist bombings in which two West Bank mayors were severely injured,[34] or the practice of firing on demonstrators[35] do not give an adequate picture of the real story of systematic degradation, humiliation, and suppression of even the most minimal form of national self-expression. The character of the occupation is revealed more clearly by these regular practices. A few examples will serve to illustrate the general picture.

In a Jerusalem suburb, the army forced hundreds of inhabitants from their homes at midnight, then "concentrating" them outdoors a kilometer away for a two-hour lecture warning against "rioting." A man of sixty-five who was ill was compelled to go by force. Inhabitants of the Daheisha refugee camp south of Bethlehem complain that on the night of December 25, 1979, the camp was surrounded by soldiers and all inhabitants between the ages of fourteen and sixty-five were compelled to stand outside in a driving rain from midnight to noon the next day while soldiers searched the houses; the governor warned of similar punishments if children continued to throw stones at Israeli cars. A man who asked why he was being arrested was beaten up while soldiers broke furniture in his house.[36] On January 29, four hundred males from ages ten to seventy were again dragged from their houses at eight P.M. and made to stand outside in a cold winter rain for thirteen hours. The same thing happened at the refugee camp of Jalazoun, where inhabitants were compelled to spend an entire night out of doors in a snowstorm: "Children had probably thrown stones at Israeli cars after the chemistry laboratory of the school was destroyed by settlers, who did this in retaliation for stones being thrown, probably following cars being sabotaged in the camp by settlers, after children threw stones, etc., etc., etc." Refugees report that "the new method, actually not so new, but much more sophisticated, is humiliation. The soldiers and the settlers want first of all to humiliate us. But they don't understand that we have lost everything and the only thing we have left is our honor and that they will never be able to take that away from us." [37] Shortly after, thousands of dunams of cultivated land were sprayed by planes with herbicides in villages near Hebron, partly within the Green Line and partly within the occupied West Bank; several weeks earlier the same punishment had been meted out by the Green Patrol, under the command of Minister of Agriculture (now Minister of Defense) Ariel Sharon, in the area of Kafr Kassem.[38]

"Residents of Silwad village, north of Ramallah, complain that during a curfew that was imposed last weekend on the village by the military government, soldiers broke into their homes, and that some of them beat up youths, humiliated adults and old people, stole vast sums of Israeli and foreign currency, and destroyed large quantities of food." The reporter, Yehuda Litani, writes that "at first I could not believe what I heard, but the details (which were also told to other reporters) were repeated again and again in all versions by different people in the village. Only one woman lodged a complaint, the others felt that it was useless to complain." Soldiers terrorized the village, beating old people and children with their hands and rifle butts. An eleven-month-old baby was taken out of a cradle and thrown on the floor. Schoolbooks and children's notebooks were destroyed. "Their whole aim was to take revenge on us and to humiliate us," one villager reported. Brutal treatment continued when some were taken away for questioning. It was later announced that investigators "had verified some of the villagers' complaints." [39]

There are many similar reports. Dani Rubinstein writes in *Davar* (May 9, 1980) that he witnessed a search in a West Bank refugee camp after two children had thrown stones at a military vehicle, during which all men and children from the camp were forced to sit out of doors for two whole days for intense questioning: "One of the officers who had conducted the questioning told me that he doesn't know whether he will find the two children, but he is sure that during the long hours of questioning under the hot sun many other children will decide to throw stones at us at the first opportunity." Amnon Kapeliouk reports that his daughter saw five soldiers "beating an Arab merchant who shut down his shop" in the Old City of Jerusalem; he reports also that all telephones in Bethlehem had been cut off for the past month and a half (*Al Hamishmar*, June 13, 1980). Knesset member Uri Avneri read in the Knesset a letter by soldiers reporting instructions concerning curfew violations given to them by a senior officer:

> Anybody you catch outside his home—first thing you beat him with a truncheon all over his body, except for his head. Don't have pity on anyone. Don't explain anything. Beat first, then, after you have finished, explain why. . . . If you catch a small child, get out the whole family, line them up and beat the father before all his children. Don't consider the beating a right; it is your duty—they do not understand any other way. [40]

It is standard practice in East Jerusalem and elsewhere for military units to compel merchants at gunpoint to open their shops, sometimes after dragging them from their homes, to break business strikes.[41] The army also arrested fifty-two members of the general committee of teachers who struck in violation of the governor's orders. Teachers report that they are beginning to think "that the military authorities and the Israeli government intend to starve the teachers in the West Bank so that in the end they shall all want to emigrate to the oil countries." [42] The purpose of the collective punishments, Amnon Kapeliouk writes, is "to make the inhabitants want to leave . . . to make life unbearable and then the inhabitants will either rebel, and be expelled by means that are prepared for this event (as General Yariv has revealed, while condemning these horrifying plans) or they will prefer to leave voluntarily." [43] The reference to General Yariv is in connection with his comment on "widely held opinions" in favor of exploiting any future war situation in order to expel seven to eight hundred thousand Arabs. Yariv stated that such opinions were circulating freely, and that he had received information that such a plan existed and that the means for its execution had been prepared.[44] Yehuda Litani writes that a retired army officer told him that in 1969–70 there was an Israeli operation sponsored not by the army but by a "governmental body" (presumably, the secret police), with the full cooperation of the military administration, aimed at getting twenty thousand people from the refugee camps to leave the country (only ten thousand left).[45]

Palestinian educational institutions have been the target of particular brutality. To cite only one example, in March 1978 Israeli troops surrounded a school in Beit Jala south of Jerusalem, "ordered the pupils, all in their early teens, to close their windows, then hurled beer-can-size canisters of U.S.-made CS antiriot gas into the packed classrooms. . . . The students in second-floor classes were so frightened that they leaped 18 ft. to the rocky ground below. Ten . . . were hospitalized with fractures; several, according to the head of the local hospital, will have lifelong limps. Though military authorities at first denied the incident, it was confirmed to *Time* Jerusalem Bureau Chief Donald Neff by a score of local residents" (*Time*, April 3, 1978). There have been many similar cases.

Constraints on political expression have reached such a ludicrous extreme that even symbolic expression is banned. Painters are forbidden to exhibit their work because the military authorities claim that they have "political themes"—e.g., a dove breaking out of prison.[46] Or because they use the colors that appear on the Palestinian flag, whatever the theme.[47] Under new laws, the curriculum of Palestinian educational institutions such as Bir Zeit College is controlled by the authorities; the college, in fact, barely functions because of regular military harassment. A Palestinian who owns a gallery from which paintings were confiscated comments that soon "they'll pass the 'Dream Law' (security) 1980 and throw us in prison for daring to dream about liberty and independence and the prisons shall be filled with Palestinians."[48] In fact, some two hundred thousand security prisoners and detainees have passed through Israeli jails, about 20 percent of the inhabitants of the territories; "this has led to horrendous overcrowding inside the jails, and to appalling human suffering and corruption."[49] Reports of beatings and torture under interrogation, random arrests, endless harassment, and, in general, a pogrom-like atmosphere created both by settlers (who have a paramilitary status) and the military forces have become so common that it is almost superfluous to cite specific examples.[50]

Long before the state was established, the labor leader Berl Katznelson warned that the Zionist movement should beware of creating a society like the one they fled in Eastern Europe, with the Jews as the Poles and the Arabs as the Jews. His fears have largely been realized. One might, incidentally, imagine the response in the West if Russian Jews were treated in the way that is now standard for Arabs under Israeli military occupation.

Occasionally, abuses by the security forces are punished. In an *in camera* trial a major received a two-year sentence for ordering soldiers under his command to beat a West Bank Arab Communist to death ("the prisoner, who had a heart disease, died").[51] A corporal was given a suspended sentence and a $100 fine for killing a high school girl on the stairs of a private home after a demonstration had been dispersed.[52] But the military government rarely takes any action against abuses by soldiers or settler-terrorists, a matter that has elicited some comment in the Hebrew press. For example, Knesset member Shulamit Aloni reports many examples of brutality by the security forces, police, and army in the West Bank which "raise painful associations to those who had lived in Fascist Europe." She continues:

> When a Jew is murdered in the West Bank, a whole town is put under curfew (not all the citizens, only the Arabs), and investigations and inquiries are held. But when Jews hit Arab citizens no inquiry file is opened and if they investigate at all, then the investigation is done in such a way and with such speed that the guilty man will never be found. Those who maltreated youths in Hebron two years ago, stripped them naked and let large dogs attack them, were not brought to court. One of the boys died since, probably as a result of that criminal incident.[53]

The religious settlers, many of whom can only be described as racist gangsters in the light of their treatment of local Arabs, are now employed as police as part of their military reserves service. Security sources say that "they are the best soldiers for this task" because of their discipline and motivation. Often they simply refuse to obey orders from the military governor, as when the governor of Ramallah demanded that they yield their arms after a violent "police action" that they undertook in Ramallah in 1980.[54] In Hebron and elsewhere, settlers have repeatedly "created facts" in violation of official orders, with impunity, gradually extending their control over the area and, with it, their regular abuse of the inhabitants. Professor Dan Horowitz, a political scientist at the Hebrew University, writes that

> Rabbi Levinger [of Hebron] and his friends realized [even before the Likud victory] that potential violence can serve as a comfortable and less dangerous replacement for actual violence and that challenging the authority of the Israeli government by creating facts illegally pays. The Likud government only made things easier for them by giving in to them more easily. . . . Today's private retaliation operations are a hint of what we can expect in the future. They are also an advance payment on account for the battle for the main target: the expulsion of all the Arabs from Judea, Samaria and Gaza.

"We are already in a cold civil war," he writes, and it may become a real civil war if any barrier is raised to the activities of the settlers and their supporters in Israel. "One of the most astonishing things heard in recent months from a senior Israeli politician came from Yigal Yadin. 'If the [Labor] Alignment returns to the government a civil war is possible,' said the Deputy Prime Minister to Amos Elon (*Ha'aretz*)."[55] With reason, "many Palestinians have now concluded that Israel's objective is to drive them out of the occupied territories altogether."[56] They know very well that Israel will never grant them even the second-class status of Arab citizens, and take quite seriously, as they should, Prime Minister Menahem Begin's statement: "There is no Green Line. It no longer exists. The Green Line is null and void!"[57] The logic seems clear.

Harassment of West Bank Arabs goes well beyond the systematic savagery of settlers and military authorities. Not only political organization and self-expression, but also social and economic development have been blocked by the Israeli authorities. "More than $1.3 million in U.S. Agency for International Development (AID) funds earmarked for community self-help projects in the West Bank and Gaza Strip have been blocked for two years by the Israeli government, according to the director of the American voluntary agency responsible for implementing the programs." Included are projects "ranging from a rural electrification project in Nablus to an agricultural marketing cooperative near Hebron." Paul Quiring, the director of the Mennonite Central Committee's development programs on the West Bank, was denied a visa by Israeli authorities. The American Friends Service Committee has been barred from providing legal aid to Arabs in the West Bank. It had been "providing counsel, among other activities, to Arab landowners who appealed to Israel's Supreme Court against the military government's expropriation of property for Jewish civilian settlements." [58]

After President Reagan stated that he regarded West Bank settlements as "legal," a huge land grab operation was set in motion on the West Bank. [59] Dani Rubinstein writes that "the chase after lands on the West Bank has recently taken on enormous proportions and is the main Israeli activity in the territories." Lands are simply stolen, with the full cooperation of the military authorities. Arab landowners who protest at the robbery of their lands are beaten or disregarded; the military governor does not even bother to respond to appeals by the village leaders. "The military government in the West Bank is enthusiastically and brutally carrying out the territorial and security policy of Arik Sharon, with one aim: grab all that you can. . . . The authorities receive permission and directions from one of the most political Chiefs of Staff the army ever had, Rafael Eitan, who openly announces that there is no difference between Jaffa and Nablus and that in accordance with his principles the Gush Emunim settlers have become an armed militia controlling the Arabs in the West Bank." [60]

There is, of course, a guise of legality, which deceives no one on the West Bank or in Israel proper but is necessary for the benefit of American supporters of Israel, who have the task of enlisting U.S. government support for the actions of the state they portray as deeply humanitarian and governed by the rule of law. The device that is used is to declare lands that have no registered ownership documents to be "state lands." Most of the land that has been worked for many generations by the local inhabitants has no valid documentation in the sense of Western law, and is therefore readily subject to expropriation under the decree of the military regime, which states that "once an area has been declared state property, the authorities may realize the ownership over it and take any measures that seem required." Hundreds of thousands of dunams of land have been taken in this fashion since late 1979, when the government began to resort to this legal deceit after being barred by the High Court from taking private Arab lands it desired at Alon Moreh. When an area is declared "state land" and turned over to Jewish settlers (never to the local inhabitants), bulldozers immediately appear to prepare the land for the new settlers. Technically, there is a right of appeal to a military tribunal, but the measures required are far beyond the capacity of the Arab villagers. "In fact, it is a simple technique of robbery and all the legal covers and the various appeal committees are merely deceit." [61]

Amnon Kapeliouk recalls the words of former Justice of the High Court Haim Cohen: "We hold Judea and Samaria only in trust. A trustee who takes for himself the property of the beneficiaries is carrying out an act of robbery—and one of the ugliest of such acts." He reports a press conference called by Minister of Agriculture Ariel Sharon "with a smile of victory." To an American reporter who asked what will happen if the Israeli army withdraws from the territories, Sharon answered: "This is our home and our land. We will not leave this place. We have arms and a half million people stand behind us, opposing any retreat." Kapeliouk comments that Minister Sharon and the Israeli government have succeeded in "constructing a wall so strong and so high that it closes off any path for settlement of the Israeli-Palestinian conflict," an achievement for which "we shall all pay dearly in the end." [62]

Meanwhile, "the authorities accept almost anything the settlers do, all their daily harassments" of the Arab inhabitants, Yehuda Litani reports. Returning to Jerusalem, after leaving the Jewish religious settlement of Kiryat Arba, "one can see the black slogans on the Arab houses surrounded by black stars of David: 'Arabs out.' " [63]

The harsh and brutal treatment of the inhabitants of the occupied territories is not only subsidized by the United States, but is also abetted by media coverage here. A *New York Times* editorial (May 19, 1976) depicts the occupation as benign—"a model of future cooperation" and a "nine-year experiment in Arab-Israeli coexistence." The characterization, which was not untypical of press commentary, was outrageously false at the time. Such commentary was a signal to Israeli authorities that they might proceed with their repressive and often savage policies in the occupied territories. By now, the major media no longer refer to the occupation in quite these terms, but deception continues in other ways. In an editorial of December 21, 1980, the *Times* writes that "Israel's Labor Party has taken a giant step toward compromise with the West Bank Palestinians and thus challenged the Arab world to reciprocate with acts of restraint and conciliation." The "giant step" to which the *Times* refers is the nomination of Shimon Peres as leader of the party, and the announcement of a program aimed at "territorial compromise" in the West Bank in place of annexation. "The Labor leaders are betting that Israelis will endorse a historic deal: land, which the present Government claims as rightfully Israel's, in exchange for security." "For the moment, it should not matter much whether a final accommodation runs along one side or another of some barren West Bank hill or even how it would affect the administration of Jerusalem. What matters is that the Israeli people, if properly encouraged, may soon elect a government that rejects domination over a million Palestinians and annexation of the land on which they live."

The program that aroused such ecstasy among *Times* editorial writers is described in the *Times,* the same day, in a report from Israel by David Shipler. Shipler notes that Labor "has expressed willingness to partition the West Bank and withdraw from segments of it as part of a peace agreement with Jordan." Peres "vehemently opposes a Palestinian state and rejects the Palestine Liberation Organization [which has repeatedly and consistently been endorsed by popular opinion and the elected leadership in the West Bank] as a negotiating partner." He also "refrains from advocating that those [settlements] in existence, inhabited mostly by armed ultranationalists, be dismantled." Earlier, Shipler notes, Peres had "criticized Mr. Begin from the right," objecting to his willingness to relinquish the Sinai to Egypt and to the idea of a "self-governing authority" on the West Bank, because this would lead to autonomy for its inhabitants, a "Palestinian state" in all but name. In fact, the Labor party program is an exercise in pure cynicism. The party does not want to assume responsibility for the Arab population of the West Bank, surely not to grant them citizenship, but it aims to maintain Israeli control over the territory and its resources. The optimal solution, then, is to grant Jordan jurisdiction over the population, or to leave them stateless, while Israel takes what it wants. By applauding this "giant step toward compromise," the *New York Times* once again declares its commitment to repression and conquest, while offering to the Palestinians nothing but the option of resort to violence, which *Times* editorials will bitterly condemn in due course.

In adopting this stance, the *Times* closely follows the official views of the U.S. government, its characteristic posture. The reality of the occupation is rarely reported; nothing remotely approximating the actual situation has ever been depicted in what might well be considered the world's leading newspaper, nor elsewhere in the U.S. press, with rare exceptions (cf. note 35 and other references above). Events that give a glimpse of the reality are quite generally overlooked or suppressed. For example, a few weeks before the *Times* congratulated Israel for its "nine-year experiment in Arab-Israeli coexistence," the Israeli press reported that thousands of Arab workers from the occupied territories are locked into factories at night, a fact allegedly known to the authorities that became public knowledge when the bodies of three Arab workers from Gaza were discovered in a locked room after the destruction of a small Tel Aviv factory by fire. Employers report that workers are locked into the factories because they are not permitted on the streets at night. Work permits have often not been obtained, because they are costly to the employer.[64] Subsequently, the Israeli press reported the arrest of Arab workers from the occupied territories who were found living in rented apartments without a permit.[65] But while a columnist for the Israeli counterpart to the *New York Times* writes, after the factory fire, that "it is unacceptable to treat Arab workers as Black slaves were treated in American cotton fields," no word of this was reported in the *Times*, then or since, though the facts were surely known.[66] The same is true of many other atrocities of the sort sampled in the preceding discussion, or many others, for example, the fact that Arab workers from the territories are kept overnight under armed guard behind barbed wire in factory detention camps (in one case, a factory half owned by Histadrut).[67] It is worth emphasizing once again that similar treatment of Jews in the Soviet Union would hardly be likely to pass with like unconcern.

The "slave market" for Arab children south of Gaza has been vividly reported, and condemned, in the Israeli press and abroad.[68] The practices continue, still unreported here, to my knowledge. In *Ha'aretz*, Avraham Zohar reports what he saw on a visit to the region: "Only Arab children workers can be seen," some about eight years old, in the fields owned by the Jewish settlements. "In Israel proper a kind of modern feudalism has been developed so that many Jewish farmers won't have to work hard." Zohar asked a senior official of the Israeli Ministry of Agriculture whether "feudalism" existed in this area. He replied, "It is worse, there is slavery there." An exaggeration, Zohar comments, "but it is not far from the truth." [69] Similarly in Jerusalem, another "model of future cooperation" after the annexation of the Old City, Arab children from age seven are employed "in garages, workshops and small shops for cleaning the factory or the shop, for carrying messages, for preparing coffee, washing dishes, delivering foodstuffs and bringing warm fresh food from the employer's house to the shop." The Child Employment Act of 1953 states that children below the age of fifteen can be employed only as trainees or if the Ministry of Education certifies that their compulsory education has been completed. But the annexation of East Jerusalem covers only the land, not foreigners who live there, so these practices, which some call "the disgrace of unified Jerusalem," continue in full accord with the law, as they have since the unification of Jerusalem.[70] None of this is observed by Western intellectuals who laud Mayor Kollek for his marvellous achievements (see Chapter 10).

Within the Green Line, the oppression of Arab citizens persists. Again, the U.S. press occasionally covers more sensational events, such as the killings during the "Land Day" demonstrations of March 30, 1976, but the regular pattern of systematic oppression goes unmentioned for the most part. One problem of increasing severity is that development funds and land are largely reserved for Jews, as described above. Consider the plight of Faradis, a village of 4,700 people near the Jewish settlement of Zichron Yaakov, of about the same population. When the state was established, half of its 4,000 dunams of land were expropriated without notice and handed over to Zichron Yaakov, which covers an area of 33,000 dunams. Most of the inhabitants of what was formerly an agricultural village now work in the wine cellar in Zichron Yaakov or for kibbutzim and moshavim (all-Jewish collectives) in the area, or in construction or in the Hadera paper factory. The development budget from the state is about one-fifth of that for Jewish settlements of equivalent size. The village lacks classrooms, there is no high school or drinking water reservoir, no drainage or roads, no medical clinic or pharmacy. The remaining farmers (about 20 percent of the villagers) receive a third the amount of water allocated to Jewish farmers in the area. "An intelligence report by the district police warns of growing nationalist extremism in the villages Faradis and Jisr-el-Zarka, both known in the past to be quiet and loyal to the State."[71]

In the village of Musmus, a branch of Um el-Fahm (which lost most of its lands through expropriation), tractors demolished newly built houses without notice while the men were at work: "The women and children and the few youngsters who were called over could not withstand these feelings of helplessness and betrayal." The houses were "illegal," without a construction permit. There are no permits, because as in all other villages of the region, "there is no approved construction plan despite the fact that the Ministry of Interior began working out such a plan for the Arab villages in 1964." Therefore the villagers build houses for the growing population without permits, and when authorities choose, they demolish them, under police guard. The owner of one demolished house in Musmus says that his eighty-one-year-old father was beaten by police when he tried to approach the ruins. There are, of course, no development towns for the rapidly growing Arab population. In some villages, authorities agree to permit construction on village lands if other lands are transferred to the state, for Jewish use. The villages are surrounded by stony hills and other lands unfit for agriculture, but these are state lands, and cannot be used by Arab citizens.[72]

These stories are quite typical. Village borders become narrower as Jewish settlements expand, taking their land. Sometimes, Arabs are given one-year land leases (Jews receive forty-nine- or ninety-nine-year leases). The district inspector of the Israeli Land Authority, "whose job is to protect national land," then visits the village and informs the inhabitants that their leases cannot be renewed, since the land is needed for Jewish settlement, even land that they have leased and worked for up to thirty years. The same provisions apply to the Druse, who have long cooperated with the state and serve in the Israeli army, but "can only rent, not buy houses in the Jewish sector and national land is not being released for construction works for them in the villages," nor can they receive permits for building.[73]

The situation is quite different for Jewish settlers. Thus, there is much concern still over the "Gentile's Galilee," where the number of Jews is regarded as insufficient (see note 48 of the main chapter, above). The secretary of Kibbutz Lotem (built on confiscated Arab land) appeared on television demanding a new road to connect the kibbutz with the Acre-Safed road "so that they will not have to pass through the Arab villages." There is concern that the Arab and Druse villages will spread, "gradually taking over lands that do not belong to them," i.e., national lands, reserved for Jews.[74] But there are fifty-nine new Jewish settlements in the Central Galilee, "one of the Likud government's most impressive achievements," established under the program "infelicitously labelled 'the Judaization of Galilee,' " most of them kibbutzim and other collectives. These are hilltop settlements, with the purpose of putting "very clear limits on Arab, and especially Bedouin, poaching on state lands in the area, which were neglected and became a target for private Arab settlement—from tent to crude shack to stone villa," a natural development given the massive expropriation of

Arab lands, the constraints on development, and the population increase. "There is surely no reason to desist from the policy of forced-pace Jewish settlement because of Arab objections. After all, none of their privately owned lands are being taken for this purpose," [75] but only "national lands," where "national," as always, means "for the Jewish nation," not for the Israeli nation, which has no legal existence.

Where the state does not act, the socialist collectives do. In the Negev, Bedouins have been rounded up and driven away by the Green Patrol, headed by Agriculture Minister Ariel Sharon, but not to an extent sufficient to satisfy the local Jewish settlers. Kibbutzniks in the northern Negev found that the cattle of the Abu Rabia tribe were left in the area after the tribe (led by an ex-member of the Knesset) was expelled by the Green Patrol. "We have decided to take the law into our own hands," the representative of twenty-six kibbutzim and moshavim in the northern Negev declared: "We shall not be restricted by the law until we finish this business. We have decided that there should be no more Bedouins here." The kibbutz and moshav members hired vans from the Green Patrol and evacuated the cattle belonging to the Bedouins, despite their legal permit to pasture, later assisted by a group from the Ministry of Agriculture. [76] In this case, there was no pretense of a legal cover. The incident is illustrative of another post-1967 development, the rise of chauvinist fanaticism within the collective settlements, again, a predictable consequence of the occupation and the state of national conflict and oppression that it engenders.

Not surprisingly, racist contempt for Arab citizens is on the increase. A survey commissioned by General Har Even, one of the directors of the Van Leer Institute in Jerusalem, reveals that 36 percent of Israeli Jews regard the Arabs as "dirty," 42 percent as "primitive," 33 percent as "not valuing human life," while 41 percent describe Israeli Arabs as "violent." Seventy-seven percent felt that the State of Israel was doing enough for the "minority groups living there," and 80 percent held that claims of discrimination were unjustified. Thirty-six percent believed that Arabs should not be given the same rights as Jews, while over 60 percent felt that Arabs should have the same duties. Most displayed "strong opposition" to granting equal opportunities to Arabs, including access to higher education, jobs in private companies, housing aid to large families, national insurance benefits, loans for agricultural development, and senior positions in government offices. Forty percent justified preventive arrest of Arabs, but only 5.3 percent justified similar forms of arrest in Russia. About one-third of Israeli Jews "are demanding that a way should be found to encourage Israeli Arabs to leave the country. A similar proportion supports the expropriation of Arab land for Jewish development requirements." [77]

These attitudes are increasingly reflected in the system of law and administration. "The officials of the Ministry of the Interior are very tough with any members of the Israeli minorities who try to change their names, because they are afraid that they may want to try 'to appear in public as Jews,' and this may bring about mixed marriages, God forbid." [78] Recent laws permit the Minister of Interior to administratively deprive a person of citizenship without trial or right of appeal "for committing an act which constitutes a breach of loyalty to the State of Israel," such "breach of loyalty" remaining undefined. [79] Another law makes it a punishable offense to express any support for or solidarity with the PLO, including waving flags or singing of "hostile anthems." [80] Still another law forbids political organizing that endangers "state security," which is similarly undefined. [81]

Violence against Arab citizens is also on the increase, particularly in the universities, where rightist student groups have gained substantial influence and power. In the Technion University in Haifa, "unknown persons" (some, at least, from the right-wing student organization *Israel Shelanu* [Israel Is Ours; *Yesh*]) broke into the rooms of Arab students in the university dormitory "in the middle of the night and beat up the Arabs with blunt instruments." [82] Attacks on Arab students at the Hebrew University by "members of 'Tehiah' and other fascist organizations" have become extremely serious, K. Amnon (Amnon Kapeliouk) reports. He cites the example of a group that broke up a private party of Arabs, " 'because Arabs shall not be happy or dance in the dwellings of the Jews'—in the words of the head of the Student Organization." Such attacks on Arab students are becoming "daily events, and the matter is becoming dangerous." [83] The left student coalition CAMPUS issued a statement condemning the Technion attack by "a gang of right-wing thugs, masked and armed with clubs," which was "clearly premeditated" and followed the shutting off of electricity in the building. CAMPUS alleges that the police pressed Arab victims (four of whom were beaten unconscious) "to 'confess' that they had attacked Jewish students." One Arab who used a pocketknife in self-defense was held by the police for a week, "the longest of all those arrested." Police also refused to investigate the right-wing organization *Yesh*, "which has continued to openly threaten violence against Arab students, and several of whose members were arrested on suspicion of having participated in the Technion attack." The university administration responded by absolving itself of any responsibility to deal with the attackers, then handing "the attackers a moral victory by banning all political activity at the Technion for a month, including even the right to protest the attack!"[84] Many other provocations by *Yesh* and attacks on Arab students with police support, as well as university punishment of Arab students and refusal to react to *Yesh* actions, are reported by Issam Makhoul, chairman of the National Union of Arab Students in Israel, who is now under administrative detention.[85]

One of the examples cited by Makhoul is the case of Rafik Badarne, a member of the Arab Students Committee at Haifa University, who was threatened by a security officer present at a meeting of April 17, 1980, called to protest against the attack by Israeli occupation forces on Palestinian students in the West Bank. The officer told him, "We shall break up your Committee." Ten days later Badarne was arrested on the charge of having written slogans on a private house six months earlier. "He was interrogated for 25 hours, non-stop, was severely beaten and lost three teeth. During the investigation his interrogators repeated their threat: 'We shall break up the Arab Students Committee.'" Beatings of students by *Yesh* members armed with clubs, chains, and knives, however, elicited no response apart from a warning to Arab Students Committee members to get away because the attackers had clubs.

Leniency for Jewish criminals who attack or plan to attack non-Jews has been harshly criticized within Israel. Eliahu Salpeter, for example, observes that "frightening questions are arising out of the enormous gap between the gravity of the offense and the lightness of the punishment meted out by the military court" in the case of a soldier and an officer given nineteen- and thirteen-month sentences after they had stolen large quantities of explosives from a military ammunition storage building ("enough equipment for a medium-size massacre"), loaded it onto a stolen army vehicle, and hidden it on the roof of the Wailing Wall Yeshiva (religious school), with the intent of blowing up mosques, Arab public buildings, and Christian missionary institutions; they were cleared of the charge of conspiracy.[86]

The persistent attitude of the State of Israel to its Arab citizens, whatever party is in power, was graphically revealed in the confidential memorandum submitted to the government by Israel Koenig, the northern district commissioner of the Ministry of the Interior, whose jurisdiction includes most of the Arabs of Israel.[87] In this memorandum, Koenig expressed concern over developments in the Arab sector that he administers. He proposed such measures as the following: "thinning the concentrations of existing Arab population"; creating a new political party for Arabs to displace Rakah (the Arab-Jewish Communist party that has become the major Arab party, not because the Israeli Arabs are Communists, but because it is willing to defend their rights) in which the government shall "maintain a covert presence and control"; eliminating the present Arab leadership, investigating the "personal habits" of this leadership "and other negative people," and circulating negative information about them and taking other "personal steps against any negative personality on all levels and by all institutions"; reducing the number of Arab employees in factories to a fixed quota far below the Arab proportion in the area; "neutralizing Arab agents"; reducing "the granting allowance to Arab families with many children" by such means as "transferring them to the Jewish Agency or the Zionist Organization which will be for Jews only"; directing "central institutions" to "prefer Jewish frameworks or individuals over Arabs"; limiting the number of Arab students in higher education and directing them to studies that will leave them less time for political activities and in which "the drop-out rate of students is high"; inducing Arabs to go abroad to study while making it "difficult for them to return and find a job—a policy that might encourage their emigration," and so on. Earlier policies of the state, he argued, "did not take into account the Arab character, which is Levantine and superficial, which contains no profundity and in which the activity of the imagination is greater than that of the reason."

In response to this remarkable document, the former adviser to the government on Arab affairs, Shmuel Toledano, characterized it as an expression of "racial discrimination." The renowned scholar Yeshayahu Leibowitz, professor at the Hebrew University and editor of the *Encyclopedia Hebraica*, went much further, stating that the document and the reactions to it reflect "values that are nothing more than fascist values."[88] Writing in *Ha'aretz* (September 10, 1976), Ran Kislev asked what the reactions would be "if it was discovered that an official in New York State, for example, had composed a memorandum on the problem of the Jewish minority there containing expressions and recommendations similar to those of Mr. Koenig with regard to the Arab minority." He questioned whether Zvi Aldorati, who was reported to have assisted in the composition of this memorandum, should be given the post of head of the Arab department of the Labor party, as recommended.[89] Kislev contrasted the Koenig position with that of "a second school," which believes, for example, that "the process of destruction of Arab agriculture, which results from the extended process of expropriation of Arab lands on the one hand and the lack of means for modernization of (Arab) agriculture on the other, should be resisted." A follow-up study in the *New Outlook* observes that Koenig "has immense power over local governments in the north, and that his policy exists not only in words, but in deeds," which the authors proceed to document, revealing extreme discrimination against Arabs. They conclude that "the matter is perfectly clear: If Koenig does not go, and quickly, it will be conclusive proof that except by a drastic change, it is impossible to change anything in this state." [90] He did not go.

This small sample—which could easily be expanded manyfold—is illustrative of the deteriorating situation both in the occupied territories and within Israel proper. Extensive information is available from public sources, much of it distributed by the Israeli League for Human and Civil Rights and its courageous chairman, Dr. Israel Shahak.[91] Once again, it must be emphasized that the United States bears direct responsibility for these ugly developments. The U.S. contribution is in part diplomatic—e.g., veto of the U.N. Security Council peace plan of January 1976—and in part material. The economics editor of the *Jerusalem Post* estimates that U.S. military aid to Israel, though not always described as such, in fact comes to $9.8 billion since 1973, covering about two-thirds of "direct and indirect defense imports." The scale of the latter is phenomenal: "Our 'investment' in defense since 1973, including locally produced equipment and construction, probably comes close to the total value of all the fixed assets in our economy, excluding housing." "In terms of our foreign policy stance since 1967, and particularly under the present [Likud] government, this means that we have to maintain an army half that of Britain, for example, which has 15 times as many people, and to spend nearly half as much on defense as Britain, although its Gross National Product is nearly 30 times ours. We maintain more tanks and combat aircraft than Britain (and France or Germany) and more armoured vehicles." "Fully 13 per cent of our total labour force, and some 24 per cent of the male labour force in the most productive age groups, consume—and produce—security." This calculation does not include police, border guards (a substantial military force noted for its brutality and used primarily for internal repression), and private security personnel. Nor does it include "tens of thousands engaged in the production of defense goods, the greatest usefulness of which lies in never having to be used." [92] But the expenditures, however astronomical, will not procure or even enhance security. For that, what is required is accommodation, not a contribution to the cycle of repression, terror, retaliation, and war. We return to the reasons for the U.S. commitment to perpetuating this system.[93] These questions should be high on the agenda for American citizens, though, as usual, they will have to extricate themselves from a web of misrepresentation and propaganda to confront them seriously.

The statement that the "greatest usefulness" of military production "lies in never having to be used" is not entirely accurate. *Business Week* observes that "despite its 150% inflation rate, Israel is in the midst of an export boom—one fueled primarily by arms sales. The export of weapons and related items is expected to soar by nearly 70% this year, raising export revenues to about $1.3 billion. And all signs are pointing to a continuation of the trend. . . . The Latin American market has developed rapidly in recent years following the Carter Administration's decision to prohibit U.S. arms sales to many right-wing regimes. Israel has become a leading supplier to such countries as Argentina, Chile, Bolivia, Colombia and Guatemala. Other major Israeli clients include South Africa, Taiwan, Nigeria, Thailand and Singapore." Though one major client disappeared with the fall of the Shah, Iran is "now purchasing Israeli weapons again through European intermediaries."[94]

The Israeli military industry is closely linked to the United States, and is part owned by U.S. corporations in partnership with Israeli corporations such as the Histadrut-owned Koor industries. While the U.S. government has imposed some barriers on the sale of Israeli arms to Latin American dictatorships, it is more than likely that it looks with some favor on the dispatch of arms to governments that it cannot support directly because of human rights legislation. Israel has sold Shafrir missiles (air-to-air infrared homing weapons) to the Pinochet dictatorship in Chile[95] and in 1978 sold a squadron of Mirage fighters to Argentina.[96] In some cases, Israel has served as a conduit for American arms to facilitate aggression and massacre (cf. Chapter 8, note 26). Israel is alleged to have supplied 98 percent of Somoza's arms towards the end of his bloody rule; recall that the Carter Administration backed Somoza until virtually the end of the civil war, but could not dispatch arms directly. And it was the major supplier of arms to El Salvador in the late 1970s, under the bloody regime of General Romero, and continues to arm the murderers whom the United States installed and has since backed in Guatemala. The director of the Latin American division of

Israel's foreign ministry, Menahem Karmi, states that "to make the industry viable, we need the revenues from arms exports." Yoram Shapira, the Israeli co-editor of *Israeli-Latin American Relations*, says that in the case of arms sales to Somoza, "We were repaying a friend"; the Somoza family "helped support the pre-state, Zionist underground movement." A representative of the Israeli foreign ministry objects to criticism of Israel on this score: "Expecting Israel to be more ethical than other nations is one way of expressing anti-Semitism." [97]

Israel's close relations and military aid to Argentina have caused some eyebrows to be raised, in the light of the virulently anti-Semitic and, some allege, neo-Nazi character of the Argentine regime. In the House Foreign Affairs Committee debate that approved the termination of the ban on U.S. military aid to Argentina, committee members "accused the Argentine Government of condoning the burning of synagogues and other anti-Semitic acts" in the face of State Department denials and reports of "significant progress in curbing human rights abuses." John Bushnell, Assistant Secretary of State for Inter-American Affairs, "noted that since the [arms] ban was imposed Argentina had bought about $2 billion in weapons, mostly in Europe and Israel." [98] The effort to depict the Argentine regime as innocent of the charge of anti-Semitism and as curbing human rights abuses[99] has not been facilitated by the publicity accorded to Jacobo Timerman's memoirs, vividly recording violent anti-Semitism and anti-Zionism along with torture and abuse. In a publication of the American Jewish Committee, we read:

Ties between Argentina and Israel were strengthened as a result of the latter's sale of planes and armaments to the former, and an increase in commercial traffic between the two countries. Israel ambassador Ram Nirgad was very much in the public eye, appearing on television and radio. He played an active role in Argentine Jewish life and maintained very privileged relations with leading figures in the Argentine military and political establishment.

There were numerous important Israeli visitors to Argentina during 1978: Generals Hod and Gur, Finance Minister Simcha Erlich, Hebrew University president Avraham Harman, Minister of Industry, Commerce and Tourism Yigal Hurvitz, M.K.'s Zina Harman and Abraham Katz. . . . During a six-day official visit to Argentina in March, Hurvitz stated that

Israel had imported 45 million dollars worth of Argentine goods in 1977, while Argentina had purchased only 5 million dollars of Israeli goods. Hurvitz indicated his desire to strengthen commercial ties between the two nations.[100]

The Israeli press provides more details. In one two-month period in 1978, three Israeli generals—Haim Leskov, Mordechai Hod, and Mordechai Gur—visited Buenos Aires. Leskov met the head of the Argentine General Staff and "conducted discussions with him and with others." Hod lectured before the General Staff of the Argentine Air Force. Gur arrived after a visit to Chile, where he was received by General Pinochet. "Gur attempted to defend Pinochet's rule saying that journalistic accounts of Chile do not reflect the reality."[101]

After the June 1980 military coup in Bolivia, the United States, Venezuela, and several European countries suspended their aid programs in protest, but the new government was recognized by Israel, Argentina, Brazil, Egypt, Taiwan, Paraguay, Uruguay, and South Africa. "Brazil has revived dormant agreements on trade and construction and Israel and South Africa have offered military and economic assistance," according to a spokesman for the regime.[102]

Israel's partnership with Taiwan and South Africa extends to other areas as well. Jack Anderson reports that "Israel, South Africa and Taiwan will soon begin joint production of strategic cruise missiles. . . . U.S. intelligence agencies have known for years that the three nations were working together on nuclear weapons development. . . . In cold, hard geographic terms, the triumvirate's new missile capability means that Israel—which already has a stockpile of 200 or more nuclear bombs—can deliver warheads from its own backyard to any of its Arab enemies in the Middle East, and even deep inside the Soviet Union," while "South Africa could annihilate targets anywhere in the southern part of the continent" and "Taiwan would be able to destroy Peking and other cities in mainland China from secure launching sites on its own soil or from naval vessels far out to sea." According to intelligence sources, "Israel, Taiwan and South Africa probably hoped to produce and deploy their cruise missiles in secrecy." The CIA "is probing the possibility that the joint development of cruise missiles by Israel, South Africa and Taiwan was aided by high-level leaks of U.S. technology to Israel" on the part of Air Force officials who "are suspected of opposing the official U.S. policy of refusing the Israelis our long-range nuclear delivery knowhow—and of taking illegal steps to circumvent this policy." [103] What the validity of these allegations may be, I do not know.

Israel's close relations with South Africa date to 1975, the London *Economist* reports,[104] though "South Africa ran an emergency service, supplying Israel with just about all the components it wanted" when de Gaulle embargoed arms shipments to Israel after the 1967 war. The new arrangements were firmed up after Kissinger "in early 1975 secretly asked the Israeli government to send troops to Angola in order to co-operate with the South African army in fighting the Cuban-backed Popular Movement" (recall that Congress had barred direct U.S. intervention). While Israel was unwilling to do this, it did send to South Africa "some military instructors specialising in anti-guerrilla warfare plus equipment designed for the same purpose." South African Prime Minister John Vorster made an official visit to Israel in May 1976 (see Chapter 10), signing "a row of economic and military collaboration agreements that centred on South Africa's willingness to finance some of Israel's costlier military projects," while "Israel was to reciprocate by supplying weapon systems and training," supplementing the contributions of France, which "was supplying South Africa with warplanes and helicopters." Extensive military relations have since been established in warship construction, armor development, military electronics, and energy. "The Americans may be wanting to use Israel as a clandestine conduit to South Africa, much as they have used it to keep a channel open to Ethiopia's Marxist leaders," a plausible surmise, in the light of earlier U.S.-Israeli cooperation in Africa (cf. Chapter 12).

Again, the Israeli press provides more details. Israeli factories, some owned by left-wing (Hashomer Hatsair) kibbutzim and by Histadrut, were carrying out successful sales to South Africa by 1976. In 1978, Treasury Minister Simha Erlich, on a visit to South Africa, proposed that Israel serve as a conduit for the sale of South African-produced goods to Europe and the United States, under a "Made in Israel" label. The Israeli aircraft industry constructed an electronic barrier between Namibia and Angola to interdict SWAPO guerrillas.[105] More recently, South Africa agreed to extend loans to Israel amounting to $200 million on terms more favorable than those obtainable on the international money market.[106]

The *Economist* (November 5, 1977) explains that Israel fears "exclusive dependence" on the United States, and felt "urgently in need of an ally to enable it to escape" such dependence in 1975, when President Ford cut off economic and most military aid to Israel in a successful bid to compel Israel to sign the second Sinai accord with Egypt. "Ideally, such an ally should not be too susceptible to American influence; should have shared geopolitical interests with Israel; and above all, should have the resources and technology needed to help build up a sophisticated weapons industry. South Africa seemed to fit the bill," and "it was more than willing" to help. The analysis is accurate. As long as Israel, backed by the United States, maintains the military occupation and refuses to consider a political accommodation with the Palestinians, it will be compelled to forge alliances with pariah states such as South Africa. The future of such alliances is not bright, as the recent history of the regimes of Somoza and the Shah indicate. But alternative options do not exist, within the framework of the policy of military occupation and confrontation.

In the course of the 1948 war, some 700,000 Palestinians fled or were expelled from the area that became Israel, and the region designated for a Palestinian state was divided between Israel and Jordan, with Egypt taking over the Gaza Strip. Several hundred thousand more fled or were expelled from the West Bank when it was conquered by Israel in 1967, and subsequently, according to U.N. commander Odd Bull, who reports expulsions many months after. Tens of thousands more were driven from the Jordanian side of the border in later attacks. From shortly after the 1949 armistice agreement, Israel pursued a policy of encroaching into the demilitarized zones and driving out the local population, while attempting to maintain border tension and to keep the refugees well away from the border areas. These policies developed in the course of an interaction of terror and reprisal, in which Israeli initiative played no small part. After 1970, the Israeli-Palestinian conflict shifted to Lebanon, as the PLO was expelled from Jordan and Sadat's persistent efforts to separate Egypt from the conflict finally met with success after the 1973 war and with the Camp David agreement.[107] Since 1975 Lebanon has been wracked by civil war, a result of internal tensions exacerbated by the Arab-Israeli conflict.[108]

In the early 1950s, the government of Israel developed plans to dismember Lebanon. Ben-Gurion in particular was much intrigued by the prospect. In his recently published diaries, Prime Minister Moshe Sharett reports the suggestion of Chief-of-Staff Moshe Dayan that

> the only thing that's necessary is to find an officer, even just a Major. We should either win his heart or buy him with money to make him agree to declare himself the savior of the Maronite population. Then the Israeli

Army will enter Lebanon, will occupy the necessary territory, and will create a Christian regime which will ally itself with Israel. The territory from the Litani southward will be totally annexed to Israel and everything will be all right.[109]

These plans had to be put in abeyance with the French-Israeli alliance of 1956, given France's role in Lebanese affairs. They have in part been realized with the establishment of Major Saad Haddad's Israeli protectorate in southern Lebanon, which he declared an independent state in April 1979, after it had been handed over to him by Israeli forces in June 1978 in defiance of the United Nations.

By mid-1976, it was clear that Israel was providing direct aid to the Lebanese Maronite Christian forces, who saw "Israel as the only potential savior—a Jewish state that would be happy to have a Maronite Christian partner as an allied island in a Moslem Arab sea."[110] Israel supplied some seventy tanks to Maronite forces and eight gunboats, and Israeli para-troops and helicopters provided direct support for Maronite forces attacking the Lebanese town of Marjayoun, while Israeli artillery along the border "provided fire support for the Christian attackers."[111] Israeli bombardment of Lebanon was significant by 1975, and in subsequent years Israeli jets, artillery, and gunboats repeatedly bombarded Lebanese towns and Palestinian refugee camps,[112] with hundreds of civilian casualties.

In March 1978, Israel invaded Lebanon in retaliation for a Palestinian guerrilla attack in which a bus was seized, leading to the death of thirty-four Israelis in an exchange of fire on a coastal road. The bus raiders had not come across the border, but by sea, from a point north of the area invaded by Israel, and the border had been relatively quiet apart from the events of November 1977, initiated by Israeli attacks. The Israeli invasion was savage, leaving "a broad path of death and destruction" with "hardly a town . . . left undamaged. Some have been all but flattened by air strikes and explosive shells. . . . The scope and sweep of the damage done here makes a mockery of Israeli claims to have staged surgical strikes against Palestinian bases and camps . . . the Israelis have used the same tactic that the Americans used in Vietnam: concentrated and heavy firepower and air strikes to blow away all before them—be they soldiers or civilians—in order to hold down their own casualties . . . throughout most of southern Lebanon, the overwhelming impression is of silence and desolation."[113] Israeli bombing reached the environs of Beirut, where "the cream of the Israeli air strike force finished off the destruction of the crowded coastal town of Damour," leaving it "mostly rubble."[114] In Uzai, a southern suburb of Beirut, "the jets did their job perfectly, leveling restaurants, bakeries, service stations and houses for five hundred yards." Cities, towns, and villages were mercilessly attacked, causing some 2,000 deaths and 250,000 refugees.[115] For an Israeli reaction, see the remarks of the commanding general, Mordechai Gur, cited in Chapter 12, below.

In the summer of 1979, the Israeli Air Force again went into action, attacking towns and villages, and eliciting a strong State Department condemnation after an attack with U.S.-supplied jets on roads "filled with motorists returning from excursions to the beaches and the mountains."[116] "People are being bombed, rocketed, shelled and shot all over south Lebanon but their sufferings have been almost entirely ignored. . . . Thousands of people are now on the move northwards to Beirut and in all two hundred thousand have been displaced by what is simply a campaign of military terror conducted against them by the Israeli army, navy and air force and its Lebanese Christian allies."[117]

Similar attacks have continued since,[118] becoming so routine that they are barely mentioned in the course of articles on Lebanon.[119] Jack Anderson reports that "in secret cables to the State Department, U.S. Ambassador to Lebanon John Gunther Dean has long argued that attacks on Lebanese civilians by Israeli forces and right-wing Christian militants have far exceeded provocations by the Palestine Liberation Organization.[120] Meanwhile, Israeli encroachments into Lebanon continue. The Israeli Army is reported to have fenced off the Wazzani River, one of the tributaries to the Jordan.[121] Israeli kibbutzim are reported to have taken land in southern Lebanon for their own use.[122] Israeli terror attacks on the Lebanese population in the south have to a significant extent succeeded in their primary goal: embittering relations between the local Shiite Muslim population and the Palestinians, whom they hold responsible for their travail. With Haddad's protectorate firmly in place, much of the south devastated and in ruins, and Lebanon caught up in hopeless strife and turmoil, Israel's northern border is now more or less under control, though the threat of war with Syria, now partially occupying Lebanon, is never remote.

Peace along Israel's northern border was shattered once again when Israeli planes struck Palestinian targets in southern Lebanon on July 10, 1981, leading to Palestinian retaliation and extensive Israeli bombardment culminating in the terror attacks of July 17–18 on Beirut and other civilian targets in which more than 300 were killed. By the time a cease-fire had been declared on July 24, about 450 Arabs—nearly all of them Lebanese civilians—and 6 Israelis were reported killed.[123] It has been speculated that the purpose of the Israeli attacks was "to drive a wedge between the US and moderate Arabs." [124] U.S. public opinion appears to have been sharply critical of the Israeli attacks and there was considerable press criticism as well, much of it mirroring U.S. government irritation that these attacks were undermining U.S. policy. One government official stated that by the terror bombing of Beirut, "Israel has lost its special moral claim it was fighting fighters while the PLO was warring on civilians," so that "Israel has now sunk as low as the PLO" [125]—a remarkable comment in the light of the ample record of earlier atrocities, not only in Lebanon, but elsewhere long before the PLO existed (see Chapters 10 and 12).

Sooner or later, Israel will probably find a pretext for another invasion of Lebanon in an effort to administer the coup de grace to the PLO and to disperse the refugees once again. Meanwhile, it is likely that creeping annexation of southern Lebanon will proceed under the guise of "saving the Christians from genocide," with the ultimate aim of attaining control of the Litani River, a Zionist objective from the earliest years. Despite much angry rhetoric, it is likely that Israel is pleased to see Syrian forces engaged in Lebanon, thus weakening the cohesiveness of the Syrian state, which faces severe internal challenges; the original intervention of the Syrians to suppress the Palestinians and their leftist Muslim allies was tolerated, probably welcomed by Israel and the United States. Disruption along its northern border is a tactic that Israel is bound to pursue. Khalidi (*op.cit.*) argues plausibly that the March 1978 invasion and Israel's earlier support for the aggressive tactics of its client Major Haddad were aimed at preventing Lebanese national reconciliation, which then appeared a fair possibility.

Efforts to intimidate and demoralize the inhabitants of the occupied territories are sure to continue, whatever the government in power. Any attempt to constrain the Jewish settlers will be resisted; serious attempts are in any event unlikely, and might, as many Israelis fear, lead to something like civil war (see above). Arab citizens within Israel will continue to be deprived of essential rights and controlled with a firm hand, while right-wing Jewish terrorism is likely to intensify. The Jewish state will be geared for war, with a dependent economy subsidized by the United States as long as it continues to serve the objectives of U.S. strategy (see Chapters 11 and 12). It will become ever more closely allied to such states as South Africa and Argentina, while its leadership attempts to wield the moral weapon of anti-Semitism and the Nazi Holocaust, averting its eyes from the pictures of Hitler in the Argentine jail cells where Jewish prisoners are tortured for alleged "Zionist plots." The Europe-oriented elites in Israel will struggle to prevent "Levantinization." Much of the educated population will continue to emigrate to the United States, along with Jews from European areas of the Soviet Union. The internal corruption of Israeli society will increase, while American visitors laud its historically unprecedented humanity and its profound commitment to socialist democracy (see Chapter 10).

After the 1967 conquests, some perceptive Israeli commentators warned that the victory would prove to be a major defeat for Israel, which might become another Rhodesia (see note 63 of the main chapter, for one of several examples). The occupied territories are held and settled not for reasons of security,[126] but because of Israel's unwillingness to tolerate Palestinian nationalism and in order to exploit its resources, human and material. As the territories are more closely integrated, the possibility of a political accommodation recedes, even if U.S. support for the occupation were to end. Conflict between the United States and its European allies is not unlikely as the latter seek to restore and extend their ties to the Arab oil producers, which now see the establishment of a Palestinian mini-state as the optimal solution to the radical nationalist threat enflamed by the unresolved Palestinian issue. Both Israel and its enemies will continue to waste their resources in an arms race of staggering proportions, with the eager assistance of the industrial societies, concerned both to compensate for the cost of oil imports and to extend their influence in a region of great strategic and economic importance. There is no area of the world where unpredictable events are more likely to escalate to nuclear war.

The United States could do a good deal to ameliorate the situation, but the opportunities, which are diminishing, are not being exploited, and there is no current indication that the foolhardy policies of the past years will be modified.

Chapter Ten

BELLOW, *TO JERUSALEM AND BACK* (1977)

S AUL BELLOW'S REPORT of his trip to Israel is subtitled "a personal account." As such, it cannot be faulted. No doubt it reflects his perceptions. But these are alleged to relate to the social and historical reality. Here, some serious questions arise.

Bellow speaks of his "American even-handedness" and "objectivity," which so irritate his Israeli hosts. In fact, he is a propagandist's delight. He has produced a catalogue of What Every Good American Should Believe, as compiled by the Israeli Information Ministry. Everything is predictable. No cliché is missing.

As for Israel, words can barely convey its magnificence. While "territorially insignificant," Israel as an idea "is immense, a country inestimably important, playing a major role in the world, as broad as all history." Its creative people "think so hard here, and so much"—"the setting is so civilized." Despite their travail, "almost everyone is reasonable and tolerant, and rancor against the Arabs is rare." "Israel has made extraordinary efforts to be democratic, equitable, reasonable, capable of change." Its people ask only to live in peace in their little postage-stamp of a state. But the iniquitous Arabs deny them even this. They "begrudge the Jews one percent" of the territories liberated from the Turks. Bellow does not consider, in contrast, the Americans, or the Germans, who have always been so willing to offer part of their ample territories for the establishment of a Jewish state.

To compound the horror, the Arabs are backed by degenerate France, which does not care "anything about liberal democracy, about freedom." And of course the Russians, who "have established themselves as the dominant power" in the Mediterranean (without a naval base or aircraft carrier), and who have "shown little interest in ending the conflict."

Review of Saul Bellow, *To Jerusalem and Back* (New York: Viking, 1976).

If only one could believe Kissinger when he says (Bellow's paraphrase) that "if the world fails to rise to the moral test of preserving [Israel's] safety, it will mean the end of our civilization" (the safety of the Palestinians, in contrast, counts for nothing, for reasons unexplained). But the world "has grown sick of the ideals Israel asks it to respect." And the Americans, who are "spreading democracy over the world," trying "to solve problems, to help, to befriend, to increase freedom"—they are unreliable as they apply "virtuous myths" to their lives with "imbecile earnestness."

Like any collection of random shots, some of Bellow's comments hit near the mark, though there is no internal evidence to determine which. Argument and evidence are not really his business. In their place, we find snippets from Proust and Baudelaire and Ruskin on Thucydides in a display of world-weary wisdom.

Bellow asserts without qualification that "the root of the problem is simply this—that the Arabs will not agree to the existence of Israel." But matters are not quite that simple. While he was writing, the Arab states brought to the U.N. Security Council a resolution calling for a settlement on the 1967 borders, with "appropriate arrangements . . . to guarantee . . . the sovereignty, territorial integrity and political independence of all states in the area and their right to live in peace within secure and recognized boundaries," including Israel and a new Palestinian state. The resolution was backed by Russia, consistent with its earlier stand. It was vetoed by the United States (January 26, 1976), supporting Israel's outright rejection. This was reported to be a serious blow to Palestinian hopes for a negotiated settlement.[1]

Nothing of this is mentioned. Instead, we learn of some Israeli proposals of May 1976 which "indicate that Israel has not become immobile, inflexible, paralyzed by stubbornness of political rivals, or lacking in leadership." These proposals offer absolutely nothing to the Palestinians and would leave Israel in control of substantial parts of the occupied territories. Bellow knows as well as anyone that there will be no peace on these terms.

Prime Minister Rabin has frequently stated his position on these matters, as have other Israeli leaders: The Palestinians have rights only as refugees, no national rights; Israel will never negotiate political issues with Palestinians, or any issues with the PLO, which Palestinians in the occupied territories as elsewhere regard as their representative; it will never withdraw from the areas that it has been developing in the occupied territories. As for the quarter-million refugees in Gaza, they should be "transferred" to Jordan, according to Rabin, while a "natural and voluntary migration" should be encouraged from "the West Bank to East Jordan." See p. 250, above.

Bellow seems to believe that Israel's solicitude for the Palestinians is not appreciated in the West because of poor public relations. A rather different interpretation comes to mind.

To attribute the continuing conflict simply to Arab and Russian intransigence has been plainly absurd for the past several years, as Bellow could have learned from established Zionist commentators. Furthermore, the earlier record is far more complex than he believes. The Israelis of Bellow's imagination do nothing but "farm a barren land, industrialize it, build cities, make a society, do research, philosophize, write books, sustain a great moral tradition, and, finally, create an army of tough fighters." In the real world they have a few other achievements to their credit. They have expelled Arab peasants from their lands, conducted murderous attacks on defenseless villages and refugee camps, invaded Egypt in collusion with France and England, settled the occupied territories and instituted a harsh and repressive military regime within them, placed 90 percent of the land within Israel under the control of an organization that is officially committed to work for the benefit of "persons of Jewish religion, race or origin." And so on.

Bellow mentions virtually nothing of this. He does report that "Israel evidently intends to hold on to [the settlements] in an eventual peace agreement" ("the government is desperately stuck with the occupation"). And he reports an allegation that settlers have taken land from the "natives" (his quotes) with army support, for example, in Pithat Rafiach, south of Gaza. But he did not trouble to investigate what has happened there since 1972, when thousands of Arab farmers were expelled to clear the area for Jewish settlement and an all-Jewish city in Egyptian territory—one of the immediate causes of the October 1973 war. Nor does he relate these programs to the expulsion of Bedouins from the region since 1950.[2] This is only one of many examples. In short, the story has never been quite so "simple" as the even-handed Mr. Bellow would have us believe.

Bellow recognizes that "the status of the Israeli Arabs is ambiguous"; "they do and do not enjoy equal rights." The respects in which one-seventh of the citizens of the state may lack "equal rights" in this "socialist democracy" are not explored, but Bellow could have learned something about the matter from English or Hebrew sources, including some that he cites.[3]

This book contains extensive accounts of conversations with Israelis and pro-Israeli commentators, including government officials, professors, and Jewish experts on Arab affairs. There is also one Arab voice, which is granted a paragraph. On this evidence, Bellow reports the attitudes and beliefs of the Arabs under Israeli control. He informs us that they are prospering and generally content. True, there are "angry demonstrations" that "challenge the occupation," but the perpetrators "are the young, many of them adolescents." Bellow ignores what the Israeli and world press had to say about the "Day of the Land" in March 1976, not to speak of innumerable other examples; say, the attempts at passive resistance by Arab shopkeepers crushed by the army on the West Bank. Like many other Western intellectuals, Bellow seems to overlook the fairly obvious fact that Jewish experts may not be the best source of evidence on Arab sentiments. How would we react if some American intellectual enamored of the Soviet Union were to discourse on the Jews in Russia on the basis of what he was told by Russian bureaucrats and specialists on Jewish affairs?[4]

Bellow observes that in 1976 "Palestinian peasants and townspeople have become aware that the attention of the world has been fastened on their political problems" by reading the world press and watching television. Previously, "many were indifferent to the question of their political future and were in effect 'self-depoliticized' " (citing the former chief of Israeli Intelligence Yehoshafat Harkabi), and were "content to leave politics to the politicians—especially those in the Arab states," as they raised their living standards under the "mild" Israeli military government. Bellow has some criticisms. He feels that this mild regime (which has been carrying out arbitrary arrests, expulsion of Palestinian moderates such as President Hanna Nasr of Bir Zeit College, destruction of houses, collective punishments, and, according to dozens of prisoners, beatings and torture in prisons),[5] should have "encouraged" the Arabs "to create political alternatives to the PLO." A curious way to express the fact that initiatives from West Bank conservatives to create anti-PLO organizations were rejected by the government and kept from the public by censorship until revealed in 1974 by the former Israeli military commander of the West Bank (see Chapter 9, note 88).

In particular, Arabs in Jerusalem are "satisfied with the Kollek administration," Bellow assures us. Admittedly, the object of Kollek's "extensive building program is evidently to make Israeli possession of the city a *fait accompli.*" But this arouses no dissatisfaction among the Arabs and does not lead them to question his "impartiality"—the latter nicely illustrated, for example, in 1971, when he objected to the program of constructing six thousand dwellings for Jews and one hundred for Arabs (he thought there should be three hundred for Arabs). Kollek, we are told, is an "irrepressible organizer of wonderful events." One of these is the reconstruction of the Jewish Quarter in Old Jerusalem. This was once a terrible place, Bellow reports, but "Kollek is building a new Jewish Quarter in the Old City" where one will no longer see "such Jews" as are described in the horrified accounts of the past. It is also true that one will no longer see such Arabs as have lived for many generations in this section. They are being forcibly evicted by the irrepressible Mr. Kollek, who always assures us that this is done for no "political purpose" but solely "for planning and building needs"—his words justifying the latest expulsion.[6] No doubt the Arabs whose homes have been demolished are much impressed.

The one Arab whose remarks Bellow reports is the editor of a Jerusalem newspaper. With a bit more enterprise, Bellow could have discovered what the Arab press reports. For example, he could have found that attorneys for the imam of an Arab mosque (one of those crazed adolescents, no doubt) protested against his sentence of thirty-seven years (sixteen at hard labor), alleging that the harshness of the sentence was intended as "revenge and warning to religious figures,"[7] along with other examples that might cast some doubt on the satisfaction of the Arabs.

Occasionally, Bellow tries to support his remarkable claims, for example, about France, which, he blandly asserts, "prefers anything to Israel." *Le Monde* is one of his pet hates. Bellow claims that it "has openly taken the side of the Arabs in their struggle with Israel" and "supports terrorists." Two bits of evidence are adduced. First, *Le Monde* did not print a letter of Bellow's or even acknowledge it (such lèse-majesté!—welcome to the human race, Mr. Bellow). The second example relates to *Le Monde's* treatment of the Entebbe affair. Bellow reports that on July 3, before the Israeli raid freeing the hostages, *Le Monde* "observed with some satisfaction that Amin, 'the disquieting Marshal,' maligned by everyone, had now become the support and hope of his foolish detractors. *Le Monde* gloated over this reversal." Bellow is referring to a brief satiric column on the way matters are presented to the public. One day, they are informed that, following Israel's example, France must refuse to yield to blackmail; Amin is "unspeakable" and "irresponsible." But the next day, *after Israel agreed to negotiate with Amin,* "everything is changed." The public is now informed that Amin "bears on his shoulders 'the honor of all Africa,' no less." Readers are "solemnly informed" one day to denounce "the disquieting Marshal," and "called upon the next day to place all their hope in the irresponsible person so harshly flogged the day before." Not precisely what Bellow reports.

Furthermore, *Le Monde* reported the same day (July 3) the communication from Giscard to Amin denouncing the taking of hostages as "a perfectly inhuman act," and reported also the condemnation of this act by the Arab League, Iraq, Syria, Jordan, and the PLO. And on July 6, in an editorial, *Le Monde* described the Israeli rescue as "one of the most magisterial operations conducted since 1945," an "immense success" which advances "the struggle against terrorism" to a new level, in "a dazzling manner." It also published lengthy commentary defending the Israeli raid under the principle of "protection of humanity" and condemning Amin's collaboration. Needless to say, all of this goes unmentioned.

If "support for terrorists" truly dismays Bellow as much as he claims, he does not have to look very far to locate authentic cases. For example, while he was free-associating about *Le Monde,* the May/June 1976 issue of the *American Zionist* appeared with an article by Mordechai Nisan of the Truman Research Center of the Hebrew University. He is concerned with the failure to understand "the major significance of terrorist groups and guerrilla tactics in the struggle for Jewish sovereignty" in the 1940s ("not excluding civilians"). "Without terror it is unlikely that Jewish independence would have been achieved when it was." He is particularly impressed with the attack on Deir Yassin, where 250 Arab civilians were massacred in April 1948, "the major effect" being "to induce a surge of Arab emigration." He notes similarities to the present, and asks whether the minority that "was instrumental in ousting the British and assuring Jewish aims in 1948 . . . [must] . . . desist today from all efforts to secure Israeli interests when— once again—the majority is incapable of the task." He suggests that a "hard-line approach" may be justified now, as it was thirty years ago.

Bellow reports that "the Jordanians built a road over Jewish graves," one of the many Arab atrocities. He fails to mention that the ancient Arab cemetery of Mamillah, where companions of the Prophet are buried, "has been swept away, a rubble of earth, tombs and the bones of their occupants, by Israeli municipal bulldozers," to create "a garden, a parking lot and a public lavatory."[8] Nor does he report that cemeteries (along with homes, wells, etc.) are routinely destroyed as Arab areas are cleared for Jewish settlement—facts that have been reported by Israeli journalists.

Bellow is outraged that the Egyptian army distributed a booklet calling on soldiers to kill the treacherous Jews, even prisoners. He is right to be outraged. He cites this as evidence that "the West does not understand the Arab world; neither does Israel." Actually, Israel should have no difficulty in understanding. The Israeli Army Chaplaincy distributed a no less appalling booklet explaining the duty of killing non-Jews, even civilians, according to rabbinic law. It was withdrawn only after exposure in the left-wing press in 1975.[9] But of this, we hear nothing. The fact is that religious fanaticism—no small problem in theocratic states—is rampant and threatening on both sides of the border.

Bellow is no less outraged that Sadat was invited to the United States. He sent to the *New York Times* "a copy of a eulogy of Hitler written by Sadat in 1953," and wonders whether the *Times* will be honest enough to print it. As Bellow was speculating about this, South African Prime Minister Vorster was being feted on a state visit to Israel. Vorster was interned as a Nazi during World War II, not to speak of his record since. But he was duly taken to the Yad Vashem Holocaust Memorial (where he laid a wreath), to Masada and the Southern Sinai, and was welcomed with honor by Israeli dignitaries (Rabin, Kollek, and others). Will Bellow be honest enough to print this? Or to report that Israel is training South African soldiers in counterinsurgency methods? The reader may determine for himself.

Not surprisingly, Nasser plays a major role in Bellow's demonology. Thus, he did not want the refugees resettled: "He kept them rotting in refugee camps and used them against Israel." More generally, the Arab states either "deliberately exploit[ed] the Palestinians for political purposes" or "were utterly incompetent" in dealing with the refugees. The facts, again, are rather more complex. Nasser bent every effort to keep the border quiet prior to the Israeli attack on Gaza in February 1955, and even after that permitted only limited response to substantial Israeli provocation. Recall that this was long after Israeli terrorists were caught placing bombs in public buildings and American and British installations in Cairo and Alexandria in an effort to poison Nasser's relations with the West. Much of this is documented in English-language sources. It has now been confirmed by Israeli studies of captured Egyptian documents.[10]

As for the Arab states and the refugees, the U.N. Relief and Works Agency (UNRWA) has taken the view that the Arab states "opposed mass schemes of direct settlement, on the grounds that this would be contrary to the interests and expressed wishes of the refugees themselves," and have extended aid to refugees "in spite of the grave difficulties which already confronted them in providing a livelihood for their own rapidly expanding populations."[11]

Another of Nasser's crimes was revealed to Bellow when he toured the Sinai in 1967 and saw the Egyptian corpses "rotting, stinking, and liquefying." He asks how Nasser, whom he holds "responsible for this slaughter," could "bear the guilt for this." Had he bothered to look into the historical record, he would have discovered that the background for the 1967 war was considerably more complex. And he would also have discovered that "when the fighting was done Israel coldly blocked a Red Cross effort to rescue the human ruins staggering and dying in the desert under the pitiless midsummer sun." [12] "How could anyone bear the guilt for this?"

Explaining the original flight of the refugees in 1948, Bellow cites without comment the conclusion of Yehoshafat Harkabi—hardly the most objective source—that the Palestinians "mostly displaced themselves"—for example, from Jaffa. Had he looked at the eyewitness reports of Zionist historians (e.g., Jon and David Kimche), he would have found that well before the Arab states entered the civil war, the Irgun and Haganah drove most of the Arab population from Jaffa by force, then indulging in an "orgy of looting and destruction," among many similar examples.

Bellow attributes to Sartre the following recipe for solving the Arab-Israeli problem: There must be a revolution in the Arab world, "an explosion of a hundred million Arabs": "After an ecstatic time of murder will come peace and justice." These are crude and ignorant slanders of a sort that one does not even trouble to refute.

When Bellow tries to deal with an argument the results are no different than on the rare occasions when he tries to touch the ground of fact. To cite one case, he is much upset by my observation that apologists for American militarism manufacture foreign enemies to mobilize a frightened population, and cynically "exploit the danger to Israel and argue that only the American martial spirit and American military power are capable of saving Israel from Russian-supported genocide"—which is quite correct (Bellow's quote is inaccurate, but the sense is conveyed). Bellow counters with a series of falsehoods and non sequiturs of which perhaps the one closest to the topic is this: He, Bellow, is frightened by the horrors of the Lebanese civil war. How this responds to my remark he does not explain. If there is any relevance, it is that once again, Bellow reveals himself to be the perfect victim of the propaganda apparatus. Bellow's other observations on the Lebanese tragedy are, incidentally, quite revealing. He discusses "the arms from Russia and Europe" and the Russian arms "used to attack the Christians." But he makes no mention of Israel's intervention (surely with American support) in training, arming, transporting, and assisting right-wing Christian groups, or Israeli bombardment of towns and refugee camps. Nor is there any reference to the ways in which Palestinians were drawn into the conflict by right-wing Christian massacres. Again, the real world bears only a faint resemblance to Bellow's constructions.

One can go on and on, but perhaps this is enough.

An ad for the book cites Philip Toynbee praising Bellow as "among the most intelligent and imaginative of living Americans." The book, he says, will remind the reader who knows Israel "of all that he found so lovable about it." That Bellow is imaginative in his reconstruction of history and social fact is no doubt correct. But it is the second statement that captures the thrust of the book most accurately. Applied to any country, the term "lovable" is outlandish. But when intellectuals speak of a state in this way, we are on familiar turf.

Bellow has an engaging ability to skim the surface of ideas. He also has a craftsman's talent for capturing a chance encounter or an odd circumstance. Beyond that, his account of what he has seen and heard is a disaster. The critical acclaim it has received is revealing, with regard to the state of American intellectual life.

Chapter Eleven

AMERICAN FOREIGN POLICY
IN THE MIDDLE EAST (1977)

IT IS WIDELY ASSUMED that the Carter Administration will pursue a settlement of the explosive Arab-Israeli conflict as one of its primary foreign policy objectives. One of its first acts was to dispatch Secretary of State Cyrus Vance to the Middle East to confer with the parties concerned—of course, apart from the Palestinians, in accordance with long-standing U.S. government policy. Shortly after, Israeli Prime Minister Yitzhak Rabin visited the United States. On this occasion, President Carter made some ambiguous pronouncements regarding the form of a future settlement. These evoked strong protest both in Israel and the Arab states. Rabin stated on American television that Carter had called on Israel to return "more territories" than "we want to give" and that "without any qualification, Israel will not return to the lines that existed before the 1967 war." A day earlier, President Anwar el-Sadat of Egypt rejected Carter's proposal in no less unequivocal terms, saying that "we will not cede a single inch of Arab land" and that "the Israelis must withdraw from all occupied lands." [1] On all sides, it is recognized that there will be no serious progress towards a political settlement unless the United States undertakes an active initiative.

Will the Carter Administration undertake such initiatives? Recognizing the crucial significance of the Arab-Israeli conflict for the peoples concerned and world affairs in general, one must nevertheless bear in mind that this is only one issue in a complex web of international and domestic American problems in which the countries and peoples of the Middle East are entangled. It is in this broader context that American policy will be determined. A consideration of this context raises serious doubts that the U.S. government will seek energetically at this time to disturb a status quo that appears to be favorable to its interests.

Since the June 1967 war, American policy with regard to the Arab-Israeli conflict has wavered between two options. One, associated with former Secretary of State William Rogers, called for a political settlement more or less respecting the pre-June 1967 borders. Under current circumstances, such a settlement will surely involve a Palestinian state organized by the PLO in the West Bank and Gaza Strip. Arabs living in these regions have left little doubt that this is their desire, when they have been able to make their voices heard. Any such proposal has been rejected out of hand by Israel, and still is, as Rabin's recent comments once again indicate.

Under Kissinger's initiative, the United States by late 1970 abandoned even a rhetorical commitment to a political settlement and was clearly supporting a very different program, namely, the Israeli program of developing and ultimately annexing substantial parts of the occupied territories, a policy that led directly to the October 1973 war. Israel's development policies as well as numerous official and semiofficial pronouncements make it clear that the goal is to realize the so-called Allon Plan, which would integrate into Israel the Golan Heights, the Gaza Strip, parts of Northeastern Sinai with a strip of the Sinai extending to Sharm el-Sheikh (Israeli "Ophira"), the Jordan valley, a large area around Jerusalem, and substantial other parts of the West Bank, excluding areas of Arab population concentration. The latter areas would be left under local or Jordanian civil administration and Israeli military control, thus alleviating what is referred to in Israel as "the demographic problem"—namely, the problem of incorporating a large Arab population into a Jewish state—while still facilitating the flow of unorganized Arab workers into Israel as a cheap labor force.

The October 1973 war led to certain adjustments in American diplomacy, but no substantial changes. Kissinger achieved a separation-of-forces agreement in the Sinai, thus effectively removing Egypt from the military conflict, for the short term at least. The United States also attempted to incorporate Egypt and later Syria into the American global system. Previously, Sadat's efforts in this direction had been rebuffed, but unexpected Arab successes in the October war with their consequences within the Arab world led to a revision of American policy in this regard. U.S. military assistance, far surpassing previous levels, reinforced Israel's position as the dominant military power in the region. The Kissinger settlement thus made it possible for Israel to continue active pursuit of the policies just described, with tacit American support.

It is evident that these policies entail a continued state of military confrontation, and quite probably, another major war. To cite only the most obvious case, it is difficult to believe that Egypt will abandon its claims to the parts of the Sinai that Israel is intent on incorporating within its permanent territory. The program of developing the Northeastern Sinai, in particular the town of Yamit, was an immediate cause of the hostilities in October 1973. Now, "Israelis have quietly extended their national water-supply network into this corner of Sinai, which they have been populating to create a security belt," and the World Zionist Organization "has requested Israeli Government authorization for 15 villages in addition to the 15 dotting the stark buff plain." The town of Yamit itself "is planned in its initial stage as an industrial and seaside resort town of 1,350 families,"[2] in an area from which Arab farmers have been forcibly removed. Given U.S. government silence on the matter, and more important, direct material support, there can be little doubt that these programs represent the current policy of the American government as well.

In January 1976 the United Nations Security Council debated a resolution supported by the Arab states calling for a two-state settlement on the pre-June 1967 borders with international guarantees for "the sovereignty, territorial integrity and political independence of all states in the area and their right to live in peace within secure and recognized boundaries," including Israel and the new Palestinian state.[3] It seems clear that this is the only realistic alternative to continued military confrontation. This resolution was strongly opposed by Israel and vetoed by the United States. By vetoing the resolution, the United States made clear its preference, for the time being at least, for military confrontation in the framework of the Kissinger-Allon Plan over a possible political settlement. The crucial question is whether the Carter Administration will join in the international consensus in support of a political settlement along the lines of the U.N. resolution, or will rather continue to back the status quo, with all of its attendant dangers, and, of course, denial of all Palestinian national rights.

The fundamental concern of the U.S. government is not Israel and its immediate neighbors but rather control over the vast reserves of energy in the Middle East. During World War II, the United States established a firm hold over Saudi Arabian reserves—hardly a great surprise, since as the State Department noted at the time, these reserves constitute "a stupendous source of strategic power, and one of the greatest material prizes in world history."[4] American intervention in Greece was in part motivated by the same concerns. By the late 1940s, the United States had succeeded in replacing Britain as the dominant power in the region and had also effectively removed France as a minor participant. Given U.S. control over Western Hemisphere resources,[5] the United States was in effective control of the major energy reserves of the non-Communist world, with all that that implied with regard to the organization of international society.

As the world shifted increasingly to an oil-based economy, in part under U.S. government pressure, it has become increasingly important for the United States to control this great material prize if it is to be in a position to dominate international affairs. The relation between the U.S. government and the energy corporations in this regard is complex. These are, of course, the major American international corporations, and their role in designing U.S. foreign policy has always been great. At the same time, the oil companies occasionally pursue interests that seem parochial from the point of view of U.S. global planning, and they must therefore be induced or compelled to serve more general long-term interests of American capitalism.

A position paper presented to the National Security Council by the Departments of State, Defense, and Interior in January 1953 noted that the "American oil operations are, for all practical purposes, instruments of our foreign policy." On grounds of "national security," Truman called for termination of antitrust actions against the companies. At the same time, this foreign policy, for which the oil companies serve as instruments, is in significant measure designed to guarantee their profits and power.

Despite the ultimate congruity of interest, conflicts have arisen in the past and still do. For several years, American oil companies operating in the Arab world have been urging the government to modify its support for Israeli occupation of the territories conquered in 1967. They have pointed out that "our government's policy in this area was causing almost intolerable aggravation from day to day in our relations with the Saudi Government" and that American interests may be imperiled (*MNOC*, 141f.). So far, the pressure has been ignored. The U.S. government has more substantial concerns than the aggravation suffered by oil company executives and has never taken very seriously Saudi threats, conveyed directly or through the oil companies, that American domination of the region would be imperiled by U.S. policies towards Israel. The future of the region will be determined to no small extent by the seriousness with which these threats are viewed.

It is not difficult to understand why the threats have been downgraded. An assessment of the precarious position of Saudi Arabia vis-à-vis its more powerful neighbors backed by American force, and a recognition of the deep commitment of the Saudi ruling elite to American hegemony as a barrier to radical nationalist currents or Russian influence, have buttressed the belief that these threats will not be implemented in any serious way, as has indeed proven to be the case, so far. Though the status quo is precarious, it is currently favorable to the basic American interests in the area.

The major military powers, Iran and Israel, are closely linked to the United States—and to one another, although "the magnitude of the Irano-Israeli program remains generally secret."[6] At present, Egypt and Syria are trying in every way to be absorbed into the American system, along with the major oil producers of the Arabian peninsula. The "radical regimes" are accommodating to American power. The largest Arab trading partners of the United States after Saudi Arabia are Algeria and Libya, and U.S. exports to Iraq are substantial.[7] Meanwhile U.S. exports to Israel, amounting to $1.4 billion in 1976, are exceeded only by those to Saudi Arabia and Iran ($2.8 billion each in 1976, with sales to Saudi Arabia projected to reach $4.8 billion in 1977).[8] American construction companies and other corporations are reaping huge profits. Furthermore, OPEC investments in the West, with the U.S. share doubling to 44 percent in early 1976, have relieved balance-of-payments problems and help "explain the dollar's strength" and "the recovery of the American stock market earlier this year."[9] Saudi Arabian investment in U.S. Treasury securities is unofficially estimated at $5 to $10 billion, though it is a closely guarded secret.[10]

As for the rise in oil prices, many observers believe that "far from penalising the American economy, the multiplication of the world oil price created a vastly expanded market for American products in the Middle East, accelerating the recovery of the United States economy into a new period of growth and more than off-setting the additional bill for imports of oil."[11] Sale of arms was a major factor in giving the United States a positive trade balance with Middle East OPEC members in 1974 and 1975, according to figures that Smart cites. The business press has been rhapsodizing over these facts, and there is little doubt that they constitute a factor in the restoration of the American power within the world of international capitalism that had been eroding in the late 1960s.[12]

More generally, it is of some interest to observe that the United States, Germany, and Japan are "leaders in the race to supply the oil-producing nations with consumer goods and equip them for rapid industrialization,"[13] and that these countries are also the leaders in the recovery from world recession.

The oil companies face local problems as a result of continued American barriers to a political settlement of the Arab-Israeli crisis in the only possible manner, that is, with a two-state settlement along roughly the 1967 borders. But the basic long-term interests of American capitalism have, so far, been adequately served by this policy. As noted before, this is not the first time that the oil companies, despite their power, have been subordinated to more general interests. After the CIA-backed coup that restored the Shah of Iran in 1953, the five major American oil companies were informed that the National Security Council had determined that it was "in the security interests of the United States that United States petroleum companies participate in an international consortium," replacing the former Anglo-Iranian Oil Company monopoly, in order to reactivate the petroleum industry, shut down by an international boycott, and "to provide to the friendly government of Iran substantial revenues on terms which will protect the interests of the Western World in the petroleum resources of the Middle East" (*MNOC*, 69). Anglo-Iranian was less than enthusiastic, preferring as the "ideal solution" that they "return to Persia alone" (*ibid.*, 67); and the American oil companies themselves were more concerned with short-term problems involving their production facilities elsewhere. But obeying the U.S. government directive, they accepted a 40 percent share in the new consortium, thus supporting the Shah and the "national interest," while incidentally displacing Britain from another part of its former empire. Not a great sacrifice to be sure (cf. also Chapter 2), but an illustration of the role of the state in serving long-term economic interests ignored even by the corporations directly involved.

American scholars typically take such incidents as support for the general doctrine that the government simply serves some abstract "national interest" and that policy is at best marginally influenced by the concerns of major corporations. Myra Wilkins, for example, notes that "the Truman Doctrine, for instance, committed the United States to defend Greece and Turkey against Communism, and in the process created security for corporate Middle Eastern oil investments; yet, Texaco's chairman of the board testified that the promulgation of the doctrine caught him by surprise,"[14] referring to Senate testimony. How literally one should take such testimony is an open question, but it may well be accurate. If so, the case simply illustrates a natural principle, quite well supported by such evidence as is available: Corporate executives are concerned with specific problems of maximizing profit, extending market control, and the like, while the state executive, largely staffed by representatives of corporate interests, is concerned with the long-term, enduring, and general interests of American capitalism. The case for the standard doctrine would be stronger if foreign policy were not so systematically directed to "creating security for corporate Middle Eastern oil investments" and the like. As long as the state uses its power to enhance "profits beyond the dreams of avarice," [15] as in the case of the oil companies, and to secure the conditions for their enhancement, it is hardly necessary for those concerned more narrowly with business operations to attempt to intervene more directly in affairs of state.

It is often argued that U.S. policy towards the Middle East is dominated by a "special relationship" with Israel that is grounded on some moral commitment or on domestic politics. That is a very dubious assumption. In fact, the relationship has varied in character over the years (cf. Chapter 12). It was cemented in its present form in 1967 when Israel won a crushing military victory. Simply to draw the obvious comparison, the American attitude was quite different when Israel invaded Egypt in 1956. Then, Dulles and Eisenhower were outspoken, only days before the presidential election, in demanding Israeli withdrawal, which they secured in the following months. The point is that on that occasion, Israel was acting in collusion with England and France, which were still operating under the illusion that they were permitted to play a major role in regulating Middle Eastern affairs. When Israel occupied the Sinai and other territories in 1967, the American reaction was entirely different. Now, Israel was closely allied not to rivals of the United States but to the imperial power itself. As basic interests safeguarded by the U.S. government evolve, policy towards Israel will change accordingly, irrespective of pluralist mythology or moralistic rhetoric, which is regularly invoked when it serves some useful purpose.

It was to be expected that the United States should have chosen to support expansionist Israeli policies after the overwhelming Israeli military victory in 1967. Apart from its military prowess, Israel is an advanced technological society which, if it weathers its current problems, will remain a major regional power. From 1967 to the October war, its prospects seemed extremely bright, and even now it remains a natural ally of the United States. American planners have regarded Israel as a barrier to Russian penetration, and have assumed that "the demise of Israel . . . likely would see increased Soviet influence." [16] The same author observes that Israeli power protected the "monarchical regimes" of Jordan and Saudi Arabia from "a militarily strong Egypt" in the 1960s, thus securing American interests in the major oil-producing regions. The Senate's ranking oil expert, Senator Henry Jackson, is only one of those who have emphasized "the strength and Western orientation of Israel on the Mediterranean and Iran on the Persian Gulf," two "reliable friends of the United States," who, along with Saudi Arabia, "have served to inhibit and contain those irresponsible and radical elements in certain Arab states . . . who, were they free to do so, would pose a grave threat indeed to our principal sources of petroleum in the Persian Gulf." [17] For such reasons, the United States has tacitly supported Israeli occupation of surrounding Arab territories as well as the takeover of Arab islands by Iran in 1971, overcoming local armed resistance. The Irano-Israeli alliance not only protects reactionary Arab states allied to the United States, but also stands as a constant threat to them, should they make unwelcome moves. More generally, Reppa argues that "the Israeli-Iranian interrelationship— wittingly or unwittingly—has contributed to" the stability of the Indian Ocean Basin: "the quiet in the eye of a hurricane," in his phrase.[18]

During the 1960s, the U.S.-Israel alliance benefited American imperial interests not only in the Middle East but in Africa as well. Recent revelations of CIA payments to King Hussein of Jordan have emphasized the role that he and other Arab leaders play "in extending American influence in the oil-rich area during the eclipse of British power there." [19] Far less attention has been paid to reports, made public at the same time, that "secret, under-the-table CIA payments amounting to 'tens of millions'—far more than any sums paid to Jordan's King Hussein—have been regularly funneled to Israel's intelligence service for control and disbursement by the prime minister's office" since about 1960. One major purpose was "to give the anti-Communist West, through the highly effective good offices of Israel, competitive equality in political penetration of newly independent states in black Africa." [20] The *Wall Street Journal* asserts that "the purpose of the Israeli payments was to finance 'foreign aid' projects in African nations." [21]

According to Evans and Novak, these "huge Israeli subsidies" were "designed to finance Israeli 'penetration' of the politics, culture, economics and military organizations of black African states rapidly moving out of colonialism into independence." They report further that "one of the best dividends from this CIA investment came in Zaire (the former Belgian Congo)," where "President Mobutu . . . might never have emerged the victor without Israel's help." General Idi Amin is another of these successes, which did not turn out too well, in this case. Edward Behr reports that CIA payments to Israel in the mid-1960s amounted to millions of dollars and that "in the late 1960s, checks for several hundred thousand dollars each were frequently delivered by U.S. government officials to the Israeli foreign ministry in Jerusalem . . . to be channeled to the African recipients," including Amin's Uganda and Bokassa's Central African Republic.[22]

These reports confirm earlier indications. In short, both in the Middle East and Africa, alliance with a powerful Israel, increasingly dependent on the United States, has been directly beneficial to U.S. government foreign policy objectives and will very likely remain so. It is reasonable to speculate that expanding Israeli relations with South Africa and Latin American dictatorships will also be exploited to the same ends.

It is important to remember that the rise in oil prices, often attributed in the popular American press to "Arab sheikhs," in fact has only a marginal relation to the Arab-Israeli conflict. As noted in *MNOC* (5), "the leadership within OPEC in raising prices has come from Iran and Venezuela, countries which have a minimal interest in the Arab/Israeli dispute." Furthermore, the oil companies have been quite satisfied with the price increases, and there is evidence that the U.S. government may also have had a hand in raising prices. Some commentators go so far as to claim that "since 1971, the United States has encouraged Middle East oil-producing states to raise the price of oil and keep it up."[23] As had been pointed out long before by Michael Tanzer in the United States and by many European commentators, this policy served the interests of the United States in restoring its position of dominance over industrial rivals that are more dependent on petroleum imports (largly from American companies) and are likely to be less successful than the United States in profiting from the new business opportunities and petrodollar flow. The business press has not been slow to observe that these predicted consequences were fulfilled in some measure,[24] although by now the rise in price is no doubt harming the American economy as well.

The rise in oil prices was accompanied by a comparable increase in the price of coal and uranium, and in fact other commodities as well. To cite only one case, "by the end of 1973, U.S. wheat exports cost three times as much per ton as they had little more than a year before."[25] As for the prospects that prices may drop, the analysis in the current *London Economist Annual Review* seems plausible enough: The consumer countries cannot organize to this end, for one reason, because "two of the most powerful of the so-called consumer countries, the United States and Britain, are now producers of high-cost oil themselves (in Alaska and the North Sea) and they would stand to lose enormous investments if the price of oil dropped substantially" (not to speak of the value of other energy reserves). Furthermore, there is "widespread acceptance among energy experts of the fairness of today's oil prices" which "are merely what had long been expected by the end of the 1970s anyway." [26] One person's "fairness," of course, is another's "cruel exploitation," but those with the power are generally in the former camp, not only in this case.

It has been a long-standing American government concern that the countries of Western Europe might undertake independent initiatives towards the Middle East and Africa. These fears were expressed quite clearly by Henry Kissinger in his important "Year of Europe" address in April 1973, in the course of his admonition to the European Community to keep to its "regional interests" while the United States pursues its "global interests and responsibilities." Specifically, he expressed concern over "the prospect of a closed trading system embracing the European Community and a growing number of other nations in Europe, the Mediterranean, and Africa," which "appears to be at the expense of the United States and other nations which are excluded." [27]

After the energy crisis erupted, Kissinger once again (in January 1974) warned against the development of bilateral arrangements with the oil producers, although the United States did not refrain from extending its own bilateral arrangements.[28] The Washington Conference of February 1974 brought the EEC powers into line on this issue. Lieber reviews the failure of France's attempt to organize an independent European policy in the face of German-American agreement "on the need for an agreed code of conduct limiting bilateral deals." The problem facing the EEC powers was that "to follow the French position meant a serious breach with the United States, which the Germans and then the British found intolerable. . . . In the end, given America's energy resources, its economic strength (particularly its limited vulnerability to international resource and financial problems), and its superpower military-political standing, the Atlantic approach seemed to offer payoffs in dealing with tangible problems which the French-led policy simply could not deliver." Simply put, American pressures to conform to U.S. "global interests and responsibilities," strongly backed by Germany, could not be resisted. Lieber further notes that "it was widely observed that the U.S. had benefited from the crisis both economically (through her multinational oil companies and the weakening of rival economies) and politically (by the reassertion of her leadership) . . . the crisis left the U.S. more dominant and the Community weakened in its influence on issues of security, finance, and economics because of its lack of a single voice." [29]

These are factors of paramount importance in assessing current and future U.S. government policy.

The Saudi refusal in December 1976 to join other OPEC countries in a 10 percent price rise was generally regarded as a move to induce the United States to move towards a political settlement of the Arab-Israeli conflict. But here too complications abound. This policy would be meaningful if Saudi Arabia were to expand its production significantly, thus driving other producers out of the international market. Early indications raise questions about Saudi intentions. Production did in fact rise rapidly in early January but was significantly reduced in the latter part of the month. Average daily production for January 1977 was lower than it was in December, before the new prices went into effect. [30] The reduction was attributed in the press to inclement weather, but Foreign Minister Prince Saud al-Feisal stated in late January that Saudi Arabia "still has not taken any decision about increasing our oil production," while the Iranian foreign minister said a few days later that he believes "what my colleague Saud has said," and the Iranian press quoted the oil minister of Qatar as saying that "as far as I know officially, Saudi Arabia will not increase its production." [31]

One of the reasons for Saudi reluctance may have been fear of Iran. The Shah announced in January that overproduction by Saudi Arabia would be considered "an act of aggression against us," and veiled threats appeared in the official Iranian press. [32] Arab oil producers had good reason to be uneasy about Iranian intentions, not only at the moment but in the somewhat longer term. What was the Iranian dictatorship, massively armed, likely to contemplate as its oil reserves face depletion, perhaps in twenty years? While a war in the Persian Gulf is the last thing that the U.S. government desires, it may nevertheless view with some favor the potential threat posed to the Arab oil producers by the military powers to which it is closely allied. A Senate report on Iran notes that "the possibility of conflict with the Arabs in the future cannot be discounted, especially if there were to be a revolution in Saudi Arabia and the present regime was replaced by more extremist anti-Western elements." [33] Even less dramatic "anti-Western" moves would no doubt have to be weighed against the same possibilities.

The American military and economic hold over the region is, for the moment, quite strong. Trade and construction are booming. The Senate report just cited estimates that "the number of official and private American citizens in Iran, a large percentage of whom are involved in military programs, has also increased from approximately 15,000–16,000 in 1972 to 24,000 in 1976; it could easily reach 50,000–60,000 or higher by 1980." There are about 30,000 Americans in Saudi Arabia, mostly Aramco employees, and American penetration of the Saudi economy and military is extensive. Israel, a rich and extremely powerful country by the general standards of the region, is virtually a dependency of the United States. There seems to be no immediate threat to American dominance.

These are only a few of the crucial factors that lie in the background of the Middle East conflicts. The United States is not likely to attempt to disturb a relatively favorable status quo. Israel is counting on this, as it proceeds with its development programs in the occupied territories. The United States does have a satisfactory "fall-back" position, namely, a political settlement along the lines of the vetoed U.N. Security Council resolution of January 1976. As matters now stand, the risk of war is not small, and given the level of armaments in the region and its economic and strategic significance, any major war would be disastrous. Nevertheless, it may well be unrealistic to expect serious U.S. government initiatives to advance the kind of political settlement that may now be feasible.

Chapter Twelve

ARMAGEDDON IS WELL LOCATED (1978)

T HE CURRENT U.N. Disarmament Session offers a suitable occasion to consider the turbulent Middle East. Nowhere has the social pathology of the arms race reached such heights, the superpowers aside. And there is a fair chance that these armaments will be used, as in the past.

Each successive war brings new levels of ferocity and destruction. In an "incursion" that will not even appear in the list of wars, yet another quarter-million Arabs were driven from their homes in Lebanon only a few weeks ago (March 1978). General Mordechai Gur was asked, in an interview in the Independence Day Supplement to *Al Hamishmar*,[1] to comment on the reported practices of the Israeli Army in Lebanon, including plunder and demolition of houses "even with no sign that they had been occupied by terrorists." His response came as a shock even to the noted Israeli military analyst Zeev Schiff, who gave this accurate summary: "In South Lebanon we struck the civilian population consciously, because they deserved it . . . the importance of Gur's remarks is the admission that the Israeli Army has always struck civilian populations, purposely and consciously . . . the Army, he said, has never distinguished civilian [from military] targets . . . [but] purposely attacked civilian targets even when Israeli settlements had not been struck."[2]

Gur recalled that during his thirty-year service the Israeli Army had looted extensively after its attacks on Jaffa and Haifa in April 1948, had bombed Arab villages and the Jordanian city of Irbid, finally clearing the Jordan Valley of all inhabitants, and had driven a million and a half civilians from the Suez Canal area during the 1970 "war of attrition." "For 30 years, from the War of Independence until today, we have been fighting against a population that lives in villages and cities."

These observations, well attested in the historical record though rarely so frankly proclaimed, give some indication of the impact on Arab civilians of the long and bitter conflict, during which the Palestinians, among others, have suffered the fate that Israel justly fears, with little reaction in the West.

During the 1973 war, when Israel's survival seemed momentarily in question, Israel threatened to resort to nuclear weapons, Nadav Safran alleges,[3] and it might well carry out this threat *in extremis*, as might its enemies. Great-power tensions in October 1973 led to a worldwide U.S. nuclear alert. Given the economic and strategic significance of the region, a local conflict might easily explode into a general conflagration. Armageddon is well located.

The imminence of catastrophe was clear enough when Israel invaded Lebanon in March 1978. A Syrian response could have had incalculable consequences. The same was true a few months earlier. In a rare factual review of what transpired in early November 1977, the London *Economist* reported that on November 4, the Lebanese town of Nabatiya "came under heavy artillery fire from Lebanese Maronite positions and also from Israeli batteries on both sides of the frontier—including some of the six Israeli strongpoints inside Lebanon." The attacks continued the next day, with three women killed among other casualties. On November 6 two rockets fired by Fatah guerrillas killed two Israelis in Nahariya, setting off an artillery battle and a second rocket attack that killed one Israeli. "Then came the Israeli air raids in which some 70 people, nearly all Lebanese, were killed."[4]

It is quite possible that these events, typically described in the United States as a Palestinian atrocity with Israeli retaliation, were the immediate cause for Sadat's sudden offer to visit Jerusalem in November. Sadat too may have asked himself, as did the *Economist*, "Could the next Middle East war, and heaven knows what else, start at Nabatiya?"

The Arab-Israeli conflict is not the only potential source of disaster in the Middle East. In Senate Hearings of September 1973, Henry Kissinger commented that the 1970 invasion of Jordan by Syrian forces "in my judgment got us closer to the brink of a war than some of the more highly publicized crises."[5] A radical Arab nationalist or Russian-backed threat to the oil-producing heartland of U.S. interest in the region will not be tolerated by the United States. The Jackson Committee report is hardly alarmist when it states that "threats to the continuous flow of oil through the Gulf would so endanger the Western and Japanese economies as to be grounds for general war."[6]

The report is no less realistic in noting that "the most serious threats may emanate from internal changes in Gulf states . . . if Iran is called upon to intervene in the internal affairs of any Gulf state, it must be recognized in advance by the United States that this is the role for which Iran is being primed and blame cannot be assigned for Iran's carrying out an implied assignment." Thus "a strong and stable Iran" serves "as a deterrent against Soviet adventurism in the region" and "against radical groups in the Gulf." [7]

But client states may still pursue their own interests or undergo internal change. Iran, the Senate report warns, may find the temptation irresistible to seize Saudi Arabian oil as its own reserves decline. "There is presently no substitute for the U.S. presence in Middle East oil," the report concludes (112), though the involvement of European states and Japan might be encouraged "in such ways as to diminish the political impact of what may well become too great a U.S. presence in the national affairs" of Iran and Saudi Arabia.

The report notes, but does not discuss, Iranian-Israeli relations, which "are conducted far from the public view," and are based on the perceived threat of "Arab radicalism." It also alleges that the Arab oil producers show some "ambivalence towards Iran's continued military build-up from the other side of the Gulf but not the total opposition often described in the Western press" (80). The analysis seems plausible. An intricate alliance linking Iran, Saudi Arabia, and Israel under the American aegis, in part tacit and in part corroded with mutual suspicion and fear, has been the basis for American control of the world's major reserves of relatively cheap and abundant energy.[8]

The U.S. military and economic involvement, and even large-scale Iranian military intervention in counterinsurgency in the Arabian peninsula, is regarded in the West as an entirely natural contribution to "stability." It has been a basic principle of international affairs since World War II that the energy reserves of the Middle East constitute an essential element in the U.S.-dominated global system. American policy towards affairs of the region cannot be understood apart from this fundamental principle.

The Senate report deals with Saudi Arabia and Iran. The books by Quandt, Reich, and Safran are concerned primarily with the U.S. relation to Israel (though Safran's has a broader scope).[9] I know of no comprehensive study of U.S. foreign policy in the Middle East with a sufficiently broad scope to render specific issues fully intelligible.

Safran is certainly correct in emphasizing that the evolution of America's relationship to Israel "has been determined primarily by the changing role that Israel occupied in the context of America's changing conceptions of its political-strategic interests in the Middle East" (571). After the Suez war of 1956, he writes, the U.S. policy of "containing [Nasser's] influence and rolling it back . . . created an obvious harmony between America's immediate objective and Israeli interests" (372). "The United States relied in large measure on Israel to check and balance the pro-Soviet Arab states" (384), and "to counter what seemed to it to be a series of challenges calculated to erode the American position in the Middle East" (449). "Israel's role as a check on forces and potential developments detrimental to American Middle East interests reached a high point in the 1967 crisis" (582). During the Jordanian crisis of 1970, "when the entire American position in the Middle East appeared . . . to be in jeopardy, the United States was able to retrieve the situation and turn it around only through the effective cooperation of a powerful Israel," an episode which "had a far-reaching effect on the American attitude toward Israel and the Arab-Israeli conflict" (455), and incidentally led to a substantial increase in U.S. aid to Israel. Two years later the United States effectively adopted the Israeli thesis "that unequivocal American support for Israel would not, in the long run, undermine the American position in friendly Arab countries and benefit the Soviets there, because those countries needed American support against their Soviet-supported, radical, sister Arab countries as much as the United States needed their friendship" (465).

We know from other sources that American analysts regarded Israel as a "protector" of Saudi Arabia against Nasserite influence during the 1960s.[10] The most advanced military and technological power in the region, Israel—along with Iran—stands as a deterrent to Russian influence and radical nationalist threats. It is important to remember, as Safran points out, that the prospect of Arab unity "appeared quite remote before 1973" (261). U.S. support for Israel was not regarded as endangering American access to (better, domination of) Middle East oil, and many specialists even believed that "there is no lack of oil elsewhere in the world."[11] Even now, despite the fabulous wealth concentrated in narrow circles in the oil-producing states, Israel, at the economic level of a European state, is rich and powerful by the standards of the region, even in comparison with Saudi Arabia, basically still a Third World country with a reported average life expectancy of forty years and a scattered population that is largely illiterate.[12]

The Saudi ruling elite has a stake in American dominance of the region, hence indirectly in Israeli strength. The United States has rarely taken Saudi threats very seriously, for this reason. So far this stance has been fairly well justified from the point of view of American global interests.

U.S. aid to Israel has been enormous. Prior to 1967, before the "special relationship" had matured, Israel received the highest per capita aid from the United States of any country, according to Safran (576), who also notes that this is a substantial part of the unprecedented capital transfer to Israel from abroad that constitutes virtually the whole of Israeli investment (110).[13] During the past four years, Vice-President Mondale recently stated, Israel has received $10 billion in U.S. aid, more than any other country. In the coming year, Israel is to receive nearly half of total U.S. military aid and 56 percent of the outright grants, a figure that would rise considerably if the standard waiving of repayment is considered.[14] More than half of U.S. credits to Israel since 1974 have been "forgiven," a unique privilege.[15] In Iran and Saudi Arabia there are tens of thousands of U.S. technicians and military advisers. The aid and direct U.S. involvement, which takes many forms, serve to tie the regimes to the United States and support them against threats, internal or external, to U.S. interests, though the system is highly unstable and rife with internal contradictions.[16]

Traditionally, one function of foreign aid has been export promotion. In the present case, military aid to Israel inspires arms purchases in Saudi Arabia, for example. The dispatch of advanced armaments to the oil producers tightens the links to the United States, which must provide technicians and advisers, helps to recycle petrodollars, and serves as an impetus for arms sales elsewhere. During the recent debate over F-15 sales to Saudi Arabia, defense analysts reported that "the precedent would almost certainly encourage other third-world countries to seek similar equipment," further stimulating the $13 billion arms export business.[17] Meanwhile a recent Commerce Department study reported that nearly all the money paid to oil exporters has returned to the United States in bank accounts and investments.[18] All of these factors are relevant for understanding American policy in the Middle East.

Given the explosive potential of the Arab-Israeli conflict, particularly since 1967, it has clearly been in the U.S. interest to reduce the threat of war. Recognition of this fact has been the cornerstone of Sadat's diplomacy since his accession to the presidency of Egypt in the fall of 1970. His policies have been based on two principles: that a comprehensive peace settlement can be achieved on the basis of the pre-June 1967 borders (the "green line"), and that the United States essentially "holds the cards." In February 1971 Sadat offered a peace plan through U.N. mediator Gunnar Jarring, including respect for Israel's "sovereignty, territorial integrity and political independence" and "right to live in peace within secure and recognized boundaries," freedom of navigation in the Suez Canal and Straits of Tiran, demilitarized zones along the borders, etc. At that time there was no mention of a Palestinian state; to this day, Sadat has made no clear commitment to Palestinian self-determination. Israel, in response, welcomed what it recognized as a genuine offer of "a peace agreement," but rejected it, stating that "Israel will not withdraw to the pre-June 5, 1967 lines," thus effectively terminating Jarring's initiative.[19]

Sadat attempted in a variety of ways to gain acceptance as an American client state but was rebuffed, until the surprising Egyptian-Syrian successes of October 1973 led to a reassessment of Egypt's potential role in the American-dominated Middle East system.

American policy for the past ten years has oscillated between a position exemplified by the Rogers Plan, calling for a peace settlement on the green line with "insubstantial" modifications,[20] and what should be called the "Kissinger Plan," namely, support for Israel's slow expansion in the occupied territories leading to ultimate integration of substantial portions within Israel. The latter programs are analyzed in an outstanding study by Amnon Kapeliouk,[21] which was unfortunately unable to obtain an American publisher. None of the books under review deal with this topic in any detail.

Sadat's misfortune was that his attempt to enlist the United States in the search for a general peace settlement conflicted with the growing perception in Washington that Israel served as a bulwark for U.S. interests. The October 1973 war was a direct consequence of the U.S. rebuff, one of the many disasters that can be attributed in part to Kissinger's narrow vision and incomprehension of international affairs.[22] A major consequence of Kissinger's "shuttle diplomacy" after the October 1973 reassessment was to remove Egypt from the conflict, thus permitting the Israeli programs of expansion to continue. Kissinger's efforts are presented in detail in several of the books under review, with much admiration, but their basic import is missed.[23] Despite rhetorical objections, the United States continues to support the Israeli programs in practice. Next year's Israeli budget proposal recommends a 30 percent increase in real terms in development beyond the green line,[24] financed, in effect, by the American taxpayer.

There is a growing international consensus that peace is possible in roughly the form outlined by Sadat in 1971—but now, with a Palestinian state in the West Bank and Gaza—but the United States stands aloof. In January 1976 the United States vetoed a Security Council resolution along these lines, backed by the USSR and the Arab states. Quandt, Reich, and Safran mention the debate but ignore its contents and significance.[25] It is fairly clear that Israeli withdrawal to something like the green line will lead to a Palestinian state organized by the PLO, which has approximately the status and legitimacy of the Zionist Organization in 1947. Within the mainstream of Israeli politics, there is a general refusal to accept any meaningful recognition of Palestinian national rights, and with the United States backing this position, it will stand. The consequence will be military confrontation, with all that it entails: the danger of war for those directly concerned and the world at large, and the corrosive effects of militarism, chauvinism, and intensifying hatred in the warring societies.

The immediate backgrounds of this situation, but not these conclusions, are discussed by Reich, Quandt, and Safran. Reich's *Quest for Peace* is a narrowly focused, well-researched diplomatic history giving a virtually day-by-day account of U.S.-Israeli interactions from 1967 to 1976. Its assumptions are the standard ones in American foreign policy studies. Thus, the "American assumption of responsibility in the Middle East" is taken as the natural order of things (would one speak in the same way of "Russian responsibility in Eastern Europe"?), and U.S. policy is generally described in defensive terms: averting "hostile domination" or a Russian "expansionary role in the Middle East" (17,36). Though there is little attempt to explore issues in any depth, the work is nevertheless useful as a reference.

Reich's final conclusion is that "the euphoria that characterized U.S.-Israeli relations in much of the period between the June [1967] and October [1973] wars has been replaced by a greater uncertainty," though the "special relationship" persists (403). That seems an accurate assessment. The reasons are easy enough to discern through the veil of alleged moral concerns and idealistic support for freedom and democracy. In an earlier footnote, Reich cites Moshe Dayan's August 1973 observation that "the total balance of forces is in our favor and this outweighs all other Arab considerations and motives." Israel will "forge ahead" in the coming years (239–40). These assumptions were shared in the United States. Quite generally, American support for Israel corresponds to perceived Israeli strength and usefulness in maintaining U.S. interests in the Middle East.

Quandt surveys the same decade, in less detail, bringing out the central issues somewhat more clearly. Currently (1978) in charge of Middle Eastern affairs on the National Security Council staff, where he also served between 1972 and 1974, Quandt relies on public sources for the most part and gives an often enlightening account of evolving American strategies. Again, the analytic perspective is limited. Quandt concentrates on "the key role of the president and his advisers." He is skeptical of analyses that do not emphasize such factors as "the psychology of decision making," about which he has nothing to say. Americans are said to value a certain "type of stability," nowhere analyzed, and the government prefers regimes "viewed as moderate, status quo powers" (16). The term "moderate," as he points out elsewhere (298), simply means "pro-American," and he does not explore the vision of the status quo that the government seeks to preserve. Presumably, it does not include the status quo in Cuba, Indochina, Angola, or Eastern Europe, for example.

Quandt is also skeptical of attempts to find "the 'real causes' behind events" and "nonobvious connections," as in what he calls "Marxist approaches," which "often fail lamentably," he claims, "from the standpoint of science and psychology" (8). It is unclear what he means by "Marxist approaches" and he tells us nothing about "the standpoint of science and psychology." Specifically, "United States support for Israel has also been difficult for Marxists to explain" (7), presumably because this support allegedly does not accord with "the concrete economic interests of the United States in the Middle East," which "lie in the Arab world, not in Israel."

This kind of rhetoric merits comment only because of its prevalence in academic social science. No "Marxists" or "Marxist approaches" are ever identified, though Quandt outlines the gyrations that "Marxists" are driven to in an effort to defend their theories, which he claims are "simply indefensible on empirical grounds." Without awareness of the self-contradiction, he himself provides empirical grounds for these theories and in fact, in scattered and unsystematic remarks, reaches conclusions akin to those he ridicules.

For example, Quandt's unnamed "Marxists" argue that U.S. policy should "try to minimize the United States relationship with Israel and to concentrate its attention on the Arab oil-producing states instead." He concedes that "American policy throughout the 1950s followed this pattern rather closely." But he thinks that a problem arises for "Marxists" in that from 1967, "despite the growing importance of Arab oil, United States support for Israel increased enormously." Quandt's "Marxists" therefore seek a "new explanation," claiming that "by defeating Nasser, Israel opened the way for the conservative Arab countries such as Saudi Arabia, Libya, and Kuwait to use their financial resources to neutralize the threat to their societies from Nasser's Egypt."

Note first that it would be a rather stupid "Marxist" who would not offer this "new explanation" as an application of the same theory to changed circumstances: The theory that the United States seeks to maximize its control over energy remains intact. What of the validity of this "new explanation"? Though Quandt seems to be dismissing it, he nevertheless notes that the chief of Israeli intelligence, visiting Washington in May 1967, gained the impression that "if Israel were to act on her own, and win decisively, no one in Washington would be upset" (57), and that was feared in Washington that "any increase in Nasser's prestige would eventually bring pressure to bear on the oil-rich Arab countries, such as Saudi Arabia and Libya" (70); evidently, Israel's victory substantially diminished Nasser's "prestige." In a backhanded way, Quandt appears to accept the "new explanation" as reasonable, thus confirming the unchanged "Marxist theory" from which it derives.[26]

Quandt also points out that "the mood of the late 1960s was one of comparative optimism regarding oil" and there was little fear of "blackmail and pressure" (13), so that presumably U.S. support for Israel did not prejudice the primary U.S. interest. By 1969, there was a "feeling that U.S.-Arab relations were growing in importance because of oil" (171), but the Jordanian crisis of 1970 led to "an unusually cooperative phase in [the] often troubled relationship" between the United States and Israel because Israel was seen as a "strategic asset," blocking threats to the oil-producing centers; he notes "nearly a tenfold increase in aid" to Israel at this point (163).[27] Again, the "Marxist theory" seems vindicated.

After the Jordanian crisis, Quandt observes, "the U.S.-Israel relationship came to be seen as the key to combating Soviet influence in the Arab world and attaining stability" (106). Later it was felt that "it was the American special relationship to Israel that compelled the Arabs to deal with Washington instead of Moscow when it came to diplomacy" (285). Why any of this should prove an embarrassment to "Marxists," Quandt does not explain. Indeed, the causes do not seem very "hidden," when ideological blinders are removed. It is unfortunate that Quandt makes no systematic effort to explore any of these issues. The causes seem particularly obvious when we decode the mystical term "stability" and recognize that the phrase

"Soviet influence" is being employed in its customary fashion (see the Introduction to this volume and Chapters 7 and 8). Then Quandt's observation translates as follows: "the U.S.-Israel relationship came to be seen as the key to maintaining U.S. dominance over the region," including its incomparable petroleum resources.

A closer reading tends to reinforce the "Marxist" analysis still further. U.S.-Israeli relations, Quandt notes, deteriorated somewhat in the late 1960s as support for Israel appeared somewhat of an embarrassment for U.S. policy, flourishing after the Jordanian events of 1970 when it was believed "that stability in the Middle East was ensured by Israeli military predominance" (120f.,200). Arab successes in October 1973 caused a modification in the "prevailing attitude" (201), with corresponding modification of policy—all as the "Marxist" theory would predict.[28]

Quandt's logic, throughout this discussion, is deeply flawed. He argues that one might suppose policies to be based on "a stable national interest" insofar as they "seem invariant," but that policy reversals defy such analysis (15). Here one must, he claims, turn to public opinion, cultural style, the psychology of decision-making, etc. But without reference to these factors, one might argue consistently that as the situation changes—e.g., after the Israeli victory of 1967 or Israel's service to American interests in 1970—the very same "national interest" perspective (itself a mystification) in favor of nebulous cultural and psychological factors is without empirical or logical grounds. His "case studies" contain much of interest, but remain in effect a collection of unanalyzed data—though their import seems rather clear.

Quandt concludes by citing the 1975 Brookings Institution study as a possible "framework for peace." This study (endorsed by Zbigniew Brzezinski, among others) called for Palestinian "self-determination" and a settlement essentially along the green line, in accord with the general international consensus, a position so far rejected by the American government, and of course Israel.

Safran's book is an ambitious review of American-Israeli relations and of the social, political, economic, and military history of Israel. Safran is less reserved in drawing general conclusions than Quandt or Reich. Some of these have already been noted. Often his conclusions seem to me to have merit, but he offers so little documentation that they carry little conviction. One would like to know more about the nature of the evidence, e.g., that the intervention of Transjordan in the 1948 war "provoked other jealous Arab countries to send in their armies as much to block its expansion as to fight the Jews" (342) or that Israel threatened to employ nuclear weapons in October 1973, raising the haunting prospect in later years that U.S. pressure might drive it "to resort to a nuclear strategy" (489, 549; see note 3).

Safran too was a signer of the Brookings Institution report, but he does not evaluate its prospects in the light of Israel's interest "in a settlement only to the extent that it would satisfy certain undefined territorial demands that it deemed essential for its national interest" (505), and its refusal to contemplate any meaningful form of Palestinian self-determination. He foresees a "severe confrontation between the Carter administration and the new [Begin] regime in Israel" (569). He does not examine the likelihood that the United States will modify its tacit support for Israel's expansionist policies, or, indeed, the opportunities available in view of possible consequences, given Israel's military capacities and options, a matter that has caused some concern in the Pentagon, to judge by recent articles in the *Armed Forces Journal*.

Safran's lack of appreciation for the plight of the Palestinians is evident throughout. Thus he writes of "the broad humanitarian impulse that had moved statesmen in London to adopt a decision of principle in favor of the Jews" in issuing the Balfour Declaration (28), and explains U.S. support for Israel on grounds of the "long tradition of sympathy for peoples striving for nationhood and independence generally and for persecuted peoples in particular" (572)—so well exemplified in Latin America and Southeast Asia, for example. Why "humanitarian" commitments and sympathy for persecuted peoples did not manifest themselves in a concern for the inhabitants of Palestine in 1917 and do not for their scattered and oppressed remnants today, he does not explain.[29] In fact, all of this talk is standard academic sentimentality and ideological claptrap.

Similarly, in discussing Israeli policy towards the Arabs, Safran notes the expropriation of Arab lands and the fact that 92 percent of the area within the green line is administered by the National Land Authority, but fails to add that this authority is, by law, under the control of the Jewish National Fund (JNF), which is committed by its charter to discriminate against non-Jewish citizens, a fact that puts matters in a rather different light.[30] He notes that JNF deeds preclude hired labor, but there is more to the story, which has been very little studied. Copies of leases have proven difficult to obtain, but it is a fact that some, at least, specifically prohibit only non-Jewish labor, a crucial difference.[31] His statement that Israel "has no masses of land-hungry peasants confronting a few big landowners" is technically correct; dispossessed land-hungry Arabs are a minority, not a mass, of the total population, and it is the JNF-controlled Land Authority, not private landowners, that they confront. But the statement is surely misleading. Safran's further claim that by the early 1960s, though Arabs "still suffered the agonies of identity and alienation," they "made up a generally free, prosperous, healthy, educated community" is difficult to reconcile with the few studies that have actually dealt with the forced proletarianization of Arabs, the complex network of devices that direct development funds and restrict land use to Jews, the state of Arab education, and other crucial matters that he ignores, though there is literature on the subject, discussed in Chapter 9, above.

Safran's investigation of international affairs, while unusual in its attempt at fairness, still is distorted by the strong pro-Israel, anti-Arab bias of most of the English-language literature. Consider, for example, his account of the events leading to the 1956 Israeli-French-British attack on Egypt. He states that Nasser's attitude shifted in 1955–56 "from one of apparent moderation to one that seemed bent on mobilizing Egypt's military resources and leading the Arab countries in an assault on Israel" (168); the apparent willingness of the Arab states "to accept a Jewish state" changed in the mid-1950s to a commitment "to eliminate that state" (225). He offers no explanation for this change in attitude. Nasser repeatedly identified the Israeli raid in the Gaza Strip in February 1955, shortly after Ben-Gurion's return to office, as the occasion for his policy reassessment.[32]

Safran does cite the "raid on Gaza in which nearly forty Egyptian soldiers were killed" (and also civilians, Love reports), but describes it as "retaliation" for the hanging of two saboteurs of an Israeli ring engaged in arson and bombing in Egypt. He states that it only became known six years later that "the spying-sabotage adventure had in fact been mounted by Israeli intelligence" (351). But surely the Israeli government knew that the Egyptian charges were valid, despite the public show of outrage. Extracts from Prime Minister Moshe Sharett's journal published in the Hebrew press in 1974 indicate clearly that he understood what had happened,[33] and surely other high government officials were aware of the facts. Safran's explanation of the Gaza raid as "retaliation" is senseless. Here, as elsewhere, the failure to cite relevant documentary evidence is a serious flaw.

Safran again ignores crucial documentary evidence when he reports fedayeen terror raids and Israeli retaliation prior to the outbreak of the 1956 war (similarly Reich, p. 32). The Israeli Arabist Ehud Yaari published an important collection of captured Egyptian and Jordanian documents which offers strong support for the thesis advanced by Love, based on Arab sources, that Egypt had been making serious efforts to prevent infiltration prior to the Gaza attack, and that the fedayeen groups, organized only after the Gaza raid, were again controlled in the summer of 1956 in an effort to calm the border.[34] This material has yet to be discussed in the English-language literature, to my knowledge, though Amnon Kapeliouk has written about it in *Le Monde*. It simply will not do merely to state, as Safran does, that the sabotage and terror attacks of the fedayeen organized by Egyptian intelligence in 1955–56 "contributed significantly to Israel's decision to go to war in 1956 and was the principal reason for its refusal to evacuate the Gaza Strip until it had obtained some international assurances that fedayeen action would not be renewed" (266). This is far from the whole story. Israeli initiatives played a major role—perhaps *the* major role—in maintaining and intensifying the level of tension and violence. These examples are typical of major flaws in the general account that Safran and many others present, ignoring crucial evidence.

Uri Davis is an Israeli anti-Zionist who was jailed in the 1960s for participating in the resistance of an Arab village in the Galilee to the expropriation of its land, under the guise of military necessity, for the establishment of the city of Karmiel, from which Arabs are excluded. He describes his book as an "anthropological study."[35] It is carefully documented from Hebrew-language and other sources, and includes a glossary with valuable information on Israeli institutions, some personalities, and other topics. He presents a revealing "kinship analysis" of leading elements in Israeli society and an analysis of industrial and economic structure.

Bitterly critical of the entire Zionist enterprise, Davis presents a scathing indictment of Zionist ideology, institutions, and culture. He describes the opposition to the rescue of European Jews except within the context of Zionist aims. (Cf. also Chapter 9, above, note 29.) The kibbutzim he regards as providing the "managerial elite of the Labour Zionist effort," relying heavily on "Oriental-Jewish hired labour from the surrounding *moshav* and development town hinterland" (28, 120), and more recently Arabs. He provides statistical data and press accounts of working conditions. He believes that the Oriental Jews are permanently relegated to second-class status, their culture and history obliterated, and sees them as potential allies for the

Palestinian movement if the latter can change its political character in a so-
cialist-internationalist direction—a doubtful prospect. Davis regards Israel
as "a completely dependable local ally to the United States," though not
necessarily a "docile" ally, because of "its position as a colonial society in
confrontation with a native Palestinian-Arab population and the neigh-
bouring Arab states" (108, 114). He expects it to play a central role if the
United States determines to intervene directly in the oil-producing regions.

Given the prevailing political culture in the United States, such studies as
this are unlikely to be granted any attention. That is a pity. Whether one
agrees with the thrust of Davis's analysis or not, it is a serious and provocative study, which will repay careful scrutiny.

David Hirst, who has been Middle East correspondent for the *Manchester
Guardian* for twenty years, intends to tell "the other side of the story," re-
dressing the balance of the English-language, particularly American, literature, "overwhelmingly Zionist in sympathy or inspiration." [36] He describes
the abortive efforts of the Palestinians to resist what they saw as a European
colonization that aimed to drive them from their homes or reduce them to a
barely tolerated minority in their native land. The book has been banned in
Jordan because of its allegation that Jordan requested Israeli cooperation
during the 1970 war,[37] and for all the attention it has received in the United
States, it might just as well have been banned here as well.

Hirst reviews the early Zionist goal of removing the native population, a
recurrent theme throughout this history, and the impact of Jewish settlement on the peasant society compelled by land sales, Arab usurers, the Jewish boycott of Arab labor and produce, and deteriorating social conditions to
flock to the cities where "many of them ended up as labourers building
houses for the immigrants they loathed and feared," living in squalor and
despair. He discusses the bitter peasant revolt of 1936–39, put down by the
British with thousands of Arabs killed, and the murderous terrorism of both
Jews and Arabs, particularly the postwar Zionist terrorism and the military
operations of 1948 that led to what Chaim Weizmann called "a miraculous
clearing of the land: the miraculous simplification of Israel's task." Safran's
more conservative estimate is that about half of the 700,000 Arab refugees
were expelled.[38] Hirst also emphasizes some further aspects of the "special
relationship" between Israel and the West, including Western willingness
to credit clumsy fabrications regarding the flight of refugees and British
government complicity in Zionist terror.

This record, partisan though documented and accurate to my knowledge,

offers a valuable corrective to the flood of propaganda about Arab terrorism—which Hirst reports and condemns—that inundates the English-
language press, journals, and books. Hirst notes that the perpetrators of the
terrorist acts of that period are now honored in Israel. He is quite correct.
The commander of the major terrorist army is prime minister, the speaker
of the Knesset was a commander of the group that assassinated U.N. mediator Folke Bernadotte, among other atrocities, and the secretary-general of
the Jewish Agency is a man who murdered several dozen Arab civilians
under guard in an undefended Lebanese village during the land-clearing
operations of October 1948—he was sentenced to seven years in prison but
was quickly amnestied, then granted a second amnesty which "denies the
punishment and the charge as well," and later granted a lawyer's licence by
the Israeli Legal Council on grounds that his act carried "no stigma."[39]

Terrorism is no invention of the Palestinians, as hypocritical commentators now pretend. The U.S.-Israel position that the PLO is no fit partner for
negotiations because it condones terror can only be dismissed with contempt.[40]

Hirst reviews the later history as well: the expulsion of thousands of
Bedouins, the terror, reprisals, and wars, the further expulsion of hundreds
of thousands from the West Bank in 1967, the growth of the Palestinian
movements with their own terror and torment. The book ends on a suitably
gloomy note with an excerpt from the *Jerusalem Post* on the "only alternative to our gradual destruction by arms race," namely, a nuclear deterrent
which "may wipe out the *entire area,* or it may not."

Hirst gives an accurate account of Zionism as perceived by its victims, a
standpoint rarely adopted, or even regarded as comprehensible, in the West.
The Palestinians have never understood the moral basis for the demand by
Americans and others that they must bear the burden of compensating the
Jews of Europe for their savage persecution. Dispersed and reviled, oppressed everywhere, their story is one of unremitting tragedy. However one
may adjudicate conflicting claims, it is callous hypocrisy to prate of "moral
impulses" and "humanitarian commitments" while ignoring their fate and
denying their claim to human and national rights.

As noted, Hirst's account is frankly partisan, intended as a corrective to an
unbalanced record rather than as a full-scale history. At times, this leads to
distortion. For example, the Jewish victory in 1948 was not so simple an affair as he makes it out to be; there were times when the survival of the Jew-

ish settlement seemed far from certain. But this is a book that Americans concerned with the Middle East should read and think about with care.

One of the sources on which Hirst relies is the study of Palestinian nationalism by the Israeli scholar Yehoshua Porath, the first volume of which appeared in 1974. The second volume carries the record through the 1936–39 rebellion and the 1939 White Paper.[41] This judicious and scholarly study breaks new ground in exploring the complex strands of evolving Palestinian nationalism. The second volume traces the abortive political effort to achieve self-governing institutions in Palestine in the face of British and Zionist opposition, and the growing opposition to Jewish immigration, leading to general strike and rebellion when it had become obvious that there was "no real chance of effecting any significant change in the British policy in Palestine through peaceful means" (159) and that Palestinian Arabs were destined to "become a minority community of no significance in the country where they had constituted the overwhelming majority" (140).

Porath observes that "the effect of the dreadful situation of the Jews in Germany and Poland on the British Parliament was totally overlooked by the Arabs" (158), which is perhaps not too surprising; we may add that this dreadful situation was ignored in the West quite generally.[42] Every effort at resistance came to naught. The general strike was exploited by the Jewish leadership to open "new horizons for the implementation of the Jewish policies of economic self-sufficiency and 'Hebrew Labour'," for what Ben-Gurion called "economic liberation" for the Jewish settlement (175). A wave of violent attacks on Jewish settlers soon became a revolt against the British, suppressed after bloody warfare and "the pan-Arabisation of the Palestine problem" (225) as the native leadership came to recognize its limitations.

The partition proposal of the 1937 Royal Commission was rejected "with deep indignation" (228). A subsequent campaign of terror against Jews, "moderate Arabs," and British officials led to Jewish reprisals and the outlawing of the Arab national organizations by the British. The Munich agreement of September 1938 allowed the British to send sufficient military force to suppress the rebellion, with ample brutality. Seriously weakened by internal struggle and unable to face the military forces arrayed against it, the revolt collapsed.

In a careful analysis, Porath concludes that "the Revolt was carried out mainly by Muslim villagers of the lower strata." It was a national revolt, "devoid of any social ideology" (264–65), though the tactics employed (e.g., cancellation of rents and a debt moratorium) reveal some "class animosities" (267). Porath concludes that the failure of the revolt confirms the Leninist thesis that there can be "no revolutionary action without revolutionary ideology and a revolutionary party" (269).

Porath estimates that no more than several thousand Arab families were evicted through land purchase, though the political repercussions were significant: "It is no coincidence then that the main centres of the 1936–9 Revolt were close to the main areas of Jewish colonisation" (297).

Porath's study is uniquely significant in the insight it provides. There is no comparable study of Zionist policies in Palestine during the same period, or the interactions between Jewish and Palestinian national movements.

One can hardly view the prospects in the Middle East without grim forebodings. The United States shows little inclination to recognize Palestinian rights, specifically, the right of national self-determination, and is, for the present at least, not under serious pressure from the Arab states to change its stance in this regard. With continued American backing, Israel will no doubt continue to temporize, on the assumption that after "seven lean years," as Prime Minister Rabin used to say, the significance of Arab oil will decline and Israel will remain as an advanced industrial society, closely tied to the Western capitalist democracies and the most viable society in the Middle East. How it will come to terms with a growing Arab minority remains to be seen. The temptation to "encourage" emigration will very likely increase. "Transfer" of the population has long been a motif of Zionist thinking, and Arab hostility and terror will continue to provide excuse and opportunity. The successive waves of expulsion, often but not only in the course of war, offer a precedent that will seem ever more appealing as the bitter conflict persists.

For the Arab world at large, the future also looks very dim. In an interview published in Beirut, French economist Maurice Guernier, one of the founders of OECD and the Club of Rome, offered a grim prognosis.[43] If the wealth of the oil states is not invested for industrial development in the next thirty years, he warned, the Arab world may not survive into the twenty-first century. This "is the region with the fewest resources in water and in cultivable land" and is even now incapable of feeding its rapidly growing population, many living in subhuman conditions. Even Saudi Arabia "will cease to exist" if current tendencies persist, while Egypt faces imminent disaster. The Arab world, and Africa as well, are "heading for tragedy." The situation is far worse even than India, where it is "catastrophic enough." A rational investment policy in the next few decades might avert disaster, but nothing of the sort is being pursued, and the persistence of the Arab-Israeli conflict, not to speak of the abominable internal social organization of the Arab states, virtually precludes the required effort. In a generation there may be a tragedy of colossal proportions as the Arab world, impoverished and lacking basic resources, will have lost its sole opportunity to enter the stage of modern history or even to guarantee survival for hundreds of millions of people.

Israeli writers have warned of a "Samson complex"; they will die with the Philistines, if need be. As the scale of the impending disaster becomes clearer in the coming years, Arab states armed to the teeth by the superpowers and probably possessing nuclear weapons may also decide to bring down the Temple walls.

Apart from considerations of simple humanity, even narrow self-interest dictates that the Arab-Israel conflict must be settled, with the recognition and safeguarding of the national rights of Palestinians and Jews. This will offer no guarantee, surely, of lasting peace or justice, or of sane policy within the few years of grace granted the Arab world. But it will at least eliminate one fundamental barrier to decent existence and to the efforts that are essential if indescribable calamities are to be avoided.

Chapter Thirteen

THE UNITED STATES AND EAST TIMOR (1980)

W HY SHOULD WE DEVOTE attention to East Timor, a small and remote place that most Americans have never even heard of? There are two reasons, each more than sufficient. The first is that East Timor has been, and still is, the scene of enormous massacres and suffering. Many of the terrible things that happen in the world are out of our control. We may deplore them, but we cannot do very much about them. This case is quite different, hence far more important. What has happened and what lies ahead are very much under our control, so directly that the blood is on our hands. The second reason is that by considering what has happened in East Timor since 1975, we can learn some important things about ourselves, our society, and our institutions. If we do not like what we find when we look at the facts—and few will fail to be appalled if they take an honest look—we can work to bring about changes in the practices and structure of institutions that cause terrible suffering and slaughter. To the extent that we see ourselves as citizens in a democratic community, we have a responsibility to devote our energies to these ends. The recent history of Timor provides a revealing insight into the policies of the U.S. government, the factors that enter into determining them, and the ways in which our ideological system functions.

The bare facts are as follows.[1] East Timor was a Portuguese colony. The western half of the island of Timor, a Dutch colony, became part of Indonesia when Indonesia gained its own independence. After the Portuguese revolution of 1974, several political parties emerged in East Timor, of which two, UDT and Fretilin, had significant popular support. In August 1975, an attempted coup by UDT, backed and perhaps inspired by Indonesia, led to a brief civil war in which two to three thousand people were killed. By early

September, Fretilin had emerged victorious. The country was open to foreign observers, including representatives of the International Red Cross and Australian aid organizations, journalists, and others. Their reactions were quite positive. They were impressed by the level of popular support and the sensible measures of agricultural reform, literacy programs, and so on that were being undertaken. The outstanding Australian specialist on East Timor, James Dunn, describes Fretilin at the time as "populist Catholic." These facts are significant, in the light of subsequent allegations to which we turn below.

The territory was then at peace, apart from Indonesian military attacks at the border and naval bombardment. Indonesian military harassment began immediately after the Fretilin victory in September, including a commando attack that killed five Australian journalists, a clear and well-understood warning to foreigners that the Indonesian military wanted no one to observe what it was contemplating. Fretilin requested that Portugal take responsibility for the process of decolonization and called on other countries to send observers, but there was no response. Recognizing that international support would not be forthcoming, Fretilin declared independence on November 28, 1975. On December 7, Indonesia launched a full-scale invasion, capturing the capital city of Dili. The attack took place a few hours after the departure of President Gerald Ford and Henry Kissinger from Jakarta. There is no serious doubt that the United States knew of the impending invasion and specifically authorized it. Ford conceded as much in an interview with Jack Anderson, while claiming ignorance of the exact circumstances.[2]

The invading Indonesian army was 90 percent supplied with U.S. arms. In congressional hearings, government representatives testified that the United States had imposed a six-month arms ban in response to the invasion, but this was so secret that Indonesia was never informed about it. Arms continued to flow, and in fact new offers of arms were made, including counterinsurgency equipment, during the period of the "arms ban," as was conceded by Administration spokesmen when the facts were exposed by Cornell University Indonesian specialist Benedict Anderson. The invasion was bloody and brutal. Subsequently, Indonesia extended its aggression to other parts of the territory, and by 1977–78 was engaged in a program of wholesale destruction including massive bombardment, forced population removal, destruction of villages and crops, and all the familiar techniques used by modern armies to subjugate a resisting population. The precise scale of the atrocities is difficult to assess, in part because Indonesia refused to admit outside observers, for reasons that are readily understood. Even the International Red Cross was excluded until 1979, and then was allowed entry only on a limited basis. But there has been ample evidence from refugees, letters smuggled out, church sources, the occasional journalist granted a brief guided tour, and the Indonesian authorities themselves. If the facts were not known in the West, it was the result of the decision not to let them be known. It appears likely that of the prewar population of close to 700,000 perhaps one quarter have succumbed to outright slaughter or starvation caused by the Indonesian attack, and that the remaining population, much of which is herded into military-run concentration camps, may suffer a similar fate unless properly supervised international assistance is forthcoming on a substantial scale. Relief officials who were finally permitted limited access to the territory after almost four years described the prevailing situation as comparable to Cambodia in 1979. The world reaction has been somewhat different in the two cases.

The U.S. government continued throughout to provide the military and diplomatic support that was required for the slaughter to continue. By late 1977, Indonesian supplies had been depleted. The Human Rights Administration dramatically increased the flow of military equipment, enabling Indonesia to undertake the fierce offensives that reduced East Timor to the level of Cambodia.[3] U.S. allies have also joined in providing the needed military and diplomatic support.

The United Nations has repeatedly condemned the Indonesian aggression and called for the exercise of the right of self-determination in East Timor, as have the nonaligned nations. But the West has succeeded in blocking any significant measures. The U.N. General Assembly met immediately after the invasion, but was unable to react in a meaningful way. The reasons are explained by U.N. Ambassador Daniel P. Moynihan in his memoirs: "The United States wished things to turn out as they did, and worked to bring this about. The Department of State desired that the United Nations prove utterly ineffective in whatever measures it undertook. This task was given to me, and I carried it forward with no inconsiderable success."[4]

Ambassador Moynihan was presumably aware of the nature of his success. He cites a February 1976 estimate by the deputy chairman of the provisional government installed by Indonesian force "that some sixty thousand persons had been killed since the outbreak of civil war"—recall that two to three thousand had been killed during the civil war itself—"10 percent of the population, almost the proportion of casualties experienced by the Soviet Union during the Second World War." Thus, in effect, he is claiming credit for "success" in helping to cause a massacre that he compares to the consequences of Nazi aggression, not to speak of the growing number of victims in the subsequent period.

Moynihan was much admired for the great courage that he displayed in the United Nations in confronting the mighty Third World enemies of the United States. Somehow, his self-congratulation in this case escaped notice.[5]

Ambassador Moynihan commented further that the Indonesian invasion must have been successful by March 1976, since "the subject disappeared from the press and from the United Nations after that time." It did virtually disappear from the press, though not from the United Nations, which has regularly condemned Indonesian aggression. The curtain of silence drawn by the press in the United States and much of the West for four years hardly demonstrates the success of Indonesian arms, though it does stand as a remarkable testimonial to the effectiveness of Western propaganda systems.[6]

Throughout, the U.S. government has pretended that it knew very little about events in East Timor, a transparent fabrication. Or else government representatives claimed at each stage that though there might have been some unfortunate excesses in the past, the situation is now calm and the sensible and humane course is to recognize Indonesian control. This was, for example, the stance taken by the government in 1977 congressional hearings, at exactly the time when Indonesia was preparing the murderous offensives of 1977–78 and the Human Rights Administration was accelerating the flow of arms for use in these military operations. The "Human Rights" reports of the State Department not only fail to consider the ample evidence of massive atrocities, but go so far as to pretend that the issue does not arise. A report prepared by the Congressional Research Service is typical of government pronouncements.[7] The report discusses the alleged improvement in Indonesia's human rights record—students of Orwell may be intrigued by the fact that in government "Human Rights" reports dealing with friendly states, the record is invariably one of "improvement," whatever unpleasant events may have occurred in the past. The November 1979 report informs us that

> Indonesia's takeover of East Timor, formerly Portuguese Timor, in December 1975 may have been an exception to this trend of improvement, but the conflicting claims and lack of access into Timor by non-Indonesians make it difficult if not impossible to ascertain the loss of life

in the heavy fighting of December 1975—March 1976. Recently, reports from Timor indicate a partial return to normalcy there although genuine self-determination for the Timorese is a dim prospect.

The latter conclusion is certainly correct, as long as the U.S. government persists in its policy of supporting Indonesian terror while denying its existence, and as long as the media loyally refrain from exposing the facts. This report is typical not only in its claim that now things are finally improving (the constant plea throughout) but also in its failure to concede that questions even arise about the period after March 1976.

The picture is a bit different when we turn to eyewitness testimony, for example, that of Father Leoneto Vieira do Rego, a sixty-three-year-old Portuguese priest who spent three years in the mountains before surrendering to Indonesian forces in January 1979, suffering from malaria and starvation. After imprisonment and interrogation, he was permitted to return to Portugal in June. His accounts of what he had observed were then reported in the world press, outside of the United States. Shortly after the appearance of the government report cited above, Father Leoneto was interviewed by the *New York Times*.[8] The transcript of the interview was leaked to the *Boston Globe*.[9] Father Leoneto said that during 1976, things were normal in the mountains where he was living, and where most of the population was, including those who had fled from Dili:

> Apart from the main towns, people in the interior weren't aware of the war. People had food commodities aplenty. It was a normal life under not-normal circumstances. Problems started in early 1977. A full-scale bombardment of the whole island began. From that point there emerged death, illness, despair. The second phase of the bombing was late 1977 to early 1979, with modern aircraft. This was the firebombing phase of the bombing. Even up to this time, people could still live. The genocide and starvation was the result of the full-scale incendiary bombing. . . . We saw the end coming. People could not plant. I personally witnessed—while running to protected areas, going from tribe to tribe—the great massacre from bombardment and people dying from starvation. In 1979 people began surrendering because there was no other option. When people began dying, then others began to give up.

Father Leoneto estimated that 200,000 people had died during the four years of war.

Of all of this, what survived in the *Times* account was the following sentence:

> He said that bombardment and systematic destruction of croplands in 1978 were intended to starve the islanders into submission.[10]

Recall that the offensives of 1977–79 reported by Father Leoneto, as by many others during this period and since, coincided with the sharp increase in arms supplies from the Human Rights Administration.

Refugees continue to report large-scale atrocities. By 1979, some foreign aid was reaching the territory, but distribution was largely under Indonesian military control. A report from Lisbon in the London *Observer* notes that "all relief work in the former Portuguese colony is being supervised by only four foreign field workers" and states that "food and medical supplies for famine hit East Timor are being diverted to Indonesian troops and shopkeepers, according to refugees arriving in Portugal."[11] The report continues:

> "We appeal to anyone left in the world with a minimum sense of human rights to ensure that relief goes directly to our people," said a refugee who preferred to remain anonymous as his family is still in East Timor. . . . Refugees insisted that there was still starvation in East Timor and that, contrary to other reports, fighting between the Indonesians and the Timorese Liberation Movement was continuing in the mountains to the east of the island. They claimed Indonesian troops were terrorising the local population with arrests, torture, and summary executions. They described the methods by which the authorities manipulated tours by visiting journalists. The Timorese claim that troops and war material are removed to give the impression of calm. One woman said that she had seen crosses taken from the local military cemetery. The authorities kept a tight control, informing their "representatives" in relief camps and placing armed plain-clothed military officers among the crowds. The growing evidence of the corruption and violation of human rights in East Timor has begun to filter out and is threatening to put the issue at the centre of a diplomatic offensive. Portugal and the US are particularly involved.

Though, it must be added, they are involved in quite different ways. Portugal, particularly the new conservative government, is seeking to gain international support to save the Timorese from final destruction and to compel

Indonesia to withdraw. The U.S. government is trying to stem the increasing flow of exposures and to guarantee Indonesian control over the miserable remnants of the U.S.-backed Indonesian assault.

In December 1979, David Watts of the London *Times* filed a report from Dili, East Timor, on "a tour supervised by the Indonesian military. He reports the success of the Red Cross relief operation in saving the lives of tens of thousands of people on "the brink of starvation." "Others will die, but at least help is coming to the innocent victims of the vicious starvation policy practised by the Indonesian armed forces against the Marxist militant and civilian alike in East Timor's little known war, which has been fought out of sight of the world since 1975." Watts's reference to the "Marxist" victims is as reliable as his statement that, on retreating to the mountains after the Indonesian invasion, Fretilin "[took] with them an estimated 100,000 lowland Timorese who were either relatives or people 'co-opted' into the movement to provide support by growing food," and presumably derives from the same source, namely, his tour guides.

Watts writes further that

the Indonesian armed forces sealed off East Timor from the rest of the world with air and naval patrols to prevent outside assistance reaching the Fretilin fighters. The civilian population was constantly forced to flee from place to place. It was impossible for the lowlanders to return to the few fertile areas around river valleys and even the highlanders were unable to practise their own, crude slash and burn agriculture. The people were reduced to stealing what they could, and when they could not get supplies they lived on leaves, mice and dead dogs, according to an official of the Indonesian Red Cross. They ate the dogs after they had died because their animist beliefs prevented them from killing them.

But the real crisis for the mountain people came in 1977–78 when the Indonesian military, tiring of the inconclusive campaign, launched a big sweep through the east of the island to eradicate the last of the Fretilin forces. Using paratroop drops and North American Rockwell Bronco counter-insurgency aircraft they fought through the island, denying the Fretilin forces sanctuaries and food supplies. . . . Here and there throughout the eastern half of the island there is evidence of what appear to have been napalm attacks by the Bronco aircraft. Made desperate by the situation in the mountains the people began to flock down to the lowlands in search of food and shelter.[12]

Like his American colleagues, Watts is silent on the role of the United States, apart from its contribution to aid for the remnants in 1979, and on the role of the press in ensuring that this would remain a "little known war" during the period when an aroused public opinion could have brought these atrocities to an end.

For four long and bloody years, the U.S. media, with very rare exceptions, kept close to the U.S. government propaganda line. During 1975, there was considerable coverage of East Timor, a reflection of the concern over decolonization in the former Portuguese empire. In late 1975, the *New York Times* was reporting Indonesia's "remarkable restraint" at the same time that Australian journalists were filing eyewitness reports of Indonesian naval bombardment of Timorese towns and military attacks along the border. An Australian journalist, the first to enter East Timor after the August-September civil war, wrote a lengthy report in the London *Times* in which he rejected allegations of Fretilin atrocities, which he attributed to Indonesian and other propaganda services. His report appeared in the *New York Times*, edited to make it appear that the charges were accurate, as *Newsweek* then reported, basing itself on the *New York Times* account. After the Indonesian invasion, reporting in the United States diminished rapidly, approaching zero (apart from occasional U.S. government and Indonesian propaganda handouts) as the U.S.-backed Indonesian assault expanded in scale and violence. Timorese refugees were scrupulously avoided, in dramatic contrast to refugees from Communist oppression. When Henry Kamm, the Pulitzer Prize-winning Southeast Asian correspondent of the *New York Times*, deigned to mention East Timor while the war raged in full fury, he did not rely on the reports of refugees, priests, or the numerous other sources available. Rather, he interviewed Indonesian generals, and on their authority presented the "fact" that Fretilin had "forced" the people to live under its "control," though now they were fleeing to Indonesian-held areas.[13] Reporting on a four-day visit to East Timor in 1980, Kamm now informs the reader that 300,000 Timorese were "displaced by persistent civil war and struggle against the invaders"—there had been no civil war, apart from U.S. and Indonesian propaganda handouts and the "news columns" of the Western press, since September 1975. He reports that "the Fretilin hold over the population" was broken by the 1978 Indonesian offensive and that Fretilin "controlled significant parts of the population at least until 1977." Nowhere is there any indication of even the possibility that Fretilin may have had popular support. These conclusions, along with reports of Fretilin savagery, are based on evidence derived from Indonesian authorities, Timorese collaborators, or Timorese who, as he notes, were so intimidated by the ever-present Indonesian military authorities that their statements were obviously meaningless.[14]

By late 1979, the truth was beginning to break through, even in the U.S. press, and a number of congressmen, notably Tom Harkin of Iowa, had become aware of the true nature of what had been concealed by the media. The *New York Times* ran an honest editorial on December 24, 1979 (see note 10), and James Markham filed the first report on the many Timorese refugees in Lisbon.[15] The press began to present some of the information that had been available for four years,[16] though much distortion persists and the crucial U.S. role is generally ignored or downplayed.

The importance of the behavior of the media and journals of opinion during these years cannot be overemphasized. The events described by Father Leoneto and many others, and the horrendous consequences that are now at last widely conceded, are the direct responsibility of the United States government, and to a lesser extent, its Western allies. Correspondingly, these monstrous acts could have been—and still can be—brought to an end by withdrawal of direct U.S. support for them.

The U.S. government has been backing the Indonesian military not because it takes pleasure in massacre and starvation, but because the fate of the Timorese is simply a matter of no significance when measured against higher goals. Since 1965, when the Indonesian military took power in a coup that led to the slaughter of perhaps half a million to a million people, mostly landless peasants, Indonesia has been a valued ally.[17] The military rulers have opened the country to Western plunder, hindered only by the rapacity and corruption of our friends in Jakarta. In this potentially rich country, much of the population has suffered enormously—even apart from the huge massacres, which demonstrated proper anti-Communist credentials to an appreciative Western audience—as the country has been turned into a "paradise for investors."[18] Given these overriding considerations, it was only to be expected that the Human Rights Administration, like its predecessor, would pour arms into Indonesia to enable it to achieve its ends in East Timor, and would attempt in every way to conceal the truth.

The importance of the deception becomes clear when we observe what happens when the system of indoctrination begins to unravel. However institutions may function, individuals are not prepared to support actions that verge on genocide. As the truth has begun to break through, a number of members of Congress and increasing segments of the population are beginning to demand an end to these atrocious acts. One result was that some aid was sent, though without adequate international supervision it is questionable how much reached those who need it, given the corruption of the Indonesian military. There is, for the first time, a real possibility that pressure will be put on the U.S. government to stop providing the military supplies that Indonesia requires, and that international efforts may be organized to induce Indonesia to withdraw, so that what is left of the population may have the opportunity to realize their long-sought right to self-determination.

It is intriguing to see how some segments of the media are reacting to the fact that information about East Timor is now beginning to reach the public. In the *Nation*—the only U.S. journal to have published a serious article on Timor from 1975 through 1978[19]—A. J. Langguth dismissed the concern over Timor with the following remarkable comment: "If the world press were to converge suddenly on Timor, it would not improve the lot of a single Cambodian." [20] The irrationality of the comment is at first startling, but the sentiment becomes intelligible on the assumption that it is only the other fellow's crimes that deserve attention. In the *Washington Journalism Review*, Richard Valeriani of NBC and Asia specialist and former foreign correspondent Stanley Karnow discussed a report on East Timor that appeared in the *New York Times* in late January 1980.[21] Valeriani said that he had read it, though "I don't care about Timor." Karnow couldn't bring himself even to read the story: "I just didn't have time. . . . There was no connection; it didn't have anything to do with me." Their point was that the *Times* was giving *too much coverage* to the insignificant fact that massacres in Timor rival those of Cambodia and that the population has been reduced to the state of the miserable victims on the Thai-Cambodian border as a direct result of U.S. policies. The *Times* is failing its responsibilities by wasting space on such trivia—but not, for example, by devoting the entire front cover and twenty-five pages of the Sunday magazine section a few days earlier (January 20, 1980) to the horrendous experiences of Dith Pran in Cambodia, recapitulating stories that had received massive media attention.

Their reactions are not unique. The U.N. correspondent of the *New York Times*, Bernard Nossiter, refused an invitation to a press conference on East Timor in October 1979 on the grounds that the issue was "rather esoteric," and in fact reported not a word on the U.N. debate, which included testimony from Timorese refugees and others on the continuing atrocities and the U.S. responsibility for them.[22] A look at the stories he did publish during those days reveals that events must be insignificant indeed to fall below the threshold for the *Times*. Thus Nossiter devoted a full-page column to the world-shaking fact that the government of Fiji had not been paid for its contingent in Southern Lebanon and, shortly after, reported a debate over a missing comma, of undeterminable import, in a U.N. document[23]—though in this case, his report is to be understood as part of the campaign of ridicule that has been directed against the United Nations, in particular its Third World membership, ever since the U.N. escaped from the control of the United States and fell under what is called here "the tyranny of the majority," or what others call "democracy." Hence the sarcastic report of the debate over the missing comma, coupled with total silence on the role of Third World nations in bringing to the United Nations the story of the U.S.-backed massacres in Timor.

Perhaps the most intriguing response to the recent breakdown of media suppression is that of the *Wall Street Journal*, which devoted an editorial to the topic.[24] The *Journal* takes note of "an interesting campaign" that "has been shaping up over the past few weeks on the issue of East Timor." It observes that a hundred thousand people may have died during the war, adding that "it sounds suspiciously like Cambodia, some people are saying. And this one is ours: Indonesia is our ally and oil supplier, it's American arms that the Indonesians used to perpetrate their atrocities." But this charge, the *Journal* continues, "tells less about Timor than it does about certain varieties of American political thinking." There are two factors that crucially distinguish Timor from Cambodia. The first is that the United States is sending some aid to Timor, and the Indonesians, "however grudgingly and imperfectly," are letting the food in, whereas "the Cambodians would be in considerably better shape if the Soviet Union undertook comparable behavior for itself and its ally"—the editors ignore the fact that the Soviet Union provided aid to starving Cambodians before the United States did, and, it appears, in substantial quantities, as well as the fact, reported by international aid workers, that their aid was let in not at all grudgingly. But the crucial distinction is this:

> But more important, it's self-deluding to talk as if the U.S. had the power any longer to determine the outcome of a situation like Timor. The violence that has cursed the place is the wholly unsurprising mark of a disintegrating world order; talk about the evils of U.S. power is likely to hasten

that disintegration, not arrest it. Those worried about the human costs of such chaos might do well to start facing up to that connection.

The reasoning is remarkable. The editors are trying to tell us that when U.S.-supplied aircraft demolish villages, destroy crops, massacre mountain tribesmen, and drive them to concentration camps, we are to understand these facts as "the mark of a disintegrating world order," not the results of U.S. actions, consciously undertaken. And if the United States were to withhold the crucial military and diplomatic support that enables Indonesia to carry out these policies, the terror might be even worse. One wonders whether *Pravda* rises to such intellectual heights when it justifies Soviet support for the Ethiopian war in Eritrea.

It is easy enough to poke fun at the *Wall Street Journal*, but that would be to overlook the more significant point. The slight exposure of U.S.-backed Indonesian atrocities during the past several months has frightened the Indonesian military, the U.S. government, and the business circles represented by the *Wall Street Journal*, all of whom want to play their games with people's lives in secret. The message is clear. By significantly extending the pressure on the U.S. government to abandon its appalling policies, and continuing to work to bring the facts to a larger public, one can contribute materially to the survival of the people of East Timor. It is rare that an opportunity arises in which a relatively small amount of effort may save hundreds of thousands of lives, and it would be criminal to allow it to pass.

AFTERWORD (1981)

IN THEIR DISPARAGING COMMENTS ON "that long story today about Timor in the *New York Times*," Stanley Karnow and Richard Valeriani agree that "99.99% of the American people don't care about Timor," just as they do not.[1] Technically, their conclusion is certainly correct; those who do not know of the enormous massacre, conducted far from view while the government and the press were congratulating themselves on their profound concern for human rights and denouncing enemy atrocities, surely do not care about Timor. But the commitment of the government and the media to conceal the facts, and the reaction when the silence was broken, suggest a rather different conclusion: that it is important to guard people against the facts precisely because they will care if they learn about the horrors that they are unwittingly supporting. The case of Timor, after all, is just one of a great many examples, unusually dramatic, perhaps, because of the scale of the slaughter, and the similarities to the simultaneous Cambodian massacre that the *Wall Street Journal* and others have found so troubling. But the example illustrates a pervasive pattern. Quite generally, "benign and constructive bloodbaths" that are favorable to U.S. global interests are ignored, suppressed, or denied, while "nefarious bloodbaths" that can be charged to enemies of the state are afforded massive publicity and, not infrequently, subjected to substantial distortion to improve the effect.[2] Such behavior is characteristic quite generally of systems of propaganda and indoctrination. The reason is, surely, that elite groups are concerned that those who know will care.

To suppress the involvement of one's government in a major massacre for four years is quite an impressive achievement, particularly when we bear in mind that the American press is not subject to state controls or centralized authority. In a genuinely free society, such journals as the *Washington Journalism Review* and others like it[3] might be concerned to explore the mechanisms and operative factors behind such remarkable subservience to the state. Since they evidently will not, others who are more concerned with the survival of free institutions should take up the task.

In his March 6, 1980, article cited above (see note 2 of the main chapter), Daniel Southerland comments that "a policy of deliberate indifference to human rights violations by Indonesia in the former Portuguese colony of East Timor is coming back to trouble the US State Department." The observation is correct. Southerland also provides the reasons for the eager U.S. participation in the Timor slaughter:

> But in deferring to Indonesia on this issue, the Carter administration, like the Ford administration before it, appears to have placed big-power concerns ahead of human rights; Indonesia is an anticommunist, largely Muslim, oil-producing nation with the fifth-largest population in the world. It commands sea lanes between the Pacific and Indian oceans. Assistant Secretary of State Richard Holbrooke recently declared it is potentially one of the great nations of the world.

As is generally the case, concern for human rights is "the Soul of our foreign policy," in President Carter's words, only when there is something to be gained by the pretense.

Southerland adds that "US policy toward East Timor has been made for the most part by the State Department's Bureau of East Asian and Pacific Affairs, headed by Mr. Holbrooke," but "Mr. Holbrooke let it be known he was too busy preparing for a trip to appear at the Feb. 6 hearing" of a congressional committee dealing with the Timor issue ("He did have the time, however, to play host at a black-tie dinner later the same day"). Holbrooke has testified before Congress on the topic on other occasions, however; for example, on December 4, 1979, when he explained that "the welfare of the Timorese people is the major objective of our policy towards East Timor," while lauding Indonesia for its "humanitarian approach to the Indochinese refugee problem," the really important matter.[4]

It was not only the loyal media that gave a wide berth to Timorese refugees who had the wrong story to tell. Southerland comments:

> The Carter administration has proclaimed human rights to be at the center of its foreign policy. To find out about human rights violations in Cambodia, the State Department has intensively interviewed Cambodian refugees. But Francisco Fernandes, a Roman Catholic priest who served

for several years as head of the Timorese refugee community, said he knew of no attempt by US officials to seek out and interview any of the more than 2,000 such refugees who have been living in Portugal for the past several years. Even today, with the magnitude of the East Timor problem better known, refugees going directly to the State Department in Washington with their stories find that most officials there give the benefit of the doubt to the Indonesians. "He acted like a lawyer for the Indonesians," said one refugee after talking with a State Department official recently.

Southerland is, of course, correct in interpreting U.S. participation in the Timor massacre within the framework of overriding concern over relations with Indonesia. As noted above, Indonesia earned its credentials as a member of the Free World in good standing with the 1965 coup and subsequent massacre of hundreds of thousands of people, mostly landless peasants. The Western reaction to this massacre was not unlike the reaction to the subsequent atrocities in Timor—or, for that matter, to the massive human rights violations in Indonesia in the intervening years, or to the fact that while the riches of Indonesia are flowing to the West when they are not appropriated by the U.S. client generals, life expectancy is forty-eight years and "real wages for agricultural labor have been declining for a decade." [5] The Western reaction is neatly conveyed by Peter Hastings, associate editor of the Sydney *Morning Herald*, in a guest column in the *New York Times* entitled "Australia's Indonesia Problem" (December 26, 1979). During the rule of President Sukarno, he explains, Australian attitudes towards Indonesia were quite negative. But the 1965 coup

> changed Australian perceptions of Indonesia overnight. *Indonesia's huge Communist Party was liquidated.* The emphasis at home was on economic rationalism; abroad it was on friendship with the West and regional cooperation. This led many Australians to believe that a special relationship was possible between the two nations after all. This belief predictably foundered on the realities of Indonesian cultural attitudes and politics. (My emphasis.)

Again, a "constructive bloodbath," though, unfortunately, not as constructive as it might have been. Freedom House statements signed by many liberal American scholars expressed a similar assessment at the time, noting the "dramatic changes" in Indonesia in the aftermath of the 1965 coup and arguing that the "sharp reversal of Indonesia's shift toward Communism" demonstrated that the United States was right to invade (or, from their perspective, to "defend") South Vietnam, so as to provide a shield behind which these constructive developments could proceed.[6]

It is revealing that such sentiments can be expressed, and even more so that they pass without notice among the Western intelligentsia, who evidently regard eradication of the class enemy as an entirely meritorious pursuit, no matter how savage and extensive the slaughter.

The U.S. government continues to assure us—as it has throughout—that the problems caused by Portuguese colonialism, the violent civil war, "the disruption of the more recent fighting," adverse geography and climatic conditions, and the Timorese family structure are now well in hand. "Developments over the past few months show that the will and the means to attack these problems are present, and I am confident that the Government of Indonesia, with help from abroad, is now on the path which will lead to a more prosperous and happy future for the people of East Timor," Ambassador Edward Masters informed Congress in December 1979 (see note 4).

Ambassador Masters's contributions to the welfare of the people of East Timor are reviewed by Benedict Anderson in congressional testimony.[7] In September 1978, Masters visited East Timor together with other members of the Jakarta diplomatic corps. Foreign correspondent Norman Peagam, who accompanied the party, wrote that "foreign ambassadors . . . including United States Ambassador Edward E. Masters, came away so shocked by the conditions of the refugees that they immediately contacted the governor of East Timor . . . to explore the possibilities for providing foreign humanitarian assistance."[8] However, more "malign neglect" followed (see note 5 of the main chapter). It was not until June 1979, nine months later, that Ambassador Masters urged that the U.S. government provide humanitarian assistance. In congressional testimony, Masters stated that at the time of the September 1978 visit, the ambassadors "did not know how bad it was—the others felt the same as I did, that the situation was not that serious." Anderson remarks that "this is another gross prevarication," citing correspondent David Jenkins of the *Far Eastern Economic Review*, who also accompanied the ambassadors, and who reported that "one ambassador said [the children he saw in one resettlement village] reminded him of victims of an African famine."[9]

Why the nine-month period of "malign neglect" from September 1978 to June 1979? Anderson offers the following plausible explanation: "From late 1977 to early 1979, the Indonesian military, bolstered by deliveries of OV-10 Broncos and other munitions [from the United States], carried out a major counterinsurgency campaign." He cites an internal State Department document which records, "It was not until the spring of 1979 that the Government of Indonesia felt East Timor to be secure enough to permit foreign visitors." In March 1979, Indonesia formally dissolved the Joint Operations Command in East Timor. In April, the International Red Cross (ICRC) was permitted to make a brief survey, the first visit permitted since the Indonesian invasion of December 1975—an unprecedented atrocity in itself (see note 10). "Only then," Anderson writes, "did Mr. Masters move," determining on June 1, 1979, "that a disaster of such a magnitude as to warrant U.S. Government assistance existed in East Timor" (the wording of the same internal State Department document).

> In other words, for nine long months, from September 1978 to June 1979, while "in ever increasing numbers the starving and the ailing, wearing rags at best, drifted onto the coastal plain," [10] Ambassador Masters deliberately refrained, even within the walls of the State Department, from proposing humanitarian aid to East Timor. Until the generals in Jakarta gave him the green light, Mr. Masters did nothing to help the East Timorese, although Mr. Holbrooke insists that "the welfare of the Timorese people is the major objective of our policy towards East Timor."

A fitting epitaph for the Human Rights Administration.

Despite the assurances of the U.S. government, press reports through 1980 indicate that some "problems" remain. Jill Jolliffe reports from Lisbon that "new fighting has erupted in Portugal's former South-East Asian colony of East Timor, according to refugees arriving here." They also claim that despite "cosmetic improvements," "the plight of civilians is deteriorating." "All the refugees interviewed claimed that suffering is increasing among the civilian population," and they reported that "some had been executed after surrendering to Indonesian authorities," as confirmed by letters they showed from early 1980. Some of those who came down from the mountains and turned themselves over to the Indonesians were shot; others were taken away by security police "and not seen again." [11]

Amnesty International urged President Suharto to order an investigation of such disappearances and possible executions, noting also "persistent reports of prisoners being beaten or tortured." [12]

In May 1980, Brian Eads reported from Jakarta that "malnutrition and disease are still more widespread than in ravaged Cambodia, but the people of East Timor are slowly struggling back to life" according to relief workers and other "reliable sources" in Jakarta, though neither Catholic Relief Services (CRS) nor International Red Cross (ICRC) teams "are allowed sufficient access to make meaningful assessments of how far their emergency aid has cut death rates" (Eads himself was denied entry). Eads continues:

> Perhaps the most telling observation came from an official who had recently visited Cambodia. By the criteria of distended bellies, intestinal disease and brachial parameter—the measurement of the upper arm—the East Timorese are in a worse state than the Khmers.[15]

Word has not yet reached the International Rescue Committee yet, however; see note 14 of the main chapter.

Eads reports that "the only evidence so far of Indonesian development plans are new villages and schools staffed by Indonesian teachers whose officially stated aim is to wash their pupils' brains of Fretilin's nationalist ideology." To restate this observation in the terminology of the U.S. embassy in Jakarta, "The educational system now being built from the first grade upward, for the first time ever in many places, will in time provide [the extremely backward population] with some means of participating in the growth and direction of their province." [14]

Eads concludes that "judging from the relentless hold of Indonesian repression and the complicity of those Western countries with influence in Djakarta, notably Australia and the United States, the prospects for a Fretilin comeback are nil."

A few weeks later a report in the Australian press (*Advertiser*, May 22, 1980) cited "new reports from East Timor" which "confirm earlier claims that the war between Fretilin guerillas and Indonesian occupying forces is continuing." The journal cites two letters, "recently smuggled from Dili to Lisbon, written by separate authors," dated March 8 and March 26, 1980. "The writers also tell of continuing executions of Timorese who had earlier surrendered to Indonesian authorities after fighting with Fretilin." The letters speak of an "intense" armed struggle with "strong resistance to tens of Indonesian battalions" and of Indonesian casualties arriving daily at Dili hospital by helicopter, alleging also that "many Timorese soldiers have left Indonesian ranks to join their compatriots in the bush." One of the letters, written to a Timorese priest, states that when a person is selected for execution, "he or she is told they have been ordered to study the Indonesian language in Jakarta, or have been summoned to Quelicai, a village 110km south-east of Dili," the correspondent of the *Advertiser* writes, quoting the letter, which states: "They have executed many, many people in Quelicai. People's hearts beat faster when Quelicai is mentioned, because it represents the terror, certain death." The same letter "says that in three separate conversations with Indonesian officials the writer was told Government policy is to eventually 'liquidate' all ex-supporters of Fretilin."

In July, James Markham reported that fighting continues, "according to newly arrived refugees and letters smuggled out of the territory." "Confirming accounts of earlier refugees, those in the new group said that when they left Dili, OV-10 Bronco reconnaissance planes took off regularly from its airport loaded with bombs, except when foreign visitors were there." The refugees also report the sale to patients of Red Cross supplies given to hospitals, robbery by Indonesian soldiers, more effective barriers to escape by bribery to Portugal, etc.[15]

The Australian press reported in November that according to secret State Department documents, "Indonesia is carrying out an intensive tribal relocation programme in its drive to integrate the former Portuguese colony of East Timor into the nation." The program has caused severe confusion and alienation from the new environment, the documents report. The bishop of Dili and much of the elite refuse to accept the inevitability of Indonesian domination, according to the Australian ambassador, but, the ambassador says, "The bulk of the population will clearly accept whatever authority exists at the time. The older people are extremely passive."[16] An encouraging indication of successful pacification.

The food situation was reported to be improving as a result of international aid operations by late 1980. "Once self-sufficient in rice, the territory is now heavily dependent on food imports. It is still unclear whether the island will be given the encouragement or opportunity to again become self-reliant."[17] Much of the population is kept in "resettlement" camps, where they are held under armed guard. Benedict Anderson notes that "the real nature of these resettlement areas was revealed by *New York Times* correspondent Henry Kamm's January 1980 interview with an agricultural specialist working with the Indonesian military in East Timor, who said that the plan for removing and concentrating these people had been drawn up 'largely for strategic reasons, placing the population where the army can control it.' He added that 'the resettlement project will make East Timor *permanently dependent on food imports*' " (Anderson's emphasis). The lucrative Timorese coffee crop "has, since the invasion, been monopolized, warlord style," by a company controlled by the commander of the Indonesian invasion forces. "If all this were not enough, the Suharto government, which has repeatedly tried to justify its actions by claiming that East Timor is not economically viable and cannot support its population, has recently designated the region a transmigration zone where peasants from Indonesia will be relocated." [18] If Timor does again become "self-reliant," in a position to exploit its coffee crop and probably offshore oil for internal development, this will be for the benefit of the Indonesian conquerors, if they finally have their way.

By the end of the year, Indonesia "declared the emergency over," Henry Kamm reports in the *New York Times*, ordering the international relief organizations to terminate their operations. "Although Indonesia imports enormous amounts of food and accepts food relief, particularly from the United States, it has emphasized to the relief agencies and the American Embassy that this will not be the case for East Timor beyond December 31. The reason offered was that the Government did not want to instill a dole mentality." [19] The "dole mentality," in its view, is appropriate only for Indonesian generals.

Kamm also reports that the U.N. General Assembly once again approved a resolution opposing the forced integration of East Timor; "the United States, as it does every year, voted with Indonesia." He also notes that "tens of thousands who might have been saved died" because of Indonesia's "long delay" after the autumn of 1978 in allowing the flow of relief to begin. He does not mention the role of the United States in implementing this "long delay," reviewed above.

One reason for "the total cutoff of the food effort and phasing out of medical relief," Kamm suggests, "is believed to be the continuation of a low level of warfare between remnants of Fretilin, East Timor's independence group, and the Indonesian Army." He reports the Fretilin raid in the capital city of Dili in June "followed by the arrest of perhaps 200 Timorese in and near Dili"; "furthermore, reliable Timorese sources reported that several hundred inhabitants of mountain areas around Dili, from where the insurgents are believed to have come, have been driven from their homes, either to camps around Dili or to banishment to the offshore island of Atauro. Their mountain shacks were reported to have been burned." But despite these reprisals, Fretilin launched another attack near Dili in July. Roman Catholic sources "reported that Fretilin's brief resurgence in the city had deepened the visible animosity of Timorese to the occupying soldiers and heightened Fretilin's residual popularity." Kamm cites "a Timorese" who states that "now many favor Fretilin" as a result of Indonesian actions, though "earlier, Fretilin was perhaps cruel to the people." The *Times* has yet to report the judgment of international observers in Timor prior to the Indonesian invasion on the popularity of Fretilin and its constructive programs.

The same Timorese says that "if the foreigners leave, it will be tragic for the Timorese people. First, they give assistance. And besides, when the foreigners are there, the military men are afraid. When they go away, warplanes will come back to Timor, and warships also." Kamm adds that "Indonesia used American-supplied OV-10 Broncos, planes designed for counterinsurgency operations, extensively in the 1978 campaign that reduced Fretilin to guerrilla bands whose total is now thought not to exceed 600."

Other reports also highlight the importance of maintaining the international presence, particularly that of the International Red Cross. To cite one example, Father W. Roetenberg, secretary of the Central Missionary Board of the Religious (the Netherlands), was interviewed by the Dutch press after his return from a trip to Indonesia where he spoke with a number of Timorese about the situation in Timor.[20] Father Roetenberg stated that

> the cruelty and corruption there are increasing rather than declining. The Indonesian army, with three battalions, is unable to bring the guerrillas in the mountains under control, and takes its anger out on the civilian population. And this in turn pushes the people to join the guerrillas. If they must die anyhow, then they'd rather die fighting. Just about everyone has a brother or sister, cousin or uncle, who has been killed by Indonesian bombs or shot by Indonesian soldiers. An entire people are being threatened and affronted in their very existence as a people and we're not taking it seriously enough. That became very clear to me there.

According to the reporter, Father Roetenberg emphasized that "the famine, which has claimed thousands of victims over the past few months, must above all be seen as a result of a deliberate Indonesian strategy of starvation." He also noted that the Netherlands continues to deliver war materials to Indonesia.

Father Roetenberg reports that Timorese view most aid "with very mixed feelings," and request that "all aid be channelled through the International Red Cross and not through the Indonesian Red Cross or the CRS [Catholic Relief Services]." The reason is that

> the government in Jakarta controls the humanitarian aid to East Timor in all respects. In the past months the biggest relief operation has come from the American Catholic Relief Services (CRS). Their contract with the Indonesian government stipulates that the CRS will provide transport to the centers and refugee camps, after which local (Indonesian) officials will supervise the distribution. This typifies the situation. CRS is in the service of the Indonesian army and the quickest possible integration imposed from the outside. The Timorese are faced with a terrible dilemma. As hunted game, they have to accept food from their own thieves in order to survive.

The role and commitments of CRS in fact raise many questions. The organization came under sharp criticism in the American Catholic press during the Vietnam war because of its cozy relations with U.S. pacification programs.[21] The funds for its Timor operations are largely provided by the U.S. government, and it sometimes appears to be virtually an arm of USAID. In an important review of the current situation in East Timor, Father Pat Walsh of Action for World Development (an Australian Catholic agency) reports a series of interviews with CRS officials, who justify their cooperation with the Indonesian military on grounds that "they had no choice but to work in East Timor on Indonesian terms," which, in the words of a CRS official in New York, means "going where the Indonesian government wants it to go and doing what the Indonesian government wants it to do."[22] Eighty percent of CRS aid passes through the Indonesian government infrastructure, which is notorious for its corruption.[23] CRS has no personnel stationed full-time in Timor, leaving the multimillion-dollar program "wide open to exploitation by corruption prone Indonesians," Father Walsh comments. The practice is defended by CRS officials. "John Donnelly, a CRS spokesman at CRS' ultra-modern office tower in New York, went so far as to argue that facilities were so backward in Dili that CRS would not want to inflict living there on any American in case they were harmed by the experience—surely a reduction ad absurdum coming from an aid official professionally committed to work in the third world."

Father Walsh adds that "CRS is generally defensive of the Indonesian government on Timor," repeating Indonesian government propaganda in its public accounts of recent history. One CRS official in New York "spoke of communism in East Timor—another polemic much used by Indonesia. Even if there is nothing in the allegation that Russia is involved in East Timor [a charge taken seriously by no competent authority], said this official, 'the fact that it's been said is enough to influence judgements around here.' " "The conduct of CRS is utterly indefensible," Father Walsh concludes.

Father Walsh's detailed report contains much other significant information. Recent Indonesian visitors to East Timor estimated the Indonesian troop level there at approximately thirty thousand. The weight of evidence "strongly suggests that the principal reason for the army's exaggerated presence in East Timor is the lack of security there." One Indonesian reports that "the Intelligence treat the people like dogs" in East Timor, which "bears all the marks of an occupied country," Father Walsh concludes from many interviews. Informants report executions of "prominent Dili Catholics." The population has largely been concentrated in "resettlement sites" in counterinsurgency measures "patterned on the practice of [Sir Robert] Thompson in Malaya and General [Maxwell] Taylor in Vietnam whose purpose was to indoctrinate the people and isolate them from the guerillas," according to an Indonesian intelligence adviser. "ICRC believes the sites are to be permanent." An Indonesian intelligence memorandum of early 1980 "urges what it calls a program of 'strategic preventive counterinsurgency' in East Timor."

An Indonesian church report of July 1980 states that "the Indonesian government controls the people by force; the people do not respond freely and voluntarily and look to the Church as their only salvation," a development reminiscent of Latin America. The population has declined by some 200,000 while "the proportion of Catholics has risen from 30% pre-1975 to more than 50%," Father Walsh reports on the basis of interviews with church officials. One Indonesian church worker states, "Non-military Indonesians are also perceived as associates of the army (which is seen by the people to be composed) of cruel people devoid of love and morality." Another Indonesian states that many Timorese "would prefer to die rather than live dependent on, and humiliated by, people of another nationality." Extensive persecution and repression is detailed by Indonesian and Timorese informants. Some of the latter estimate that only about 300,000 of the population are still alive and about half of these "are vulnerable because many are sick and will die of hunger and lack of care" (as reported by an Indonesian Catholic priest).

The Vatican's permanent observer to the United Nations "surmised the people were being kept half-starved and confused to lessen their resistance," but the Vatican accepts Indonesian annexation as a fait accompli, though its official position remains ambiguous; it hopes that "freedom of the Church in East Timor" might "ensure that East Timor [play] in the Indonesian region a civilising role analogous to that played by colonised Greece in ancient Rome and modern Israel in the Middle East."[24]

Father Walsh concludes that "the Biafra-like crisis of 1978–80 has passed," though "the situation remains precarious" and "might very well regress to the catastrophic state" of this period "were the [international] agencies on whom the bulk of the population depend, to leave." They have since been forced to leave, apart from an intermittent presence. An estimate of the casualty rate is suggested by the fact that enrollments at the junior seminary in Dili, which were over one hundred before 1975, are now thirty-seven, of whom twenty have parents missing. "The precise death-toll and the long-term damage to countless minds and bodies may never be known." There are development projects, but most of the funds appear "to have been spent, 'showcase style,' on cosmetic improvements" such as traffic lights in Dili, TV, and a new airport terminal. The July 1980 report of the Indonesian Church states that "already there are signs that large-scale projects will be exploited for large profits by those involved in corruption," not a great surprise to those familiar with the practices of the Free World clients who rule Indonesia. The church report considers it likely that "the Timorese will certainly become mere coolies."

One interesting fact that Father Walsh notes is that "there are some 180 Portuguese citizens in East Timor whose plight resembles that of the US hostages in Iran"—although, once again, the U.S. and world reaction to their plight has not been exactly comparable. "According to informed observers the Indonesian government is detaining these forgotten would be refugees in the hope of extracting political concessions from the Portuguese Government in return for their release." One might add that the remnants of the Timorese people are, *in toto*, being held hostage by Indonesia. As Henry Kamm (December 9, 1980) and many others have observed, one reason for Indonesian refusal to permit free access (or by now, virtually any access) to international relief workers is "discomfiture" over international refusal to accept its incorporation of East Timor. If the world will accept the annexation, then perhaps aid to the miserable victims who still survive may be permitted. Holding of an entire population hostage—hostage-taking on a grand scale—is not considered a deplorable act of international terrorism by the civilized communities of the world, and elicits no outrage or indignation. Particularly in the United States, "retail terrorism" (e.g., by the PLO) is regarded as an unforgivable sin which evokes memories of the Nazis, while "wholesale terrorism" (e.g., Israeli bombardment of Palestinian refugee camps and Lebanese villages) is taken to be a perhaps unwarranted but surely understandable act of self-defense. The holding of American hostages in Iran is an international crime of the first magnitude. But it is not a crime for the United States to hold the starving population of Laos hostage, refusing food aid to a country where the agricultural system was demolished by American bombers in an effort to bring about a change of government, or at least to maximize suffering as retribution for the refusal to bend to American will. Similarly, the United States holds the population of Cambodia hostage, supporting the Pol Pot army (via Thailand) surely not out of concern for Cambodians, but in order to punish Vietnam.

All of this is entirely natural. What arouses the outrage of the civilized is resort to the weapons of the weak; the weapons of the strong may be wielded with impunity (with the exception, of course, of official enemies, as in the case of the Russian invasion of Afghanistan). None of this should occasion the least surprise, nor would it merit even a word of comment were it not for the remarkable success of Western systems of indoctrination in obscuring the obvious.

Returning to Timor, Father Walsh reports that one Indonesian source, "quoting military sources in Dili and BAKIN [the Indonesian Intelligency Agency] in Jakarta, was convinced the military was planning a major final offensive against Fretilin and would move in a large number of fresh combat battalions for this purpose—possibly towards the end of 1980." In March 1981 the Indonesian armed forces held extensive joint exercises in East Timor, "using airborne Kopassandha units dropped from helicopters in the wake of a rocket bombardment by counter-insurgency OV-10

'Broncos,' " and with airdrops of a battalion "from eight Hercules aircraft backed up by counter-insurgency OV-10 'Broncos' pouring in fire-power for 'mopping-up' purposes," along with amphibious landings.[25] The ACFOA (Australian Council for Overseas Aid) sub-committee on East Timor issued a statement on May 4, 1981, expressing its conviction "that the Indonesian armed forces have recently launched a major offensive in East Timor aimed at wiping out the remaining nationalist resistance in the interior of the island," under the cover of the March exercises, which took place (with ten thousand troops) in regions of East Timor where the resistance is known to be active. "Furthermore, the departure in mid-April of the only effective outside organisation in East Timor, the International Red Cross, has cleared the way, ACFOA believes, for the Indonesian army to conduct an offensive free of foreign constraint." The statement continues:

> It should be emphasized that an offensive of this nature is completely consistent with the reality in East Timor. Timorese resistance, military and otherwise, is continuing as are Indonesian attempts to suppress it. Wholesale arrests of thousands of people have been made since late last year. Some 5000 prisoners are confined on the off-shore island of Atauro alone, one of the four prisons known to exist. Perhaps the ugliest brutality learnt of recently was the execution in February this year of five Timorese whose heads were subsequently displayed in the market place of Laga.
>
> Frustrated by continuing internal resistance to its plans and continuing international censure of its takeover (at the UN in particular), the Indonesian military is absolutely determined to "solve" the East Timor problem. If necessary, it appears, it will engage in genocide to subjugate the East Timorese.

As usual, nothing of this appeared in the U.S. media. ACFOA expresses its plausible belief "that only the most forceful public protest coupled with requests to visit the territory and support for the current [spring 1981] Portugal-UN initiative,[26] will offset the terrible consequences for the long-suffering Timorese." But there can be no public protest in the country that counts the most, as long as the public is kept in ignorance of the facts, that is, as long as the free press performs its task.

The departure of the ICRC from Timor was briefly noted in the U.S. press. The following item is quoted, *in toto*, from the *Christian Science Monitor*, May 22, 1981:

THE PLIGHT OF THE EAST TIMORESE GROWS MORE DESPERATE

Never as visible as the starving people of Cambodia, the Timorese now have lost the international food aid that lasted 20 months. An estimated 60,000 of them are seriously malnourished.

Half the food in East Timor is imported. The island has only 16 miles of paved roads. All the water buffalo are gone, and the task of restoring dry and denuded lands could take years. Meanwhile, fewer and fewer countries endorse the yearly UN resolutions condemning Indonesia for its forcible takeover of East Timor.

Indonesia claims it will put more money per-capita into Timor than any of its 13,000 other islands.

I came across no other reference.

Some members of Congress have continued to press for a change in the U.S. policy of supporting aggression and massacre in East Timor. In an important article, Representative Tom Harkin of Iowa, who has been in the forefront of these and other human rights efforts, writes:

> The State Department's cover-up of the invasion, its failure to respond to the burgeoning famine when it first became evident, and its excessively cordial posture towards Indonesia today, demonstrate callous indifference to the tragic implications of East Timor's annexation. Our uninterrupted and increased military assistance to Indonesia has had criminal consequences in East Timor. We have the moral obligation to take action now which may benefit the East Timorese people.[27]

He calls for suspending non-humanitarian foreign assistance and commercial arms sales to Indonesia, as required by U.S. law in the case of severe human rights violations,[28] and for pressures to compel Indonesian withdrawal and opening of the area to church, human rights, and relief groups. "And finally, Congress should subject the history of our involvement in this tragedy to comprehensive scrutiny, in the hopes that the United States can avoid complicity in future 'East Timors' "—vain hopes, unfortunately.

Senator Paul Tsongas of Massachusetts was one of ten senators who called on Secretary of State Muskie in October 1980 to act to ensure that an independent international presence would remain in East Timor full-time—in vain, as we have seen. In April 1981 he introduced into the *Con-*

gressional Record a letter sent in late 1980 by a Roman Catholic priest living in East Timor.[29] The letter points out that while the military struggle continues, "the presence of the International Committee of the Red Cross has apparently had a moderating influence on the level of violence: the Indonesian Air Force has stopped its policy of heavy bombardments of areas where Fretilin is active." From June 1980, the priest reports, "the prisons have been overflowing. The island of Atauro, in particular, has been turned into a penal colony for political prisoners." In one region, "Almost all the teachers . . . have been imprisoned." "Dozens of prisoners are reported to have disappeared." The material situation is "desperate." "Hunger and disease continue to decimate the population. Several villages have been burned to the ground and their inhabitants sent to concentration camps." Indonesian military authorities sell food, clothing, and medicines donated by the ICRC and CRS for high prices.

> Freedom of speech and association do not exist in East Timor. All mail is censored. The torture in the prisons is indescribable, especially for women and children. The confiscation of property belonging to prisoners is commonplace.
>
> The Indonesians appear determined to destroy the educated class in East Timor. Almost all the educated Timorese have been killed or are in constant danger.

Meanwhile, the U.S. government assures Congress of its confidence "that the Government of Indonesia, with help from abroad, is now on the path which will lead to a more prosperous and happy future for the people of East Timor" (Ambassador Masters; see above, p. 373) while the United States "will continue to play a constructive role in helping resolve the humanitarian problems which grew out of the tragic history of East Timor since 1975" (Assistant Secretary of State Holbrooke; see note 28), and the press remains silent while press pundits assure us that "99.99% of the American people don't care about Timor" (see p. 370, above).

While the current situation is unreported, there has been some exposure of the earlier record. There was a brief flurry of interest in this topic in late 1980, when the Australian High Court attempted to ban a new book containing secret cables from the Australian ambassador to Indonesia on the topic of Timor in late 1975, among other documents.[30] The U.S. press referred to "newly available Australian documents" (Southerland), including

a secret cable of August 17, 1975, in which Australian Ambassador Woolcott
stated the following:

> The United States might have some influence on Indonesia at present as
> Indonesia really wants and needs United States assistance in its military
> re-equipment programme. But [U.S.] Ambassador [David] Newsom told
> me last night that he is under instructions from Kissinger personally not
> to involve himself in discussions on Timor with the Indonesians on the
> grounds that the United States is involved in enough problems of greater
> importance overseas at present. The State Department has, we under-
> stand, instructed the embassy to cut down its reporting on Timor. . . .
> [Newsom's] present attitude is that the United States should keep out of
> the Portuguese Timor situation and allow events to take their course. His
> somewhat cynical comment to me was that if Indonesia were to intervene
> the United States would hope they would do so "effectively, quickly and
> not use our equipment."

Jack Anderson describes this as "one of the most damning pieces of evidence" concerning U.S. complicity in the forthcoming invasion—concerning which U.S. officials continually pretended, before Congress, that they
knew very little. Other documents in the collection make it clear that the
Indonesian intention to take over East Timor was well understood and that
the United States had decided to "avoid any involvement in the Portuguese
Timor issue although Ambassador Newsom considers that Indonesia's need
for United States military equipment and likely congressional disquiet
about Indonesian intervention could, in itself, exercise an influence on the
President to move towards the incorporation of Timor as cautiously and as
subtly as possible unless there is a total breakdown of law and order in the
colony." What concerned the United States was its relations with Indonesia,
as Ambassador Newsom explained in an "authoritative statement" based on
instructions received from Washington on August 19. Newsom notified
General Yoga Sugama of Indonesian intelligence that "it was not intended
to pressure the outcome in one way or the other but the Indonesian government should be aware that if United States equipment were used this could
call into effect sections of the foreign assistance act and could place the
United States military assistance programme in Indonesia in jeopardy."
Yoga explained that he understood the problems that might be raised by
Congress, and informed Newsom that Indonesia "had not gained more sup-

port" in Timor and that only APODETI (a tiny pro-Indonesian party) "favoured integration with Indonesia." Indonesia then proceeded to invade, using American arms (which were virtually all it had), with the full knowledge and understanding of the United States government, which then proceeded to accelerate the flow of armaments as needed to suppress the resisting population, while blocking U.N. efforts to stop the massacre, as discussed earlier.

These documents are no doubt important in demolishing what little was left of the U.S. government's case (which, it must be recalled, was loyally repeated without serious question by the major media throughout the war until late 1979). But it is hardly accurate to state that these "damning pieces of evidence" are "newly available." In fact, the most "damning" of them were published in the Australian press in May 1976, and appear in a book that was published in the United States in mid-1979.[31]

In February 1981, Henry Kamm published a major article entitled "The Silent Suffering of East Timor" in the *New York Times Magazine* (February 15, 1981). The article is an important one, though it would have been far more important years earlier, when the Ford and Carter Administrations were creating the situation that Kamm describes ("I walked among thousands of people huddled together, from the outskirts of the village to its ravaged center. Men, women, children—all shared the look and scent of deprivation to the limits of human endurance: frail bodies clothed in rags, gaunt faces uttering mute pleas. The bloated bellies of children protruded over waists so scrawny that the smallest ones had to hold up their shorts or lose them"; this in January 1980, when, Kamm states, "The war was over").

While the article is undoubtedly important, it raises a number of questions. First, consider the title. Why the "silent suffering" of the people of East Timor? Was their suffering silent because they did not try to be heard? Or was it because their now "mute pleas" were ignored by the free press when they voiced them, as they did, from the outset, in an ample record? Was the suffering silent because, for example, the Southeast Asia correspondent for the *New York Times*, Henry Kamm, chose to ignore these pleas, preferring the "facts" provided to him by Indonesian generals about how Fretilin "forced" the population to live under its "control" in the mountains, though now (1977) they were fleeing to the protection of the Indonesians, escaping their fierce captors—related as fact in the *New York Times* "news" columns? A word about these matters might have been in order.

The subheading too raises questions. It reads: "Since it was abandoned by

Portugal in 1975, East Timor has undergone revolution, civil war, invasion by neighboring Indonesia and famine. The tragic toll of Timorese lives lost is estimated to be upward of 100,000." There was, in fact, little in the way of "revolution," and the civil war lasted for less than a month and left a toll of two to three thousand dead. A more accurate subheading would read: "Since East Timor was invaded by Indonesia with U.S. support, over 100,000 Timorese are estimated to have lost their lives."

Kamm notes that the Indonesian invasion "never became a major issue in the world, but in the United States and Australia small groups centered in universities continued to protest their Government's acquiescence in the act of force." In the United States the numbers were so few that it would not have been difficult to list the names: Arnold Kohen, Richard Franke, Sue Nichterlein, Roberta Quance, Michael Chamberlin, Jeremy Mark, and a handful of others, several of them at Cornell University, where they had the support of Professor Benedict Anderson. This tiny group deserves full credit for the fact that there is any awareness at all of the Timor tragedy and the U.S. role in it in the United States, for the fact that the story did finally break through and reached the press and Congress and large parts of the loosely structured "peace movement." They also deserve credit for the fact that some international relief did finally reach the silently suffering people of East Timor, saving tens of thousands of lives. There is no doubt that they would receive the Nobel Peace Prize, if that award had any meaning. Again, these are facts that are familiar to the author and his editors, and that might have been recounted.

Kamm agrees that "there is substance to these protests, even if, at their most extreme, they degenerate into hyperbole," for example, accusations "of American complicity rather than acquiescence." The admission is too grudging. The protests were quite accurate throughout the period that the *Times* and its colleagues were ignoring or distorting the facts, and it is no "hyperbole" to speak of American "complicity," as is evident from the record reviewed here and in more detail elsewhere (see note 1). In support of his objection, Kamm claims that "there is no evidence" that Ford and Kissinger discussed with Suharto "the impending attack" which took place a few hours after they left Jakarta. True, no documentary record of their discussions is currently available; it hardly could be. But the evidence that they knew of the impending attack and gave their approval is substantial, as already discussed. Fifteen months before Kamm's article appeared, Jack Anderson had reported that in an interview, President Ford conceded as much.

The intelligence record leaves hardly any doubt of American complicity, from well before the outright invasion following three months of border attacks and naval bombardment.[32] It takes quite an act of faith to believe that the invasion was not discussed. Furthermore, the subsequent record of accelerated arms shipments and diplomatic support, including Moynihan's disruptive tactics at the U.N. of which he is so proud, surely amount to "complicity"; recall Moynihan's statement that "the United States wished things to turn out as they did, and worked to bring this about." Rather than considering the protests to be "hyperbole," it would be more accurate to characterize Kamm's stance as "apologetics for massacre."

Kamm states categorically that the United States "intended" that the weapons it sent to Indonesia "be used only for Indonesia's self defense." More apologetics, in this case, of a particularly disgraceful kind. The State Department has conceded that no constraints were placed on how Indonesia would use the weapons that were sent, in an accelerating flow, in the course of the invasion (see note 3 of the main chapter). Furthermore, even without this admission, it was surely obvious to any sane person that the OV-10 Broncos and other counterinsurgency equipment would be used exactly as they were used, with exactly the consequences that Kamm graphically describes. As Benedict Anderson observed in congressional testimony, this equipment is useless for Indonesia's "self-defense." See also the Newsom-Yoga interchange described above, page 386.

Kamm claims that "little is known about events in East Timor since the invasion," and that "the bulk of the testimony has come from highly partisan members or supporters of Fretilin." This is false. The refugees in Lisbon whose testimony on Timor the *Times* systematically ignored until January 1980 are mostly supporters of UDT, not Fretilin; their reports were of no interest to the U.S. press. Nor did the *Times* show any interest in the refugee studies carried out by others, specifically the Australian specialist on Timor James Dunn, who testified before Congress on the subject in 1977. Father Leoneto, whose eloquent testimony the *Times* largely suppressed (see pp. 362–63), is hardly a Fretilin partisan, and the same is true of the many other sources that Kamm and others pretend do not exist; see the references of note I of the main chapter.

Kamm cites reports of "waning Fretilin control" in early 1978, presenting them as fact. It is a matter of dogma, requiring no evidence and admitting of no argument, that the relation of Fretilin to the population is one of "control." It is by such means as this that the doctrines of state propaganda are insinuated, without direct assertion, in what pretend to be objective, nonpartisan accounts.

Kamm observes correctly that "crucial questions remain unanswered" about the East Timor story. It is enlightening to survey his list: "Why did the East Timorese elite, whatever its political differences, drive the colony so quickly into murderous civil war? Why did Portugal abandon East Timor before any pressure had been exerted on its administration and forces? Why did Indonesia intervene so heavy-handedly?" Putting aside what is known about these questions, it is striking to see what does not qualify as a "crucial question": for example, why is it that "the United States wished things to turn out as they did and worked to bring this about" (Moynihan)? Why did Henry Kamm and his colleagues commit themselves to suppressing the facts, thus contributing to the death of over a hundred thousand people, by the *Times* estimate? What do we learn from these facts, and facts they are, about the functioning of our free institutions, a question that should be of some concern to us, perhaps even of "crucial" concern? These questions cannot be raised.

Kamm comes perilously close to raising them, however, when he cites the "recent publication of a series of secret diplomatic documents"—of which, it will be recalled, the most crucial were published in mid-1976 and in the United States in mid-1979. He cites the August 17 dispatch from Ambassador Woolcott quoted above, omitting the crucial first sentence of the paragraph: "The United States might have some influence on Indonesia at present as Indonesia really wants and needs United States assistance in its military re-equipment programme." This crucial fact is significant in highlighting the "complicity" that Kamm denies.

Kamm states that the post-invasion American position "was limited to halting the weapons flow for six months." In fact, as the Administration conceded, the arms flow was not halted, and new offers of weapons, including counterinsurgency equipment, were made during the period of the alleged "arms halt," of which Indonesia was never even informed.

"The Moslem fasting month, when many services cease function in Indonesia, and what Mr. Carlin [of CRS] termed 'internal delays' between Catholic Relief and the United States Government (which underwrote most of the assistance), kept aid from arriving until September, a year after the ambassadors, including Mr. Masters, had seen the first victims," Kamm reports. As related earlier, the facts are a bit different. Ambassador Masters delayed nine months before initiating a request for aid even through internal channels, apparently awaiting a "green light" from the Indonesian generals, and subsequently misinformed Congress about the conclusions of the ambassadors on the September 1978 visit.

Finally, consider Kamm's description of the Indonesian invasion as "a typical Southeast Asian war—in which cruelty knew few bounds and both sides pushed and pulled a largely unpolitical people in order to deny them to the 'enemy.' " Three points deserve special notice. First, Kamm provides no evidence to indicate that the Timorese were more "unpolitical" in his sense than, say, the American colonists in 1776.[33] He simply ignores sources that deal with this question, including anthropologists who worked in East Timor, international observers during the brief period of independence, and others (see the references of notes 1 and 38). Secondly, he flies in the face of the available facts when he implies that cruelty to the population was shown in more or less equal measure by the Indonesian invaders and the Fretilin resistance. But more significant is his reference to "a typical Southeast Asian war." Is it "untypical" of Western wars to place few bounds on cruelty? Limiting ourselves just to the United States—our prime concern, one might imagine—what bounds on cruelty are revealed by the terrible bombing of the civilian population of Japan and Germany in the final stages of World War II, or in Korea? Or in the war directed by the United States in Greece in the late 1940s (see Chapter 7)? Or in Indochina? And is the war in East Timor correctly described simply as a "Southeast Asian war"? Was there no role played by Washington in intensifying its savagery? Or by the American press? Kamm's observation can only be described as racist in the extreme, and yet another contribution to apologetics for the U.S. government commitment to terror and violence in the Third World, when higher strategic or economic interests are at stake.

Nevertheless, the article remains an important contribution, when measured against the general performance of the press throughout this sordid affair, and the *Times* is to be complimented for rejecting the Karnow-Valeriani criticism that the massacre of upwards of 100,000 people in the course of U.S.-backed aggression is too insignificant a matter to deserve comment.

If the past is any guide, the "silent suffering of East Timor" will continue, and will intensify, with the withdrawal of foreign aid and the marginal full-time international presence.[34]

But we may, perhaps, end on a slightly more hopeful note. As a result of the dedicated efforts of a handful of young people who have devoted themselves to the welfare of the people of East Timor, the veil of self-imposed censorship has been partially lifted, and for a time, some assistance did reach the victims of U.S.-backed Indonesian aggression, saving many lives. While there is nothing remotely comparable to what a minimal commitment to human rights would dictate, nevertheless the terrible story is slowly coming to be generally known, and there remains a possibility that substantial elements of public opinion can be mobilized in the United States to save the miserable remnants who have survived, and to compel the U.S. government to terminate its support for these atrocities, so that the people of East Timor may enjoy the right of self-determination that they have demanded, with the regular and insistent support of the majority of the members of the United Nations—always excluding the United States and its allies,[35] whose policies have been guided by the following principle expressed by a State Department official and reported in the Australian press:

> We regard Indonesia as a friendly, nonaligned nation—a nation we do a lot of business with.[36]

How many Third World victims have suffered and died as a result of our commitment to this overriding doctrine?

NOTES

Foreword

1. Noam Chomsky, *The Chomsky Reader*, ed. James Peck (London: Serpent's Tail, 1987).
2. Milan Kundera, *The Book of Laughter and Forgetting* (London: Penguin, 1983), p. 5.
3. This quotation is from an interview similar to that in *Language and Politics* (Montreal: Black Rose Books, 1988), p. 700.
4. Noam Chomsky, *The Culture of Terrorism* (Boston: South End Press, 1988), p. 95.
5. Chomsky's extended sense of Isaiah Berlin's term, "secular priesthood," is developed in his major essay "Intellectuals and the State" (1977), reprinted in this volume.
6. Noam Chomsky, *The Culture of Terrorism*, p. 24; also *Language and Politics*, p. 693.
7. In conversation with John Pilger, *The Late Show*, BBC Television, December 12, 1992.
8. Cited in *The Late Show*.
9. *Radical Philosophy*, no. 53 (autumn 1989): pp. 31–40.
10. Norman Mailer, *The Armies of the Night: History as a Novel, the Novel as History* (New York: New American Library, 1968), p. 203.
11. *The Late Show*.
12. E-mail correspondence, March 2003.
13. *The Late Show* (and all quotes that follow).

Introduction

1. *Business Week*, "The international forces dictating U.S. economic policy," November 5, 1979. The specific reference is to the erosion of hegemony in "the sphere of economic affairs," but the point is more general, and had evoked much concern well before. See, e.g., Chapter 2, p. 106, for similar concerns in the same journal several years earlier.
2. See Chapter 7 at note 31.
3. *Business Week*, "U.S. ineffectiveness frays the alliance network," March 24, 1980. On the misuse of the concept "Finlandization," see Fred Singleton, "The myth of 'Finlandization,' " *International Affairs* (Spring 1981).
4. *The Credibility of the NATO Deterrent: Bringing the NATO Deterrent Up to Date*, Report of the Working Group of the Atlantic Council of the United States on the Credibility of the NATO Deterrent, Kenneth Rush and Brent Scowcroft, Co-Chairmen, Joseph J. Wolf, Rapporteur, Policy Papers, Security Series (May 1981).
5. "In Senate testimony yesterday, Eugene V. Rostow, the nominee for the post of director of the Arms Control and Disarmament Agency [a remarkable choice, given Rostow's record], said the United States probably would not be ready to begin formal arms talks before March 1982"; John F. Burns, "Brezhnev Says U.S. Is Evading Arms Talks," *New York Times*, June 24, 1981. See also "Vance Assails Policy on China Arms Sales," *New*

York Times, June 24, 1981, reporting former Secretary of State Cyrus Vance's criticism of the Reagan decision to provide "lethal weapons" to China though, Vance alleges, there was no pressure from Peking for arms: "It seems to me that we were pushing these arms on them rather than any felt need on their part to have lethal weapons," Vance said. Vance pointed out further that the decision was not only a "needlessly provocative" form of "bear-baiting," but that it would also lessen U.S. restraints on potential Soviet moves, perhaps in Poland.

6. *Economist,* "Did you say allies?," June 6, 1981.

7. As a sign of the times, consider the observations by Richard E. Morgan on "the attack on the American intelligence community by liberal and radical intellectuals and by their outriders in the media and Congress." Morgan comments on "the low intellectual level at which the debates over intelligence have been carried out," as illustrated, for example, by the fact that "the critics *assumed* that it was wrong for the agency [CIA] to engage in certain sorts of activities such as assassinating foreign leaders and destabilizing governments" (his emphasis) without undertaking "serious consideration" of "the underlying questions of morality in politics." He fails to add that the response to Soviet intervention (there is no debate in this case) has been marked by a similarly "low intellectual level." Review of Ernest W. Lefever and Roy Godson, *The CIA and the American Ethic,* Ethics and Public Policy Center of Georgetown University (1980), *Political Science Quarterly* (Spring 1981).

8. For extensive discussion of this matter, see N. Chomsky and Edward S. Herman, *The Political Economy of Human Rights,* two volumes (Boston: South End Press, 1979).

9. See, for example, the discussion in *Fortune* of how dictates of Western bankers helped "trigger the worker's revolt that swept across Poland," much to their consternation ("What the Bankers Did to Poland," September 22, 1980). The Western banks wanted "to play an IMF role," one banker explained, and demanded austerity measures and economic changes of the sort that the IMF typically imposes on such states as Jamaica. "Most of the bankers were pleased when the Polish government—although without warning—doubled the price of sugar in June and raised the price of meat on July 1. But many were shocked by the ensuing strikes, which they hadn't foreseen." In short, the Polish workers did not behave in the manner required by those who control the world's major capital resources, and there was no way to undertake the coercive measures applied in U.S. domains; one wonders whether in private the Western bankers are not hoping that the Russians "send in the Marines" to suppress the intolerable behavior of Solidarity.

Alexander Cockburn and James Ridgeway point out that though "enthusiasm for the Polish strikers has been unbounded in the United States," even in conservative publications, their actual demands and subsequent agreements with the government "are hard to find in U.S. publications" ("Love at Long Distance: Polish Workers and the U.S.," *Village Voice,* December 17, 1980). Cockburn and Ridgeway give a detailed survey (the only one in the U.S. media, to my knowledge) of demands "calling for an expansion of unionism and workers' control in Poland," noting that Western bankers "must view the Gdansk agreements with horror." They conclude that "it is hard to imagine the Gdansk demands being deeply mourned by Washington, if they vanish beneath the tracks of a Soviet tank."

The Gdansk Agreement and other documents appear in *Radical America* (May–June 1981).

10. Interview with Bill Moyers on Public Broadcasting; excerpts appear in the *Boston Globe*, June 7, 1981. Timerman's denunciations of the Argentine regime have evoked harsh attacks on the part of so-called conservatives, a highly misleading term for those committed to an enhancement of state power and violence. For discussion of attacks by William Buckley and Irving Kristol, see Alexander Cockburn, "Timerman, American Jews and the Neo-Conservatives," *Village Voice*, June 3, 1981; "Israel and the Effort to Discredit Timerman," *Wall Street Journal*, June 4, 1981. See also Colin Campbell, "Timerman's Views Bring Debate on Rights Policy and Argentina," *New York Times*, June 8, 1981; and Anthony Lewis, "The Timerman Affair," *New York Times*, June 14, 1981.

11. For references and discussion, see *Political Economy of Human Rights*, vol. 1, section 4–5.

12. See *Political Economy of Human Rights*, vol. 2, chapter 5, note 44, pp. 326–27; and Chapter 11, note 22, below.

13. See *Political Economy of Human Rights*, vol. 1, for discussion.

14. *Latin America Regional Reports Southern Cone*, May 22, 1981.

15. For discussion, see chapter 2 of my *American Power and the New Mandarins* (New York: Pantheon, 1969).

16. Christopher Eastwood, head of the General Department of the British Colonial Office, April 1943, cited in Wm. Roger Louis, *Imperialism at Bay: The United States and the Decolonization of the British Empire, 1941–1945* (New York: Oxford University Press, 1978), p. 247. Eastwood added that "independence is a political catchword which has no meaning apart from economics." Another official, Sydney Caine, observed: "The Americans themselves are not really interested only in the welfare of colonial peoples but also in the exploitation of natural resources in colonial territories," to which the British imperial system posed a barrier. Louis adds: "The Americans talked much about welfare and development in the colonies, but if one looked at their idealism in relation to their economic investments the problem assumed another dimension" (402); President Roosevelt's "interest in trusteeship schemes as a means of stabilizing unsettled areas and opening the door to American commerce remained constant" (449). Another British official, M. E. Dening, observed: "At present American imperialism is in the forefront in the conduct of affairs in the Far East," attempting "to elbow us out" (550).

    Churchill, in particular, "viewed American trusteeship schemes as mainly a cover for annexationist plans in the Pacific" (349). But as Abe Fortas explained in internal U.S. government discussion: "When we take over the Marianas and fortify them we are doing so not only on the basis of our own right to do so but as part of our obligation to the security of the world. . . . These reservations were being made in the interest of world security rather than of our own security . . . what was good for us was good for the world" (481) (to which we may perhaps add Charles Wilson's famous remark that what is good for General Motors is good for the country, so that . . .). As for the domains of U.S. influence: "Conditions were sufficiently 'different' in the Western hemisphere to warrant its exclusion" from the principles of trusteeship, Louis notes, referring to Sumner Welles's rejection of "all proposals to place any territory in any part of that hemisphere under international supervision. Indeed he viewed all of the Americas as almost a sole United States responsibility" (184).

    Many Europeans were unimpressed with this "idealism," asking, in Louis's paraphrase: "*Why should the question of dependent peoples be restricted to the European overseas empires?* Why should trusteeship not apply to the Indian tribes of North America? Or for that matter to the dependent peoples within Russia?" (his emphasis, 570). Or to Puerto Rico, Hawaii, Guam, or Alaska? The reference to the American Indians is not out of place. On this matter, see Michael A. Dorris, "Contemporary Native Americans," *Daedalus* (Spring 1981), who discusses the regular violation and abrogation of treaties that gave the native tribes the powers of any sovereign state, "a status higher than that of states" of the union, according to the U.S. courts. Dorris also points out that the Indian population was reduced from about 12 to 15 million north of the Rio Grande in 1491 "to a low of 210,000 in the 1910 census," a case of protracted genocide that arouses little notice.

Welles drew the line for his "idealistic experiments" elsewhere too. He felt that in the case of the Belgian Congo, self-government would not come for more than one hundred years. In the case of Portuguese Timor, "it would certainly take a thousand years" (Louis, p. 237)—an interesting foretaste of subsequent U.S. policy; cf. Chapter 13.

17. Cf. Gabriel Kolko, *The Politics of War* (New York: Random House, 1969); Joyce and Gabriel Kolko, *The Limits of Power* (New York: Harper & Row, 1972); Fred L. Block, *The Origins of International Economic Disorder* (Berkeley: University of California Press, 1977).

18. Lennox S. Hinds, *Illusions of Justice: Human Rights Violations in the United States*, School of Social Work, University of Iowa, Iowa City (1978). The foreword notes that since the filing of the petition, "international interest in its allegations has far surpassed domestic concern." Perhaps it is a best-seller in the Soviet Union.

19. On Carter's refusal and the circumstances, see my *'Human Rights' and American Foreign Policy*, chapter 2 (Nottingham: Spokesman, 1978). See also Mary McGrory, "Carter's human rights charity begins abroad," *Boston Globe*, December 17, 1977, discussing the refusal of "Mr. Human Rights" to "say anything about oppression in his own backyard" since, in his words, the case of the Wilmington Ten "is a state matter, I would have no jurisdiction"—in contrast to the case of Russian dissidents, where he was always quite willing to issue sharply critical statements.

20. See *Political Economy of Human Rights*, vol. 1, chapter 1, sections 15 and 16, for further discussion of this important but generally neglected question.

21. On this phenomenon, see *'Disappearances': A Workbook*, Amnesty International USA (1981). The case of Guatemala is "unique, because in no other country have 'disappearances' occurred so regularly for such a long period of time." Furthermore, the scale is enormous, amounting to tens of thousands, "mainly peasants and rural workers": From 1968, "as so many Guatemalans have lamented, there have been virtually no political prisoners but only 'dead men.' "

Disappearances began in 1963, originally in response to guerrilla movements that arose "with considerable support from the urban middle class" after the U.S.-backed military coup brought to an end "ten years of civilian and reformist government" in 1954. A 1968 report of the Guatemalan Committee for the Protection of Human Rights "listed 277 individuals—most of them Guatemalan military and police officials, and North American advisers—who were believed to be responsible for the deaths and 'disappearances' during this period." In the period of "Official Terrorism" from 1970 to 1974, when disappearances may have amounted to about fifteen thousand, a human rights group estimated that "over 75 percent could be attributed directly to the government's security forces." "In 1979 over two thousand 'disappearances' and killings occurred in which the evidence shows that the government of Guatemala exercised an illegal and largely arbitrary form of the death penalty." Victims include religious and cooperative leaders, labor leaders, lawyers, professors and students, political leaders of the centrist parties, and others. The "death squads" appear to operate under orders delivered from the presidential palace.

On the direct involvement of U.S. Green Berets, U.S. pilots dropping napalm on peasants, USAID, and the U.S. military mission in the slaughter of thousands of Guatemalan peasants in 1966–68, see Penny Lernoux, *Cry of the People* (Garden City, N.Y.: Doubleday, 1980). Also my *American Power and the New Mandarins*, pp. 249, 285–86, citing *Le Monde* and the *New Statesman*. Evidence on this matter was repeatedly brought to the attention of the *New York Times* but was not published. See also *Political Economy of Human Rights*, vol. 1, and note 189, below; and Chapter 7, below, for discussion of atrocities in Guatemala for which the United States bears major responsibility that exceed by a substantial margin those inflicted by the government's "death squads."

22. See, however, my introduction to N. Blackstock, ed., *COINTELPRO* (New York: Vintage, 1976) and sources cited there, among others. See also note 43, below.

23. Commenting on "the invective used to condemn the Soviet intervention," Robert Fisk writes from Kabul in the *Christian Science Monitor* (March 5, 1980) that "things are not that simple." The country "never really existed" as a nation-state, but was bandit-infested and torn by factional wars under an unpopular king. The revolt led by mullahs who "resented the new regime's attempt to impose land reforms and its efforts to educate women," involves hill tribesmen who fight each other and rob civilian travelers out of "prosaic greed." Prime Minister Hafizullah Amin, whom President Carter referred to as "the legal ruler of Afghanistan" and who was overthrown by the Russian invasion and killed, was a "brutal despot" who carried out "a bloody purge of all political opposition," while the current Russian puppet President Karmal, is "a philosophical Marxist of considerable intelligence and even charm." Fisk does not justify the Soviet invasion on these grounds, though perhaps Communist propaganda does. One can change a few names and derive familiar justifications for U.S. aggression and subversion.

Charles Fenyvesi reports that the Soviet invasion may have been triggered by "the massacre of a Soviet military delegation" of thirty-five to fifty officers, many of them generals and colonels, by Afghan tribesmen, with "decapitation and worse," subsequent to an earlier massacre and mutilation of twenty Soviet military advisers and civilians (*Manchester Guardian Weekly*, April 19, 1981). He compares the Russian response to the "British reaction in 1756 to losing 123 of their own in the Black Hole of Calcutta—a massacre that led to eventual British rule over India." One wonders how the United States would respond to similar massacres of U.S. civilians and advisers. See note 26.

A Western diplomat unsympathetic to the Soviets suggests that the Soviet invasion was triggered in part by the NATO decision to install Pershing II missiles in Western Europe and the "ever-growing Sino-American alliance." "There are no more dividends for the Soviet Union in détente," he says. And furthermore, "Soviet jockeying for power cannot be understood without being linked to American initiative. Indonesia, Egypt, Ghana, and Sudan have been snatched back by the United States. . . . This geopolitical game of monopoly must be put into perspective" (Louis Wiznitzer, *Christian Science Monitor*, February 7, 1980).

Jill Tweedie contrasts the "incomparably better" conditions in southern Russia and those in Kabul, not many miles away, noting that the "barbarity" that had "occurred under British rule" has been overcome in southern Russia; she suggests that the same may prove to be the case in Afghanistan. She suggests further that the alternatives for Afghan women may be "a healthy body and an educated mind for yourself or your children under foreign occupation, or a bestial existence in what the West likes to call 'freedom,' " adding that "it is easy to sit in comfort, in London, and deplore the Soviet presence in Afghanistan, on principle" (*Manchester Guardian Weekly*, August 17, 1980). In a similar vein, the editor of the *Observer*, Conor Cruise O'Brien, notes "the sense of contrast between the modernity of Soviet Tadjikistan [adjacent to Afghanistan] and the continuing backwardness of independent Afghanistan . . . ," regions that were comparable sixty years ago, though now the capital city of Tadjikistan "is a bit of a marvel" by Third World standards. He also suggests that "British and American people, before coming loudly, though figuratively, to the rescue of Afghans from Russian 'imperialism,' should reflect a little on their own comparative historical record in dealing with less-developed peoples. . . . The British ruled much of Africa for a period of time slightly longer than the period of Soviet rule in Central Asia to date—effectively 60 years. If you look at many of Britain's former African possessions and at Soviet Asia, the contrast is cruel—and not to the Soviets." (Americans might add a comparison to blacks and native Americans in 1840, or even somewhat later.) Cited by Alexander Cockburn, *Village Voice*, April 28, 1980.

Others report that the current guerrilla groups had been raiding Afghanistan with Pakistani support since the early 1970s (see Chapter 2, pp. 93–94), and that the Russians won out in early 1978 in a complex series of manipulations involving Western intelligence and the Shah as well.

Note again that none of these commentators make any effort to justify the Soviet invasion of Afghanistan. In contrast, much weaker arguments are standardly used to justify U.S. invasions—e.g., the 1965 invasion of the Dominican Republic, commonly justified on grounds that it led to "democracy." See note 67, below.

24. "Don't forget Afghanistan," *Economist*, October 25, 1980.

25. See Chapter 5, below; Chapter 3, note 30. For further references from the Pentagon Papers see *Political Economy of Human Rights*, vol. 2, pp. 63–64; and my *For Reasons of State* (New York: Pantheon, 1973), chapter 1.

26. The pretext for the simultaneous bombing of the North, at about one-third the level of the southern bombardment, was the Pleiku incident, in which several American military advisers were killed in an attack by southern guerrillas, a minor variant of the ambush that may have provoked the Russian invasion of Afghanistan; see note 23. The bombing of the North had been planned in 1964. Its major purpose was the hope that punishment of the North might lead Hanoi to use its influence to call off the southern guerrilla movement, although, planners anticipated, the bombing might draw the North into the southern war. For discussion, based largely on the Pentagon Papers, see *For Reasons of State*, chapter 1; also Chapter 5, below, and references cited there.

27. Analyst, *The Pentagon Papers*, Gravel Edition, vol. 2, p. 22 (Boston: Beacon Press, 1971). The actual quote reads: ". . . we must note that South Vietnam (unlike any of the other countries in Southeast Asia) was essentially the creation of the United States. Without

U.S. support Diem almost certainly could not have consolidated his hold on the South during 1955 and 1956. Without the threat of U.S. intervention, South Vietnam could not have refused to even discuss the elections called for in 1956 under the Geneva settlement without being immediately overrun by the Viet Minh armies. Without U.S. aid in the years following, the Diem regime certainly, and an independent South Vietnam almost as certainly, could not have survived."

28. See Chapters 4 and 5.

29. Josef Joffe, "European-American Relations: The Enduring Crisis," *Foreign Affairs* (Spring 1981).

30. Michael Howard, "Return to the Cold War?" *Foreign Affairs, America and the World 1980* (Winter 1980–81), Daniel Yankelovich and Larry Kaagan, "Assertive America," *ibid.* In the latter article, the authors also refer to "the knife-twisting which Castro has learned to administer so skillfully to the United States," which is so "distressing." More distressing, apparently, than the twenty years of embargo, terrorism, crop poisoning, etc., which the United States has administered to Castro's Cuba, which go unmentioned. See below, pp. 49–50. On Howard's justification for the 1972 Christmas bombing of Hanoi and Haiphong, see Chapter 6, below, p. 181.

31. Not entirely, however. There are occasional exceptions, though they hardly count as more than statistical error. See, e.g., David G. Marr's review in *Pacific Affairs* (Spring 1981) of a RAND Corporation study of the reactions of Vietnamese (GVN) military and civilian leaders to the collapse of their regime in 1975 (Stephen T. Hosmer, Konrad Kellen, and Brian M. Jenkins, *The Fall of South Vietnam* [New York: Crane, Russak, 1980]). Marr discusses the record of corruption, incompetence, cowardice, blind dependency on the foreign master, and total lack of concern for the population (one general deplored the failure of the United States to bomb the environs of Saigon with B-52s, "quite ignoring the fate of hundreds of thousands of refugees who had crowded into the intended drop-zones") on the part of the "compliant, devious men" whom the United States had installed in power in South Vietnam ("Vietnamese daring to voice serious disagreement with their foreign mentors had already been shunted aside in previous decades"; cf. Chapter 4, note 7). He concludes that the book should be read "as a lesson in how foreign aggressors often get exactly the local clients they deserve."

David Marr, formerly a U.S. Marine Corps intelligence officer in Vietnam is a distinguished Vietnamese historian who is professor at Australian National University. The journal is published by the University of British Columbia.

32. Interview, "All Things Considered," National Public Radio, May 15, 1981.

33. "60 Minutes," CBS Television, April 6, 1980.

34. *New Republic*, editors, January 31, 1981; June 30, 1979.

35. Morton Kondracke, editor, *New Republic*, January 31, 1981. This unvarnished nonsense is a staple of the propaganda system, quite resistant to the overwhelming evidence to the contrary because of its utility in disguising state violence and aggression under the neutral category of "error." See Chapter 1, note 33; also p. 167.

Kondracke also ridicules the idea that "President Carter's Latin American policy was not the result of naiveté and excessive devotion to human rights considerations"; for example, his support for Somoza until virtually the end of his bloody rule, which was not sufficient for the editors of the journal—see Chapter 8, p. 226. Elsewhere, the editors "give Reagan & Co. good marks for their performance (so far) in . . . El Salvador," where Reagan, Haig, et al. overcame Carter's obsessive concern for human rights; though they are critical of the Reagan Administration for going too far in rejecting human rights "as the preoccupation of US foreign policy," which "only signals to the world that the United States is no longer an advocate of justice," as it has been for so many years, throughout the world (editorial, May 2, 1981). On the performance that merits their "good marks," see below, pp. 35f., 228–9.

36. The actual passage reads: "For a segment of Western Europe's left, El Salvador is a windfall. Exotic, blessedly far from home and potentially confirming a post-Vietnam generation's notions of the misuse of United States power, the controversy over the little war is packed with possibilities for simplistic portrayal. Also, it drowns out more than a year's discomfort about Afghanistan, distracts attention from Poland . . . and tends to confirm fond suspicions that superpowers behave alike. . . . [It] offers Europeans the luxuries of distance and vagueness" (John Vinocur, "For Europe's Left, Salvador Helps to Fuel U.S. Distrust," *New York Times*, February 22, 1981).

37. Editorial, "What Needs Containing in El Salvador?," February 19, 1981; Bernard Gwertzman, "Key Legislators Support Increases in Aid for Salvador," February 18, 1981. The remarks are fairly typical. For example, *Business Week* sternly admonishes the Socialist International for "supporting the fictional Social Democratic Party and the guerrillas against the *reformist junta* backed by the U.S." ("A tilt left among Europe's Socialists worries Washington," July 6, 1981, my emphasis). See below for additional examples.

   In contrast, in the foreign press we find, quite typically, such statements as the following: "The country's powerful oligarchy finances a score of far-right 'death squads.' But most of the killings are carried out by the army, the brutal national guard and the national police. American diplomats in San Salvador believe that nine-tenths of rightwing violence is carried out by these security forces. Their commanders, who are probably also in the pay of wealthy families, fervently believe that the answer to the crisis lies in wiping out tens of thousands of 'communists' " (*Economist*, December 20, 1980).

   One can find exceptions to the tendencies illustrated, but the tendencies are clear nonetheless.

38. See below for discussion, pp. 35f.

39. "The Pulitzer Lie," *New York Times* editorial, April 17, 1981. The case aroused great indignation in the nation's press. The National News Council condemned the *Post* for "a monstrous miscarriage of journalism" and as "negligent in its editing process" (AP, *Boston Globe*, June 13, 1981). The council did not condemn the *Post* when, for example, it devoted a page to photographs of Khmer Rouge atrocities that had apparently been fabricated by Thai intelligence, refusing to publish a letter stating the facts, nor did it condemn *Time* and *Newsweek* when they repeated the same farce well after the facts had been exposed. Nor did they condemn the *New York Times* for suppressing the "secret bombing" of Northern Laos. See *Political Economy of Human Rights* for discussion of these and innumerable other examples of somewhat greater significance than "the Pulitzer lie."

40. See the books cited above, in particular, *Political Economy of Human Rights* and references cited there.

41. See Chapters 3 and 4. See in particular the reference of Chapter 4, note 35. On Watergate, see the reference of note 22, above.

42. For discussion of these factors, see *Political Economy of Human Rights*, vol. 1, chapter 2, section 2.1. See also the discussion by Thomas P. McCann, vice-president in charge of public relations for the United Fruit Company for twenty years, on the success of the corporation in using the free press as a means for creating a climate of opinion supporting U.S. intervention in Guatemala. He writes: "It is difficult to make a convincing case for manipulation of the press when the victims proved so eager for the experience." *An American Company* (New York: Crown, 1976). His comments have much broader applicability.

43. Consider, for example, the recent series of malicious attacks on the Institute for Policy Studies. It is interesting that of the many "think tanks" in the United States, this one alone has been subjected to such attacks in the press (e.g., the *New York Times Magazine*) and elsewhere, hardly because of its unique power and wealth.

   The penalties for significant departure from standard dogma may go beyond the normal slander, insinuations, and lies that anyone who holds unpopular views comes to expect as a matter of course. See the reference of note 22, above. Or consider the case of Ngo Vinh Long, the author of important studies on Vietnam (*Before the Revolution: the Vietnamese Peasants Under the French* [Cambridge, Mass.: MIT Press, 1973]; *Peasant Revolutionary Struggles in Vietnam in the 1930s*, Harvard University Ph.D. dissertation, 1978; and many articles), now engaged in a village study based on a seven-month stay in Vietnam. Long has been asked to speak at Harvard representing the Hanoi government, and has refused, on the grounds that he is an independent scholar, not a representative of Hanoi. He agreed to take part in a Harvard panel on Vietnam on April 23, 1981, where, according to observers present, he was subjected to considerable abuse by panelists and a group of ninety Vietnamese refugees who were notified of the event in a letter calling him an agent of the Hanoi government. After the talk, a gasoline bomb was thrown as he approached his car, injuring two policemen who were accompanying him because of the threat of violence. The Harvard administration has refused to make a statement to the effect that assassination of political dissidents (in this case, one who is a research associate of the East Asia Center) is improper at Harvard University. The faculty, apart from a few individuals, has issued no statement of protest (consider, in contrast, the response to a much less violent act by the faculty of the Technion University in Haifa; Chapter 9, Afterword, note 84.).

   The *New York Times* reported the incident (May 6, 1981) under the headline "Vietnamese Who Supports Hanoi Angers Refugees." The report notes that Long "identifies himself as an 'independent scholar,' " not a supporter of Hanoi, but the free press knows better. In my view, the report reads as a thinly veiled justification for the attack. For a report meeting professional standards of journalism, see Robert Levey, "For these refugees, Viet war goes on," *Boston Globe*, May 7, 1981.

44. *Manchester Guardian Weekly*, March 2, 1980; also May 18, 1980.

45. On the situation under the Romero government, see *Report on the Situation of Human Rights in El Salvador*, Organization of American States, General Secretariat, Washington, D.C., November 17, 1978. See also Baloyra and Schoultz (full citation in note 159).

46. Alan Riding, "U.S. Aid to Salvador Army: Bid to Bar 'Another Nicaragua,' " *New York Times*, February 23, 1980, reporting the official interpretation. The idea that U.S. training has a moderating effect is a familiar pretense, maintained in blissful disregard for the regular and systematic contribution of U.S. training to reinforcing the most sav-

age and brutal tendencies among the Latin American military. For discussion, see *Political Economy of Human Rights*, vol. 1, and references cited there; Lernoux, *op. cit.* For the case of El Salvador, see p. 41, below.

47. Riding, *op. cit.*

48. See *Political Economy of Human Rights*, vol. 1, p. 292.

49. *Ibid.* See also an important series by Scott Armstrong in the *Washington Post*, October 25, 26, 27, 28, 29, 30, 1980. Relying in part on government documents obtained by the *Post*, Armstrong gives an enlightening account of U.S. policy from 1977 through 1979. He notes that "the Shah, notwithstanding his reputation as a bloodthirsty tyrant, disregarded eleventh-hour advice from Washington to get tough with street demonstrators and opposition leaders. . . . In fact, Carter still hoped to preserve the Shah's power long after intelligence reports and top foreign policy advisers insisted, as a matter of realism, the United States must assist the orderly transition to whatever political forces were going to displace the peacock throne." National Security Adviser Zbigniew Brzezinski was particularly intransigent, continually urging the use of military force to crush the mounting opposition to the Shah. Among other contributions, he drafted a letter to be sent to the Shah (according to State Department sources) "which unambiguously urged him to use force to put down the demonstrations," an act that some State Department aides thought might lead to tens of thousands of deaths. Ambassador William H. Sullivan feared that the Shah "was becoming unhinged," Armstrong reports, though "American policymakers viewed the Shah's willingness to use force [after the September 1978 massacre of demonstrators on "Black Friday"] as a good sign." Brzezinski proposed sending the USS *Constellation* with its eighty aircraft and five thousand sailors and aviators to demonstrate U.S. commitment to the Shah. Ambassador Sullivan, who referred to dissident groups as "students and other miscreants" and regarded freedom of expression as an aspect of "permissiveness," was concerned that "the Shah's new directives to his security forces, such as instructions to desist from torture . . . are disorienting," with unfortunate effects on those who are "being prevented from using the time-honored methods of arrest, long imprisonment and manhandling—if not worse—to get at the threat" (report of June 1, 1978). In January 1979, General Robert Huyser was sent to Teheran to consult with Iranian generals, urging them to proceed to a military takeover of the oil fields, while General Haig also urged "that the military should be pushed into action," but to no avail.

50. See Chapter 7.

51. One minor indication of the nature of Reagan's domestic program is that "there is more money in the 1982 Administration budget for military bands than for all of the music, art, dance, literature, theatre, film and other National Endowment for the Arts (NEA) programs together" (*Boston Globe*, May 24, 1981), an indication of the nature of the society and culture towards which we are evolving. The real targets, however, are social programs that benefit the poor. For an analysis of the real significance of the Reagan program, see Edward S. Herman, "Reaganomics: Class Warfare as 'Economic Policy,' " manuscript, Wharton School, University of Pennsylvania, 1981; and for an assessment of its prospects, see the articles by Robert M. Solow, James Tobin, Joseph A. Pechman, Henry Aaron, and Kenneth J. Arrow in Federation of American Scientists (FAS) *Public Interest Report*, "Reagan Economic Program" (June 1981); also Lester Thurow, "How to Wreck the Economy," *New York Review of Books*, May 14, 1981.

52. *An-Nahar Arab Report and Memo*, Beirut, February 23, 1981.

53. In a response to a query of the *Jornal do Brasil*, cited by Luis Maira, *Nexos* (Mexico; May 1981). A similar quote is given by Clifford Krauss, "Guatemala's Indian Wars," *Nation*, March 14, 1981.

54. Fontaine was speaking of economic aid and national reconciliation, a curious way of referring to what the United States did in Greece in 1947 under the Truman Doctrine; see Chapter 7.

55. John Lewis Gaddis, *The United States and the Origins of the Cold War, 1941–1947* (New York: Columbia University Press, 1972). Gaddis believes that the Truman Administration did not intend this universalistic interpretation, but that American leaders were later "trapped in their own rhetoric." A dubious interpretation, I believe, even on the evidence he presents.

56. On this planning, see Chapter 2 and references cited there; also Louis, *op. cit.*

57. Cited by Richard J. Barnet, *Intervention and Revolution* (New York: World, 1968).

58. See Louis, *op. cit.* Also John W. Dower, "Occupied Japan and the American Lake, 1945–50," in Edward Friedman and Mark Selden, eds., *America's Asia* (New York: Pantheon, 1971). See also the references of note 17.

59. Paul A. Samuelson, "The World Economy at Century's End," *Bulletin* of the American Academy of Arts and Sciences (May 1981). The U.S. share of world output has now fallen to about 25 percent, Samuelson estimates, a sign of the "Declining World Role of the U.S." The figures are, however, somewhat misleading in that they do not take account of U.S.-owned production abroad.

One might also take note of Samuelson's rather grim prediction that "if you want to read the shape of things to come, perhaps you should turn your gaze from Scandinavia and toward Argentina," for a glimpse of the "capitalistic fascism" that the future may bring into being. See also Edward S. Herman, *Corporate Control, Corporate Power* (Cambridge: Cambridge University Press, 1981), where it is suggested that if current tendencies persist, the "New Conservatism" in the United States may "look toward the Brazilian or Chilean models rather than toward the more benign models of the industrialized world"; also Bertram Gross, *Friendly Fascism: The New Face of Power in America* (New York: Evans, 1980). On this matter, see the important study by Robert Brady, *Business as a System of Power* (New York: Columbia University Press, 1943).

60. Fred Block, "Economic Instability and Military Strength: The Paradoxes of the 1950 Rearmament Decision," *Politics and Society*, vol. 10, no. 1 (1980). See also his *Origins of International Economic Disorder* (see note 17).

61. The document has long been referred to as a central document in U.S. foreign policy planning. It was declassified in 1975 and published in the *Naval War College Review* (May–June 1975), from which I quote, and subsequently in *Foreign Relations of the United States 1950*, I (Washington, D.C.: Government Printing Office, 1977); reprinted in Thomas H. Etzold and John Lewis Gaddis, *Containment: Documents on American Foreign Policy and Strategy 1945–1950* (New York: Columbia University Press, 1978). For a discussion of its import, see Block, "Economic Instability and Military Strength." Also Gregg Herken, *The Winning Weapon* (New York: Knopf, 1980). Herken notes that NSC 68 was adopted on September 30, 1950, approved by President Truman "as a statement of policy to be followed over the next four or five years."

62. To cite only one obvious example, compare the rhetoric of the Atlantic Council report cited in note 4 with its invocation of the Soviet threat "of truly global proportions" (coupled with a recognition that the Soviet military posture is defensive), of the subtle

Soviet strategy of inducing relaxation of tension against which we must be perpetually on guard, etc. This report also mimics NSC 68 in its fantasies about the West ("Western civilization has evolved beyond a belief in the use of armed force as an instrument of policy; the Kremlin has not"). It perhaps even transcends NSC 68 in bewailing the incomprehensible fact that "Moscow's propaganda has somehow managed to portray the Western allies solely as militarist and imperialist, as the champions of oppressive political systems, and the opponents of change and development." Surely there is nothing in the historical or contemporary experience of Third World peoples that could support this outrageous view, implanted by the clever and formidably effective machinations of Moscow propaganda.

A check through the list of people who were willing to have their names signed to this document gives a certain insight into the dominant intellectual culture.

63. Thomas Powers, *The Man Who Kept the Secrets: Richard Helms & the CIA* (New York: Knopf, 1979). This is not the whole story, however. On U.S. saboteurs in North Vietnam from the late 1950s, see *For Reasons of State*, pp. 103 and 163, and references cited there.

64. See the references of Chapter 7, notes 12 and 13. Also Douglas S. Blaufarb, *The Counterinsurgency Era* (New York: Free Press, 1977), a study that is particularly noteworthy for the assumptions on which it is based.

65. Cited by Jan Knippers Black, *United States Penetration of Brazil* (Philadelphia: University of Pennsylvania Press, 1977). On the economic programs of the Brazilian generals, see Peter Evans, *Dependent Development* (Princeton: Princeton University Press, 1979); Sylvia Ann Hewlett, *The Cruel Dilemmas of Development* (New York: Basic Books, 1980).

66. Cf. Black, *op. cit.;* Lernoux, *op. cit.,* A. J. Langguth, *Hidden Terrors* (New York: Pantheon, 1978). See *Political Economy of Human Rights*, vol. 1, for extensive discussion.

67. See *Political Economy of Human Rights*, chapter 4, section 4; Lernoux, *op. cit.,* pp. 236ff; Lisa Wheaton, " 'Democratization' in the Dominican Republic," in Holly Sklar, ed., *Trilateralism* (Boston: South End Press, 1980). One familiar consequence of the U.S. invasion is that production of food for local consumption has declined sharply, while almost two-thirds of the agricultural production is now exported, largely for the benefit of Gulf & Western, which moved in to take over much of the country in the wake of the invasion. Gulf & Western is able to produce sugar for export cheaply now that state terror and the U.S. labor movement's American Institute for Free Labor Development (AIFLD) have succeeded in destroying the unions, replacing them with company unions; or still better, with starving Haitians who work as virtual slaves. Malnutrition is so severe that infant mortality is to percent of live births, while of the survivors, half suffer chronic malnutrition. Four hundred thousand Dominicans have fled to the United States; one Dominican out of four depends on U.S. food supplies distributed by private charities. "Bishop Roque Adames, whose diocese spans the country's central mountain range, reported that were it not for the monthly remittances of Dominicans in the United States, half the people in his diocese would be starving to death" (Lernoux, p. 243–44).

One reads virtually nothing about this in the U.S. media—on the contrary, the Dominican Republic is frequently invoked as an illustration of the benign influence of the United States—but occasionally there is a report. See, for example, Jo Thomas,

"U.S. Good-Will Visit Brings Tragedy to Dominicans," *New York Times,* April 11, 1981, reporting "student demonstrations set off by a good-will visit of two United States naval vessels and fueled by labor strife and charges of police brutality," which led to many injuries and arrests, with four shot dead by the police. "Mr. Guzmán's Government, the first successful experience in democracy in a nation cursed with coups and dictatorships [not to speak of U.S. Marines], has been friendly with the United States, and the vehemence of the student opposition to last week's visit of the American ships apparently caught Dominican leaders and American officials by surprise.... The choice of April, the month in 1965 when 42,000 United States Marines landed here, was seen by many Dominicans, however, as inopportune at best and at worst a national affront. Thirty-nine Dominican labor leaders signed a protest that noted that 3,000 Dominicans died in 1965" in the course of this "landing." At a news conference called by the visiting U.S. admiral to reiterate "the friendly nature of the visit" and to stress the "common threat" posed by the Soviet Union to both the United States and the Dominican Republic, "a Dominican reporter observed that the Soviet Union had never invaded the Dominican Republic but that the United States had done so twice" (Dominican reporters, not yet properly acculturated, use such terms as "invasion" to refer to American invasions). The visitors were greeted warmly by the Dominican military and high government officials, "but the protests continued, spreading to other cities." Municipal workers went on strike "because they had not been paid for a month," following "stoppages by truck drivers and doctors working for the Government." "Violence broke out in northern neighborhoods of Santo Domingo, the same neighborhoods that were papered with posters saying 'Yankee get out.' " Thomas interviewed the mother of a slain newsboy as "she sat weeping as a relative mopped up a flood of rainwater that had flowed into the tiny house, which is, in many places, open to the elements" in a neighborhood which, "like many in which the disturbances occurred, is desperately poor, burdened with unemployment, inflation, a scarcity of funds in public coffers and now also with sorrow and fear" in the country's "first successful experience in democracy."

As is standard, no word is said about the U.S. role in all of this. No doubt the Atlantic Council would describe the protests over this "good-will visit" as one of those examples of how "Moscow's propaganda has somehow managed to portray the Western allies solely as militarist and imperialist, as the champions of oppressive political systems, and the opponents of change and development." See note 62.

Jeane Kirkpatrick, currently U.N. Ambassador, explains that "authoritarian" regimes such as the Dominican Republic (or perhaps this state has now advanced to the rank of "democracy" in terms of contemporary theology) "create no refugees," because "the miseries of traditional life are familiar," hence "bearable to ordinary people." It is only totalitarian regimes that "create refugees," as a survey of the Latin American population in the U.S. and Europe will quickly demonstrate. Jeane Kirkpatrick, "Dictatorships and Double Standards," *Commentary,* November 1979.

68. See above, note 21, and references cited there. Also note 189 and Chapter 7, below.
69. The phrase is from the report of the Linowitz Commission. See p. 206.
70. See Stephen Rousseas, *The Death of a Democracy: Greece and the American Conscience* (New York: Grove Press, 1967).
71. Sheilah Ocampo, "A united opposition—but only up to a point," *Far Eastern Economic*

Review, October 17, 1980. On Indonesia, see Chapter 13, below. See *Political Economy of Human Rights,* vol. 1, chapters 3 and 4, on Indonesia, the Philippines, and also Thailand, where the story is similar. Other references will be cited below.

72. For discussion of this matter, see *Political Economy of Human Rights,* vol. 2, chapter 1.

73. John Pilger, "From Vietnam to El Salvador," *New Statesman,* May 22, 1981. He also reports an interview with the wounded veteran who heads Vietnam Veterans of America, who describes how "he watched Vietnamese prisoners interrogated, then thrown out of helicopters and others laced together with a detonating cord which, when pulled, blew their heads off." His battalion commander "issued all of us with hatchets and offered a case of whisky to the first man to chop somebody's head off. And, sure enough, a head got chopped off. Some of his boys are right here now crazier than bed bugs." The commander is now a general. Neither he nor his civilian superiors are considered war criminals. See Chapter 5.

Pilger alleges that the "landbridge" from Thailand to Cambodia had just been reopened, "allowing Western, chiefly American sustenance to flow more conveniently to Pol Pot's Khmer Rouge and thus to accelerate the 'de-stabilization' of Cambodia and Vietnam and to push both countries deeper into the arms of the Soviet Union, which neither wants." At the same time, while rations in Vietnam are lower even than during the war years, aid has been cut off. See below.

On U.S. support for Pol Pot, see also Pilger, "America's second war in Indochina," *New Statesman,* August 1, 1980. See also Michael Vickery, "Ending Cambodia—Some Revisions," manuscript, Australian National University (June 1981), submitted to the *New York Review* but not published. Basing himself on extensive refugee interviews by him and others after the fall of the Pol Pot regime in January 1979, Vickery—one of the handful of authentic Cambodia scholars in the world—concludes that the worst massacres of the Pol Pot regime were in mid-1978 and writes:

Thus the CIA, who in 1975–76 had set out to exaggerate derogatory information about Cambodia in order to discredit what appeared to be a new and threatening socialist regime, finally moved to the position of tacitly abetting the Pol Pot clique in their worst crimes. The reason is clear. By 1978 it was apparent that Democratic Kampuchea was not going to be a Marxist success which would attract the peasantry of neighboring countries. In fact, it had lost any Marxist coloring it may have once bad, and bad become a vehicle for hyper-chauvinist, poor peasant populism, and considered its most important task to be a life and death struggle with the "hereditary enemy," Vietnam. Pol Pot's worst massacres were for traditionalist, racist, anti-Vietnamese reasons. At last his regime was becoming bloody enough to attract the American support which has continued up to the present time in the hope of making use of him to roll back revolution in Indochina.

On the historical backgrounds for the policies that Pilger describes in Cu Chi, see Arthur Westing, "Crop destruction as a means of war," *Bulletin of the Atomic Scientists* (February 1981). He reviews the policies of "agricultural devastation" employed by the American colonists since the early seventeenth century, which "earned [George] Washington the permanent epithet of 'destroyer' " among the Iroquois. He also discusses the use of the same tactics subsequently, including the conquest of the Philippines at the turn of the century and extensively in Vietnam, where crop destruction programs, Rome Plow devastation, obliteration of agricultural land, dikes, farming hamlets, etc., had a terrible and lasting impact. See also Chapter 2.

74. Ngo Vinh Long, "View from the Village," *Indochina Issues*, Center for International Policy, Washington, D.C. (December 1980). Bombing of dikes was reported by the U.S. press without comment during the war, recalling to some the fact that Nazi criminals were hanged for opening the dikes in Holland under the postwar "victor's justice." See Gabriel Kolko, "Report on the Destruction of Dikes: Holland 1944–45 and Korea 1953," in John Duffet, ed., *Against the Crime of Silence* (Flanders, N.J.: O'Hare Books, 1968). Also *For Reasons of State* (New York: Pantheon, 1973), pp. 225–26; Chapter 2, below.

75. Chris Mullin, "Unexploded U.S. bombs sabotage recovery in Laos," *In These Times*, June 3, 1981. Senator S. J. Hayakawa has advocated assistance to Laos to remove live bombs, but not to Vietnam: "We hope they kill some Vietnamese still." He is merely more honest than most. UPI, Rutland (Vermont) *Herald*, September 4, 1981.

76. "Mass starvation looms in Vietnam with no aid in sight," *Business Week*, May 4, 1981.

77. Martin Woollacott, *Manchester Guardian Weekly*, June 15, 1980. It is not clear why it should be "humiliating" to offer reparations for criminal destruction. Was it humiliating for the postwar German government to offer reparations to Jews for Nazi crimes? Would it have been humiliating for the Nazi government itself to have done so, had it survived?

78. In an interview with the *Far Eastern Economic Review*, May 9, 1980.

79. As late as the late 1960s, high State Department officials appear to have been hoping that China would break up into warring constituencies under the impact of the cultural revolution, leaving the way open to a more direct assertion of U.S. control. It is not unlikely that such thinking played some part in the decision to hold on in Indochina, giving the United States a base for the projection of its power onwards. On the debates over policy towards China in the mid-1950s between those whom Michael Klare was later to label "the Prussians" and "the traders," see my *At War with Asia*, chapter 1.

80. See Chapter 7, at note 38. Also Chapter 1, at note 29. Pilger reports that an official from the Asian Development Bank informed him that "the Americans have told us to lose the file on Vietnam" (*New Statesman*, May 22, 1981).

81. Louis Wiznitzer, "US tries to punish Vietnam by paring UN assistance," *Christian Science Monitor*, May 26, 1981. This U.S. effort failed, however. See Ted Morello, "The U.S. loses a Vietnam battle," *Far Eastern Economic Review*, July 10, 1981.

82. Daniel Southerland, "US squeezes Vietnam's economy," *Christian Science Monitor*, May 14, 1981; also UPI, *Christian Science Monitor*, May 13. See pp. 209–10.

83. Daniel Southerland, "US blocks private shipment of wheat to Vietnam," *Christian Science Monitor*, May 13, 1981. According to Elizabeth Becker, this decision was reversed after lobbying by religious groups. She also alleges that the EEC decision to withhold food from UNICEF for Vietnam was taken under strong U.S. pressure ("Milk for Vietnam," *New York Times*, Op-Ed, July 3, 1981).

84. François Nivolon, "Debt shackles Vietnam," *Far Eastern Economic Review*, May 22, 1981. See also Ted Morello, "Reagan's aid weapon: the axe hangs over UN agencies as Washington seeks revenge over Kampuchea," *Far Eastern Economic Review*, May 1, 1981; Murray Hiebert, "The Food Weapon: Can Vietnam be Broken?," *Indochina Issues* (April 1981).

85. Wiznitzer (see note 81). He also notes that UNICEF adopted a relief plan for Cambodia "despite an attempt by the US to restrict it."

86. There have, however, been repeated accusations that "the Vietnamese are now conducting a subtle 'genocide' in Cambodia," François Ponchaud's charge as presented by William Shawcross, "The End of Cambodia?," *New York Review,* January 24, 1980. For analysis and refutation of charges by Shawcross and Ponchaud, see Vickery, *op. cit.*

87. On the remarkable cynicism of the Human Rights Administration in this regard, see *Political Economy of Human Rights,* vol. 2, chapter 5. See also Chapter 7.

88. There was undoubtedly an element of irresponsibility in these far too limited demands, but that of course was not what Mansfield had in mind. For discussion, see my *At War with Asia,* chapter 1.

89. See Chapter 4, note 11. Also Chapter 1.

90. *New York Times,* December 27, 1979; *Dissent* (Fall 1979).

91. See, e.g., my *At War with Asia,* p. 286; see Chapter 7.

92. The bombings "created the Khmer Rouge," according to Sihanouk; see Chapter 4, note 11. See the reports at the time by Richard Dudman, relying in part on his personal experience while a captive of the Khmer Rouge: *Forty Days with the Enemy* (New York: Liveright, 1971); "The Cambodian 'People's' War," *Washington Post,* April 24, 1975. Also William Shawcross, *Sideshow* (New York: Simon & Schuster, 1979). For evidence from U.S. government sources (and assessment by Cambodia specialists) on the brutalizing impact of the U.S. bombing on the Khmer Rouge, see *Political Economy of Human Rights,* vol. 2, chapter 7. For a valuable eyewitness account of the Khmer Rouge in the period prior to the murderous 1973 bombings, see Serge Thion, "Journal de marche dans le maquis," *Le Monde,* April 26, 27, 28, 1972; reprinted in Serge Thion and Ben Kiernan, *Khmers rouges!* (Paris: Albin Michel, 1981); for some excerpts, see my *For Reasons of State,* pp. 190f. Another success of American policy is revealed by a USAID report of April 1975 which concluded that widespread starvation was imminent and "slave labor and starvation rations for half the nation's people . . . will be a cruel necessity for this year, and general deprivation and suffering will stretch over the next two or three years"; cited by Shawcross, *Sideshow,* p. 375. On the situation at the war's end, see George C. Hildebrand and Gareth Porter, *Cambodia: Starvation & Revolution* (New York: Monthly Review Press, 1976); and other sources cited in *Political Economy of Human Rights,* vol. 2, chapter 6.

93. It is rarely appreciated how ready U.S. Presidents have been to wield the nuclear weapon. As Daniel Ellsberg has emphasized, the use of nuclear weapons has been regarded as a live policy option by every Administration. For a review of the remarkably frequent resort to nuclear alerts, see Barry M. Blechman and Stephen S. Kaplan, *Force without War: U.S. Armed Forces as a Political Instrument* (Washington, D.C.: Brookings Institution, 1978), particularly p. 48. Some of the "incidents in which strategic nuclear forces were involved"—they record nineteen between 1946 and 1973—are quite astonishing, for example, the inauguration of a president in Uruguay in February 1947 and the Guatemalan intervention of 1954, when bombers of the Strategic Air Command were dispatched to Uruguay and Nicaragua, respectively. They also count "215 incidents in which the United States employed its armed forces for political purposes between 1946 and 1975."

94. Wilbur Crane Eveland, *Ropes of Sand* (New York: Norton, 1980). Eveland, who was working under cover for the CIA, was in Turkey at the time of the invasion, and had

difficulties in following Allen Dulles's instructions to return to Beirut because of the banning of non-military traffic.

95. See Chapter 7, at note 30. For discussion of the origins of trilateralism after the bitter attacks by spokesmen for transnational corporations on the neomercantilist measures adopted by Nixon in 1971, which they saw as threatening the collapse of the international economic system in which they flourished, see Sklar, *op. cit.*, particularly the editor's overview and the articles by Jeff Frieden and by Fred Block, the latter discussing the failure of the system as the neomercantilist policies of the state managers came into conflict with the goals and interests of internationally oriented business.

96. By that time, it was becoming quite impossible to maintain the pretense that the Sino-Soviet split did not exist. See also note 79. On Kissinger's fantasies, see Chapter 6.

97. Yankelovich and Kaagan, *op. cit.*

98. Scott Armstrong, "Carter Held Hope Even After Shah Had Lost His," *Washington Post*, October 25, 1980; see note 49.

99. See Lernoux, *op. cit.* It is arguable that Carter's policy helped to secure the release of some political prisoners as well. See John Lieber, "Kristol Unclear," *New Republic*, June 27, 1981, for an argument to this effect in the case of Jacobo Timerman in Argentina and Huber Matos in Cuba.

100. Bernard Gwertzman, "New Policy on Aid for Caribbean Wins Reagan's Approval," *New York Times*, June 4, 1981.

101. See below, p. 54.

102. Juan de Onis, "Cuba Warned Direct U.S. Action Against It on Salvador Is Possible," *New York Times*, February 23, 1981.

103. Ferdinand Mount, "Another little Vietnam?," *Spectator* (London), March 7, 1981. There are, of course, contrary views; see the *Economist*, editorial, June 6, 1981; see note 6.

104. Richard Halloran and Bernard Weinraub, *New York Times*, September 21, 1980.

105. For data, based on Pentagon figures, see *The Defense Monitor*, vol. 10, no. 3 (1981).

106. See Chapter 7. Also Arthur Macy Cox, "The CIA's Tragic Error," *New York Review*, November 6, 1980. The error to which Cox (a former CIA analyst) refers was the near-doubling of the estimate of GNP that the USSR spends on defense, interpreted here as rectification of an "intelligence blunder" (Nixon) that vastly underestimated the scale of the Soviet military. In fact, as Cox points out, the rectification was based on the discovery that Soviet military industry is far less efficient than had been believed: "What should have been cause for jubilation became the inspiration for misguided alarm." It is not clear that "tragic error" and "misguided alarm" are the correct terms to use. In fact, the gross misinterpretation of the facts that Cox records falls into place as part of the technique for overcoming the "Vietnam syndrome."

A number of commentators have observed that U.S. military spending on high-technology armaments may not increase military capacity—it may even reduce it. This would be properly regarded as paradoxical, if the primary goal of military expenditures were to enhance the nation's military capacities, but not if the goal is military Keynesianism—basically, a subsidy to high-technology industry—and enhancement of the power of military bureaucracies. In general, one should not be too quick to explain policies and pronouncements in terms of error before exploring the possibility that they develop from systematic and quite intelligible commitments.

107. *Nation*, May 9, 1981.

108. Frank C. Carlucci, remarks delivered to a military policy conference in West Germany, *New York Times*, February 22, 1981. In fact, the United States has on occasion relied on its allies for what Carlucci calls "the defense of freedom," e.g., French and Belgian forces in Africa. "Indeed, an 11,500-man force of French marines and Foreign Legionnaires, augmented by light armor and tactical aircraft, helps keep West Africa safe for French, American, and other foreign oilmen," so *Business Week* exults (August 10, 1981).

109. See the Arab-American journal *Action*, "Economic News Related to the Arab World," October 13, 1980.

110. According to figures cited from the *Middle East Economic Digest* in *Action*, February 16, 1981.

111. David Fouquet, "European Community jumps back into Mideast's geopolitical whirlpool," *Christian Science Monitor*, January 26, 1981.

112. Tom Heneghan, Reuter, "US lambasts Europe on defense spending," *Boston Globe*, June 28, 1981, reporting on a conference in Austria on U.S.-West European relations.

113. For the figures, see John Judis, "NATO allies have their own opinions," *In These Times*, June 3, 1981.

114. See, e.g., the report in *Time*, April 20, 1981, on Defense Secretary Caspar Weinberger's trip to Europe, where he "raised eyebrows and hackles . . . by portraying détente as an unmitigated failure for the West from the very beginning." Also John Vinocur, "Lag in Bonn's Arms Outlays Foreseen," *New York Times*, November 8, 1980; "Bonn Cuts Back on Developing Arms for Future," March 8, 1981; Gerald F. Seib, "NATO Foreign Ministers Pledge Support for Reagan Push to Strengthen Defense," *Wall Street Journal*, May 6, 1981, reporting, contrary to the headline, that "turning the words into action" may prove a "difficult task." The report describes the concern of European officials over "pacifist sentiment" in Europe and their suggestion that arms-control talks "will help defuse growing antimilitary sentiment"—what other purpose could they serve? Europeans "generally take a milder view than the Reagan administration of the Soviet military buildup. They also have a stronger desire for détente with the Soviet Union, which represents a potentially important economic partner." See also pp. 2–3 above and note 5.

115. See, among others, Geoffrey Murray, "Japan-US 'alliance' costs Suzuki an aide—and he could be the next to go," *Christian Science Monitor*, May 18, 1981.

116. *Economist*, May 16, 1981.

117. Donald Kirk, "Japan's 'situation': Tokyo wants more 'understanding' from the US on defense spending," *Boston Globe*, June 28, 1981. See also Richard Halloran, "Japan's Defense Chief Resists U.S. Pressure," *New York Times*, June 30, 1981.

118. *Time*, April 20, 1981. See also Pranay B. Gupte et al., "Reagan and the Gulf," *New York Times*, February 23, 1981, noting the tendency among traditional pro-American and conservative Gulf states to distance themselves from American ties and avoid superpower alliances; James Dorsey, "Six oil-rich Gulf states seek unity and security," *Christian Science Monitor*, May 26, 1981: "Contrary to the perception of the Reagan administration, most council members see the threat to their security as an internal one, stemming mainly from the Arab-Israeli conflict." See Chapter 9, Afterword.

119. Mohammed Heikal, "Encircled Nationalisms," *New York Times*, Op-Ed, April 2, 1980.

120. Secretary of State Alexander M. Haig, briefing on El Salvador presented to representatives of NATO and other countries, *New York Times*, February 21, 1981. An article on

the same page of the *Times* reports that Reagan's emissary, General Vernon Walters, was refused an audience with the president of Mexico, who, however, concluded a discussion on economic cooperation with a visiting Cuban minister by offering his "very fraternal salute to the people of Cuba" (Alan Riding, "Mexico Stresses Ties with Cuba in an Apparent Rebuff to Reagan"). General Walters's visit was kept secret at the request of the United States, "apparently to avert anti-American demonstrations here." Walters then proceeded on his way to Brazil, Argentina, and Chile, where he also appears to have won few converts. Walters was an interesting choice as emissary, given the widely held suspicions in Brazil and elsewhere in Latin America about his role in the 1964 Brazilian military coup. See Black, *op. cit.* See also *Latin America Weekly Report*, February 27, 1981, on Walter's reception in Mexico.

121. Alan Riding, "Mexico and Venezuela Plan to Counter Outside Intervention in Caribbean," *New York Times*, April 9, 1981.

122. *Washington Post*, March 27, 1981, cited in *Inquiry*, May 11, 1981; *Latin America Weekly Report*, April 10, 1981, citing a Gallup Poll that revealed that only 2 percent of the public thought the United States should send troops to El Salvador while less than 20 percent favored the sending of economic aid, military supplies, or military advisers.

123. For some indication, see the comparison of the *New York Times* and the *Economist*, note 37; and comments below, and references cited. The reporting of El Salvador was sufficiently biased and inadequate as to win the award as "Top 'Censored' Story of 1980" in *Project Censored*, a nationwide media research project conducted by Carl Jensen and David Holmstrom at Sonoma State University, California. The panel of jurors consisted of Donna Allen, editor and publisher of *Media Report to Women;* Ben H. Bagdikian, Graduate School of Journalism, University of California, Berkeley; Hodding Carter, President Carter's press secretary; Noam Chomsky; Robert Cirino, author and teacher; Ann Crittenden of the *New York Times*, David Cohen; Joel Dreyfuss, editor, *Black Enterprise Magazine;* Nicholas Johnson, chairman, National Citizens Communications Lobby; Mary McGrory, nationally syndicated columnist of the *Washington Star;* Jack Nelson, professor, Rutgers University; Sheila Rabb Weidenfeld, writer and TV producer and moderator. See Press Release, Office of Public Affairs, Sonoma State University, May 27, 1981. I noticed no press coverage apart from the *Guardian* (Marxist-Leninist, New York, June 24, 1981).

The nomination that went to the jurors observed that while the civil war received "ample attention by the US media in 1980," the reporting was "dangerously misleading" through either "willful misinformation" or "ignorance," giving a number of striking examples, some discussed below.

There were, however, some important exceptions, among them articles in *Inquiry* by Anne Nelson ("The Continuing Calamity of El Salvador," May 5, 1980; "Central American Powder Keg," November 10, 1980) and in the *Nation* by Penny Lernoux ("El Salvador's Christian Democrat Junta," December 13, 1980) and James Petras ("The Junta's War Against the People," December 20, 1980). And regularly in the left-wing press (*Guardian, Militant, In These Times,* and others) and church-based publications such as *Overview Latin America,* which regularly reported material that sometimes found its way into the mainstream press long after. And in early 1981, T. D. Allman, "Rising to Rebellion," *Harper's* (March 1981); Alexander Cockburn and James Ridgeway, "The U.S. in El Salvador: The Plan, the Terror, the Opposition," *Village Voice,* March 4, 1981; among a few others.

For critical discussion of the "functionally illiterate" U.S. press in comparison with the foreign press, see Jonathan Evan Maslow and Ana Arana, "Operation El Salvador: The administration dusted off the domino theory. The pushover press fell into line," *Columbia Journalism Review* (June 1981); also Alexander Cockburn, "Blood and Ink: Keeping Score in El Salvador," *Harper's* (February 1981); also the references of note 125.

124. On the success of land reform adviser Roy Prosterman and former U.S. Ambassador to El Salvador Robert White in using the "Pol Pot left" comparison in lobbying Congress for economic and military aid for the military junta that was massacring the peasantry, see Laurence R. Simon and James C. Stephens, Jr., *El Salvador Land Reform 1980–1981*, Impact Audit, Oxfam America (February 1981), p. 51. See also Chapter 7, at note 44, for one of many examples illustrating how the ground was prepared for this contribution to massacre in El Salvador.

125. See Cynthia Brown and Fernando Moreno, "Force-Feeding the Press on El Salvador," *Nation*, April 25, 1981, and *Latin America Weekly Report*, February 20, 1981, for discussion of studies comparing U.S. and foreign press coverage. Also the interview with a Panamanian reporter who worked with UPI (Alexander Cockburn, *Village Voice*, April 8, 1981), who describes home-office manipulation of his reports and the practices of U.S. correspondents; and William Wipfler, "El Salvador: Reform as Cover for Repression," *Christianity and Crisis*, May 12, 1980, also describing editorial manipulation in the *New York Times* as described by a wire service correspondent. See note 123; also, note 208.

126. Cited from the report and the January 5, 1981, press release of the Council on Hemispheric Affairs, in *Human Rights Internet Reporter* (February-March 1981).

127. *New York Times*, December 7, 1980; interview moderated by Juan de Onis.

128. Editorial, "Reform in El Salvador," reprinted in the *Manchester Guardian Weekly*, February 22, 1981.

129. "Salvador rightists accused of raiding Honduran sites," *Christian Science Monitor*, March 23, 1981, a ninety-word item. This report only refers to ORDEN raids; others, cited below, to attacks by the military forces themselves.

130. Again, there are exceptions; e.g., Allman, *op. cit.*

131. Representative Gerry E. Studds (Mass.), *Central America, 1981*, Report to the Committee on Foreign Affairs, U.S. House of Representatives, March 1981 (Washington, D.C.: Government Printing Office, 1981).

132. Transcripts of some of the interviews were played on WMUA radio, Amherst, Mass., February 22, 1981; Robbie Leppzer, producer. Virtually nothing of this appeared in the press, to my knowledge. Cf. Chapter 8, note 22.

   Compare W. Scott Thompson, professor of international politics at the Fletcher School of Law and Diplomacy, Tufts University, "Choosing to Win," *Foreign Policy* (Summer 1981): "True, right-wing forces strike back, often without government sanction. In the past year they have perhaps caused even more than the 6,000 deaths the left takes credit for—but not with weapons supplied by an international power overtly hostile to the United States and not to overthrow an established government."

   The "6,000" figure appears regularly in U.S. government propaganda, but with no source cited, to my knowledge. If a source exists, it probably refers to guerrilla claims concerning soldiers killed in combat, but in the absence of any reference, one can only speculate. On assessments by the Catholic Church of responsibility for massacres, see below.

In general, caution is in order with regard to statements attributed to enemies of the state, given the tendency of many foreign correspondents to rely on U.S. government handouts. For example, the U.S. press regularly referred to the "final offensive" announced by the guerrillas in January 1981. Since the government still stands, that proves that the guerrillas failed because of lack of popular support. The generally well-informed *Latin America Weekly Report*, however, maintains that although "the US press has been full of stories about a supposed 'final offensive' by the FDR at the beginning of January, launched in the hope of achieving victory before President Reagan's inauguration on 20 January," in fact there was no such announcement; rather, "opposition spokesmen are cautiously describing the wave of attacks, launched on 10 January, as a 'general offensive in preparation for the final onslaught' " (*Latin America Weekly Report*, January 16, 23, 1981).

133. "Col. Arnoldo Majano, an outspoken liberal who has been in hiding since he was ousted as head of the ruling junta here two months ago, has been held under arrest by Government authorities since last Wednesday, according to informed sources. The Government has refused to release any details of the arrest or the charges against the colonel, who, until an assembly of army officers voted him out of the junta, had been the symbol of American policy in this country. Colonel Majano was the leader of a group of young army officers who overthrew a right-wing military dictatorship 16 months ago and began to institute land and economic changes. . . . He had been releasing statements, for example, that were harshly critical of the continued assassinations of leftists and moderates by right-wing and corrupt elements in the armed forces, which neither he nor the present junta has been able to control [the reporter's conclusion, not Majano's]. His successor, however, José Napoleón Duarte, a civilian Christian Democrat who is equally liberal, says that the number of such incidents is declining" ("Salvadoran Liberal Ousted by Junta Is Under Arrest," *New York Times*, February 22, 1981). The report assures us that despite Majano's ouster, the government "has continued with most of the changes."

134. This massacre of six hundred peasants in a joint operation of the armies of El Salvador and Honduras was reported by AFP in June 1980, and in *Overview Latin America* (9 Sacramento Street, Cambridge, Mass. 02138, a church-based group) in midsummer 1980, on the basis of a communiqué from the Diocese of Santa Rosa de Copan in Honduras. It was also reported in *Inquiry* (November 10, 1980) by Anne Nelson. There is a detailed study by David Blundy, "Victims of the massacre that the world ignored," *Sunday Times* (London), February 22, 1981. It was apparently not mentioned by the mainstream U.S. press. I found no reference in the *New York Times* prior to an article by Warren Hoge, *New York Times*, June 8, 1981, reporting a similar massacre on March 17 at the Lempa River. See Chapter 8, note 28. Also note 149, below.

135. Édouard Bailby, "Terreur dans les campagnes d'El Salvador," *Le Monde diplomatique* (January 1981). Similar reports of Pol Pot massacres in the French press were immediately translated and given wide publicity in the U.S. press, side-by-side with the extensive accounts of American journalists on the Thai-Cambodian border. See *Political Economy of Human Rights*, vol. 2, chapter 6, and Vickery, *op. cit.*, who discusses apparent collusion of the CIA and "independent journalists" (John Barron and Anthony Paul) in fabricating statistics, among other related matters; see his forthcoming book *Cambodia* (Boston: South End Press) for much further detail.

136. David Blundy, "The innocents caught in Lempa River massacre," *Sunday Times* (Lon-

don), April 26, 1981. See also Alex W. Drehsler, *Boston Globe*, March 26, 1981, and Hoge, *op. cit.*, and *Latin America Weekly Report*, April 3, 1981. A March 25 letter to journalist Anne Nelson from an American who participated in the rescue of some of the thousands of fleeing peasants gives a vivid picture of this mid-March massacre which made it to the *New York Times* by June. Refugees had been hiding in caves for three days under daily bombardment before fleeing to the river. The river was deep, there were few swimmers, the refugees, including many women and children, had been without food for three days, many were seriously wounded; helicopters of the Salvadoran army machine-gunned and bombed the river trying "to systematically massacre us all." Only a little more than half of the announced seven thousand refugees were able to cross the river to Honduras, where they remain in "heart-rending" misery in an area sealed off by the Honduran army. Many of the surviving children are seriously ill, many with pneumonia, as a result of the harsh crossing and lack of care.

137. "Central American Watch," *Nation*, April 18, 1981. The Legal Aid Office of the San Salvador archdiocese was established by twelve Catholic lawyers and invited to become part of the archdiocesan services by the assassinated Archbishop Oscar Romero.

138. Edward Schumacher, "Duarte, Three Months in Power, Bringing Change to El Salvador," *New York Times*, March 30, 1981. Schumacher notes that assassinations "continue," despite the alleged decline.

139. Edward Schumacher, "Program in Salvador to Redistribute Land Prospers in First Year," March 15, 1981; "For Salvador Peasants, Fruits of Change Seem Good," March 16, 1981.

140. Edward Schumacher, "Salvadoran Peasants Flee War-Ravaged Villages," *New York Times*, February 19, 1981. Some light on the "killing from both sides" is given by a "conservative priest" who states: "The difference in the violence is that the left kills selectively—members of ORDEN and Government security forces. Killing by the right and the army is more indiscriminate. When they sweep through a village looking for leaders and leftist sympathizers, they kill a lot of innocent peasants" (Raymond Bonner, "The Agony of El Salvador," *New York Times Magazine*, February 22, 1981). If this is an accurate statement of general tendencies, as numerous other reports indicate, then what it means is that the guerrillas are at war with the army that is seeking to destroy them and what peasants and independent scholars refer to as "the popular organizations," while the government is at war with the people.

141. "U.N. Official Claims Refugees Fleeing Government Forces," *Los Angeles Times*, April 2, 1981. The same report, from the Honduran border, states that 99 percent of the refugees in Honduras were farm laborers who fled the government soldiers: "This is the answer that virtually all the refugees give when they are asked who is behind the violence that drove them out of their country." See also Al Kamen, "Question in El Salvador: Who Kills Noncombatants?," *Washington Post*, April 9, reporting that in private conversations peasants in urban slums and rural cooperatives blame the army for the killings, and quoting a businessman who "scoffed at the suggestion that the government could not stop the random killing" by the paramilitary organization ORDEN, which theoretically no longer exists: " 'Are you kidding?' he asked rhetorically. 'ORDEN *is* the government.' " Also Kamen, "Land Reform and Repression," *Washington Post*, April 5, 1981, reporting that board members of an agricultural cooperative blamed the left for the murders, but: "In a pattern repeated again and again, a resident who was not on the board of directors later approached a group of visitors as they were

leaving and whispered that he and everyone else knew that the killings were almost all the work of the government security forces," an allegation with which "many U.S. officials and AFL-CIO advisers here agree." Cited from CISPES *Central America Monitor*, May 11, 1981. Apparently the *New York Times* correspondent picked up no such whispers.

14.2. For a detailed accounting, see "Documents of Repression in El Salvador," *Overview Latin America* (February 1981); Vicente Navarro, "Genocide in El Salvador," *Monthly Review* (April 1981). Also Petras, *op. cit.*

It would be a useful exercise to compare these regular reports of the Archdiocese Legal Aid Office with reports at the same time in the U.S. press; see pp. 13, 36, for examples. These reports are certainly known to the press, and one finds an occasional mention; e.g., "Salvadorans Fear Revenge Attacks After 5 Leftist Leaders Are Killed," UPI, *New York Times*, November 29, 1980, the last paragraph: "The Roman Catholic Church has blamed the right-wing paramilitary groups for 80 percent of the 9,000 political killings reported in El Salvador since Jan. 1 and has accused the junta of covertly backing them"; see also Alan Riding, "Rightist Offensive Seen in Latin Region," *New York Times*, November 30, 1980, in the latter part of a column. "But United States officials believe much of the right-wing violence is carried out by two special forces, the National Guard and the National Police." But in general, the press kept to the official picture of a centrist government unable to constrain right-wing "death squads" or soldiers out of control, with responsibility for the killings shared by left and right. The press generally mirrors the U.S. government, which is "incapable of grasping [a charitable interpretation] that in El Salvador, as in Nicaragua before it, the centrist forces which the United States perceives as its natural allies have joined with the very forces which the United States perceives as its natural enemy—the radical Left" (William M. LeoGrande and Carla Anne Robbins, "Oligarchs and Officers: the Crisis in El Salvador," *Foreign Affairs* [Summer 1980]). See also Chapter 8. Alan Riding alleges that "under the Carter Administration, United States officials said security forces were responsible for 90 percent of the atrocities," not " 'uncontrollable' right-wing bands" (*New York Times*, September 27, 1981). If this is correct, it provides an enlightening commentary on the behavior of the media at the time.

A good place to begin such a comparison would be with the accounts of the killings of the five "leftist" leaders on November 27, 1980, aborting the possibility for a negotiated settlement. The most prominent of these "leftist" leaders was Enrique Alvarez, "a certified member of the country's long dominant economic oligarchy," "a millionaire cattle rancher" who "had served in previous governments," as the *New York Times* noted in an editorial (November 29) condemning the killings. The UPI story, describing the dilemmas of the junta ("besieged by leftist guerrillas and rightist paramilitary groups"), reports that the "five leftists" were abducted "from a Jesuit-run high school three blocks from the United States Embassy by a band of nearly 200 men who raided the school"; the Legal Aid Office, whose offices are in the school, issued a statement reporting that "Some 200 *soldiers and police* had surrounded the high school" (my emphasis). The same statement notes that the high school watchman was kidnapped and taken "to the premises of the Salvadoran Institute for Social Security" and that the vehicles that surrounded the school had license plates identifying them "as belonging to official organizations." "Another revealing piece of information," the statement continues, "is the total immunity with which the operation was carried out: in full daylight, at the largest secondary school in the country, along one of the most heavily-traveled roads of the capital, and three blocks from the most guarded building, the Embassy of the United States. Given these elements, it seems incredible that no authority came to the scene of the events during the operation," which lasted for more than twenty-five minutes. It also cites an AP cable sent "moments after the events" from San Salvador, which appeared in the local press on the front page, stating: "The authorities today announced that they had captured the highest leaders of the FDR, who were offering political leadership for leftist organizations."

Little reference to these facts (and, to my knowledge, no reference to the Legal Aid Office statement) is found in the national press, though the facts were known; e.g., in the Riding column cited above, the quote given is followed by this comment: "Witnesses said uninformed troops had surrounded the Jesuit-run San José High School Thursday before plainclothed gunmen seized the opposition leaders" (gunmen who were in radio communication with the Salvadoran Institute for Social Security, according to witnesses reported by the Legal Aid Office statement).

This pattern of general suppression, stories framed in accordance with state propaganda, and occasional glimpses of the facts, is quite typical.

143. U.S. Agency for International Development, *Phaseout Study of the Public Safety Program in El Salvador* (Washington, D.C.: Government Printing Office, 1974); cited by Cynthia Arnson, "Background Information on the Security Forces in El Salvador and U.S. Military Assistance," Institute for Policy Studies *Resource* (March 1980).

144. *Communist Interference in El Salvador,* Special Report no. 80, February 23, 1981, United States Department of State, Bureau of Public Affairs, Washington, D.C.

145. Sol W. Sanders, "The Vietnam shadow over policy for El Salvador," International Outlook, *Business Week,* March 16, 1981. Sanders deftly refutes "the Communist line," which is "that Central American revolutionary movements are local, indigenous, and as one Soviet spokesman in Washington puts it—ideologically Roman Catholic rather than Communist-oriented. This argument parallels the argument used in Vietnam that the revolt against President Ngo Dinh Diem in the early 1960s was a local South Vietnamese movement. The conquest of Saigon in 1975 by northern forces never dissipated this canard."

On the press response to the White Paper, see Maslow and Arana, *op. cit.*

146. John Dinges, "White Paper or Blank Paper?," *Los Angeles Times,* March 17, 1981; also *In These Times,* April 1, 1981.

147. Hodding Carter III, "The El Salvador Crusade," *Wall Street Journal,* March 19, 1981. Carter was Assistant Secretary of State for Public Affairs, department spokesman for the press, under the Carter Administration.

148. Elsewhere, hard questions were raised, for example, by James Petras ("White Paper on the White Paper," *Nation* [March 1981]; reprinted in *El Salvador: The Roots of Intervention,* by the Nation Associates). See also the detailed analysis by Philip Agee in *White Paper? Whitewash!: Philip Agee on the CIA in El Salvador,* Werner Poelchau, ed. (New York: Deep Cover Publications, 1981). Also Maslow and Arana, *op. cit.,* and Konrad Ege, "El Salvador White Paper?," *Counterspy* (May 1981).

149. Jonathan Kwitny, "Apparent Errors Cloud U.S. 'White Paper' on Reds in El Salvador," *Wall Street Journal,* June 8, 1981. An accompanying story indicates that the next attempt will implicate religious and charitable organizations as supporters of "the Communist war effort in El Salvador, with or without the charities' knowledge" ("A New

White Paper Is Expected Soon; Leaks of Its Contents Distress Churches"). Subsequently, the U.S. embassy in Honduras "sharply criticized" Catholic and Protestant relief organizations, accusing them "of delivering more than 50 percent of their assistance to the Salvadoran guerrillas" ("El Salvador Says 30,000 Refugees May Be Moved from Its Border," *New York Times*, June 27, 1981). The latter *Times* report speaks coyly of "several alleged massacres of refugees by Government troops as the refugees attempted to cross the border into Honduras," presumably referring to the Sumpul and Lempa River massacres, which are still only "alleged."

According to the *Latin America Weekly Report*, June 19, 1981, Agee's then forthcoming book (see note 148) was an unacknowledged source for the *Wall Street Journal* story.

150. Robert G. Kaiser, "White Paper on El Salvador Is Faulty," *Washington Post*, June 9, 1981.

151. Juan de Onis, "State Dept. Defends Report on Salvador," June 9, 1981; "U.S. Officials Concede Flaws in Salvador White Paper but Defend Its Conclusions," June 10, 1981. See also Juan de Onis, "U.S. Defends Report on Salvador Arms," *New York Times*, June 19, 1981; Robert G. Kaiser, "U.S. Issues Rebuttal to Critics in Press of Salvador Aid Report," *Washington Post* Service, *International Herald Tribune*, June 20–21, 1981.

152. Cynthia Arnson, "El Salvador: There's more to the disturbing story," *Boston Globe*, April 23, 1981; also Arnson, "White's Papers," *Nation*, May 9, 1981.

153. "Leftists' Offensive in El Salvador Stalls," *New York Times*, January 26, 1981.

154. AP, *Boston Globe*, April 15, 1981.

155. Philip Jacobson, "Why El Salvador's civil war raises ghosts of Vietnam—whatever Washington says," *Sunday Times* (London), March 8, 1981. There were many similar reports in the foreign press at the time. See, *inter alia*, *Latin America Weekly Report*, February 27, March 20, 1981.

156. Kenneth Freed, "Venezuela now leads opposition to leftists," *Los Angeles Times-Boston Globe*, February 18, 1981. The same page of the *Globe* carries a story by Tom Fiedler, "US aides lay ground for hike in military aid to El Salvador," Knight-Ridder service, describing Reagan Administration efforts "laying the groundwork to request that the embattled government of El Salvador be given a big increase in US military aid to defeat leftist revolutionaries"—efforts that reached their peak with the issuance of the White Paper a few days later. Fiedler reports that Congress was "given documents showing that Salvadoran guerrilla leaders were given money by Cuba to carry on their revolution." This shows that Cuba is engaged in Soviet-sponsored aggression. Hundreds of millions of dollars given to the junta by a U.S. ally, however, do not imply that it is engaged in a U.S.-sponsored massacre of the peasant population.

157. Stephen L. Vaughn, *Holding Fast the Inner Lines* (Chapel Hill: University of North Carolina Press, 1980), p. 194.

158. Edward Schumacher, "From Washington and Salvador, Differing Views on Fighting Rebels," *New York Times*, February 21, 1981.

159. On the backgrounds of ORDEN, "in essence . . . an irregular militia enjoying government patronage and local privilege," often drawn from the poorest sectors and commanded by the army, see *'Disappearances,'* p. 101f. (see note 21). For more extensive discussion of the historical background for the development of the popular organizations and ORDEN, and for the present crisis, see Federico G. Gil, Enrique A. Baloyra, and Lars Schoultz, *The Failure of Democratic Transition in Latin America: El Salvador*

(December 1980); draft submitted to the State Department under contract. This study alone suffices to make nonsense of State Department claims about the origins of the current crisis. It received some notice in the press; see Robert Parry, "Study hits US path in Salvador," AP, *Boston Globe*, February 22, 1981.

160. Allman, *op. cit.*

161. On the peasant uprising of 1932 and its bloody suppression, see Thomas P. Anderson, *Matanza: El Salvador's Communist Revolt of 1932* (Lincoln: University of Nebraska Press, 1971). Anderson estimates that about one hundred people were killed by the rebels, about half of them soldiers and police. His rather conservative estimate is that about ten thousand people were then killed in the *matanza*, which "means that the government exacted reprisals at the rate of about one hundred to one." Anderson concludes that "the whole political labyrinth of El Salvador can be explained only in reference to the traumatic experience of the uprising and the *matanza*."

162. AP, *New York Times*, March 13, 1981, a fifteen-line report of Gómez's press conference under the general heading: "Salvador Leftists Accused of Raid." In this press conference, Gómez stated that promises of free elections are worthless, since "all meaningful opposition is either dead or outside the country."

163. Steven Kinzer, "Salvador activist Gómez finds it pays to stay one step ahead," *Boston Globe*, February 25, 1981, a lengthy interview with Gómez.

164. Daniel Southerland, "New allegations against rightists in El Salvador," *Christian Science Monitor*, March 4, 1981.

165. Kinzer, *op. cit.*

166. *Latin America Weekly Report*, February 13, 1981.

167. Leonel Gómez and Bruce Cameron, "El Salvador: The Current Danger: American Myths," *Foreign Policy* (Summer 1981).

168. Simon and Stephens, *op. cit.* (see note 124). See also Mac Chapin, "A few comments on land tenure and the course of agrarian reform in El Salvador" (June 1980) (Chapin is an AID official). On the role of the U.S. labor movement's AIFLD, see Carolyn Forché and Philip Wheaton, *History and Motivations of U.S. Involvement in the Control of the Peasant Movement in El Salvador*, Ecumenical Program for Interamerican Communication and Action (EPICA), n.d.

169. Correspondingly, the media too began to decide that there might be reason for a diagnosis of the El Salvador affair that differs from the standard government line that a centrist regime is being attacked from the left and is unable to control the right. See, among other articles, Philip Geyelin, "Time for a second opinion on El Salvador," *Washington Post-Boston Globe*, May 17, 1981, discussing the opinions of a Christian Democrat economist who quit his position in the agrarian reform program and fled the country in January when he noticed armed men parked in front of his apartment, drawing the obvious conclusions. According to Geyelin, who regards him as "rather more like a rising young banker than, say, Che Guevara," he "sees a harshly repressive right-wing military government, under the tight thumb of a rich and ruthless oligarchy, with only the thin facade of Christian Democracy in Duarte's presence as its nominal leader," and "he sees the guerrilla forces as the home-honed military cutting edge of a political opposition movement whose representation—peasant organizations, labor unions, the clergy, businessmen, technocrats—reflects a wider consensus and a tighter cohesion than that of any comparable movement in Latin America." Not

unlike a rather standard interpretation outside of the United States, though credence might be given to the Gómez view that a brutal and corrupt military is to some degree replacing the traditional oligarchy.

A few months earlier, Geyelin had been writing that "the so-called central [sic] government, a coalition of Christian Democrats and the military, remains perilously threatened by extremists from the far right and the far left" ("El Salvador: Proving Ground," *Washington Post*, February 10, 1981).

I believe that one can plausibly account for a detectable shift in the character of media coverage of El Salvador in spring 1981, in part indicated above, as a reflection of the partial abandonment of a militant public posture by the government, in response to domestic and international failures. See note 142.

170. Claire Sterling, *The Terror Network: The Secret War of International Terrorism* (New York: Holt, Rinehart & Winston, 1981).

171. Review in *The New Yorker*, May 11, 1981.

172. Claire Sterling, "Terrorism: Tracing the International Network," *New York Times Magazine*, March 1, 1981, a few days after the release of the White Paper on El Salvador.

173. Which is not to say, of course, that Sterling's book is merely a compendium of absurdities. It would be remarkable indeed if the Soviet Union were not engaged in "international terrorism" along with other major actors on the international scene. For a judicious review, noting the plausible elements of the book along with its manifest absurdities, see Jonathan Marshall, *Inquiry*, May 11, 1981. See Diana Johnstone's review in *In These Times*, May 20, 1981, for extensive discussion of gross misuse of evidence and falsification of crucial facts.

For a few other examples of widespread awe and commendation for books, however ridiculous, that convey a desired message, see Chapters 5, 6, and 10, below. Also Chapter 1, note 34, on one of the most startling cases, Peter Braestrup's Freedom House study, *Big Story*, which "demonstrated" the complicity of the press in American failures in Vietnam on the basis of fabrication of evidence and absurd argument so transparent that even a casual reader could hardly miss it. What is particularly interesting, in this case, is the reception of the book by scholars of international affairs, for example, Scott Thompson, professor of international politics at the Fletcher School of Law and Diplomacy, who swallows it whole (*op. cit.*), or John Roche, academic dean of the Fletcher School, whose response verged on ecstasy.

174. Ronald Taggiasco, review of *The Terror Network*, *Business Week*, April 27, 1981.

175. William P. Bundy, editor, *Foreign Affairs* (Spring 1981). The journal almost never publishes signed reviews. This one is about four times the length of the standard book notes.

176. See Alfred M. Lilienthal, *The Zionist Connection* (New York: Dodd, Mead, 1978), for extensive documentation of this and many other examples of the double standard employed in treating Israeli and Palestinian terrorism; see also Chapter 9 through 12, below. Marshall also discusses this point.

177. *New York Times Magazine*, March 1, 1981.

178. Walter Laqueur, review of *The Terror Network*, *Wall Street Journal*, April 9, 1981. As other examples of "multinational terrorism" Laqueur cites the Polisario independence movement in the western Sahara (which might "further weaken the Moroccan regime

and ultimately bring down the monarchy") and terrorism in "some Central American countries." It is evident from the context that the latter reference is not to state terrorism.

179. *New York Times Book Review*, May 17, 1981. According to the CIA, the United States is the "most victimized" nation with regard to international terrorism. Its 1981 international report counts 6,714 international terrorist incidents from 1968 through 1980, including 760 in 1980. Included are 1,008 threats, 58 hoaxes, and 121 cases of "conspiracy." These are new categories, added in a transparent effort to inflate the significance of "international terrorism" in accordance with the needs of the Reagan Administration. The "most victimized nationalities," according to the CIA report, are, in order: Americans, Israelis, Soviets, Turks, Iraqis, and Libyans, "a notable change from 1979, when the favorite targets were Americans, British and French" (George Lardner, Jr., *Washington Post-Boston Globe*, June 16, 1981). The report cites ten American deaths in terrorist attacks in 1980, six in El Salvador, including the three Maryknoll nuns and the woman Catholic lay worker assassinated, it appears, by the Salvador military. Even if we take the CIA report at face value, it hardly substantiates the Sterling thesis.

180. For discussion of the backgrounds for these and numerous other attacks, mostly coordinated in Miami, see the article by an anonymous Cuban-American professional, "Miami, Haven for Terror," *Nation*, March 19, 1977. The author also discusses the "extremely friendly" attitudes (and actions) of the governor of Florida and the mayor of Miami towards terrorists, concluding: "Terror's shield of respectability—that is the still untold story of Miami and of the anti-Castro movement abroad."

181. Powers, *op. cit.*, citing "several sources." He notes that "the CIA carried out at least six major operations against Cuba, along with a host of lesser ones" in 1963.

182. Bradley Earl Ayers, *The War that Never Was* (Indianapolis: Bobbs-Merrill, 1976). A U.S. Army captain, Ayers is bitter at the fact that after the Kennedy assassination, attention shifted to Southeast Asia, aborting plans then underway to carry out the bombing of Cuban oil refineries, petrochemical facilities, and telephone/telegraph installations, a shame, after the "pronounced increase in exile raids and bombings" in May–June 1963. The first general book on U.S. terrorism against Cuba is Warren Hinckle and William Turner, *The Fish Is Red* (New York: Harper & Row, 1981).

183. See *Political Economy of Human Rights*, vol. 1, p. 379 and references cited there.

184. Taylor Branch and George Crile III, "The Kennedy Vendetta: Our Secret War on Cuba," *Harper's* (August 1975).

185. It would be unfair to leave the impression that U.S. attacks on Cuba are never reported in the press. See, for example, Tad Sculz, "Confronting the Cuban Nemesis," *New York Times Magazine*, April 5, 1981. Sculz notes in passing that "for years, the United States continued to send in C.I.A. teams who would burn crops and sabotage industrial projects in Cuba." See also the references cited in note 183.

186. In fact, a number of Palestinians were killed in earlier years by the Israeli secret services as part of a campaign of mutual terrorism conducted by Israel and the PLO in Europe. Of course, "deadly terrorist attacks" by national governments long antedate 1980, the "secret war" against Cuba being a prime example.

187. See *Political Economy of Human Rights*, vol. 1, and references cited there.

188. Alan Riding, "Rightist Exiles Plan Invasion of Nicaragua," *New York Times*, April 2, 1981.

189. Philip Taubman, "U.S. Tries to Back Up Haig on Terrorism," reporting the annoying

inability of intelligence to substantiate government allegations against the USSR; Warren Hoge, "Repression Increases in Guatemala as U.S. Tries to Improve Relations," *New York Times*, May 3, 1981. The latter article explains that "complicating the State Department's task, however, is a campaign being conducted by the Lucas Garcia Government . . . to eliminate centrist politicians that Washington could ultimately identify with."

> *Killings of people in opinion-making positions have decimated university faculties, student groups, moderate and left-of-center political organizations, rural cooperatives, newspaper and radio staffs, peasant leagues, unions and churches. In recent weeks there have been massacres in Indian villages aimed at frightening residents into ignoring guerrilla calls for support. . . . The number of killings in the Lucas Garcia years now exceeds 5,000, but there have been no arrests or investigations. . . . From the evidence, killing alone does not satisfy the vengeful motives of the security forces. The coroner in one of the capital's four morgues said that two of every three bodies brought to his morgue bore signs of torture. Virtually all of the murder victims found in the countryside are manacled and indicate beatings, facial disfigurements or violence to sexual organs. Leftist guerrilla tactics include ambushes of army convoys and killings of suspected informants, business leaders and doctors who refuse to treat wounded rebels. Victims of the guerrillas are usually not tortured. The insurgents often occupy villages briefly, explain their cause and then melt back into the hills before the security forces arrive.*

The former press secretary to President Lucas Garcia, now in hiding, informed Amnesty International that the "Secret Anti-Communist Army," which is responsible for the worst atrocities, is controlled by the army chief of staff in the National Palace. The force is "openly associated with the regular army." See Chapter 7.

But the only relation that this has to the United States is that it "complicates" attempts to establish better relations (meanwhile, U.S. corporations enjoy fine relations with the government). And all of this has nothing to do with the "terrorism" that Laqueur and others lament in "some Central American countries"; see note 178.

190. John M. Goshko, "Reagan Quietly Approves Guatemala Military Sale," *Washington Post-International Herald Tribune*, June 20–21, 1981.

191. The Bavarian Ministry of the Interior "suggested that Mr Hoffmann's group [which was responsible for the massacre] financed itself through trade deals with other Arab groups—notably right-wing Christian militants in Lebanon." Links with the PLO were also "suspected" (*Economist*, October 11, 1980).

192. Which sometimes yield odd consequences. For example, Eveland (*op. cit.*) writes that a CIA attempt to overthrow the government of Syria, for which he was bagman, came to grief because the Israeli Mossad neglected to inform the CIA that the day of the attempted coup was the very day of the Israeli attack on Egypt in 1956. This curious oversight apparently did not cause the CIA to review its policy of relying on the Mossad for its intelligence concerning Israel.

193. Kevin Klose, "Probers allege terrorist network," *Washington Post-Boston Globe*, May 20, 1981.

194. Kathleen Teltsch, "400 Intellectuals Form 'Struggle for Freedom' Unit," *New York Times*, February 19, 1981. On the composition of the group and its origins in a meeting

in Jerusalem, see Chapter 12, note 39, where an unfortunate coincidence, fortunately ignored by the *Times*, is also noted.

195. The dots represent hesitation, not omission. For some counterpoint to this soulful comment, see, among innumerable examples, the report by *Manchester Guardian* correspondent Irene Beeson, "The Agony and Death of Khiyam," *AJME*[Americans for Justice in the Middle East] *News* (April 1981), which appeared as the ABC documentary was aired. I quote some excerpts:

> *Khiyam [in Southern Lebanon] has been jointly occupied by Israeli forces and the right wing separatist militia of Major Saad Haddad since 1978. . . . Khiyam is one among 150 or more towns and villages in South Lebanon that have been repeatedly savaged by the Israeli armed forces since 1968 and, in the last three years, jointly by the Israelis and the Haddadists.*
>
> *It stands out as a particularly tragic example of the suffering Israel has inflicted on the people and land of Lebanon. Here the Israeli army has subjected the town and its people to the full range of methods it has used so effectively in the past three decades in Palestine and neighbouring countries—"softening up" by land and air attacks followed by invasion, devastation, depopulation through terror, and as a last resort, cold-blooded massacre.*
>
> *It was shortly after the June 1967 war that Khiyam and other villages in the area became targets for what Israel refers to as "preventive action."*
>
> *Migration from Khiyam and other border villages started in 1968, when the townspeople came under repeated Israeli attacks: aerial bombardment, shelling, assaults by land and from the sea, the blowing up of houses and kidnapping of inhabitants.*
>
> *Israel alleged that these military operations were in retaliation for Palestinian "terrorist attacks" from Lebanon. This prompted the Beirut correspondent of Le Monde at the time to comment that "this Israeli declaration might seem surprising, especially since no violation of the ceasefire from the Lebanese border has been reported. But," he added with a touch of irony, "Israeli observers consider that the calm might be concealing something" (Le Monde, January 7, 1969).*
>
> *. . . Israeli attacks continued through 1969. On December 14 the suburbs of Khiyam were shelled. One villager was wounded and five houses destroyed (Beirut's Al Nahar, December 15, 1969). A week later the town itself came under shell fire for two consecutive hours. One Lebanese civilian was killed and five injured. Five houses were destroyed and several others, along with electric power lines and water works, were damaged (Beirut's Daily Star, December 24, 1969).*
>
> *At the same time Israeli Minister of Defence Moshe Dayan sent a warning to the Lebanese authorities advising them to visit the Jordanian villages and Egyptian towns along the Suez Canal to assess the destruction with which their own villages were threatened at the hands of the Israelis (Le Monde, December 30, 1969).*
>
> *Dayan was true to his word. Attacks on the area were stepped up in frequency and ferocity. By early 1970 a mass exodus from Lebanon's South began. Israeli tactics had "improved" from aerial and land bombardment and shelling and "blitzkrieg" assaults to invasion and occupation (for "mopping-up operations") lasting from several hours to several days.*

In May 1970 it was estimated that 30,000 Lebanese villagers had already fled from South Lebanon. By June the number had risen to 150,000 (Newsweek, June 8, 1970). Another 25,000 or so fled in early September of that year when the Israeli airforce bombed and strafed Arkoub while ground armour moved into the villages causing a major exodus (The Guardian, September 7, 1970).

For Israel, attacking defenceless South Lebanon became a routine job. For the inhabitants life in their ancestral villages became a calvary. They were faced with the alternatives of living under siege and a reign of terror or fleeing to seek refuge in Beirut or elsewhere in North Lebanon. The majority fled. Even those who were initially determined to stay put and brave the daily onslaughts were forced to leave when the devastation caused by the Israeli war of attrition not only left them homeless, but also deprived them of the means to earn a living.

The coup de grace for a large area of the South came in February 1978, when a force of Israelis of about 20,000 strong, supported by warplanes and covered from the sea by missiles and gunboats, invaded the South to "empty" an area in which to set up what Tel Aviv referred to as a "security belt." ... When the Israeli guns fell silent, thirty-two inhabitants out of a population of 30,000 remained in Khiyam. All thirty-two were between the ages of 60 and 80. They were massacred in cold blood [by Haddadists; some witnesses claim Israelis were present].

Khiyam was added to the list of martyr villages—Deir Yassin (1948), Kafr Kassem (1956), Qibya (1953), Al Samu' (1966) and others, where defenceless villagers—men, women and children—were killed in wanton acts of savagery.

... For the people of South Lebanon one cannot speak of an "exodus." One would have to coin a new word to describe the tragedy of peaceful citizens kept perpetually on the run from the horrors of armed retaliation inflicted upon them by a power that has arrogated to itself the right to strike, invade, conquer, devastate and kill at will. ...

For background and further information, see the Afterword to Chapter 9. The basic facts are well known to ABC News.

The ABC documentary surpasses the norm, but not by a wide margin. Since the overwhelming Israeli military victory of 1967, Israel has occupied a unique position for many American intellectuals, who treat it not as a normal state and society, but as an object of reverence and awe. They have succeeded in constructing an image of Israel and its problems and conflicts that is a crude distortion of a much more complex reality. Under the guise of "support for Israel" (a more accurate term, in my view, would be "support for Israeli intransigence and the corruption and probable ultimate destruction of Israel"), an atmosphere of fanaticism has been engendered in which discussion of the reality has been difficult or impossible, a fact that has been of some concern to Israeli doves (see Chapter 9, Afterword, at note 30). One characteristic pose of "supporters of Israel" in this curious sense of the term is that those who hold that Israeli Jews and Palestinian Arabs have comparable individual and national rights reveal a "double standard," or are "pro-PLO," or "anti-Israel," or even "anti-Semites." On such assumptions, it is possible to "prove" the ridiculous thesis that substantial parts of the U.S. press are pro-Palestinian and anti-Israel because of their occasional recognition that Palestinians are human and may even have a claim to the national rights that are accorded as a matter of course to Israeli Jews, and their occasional reporting of Israeli atrocities alongside of the spotlight focused on Palestinian terror. Another characteristic feature has been the remarkable success of "supporters of Israel" in suppressing the basic facts about Israel's treatment of its non-Jewish citizens, an effort that is not novel in the annals of state worship, though the level of achievement is surely unequaled.

For some discussion, see my paper "Israel and the New Left," in M. S. Chertoff, ed., *The New Left and the Jews* (New York: Pitman, 1971), and chapter 5 of my *Peace in the Middle East?* (New York: Pantheon, 1974). Among other striking phenomena, these papers document falsification of positions of those who did not toe the line and a degree of fabrication and deceit that would be regarded as outrageous in other contexts, but that are regarded as quite acceptable in "support of Israel," again, hardly a novelty in such cases. See also Chapters 9, 10, and 12, below. The topic deserves a much more extended treatment.

196. Media Transcripts, Inc., for ABC News, Program 20/20, April 2, 1981.

197. Charles Mohr, "Soviet Said to Ease Its Views on Terror: Experts Predict That a Revision of Marxist Theory May Increase Global Political Violence," *New York Times,* May 31, 1981.

198. See Herman, "Reaganomics." See note 51.

199. Cited in Gary Orren and E. J. Dionne, "The Next New Deal," *Working Papers* (May–June 1981), an interesting analysis and debunking of the alleged Reagan "landslide." See also the contribution by Walter Dean Burnham to Thomas Ferguson and Joel Rogers, eds., *The Hidden Election* (New York: Pantheon Books, 1981).

200. Demetrios Caraley, "Do Congressional Liberals Really Need to Tremble?," *Political Science Quarterly* (Spring 1981).

201. See Chapter 2, below; and Herman, *Corporate Control, Corporate Power,* particularly pp. 294ff.

202. Compare Poland; see note 9.

203. See note 59, and the references cited there. Samuelson actually suggested the less plausible Argentine model.

204. Conor Cruise O'Brien's term. For discussion of this topic, see my essay "Objectivity and Liberal Scholarship," in *American Power and the New Mandarins.*

205. See, e.g., Barry Siegel, "Revisionism: A New Look at Vietnam," *Los Angeles Times,* November 16, 1980, a study of "a small but increasingly vocal minority of scholars" who lend support to Ronald Reagan's characterization of the American war as a "noble cause." The article is noteworthy for the complete inability it reveals to understand what led many people (though only a tiny minority of the intelligentsia) to oppose the war on grounds of principle, not merely because it wasn't working or was proving too bloody. A typical assessment is that of Samuel Popkin, who states that "in Vietnam, if you despised Thieu, you supported the communists"—i.e., no one opposed the war on grounds that aggression is wrong, even if carried out by the United States; a serious misrepresentation of the facts, but a standard one in the media and scholarship, which serves to reinforce the basic dogma that principled criticism of U.S. actions is illegitimate, or more accurately, unthinkable.

206. See the books of mine cited above, among other sources.

207. On this topic, with primary focus on Latin America and Southeast Asia, see *Political Economy of Human Rights.*

Chapter One. Intellectuals and the State

1. The quotes that follow are taken from several of Bakunin's later essays, translated by Sam Dolgoff, *Bakunin on Anarchy* (New York: Knopf, 1972); in order, pp. 319, 295, 332, 284, 275, 329, 337, 338, 284. Another excellent collection in English is Arthur Lehning, ed., *Michael Bakunin: Selected Writings* (London: Jonathan Cape, 1973).

2. David Noble, *America by Design* (New York: Knopf, 1977).

3. Anton Pannekoek, *Lenin as Philosopher* (New York: New Essays, 1948), translated from the 1938 German original; *Workers' Councils*, Melbourne, 1950, reprinted in part as *Root & Branch* Pamphlet #1, Left Mailings, 275 River Street, Cambridge, Mass. 02139 (1970).

4. Daniel Bell, "Notes on the post-industrial society (I)," *The Public Interest* (Winter 1967). He goes on to say that "the leadership of the new society will rest, not with businessmen or corporations as we know them (for a good deal of production will have been routinized), but with the research corporation, the industrial laboratories, the experimental stations, and the universities. In fact the skeletal structure of the new society is already visible." To some perhaps, but not to me.

5. John K. Galbraith, *The New Industrial State* (Boston: Houghton-Mifflin, 1967).

6. Cited by Maurice Brinton, *The Bolsheviks and Workers' Control* (London: Solidarity, 1970).

7. Robert S. McNamara, *The Essence of Security* (New York: Harper & Row, 1968).

8. Cited by Clarence J. Karier, "Testing for Order and Control in the Corporate Liberal State," *Educational Theory,* vol. 22, no. 2 (Spring 1972). On Berlin's usage of the term "secular priesthood," see Chapter 2, note 17.

9. Harold D. Lasswell, "Propaganda," *Encyclopaedia of the Social Sciences,* vol. 12 (New York: Macmillan, 1933).

10. James P. Selvage, "Selling the Private Enterprise System," *Vital Speeches of the Day* (November 1942).

11. Cf. Alex Carey, "Reshaping the Truth: Pragmatists and Propagandists in America," *Meanjin Quarterly* (Australia), vol. 35, no. 4 (1976); Carey and Trudy Korber, *Propaganda and Democracy in America* (unpublished ms); see Carey, *Taking the Risk Out of Democracy: Corporate Propaganda Versus Freedom and Liberty,* ed. Andrew Lohrey (Urbana and Chicago: University of Illinois Press, 1997).

12. Cf. Carey, *op. cit.,* for discussion of his role. Also Thomas P. McCann, *An American Company* (New York: Crown, 1976). See Introduction, note 42.

13. Earlier, Walter Lippmann had written of "the manufacture of consent," an art which "is capable of great refinements," leading to a "revolution" in "the practice of democracy" which is "infinitely more significant than any shifting of economic power," as "persuasion has become a self-conscious art and a regular organ of popular government." *Public Opinion* (London: Allen & Unwin, 1932), p. 248; originally published in 1921.

14. Cited by Carey, *op. cit.*

15. M. J. Crozier, S. P. Huntington, and J. Watanuki, *The Crisis of Democracy: Report on the Governability of Democracies to the Trilateral Commission* (New York: New York University Press, 1975).

16. Ithiel Pool, "The Public and the Polity," in Pool, ed., *Contemporary Political Science: Toward Empirical Theory* (New York: McGraw-Hill, 1967).

17. Johan Huizinga, *The Waning of the Middle Ages* (London: Arnold, 1924).

18. Henk L. Wesseling, "Reluctant Crusaders: French Intellectuals and the Dreyfus Affair," *Stanford French Review* (Winter 1977).

19. The quotes that follow are cited by Clarence Karier, "Making the World Safe for Democracy," *Educational Theory*, vol. 27, no. 1 (Winter 1977).

20. Later published as a book: Michael Charlton and Anthony Moncrieff, *Many Reasons Why: The American Involvement in Vietnam* (New York: Hill & Wang, 1978).

21. Cf. H. C. Peterson, *Propaganda for War: the Campaign against American Neutrality* (Norman: University of Oklahoma Press, 1939), for discussion of the gullibility of the intelligentsia and their rush "to join a cause that was intellectually fashionable" as they "repeated with a great show of wisdom" material prepared for them by the British propaganda services, while "in contradistinction to the easy surrender of American leaders was the stubborn pacifism of the great mass of the people."

22. Carol S. Gruber, *Mars and Minerva: World War I and the Uses of the Higher Learning in America* (Baton Rouge: Louisiana State University Press, 1975). See also the (rather sympathetic) account of the Creel Commission by Stephen L. Vaughn, *Holding Fast the Inner Lines* (Chapel Hill: University of North Carolina Press, 1980).

23. Jesse Lemisch, *On Active Service in War and Peace: Politics and Ideology in the American Historical Profession* (Toronto: New Hogtown Press, 1975). Lemisch cites another clear evocation of the necessity for the engineering of consent, by historian Thomas A. Bailey in 1948: "Because the masses are notoriously short-sighted and generally cannot see danger until it is at their throats, our statesmen are forced to deceive them into an awareness of their own long-run interests. Deception of the people may in fact become increasingly necessary, unless we are willing to give our leaders in Washington a freer hand."

    Lemisch himself was dismissed from the University of Chicago on the grounds that his "political concerns interfered with his scholarship." Comment on those who have not been subjected to this interesting judgment would be superfluous.

24. Compare Robert Keohane's criticism of Richard Barnet's "naïve notion that U.S. military forces are necessarily a source of disruption and conflict"; the "real lessons of the Vietnam war" were, rather, "that military power has only limited usefulness, and should not be employed to fight revolutionary social change"—"the use of military force must be carefully circumscribed and tightly controlled if it is to be effective," so we learned from the failure in Vietnam. *New York Review*, November 6, 1980.

25. Discussing Dewey's social science project aimed at socializing the Polish-American community along lines that he felt appropriate ("a precursor of the think-tank operationalism with which the liberal intellectual has been engaged throughout the twentieth century"), Karier argues that Dewey conceived of democracy as "a process by which the intelligent minority can become a majority in influence," a standard doctrine of the new class.

26. For one example, see Chapter 2. For further discussion of historical backgrounds, see Introduction.

27. Hans J. Morgenthau, *The Purpose of American Politics* (New York: Vintage, 1964), reprint of 1960 edition with new introduction dated December 1963.

28. Cf. Chapter 2, note 53.

29. Cf. Nayan Chanda, "New Delhi Wants to Offer Help," *Far Eastern Economic Review*, February 25, 1977. See also Chapter 7 and the Introduction.

30. Cf. Chomsky and Edward S. Herman, *The Political Economy of Human Rights,* vol. 2 (Boston: South End Press, 1979).

31. Charles Kadushin, *The American Intellectual Elite* (Boston: Little Brown, 1974).

32. For references, see my *For Reasons of State* (New York: Pantheon, 1973), p. 25.

33. Edwin S. Reischauer, "Back to Normalcy," *Foreign Policy* (Fall 1975). Reischauer is generally regarded as a "dove" on Vietnam, and accurately, as the term is generally used.

    Reischauer's Harvard colleague John K. Fairbank, perhaps the most distinguished China scholar in the United States, took a stronger and more consistent stand in opposition to the American war, and was one of the few senior scholars in the field who gave encouragement to young dissident voices, much to his credit. His own analyses, however, fall strictly within mainstream ideology, a fact that reveals very clearly how narrow is the spectrum of tolerated opinion in American academic circles (though rare exceptions may be found). Thus in his December 1968 presidential address to the American Historical Society, which was far from uncritical of U.S. foreign policy, he characterized the Indochina war in these terms: This is "an age when we get our power politics overextended into foreign disasters like Vietnam mainly through an excess of righteousness and disinterested benevolence." "Assignment for the '70's," *American Historical Review,* vol. 74, no. 3 (February 1969).

    Later, in discussing "the reason for our failure" in Vietnam, Fairbank explains that one factor "was the absence in our minds of an historical understanding of the modern Vietnamese revolution. By degrees, when it was too late, we began to realize that it was a revolution inspired by the sentiment of nationalism while clothed in the ideology of communism as applied to Vietnam's needs. . . . The result was that in the name of being anti-communist, vague though that term had become by 1965, we embarked on an anti-nationalist effort," a serious "error," one of many: "Our role in defending the South after 1965 was first seen as an equivalent of our defense of South Korea fifteen years before. It was also aimed at forestalling a southward expansion of Chinese communism. . . . Having so inadequate a picture of our role on the scene, we had great trouble in convincing ourselves that it had a purpose worthy of the effort."

    There are three comments to be made about this analysis. First, with regard to the factual claims: Policy planners knew perfectly well in the late 1940s that they were combating the forces of Vietnamese nationalism; our anti-Communist effort hardly began in 1965; it is absurd to say that we were "defending the South" after 1965, or ever—rather, we were at war with the rural society that comprised the large majority of the South; and there is no evidence that the United States thought it was "forestalling a southward expansion of Chinese communism," though that claim was naturally invoked in propaganda that is to be taken as seriously as comparable Soviet propaganda about forestalling Western aggression in Afghanistan. Second, with regard to the moral level of the presentation: Are our acts properly described merely in terms of "failure," "error," the result of a meager understanding of history? Was the problem really that the Bundy and Rostow brothers hadn't had good college courses in Vietnamese history? Or are stronger words in order? A third comment has to do with the time and place of these statements, which appear in the *Newsletter* of the Harvard Graduate Society for Advanced Study and Research (June 1975) under the title "Our Vietnam Tragedy" (is it properly described as "our" Vietnam tragedy?), announcing a new professorship of Vietnamese Studies to be named for Ambassador Kenneth T. Young, who presided over the early stages of the American war in the 1950s, when the Diem regime was conducting a merciless campaign of terror and violence that virtually decimated the anti-French resistance, finally eliciting a response that then brought on the full-scale U.S. attack in the 1960s. Surely Fairbank, of all people, should see that there is something obscene in this, even if it is beyond the comprehension of most of his Harvard colleagues.

34. The examples most frequently offered in defense of this view are the reporting of the Vietnam war and Watergate. Both examples demonstrate the opposite, as does the regular behavior of the media on other issues, despite occasional exceptions. For ample documentation, see the reference of note 30 and earlier books by the same authors, among many other sources. It is a striking and important fact that even the examples offered as the "strongest case" in favor of media independence clearly undermine the thesis. On Watergate, see references of Chapter 2, note 7. As for the Vietnam war, the general behavior of the media was exactly as described in the case studies that follow in Chapters 3 and 4. See also Chapter 13 and the sources cited.

One institution that has been much exercised over the alleged adversary character of the press is Freedom House, which published a two-volume study by Peter Braestrup (one volume of analysis, a second volume of supporting documentation) demonstrating that by the standards of Freedom House, the press was too critical of the American war in Vietnam, contributing to the failure of the United States to achieve its (by definition) noble aims; Peter Braestrup, *Big Story: How the American Press and Television Reported and Interpreted the Crisis of Tet 1968 in Vietnam and Washington*, two vols. (Boulder, Colorado: Westview Press, 1977, Praeger), published in cooperation with Freedom House. Braestrup's study has impressed many commentators, who describe it as "conscientious" and "painstakingly thorough" (Edwin Diamond, *New York Times*); with its "endless attention to accuracy," it constitutes "one of the major pieces of investigative reporting and first-rate scholarship of the past quarter century" and should lead to a congressional investigation of the press (John P. Roche, *Washington Post*). See also Introduction, note 173.

In fact, Braestrup's analysis in volume 1 grossly misrepresents even his own documentation, while omitting obviously relevant material from the media and government sources. When the amazingly shoddy and incompetent treatment of documentary evidence is corrected, nothing remains of his case, which is a very narrow case to begin with. What Braestrup's evidence demonstrates is that the media accepted the framework of state propaganda without serious question, including the legitimacy of the U.S. attack on South Vietnam, both in editorials and, more importantly, in the implicit editorializing in news reporting. Braestrup's basic criticism is that the press was too pessimistic about the likelihood of success for American arms—though the media tended to be less pessimistic than internal government documents or U.S. intelligence, a fact that Braestrup never mentions, and one that is hardly surprising when we observe, as the documentary record shows, that the media tended to rely uncritically on the more optimistic public pronouncements of the state propaganda system. By the standards of Freedom House, then, the press must not only adopt the basic assumptions of state propaganda without critical analysis in its news reporting and editorial comment, but it must also display a proper degree of enthusiasm and optimism for the noble cause of advancing freedom by demolishing the rural society of South Vietnam.

This study in itself provides dramatic evidence of the subservience of the media to the state, and the remarkable standards of Freedom House.

For details, see my review in *Race and Class*, vol. 20, no. 1 (1978), and an abbreviated version, in *More* (June 1978).

35. Cf. references of Chapter 2, note 7.

36. For details, see *The Political Economy of Human Rights*, vol. 2, pp. 288–89; and on Laos, *ibid.*, chapter 5 and sources cited there; see also Chapter 6, below.

A. J. Langguth, formerly bureau chief of the *New York Times* in Saigon (where, incidentally, he was responsible for some outstanding reporting), offers a defense of the failure of the *New York Times* to report the savage bombing of the peasant society of Northern Laos in his review of *The Political Economy of Human Rights, Nation*, February 16, 1981. He argues that this charge is false, because the *Times* did report the bombing of the Ho Chi Minh trail in southern Laos, concluding that "The *Times* is in the business of selling news, not suppressing it." The example however, demonstrates the real commitment of the *Times* quite precisely. The bombing of northern Laos, and its ferocious character, were not in doubt after the eyewitness reports of *Le Monde*'s Southeast Asia correspondent Jacques Decornoy, which was repeatedly brought to the attention of *Times* editors and others, who also refused to print the facts. It is quite true that the *Times* reported the bombing of southern Laos. The latter, an extension of the Vietnam war, was tolerable to the propaganda system on the generally accepted assumption that the U.S. intervention in South Vietnam was legitimate, in which case bombing of the enemy's supply trails was arguably legitimate as well. But the bombing of northern Laos was much harder for the system to assimilate, since it was—as the government acknowledged—basically unrelated to the war in South Vietnam (or Cambodia) and involved the destruction of a defenseless peasant society by extraordinarily brutal means. The difference in treatment by the press is quite instructive.

37. Reprinted in the *Boston Globe*, March 13, 1977.

38. Cf. John Ehrman, *History of the Second World War, Grand Strategy*, vol. 5 (London: Her Majesty's Stationery Office, 1956).

39. Robert Aron, *France Reborn: The History of the Liberation* (New York: Scribner's, 1964), chapter 5; translated from the French. See *The Political Economy of Human Rights*, vol. 2, chapter 2, for further discussion.

40. Robert Paxton, in his study of Vichy France, concludes that probably about "as many Frenchmen participated in 1943–4 in putting down 'disorder' as participated in active resistance"; earlier, Vichy had actively sought to become a partner in the creation of Hitler's New Order, though it was continually rebuffed (Paxton observes that "Vichy was more the creation of experts and professionals than of any other social group, and to judge Vichy is to judge the French elite"). He estimates that resistance participation at its peak, "at least as officially recognized after the war," involved about 2 percent of the French adult population, while perhaps 10 percent were willing to read a resistance newspaper. The Nazis were pleased with the French refusal to offer resistance. For example, after the failure of the Canadian landing at Dieppe, Germany freed all citizens of Dieppe who were prisoners in POW camps "in recognition of their city's failure to rise in support of the Canadians." No doubt the Nazi press exulted in this demonstration of the lack of popular support for de Gaulle's "Free French," merely the puppets of Anglo-American aggressors. The reader may supply current analogies. Robert Paxton, *Vichy France* (New York: Knopf, 1972).

41. *Boston Globe,* October 19, 1977. Japan had "condemned the show attack as being in bad taste and offensive to the Japanese people" the preceding year, but to no effect.

42. For extensive discussion, see *The Political Economy of Human Rights.*

43. Martin Woollacott, *Manchester Guardian Weekly,* September 18, 1977; excerpts in the *Boston Globe,* October 2, 1977.

44. Ngo Vinh Long, *Before the Revolution: the Vietnamese Peasants Under the French* (Cambridge, Mass.: MIT Press, 1973); see also his *Peasant Revolutionary Struggles in Vietnam in the 1930s,* Harvard University Ph.D. dissertation (May 1978). On French "humaneness" in Cambodia, see, for example, the comments by Milton Osborne, *Before Kampuchea: Preludes to Tragedy* (London: Allen & Unwin, 1979): "In a way that I believe goes far beyond the attitudes adopted by the British in India or Malaya, to take only two 'Anglo-Saxon' examples, the French thought of themselves as not only ruling but also as possessing Indochina. It was *theirs* and this allowed them to adopt a clear-eyed view that they were present as colonisers essentially for *their* own benefit. . . . In the late nineteenth and early twentieth centuries French officials had seen nothing extraordinary in the pursuit of policies that they judged would lead to the extinction of a Cambodian national identity as the result of Vietnamese immigration into Cambodia. It was the same cast of mind that allowed French observers—devotees of Cartesian thought, supposed connoisseurs of Angkorian civilisation—to dismiss Cambodians as a force to be seriously reckoned with in terms of a history that had led them to think like slaves." The record of French rule adequately reflects this perception of their victims.

For an interesting view on French racist attitudes towards the "insufferable Annamites," particularly de Gaulle's delegate Jean Sainteny, in the early post–World War II period, see Archimedes L. A. Patti, *Why Viet Nam? Prelude to America's Albatross* (Berkeley: University of California Press, 1980).

45. According to Paxton (*op. cit.*), Louis Darquier de Pellepoix, perhaps the most virulent anti-Semite of the interwar years, was appointed French Commissioner for Jewish Affairs from 1942 to 1944.

Meanwhile, President Roosevelt approved General Eisenhower's dealings with Admiral Jean Darlan, who happened to be in Algiers at the time of the American invasion of North Africa, recognizing him as head of the French North African Government. Stephen Ambrose observes that "Darlan was bitterly anti-British, author of Vichy's anti-semitic laws, and a willing collaborationist. . . . The result was that in its first major foreign-policy venture in World War II, the United States gave its support to a man who stood for everything Roosevelt and Churchill had spoken out against in the Atlantic Charter. As much as Goering or Goebbels, Darlan was the antithesis of the principles the Allies said they were struggling to establish. . . . [In French North Africa after "liberation"], Jews were still persecuted, unable to practice professions, attend schools, or own property; Arabs continued to be beaten and exploited; the French generals who had co-operated with the Nazis and fought the Americans lived in splendor amid the squalor that surrounded them." Stephen E. Ambrose, *Rise to Globalism,* vol. 8 of the Pelican History of the United States (Baltimore: Penguin, 1971).

This was, incidentally, typical of the behavior of the Anglo-American conquering forces when it was found necessary as a means to restore the desired social order and to destroy the popular forces that had resisted fascism. For example, in Italy, the United States immediately restored the fascist regime in 1943. In Greece, the British invaded after the Nazis had evacuated the country, imposing the rule of royalist elites and Nazi collaborators and initiating a "white terror" against the Communist-led anti-Nazi resistance, which was taken over by the United States under the aegis of the Truman Doctrine when the British proved unequal to the task (see Chapter 7). The same was true in Asia, where the United States backed the Japanese collaborator who had declared war on the United States in Thailand, undermining a democratic government; and in the Philippines, reinstated the rule of Japanese collaborators while organizing and arming them to suppress the anti-Japanese peasant organizations. In Indochina, the British took the first steps in overcoming the nationalist movement that had cooperated with the United States during the war, then turning the task over to the French, backed by the United States. On Europe and Asia see Gabriel Kolko, *The Politics of War* (New York: Random House, 1968), and Joyce and Gabriel Kolko, *The Limits of Power* (New York: Harper & Row, 1972). On Thailand and the Philippines, see *The Political Economy of Human Rights*, vol. 1, and sources cited there; also my *American Power and the New Mandarins* (New York: Pantheon, 1969), chapter 1. On the Philippines, see Stephen Rosskamm Shalom, *The United States and the Philippines: A Study of Neo-Colonialism* (Philadelphia: ISHI, 1981). On Indochina, see Patti (*op. cit.*), among many other sources.

46. William Y. Elliot, ed., *The Political Economy of American Foreign Policy* (New York: Holt, Rinehart & Winston, 1955). For further discussion of this revealing study, see my *At War with Asia* (New York: Pantheon Books, 1970).

Chapter Two. Foreign Policy and the Intelligentsia

1. For references and further comment, see my *For Reasons of State* (New York: Pantheon, 1973). Cf. also the description of refugees in South Vietnam by Leo Cherne, chairman of the executive committee of Freedom House and chairman of the board of directors of the International Rescue Committee: "There are more than 700,000 additional refugees who have recently fled the countryside dominated by the Vietcong and with their act of flight have chosen the meager sanctuary provided by the government of South Vietnam" ("Why We Can't Withdraw," *Saturday Review*, December 18, 1965). On U.S. programs of forced generation of refugees at that time and later (and indeed, since 1962), see *For Reasons of State*, see also Chapter 5 of the present volume. To cite one example, as Cherne wrote about the refugees fleeing the Vietcong, a government-sponsored study explained that U.S. air and artillery bombardment impel the villagers "to move where they will be safe from such attacks . . . regardless of their attitude to the GVN [the U.S. client government]." No doubt some Soviet Cherne is now writing about how refugees are fleeing to the meager sanctuary of Kabul, trying to escape the murderous terrorists who dominate the countryside, agents of Western imperialism.

To show that there are no limits to cynicism, Cherne adds that "the South Vietnamese ask only to be left in peace to overcome" the defects of the GVN, "its instability, the imperfections of its democratic institutions, and the inadequacy of its economic and social programs." With as much justice, his Soviet counterpart could now explain how the people of Afghanistan ask only to be left in peace to overcome the similar problems of their struggling nation, defended from aggression by Soviet benevolence. The extent to which such remarkable assertions pass without arousing horror and indignation, even comment, is a fair measure of the extent to which Bakunin was correct in describing "worship of the state" as the malady of the intellectuals.

2. *New York Times*, February 6, 1966.

3. *New York Times*, September 28, 1974. See Chapter 1, note 33, for a similar example from liberal scholarship. Examples are legion.

4. Peter L. Berger, "When Two Elites Meet," *Washington Post*, April 18, 1976, reprinted from *Commentary* (March 1976).

5. Samuel P. Huntington, in M. J. Crozier, S. P. Huntington, and J. Watanuki, *The Crisis of Democracy: Report on the Governability of Democracies to the Trilateral Commission* (New York: New York University Press, 1975). See also Chapter 1, note 34.

6. See Chapters 3 and 4 for some specific examples, and N. Chomsky and E. S. Herman, *The Political Economy of Human Rights*, 2 vols. (Boston: South End Press, 1979), for extensive documentation and discussion.

7. See my articles "Watergate: A Skeptical View," *New York Review* (September 20, 1973); editorial, *More* (December 1975); and introduction to N. Blackstock, ed., *COIN-TELPRO* (New York: Vintage Books, 1976).

8. On the limited nature of opposition to the Vietnam War among the intelligentsia, see Chapter 1. For some acute commentary on critique of the student movement and the refusal to join popular opposition to the war, see Julius Jacobson, "In Defense of the Young," *New Politics* (June 1970).

9. *Boston Globe*, October 18, 1976. Variants of this argument are common. Recall the observation by Martin Peretz, editor of the *New Republic*, cited in Chapter 1: "The American collapse [in Indochina] will read in history as among the ugliest of national crimes" (June 11, 1977). Peretz makes an interesting contribution to the new version of history now being created. He states that the book he is reviewing "stakes out significant independent ground—implicitly against the peace movement" by arguing "that a political settlement was possible," thus implying that "the peace movement" was against a political settlement. Of course, everyone on every side was in favor of a political settlement, but they differed on the terms: Crucially, should the National Liberation Front, which the United States government always knew to be the only mass-based political force in South Vietnam, be permitted to share in (hence presumably to dominate) the governance of the South? The "peace movement," to the extent that such an entity can be identified, argued for a political settlement on these terms, which the United States government rejected on the grounds that if the group it supported were to enter a coalition with the NLF, "the whale would swallow the minnow," in the picturesque phrase of government expert Douglas Pike. Until it committed the ugly crime of failing, the United States government was committed to blocking any such political settlement. Placed against the background of the actual history, which he knows well enough, Peretz's argument that it was criminal for the United States to desist can be understood in its full significance.

10. See Chapters 3 and 6 of the present volume.

11. Bruce Andrews, *Public Constraint and American Policy in Vietnam*, SAGE Publications, International Studies Series, vol. 4 (1976). Note that the facts are somewhat ambiguous, as Andrews explains, in that much of this opposition was of the "win or get out" variety.

12. *Crisis of Democracy* (above, note 5). See Chapter 1, above.

13. For particularly inane musings along these lines, see Sandy Vogelsang, *The Long Dark Night of the Soul* (New York: Harper and Row, 1974).

14. Nathan Glazer, "American Jews and Israel: The Last Support," *Interchange* (November 1976).

15. Gordon Connell-Smith, *The Inter-American System* (Oxford: Royal Institute of International Affairs, 1966), p. 343.

16. Consider Henry Kissinger's characterization of the "statesman": "He judges ideas on their utility and not on their 'truth.' " The word "truth" is placed in quotes, reflecting the contempt that Kissinger has always felt for this concept. In the same essay he complains of the difficulty of dealing with the "ideological leadership" of the Communist states: "The essence of Marxism-Leninism . . . is the view that 'objective' factors such as the social structure, the economic process, and, above all, the class struggle are more important than the personal convictions of statesmen. . . . Nothing in the personal experience of Soviet leaders would lead them to accept protestations of good will at face value," as we do all the time. "Domestic structure and foreign policy," in *American Foreign Policy* (New York: Norton, 1969).

A few pages later Kissinger identifies "the deepest problem of the contemporary international order": It is nothing like starvation, war, oppression, or other trivia that occupy superficial minds, but rather the fact that current debates are peripheral to the "basic division" between two styles of policy and a "difference of philosophical perspective" that separates the West, which "is deeply committed to the notion that the real world is external to the observer," from "cultures which escaped the early impact of Newtonian thinking," and still believe "that the real world is almost completely *internal* to the observer." The French Revolution, Lenin, Mao, and others failed to cross this philosophical barrier (though Russia, he concedes, has partly come to recognize that there is a real world outside of our heads). Just how this squares with the idea that the Communists are difficult because of their absurd concern for objective reality is not easy to determine, but perhaps this all-too-typical nonsense should simply be dismissed as a parody of the academic intellectual, which was in fact quite effective with the media and, remarkably, with the academic world as well. See Chapter 6.

17. The term is used by Isaiah Berlin, "The Bent Twig," *Foreign Affairs* (October 1972). The context suggests that he has in mind primarily the subservient intelligentsia of the state socialist societies, an apt but insufficiently general usage.

18. It is worth noting Kissinger's uncritical acceptance of the legitimacy of this concept of "the expert" as someone who grovels before authority, whatever may be the truth—or as he would say, the "truth" (see note 16).

19. In the essay cited in note 16, Kissinger observes that "law and business . . . furnish the core of the leadership groups in America." So far, he is correct. But which lawyers? Those who defend civil rights of blacks? Obviously not. Rather, overwhelmingly, those linked to corporate power. And which businessmen? The corner grocer? Evidently it is the "business élite," whose special talent, Kissinger adds, is their "ability to manipulate the known"—an ability that they share with carpenters and the peasants who have yet to learn about the existence of the external world. Putting aside the typical obfuscation, the fact that Kissinger carefully skirts is that foreign policy is largely in the hands of those with private power. Some ideologists are more straightforward, e.g., Huntington, who writes (in *The Crisis of Democracy*) that "Truman had been able to govern

the country with the cooperation of a relatively small number of Wall Street lawyers and bankers," though he fears that these happy days are gone, since other groups have been "mobilized and organized" to advance their own interests, leading to a "crisis of democracy." See Chapter 1.

20. *Trialogue* (Fall 1976).

21. For example, Leon Wieseltier explains that my political writings "are a monument to left-wing paranoia, devoted as they are to demonstrating that the press in this country is 'a system of state-supported propaganda'; nothing that Chomsky wrote about the slaughter in Cambodia was quite as angry as his attack on Jean Lacouture for misquoting the number of its victims" (*New Republic*, September 23, 1981). Turning to the facts, the alleged quote is simply a fabrication. Secondly, the nature of my "attack" on Lacouture is accurately illustrated in this summary passage: "In what passes for intellectual discourse in the West, political discussion included, correction of errors is rare indeed, as a glance at review journals will indicate. Lacouture deserves credit for departing from the general norm. We think that his corrections are inadequate and disagree with some of the conclusions expressed in them, but we want to stress that it is no crime to misread—it is a rare review that avoids error—and it is only proper to issue corrections when errors are discovered" (*Political Economy of Human Rights*, vol. 2, p. 377). In contrast, we described "the record of atrocities" of the Khmer Rouge as "substantial and often gruesome," etc.

Wieseltier does believe that some criticism of the press is not paranoid: "There is a scandal, and it is the moral and political prestige of the PLO [in media] coverage of the Middle East," something that will be apparent to every reader of the American press.

Since my "attack on Lacouture" has taken on a mythical life of its own, perhaps a word about the facts is in order (*ibid.*, for details). Lacouture's review of François Ponchaud's *Cambodge année zéro* appeared in the *Nouvel Observateur* and the *New York Review* in early 1977, and was widely quoted in the press here as an authoritative account of Ponchaud's work. I read the book and found that there was scarcely a reference to it in the review that was even near accurate. In the case to which Wieseltier alludes, Lacouture claimed that the Khmer Rouge had "boasted" of having murdered some 2 million people, apparently basing himself on Ponchaud's estimate that 800,000 had been killed during the war and that some 1.2 million had died from all causes since. I wrote Lacouture a personal letter, pointing out a series of such errors and suggesting that he issue corrections. In publishing partial corrections in the *New York Review* (never in France), Lacouture posed to me the question whether it is an important matter "whether the regime has murdered thousands or hundreds of thousands of wretched people" (the original claim was a "boast" of 2 million murdered). In a review-article in the *Nation* in which we recommended Ponchaud's book as "serious and worth reading," noting his "grisly account of what refugees have reported to him about the barbarity of their treatment at the hands of the Khmer Rouge," E. S. Herman and I responded to Lacouture's rhetorical question, stating that we felt that facts do matter, and that a factor of 100 or 1000 in estimates of killings is not insignificant. We also noted that there was wide disparity in estimates of killings, ranging from the *Far Eastern Economic Review* ("possibly thousands" killed) to Lacouture's original 2 million figure, adding that we were in no position to determine which estimates were correct; Lacouture himself oscillated from a boast of 2 million murdered to possibly thousands killed, within a few months. This was followed by a remarkable campaign of deceit and outright prevarication in the international press, alleging that I was denying Pol Pot crimes; some of the press (including the *New Republic,* repeatedly) refused the normal right of reply. To mention only one example, in the author's preface to the American edition of his book, Ponchaud cites my praise for it and in turn praises me for "the responsible attitude and precision of thought" shown in what I had written about Cambodia (which in fact includes everything that appeared during the Pol Pot period). In the author's preface to the world edition, dated the very same day, these passages are eliminated and replaced by the allegation that I "sharply criticized" his book, claim that there were "no massacres," and insist that one rely on "deliberately chosen official statements" of the regime while excluding the testimony of refugees—all falsehoods, as Ponchaud knew very well; compare the simultaneous American edition, which is not available elsewhere while the world edition is unavailable in the U.S. His allegations in the world edition were widely repeated and in fact seeped back to the United States, while his comments here were ignored, as was the exposure of this deception. This is not the place to review the record, which provides an intriguing insight into the attitude of much of the intelligentsia towards the curious idea that one should try to keep to the truth, even when joining in the chorus of condemnation of an official enemy.

22. The following remarks on the War-Peace Studies Project relies on Laurence H. Shoup, "Shaping the Postwar World," *Insurgent Sociologist,* vol. 5, no. 3 (Spring 1975), where there are explicit references for the quotes that appear below. See now also the important study by L. Shoup and W. Minter, *Imperial Brain Trust* (New York Monthly Review Press), to my knowledge the first serious study of this project, issued in early 1977 to a resounding silence, apart from ritual denunciation in the journal of the CFR by William Bundy (*Foreign Affairs,* October 1977).

23. Cf. Gabriel Kolko, *The Politics of War* (New York: Random House, 1968), and David P. Calleo and Benjamin M. Rowland, *America and the World Political Economy* (Bloomington: Indiana University Press, 1973). Kolko is, to my knowledge, the first historian to have seriously investigated this question. Calleo and Rowland conclude that "the war had exhausted British economic power. To a considerable extent, the United States was responsible. Throughout the War, Hull, determined to break up the British bloc, had used the leverage of Lend-Lease skillfully and systematically to reduce Britain to a financial satellite." The British, of course, were aware of what was going on; Calleo and Rowland quote an "outraged" communication from Churchill to Roosevelt on the subject. See also Introduction, note 16.

24. There has been much debate over the question of how or whether Western policy deliberately contributed to this outcome. Albert Speer recalls "one single case" of direct cooperation between Hitler and the West—namely, an arrangement for the transfer of German troops cut off by the British fleet on a Greek island to the Russian front, to allow the British, rather than the Russians, to take Salonika. Albert Speer, *Inside the Third Reich* (New York: Macmillan, 1970; Avon Books, 1971), p. 509.

25. Cf. Chapter 11, note 4.

26. Cf. Kolko, *op. cit.,* pp. 302f.

27. The Western Hemisphere was then and for many years after the major producing area. Until 1968 North America surpassed the Middle East in oil production. Cf. John Blair, *The Control of Oil* (New York: Pantheon, 1976).

28. For discussion of how this principle was applied or abrogated to extend the power of the American oil companies, see *Multinational Oil Corporations and U.S. Foreign Pol-*

icy (henceforth, *MNOC*), Report to the Committee on Foreign Relations, U.S. Senate, January 2, 1975 (Washington, D.C.: Government Printing Office, 1975).

29. Cf. Michael Tanzer, *The Energy Crisis* (New York: Monthly Review Press, 1974), in particular, his discussion of the devices used to shift other countries to an oil-based economy. Cf. also Joyce and Gabriel Kolko, *The Limits of Power* (New York: Harper & Row, 1972).

30. This plan was actually imposed on the oil companies by the government, naturally over the strong objections of the British. This is one of several instances that reveal how the government may disregard the parochial short-term interests of even major segments of the corporate system in order to safeguard the more general interests of American capitalism. For discussion, see Chapter 11.

  The 40 percent American share was distributed among the five major American companies, who were persuaded to relinquish 1 percent each to American independent companies for "window dressing," according to the Middle East coordinator for Exxon (*MNOC*, p. 71). It should be remembered that this was shortly after President Truman had killed a grand jury investigation of the oil cartel on grounds of "national security," on recommendation of the Departments of State, Defense, and Interior, who advised that the "American oil operations are, for all practical purposes, instruments of our foreign policy"—and who might have added, reciprocally, that our foreign policy is to a significant extent guided by long-term oil company interests.

31. Yoshio Tsurumi, "Japan," in "The Oil Crisis: In Perspective," *Daedalus* (Fall 1975). Discussing the prewar period, the same author has commented on "the American myth that the government and business circles of the United States operate at arms-length, if not in outright adversary relationships"—Reviews, *Journal of International Affairs* (Spring/Summer 1976). It should be noted that under the conditions cited in the preceding note, local conflict may occasionally arise, since, insofar as it functions as a generalized agency of American capitalism, the government may have concerns different from those of some particular segment.

32. For a review of the contents of these memoranda, see Richard B. Du Boff, "Business Ideology and Foreign Policy," in N. Chomsky and H. Zinn, eds., *Critical Essays*, published as volume 5 of the Gravel edition of the Pentagon Papers (Boston: Beacon Press, 1972). For further analysis of the contribution of the Pentagon Papers to the understanding of United States imperial planning, see John Dower, "The Super-domino in Postwar Asia," in the same volume, and my *For Reasons of State*, particularly pp. 31–66.

33. *Annals of the American Academy of Political and Social Science* (March 1976).

34. Robert L. Gallucci, *Neither Peace nor Honor: the Politics of American Military Policy in Vietnam* (Baltimore: Johns Hopkins University Press, 1975). The limitation to "military policy" is crucial; basic decision-making with regard to the American involvement in Vietnam is nowhere discussed.

35. Largely as a result of the impact of the student movement, it became difficult to ignore completely the so-called radical critique—though, as noted, it is not obvious why the assumption that the United States behaves much as all other great powers do should be considered particularly "radical." There are, in fact, several publications attempting to deal with it. The most serious, to my knowledge, is Robert W. Tucker, *The Radical Left and American Foreign Policy* (Baltimore: Johns Hopkins University Press, 1971). For a discussion of gross errors of fact and logic that entirely undermine his analysis (and

others), see my *For Reasons of State*. For a very penetrating discussion of critical literature on the "radical critique," see Stephen Shalom, "Economic Interests and United States Foreign Policy," unpublished, adapted from the author's Boston University Ph.D. dissertation: "US-Philippine Relations: A Study of Neo-Colonialism" (1976).

An interesting example of the evasion and misrepresentation of the "radical critique" appears in the study by Leslie H. Gelb, who was director of the Pentagon Papers project (*The Irony of Vietnam: The System Worked*, with Richard K. Betts [Washington, D.C.: Brookings Institution, 1979]). He begins by outlining nine "wide-ranging explanations of U.S. involvement given in the Vietnam War literature." The first two of these are "idealistic imperialism" and "economic imperialism" (the latter explanation is allegedly mine; for comment, see *For Reasons of State*, pp. 63–65). Gelb then explains why these "stereotypes fail," including the first two, and crucially the second, which, when presented without his distortion, is the thesis that is documented in the Pentagon Papers and elsewhere, a fact that Gelb systematically ignores. Curiously, his analysis of defects covers all of the theories presented with the exception of the first two theses, which are ignored in this analysis of defects and subsequently. The only comment that has even marginal bearing on the alleged failure of this "stereotype" is this: "But however these explanations are combined, they are better as answers to the question of why the United States originally became involved and committed in Vietnam than as analyses of the process of involvement, the strategy for fighting the war, and the strategy for ending it." Even that statement is false: In fact, the "radical" thesis documented in Gelb's Pentagon Papers study and ignored in his book provides quite a convincing explanation for the evolution of U.S. strategy throughout Indochina and also for the Nixon-Kissinger effort to salvage victory from defeat (cf. Chapter 3), and furthermore for the postwar policy of exploiting and maintaining the quite substantial, even if only partial, U.S. victory—namely, the destruction of Indochina, which succeeds in deflecting the dread "domino effect" of successful development that might be emulated elsewhere (cf. Chapter 4, note 1). But even assuming Gelb's comment to be accurate, note the implications. A study of the sources of U.S. policy is dismissed as irrelevant and beside the point; we must restrict attention to the execution of this policy. When Gelb refers to "doves," he restricts attention to "pessimists," who thought that the United States would fail, and who "were not ignored," Gelb observes, which shows that "the system worked." The only analyses of U.S. policy that can be seriously considered are those that sought to explain why "the United States failed in Vietnam," not those that reject the assumption that the United States had a right to succeed.

Gelb is one of those who regard concern for French sensibilities and the French role in Europe as being of paramount importance in guiding U.S. policy in the early years. While this may have been a minor factor, the documentary record shows clearly that imperial strategy concerning the Far East was a far more predominant one. Gelb is not unaware of the latter factor, but misrepresents it, without providing any evidence, as "an inversion of Marxist theory," in which "economic interest was used as a cloak for political interest." The popularity of the former thesis (which is widely regarded as the "sophisticated" theory) can easily be explained by the fact that it is far less threatening to the state religion than the actual record of planning revealed in considerable detail in the Pentagon Papers.

Even on the narrow issue of strategy for realizing the objectives that Gelb misstates, his use of documentary evidence is worth careful investigation. For example, in discussing the aftermath of the Geneva Accords in 1954, he does not so much as mention the National Security Council response (NSC 5429/2, August 20, 1954); for good reason, as we see when we consider the contents of this document, which laid plans for U.S. subversion and aggression throughout East Asia in response to the dangerous threat that peace might be brought to Indochina. Cf. *For Reasons of State*, pp. 100f. (Also p. 150, below) Interestingly, this document is even severely misrepresented in the Pentagon Papers study itself, as noted in *For Reasons of State*.

36. Laurence B. Krause, "The International Economic System and the Multinational Corporation," in *The Multinational Corporation, Annals of the American Academy of Political and Social Science* (September 1972).

37. Ray, "Corporations and American Foreign Relations."

38. Gaddis Smith, "The United States as Villain," *New York Times Book Review*, October 10, 1976.

39. Cited in Charles B. Maurer, *Call to Revolution* (Detroit: Wayne State University Press, 1971), p. 174.

40. A fact of which the business press is not unaware, though businessmen constantly whine of their difficulties in reaching public opinion with their "message." See Chapter 1.

41. See Chapter 11.

42. "International Economics," *Business Week*, March 29, 1976.

43. *Winning the Cold War: The U.S. Ideological Offensive*, Hearings before the Subcommittee on International Organizations and Movements of the Committee on Foreign Affairs, House of Representatives, 88th Congress, second session, Part VIII, U.S. Government Agencies and Programs, January 15 and 16, 1964 (Washington, D.C.: U.S. Government Printing Office), pp. 953f.

44. In much of Latin America and Asia, the AID-trained police have proven to be among the most vicious torturers and murderers. El Salvador is a recent example. See Introduction. The U.S.-trained military have been no less adept at repression and slaughter. On this topic, see *The Political Economy of Human Rights*, vol. 1, and references cited there.

    To cite only one example, consider Somoza's Nicaragua. A National Guard offensive resulted "in thousands of deaths in the countryside, where whole villages suspected of harboring guerillas were destroyed," and villagers describe "aerial bombings, summary executions and gruesome tortures . . . it is also believed by many that an ongoing American-backed 'peasant welfare' program [heavily financed by AID] is actually a cover for anti-guerilla activities" in the north, where these military exercises were being conducted. Furthermore, "about 85 percent of the National Guard leadership is directly trained in anti-guerilla warfare by the United States" in Nicaragua, which is "the only country which sends the entire annual graduating class of its military academy for a full year of training" at the United States Army school in the Panama Canal Zone. Stephen Kinzer, "Nicaragua, a Wholly Owned Subsidiary," *New Republic* (April 9, 1977). In a pastoral letter the seven principal Catholic prelates of Nicaragua denounced the "atrocious climate of terror" that reigned in the country. Jean-Claude Buhrer, "Les droits de l'homme en Amérique centrale," *Le Monde diplomatique* (May 1977). Even the generally ludicrous State Department *Human Rights Reports* concede that there may have been a few problems in Nicaragua (primarily, as a result of Cuban-supported guerrilla activities), while naturally ignoring entirely the United States role.

Cf. *Human Rights Reports*, submitted to the Subcommittee on Foreign Assistance of the Committee on Foreign Relations, of the U.S. Senate, March 1977 (Washington, D.C.: U.S. Government Printing Office, 1977). For discussion of these reports, see *Political Economy of Human Rights*, vol. 1.

45. Otto H. Kahn, *The Myth of American Imperialism*, publication of the Committee of American Business Men, an address given December 30, 1924, at a meeting on the subject of American imperialism organized by the League for Industrial Democracy, p. 4, section entitled "The Allegation of Political or Military Imperialism."
46. For references, see chapter 4.
47. James Chace, "American Intervention," *New York Times*, September 13, 1976.
48. Chace, "How 'Moral' Can We Get?" *New York Times Magazine*, May 22, 1977.
49. To be sure, the contradiction can easily be resolved. We can take these statements as an indication of what is really meant by the term "stability" in the rhetoric of American political analysis.
50. Norman A. Graebner, *Cold War Diplomacy: 1945–60* (New York: D. Van Nostrand, 1962).
51. Sixto Lopez, "The Philippine Problem: A Proposition for a Solution," *The Outlook*, April 13, 1901.
52. "How 'Moral' Can We Get?" The word "often" is a bit of an understatement.
53. News conference, March 24, 1977; reprinted in the *New York Times*, March 25.
54. Commencement address at Bentley College. *Boston Globe*, May 18, 1975. See Chapter 4.
55. William Beecher, "US show of force impressed N. Korea," *Boston Globe*, September 3, 1976.
56. Quarterly Review Staff Study, "The Attack on the Irrigation Dams in North Korea," *Air Universities Quarterly Review*, vol. 6, no. 4 (Winter 1953–54). Cf. also Robert Frank Futrell, *The United States Air Force in Korea, 1950–1953* (New York: Duell, Sloan and Pearce, 1961), pp. 623f.
57. John Osborne, *New Republic*, June 7, 1975. See Chapter 4 for the further thoughts of this courageous defender of the nation's honor.

Chapter Three. Indochina and the Fourth Estate

1. Henry Kissinger, *American Foreign Policy* (New York: Norton, 1969), p. 62.
2. *Ibid.*, p. 97.
3. Dana Adams Schmidt, reporting the views of "the highest level of officials at the Pentagon," and Courtney R. Sheldon, on the "new wave of uncertainty over President Nixon's intentions in Vietnam sweep[ing] across Washington," *Christian Science Monitor*, March 23, 1973.
4. Wendell S. Merrick and James N. Wallace, *US News and World Report*, April 2, 1973.
5. *Boston Globe*, April 2, 1973. Kraft adds that "to that end the Communists have staged military actions in South Vietnam, and sent down equipment on a large scale." An editorial comment in *US News and World Report* concurs: "In South Vietnam, massive infiltration from the North and a dangerous surge in Communist warfare eroded the truce" (April 23, 1973). These opinions, which bracket the "responsible mainstream of opinion," are typical. On military actions, neither commentator cites evidence. I will return to the facts.

6. The full text appears in Douglas Pike, *Viet Cong* (Cambridge, Mass.: MIT Press, 1966), pp. 350–51. Pike was a USIA expert on the NLF. On the political premises of his work, see my *American Power and the New Mandarins* (New York: Pantheon, 1969), pp. 365–66. For further information on Pike's role as a government propagandist, see D. Gareth Porter, "U.S. Political Warfare in Vietnam—the 1968 'Hue massacre,' " *Indochina Chronicle*, no. 33, June 24, 1974.

7. Pike, *op. cit.*, p. 359. For discussion of the neutralization option and the fears it engendered in Washington, see my *For Reasons of State* (New York: Pantheon, 1973), chapter 1. See also Marek Thee, *Notes of a Witness* (New York: Random House, 1973), pp. 283f. and Georges Chaffard, *Les deux guerres du Vietnam* (Paris: La Table Ronde, 1969), which discuss the hopes of all major parties in Indochina apart from the GVN that the Laos agreements would serve as a model for South Vietnam.

8. Pike, *op. cit.*, p. 361.

9. *Ibid.*, p. 362. Pike assessed indigenous support for the NLF in 1962 at 50 percent of the population, a phenomenally high level of support for a revolutionary movement under such conditions; *War, Peace and the Vietcong* (Cambridge, Mass.: MIT Press, 1969), p. 6. George Washington could not have claimed as much, under far more favorable conditions. High officials in the U.S. Mission agreed; see Robert Scigliano, *South Vietnam: Nation under Stress* (Boston: Houghton-Mifflin, 1964), p. 145. U.S. officials were well aware that the Diem regime, in comparison, had little indigenous support, and its successors, still less. As Ambassador Lodge pointed out in January 1964, "It is obvious that the generals are all we have got" (Gravel Edition, *Pentagon Papers*, Boston: Beacon Press, 1971, vol. 2, p. 304). Even the generals were opposed to American efforts at the time to take over the war and local administration, complaining that in their "worst and clumsiest days" the French never went so far as the United States was then doing. *Ibid.*, pp. 307–8. See Chapter 4 of the present volume, note 7.

10. *Ibid.*, p. 376.

11. *Ibid.*, pp. 337–38.

12. *Ibid.*, p. 384. These measures included systematic exclusion of all persons connected with the Buddhist "struggle movement," and, obviously, the NLF. As the Pentagon Papers analyst remarks, "If we could not have the reality [of democracy], we would start with appearances" (p. 284).

13. Kissinger's press conference appears in the *New York Times*, January 25, 1973, and, with slight modifications, in the *State Department Bulletin*, February 12, 1973.

14. *New York Times*, December 17, 1972.

15. *New York Times*, October 27, 1972.

16. *Ibid.*

17. In a CBS interview of February 1, Kissinger described the American dilemma in December as he would like it to be perceived. The North Vietnamese were not serious, and "the more difficult Hanoi was, the more rigid Saigon grew." The United States feared it "would be caught between the two contending Vietnamese parties." In order "to bring home really to both Vietnamese parties that the continuation of the war had its price," the United States bombed Hanoi and sent General Haig to placate Saigon; "so we really moved in both directions simultaneously." Putting aside the matter of the even-handedness of the U.S. response, as Kissinger outlines it with his engaging cynicism, his account suffers from a few omissions: specifically, that Hanoi was publicly calling for signing of the October plan, which the United States then accepted in the

Paris Agreements after the failure of the Nixon-Kissinger terror bombings of late December. For lengthy excerpts from Kissinger's remarks, see *Monthly Review* (March 1973).

18. *Newsweek*, February 5, 1973.

19. *New York Times*, March 1, 1973. Similarly, Stanley Karnow comments in the *New Republic*, February 17, 1973, that "the Vietcong considers [the PRG] to be a parallel administration," failing to add that it is the Paris Agreements signed by the United States and the GVN that assign to the PRG a status exactly equivalent to the GVN.

20. John F. Kennedy, quoted in Roger Hilsman, *To Move a Nation* (New York: Delta, 1967), p. 439.

21. *New York Times*, March 29, 1973.

22. Quite apart from the physical condition of the POWs, there are problems with their testimony that have passed without press comment. They have repeatedly denounced visitors to Hanoi for contributing to torture of prisoners forced to meet them, failing to note that if the visitors are culpable as alleged, then the U.S. government and the prisoners who had already returned are still more culpable, since they never indicated to visitors that they should refrain from meeting prisoners. In fact, visits to Hanoi were expedited by U.S. government officials. Or consider the charge that the peace groups that transmitted mail were blackmailing POW families into cooperating with them. To prove this charge, it would suffice to produce some family whose mail was rejected because of refusal to cooperate. Of course, no such evidence is produced, there being none.

23. *New York Times*, April 1, 1973.

24. "Five years later, My Lai is a no man's town, silent and unsafe," AP, *New York Times*, March 16, 1973.

25. *Le Monde*, January 4, 1973. The two Frenchmen state explicitly that a November 9, 1972, story in the *New York Times* on the treatment of prisoners "is false," citing evidence directly refuting it. To my knowledge, the *New York Times* carried neither the AFP report of the Paris press conference nor any other news report of the two French prisoners who toured the United States in March 1973. The latter was discussed on the Op-Ed page, but with no mention of the U.S. role. The impression given was that the tortures and assassinations are just another example of Vietnamese savagery. For a recent summary of the American role, the deception concerning it, and the consequences for the Vietnamese, see Holmes Brown and Don Luce, *Hostages of War*, Indochina Mobile Education Project, 1973.

26. March 26, 1973.

27. *Far Eastern Economic Review*, "A sudden increase in criminals," April 9, 1973. George notes also that the Thieu Administration had not returned any military personnel to the PRG, in direct violation of Article 8(c) of the Paris Agreements, according to a PRG statement which alleges as well that "many prisoners had been taken to unknown places or secretly disposed of, while dossiers had been changed to turn military personnel into 'common law prisoners in a bid not to return them.' " There has been a substantial flow of information from the prisons on torture and murder since the cease-fire, and some reporting in the American press, particularly, from prison hospitals. Cf. Jacques Leslie, *Los Angeles Times*, March 8, 1973, on "violent seizures" of women prisoners in reaction "to being tortured with electricity at South Vietnamese police interrogation centers," and elaborate descriptions of torture by prisoners.

28. Editorial, *New York Times*, April 8, 1973.

29. In 1962, as part of the Strategic Hamlet program, "open zones" were declared for "random bombardment by the newly-arrived artillery and aircraft so as to drive the inhabitants into the safety of the strategic-hamlet belt"; this "was the principal cause of a huge migration of tribesmen in the summer of 1962, which gave the President [Diem] the personal satisfaction of being voted for by about a quarter of a million feet" (Dennis J. Duncanson of the British "aid" mission, *Government and Revolution in Vietnam* [New York: Oxford University Press, 1968], p. 321). Roger Hilsman witnessed bombing of a Vietnamese village by U.S. planes in January 1962 (after a Cambodian village had been bombed by mistake) and describes the "continued and excessive use of air power and crop destruction" reported to the President in 1962 (*op. cit.*, pp. 437, 452). Defoliation missions were first authorized by the President in November 1961. By October 1962, U.S. planes were flying about 30 percent of the combat missions in South Vietnam, excluding helicopter flights; *New York Times*, October 17, 1962. See also Chapter 5 of the present volume.

30. *New York Times*, May 6, 1972.

31. *Christian Science Monitor*, March 30, 1973.

32. For a careful review and analysis of press reports, see Dave McFadden, "We Call this War a Ceasefire," NARMIC, 112 S. 16th Street, Philadelphia (April 1973). In the first eight weeks of the cease-fire, he found more than thirty firsthand reports of cease-fire violations by the GVN, and not a single report of a PRG- or DRV-initiated violation that had actually been observed. Note that the reporters are all in GVN areas, and thus in a poor position to detect GVN-initiated actions.

33. *Christian Science Monitor*, February 8, 1973. It is unclear from his account whether the "penetration" by Communist troops, apparently without combat in some cases at least, was before or after the cease-fire.

34. Neil Davis, Reuters, *New York Times*, February 9, 1973.

35. *Christian Science Monitor*, March 16, 1973. "We like the Americans very much," one old woman said. "We like them because they are leaving."

For further discussion of U.S.-GVN efforts to undermine the accords by military action, finally evoking a North Vietnamese military response (denounced, naturally, as unprovoked aggression from Hanoi), including U.S. government reports that "the GVN has fared well during the post-cease-fire maneuvering; since January 1973 it has added 770 hamlets to the list of those over which it has dominant control" (an achievement not unrelated to the fact, proudly announced by the U.S. and Saigon military, that the "countryside ratio of the number of rounds fired by South Vietnamese forces [since the Paris Agreements] to that fired by Communist forces was about 16 to 1"), see N. Chomsky and Edward S. Herman, "Saigon's Corruption Crisis: The Search for an Honest Quisling," *Ramparts* (December 1974). See also Maynard Parker, "Vietnam: The War that Won't End," *Foreign Affairs* (January 1975), among other sources, particularly, Gareth Porter, *A Peace Denied* (Bloomington: Indiana University Press, 1975).

36. David Hotham, commentary, in R. W. Lindholm, ed., *Vietnam: The First Five Years* (East Lansing: Michigan State University Press, 1959), p. 359.

37. Joseph Buttinger, "Lösung für Vietnam," *Neues Forum*, Vienna (August-September, 1966), translated in Edward S. Herman, *Atrocities in Vietnam* (New York: Pilgrim Press, 1970).

38. Memorandum after a visit to Vietnam in January 1961; U.S. Department of Defense

United States—Vietnam Relations, 1945–67, book 2, tab 4, pp. 66–77 (Washington, D.C. U.S. Government Printing Office, 1971); the government edition of the Pentagon Papers.

39. Gravel Edition, *Pentagon Papers*, vol. 1, p. 259.

40. Henry Kamm, *New York Times*, March 28, 1973. Malcolm Browne reports that according to official American sources in Phnom Penh, "there has been no documented evidence that Vietnamese Communist troops are serving in combat roles in Cambodia," in "direct contradiction of the official Cambodian Government position" and also in conflict with the justification given by Washington for continued American bombing. Browne concludes, "It is clear, therefore, that American bombing has been intended not so much to drive out the Vietnamese as to sustain the feeble resistance offered by the forces of President Lon Nol to an indigenous insurgent army dominated by Communist-led units." *New York Times*, April 21, 1973.

41. UPI, *Boston Globe*, April 1, 1973: "Refugees swarming into the capital from target areas report dozens of villages, both east and southeast of Phnom Penh, have been destroyed and as much as half their population killed or maimed in the current bombing raids by B-52s and F-111 tactical fighter-bombers." Elizabeth Becker reports in the *Far Eastern Economic Review*, April 16, 1973, that "according to military reports, the targets of these devastating missions [by Thailand-based bombers] are in heavily-populated areas."

42. Dana Adams Schmidt, *Christian Science Monitor*, April 5, 1973.

43. *Boston Globe*, April 8, 1973.

44. UPI, *Boston Globe*, April 7, 1973. Bankrom was a town sixteen miles from Phnom Penh.

45. James N. Wallace, *US News and World Report*, February 26, 1973.

46. See *Aerospace Daily*, November 6, 1972. Friedheim said "that the Vietnamese could bridge the [pilot] gap by hiring 'contract personnel' which could either be active duty U.S. pilots loaned to them or recently retired U.S.A.F. fliers." For more on these matters, see D. Aftergut and D. Roose, "Civilianizing the War," *American Report*, March 12, 1973, and *The War Is Not Over*, Indochina Resource Center, 1973.

47. *Time*, March 19, 1973. For an analysis of the aid program, see Guy Gran, "American welfare abroad—aid to South Vietnam," Indochina Resource Center, April 8, 1973. The Indochina Resource Center, by providing information to Congress and the public, contributed significantly to compelling the Administration to terminate its devastating bombing of Cambodia, as it had done earlier in the case of the "secret war" against the peasants of Laos. The center's work is described by William Shawcross as "dedicated support for the communist cause in Indochina" (*Inquiry*, December 7, 1981). Apparently, his view is that it was only proper to condemn these atrocities long after they had ceased, not to work to stop them. In the same article, he writes, with unintended irony, that "those who were most right about the war have been the least honored." On the character of Shawcross's style of argument, see Chomsky and Herman, *Political Economy of Human Rights*, vol. 2, pp. 232f. See Introduction, note 205.

48. See *Business Week*, January 27, 1973, the day of the signing of the Paris Agreements. This upbeat analysis virtually recapitulates the plans described in business journals, government-financed studies, and academic journals prior to the spring 1972 offensive. For details, see my *For Reasons of State*, chapter 4.

49. *Asahi Evening News* (Tokyo), March 31, 1973.

50. *New York Times*, March 16, 1973.

51. *New York Times*, March 18, 1973.

52. Daniel Southerland, *Christian Science Monitor*, April 14, 1973. He also reports, to no one's surprise, that "what struck us first about the Liberation Front Zone was the appalling destruction" (*ibid.*, April 13), resulting from some of those minor flaws in the American record that trouble the *New York Times* editors. See pp. 137.

53. *Op. cit.*

54. William Beecher, *New York Times*, April 12, 1973.

Chapter Four. The Remaking of History

1. See *At War with Asia* (New York: Pantheon, 1970), chapter 1; *For Reasons of State* (New York: Pantheon, 1973), chapter 1, section 5. On the dangers posed by Communist successes in South Vietnam, see Douglas Pike, *Viet Cong* (Cambridge, Mass.: MIT Press, 1966). See also the important study by Jeffrey Race, *War Comes to Long An* (Berkeley: University of California Press, 1971). Also William A. Nighswonger, *Rural Pacification in Vietnam* (New York: Praeger, 1967); Robert L. Sansom, *The Economics of Insurgency in the Mekong Delta of Vietnam* (Cambridge, Mass.: MIT Press, 1970).

It is this concern over the dangers of Communist successes in organizing the rural population that explains the savagery of the U.S. attack on the rural societies of South Vietnam and Laos, compounded in the case of South Vietnam by the fear that the NLF might realize its efforts to neutralize South Vietnam, along with Laos and Cambodia. It is important to recognize that in terms of its basic objectives, the United States won the war in Indochina, despite the major defeat it suffered. The National Liberation Front of South Vietnam was destroyed, particularly in the post-Tet accelerated pacification campaigns, along with the rural society in which it was embedded. All of Indochina was reduced to a level of bare survival from which it may never recover. Postwar U.S. policy has been designed to ensure that the prospects for recovery are slight. For further discussion of the substantial, though not complete U.S. victory in Indochina, and the ways in which the facts are presented to the public in the free press, see Chomsky and Herman, *The Political Economy of Human Rights*, volume 2.

2. Robert W. Tucker, *The Radical Left and American Foreign Policy* (Baltimore: Johns Hopkins University Press, 1971); "Vietnam: The Final Reckoning," *Commentary* (May 1975).

3. Equally faulty is Tucker's argument that since "the costs of imperialism may prove harmful to the greater economy, thus creating dissension among the corporate rulers" (as happened in Vietnam, by early 1968), there must be a fallacy in the "radical critique" that attributes the main thrust of U.S. imperial intervention to "benefits . . . calculated primarily in terms of the interests of America's 'corporate rulers.' " In fact, as the "radical critique" he is discussing consistently observed, it was just this reassessment of costs that led to a shift towards less "costly" tactics, including greater reliance on surrogate forces and a more capital-intensive war, and finally towards liquidation of the enterprisé. By Tucker's logic, one could prove that corporate managers do not pursue the maximization of profit, since sometimes they shut down an inefficient plant. For further discussion of errors of fact and logic in Tucker's critique, see my *For Reasons of State*. This is, nevertheless, the best and most serious effort in mainstream schol-

arship to come to terms with the so-called radical critique, to which the term "radical" hardly applies, in my view.

4. Arthur M. Schlesinger, *The Bitter Heritage* (Boston: Houghton-Mifflin, 1967).

5. There is an enlightening account of the early days, and the lost opportunities, in Archimedes L. A. Patti, *Why Vietnam: Prelude to America's Albatross* (Berkeley: University of California Press, 1980). Many important documents bearing on this and later periods are assembled in Gareth Porter, *Vietnam: the Definitive Documentation*, 2 vols. (New York: Coleman, Stanfordville, 1979). See my *For Reasons of State*, chapter 1, for discussion of the record in the Pentagon Papers. See also Richard B. Duboff, "Business Ideology and Foreign Policy: The National Security Council and Vietnam," in N. Chomsky and Howard Zinn, eds., *Critical Essays*, volume 5 of *The Pentagon Papers* (Gravel ed.) (Boston: Beacon Press, 1972). On the post-Geneva period, see particularly Race, *op. cit.*

6. Roger Hilsman, *To Move a Nation* (Garden City, N.Y.: Doubleday, 1967).

7. On this period, see George McT. Kahin, "Political Polarization in South Vietnam: U.S. Policy in the Post-Diem Period," *Pacific Affairs* (Winter 1979–80). As Kahin observes, the group of South Vietnamese generals and civilians who ousted the Diem regime "had a set of priorities that differed markedly from those of the administration in Washington and hinged on a political rather than a military solution. . . . They looked towards a negotiated agreement among the Vietnamese parties themselves without American intervention." But this view was intolerable to the United States because, as Under-Secretary of State George Ball explained, "Nothing is further from USG mind than 'neutral solution for Vietnam.' We intend to win." Ball is widely regarded as a "dove," since he was later opposed to a full-scale invasion beyond the level of about 75,000 men. The post-Diem Vietnamese leadership regarded the NLF as "overwhelmingly non-communist, with the PRP [People's Revolutionary Party—its avowedly Communist component] still having no dominance and indeed only a minor position within the organization," and "sufficiently free of Hanoi's control to have made [a peaceful settlement in South Vietnam] quite possible," with a pro-Western neutralist government: "Unfortunately there were leaks of our plans [for a negotiated settlement among South Vietnamese] and it is apparent that the American government got wind of them" (Nguyen Ngoc Tho, the civilian prime minister, in 1969). The South Vietnamese generals were also opposed to the American plan to bomb North Vietnam, put into operation a year later. For these reasons, the post-Diem government was overthrown in a U.S.-organized coup placing General Khanh in power, to be overthrown a year later in another U.S.-backed coup. At each stage, the United States imposed a regime that could then "invite" the United States to "defend it" against aggression (sometimes, the United States failed even to notify its client of these steps, so that the "request" was subsequent to them). The great fear of the United States that there might be neutralization of South Vietnam in 1964, in accordance with the official program of the NLF, is well documented in the Pentagon Papers; cf. *For Reasons of State*.

8. Maxwell D. Taylor, *Swords and Plowshares* (New York: Norton, 1972).

9. See Chapter 3, above.

10. See the references cited in Chapter 3, note 35.

11. *New York Times*, April 21, 24, May 1, 1975. Subsequently, Lewis has repeatedly made clear his evaluation of the U.S. war in Indochina, with such references to it as the fol-

lowing: Regarding Rhodesia, America should do nothing, because "if we remember Vietnam, we know that intervention, *however well-intended*, may do terrible harm if it is uninformed" (*New York Times*, February 1, 1979); in Cambodia, the United States dropped three times the tonnage of bombs that fell on Japan in World War II, with the result that "thousands of square miles of what had been fertile land, dotted with villages, were devastated," meanwhile "creat[ing] the Khmer Rouge" (citing Sihanouk)—"in short, the policy, *however sincerely intended*, had disastrous results" (September 24, 1979); the argument against the war "was that the United States had misunderstood the cultural and political forces at work in Indochina—that it was in a position where it could not impose a solution *except at a price too costly to itself*" (December 27, 1979); the Christmas bombing of Hanoi "was the symbol of a much larger failure: the continuation of the war for four years after every informed person knew *it could not be won*. The price of that failure was and still is enormous. From 1969 through 1972 the United States spent $50-billion on the Indochina war, dropped 4 million tons of bombs, lost 20,492 American lives. But *the highest cost* was not measurable in figures. *It was the further polarization of this country, the political embitterment*" (December 22, 1980); "what we learned in Vietnam, and have to keep recalling, is that there are limits to what the greatest power can do" (December 27, 1979); etc. (my emphases).

Recall that I am quoting from one of the most outspoken critics of the war in the mainstream American press, a person who in some cases was almost alone in refusing to join the chauvinist consensus (see below). It would be a sad enough commentary on the United States and its ideological institutions if such sentiments as these had been quoted from the jingoist extreme of the spectrum of mainstream opinion.

With tedious predictability, Lewis unquestioningly repeats the government propaganda line on the Christmas bombings: Thieu and his Saigon colleagues "blocked" the October agreements after "Kissinger declared that peace was 'at hand,' " and thus "forced the last bloody chapter," namely, the bombing of Hanoi. On the facts, see Chapters 3 and 6.

12. Bernard Fall, "Vietcong—the Unseen Enemy in Vietnam," *New Society*, April 25, 1965. Reprinted in *The Vietnam Reader*, Fall and M. G. Raskin, eds. (New York: Vintage, 1965).

13. Cited from the Nuremberg Documents by Karl Dietrich Bracher, *The German Dictatorship* (New York: Praeger, 1970), p. 423.

14. For discussion, based on research by Kevin Buckley and Alex Shimkin, see *The Political Economy of Human Rights*, vol. 1, chapter 5, section 1.3. See also Chapter 5 of the present volume.

15. Charles E. Bohlen, *The Transformation of American Foreign Policy* (New York: Norton, 1969).

16. Charles Kadushin, *The American Intellectual Elite* (Boston: Little, Brown, 1974); see Chapter 1, above. On the polls, see Andre Modigliani, *American Political Science Review* (September 1972).

17. Evelyn Keene, *Boston Globe*, May 18; commencement address at Bentley College.

18. James McCartney, *Boston Globe*, May 29, 1975.

19. See Chapter 8 of the present volume.

20. Editorial, *New Republic*, February 1, 1975. The editors warn against the kind of "arbitrarily consistent policy" that would have us eschew the use or threat of force (as re-

quired by law). They reassure the Pentagon that it is "wrong to assume that those who opposed the Vietnam horror are blindly bound to permanent opposition to military action"—rather, "they will be receptive to arguments about national interest and for that matter about ethical obligations to democratic allies threatened by terror and aggression" (read: "Israel, threatened with loss of control over the occupied territories"). They stress, of course, the benevolent purposes of our military intervention in the Middle East, if we are driven to such steps.

The reader may check to see when U.S. actions in Indochina were described as "aggression" by these editors, or when they have soberly discussed invading Canada, England, Venezuela, Iran (during the period when it was a client regime), countries that also committed "aggression" by supporting the rise of oil prices.

21. Cf. Jonathan Power, *New York Times,* March 15, 1975; several articles in *Middle East International* (April 1975); the analysis by the Pakistani director of policy planning and program review at the World Bank, reported by David Francis, *Christian Science Monitor,* May 5, 1975; and many other sources.

Chapter Five. On the Aggression of South Vietnamese Peasants Against the United States

1. Diem was a direct import from the United States and owed his original status as a "leader" and his subsequent capacity to withstand his lack of indigenous support to the backing of his godfather. One of his replacements, General Khanh, claimed that "in January 1964, Wilson [his U.S. advisor] told me a coup d'état was planned in Saigon and that I was to become President. . . . On 8 February 1964 I took over as Premier." (Interview with the German magazine *Stern* reprinted in the *Los Angeles New Advocate,* April 1–15, 1972.) General Maxwell Taylor, in a briefing of November 27, 1964, speaks with assurance about our "establishing some reasonably satisfactory government" in South Vietnam, indicating that if we were not satisfied with the way things were going, "we could try again with another civilian government. . . . Another alternative would be to invite back a military dictatorship on the model of that headed of late by General Khanh." (*Pentagon Papers,* Gravel ed. [Boston: Beacon Press, 1972], vol. 3, p. 669.) From Diem to Thieu each government was chosen by or with the approval of the United States and continued to exist only by U.S. sufferance. This is clearly assumed in internal government documents, but for PR purposes these client governments were regularly put forward as independent and possessing all authority. See Chapter 4, above, particularly note 7. For one of many demonstrations of the irrelevance of mere fact, cf. Daniel P. Moynihan: "It was simply not the case that the United States in the middle 1960s was trying to control events 'within' South Vietnam" (*Washington Post,* March 31, 1979).

2. See Chapter 4, above, note 1.

3. Chomsky, *For Reasons of State* (New York: Pantheon, 1973), p. 19.

4. See Chomsky and Herman, *The Political Economy of Human Rights,* vol. 1 (Boston: South End Press, 1979), for discussion and references.

5. Race, *War Comes to Long An* (Berkeley: University of California Press, 1971).

6. Buttinger, *Vietnam: The Unforgettable Tragedy* (New York: Horizon, 1977). Buttinger

also observes that "it required a tidal wave of falsehood to persuade Americans into accepting the myth that not French, but Communist, aggression was responsible for the first Indochina war."

7. Douglas Pike, *Viet Cong* (Cambridge, Mass.: MIT Press, 1966).

8. Chomsky, "The Pentagon Papers as History and Propaganda," in N. Chomsky and H. Zinn, eds., *Critical Essays, The Pentagon Papers* (Gravel ed.), vol. 5 (Boston: Beacon Press, 1972).

9. *Ibid.;* also, *For Reasons of State*, for extensive documentation from U.S. government sources.

10. Cf. *The Political Economy of Human Rights*, vol. 1, chapter 5.

11. *Ibid.,* for discussion and references.

12. *Ibid.*

13. *Ibid.,* vol. 2, p. 154.

14. See Chomsky, "U.S. Involvement in Vietnam," *Bridge* (October 1975); also *Vietnam Quarterly*, vol. 1, no. 1 (1975).

15. *Ibid.* and Chomsky and Herman, *op. cit.,* vol. 1, chapter 5.

16. For a postwar eyewitness description, see John Pilger, "Vietnam: The Children's Inheritance," *New Statesman*, September 15, 1978. There have been many others, during the war and since.

Chapter Six. Kissinger, *The White House Years*

1. Seyom Brown, *The Crises of Power* (New York: Columbia University Press, 1979), pp. 17, 11.

2. On the profundities of Kissinger's academic contributions, see Chapter 2, above, notes 16, 19.

3. Consider, for example, the geopolitical analyses developed in the War and Peace Studies group of the Council on Foreign Relations and the State Department from 1939 to 1945, concluding that the United States must dominate a "Grand Area" including at a minimum the Western Hemisphere, the Far East, and the former British Empire, to be developed as an integrated economic system responsive to the needs of the American economy—or more precisely, those who own and manage it. See Chapter 2, above. In fact, geopolitical analysis is standard in high-level planning documents, though in the serious sense of the term, not Kissinger's trivialized and sanitized version of it.

4. For an analysis of Kissinger's assumptions, see V. Brodine and M. Selden, eds., *Open Secret: the Kissinger-Nixon Doctrine in Asia* (New York: Harper & Row, 1972).

5. See William Shawcross, *Sideshow* (New York: Simon & Schuster, 1979). On Kissinger's revision of his memoirs (and denial of same) after the appearance of Shawcross's book, see Wolfgang Saxon, "Kissinger Revised His Book More Than He Reported," *New York Times*, October 31, 1979. Also Shawcross, *Far Eastern Economic Review*, January 2, 1981.

6. *Supplemental Foreign Assistance, Fiscal Year 1966—Vietnam*, Hearings before the Committee on Foreign Relations, U.S. Senate, 89th Congress, 2nd Session, 1966, p. 433; cited in Gareth Porter, *A Peace Denied* (Bloomington: Indiana University Press, 1975), p. 36.

7. For details, see especially the articles by R. B. Du Boff and John Dower in *The Pentagon*

Papers, vol. 5, *Critical Essays*, N. Chomsky and H. Zinn, eds. (Boston: Beacon Press, 1972); and my *For Reasons of State* (New York: Pantheon, 1973), chapter 1, section 5.

8. Cf. Vann's internal memorandum of 1965 explaining how the United States must conduct "effective political indoctrination" of the "unsophisticated, relatively illiterate rural population" in South Vietnam under a U.S.-instituted "autocratic government," since these naive souls do not understand the evils of Communism as we do and thus have identified with the National Liberation Front instead of the government we back, which is "oriented toward the exploitation of the rural and lower class urban population." Cf. *For Reasons of State*, pp. 232–33. See also the analysis of the State Department in 1948 concerning our dilemma, given "the unpleasant fact that Communist Ho Chi Minh is the strongest and perhaps the ablest figure in Indochina and that any suggested solution which excludes him is an expedient of uncertain outcome," an analysis that coincided with the decision to back France in overcoming the nationalist movement led by Ho. *Ibid.*, p. 32. The documentation in this regard is substantial.

9. See Chapter 7 of the present volume, and Introduction.

10. See *For Reasons of State*, pp. 84–94, for a review of some of Komer's contributions to resisting aggression.

11. A corollary of the underlying principle concerning academic freedom is that they should not be granted high-level appointments for which they lack academic qualifications on political grounds, i.e., on the basis of their actions as state managers and their influential connections. Not infrequently, this principled commitment to the independence of the university has been absurdly misrepresented as a rejection of the principles of academic freedom.

12. For a concise review, see Nikki R. Keddie, "Oil, economic policy and social conflict," *Race & Class* (Summer 1979).

13. Testifying before the Senate Foreign Relations Committee, April—May 1971, p. 502 of *Hearings;* cited in Allan Goodman, *The Lost Peace* (Stanford: Hoover Institution Press, 1978), p. 70. The general character of this book is revealed by its initial premise, that "in 1965, the security of the free world and the credibility of American power required our presence in Vietnam" (xvii). It contains many false claims (e.g., that Johnson sought negotiations in 1964–65), but is useful in showing how a strongly pro-government scholar views the negotiations history.

14. Terence Smith, "New U.S. Tactics Intensified Fighting," *New York Times*, March 23, 1969.

15. For extensive quotes from Buckley's article and original notes, see N. Chomsky and E. S. Herman, *The Political Economy of Human Rights*, vol. 1 (Boston: South End Press, 1979), pp. 313ff. See also Chapter 5, above.

16. Peter Arnett, *New York Times*, April 15, 1969. He estimates that 90 percent of the "enemy forces" were locally recruited.

17. For extensive citations, see N. Chomsky, *At War with Asia* (New York: Pantheon, 1970), pp. 127–28. Only a few sentences appeared in the U.S. press, to my knowledge.

18. *Pentagon Papers*, Gravel ed. (Boston: Beacon Press, 1971), vol. 4, p. 479. For a comprehensive review of the *Pentagon Papers* record on Cambodia, see *For Reasons of State*, chapter 3, pp. 202f.; see also *At War with Asia*, chapter 2, for other sources, and *The Political Economy of Human Rights*, vol. 2, pp. 268f.

19. For sources and further details, see *The Political Economy of Human Rights*, vol. 2, p. 288f. See pp. 32, 94, above.

20. See *At War with Asia*, pp. 122f.
21. See *At War with Asia*, pp. 160f., for a sample.
22. See *At War with Asia*, chapter 2, for details concerning this and many other relevant reports, generally ignored in the U.S. press.
23. *Life*, April 3, 1970, cited with other reports in *At War with Asia*, p. 214. Most of the press, however, simply repeated Nixon's claim, despite their knowledge of the facts. The same was true of the scholarly literature. Cf. *For Reasons of State*, p. 179.
24. See *At War with Asia*, chapter 3; *For Reasons of State*, chapter 2; and sources cited there.
25. See Chapter 4, above, note 7.
26. See Goodman, *op. cit.*, p. 156; and for substantial detail, Porter, *op. cit.*; Chomsky and Herman, "Saigon's Corruption Crisis," *Ramparts* (December 1974); Maynard Parker, "Vietnam: The War That Won't End," *Foreign Affairs* (January 1975); also Chapter 3, above.
27. For details, see Chapter 3, above. Also N. Chomsky, "The Peace Hoax," *Liberation* (January 1973); "Endgame: The Tactics of Peace in Vietnam," *Ramparts* (April 1973); N. Chomsky and S. E. Luria, letter, *New York Times*, February 12, 1973.
28. For explicit references, see *The Political Economy of Human Rights*, vol. 2, chapter 7.
29. Cited by Shawcross, *Sideshow*, p. 363, along with Kissinger's response.
30. Yitzhak Rabin, *The Rabin Memoirs* (Boston: Little, Brown, 1979).
31. William B. Quandt, *Decade of Decisions* (Berkeley: University of California Press, 1977), p. 124. On these matters, see Chapter 12 of the present volume.
32. See *Multinational Oil Corporations and U.S. Foreign Policy*, report to the Committee on Foreign Relations, U.S. Senate, by the Subcommittee on Multinational Corporations, January 2, 1975 (Washington, D.C.: U.S. Government Printing Office, 1975).
33. See Chapters 10, 11, 12, and my article "The Interim Agreement," *New Politics* (Winter 1975).
34. Margaret Manning, *Boston Globe*, October 28, 1979.
35. See Chapter 2, above, note 16, for a more extensive quote.

Chapter Seven. Towards a New Cold War

1. Text of press conference, *New York Times*, December 1, 1978. This and the next reference are cited in Robert C. Johansen, *Jimmy Carter's National Security Policy*, Working Paper number 14, World Order Models Project, Institute for World Order, New York, 1980.
2. *State Department Bulletin* (March 1980).
3. *New York Times*, November 16, 1978, cited by Michael T. Klare, *Resurgent Militarism*, Institute for Policy Studies Issue Paper, Washington, D.C., 1978. This and Johansen, *op. cit.*, provide a useful picture of one aspect of the policies cloaked by human rights propaganda. For one example of another aspect, see Chapter 13, below. See Chomsky and E. S. Herman, *The Political Economy of Human Rights* (Boston: South End Press, 1979), for much further discussion, in the recent historical context of U.S.-Third World relations that is often ignored or obscured.
4. According to Klare, U.S. arms exports rose 20 percent during the first two years of the Carter Administration, reaching record levels in 1979. Cited by Johansen, *op. cit.*, from

Klare, "The Arms Overstock," *Harper's* (November 1979). In *Resurgent Militarism,* Klare estimates the U.S. share of the international market in 1978 at 49 percent, followed by the USSR at 28 percent, France at 5 percent, and Britain at 4 percent. Smaller countries are fighting for their share of the international market, including Israel, which has become a major supplier for the murderous dictatorships backed (often installed) by the United States; it would not be unrealistic to regard this as part of the U.S. contribution to world order, given the unprecedented dependence of Israel on U.S. aid. (See Chapter 12.) Arms exports provide one index of the contribution of a state to international terrorism. Perhaps the most notorious example of this sort was the substantial increase in arms to Indonesia to expedite the huge massacre in Timor, abetted, in this case, by the convenient silence of the media. See Chapter 13.

5. Hedrick Smith, *New York Times,* December 2, 1975.

6. *New York Times Magazine,* December 16, 1973. See Chapter 8.

7. Drew Middleton, *New York Times,* March 20, 1980.

8. See Thomas M. Franck and Edward Weisband, *Word Politics: Verbal Strategy among the Superpowers* (New York: Oxford University Press, 1971) for discussion of how the Khrushchev and Brezhnev doctrines mirrored, respectively, the earlier Eisenhower and Johnson doctrines in the rhetoric adopted to justify military intervention in satellite states.

9. Thomas Powers, *The Man Who Kept the Secrets* (New York: Knopf, 1979), p. 306. Cf. also Basil Davidson, "South Africa's Border Wars," *New Society,* March 19, 1981, and for the general background, John Marcum, *The Angolan Revolution,* vol. 2 (Cambridge, Mass.: MIT Press, 1978). Also John Stockwell, *In Search of Enemies* (New York: Norton, 1978). The French role in Africa is also consistently underplayed in U.S. commentary. See Daniel Volman, "Gendarme of Africa," *Progressive* (March 1981), for a rare exception. Attention in the United States is generally focused not on intervention by France or South Africa, or Belgium, Egypt, and Morocco (in Zaire, as U.S. proxies), or Zaire (in Angola), etc., but rather on the Cuban role, interpreted as Kremlin-inspired aggression. Whatever one thinks of Cuba's activities in Africa, it is well to recall that in Angola, Cuba's intervention in support of the MPLA (whose government is now recognized by black Africa and the West apart from the United States) "followed upon substantial intervention by others, including Zaire and South Africa . . . there is no question that Cuba's intervention was partly an improvised response to South Africa's" (Marcum, *op. cit.*). Furthermore, the country remains under regular attack by South African forces and mercenaries. On this matter, see Jonathan Steele's report from Angola (*Manchester Guardian Weekly,* February 8, 1981), concluding that "it is clear that South Africa is conducting a systematic policy of striking economic and military targets in Angola" and that "there can be no more doubt that the broad thrust of Angola's complaints that it is facing South African aggression is true, despite South African denials." Steele also gives a detailed account of the savagery and brutality of South African mercenaries (and their contempt for Savimbi's UNITA guerrillas, described as "a lot of crap"; Savimbi, widely touted as a freedom fighter in the United States, had made his peace with South Africa by mid-1975, shortly before he began receiving U.S. arms; see Marcum, *op. cit.,* who notes that American arms also "poured in on C130s from Zaire to the FNLA's staging areas," while this group too was being helped by South Africa). The latter account is based on an interview with a British

mercenary who explains how his colleagues "love killing," particularly, "killing women, hanging them and things." "They don't see them as people, just as things that are there." See also Introduction, note 108.

As for Cuba serving as a Soviet proxy, while it is obvious that the USSR foots the bill, Cuba has its own reasons for involvement in Angola. The majority of the population of Cuba is African in origin, many from what is now Angola, and relations would no doubt be close even apart from South African aggression and terror, motivated in large part by South African efforts to defy U.N. decisions on independence for mineral-rich Namibia.

Angola has stated publicly that Cuban forces will withdraw when South African aggression ceases and Namibia gains independence, in accordance with U.N. resolutions. *Washington Post,* April 25, 1981.

For detailed analysis of the U.S. press on Angola and its close adherence to official doctrine, see Marsha Coleman's forthcoming Ph.D. dissertation, MIT, Political Science Department.

10. See, for example, Franklyn Holzman, "Are the Soviets Really Outspending the U.S. on Defense?" *International Security* (Spring 1980).

11. Holzman estimates this gap at perhaps $400 billion in the past decade; "The Military Expenditure Gap—Fact or Fiction," manuscript, Tufts University, 1981. See Introduction, notes 105, 106.

12. See Richard B. Duboff and Edward S. Herman, "The New Economics: Handmaiden of Inspired Truth," *Review of Radical Political Economics* (August 1972). See also their review of James Tobin, *The New Economics One Decade Older* (Princeton) in *Commonweal,* December 20, 1974.

13. These events, and the way they are commonly treated here, merit careful consideration. It will be recalled that at a crucial stage of the missile crisis, the Kennedy Administration was faced with what it regarded as a serious dilemma: whether to accept Khrushchev's offer to arrange a mutual withdrawal of Soviet missiles from Cuba and American missiles from Turkey (obsolescent missiles, for which a withdrawal order had already been given since they were being replaced by Polaris submarines), or to reject this offer and face a probability of nuclear war that top-level Kennedy advisers estimated at 1:3 to 1:2. The latter course was chosen, so as to establish the principle that we have the right to maintain missiles at their borders (but not conversely), and to ensure that there would be no challenge to the machismo image that the Kennedy Administration endeavored so desperately to project. On the general character of Kennedy's much-admired statesmanship during this period, see Richard J. Walton, *Cold War and Counter-Revolution* (Baltimore: Penguin, 1972). The memoirs of the participants make sufficiently chilling reading.

14. Cited from the *Forrestal Diaries* in Joyce and Gabriel Kolko, *The Limits of Power* (New York: Harper & Row, 1972), which remains the most important analytic study of evolving U.S. policy in this period, though there has been much useful work since.

15. *Ibid.,* p. 341. The all too common incapacity of mainstream scholarship even to comprehend what is being said in work that departs too far from the chauvinist consensus is evident in the discussion of the Anglo-British conflict during this period. Consider, for example, John C. Campbell's review in *Foreign Affairs* (Spring 1981) of Barry Rubin's *The Great Powers in the Middle East, 1941–1947* (London: Frank Cass, 1980), a book that provides documentation generally supporting the account by the Kolkos and

other "revisionists," while typically disparaging the revisionist literature without serious argument. Campbell writes that the message of Rubin's book "brings no comfort to the revisionist school of cold-war historians" because it shows that U.S. policy was antiimperialist ("Wilsonian") and "anti-British, and only anti-Soviet after the Russians began to subvert the independence of Middle East states." The anti-British element in U.S. policy and its "anti-imperialism" (i.e., opposition to imperial prerogatives that blocked the expansion of U.S.-based economic interests) is a major thesis of the revisionist literature—apart from the fact that Rubin's book hardly demonstrates any great success of the Russians in subverting the independence of Middle East states, a task that was then and subsequently a prerogative of the West, primarily.

16. Dean Acheson, *Present at the Creation* (New York: Norton, 1969), p. 219.

17. See Chapter 8 for further discussion.

18. *An-Nahar Arab Report & Memo,* Beirut, February 4, 1980.

19. See, for example, Bernard Lewis, *New York Times,* March 29, 1980.

20. *Manchester Guardian,* weekly edition, January 20, 1980.

21. Peter Niesewand, *Manchester Guardian,* February 17, 1980.

22. For documentation and discussion, see *The Political Economy of Human Rights,* vol. 2, chapter 2.

23. The material just reviewed is from Lawrence S. Wittner, "The Truman Doctrine and the Defense of Freedom," *Diplomatic History* 4 (Spring 1980), largely drawn from government documents. See also Secretary of Commerce Maurice Stans, quoted in the *New York Times,* April 24, 1971, on "the welcome that is given here to American companies and the sense of security the Government of Greece is imparting to them" under the fascist regime of the U.S.-trained colonels.

24. Anthony Wild, *Manchester Guardian,* March 31, 1980.

25. Amnesty International provides evidence that the systematic massacre of the population and the regular "tortures and murders are part of a deliberate and long-standing program of the Guatemalan Government," and that the "selection of targets for detention and murder, and the deployment of official forces for extra-legal operations, can be pin-pointed to secret offices in an annex of Guatemala's National Palace, under the direct control of the President of the Republic"; *Guatemala; a Government Program of Political Murder* (London: Amnesty International, 1981). AI began its campaign "focusing attention on the political murder encouraged by the Guatemalan Government" in September 1979 (*Amnesty International Report 1980,* which adds many further details). The reports of atrocities received some mention in the U.S. press, though analysis of the U.S. government role in placing these gangsters in power and supporting them is rarely noted. The latter topic is not part of AI's mandate, and it is legitimate for them to avoid the issue. The same cannot be said about the U.S. press and scholarship, which have the moral and intellectual duty to make this a primary topic of publicity and concern. For more on Guatemala, see *The Political Economy of Human Rights,* vol. 1, pp. 274ff. Note that while the tortures and murders are sometimes noted, the far more significant topics discussed briefly above are generally—though not totally—ignored.

See also the Introduction to this volume, notes 21 and 189. On the military coup organized by the United States, which inaugurated the current era of horror, see Blanche W. Cook, *The Declassified Eisenhower* (Garden City, N.Y.: Doubleday, 1981); Stephen Kinzer and Stephen Schlesinger, *Bitter Fruit* (Garden City, N.Y.: Doubleday, 1981).

26. Anti-Slavery Society for the Protection of Human Rights, Report for 1980 to the United Nations Working Group of Experts on Slavery: *Guatemala—Deprivation of Indigenous Peasants' Land, Livelihood, Liberty and Lives, 1978–1980,* London.

It is a useful exercise to compare the reports of AI and the Anti-Slavery Society with the tempered account in the State Department's Human Rights report (*Country Reports on Human Rights Practices,* Report submitted to the Committee on Foreign Relations, U.S. Senate, and Committee on Foreign Affairs, U.S. House of Representatives, by the Department of State, February 2, 1981). The report notes the increase in violence in 1980, estimating politically motivated deaths at seventy-five to one hundred each month, far lower than the estimates by human rights groups, including church groups. The State Department, as distinct from human rights groups, notes merely that "reportedly these acts were carried out by armed extremists of the left and right and by elements of the official security forces. The government has not taken effective steps to halt abuses or carry out serious investigations," which is hardly surprising if the massacres are being organized from the presidential palace. The report continues: "Victims of the violence in 1980 included military and police personnel, government officials, pro-government politicians, businessmen, opposition political leaders, peasants and large numbers of students, academics and trade union activists." No distribution of killings is presented, just as the agent for the vast majority of them is suppressed. Nothing is said about the conditions of "virtual servitude" of the majority of the work force, though there is much discussion of the progressive programs planned by the government, and the new labor code, which "could theoretically strengthen trade unions." The report notes that "the government supports the dynamic industrial and well diversified, export-oriented agriculture sectors," but has nothing to say about the effect of export-oriented agriculture on the domestic population. On the various ways in which the State Department human rights reports conceal the true nature of governments placed and maintained in power by the United States, see *The Political Economy of Human Rights,* vol. 1.

27. Stephen Kinzer, *Boston Globe,* February 18, 1980.

28. *London Financial Times,* December 4, 1979.

29. See also David Hayes, "One-way Ticket to Misery," *Far Eastern Economic Review,* October 3, 1980, on child slavery in Thailand, another beneficiary of U.S. intervention since the early postwar years; for background, see *The Political Economy of Human Rights,* vol. 1, chapter 4, and my *American Power and the New Mandarins* (New York: Pantheon, 1969), pp. 61f.

On slavery in the United States, see John M. Crewdson, "Thousands of Aliens Held in Virtual Slavery in U.S.," *New York Times,* October 19, 1980, an important exception to the general rule.

30. Henry Kissinger, *American Foreign Policy,* expanded ed. (New York: Norton, 1974).

31. Samuel P. Huntington, in his contribution to M. J. Crozier, S. P. Huntington, and J. Watanuki, *The Crisis of Democracy* (New York: New York University Press, 1975).

32. *Defense Monitor* (January 1980).

33. This and the preceding quote are cited in the important study by Jan K. Black, *United States Penetration of Brazil* (Philadelphia: University of Pennsylvania Press, 1977).

34. Cited in *ibid.*

35. Peter Winn, *Nation,* June 2, 1980. Recall the explanation by the current U.N. Ambas-

sador Jeane Kirkpatrick as to why "such societies create no refugees." See Introduction, note 67.

36. *Foreign Affairs*, vol. 58, no. 3, 1980.

37. See *The Political Economy of Human Rights*, vol. 2, chapter 5.

38. *Far Eastern Economic Review*, November 16, 1979; May 9, 1979; *Christian Science Monitor*, November 5, 1979, the only mention of these incidents that I noted in the U.S. press.

39. See *The Political Economy of Human Rights*, vol. 1, chapter 3, section 4-4, for extensive documentation. See also Chapter 13 of the present volume.

40. See, for example, my *At War with Asia* (New York: Pantheon, 1970), p. 286: if the United States is able to "destroy the National Liberation Front of South Vietnam, by employing the vast resources of violence and terror at its command," and to "break the will of the popular movements in the surrounding countries," then "it will create a situation in which, indeed, North Vietnam will necessarily dominate Indochina, for no other viable society will remain." Essentially what happened in Vietnam. In Cambodia, subsequent U.S. atrocities played a major role in "creat[ing] the Khmer Rouge" in Sihanouk's phrase (cf. Chapter 4, note 11); on the subsequent hostilities between Cambodia and Vietnam, leading to the Vietnamese takeover of Cambodia in December 1978-January 1979, see references cited in *The Political Economy of Human Rights*, vol. 2, Chapter 6. See the same chapter and references cited there for discussion of the "major atrocities and oppression," documented largely "from the reports of refugees" in a society that was "almost entirely closed to the West," focusing on the extensive fabrication of evidence as part of a more general study of Western propaganda. On Laos, see chapter 5, and on Vietnam, chapter 4, of the same volume. Forthcoming books by Michael Vickery (*Cambodia* [Boston, South End Press]) and Ben Kiernan and Chanthou Boua (eds., *Peasants and Communists in Kampuchea* [London, Zed Press]) add valuable information about the Pol Pot years and discuss the situation in Cambodia since, as do several important studies by Stephen Heder: *Kampuchean Occupation and Resistance, Asian Studies Monographs* No. 27 (Bangkok: Chulalongkorn University, 1980); "Kampuchea October 1979–August 1980," unpublished manuscript, Bangkok, November 1980, based on extensive refugee interviews. See also Laura J. Summers, "Co-operatives in Democratic Kampuchea," paper prepared for annual meeting of the Political Studies Association at the University of Hull, April 1981; Department of Politics, University of Lancaster, 1981.

See also the CIA research paper *Kampuchea: A Demographic Catastrophe* (Springfield, Va.: National Technical Information Service, 1980). The CIA estimates the population decline during the Pol Pot years at about 1.5 million, based on a December 1979 population estimate of about 5.2 million (the mid-1975 population is generally estimated at about 7.5 million; the CIA research paper gives an estimate of about 700,000 deaths from the 1979 famine after the fall of the Pol Pot regime). International relief personnel estimate the 1980 population at about 6.5 million (*Report of the FAO Food Assessment, Kampuchea*, Office for Special Relief Operations, Rome, November 1980). See also *Nation Review*, Bangkok, November 10, 1980, for an AP report on the release of a United Nations study (perhaps the same one) by the special coordinator for Kampuchea Sir Robert Jackson, estimating the population at 6.4 million. These are stated to be revisions of earlier estimates upwards by over 25 percent. See Vickery, *op. cit.*, for evaluation of this and other material. See also Carlyle A. Thayer (of the Royal Military College, Australia), review-article, *Problems of Communism* (May-June, 1981; and Chapter 1 above, notes 73, 92, 135.

As one indication of the reliability of earlier estimates, compare the *Asia 1979 Yearbook* and the *Asia 1980 Yearbook* of the *Far Eastern Economic Review.* The former estimated the population at the end of the Pol Pot regime (December 1978) at 8.2 million (figures "mostly based on CIA estimates"). The latter estimated the December 1979 population at 4.2 million. A common estimate in the Western press has been that the population was reduced from 7 to 4 million during the Pol Pot years, figures apparently derived from Hanoi.

41. See *The Political Economy of Human Rights*, vol. 2, chapter 6, for references and discussion.

42. Peter Kovler, *New York Times*, April 30, 1980. See also Chapter 2.

43. Ben Bradlee, "Russia's Vietnam," *Boston Globe Magazine*, May 11, 1980.

44. Dennis Bloodworth, "The Man Who Brought Death," *Observer Magazine* (London), January 20, 1980.

45. Anthony Hartley, *Encounter* (May 1980).

46. Jawaharlal Nehru, *The Discovery of India* (Bombay: Asia Publishing House, 1961), p. 326.

47. British Middle East specialist Elie Kedourie, *New Republic*, June 7, 1980.

48. *Encounter* (December 1976).

49. Alain Besançon, *Encounter* (June 1980), an article presented under the rubric "Are Intellectuals 'Betraying' Again?," presumably without irony in a journal that has been committed since its origins to intellectual betrayal of the classic sort. On the process of acculturation that was used to overcome the "curse," see the documentation of state terrorism in my introduction to N. Blackstock, ed., *COINTELPRO* (New York: Vintage, 1976); Morton H. Halperin et al., *The Lawless State* (New York: Penguin, 1976); Robert J. Goldstein, *Political Repression in Modern America* (New York: Schenkman, 1978); Lennox S. Hinds, *Illusions of Justice* (Iowa City: School of Social Work, University of Iowa, 1978); Christy Macy and Susan Kaplan, eds., *Documents* (New York: Penguin, 1980).

Chapter Eight. Resurgent America

1. Robert W. Tucker, *The Radical Left and American Foreign Policy* (Baltimore: Johns Hopkins University Press, 1971). For analysis of his argument, see my *For Reasons of State* (New York: Pantheon, 1973). For a few examples of silence or caricature, see, in the present volume, Chapter 2, note 35; Chapter 7, note 15. See also Chapter 2. It is an interesting commentary on the ideological disciplines that although the errors of fact, and more strikingly the gross errors of reasoning, in Tucker's critique are quite transparent, they cannot be perceived even by serious scholars. See, for example, Alfred Grosser, *The Western Alliance* (New York: Continuum, 1980), translated from the 1978 French original, p. 360. He describes Tucker's book as "a remarkable work whose critical but calm analysis makes it almost unnecessary to read such aggressive books as Harry Magdoff, *The Age of Imperialism. The Economy* [sic] *of U.S. Foreign Policy* (New York: Monthly Review, 1969)." When matters of doctrine are at stake, questions

of fact and logic are irrelevant. The fact that Tucker's book exists suffices to overcome any lingering doubts about the possible utility of the "aggressive" books of the "radical left," and it is quite unnecessary to evaluate either Tucker's argument, such as it is, or the critical analysis of it. See also Chapter 4, note 3, and p. 136, above.

2. Thomas H. Etzold and John Lewis Gaddis, eds., *Containment: Documents on American Policy and Strategy*, 1945–50 (New York: Columbia University Press, 1978).

3. See his article "Oil: The Issue of American Intervention," *Commentary* (January 1975), which bemoaned the "rationalizations of political incompetence and the failure of will" which led to "the absence of the meaningful threat of force," an "astonishing" feature of the crisis implying "a revolutionary change in the very nature of international relations," as well as being "a rather demeaning way for a great power to behave," and one with grave implications: "Why should men be 'reasonable,' according to Western lights, when they have come so far and so fast by being unreasonable?" Tucker asks. American military intervention should, of course, lead to "an equitable allocation of the oil on a cost-plus basis," the standard U.S. practice with regard to resources it controls. For other contemporary proposals along similar lines, see Miles Ignotus, "Seizing Arab Oil," *Harper's* (March 1975); Josiah Lee Auspitz, "Oil: The Strategic Utility," *New Republic*, April 26, 1975; Walter Laqueur, "Détente: What's Left of It?" *New York Times Magazine*, December 16, 1973; Irving Kristol, "Where Have All the Gunboats Gone?" *Wall Street Journal*, December 13, 1973, which warns that "insignificant nations, like insignificant people, can quickly experience delusions of significance . . . smaller nations are not going to behave reasonably—with a decent respect for the interests of others, including the great powers—unless it is costly to them to behave unreasonably." I return to some more current expressions of the spirit of Western humanism in this regard.

4. See my article "The Interim Agreement," *New Politics*, no. 3 (1976). Also see Chapter 11 of the present volume.

5. On this matter, see James Petras, "La social-démocratie en Amérique latine," *Le Monde diplomatique* (June 1980).

6. In Richard M. Pfeffer, ed., *No More Vietnams? The War and the Future of American Foreign Policy* (New York: Harper & Row, 1969).

7. For references from the Pentagon Papers, see my *For Reasons of State*, p. 74. See also Chapter 5, above.

8. See Amnon Kapeliouk, *Israël: la fin des mythes* (Paris: Albin Michel, 1975), an excellent study of the topic that was unfortunately unable to obtain an American publisher. For further information, see Chapter 6, above, Chapters 9–12, below, and "The Interim Agreement."

9. For some discussion of this topic, see chapter 5 of my *Peace in the Middle East?* (New York: Pantheon, 1974), which deserves considerable amplification, I believe. See also Tucker's article "Israel and the United States: From Dependence to Nuclear Weapons," *Commentary* (November 1975). Here, Tucker advocates a nuclear strategy for Israel, judiciously deflecting all objections save one, that there would be little to "prevent Israel, once delivered from these dangers, from pursuing a hawkish policy and employing a nuclear deterrent to freeze the status quo." But even the best-crafted policy cannot be perfect.

10. *Business Week*, April 7, 1975. See Chapter 6, p. 106, for fuller quotations.

11. Samuel Huntington; see Chapter 7, above, note 31.

12. See Chapter 7, above, and Introduction.

13. J. B. Kelly, *New Republic*, October 11, 1980.

14. D. C. Watt, *Times Literary Supplement*, July 18, 1980.

15. A standard complaint against Carter by New Cold Warriors is that with his weakness and indecision, he "lost Nicaragua," abandoning Somoza to the Communists. In fact, Carter backed Somoza fully until and even past the point when the natural allies of the United States, the local business community, had turned against him with a surprising degree of unanimity because his corruption and power-madness had made it virtually impossible for them to continue to function. Similarly, when its man Trujillo got out of hand, the United States turned against him, even attempting to use the CIA to eliminate him. Hardly a sign of being soft on Communism, in either case. The same may be said about the dismissal (and unintended assassination) of Diem when his regime had lost its value and was even apparently dickering with the National Liberation Front, among other cases.

16. John Huey, *Wall Street Journal*, September 19, 1978.

17. *New Republic*, November 29, 1980.

18. *New Republic*, January 31, 1981.

19. Maurice Duverger, *Le Monde*, January 15, 1981; translated in the *Manchester Guardian Weekly*, January 25.

20. "A Bloody Metaphor," *Wall Street Journal*, November 25, 1980.

21. Jorge Domínguez, *Daedalus* (Fall 1980), reporting poll results in Caracas. One wonders what the results would be if peasants in Guatemala or El Salvador were similarly polled.

22. *Boston Globe*, January 22, 1981, p. 56, and the more extensive report in *The Cape Codder*, January 27, 1981, a local newspaper in Studds's congressional district. See also UPI, *Boston Globe*, January 20, 1981. In our book *The Political Economy of Human Rights* (Boston: South End Press, 1979), E. S. Herman and I distinguish three types of bloodbath: benign, constructive, and nefarious. The massacre in El Salvador is constructive, serving a significant U.S. interest. Therefore one must put forth some effort and trace exotic sources to become informed of significant evidence, such as the reports of a congressional fact-finding group. The massacres in Cambodia, in contrast, were nefarious, hence meriting far more substantial coverage and enormous outrage, notably lacking in this case, except when American nuns are murdered. See Introduction for more extensive discussion.

23. Édouard Bailby, "Terreur dans les campagnes d'El Salvador," *Le Monde diplomatique* (January 1981).

24. See *The Political Economy of Human Rights* for substantial documentation illustrating the point in a wide variety of examples. See pp. 35ff., above.

25. For discussion of comparative response to the plight of refugees in the 1975–78 period under review, see *The Political Economy of Human Rights*, vol. 2, chapter 3. Note that the population of Vietnam is ten times that of El Salvador, and that the boat people were not fleeing a murderous army employing measures that Bailby does not hesitate to compare to those of Hitler's SS, in an article that will not be widely publicized in the United States. To my knowledge, no American reporter has as yet (March 1981) visited the Honduran border areas, though it is obvious that that is exactly where one would go to discover what is happening in areas of El Salvador where the most brutal repression is taking place, and where reporters can rarely visit except under the guidance of the military. The situation is reminiscent of Timor; the United States-backed war was

waged for over four years before an American reporter ventured to seek Timorese refugees, who were readily accessible (see Chapter 13, below). The same can be said in many other cases.

By mid-1981, the U.N. High Commission on Refugees estimated the number of Salvadorean refugees in Central America at more than 180,000, along with 150,000 in the country itself. *Overview Latin America* (Cambridge, Mass.), July 1981.

26. *World Armaments and Disarmament SIPRI Yearbook 1980* (New York: Crane Russak, 1981). The figures are from the mid-1970s, when El Salvador was ruled by the brutal General Romero, who was overthrown in the military coup of October 1979, not to the displeasure of the United States, which was concerned at the time that his murderous rule might lead to an uncontrollable revolt of the Nicaragua variety.

Supply of arms to Latin American dictatorships from Israel is a particularly significant question for Americans to consider, given that Israel receives unprecedented quantities of U.S. aid, including military aid, and that its military industry has close links to U.S. counterparts. Correspondingly, we find that this topic is rarely discussed in mainstream U.S. media, not because they are unaware of the facts; they are well aware of them.

Foreign journals are less circumspect. See, e.g., Tim Coone, "Israel's dangerous exports," *New Statesman*, May 9, 1980, citing the SIPRI report on Israel's arms supplies to El Salvador. Coone notes that "sales of small arms, artillery, ammunition and electronic equipment which can be employed directly against a country's own people, are rarely publicised—primarily because of the adverse effect this would have on Israel's image. These tend to come to light during civil uprisings when arms are captured. At the height of the Guatemala-Belize dispute in 1977, a 65-ton shipload of Israeli guns and ammunition en route for Guatemala was seized at Barbados." Coone goes on to point out that Israel "has had major military contracts with South Africa, Argentina, Chile, El Salvador, Nicaragua [under Somoza], Guatemala, Ecuador, Indonesia, to name but a few. . . . It has wittingly supplied weapons to regimes such as South Africa, Nicaragua and El Salvador, where human rights considerations have prompted even Western countries to cancel or refuse arms deals." The latter comment should be taken with a large grain of salt.

In some cases, at least, Israel has simply been serving as a conduit for U.S. arms, e.g., Indonesia, when it needed military aircraft for the massacre of Timorese; George C. Wilson, *Washington Post*, October 5, 1979. See Chapter 13 in the present volume. Some aerospace executives were reported by Wilson as annoyed that Israel is "getting U.S. planes at a discount and then selling them at world market prices," thus cutting into their market, as in this case. See pp. 290–94.

27. *Dissent Paper on El Salvador and Central America*, November 6, 1980, written by current and former analysts and officials of the National Security Council, the Department of State, the Department of Defense, and the CIA. While the authenticity of this paper has been challenged by the State Department, it is generally agreed that it was written by people with a close knowledge of U.S. government actions, from the inside. The *Dissent Paper* alleges that "Argentina has become the second largest trainer of Salvadorean officers after the U.S.," and that "Argentina, Chile and Uruguay provide training and advisors on intelligence, urban and rural counter-insurgency, and logistics" to the junta. The *Dissent Paper* is reprinted in Warner Poelchau, ed., *White Paper Whitewash* (New York: Deep Cover, 1981), interviews with Philip Agee.

28. The most notorious example is the May 15, 1980, Rio Sumpul massacre in which hundreds of peasants were murdered in a combined military operation of the armies of El Salvador and Honduras on the border. Church sources, including an American priest (Father Earl Gallagher) who had investigated the massacre, attempted to publicize it, but with little success. The mainstream U.S. press published nothing, to my knowledge. The story was reported by Agence France Presse, June 23, 1980; cf. Institute for Policy Studies Resource, Update: Background Information on El Salvador, prepared by Cynthia Arnson and Delia Miller (June 1980). See Introduction, pp. 35ff., for fuller discussion.

Chapter Nine. Israel and the Palestinians

1. Cf. Christopher Sykes, *Crossroads to Israel* (Cleveland: World Publishing Company, 1965), pp. 305–6.
2. I will return below to the American scene and the claim by left-liberal American Zionists that Israel already is a democratic secular state. On the tendency in left-liberal American circles to identify, if only tacitly, with the Israeli right, see my *Peace in the Middle East?* (New York: Pantheon, 1974).

   The editors (of *Socialist Revolution*) have suggested to me that the comparison in the text is unfair to the PLO, in that I give no reason to doubt their commitment to a true democratic secularism. A careful look at the documents will show, however, that the PLO speaks only of a democratic secular state within the framework of "comprehensive Arab unity," offering to Israeli Jews no prospect other than that of a tolerated minority within an "Arab nation." While the PLO is willing to administer territories released from Israeli occupation, it remains opposed to any plan that involves recognition of Israel, conciliation with it, renunciation of the national rights of Palestinians (as part of the Arab nation) anywhere in the former Palestine (Political Program, Palestinian National Council, June 1974). Officially, "The aim of the Palestinian revolution is to liquidate [the Zionist] entity in all its aspects, political, military, social, trade unions and cultural, and to liberate Palestine completely," so that all its citizens may "coexist with equal rights and obligations within the framework of the aspirations of the Arab nation to unity and progress" (Unified Command of the Palestinian Resistance Movement, May 6, 1970; still in force). Jews, in contrast, are denied any national rights within this scheme; only Arabs constitute a "nation." In what Fatah has described as "transitional collective accommodations immediately after liberation," Jews "would have the right to practice their religion and develop culturally and linguistically as a group, besides their individual political and cultural participation" ("Towards a Democratic State in Palestine," Second World Congress on Palestine, September 1970). Thus even the rights taken for granted under any system that pretends to democracy are regarded only as "transitional" as regards Jews in the future Arab state. Evidently, this program entails that all segments of Israeli society will be united to resist the liquidation of all their political, social, and cultural institutions, and the abrogation of any national rights within an Arab state, part of the Arab nation. Thus the only program offered is suicidal, as well as objectionable.
3. For more extensive discussion of this and other issues touched on here, see my *Peace in the Middle East?*

4. "Israel, Jordan and the Palestinians," Consulate General of Israel, Philadelphia (September 1974).

5. Interview, July 1974. This and Allon's statement, and other expressions of Israeli government policy, can be found in the background memorandum "The Palestine Question and Its Implications," American Jewish Committee (October 1974). On the evolution of Israeli attitudes towards the Palestinians, and the matter of the "historic rights" of the Jewish people and their scope, see Yeshayahu Ben-Porat, *Yediot Abronot*, July 19, 1974.

Allon subsequently developed his own view of "historic rights" in the following terms:

> *It is the historic right of the people of Israel to the land of Israel; that is my point of departure, morally. I reject the currently fashionable notion of the right to self-determination according to which it is enough to have lived in a territory for a certain number of years to have a justified claim to such right.*

Cited by Amnon Kapeliouk in a review of a book of conversations in Hebrew with Allon, who was generally regarded as one of the Labor "doves," in *New Outlook*, Tel Aviv (June 1977).

Efforts to come to terms with the problem of "historic rights" have led to some strange forms of mysticism and self-delusion. Some have denied that the Palestinians were really native to the region, or even that they had formed a majority (see below). Others have pointed to the existence of a small Jewish settlement, neglecting to add that these largely orthodox groupings could hardly be called supporters of Zionism (see Chapter 12, note 29). David Ben-Gurion was bemused by the idea that some Arabs of Palestine were Jews by "racial origin," who had converted to another religion to hold on to their lands and avoid exile, and even undertook efforts to convert Bedouin tribes to Judaism along with General Gad Navon, now the chief military rabbi, apparently on the grounds that this was really a form of "re-conversion" (cf. Reserve-General Yoseph Geva, *Ma'ariv*, July 13, 1980). Actually, those who adopt some form of racialist mythology might well argue that the Palestinians are in part descendants of the original Jews (peasants were less likely to be exiled by the Romans than elites), who are now resisting a European takeover. Such matters would be unworthy of discussion, were the assumptions not so close to the core of various ideological claims.

6. For some discussion of Palestinian opinion in these territories, based on extensive interviews, see Ian Lustig, "What the Palestinians Want?" *New Outlook*, Tel Aviv (February 1974), and another version distributed by the Jewish Student Press Service, Israel Bureau (1974). Lustig (elsewhere, Lustick) concludes from his interviews that "many, perhaps a majority, of Palestinians in the West Bank, Jerusalem and the Gaza Strip . . . consider the Palestine Liberation Organization to be their sole legitimate representative." More recent events certainly substantiate this surmise. He also describes the intensified repression: mass arrests, administrative detention, deportation, school closings, demolitions, night searches, sudden interrogations, heavy censorship, refusal of any public expression of discontent, warnings of further arrests and deportations, and other pressures of a sort feasible for a military government.

7. Arie Lova Eliav, *Land of the Hart* (Philadelphia: Jewish Publication Society, 1974), pp.

144–45. This post-October 1973 revision of a Hebrew original appears with the comment that it expresses an "extraordinary anti-Establishment position." Eliav has been regarded in the West as a leading voice of protest against the annexationist policies of the recent past.

8. *Jerusalem Post*, October 17, 1974; cited in SWASIA, vol. 1, no. 40, November 1, 1974, National Council of Churches. The most recent example is the plan for a new industrial center between Jerusalem and Jericho. Cf. Terence Smith, *New York Times*, November 25, 1974.

9. On Kissinger's takeover of Middle Eastern affairs at this time, see Marvin and Bernard Kalb, *Kissinger* (Boston: Little, Brown, 1974). According to their account, which must be taken with a grain of salt since it seems to derive largely from Kissinger himself, "Rogers and Sisco tried to hold on to their mandate [in mid-1970], but Kissinger snapped it away" (p. 190). See Chapter 6, above.

10. It is somewhat ironic that Kissinger has been lauded for his conduct of the peace negotiations after October 1973, with no mention of the fact that this dangerous and confused man is probably as responsible as any single individual for the outbreak of the October war. The Rogers Plan, whatever its faults (and these were many), would nevertheless probably have maintained stability and peace for some period at least. Kissinger's support for Israeli annexation and his refusal to respond to Sadat's initiatives, on the contrary, prepared the ground for the October war. See Chapter 6.

11. *Ha'aretz*, July 24, 1974.

12. *Davar*, August 21, 1974. Cited in *Israleft* News Service, no. 46, September 15, 1974, POB 9013, Jerusalem. Yamit is a new deep-water port to be developed west of Gaza.

13. Cf. Eliav, *op. cit.*, p. 238. "The Americans agree with us . . . that the Gaza Strip should not be returned to Egypt or have a common border with Egypt." That the Strip should not be returned to Egypt is fair enough; it is Palestinian, not Egyptian or Israeli territory. For it to be separated from Egypt by Israeli settlement entails that any Palestinian entity including the Strip will be separated from the Arab world (apart from Jordan, at present, in effect an ally of Israel with respect to the Palestinians at least). It also significantly increases the risk of war, since it is doubtful that Egypt will agree to be excluded permanently from the Mediterranean region west of Gaza.

14. Francis Ofner, "Sketching Rabin's Plan for Peace," *Christian Science Monitor*, June 3, 1974, dispatch from Tel Aviv.

15. *Yediot Ahronot*, July 23, 1974. Emphasis added.

16. *Ma'ariv*, February 16, 1973.

17. Ofner, *op. cit.*

18. *Ha'aretz*, July 24, 1974.

19. Mattityahu Peled, "The imagination is dwarfed by the reality," *Ma'ariv*, August 9, 1974.

20. Cf. Susan Lee Hattis, *The Bi-National Idea in Palestine During Mandatory Times* (Haifa: Shikmona, 1970), and Aharon Cohen, *Israel and the Arab World* (New York: Funk & Wagnalls, 1970), for some of his views. For some quotes, see my *Peace in the Middle East?*, pp. 33–34.

21. Cited by the Israeli novelist Moshe Shamir, a spokesman for the maximalist Greater Israel Movement, in *Ma'ariv*, August 9, 1974, from Katznelson's *Writings*, vol. 12, p. 361, on the occasion of the thirtieth anniversary of his death.

22. Cf. Efraim Orni, *Agrarian Reform and Social Progress in Israel* (Jerusalem: Keren Kayemeth Leyisrael [Jewish National Fund], 1972).

23. For fuller quotes and references, see my *Peace in the Middle East?*, pp. 109, 130–31; and Walter Lehn, "The Palestinians: Refugees to Guerrillas," *Middle East Forum* (Spring 1972).

24. Michael Walzer, "Nationalism, internationalism, and the Jews: the chimera of a bina-tional state," in Irving Howe and Carl Gershman, eds., *Israel, the Arabs & the Middle East* (New York: Bantam, 1972).

25. Shulamit Aloni, *Yediot Abronot*, August 9, 1974; translated in SWASIA, vol. 1, no. 33, September 13, 1974. By the "Land of Israel" she must be referring to all of the territory west of the Jordan.

26. One might ask whether the summer 1974 events in Cyprus constituted a "failure," or rather a success for the American policy of eliminating the neutralist Makarios gov-ernment, replacing the tottering Greek fascist regime by a more stable conservative government, and partitioning Cyprus along the lines proposed by the United States to the Papandreou government (the "Acheson plan") and rejected in 1964. Kissinger's policy of tacit support for the Greek officers' coup that overthrew Makarios followed by a "tilt" towards Turkey as the bigger battalions entered the fray may prove a marked success, along the lines of the "Acheson plan," with its obvious purpose of opening Cyprus up as a NATO and U.S. base in the eastern Mediterranean.

27. Hagi Eshed, *Davar*, September 12, 1974; cited in *Viewpoint* (November 1974), Jerusalem, Israel. The same issue also contains the Aloni article cited in note 25.

28. *New York Times*, October 31, 1974.

29. According to the American Jewish press, 5 percent of the ninety thousand Jews who had immigrated to Israel from the USSR since the inception of large-scale emigration have left for other countries. "The figures are not that reassuring, however, when it is considered that a larger and larger percentage of Jews who leave Russia and reach the staging area at Vienna opt not for Israel but for the United States, Canada, and other western havens. This figure has been put at as large as 22 percent." The Russian emi-grants from Israel are provided no help by the JDC, "the arm of the world Jewry that is entrusted with the task of providing assistance for Jews leaving countries where they are in distress." They are cared for by Catholic charities, a fact "which raises a number of questions." *Jewish Post and Opinion*, New York, October 18, 1974. In Sep-tember 1974, Belgium, "faced with a mounting flood of refugees from Israel, yesterday began enforcing immigration regulations that prevent the entry of Soviet Jews who do not have Israeli passports," i.e., recent immigrants. Belgium had been "the last remaining European refuge for westward-bound Jewish refugees from Israel" after other European countries had effectively closed their borders. Reportedly, "several hundred Jewish refugees from Israel who want to go back to the Soviet Union are stranded in Austria, some for as long as three years." Douglas Ramsey, *Washington Post*, September 18, 1974 (the latter report is denied in the *Jewish Post and Opinion* article). The numbers are not large—in the hundreds—but the problem is potentially quite serious.

In subsequent years, the proportion of Russian émigrés choosing to go to Israel dropped dramatically, and by now (1981) the overwhelming majority of those of Euro-pean Russia (as opposed to Georgia, etc.) are choosing to come to the United States. The government of Israel and the World Zionist Organization have attempted in various ways to prevent an exercise of free choice by the Jews leaving Russia, so that they will be compelled to go to Israel. One device has been pressure on American Jewish communities (some of which have accepted, some not) to refuse Russian Jews the normal aid services to Jewish immigrants. Procedures at the Vienna transfer point have been arranged so that Jewish Agency representatives have a first opportunity to direct refugees to Israel before they are permitted to contact the Hebrew Immigrant Aid Society and other organizations that are simply devoted to aid to refugees, not to the task of directing them to Israel.

It has been reported that the "unilateral decision" of the chairman of the Jewish Agency, Leon Dulzin, "to force all Russian emigres reaching Vienna to go to Israel unless they have parents or children or brothers or sisters already in the West, has won support by HIAS [the Hebrew Immigrant Aid Society] and the JDC [the Joint Distribution Committee]," hence in effect by the American Jewish community (*Jewish Post and Opinion*, September 11, 1981). The arrangement is for a three-month "trial period."

30. *Op. cit.* Cf. note 24.

31. Correspondence, *New York Times Book Review*, December 1, 1974. Walzer also claims not to know of any "legal segregation," surely nothing "comparable to the sort of thing that phrase will call to mind among American readers." He seems oblivious to the legal segregation on JNF lands, to cite only the most obvious example. Cf. also note 50. Also interesting is Walzer's characteristic complaint that while I criticize discrimination against Arabs in Israel, I do not write on "the treatment of the Copts in Egypt," which "is far worse, on any measure, than that of the Arabs in Israel." Suppose we grant his claim about the Copts in Egypt. Then, if journals of intellectual opinion in the United States were flooded with applause for Egyptian democracy, with endless falsehoods about the fair treatment of the Copts, it would be important to refute these vulgar apologetics. Under the circumstances that actually exist, Walzer's analogy is worthless, though revealing. One recalls the Stalinist apologists of a generation ago with their slogan "What about the lynchings in the South?"

32. Carl Cohen, "Democracy in Israel," *Nation*, July 20, 1974.

33. Rubinstein is regarded in the United States as a civil libertarian, but his writings in Israel show that this reputation is undeserved. See his slanderous attack on Professor Israel Shahak, chairman of the Israel League for Civil and Human Rights (*Ha'aretz*, October 10, 1974); *Ha'aretz* refused to grant Shahak any opportunity to reply. Rubinstein's attack appears in translation, with several responses from the Israeli press exposing Rubinstein's lies and deploring his repressive principles, in SWASIA, vol. 1, no. 42, November 15, 1974, and *Israleft* news service, no. 49, November 1, 1974. Shahak, an outspoken opponent of all terrorism and violence and a courageous defender of civil rights, has also been the target of much abuse and outright falsification by American Zionists; for one example, see my *Peace in the Middle East?*, p. 197, discussing false accusations by Professor Alan Dershowitz of the Harvard Law School. Though Shahak's colleagues at the Hebrew University have been forthright in defense of his right to express himself on political issues, the attacks in the Israeli press continue. The most scandalous of these is an article by Lea Ben Dor, *Jerusalem Post*, November 8, 1974, which ends by asking: "What shall we do about the poor professor? The hospital? Or a bit of the terrorism he approves? A booby-trap over the laboratory door?"

34. Jean-Claude Guillebaud, *Le Monde*, April 20, 1974; translated in the *Manchester Guardian Weekly*, April 27, 1974.
35. Leonard J. Fein, *Israel: Politics & People* (Boston: Little, Brown, 1967), pp. 77–80.
36. Amos Elon, *The Israelis: Founders and Sons* (New York: Holt, Rinehart & Winston, 1971). Elon, who is generally skeptical and sophisticated, does devote a few pages to the Arab mind, uncritically repeating some fatuous remarks about Arab society as a "shame society." For discussion, in the context of a general analysis of racism and Orientalism, see Edward Said, "The war and Arab society: the shattered myths," unpublished manuscript, 1974. See now his *Orientalism* (New York: Pantheon, 1978).
37. See, e.g., Alan Dershowitz, "Civil Liberties in Israel," in Howe and Gershman, eds., *op. cit.* Dershowitz asserts that the Israeli Arab poet Fouzi el-Asmar was the "commander" of a group engaged in "terrorist activities." While no credible evidence was ever presented to justify his preventive detention for fifteen months in an Israeli prison, or his confinement to Lydda afterwards, Dershowitz states that it is his "personal conviction," on the basis of evidence prevented to him by Israeli counterintelligence, that the charges are true. Dershowitz's casual attitude towards the facts in this regard is a matter of record. See the reference of note 33. It would seem appropriate, in the absence of any credible evidence, for him to desist from such slanders. See the responses to Dershowitz's article, which originally appeared in *Commentary*, in *Commentary* (June 1971).
38. These laws were described by the first Knesset as "incompatible with the principles of a democratic state." They are still in effect, apart from provisions relating specifically to Zionist institutions and activities, which were rescinded immediately upon the establishment of the State of Israel. It is noteworthy that in 1946, Y. S. Shapira, later to be Attorney-General of Israel and Minister of Justice, described these laws as "unparalleled in any civilized country; there were no such laws even in Nazi Germany." For Jiryis's investigations, see his monographs *The Arabs in Israel*, 1968, translation from the Hebrew edition, and *Democratic Freedoms in Israel* (Beirut: Institute for Palestine Studies, 1972). The former has since been published by Monthly Review Press, New York, 1976.
39. Fouzi el-Asmar, "*I Will Remember the Land*," undated (1973–74), American Jewish Alternatives to Zionism, Inc., Suite 404, 133 E. 73rd Street, New York.
40. The *Journal of Palestine Studies*, Beirut, has had several articles dealing with some facets of these matters. Cf. also Nathan Weinstock, *Le sionisme contre Israël* (Paris: Maspéro, 1969); Ibrahim Abu-Lughod, *The Transformation of Palestine* (Evanston: Northwestern University Press, 1971); and other publications of the Institute of Palestine Studies. See now also the excellent study by Ian Lustick, *Arabs in the Jewish State* (Austin: University of Texas Press, 1980).
41. Elias H. Tuma, "The Arabs in Israel: an impasse," *New Outlook*, Tel Aviv (March–April 1966). Parts are reprinted in his *Peacemaking and the Immoral War* (New York: Harper Torchbooks, 1972), pp. 63ff., from which these quotes are taken.
42. Henry Kamm, "Most Arabs boycott Jerusalem election," *New York Times*, January 1, 1974.
43. Charlotte Saikowski, "Jerusalem: crux of peace," *Christian Science Monitor*, December 27, 1973. For more on this subject, see David Hirst (Middle East correspondent for the *Manchester Guardian*), "Rush to annexation; Israel in Jerusalem," *Journal of Palestine Studies* (Summer 1974).

44. Or in this profession, if they appear too independent or critical of official ideology. Cf. Tuma's report (note 41), which is borne out by observations of others who have had contact with Israeli Arabs. Cf. also the reference of note 45.

Development programs within Israel are largely in the hands of quasi-governmental organizations such as the Jewish Agency, with the obvious and intended result that there is an enormous disparity between Jewish and Arab settlements. See below. Thus, "90,000 Arab villagers in the Galilee receive a water allocation identical to that authorized for a single Jewish village . . . and 60% of the Arab villages are still without electricity" (Dan Bavli, *Davar*, June 29, 1975, translated in *Israleft*, July 15, 1975). Such facts are a natural consequence of the control of electrification and water allocation by organizations devoted in principle to the welfare of Jewish citizens. Thus we read, in an official publication of the government, that the Mekorot water company, the national company in charge of water, is controlled by the state, the Histadrut, and the "national institutions (the Jewish Agency and the JNF)" (*Hamayim Beyisrael* (Water in Israel) [Jerusalem: Government Information Center, 1973]). The term "national," in its Israeli context, means "Jewish," not "Israeli." There is no Israeli nation, as the courts have insisted in explicit terms. See note 56.

For more information on the striking disparity in the treatment of Arab and Jewish settlements, see Amnon Kapeliouk, *Le Monde diplomatique* (February 1981). For backgrounds and analysis, see also Elia T. Zureik, *The Palestinians in Israel* (London: Routledge & Kegan Paul, 1979).

45. Ian Lustick, "Israeli Arabs: Built-in inequality," *New Outlook* (July 1974). The publications of the Jewish-Arab Communist party, Rakah, give some indication of how many Israeli Arabs really feel about their status in Israel. One might usefully compare this record with Cohen's impressions about the matter. See, for example, the discussion of educational policy by Knesset member Tawfiq Zayyad, reported in the *Information Bulletin: Communist Party of Israel* (September 1974). Zayyad complains of severely discriminatory policies in education that have led to a sharp decline in students above the elementary levels, a "tremendous shortage in teachers, in addition to the unbearable conditions in the classrooms," closing off of educational opportunities so that Arabs "remain under control" as laborers, and, in general, conditions in the middle and high schools which "are an appalling tragedy." He cites Ministry of Education statistics that indicate that the percentage of Israeli Arabs "in the above medium stages" is a tenth that of Jewish students, and a third of that found in parts of the Arab world.

See *New Outlook*, correspondence (October 1974), for an interesting response to Lustick by Erwin Fuchs, a resident of Kiryat Siegal. He states that he can conceive of no legal or moral reason why Jews should contribute to electrification of Arab villages. Since "an Israeli Arab is no less an Arab than an Egyptian, Jordanian or Syrian," they should ask their "rich brothers" in the Arab states for help if they "feel deprived."

46. Figures from *Statistical Abstracts of Israel*, Central Bureau of Statistics, Israeli Government, Jerusalem. Cf. also Yechiel Harari, ed., *The Arabs in Israel: Statistics and Facts* (Givat Haviva: Center for Arab and Afro-Asian Studies, 1970). It is asserted here that the disparity in cultivated land under irrigation results from "the geographical position of most of the Arab lands" (p. 27). The statistical tables in the *Abstracts* are subdivided into Jewish, non-Jewish, and "mixed settlements" in which both Jews and Arabs live (Jerusalem, Tel Aviv-Yafo—a bit misleading, since few if any Arabs live in Tel Aviv—Haifa, Akko, Lod, and Ramla); but there are no "mixed farms," since Jewish

farms are generally on land reserved by law for Jews. We thus have the additional irony that the kibbutzim, the purest model of socialist democracy in existence, are subject to discriminatory land laws, to which I return. The *Statistical Abstracts* give other relevant figures. Thus, the death rate for non-Jewish infants in the "mixed settlements" is almost three times as high as for Jewish infants (and considerably higher than in Arab towns and villages); *Abstracts,* 1971, p. 64.

47. For analysis, see the works by Jiryis, cited earlier. Also, Weinstock, *op. cit.* I have found no discussion in Zionist sources.

48. For an informative account of these events and the protests against them, see Uri Davis's contribution to Martin Blatt, Uri Davis, and Paul Kleinbaum, eds., *Dissent and Ideology in Israel* (London: Ithaca Press, 1975). Davis was sentenced to eight months in prison for entering a military zone without a permit, as part of the protests against expropriation of land of Arab villages for the establishment of Karmiel. Some relevant documents are collected in "Din Vecheshbon Karmiel," by Uri Davis and Shimon Shereshevsky.

An official publication of the Jewish Agency, which is in charge of settlement programs within the State of Israel, describes long-term plans for "the Judaization of the Galilee" (*Hatsa 'a Letichnun Eyzori Kolel Beharey Hagalil* [Proposal for a General Development Program in the Galilee Hills], Jewish Agency, Safed, August 1973). It notes that the Jewish population in some regions of the Galilee is far too low. Planners must therefore determine "the size of the desired Jewish population" and undertake a program of development to "convert the territory to a region with a large Jewish population and drawing power" (for Jews), with all-Jewish urban centers, Jewish agricultural settlements, all-Arab settlements; the program of "Yihud Hagalil," "Judaization of the Galilee." Detailed plans are laid out for the next several decades. Those who write with such awe about the profound commitment to democracy and equality of citizens in a state that is a virtual dependency of the United States might ask how they would react to an official program of a similar nature devoted to increasing the white or Christian population of New York.

It should not be supposed that ethnic separation is undertaken to satisfy the demands of local Arabs. On the contrary, when Arabs attempt to move into areas intended to be all-Jewish, purchasing apartments (e.g., in Upper Nazareth, the all-Jewish suburb of all-Arab Nazareth, which naturally receives a far higher per capita state development budget than the main city, leasing land, or attempting to establish businesses, there is a great hue and cry and measures are taken to put an end to this "plague." For some references, see pp. 251, 449, and my articles "The Interim Agreement," *New Politics* (Winter 1975), and "Against Apologetics for Israeli Expansionism," *ibid.* (Winter 1979). See the same sources for data on the scale of expropriation from Arab villages to realize such programs as "Judaization of the Galilee."

The latter program has been impeded by the fact that Jews prefer to stay in towns— most new Jewish agricultural settlement is in the occupied territories, not within Israel. At the same time, the increasing Arab population, constrained by expropriation and application of laws preventing new construction, are unable to maintain themselves except by working in Jewish-owned industrial developments (there is virtually no Arab-owned industry). To meet this problem, a new program has been developed, the establishment of small hilltop "lookout" settlements throughout the Galilee "in order to govern the state lands that are now free for any invader . . . [and] . . . to ensure

the Jewish hold over thousands of dunams in the area"; the purpose of agricultural settlement is "to spread Jews in the area and guard those state lands that have not yet been
invaded by the Arabs" ("The Gentiles' Galilee Yearns for Jews," *Davar*, April 25, 1979).
The "land robbery" by Arab citizens of Israel must be stopped, in particular, the care-
lessness of authorities in permitting Arab farmers "to cultivate parts of their own lands
that have been expropriated." One difficulty is that when Arab shepherds come
too close to the fences around the Jewish hilltop lookouts, "friendships develop," so that
it has been necessary to "ask them not to come near the gates" (Avshalom Ginat,
Hotam, June 8, 1979). Another problem is the unwillingness of Jews to do the "difficult
work" in new enterprises that are established, so that "most of the workers today are
Arabs" (*Davar*, April 27, 1979). On the concern by old Jewish settlers over the "New
Zionism" of the Arabs, who devote themselves to agricultural development, replacing
Jews, see my articles cited above and the Afterword to this chapter, note 74. See also
pp. 284f.

49. Daniel Dagan, *Ma'ariv*, August 29, 1974. For a vivid account of this extraordinarily
brutal operation of expulsion and destruction of Arab communities, see Amnon Kapeliouk, *Le Monde*, May 15, 1975 (translated in *Middle East International*, July 1975). For
extensive quotes, see my articles cited in the preceding footnote, along with material
from the Hebrew press on the miserable conditions of those expelled and the problem
noted by government officials, when some of the remnants stay in areas planned as resorts for Jewish tourists from Israel.

50. The fraudulence of these grounds has repeatedly been exposed in the Israeli press. Cf.
Peace in the Middle East?, p. 47; also pp. 41, 125. See also Lea Ben Dor, *Jerusalem Post*,
November 8, 1974, reporting (with much disdain) the Knesset debate in which Meir
Pail, former Commander-in-Chief of the Central Officers' School of the Israeli Army,
points out that no question of security was involved in the displacement of the
Bedouins (he gives the figure of 300,000 dunams of land from which they had been
expelled). In fact, "the army had moved out to take Beersheba in 1948, from the house
of a sheikh of one of the dozen or more tribes involved" (Ben Dor). Although the security arguments are ridiculed by knowledgeable Israelis, in the press and elsewhere,
they are accepted as gospel by American Zionists. To take one case, Walzer claims that
"there is no 'systematic pattern' of expulsions of Arabs from Arab lands except in militarily sensitive areas" (Correspondence, *New York Times Book Review*, December 1,
1974). It would be interesting to know which areas Walzer regards as not "militarily
sensitive."

51. *Report on the Legal Structure, Activities, Assets, Income and Liabilities of the Keren
Kayemeth Leisrael*, Keren Kayemeth Leyisrael Head Office, Jerusalem, 1973; pp. 17, 19,
21, 56–58.

52. *Ibid.*, p. 5.

53. *Ibid.*, pp. 18, 86.

54. *Ibid.*, p. 6. The 1961 Covenant, cited earlier, appears as Appendix D.

55. *Seventy Years in Facts and Figures*, Keren Kayemeth Leisrael, Jerusalem, 1971. Taking
the official *Report* to be reliable, I wrote in *Peace in the Middle East?*, p. 14, that "in
1960, the Knesset . . . enacted the *Basic Law: Israel Lands*, extending to state lands the
principles of the Jewish National Fund," noting that official figures give the territory
covered as 92 percent of the state's surface (pre-1967); this would entail that non-Jews
are excluded from living or working on nine-tenths of the state's surface. As we shall

see directly, however, the JNF *Report* is not accurate in its account of the wording of the law. I have found only one serious study of the JNF, namely, Walter Lehn, "Zionist land: the Jewish National Fund," *Journal of Palestine Studies* (Summer 1974). Lehn concludes that under the Basic Land Law and the Covenant, "JNF restrictive policies regarding the sale and leasing of land were applied to all state lands, which together with JNF lands constitute 90% of the land in Israel." In a footnote, he cites additional laws which, according to his analysis, lead in practice to restriction of these lands to Jews. I have found very little discussion of this topic in Israeli or Zionist sources. Professor Uzzi Ornan of the Hebrew University has discussed the matter. He concludes that by virtue of the laws and Covenant cited, "the principles of the JNF apply to all the lands for which the State Land Authority is responsible," thus restricting these lands (he gives the figure of 95 percent within the pre-1967 borders) to Jewish use (*Ma'ariv*, January 30, 1974). Elsewhere, he writes that a Jew can obtain a residence on state land, but that a non-Jew requires an official "agreement" that is given only with several "residence limits" (*Ha'aretz*, March 18, 1971).

Subsequent to the publication of this article in 1975, a study appeared by Uri Davis and Walter Lehn giving substantial detail beyond what is discussed here ("And the Fund Still Lives," *Journal of Palestine Studies*, Summer 1978; for a fuller discussion, see their forthcoming book *The Jewish National Fund*, to be published by Routledge & Kegan Paul, London). Their investigation of background documents makes it quite clear that the intention to restrict land use to Jews by various devices was quite explicit, as was the intent to extend the JNF principles of ownership and use of the land by the Jewish people to state lands, whatever the precise wording of the highly convoluted legal phraseology may be.

56. The court decisions are cited in Ronald Segal, *Whose Jerusalem? The Conflicts of Israel* (London: Jonathan Cape, 1973), p. 132. Cf. also *Al Hamishmar*, January 21, 1972, cited in *Peace in the Middle East?*, p. 128, from *Tadmit* newsletter, February 1, 1972. For a similar position taken by the courts on another occasion, see my *Peace in the Middle East?*, p. 174 and note 30. In the Eichmann Trial Judgment, the courts were still more explicit, as indicated by the following excerpt:

> *The connection between the State of Israel and the Jewish people needs no explanation. The State of Israel was established and recognized as the State of the Jews. . . . It would appear that there is hardly need of any further proof of the very obvious connection between the Jewish people and the State of Israel: this is the sovereign State of the Jewish people.*

Cited by W. T. Mallison, in J. N. Moore, ed., *The Arab-Israeli Conflict*, vol. 1 (Princeton: Princeton University Press, 1974), p. 148.

Thus the courts have established the doctrine that Israel is not the state of its citizens, but the state of the Jewish people, those who are its citizens and those in the diaspora. At the foundations of the legal system, then (Israel has no constitution), Israel makes no pretense of being a democracy.

57. *Op. cit.* (cf. note 22), p. 36. Under the 1961 Covenant, the JNF is responsible for "informational and Zionist-Israel educational activities," and is to receive government assistance to this end.

58. Cited by Lehn, "Zionist land." Cf. now Davis and Lehn, *op. cit.*

59. *Ha'aretz*, November 5, 1971.

60. David Caploe, "Discrimination by law," *Middle East International* (July 1974). On measures used to compel Arabs to agree to expropriation, see also Hirst, *op. cit.* (cf. note 43).

61. E. D. Morel, *The Black Man's Burden* (New York: Monthly Review Press, 1969), p. 116; cited in Chinweizu, *The West and the Rest of Us* (New York: Random House, 1975).

62. J. A. Hobson, *Imperialism* (Ann Arbor: University of Michigan Press, 1965), p. 265; cited in Chinweizu, *op. cit.*

63. Left-liberal Israeli commentators have pointed out, however, that the comparison is far from absurd. Thus, Michael Bruno, a Hebrew University economist who is director of research of the Bank of Israel, points out that if the occupied territories are retained, Israel will become "either a binational state or another Rhodesia." Cf. Michael Bruno, "Israeli policy in the 'administered territories,' " in Howe and Gershman, eds., *op. cit.* On parallels to White Africa, see Segal, *op. cit.*

64. *Op. cit.*, p. 64.

65. Figures from Lehn, "Zionist land," from JNF sources.

66. Cf. Orni, *op. cit.*, p. 64. Orni gives the figure for lands owned by the JNF in 1970 as 2,586 sq. km., with another 500 sq. km. placed at its disposal by the government. The territory within the pre-1967 borders is 20,700 sq. km., of which 445 sq. km. is water. He says that over 15,000 sq. km. additional is state land. The various figures cited are not precisely consistent, but are rather close.

67. Cited in Hattis, *op. cit.*, pp. 48–49.

68. Nathan Khofshi, in Blatt, Davis, and Kleinbaum, *op. cit.*

69. Cf. Sykes, *op. cit.*, pp. 89–93.

70. Cf. Y. Ts. Kolton, *Lesheelat Hayebudim Ufitrona* (On the Jewish Question and Its Solution), Tel Aviv, 1932. He also shows how the policy of land acquisition gave the Zionist movement a stake in the feudal system and led to opposition to land reform and economic development; and how the policy of "conquest of labor" and open immigration led the Jewish labor movement to oppose such measures as employment relief for Arabs, and stood in the way of efforts by Arab workers to organize and fight for higher wages.

　　See also Leopold Trepper, *The Great Game: Memoirs of the Spy Hitler Couldn't Silence* (New York: McGraw-Hill, 1977), chapter 3. Trepper, a Polish dissident now in the United States, was a Communist party activist in Palestine in the 1920s, attempting to organize Jewish and Arab workers. He describes how "Zionist organizations and Arab reactionaries helped the police to hunt us down. . . . The influence the movement was beginning to have in the kibbutzim worried the leaders of the Histadrut [the socialist Jewish labor movement]; they could not seem to understand how Jews and Arabs could join forces. At the end of 1926 the first general meeting of the movement ["Ichud," "Ittihad," "Unity"] was held; more than one hundred delegates were there, including forty Arabs. On the evening of the first day, the delegates were amazed by the arrival of Ben-Gurion, the national leader of the Histadrut, and Moshe Shertok [later, Sharett], the specialist in Arab questions, who stared at the spectacle of Jews and Arabs sitting in the same room." Trepper was later arrested by the Jewish police, controlled by the British, in a raid during a meeting in Tel Aviv, and jailed for several months. Later, Trepper was jailed by the Nazis (and escaped, during the war), and by Stalin, after the war.

71. Cf. Michael Walzer, review of *Peace in the Middle East?, New York Times Book Review,* October 6, 1974.

72. Cf. Walter Schwarz, "Israel's new horizons," *Manchester Guardian Weekly,* April 8, 1972. Also Ben-Porat, *op. cit.* On the rise of religious mythology in Israel since 1967, even among socialists, see Benjamin Beit-hallahmi, "Religion and nationalism in the Arab-Israeli conflict," *Il Politico,* University of Pavia, vol. 38, no. 2. The forms that this takes are often remarkable, for example, in terms of discriminatory practices against Jews who do not adhere to the orthodox version of the established religion. There is no space to go into this topic properly here. To cite one example that reflects the tenor of this discrimination, see the letter in the *Jerusalem Post* (January 4, 1981) signed by over sixty members and staff of the World Union of Reform Jews, expressing "disappointment at the defeat of the bill introduced in the Knesset which would have provided equal rights for the Conservative and Reform movements in Israel." They complain that Reform and Conservative Jews are unable to observe fully their version of traditional laws and practices, their rabbis cannot perform marriages, individuals they convert are not considered Jews, and "all money for religious institutions goes to Orthodox ones." They note further that Foreign Minister "Yitzhak Shamir did not attend a memorial ceremony for the Jews who died in the Paris synagogue bombing and the Israeli rabbinate refused to send condolences to the bereaved solely because the bombing took place in a Reform synogague," a fact not mentioned in the many condemnations of the rise of anti-Semitism in France, of which the rue Copernic bombing is taken to be an example (on dubious evidence, to my knowledge).

   We thus have the curious phenomenon that in the Jewish state, alone among the Western industrial democracies, there is official discrimination against Jews and Jewish practices and observances.

73. Michael Deshe, "The source of the conflict—the terrible mistake of the Arabs," *Ma'ariv,* September 3, 1974.

74. Amos Ben-Vered, "An undefined right," *Ha'aretz,* September 9, 1974.

   See also the JNF-sponsored publication by Y. Shur, *On the Roots of Our Problems,* published "through the aid of the [JNF] in Jerusalem and friends in the U.S.A. and Israel," Kibbutz Ashdot Yaakov (July 1974), which explains "the origin of Jewish-Arab conflict" in the following manner. It describes "the overwhelmingly sorrowful scene of the country as we found it in the earlier decades of this century," as the "thinly scattered population . . . survived on a meager sustenance, . . . on a constant decline," with "no stable economy whatsoever" and "no organized forms of social relationship or communications." Then, the Jews came to make the desert bloom in this land where a few people remained in "once prosperous cities" but "the majority roamed the countryside as nomads," overgrazing and searching grass after the winter rains. However, "even the austere conditions in which we fought for our cause seemed like a paradise for the then starving masses in surrounding Egypt, Syria, Jordan and Lebanon," and "what is now Israel" became "a fancy spot into which their massive influx could not be prevented or stopped." There was "an uncontrolled flow of those poverty-beaten close neighbors" who "filled every hole and every corner as pretendents for work, for housing. . . ." Some settled in cities, while "many of them settled on the land, becoming self-supporting farmers and villagers." Thus "the Arab community grew in numbers and *became a majority*" (my emphasis), leading to "political discord."

   It should be noted that this mythology—put forth by one of the early settlers, who has lived for fifty years in the kibbutz where this document is published—is rejected out of hand by reputable Israeli scholars, though not by Western Zionists. Cf. Yehoshua Porath, *The Emergence of the Palestinian-Arab National Movement* (London: Frank Cass, 1974): The Arab population, which was of course always an overwhelming majority, "also grew . . . due for the most part to natural increase" (as of 1931, where this study ends; p. 19). Elsewhere he has commented on the erroneous census figures and other "pointless legends" that have been invoked to explain the growth of the Arab population in terms of immigration (*Yabadut, Tsionut u-Medina,* Jerusalem, Symposium published by the Government Information Center, January 1975). In contrast, Bernard Avishai asserts that "most Arabs were attracted to Palestine during this period because of the vigorous commercial and industrial life developed by Jewish immigrants and because of the lucrative Jewish market" (*Dissent,* Spring 1975). He gives the 1947 Arab population as 1,200,000; Porath estimates it as close to 900,000 in 1931 (*Yabadut,* p. 117), increasing at a natural rate of 2.5 percent a year. The 1931 census gives a Jewish population of 175,000.

There are also many travelers' reports in the nineteenth century describing the quite successful, sometimes flourishing Arab agriculture, though there is no doubt that Palestine was for the most part an impoverished country. Such "pointless legends" as Shur's are, however, not uncommon in Western Zionist literature.

See also the study of the Government Information Center demonstrating, to its satisfaction, that "on political and legal grounds the Sinai peninsula is not included within the boundaries of Egypt" (*Dapey Sinai,* second edition, Government of Israel Information Center, February 1975). It must be a great comfort to the families of Israeli soldiers killed in the Sinai to know that "the land of Goshen" was offered to Joseph and his brothers by Pharoah in the seventeenth century B.C. in a passage from *Genesis* misquoted by the Information Ministry (p. 23), or that Herodotus placed the border well to the west of the internationally recognized line.

Such forms of irrationality are extremely dangerous in a state that survives in such precarious circumstances, particularly when they are combined with the kind of racist arrogance—no other term is appropriate—that contributed to the initial setbacks, ominous in their import, suffered by Israel in the early stages of the October 1973 war. For some examples, see my *Peace in the Middle East?;* also, Amnon Kapeliouk, *Israël: la fin des Mythes* (Paris: Albin Michel, 1975), particularly his remarks on the contribution of Israeli Arabists. The belief that "war is not the Arabs' game" (Yehoshaphat Harkabi, a leading Israeli Arabist and former director of intelligence), one of Kapeliouk's "myths," persists after 1973. Thus in the supplement to *Al Hamishmar,* organ of the socialist Mapam, we read that "the superiority of human qualities of the Israeli fighter" can be explained by "researches conducted in the U.S.," which prove that "Negroes are not inferior to whites in associative intelligence, but only in the more complex cognitive intelligence." Hence they cannot succeed in enterprises that require calculating and planning, like long-distance running (note the regular failure of Africans in this regard) or aerial combat (*Hotam,* April 18, 1975). We may compare this with Moshe Dayan's recent criticism of the quality of the U.S. armed forces in an Israeli television interview in which he pointed out that the lower ranks are made up "mostly by blacks who have low intelligence and low education." *Boston Globe,* November 15, 1980; Carl Rowan, *Dallas Morning News,* December 7, 1980.

Fantasies about Israeli military prowess are still expressed, as before (cf. *Peace in the*

Middle East?), at the highest level of the military command. See for example the remarks by the Chief of Staff, General Rafael Eytan, in the official army journal *Bamahaneh:* "If the Russians start a war against Israel, the Israeli Defence Forces will win." The reason is that the Russians will be fighting on foreign territory, while the IDF will be defending its own land. Quoted in *Ma'ariv,* December 27, 1979; *Ha'aretz,* December 28, 1979. A similar assessment is presented by Air Force Commander General Bennito Peled, who "mocks the 'chickens' who fear Soviet intervention and therefore oppose an Israeli initiative. He describes the Soviet threat as a lie. As he sees it, the Soviet Union would have to send over a million and a half soldiers in order to join into the battle, and even then 'the Israeli army would defeat its enemies' " (Yair Kotler, *Ma'ariv,* August 29, 1980). Peled also urges that "we must take over Saudi Arabia" so that Israel will have its own sources of energy, presumably not a difficult task if the Israeli military forces can defeat the Soviet Union (Nahum Barnea, *Davar,* April 10, 1981). The last two articles are translated in *Israeli Mirror,* SUNI News Service, 21 Collingham Road, London, April 16, 1981.

75. Abba Eban, Interview, *New Republic,* March 23, 1974.
76. There has, I think, been a notable growth of racist attitudes in Israel since 1967. The press provides many illustrations. For example, during a labor conflict in the Port of Ashdod, a labor leader complained that "the border guards think that we are pigs or Arabs from the territories. They behave towards us as if we were workers from Gaza or Rafiah" (i.e., Arabs; *Ma'ariv,* July 10, 1975). Such statements pass without notice, as does the implication concerning the treatment of Arab workers.
77. Nahum Sokolov, as he was elected president of the World Zionist Organization in 1931, Cf. Aharon Cohen, *op. cit.*
78. David Ben-Gurion. For discussion of this period and changes of attitude later, see my *Peace in the Middle East?,* foreword, introduction, chapter 1, and literature cited there.
79. Cf. Sykes, *op. cit.* Similarly, Eliav argues that at no time could there have been any doubt that the purpose of Zionism was the establishment of a Jewish state (*op. cit.,* p. 27). See also John Galvani's review of *Peace in the Middle East?,* MERIP Reports, no. 32 (November 1974). Galvani argues that the commitment to binationalism was indeed sincere, but on cynical grounds: namely, that was the most that could be hoped, since there were no grounds for Jewish sovereignty. Galvani also argues that I give no theoretical justification for Jewish nationhood or its demands. That is true; I have little faith in such exercises, and know of no criteria for "legitimate nationhood" apart from self-identification in national terms. As for "national rights," their justification is also largely subjective. I am neither aware of, nor prepared to contribute to, a significant theory of such rights. On attitudes of Palestinians during this period, see Porath (*op. cit.*). He demonstrates that Palestinian opinion was at all times strongly anti-Zionist, for perfectly understandable reasons. Palestinian nationalism emerged at about the time of World War I. After a brief period of interest in union with Syria, largely motivated by the hopes that an independent Syria incorporating Palestine could block Zionist initiatives, Palestinian opinion, insofar as it received overt expression, was generally committed to the independence of Palestine as an Arab state.
80. *The Autobiography of Nahum Goldmann* (New York: Holt, Rinehart & Winston, 1969), pp. 101–2.
81. Ben-Gurion, 1931, before the World Zionist Congress. See my *Peace in the Middle East?,* p. 36, and references cited there.

82. Hattis, *op. cit.*, p. 91.

83. *Ibid.*, p. 97.

84. *Ibid.*

85. *Ibid.*, p. 46.

86. Shmuel B'ari, *New Outlook* (November 1969), in a critical commentary on an article of mine that appears in the same issue.

87. Elie Eliachar, "The road to peace: Israel is an integral part of the Middle East," *New Outlook* (February 1974). Cf. also Trude Weiss-Rosmarin, editorial, *Jewish Spectator* (Fall 1974), New York.

88. It is worth noting that after the 1967 war, the military commander of the West Bank, General Haim Herzog, proposed that some Palestinian formation be encouraged on the West Bank "to work against the PLO," and that he was approached by West Bank notables with a request that such political organization be permitted on the West Bank. Even this was not allowed by the allegedly "enlightened" Israeli military occupation, and in fact, Herzog states, government censorship prevented the Israeli press from reporting his proposal. See *Emda*, no. 3 (December 1974), Tel Aviv. Plainly, the objection to political organization by West Bank anti-PLO conservatives was not based on considerations of security. Rather, it indicates that even at that early stage, the government of Israel was contemplating some long-range plan for incorporation of the occupied territories.

89. AP, *Boston Globe*, November 19, 1974. Information Minister Aharon Yariv followed with some remarks suggesting that local autonomy on the West Bank, excluding the PLO, might eventually "lead to a federated status for the area." Terence Smith, *New York Times*, November 24, 1974.

90. For discussion, see the works by Aharon Cohen and Hattis cited in note 20. Also, references of note 78. See also Don Peretz, "A binational approach to the Palestine conflict," *Law and Contemporary Problems,* Duke University School of Law (Winter 1968) (reprinted by the Jewish Peace Fellowship, Box 271, Nyack, New York); Norman Bentwich, "The bi-nationalist solution," *New Outlook* (March–April 1970). Outside of the United States, it is possible to discuss the issue in a rational way. Thus, even such a relatively orthodox British Zionist as T. R. Fyvel can criticize American Jewish academics because they have not "turned out studies in bi-nationalism designed to help solve this Middle East conflict." Letter, *New Middle East* (February 1970).

Afterword to Chapter Nine

1. See, e.g., the announcement by Meir Zarmi, secretary-general of the Labor party, at a kibbutz conference, giving a "clear, final map" along lines just described; David Lancashire, AP, *Boston Globe*, June 20, 1975; Yuval Elizur, *Washington Post*, June 21; and a brief note in the *New York Times*, June 20. For earlier statements to the same effect, see above; also Emanuel Farjoun, "Zionism after the 1967 war," *New Politics* (Fall 1970), and my *Peace in the Middle East?*

2. *Ma'ariv*, September 26, 1971; cited by Kapeliouk, *Israël: la fin des Mythes.*

3. See, for example, the remarks of the former president of the Jordanian Parliament, cited by Eric Rouleau, *Le Monde*, May 21, 1975 (translated in SWASIA, July 11, 1975).

4. The text appears in SWASIA, June 13, 1975.

5. See *New Outlook*, Tel Aviv (September 1975).
6. *Ibid.* (March–April 1975). Hammami was subsequently assassinated, apparently on Iraqi initiative.
7. Zvi al-Peleg, *New Outlook* (September 1975).
8. See, e.g., the statement by Minister Israel Galili, reported in the *New York Times*, April 17, 1975. See also the remarks by Yigal Allon, the leading cabinet dove in the Labor government, who described the PLO before the United Nations General Assembly as "a congerie[s] of feuding terrorist gangs whose principal victims are the Arabs of Palestine themselves, and whose primary aim is the annihilation of the State of Israel and the genocide of its people" (*New York Times*, October 1, 1975). When Allon went on to reject the "absurd pretensions of the so-called Palestine Liberation Organization to speak in the name of the Palestinian Arabs," he was simply reiterating his government's rejection of Palestinian national rights, for he knew full well that the pretensions of the PLO are no more absurd than those of the Zionist movement before the establishment of the State of Israel, and that any relaxation of Israeli repression in the occupied territories quickly demonstrates the reality of these "pretensions." In reiterating the "long-standing Israeli position that King Hussein of Jordan was the proper interlocutor," Allon had not, as a *New York Times* editorial claimed, "opened the door to a discussion . . . over the status and aspirations of the Palestinian Arabs" (October 6, 1975). Quite the contrary, what the *Times* editorial called his "carefully measured words" were designed to keep that door nailed tightly shut. It may be, in fact, that this former Palmach commander was not too happy to be playing a role, with respect to the Palestinians, that recalls the role of British imperial force with respect to the "absurd pretensions" of "Zionist terrorists" not many years earlier. Allon's rhetoric has remained the standard for both the Labor party and the Begin Likud government.
9. *Ha'aretz*, April 14, 1975. Translated in *Israleft News Service*, May 4, 1975.
10. *New York Times*, December 10, 1976.
11. *Ibid.*
12. Yuval Elizur, *Washington Post*, December 6, 1975, quoting an interview with Prime Minister Rabin in *Ma'ariv*, December 5.
13. *Newsweek*, December 15, 1975.
14. *New York Times*, December 2, 1975.
15. *Davar*, July 4, 1976.
16. *Le Monde*, December 1, 1976; cited in SWASIA, December 24, 1976. See also Kaddoumi's U.N. interview of November 17, 1976, in which he stated, "We accept establishment of a state in the West Bank and Gaza Strip" (AP; cited in SWASIA, November 26, 1976).
17. David Hirst, dispatch from Beirut, "PLO reaches Limit of Moderation," *Manchester Guardian Weekly*, August 7, 1977.
18. Henry Tanner, "Arabs to Negotiate a West Bank State," *New York Times*, December 4, 1976. This conclusion is regularly denied by American commentators. See, e.g., p. 224 above.
19. Both the letter and the vote are cited in SWASIA, September 16, 1977.
20. Sartawi's letter and the AFP statement appear in the *New Outlook* (February–March 1981).

Sartawi resigned from the Palestinian National Council after objections to "his controversial—and officially encouraged—meetings with Israeli dissidents" (Jonathan C.

Randal, *Washington Post;* reprinted in *Manchester Guardian Weekly,* May 3, 1981). According to Randal, Arafat "did nothing to prevent" his resignation. *Le Monde* correspondent Lucien George, reporting on the same council meeting, states that Arafat "vigorously defended" Sartawi and that his dealings with Israeli doves were defended and confirmed in the council resolutions, *Le Monde,* April 22, 1981.

21. Mattityahu Peled, "PLO and the Israeli Peace Camp," *New Outlook* (February—March 1981). The last passage is quoted from the Spanish-Italian resolution, supported also by Austria, Sweden, Senegal, Venezuela, and others.

22. See the analysis of the program by Eric Rouleau, *Le Monde,* January 22, 24, 1981. Rouleau comments that "the foreign ministers of 38 African, Asian and Middle Eastern states (most reputed to be 'moderate' and 'pro-Western') strongly denounced the United States alone, going so far as to threaten it with sanctions. The Soviet Union is only condemned in 1 of the some 20 documents adopted and even then in carefully weighed terms on the subject of the Afghan crisis. . . . We must conclude that the Soviet Union is less intimidating than the United States or else inspires less hostility owing to the Palestinian conflict, on which the Muslims are particularly touchy." (FBIS, January 30, 1981). It is remarkable that American commentators continue to insist that there is no consensus among the Arab states on the Palestine issue, and that it is the Soviet Union that they primarily fear.

23. FBIS, January 29. See also *Journal of Palestine Studies,* Spring 1981.

24. Rouleau, *op. cit.* In connection with the Camp David agreements, Rouleau notes that "Washington has been singled out several times in this document, notably in connection with the Camp David agreements and its 'collusion' with the Egyptian regime which is described as a 'direct attack on the Palestinian people, their homeland and their future.' "

25. Eric Rouleau, *Le Monde,* January 29, 1981; FBIS, January 30.

26. Prime Minister Yitzhak Shamir, on Tel Aviv IDF Radio, February 2, 1981; FBIS, February 3.

27. Cited in the *New Outlook* (April 1977), from Ben-Gurion's *Memoirs.* The same issue contains an interesting comparison of PLO strategy and that of the Zionists in the 1940s. "The boundaries of Zionist aspirations," according to Ben-Gurion, were quite extensive. He held that "the Land of Israel" ("Eretz Israel") included southern Lebanon (which he called "the northern part of western Israel"), southern Syria, Transjordan (today's Jordan), Palestine ("the territory of the Mandate in the Western Land of Israel"), and Sinai ("On Ways of Our Policy," Report of the Congress of the World Council of Poalei Zion [the forerunner of Mapai, the major constituent of the Labor party], Tel Aviv [1938], pp. 206–7; cited by Israel Shahak, "The 'Historical Right' and the Other Holocaust," *Journal of Palestine Studies* [Spring 1981]).

28. The Principles of the Jewish Liberation Movement, established by Herut; June 1948. Included in an anthology of Herut documents prepared by Israel Shahak, Jerusalem (1977). Similar views were expressed in subsequent years.

29. Menahem Begin, *The Revolt: Story of the Irgun* (New York: Schuman, 1951), p. 335. This is "the credo of the underground fighters," asserted in response to the November 1947 UN partition recommendation, reasserted with evident approval in Begin's subsequent book.

30. Mattityahu Peled, "American Jewry: 'More Israeli than Israelis,' " *New Outlook* (May—June 1975).

31. See my *Peace in the Middle East?*, chapter 5, for discussion.

32. See Kapeliouk, *Israël: la fin des mythes*, for a discussion of Israeli policies in the early post-1967 period. See also Jon Kimche, *There Could Have Been Peace* (New York: Dial, 1973), on Israel's failure to exploit diplomatic opportunities for a settlement in this period.

33. Among other sources, see Amos Elon, *Ha'aretz*, February 5, 1971, describing "aimless brutality," beatings, destruction of property, stealing from poor refugees, exile of families of suspected Fatah members to the southern Sinai desert, etc.; translated in Uri Davis and Norton Mezvinsky, *Documents from Israel* (London: Ithaca Press, 1975). See also the account of torture, beating of children in classrooms with clubs so that they will "fear us like death," and so on, by an Israeli soldier in Gaza in 1969; Amnon Dankner, *Ha'aretz*, December 26, 1980. On the brutal treatment of Bedouin farmers in the region, expelled by force to prepare the area for Jewish settlement, see the references of note 49 of the main chapter, above.

34. The *Washington Star* reported (August 7, 1980) that "the head of Israel's internal security service has resigned in protest over what he considers stonewalling by Prime Minister Menachem Begin on the investigation of the terrorist bombings against three West Bank mayors two months ago, according to highly placed Israeli sources." It reports further that according to Israeli internal security (Shin Beit), the bombings were carried out by members of Gush Emunim who were veterans of elite Israeli commando forces. A spokesman for the prime minister denied that the Shin Beit director, Avraham Achituv, had resigned. See also Eric Silver, "Security chief to resign," *Manchester Guardian Weekly*, August 17, 1980, reporting the resignation "amid persistent rumors of differences with the Prime Minister about the investigation into the June assassination attempt on three West Bank Arab mayors," along with a government denial that the resignation was "in protest at foot dragging by the Prime Minister in the investigation." Silver reports also that one of the mayors targeted for assassination, Ibrahim Taweel, was one of seven West Bank nationalist leaders "banned last week from leaving their home town for an indefinite period," which "completes the dismantling of the 21-member National Guidance Council," which had "provided the most disciplined and cohesive leadership the occupied Palestinians had known since the 1967 war," and like virtually all other manifestations of West Bank opinion, was pro-PLO.

On the failure of the authorities to conduct a serious investigation of the assassination attempt against the Arab mayors, see K. Amnon (Amnon Kapeliouk), *Al Hamishmar*, June 11, 1980; also Amnon Kapeliouk, *Al Hamishmar*, June 27, 1980. He points out that family members were not interrogated, though they had much to report; for example, that military authorities wiped away footprints outside the bombed house, that army units patrolling the streets ordered residents of Ramallah to return home the night before the attack, and that Mayor Bassam Shak'a's phone service was cut off just before the attack and restored a few minutes after it. He also comments that it should be easy enough for authorities to identify those who had been trained by the Israeli Army to use explosives of the kind employed in the bombings. Kapeliouk also discusses the failure of the authorities to investigate seriously the killing of a young Arab woman by Israeli soldiers. In comparison, when an Arab child throws a stone at a military vehicle "they at once put in force collective punishments" and other operations of the sort reviewed below. See also Tim Coone, *New Statesman*, August 15, 1980.

Amnon Kapeliouk also discusses the attack on the West Bank mayors in the *New Outlook* (June 1981). He writes that "the investigation, if indeed there is one, is so secret that no one knows of its existence. . . . I cannot remember ever coming up against such a stone wall in my entire career as a journalist." He points out that the most obvious leads have not been pursued, and that it should hardly be difficult to find the "top professionals" who must have been responsible, "according to the testimony of experts in the field."

35. See, e.g., Trudy Rubin, "Palestinian youths reap bitter harvest," *Christian Science Monitor*, March 28, 1978; William Claiborne, "Israeli Troops Wound Nine in Protests on West Bank," *Washington Post*, November 19, 1980; also "Israelis Are Said to Beat Students in West Bank as Parents Watch," *New York Times*, December 10, 1980. See William Claiborne and Edward Cody, "Israel Shapes Immutable Future for West Bank," *Washington Post*, September 7, 1980, and "A Sad West Bank Stops Struggling," September 8, 1980, for a rare comprehensive account of Israeli tactics and goals in the West Bank in the U.S. press.

36. *Ha'aretz*, May 12, 1977. K. Amnon, *Al Hamishmar*, December 31, 1979.

37. Amnon Kapeliouk, *Al Hamishmar*, March 31, 1980.

38. K. Amnon, *Al Hamishmar*, April 14, 1980. Kafr Kassem was the scene of an unprovoked army massacre of 47 Arab civilians in 1956; see Chapter 12, note 40.

39. Yehuda Litani, *Ha'aretz*, December 12, 1981; *Jerusalem Post*, December 17; in *Israleft News Service*, January 4, 1981. See also *New York Times*, December 18, 1980, reporting beatings and vandalism in Silwad by Israeli soldiers, and a comment by an Israeli officer that "it's a village of murderers."

40. Tzvi Lavi, *Ma'ariv*, May 22, 1980 (*Israeli Mirror*). Reported also by *Newsweek*, June 9, 1980; Edward Mortimer, *Spectator*, June 14, 1980. In *Haolam Haze*, February 4, 1981, Avneri reprinted a letter he distributed to all members of the Knesset reporting testimony of soldiers in the West Bank on beating of children, forced labor, locking of children in a storehouse without food, etc.

41. See *New Outlook Newsletter* (August 1980), for one of many cases.

42. Yehuda Litani, *Ha'aretz*, February 6, 1981. David Richardson, *Jerusalem Post*, March 1, 1981.

43. Amnon Kapeliouk, *Al Hamishmar*, June 6, 1980.

44. *Ha'aretz*, May 26, 1980.

45. Yehuda Litani, *Ha'aretz*, October 28, 1980.

46. Yehuda Litani, "Art in the light of struggle," *Ha'aretz*, October 14, 1980.

47. *Haolam Haze*, " 'It is permitted to paint—but with natural colors, not the colors of the Palestinian flag'! commanded the Military Government," September 8, 1980; "Art Show in Jerusalem—But No Windows for West Bank Artists," *Al-Fajr* (Jerusalem), December 14–20, 1980; Yehuda Litani, "The Military Authorities Closed Down the '79 Gallery in Ramallah," *Ha'aretz*, September 22, 1980.

48. Amnon Kapeliouk, *Al Hamishmar*, September 5, 1980.

49. Mattityahu Peled, *Ha'aretz*, August 8, 1980. Peled also notes the obvious comparison: to the Jewish underground fighters held by the British in the pre-state period.

On the conditions of Arab political prisoners, see H. D. S. Greenway, *Washington Post*, March 20, 1977: "They live cramped together, 10, 20, sometimes 30 to a cell, so closely packed that there is little room to step between them when they are sleeping. There are no chairs, tables, not even beds. They sleep on rubber mats less than a third of an inch thick. . . . The prisoners are brought buckets of food, which they eat on the floor of their cells"—where they spend twenty to twenty-two hours a day (report from Ashkelon, where there was a long hunger strike in protest). See also Greenway's account the same day of the vicious attack by security forces on demonstrating students, largely censored in Israel; on this, also *New York Times*, March 25, 1977. On prison conditions, see also Christopher Wren, *New York Times*, August 6, 1980, reporting on the strike at Nafha prison where two prisoners died after force-feeding; also *The Times* (London), July 20, 1980. The latter report cites "claims by senior members of the prison service that the 6,000 prisoners held in Israeli jails endure worse conditions than any in the Western world," citing some supporting facts. There have been repeated protests by prisoners, including frequent hunger strikes, as in Nafha, where indications are that the conditions and treatment of prisoners verge on sadism (see *Al Hamishmar*, May 30, 1980; July 23, 1980). See also *Washington Post*, July 25, 1980; Trudy Rubin, *Christian Science Monitor*, July 25, 1980, reporting "prison-service sources" who told the Israel press that "conditions in Israeli prisons were the 'worst . . . in the Western world' for 6,000 Jewish and Arab inmates, half criminal and half security prisoners, the latter nearly all Arabs"; Michael Precker, *Boston Globe*, July 28, 1980, noting that "Israeli prison officials confirm many of the prisoners' complaints" and quoting Prison Commissioner Haim Levy who says that "they continue to work against the state, and I see them as a dangerous group. I must maintain certain conditions to prevent mass breakouts or revolts."

The ABC television documentary of Palestinian terrorism discussed in the Introduction (pp. 53–55) found prison conditions "adequate, certainly when compared to prisons in our country" (which, if true, is an interesting comment on U.S. prisons) and found PLO prisoners "well treated."

50. On torture, see the London *Sunday Times,* June 19, 1977, reporting the results of a five-month investigation by the Insight team that produced evidence of torture of Arab prisoners so widespread and systematic that "it appears to be sanctioned at some level as deliberate policy," perhaps "to persuade Arabs in occupied territories that it is least painful to behave passively." This study was offered to the *New York Times* and *Washington Post,* but rejected for publication.

See also the report of the study mission of the Swiss League for the Rights of Man (June 26–July 2, 1977), presented to the U.N. secretary-general, published in *An-Nahar Arab Report & Memo* (Beirut), October 10, 1977, with many reports of torture among other human rights violations detailed. See also the report of five months of torture and abuse followed by expulsion in the *Christian Science Monitor*, March 1, 1977 (and a follow-up letter by a former Israeli soldier describing merciless beatings and the wanton murder of an old man by a military commander that he had witnessed in the occupied territories; March 11, 1977); and Victor Cygielman, *Nouvel Observateur,* March 22, 1976. Or consider the gruesome tale of Muhammad Akel, who reports that he was severely beaten and tortured before he was sentenced to three and a half years for belonging to the Palestine National Front, flying a Palestinian flag, and distributing pamphlets calling for protest strikes against the occupation (London *Times,* April 25, 1977). Or the report by Amnon Kapeliouk, *Al Hamishmar,* February 22, 1980, on the case of Nader el-Afuri, whose treatment under administrative detention was so harsh that he lost his sanity. After a year of these horrors, and after intervention by Amnesty International, the government released him to a mental hospital. Kapeliouk writes:

"In our travels on the West Bank we have heard too many hair-raising stories about torture and we are unwilling to react with total disbelief, as do the Minister of Justice or
the Minister of the Interior when they are queried on the subject." See also Chapter 10,
note 5.

51. *Yediot Abronot,* October 13, 1976; *Ha'aretz,* October 17, 1976.
52. *Yediot Abronot,* January 26, 1977.
53. *Davar,* March 4, 1980.
54. Yehuda Litani, *Ha'aretz,* May 16, 1980
55. Dan Horowitz, *Yediot Abronot,* June 11, 1980.
56. *Newsweek,* June 9, 1980.
57. Quoted by Misha Louvish, *Jerusalem Post,* March 24, 1981.
58. *Washington Post,* September 8, 1980. One major component of this policy of blocking
development has to do with water supplies. Michael Widlanski reports in the *New York
Times* (December 28, 1980) that "according to American officials, Palestinians are not
being allowed to draw more than the 1967 levels. . . . An American official noted, however, that the availability of water was a primary consideration in the location of Israeli
West Bank settlements and that any new water sources discovered by Israel since 1967
are being restricted to Israeli use." This has been regular practice since 1967, and is a
factor in the decline of Arab agriculture and proletarianization of the population. The
West Bank water reserves are being used not only for Jewish settlers but also for Israel
proper, as noted above. Mayor Bassam Shak'a hardly exaggerates when he says that
"the West Bank has become little more than a water reservoir for Israel." He claims
that "they siphon off 80 percent of the Palestinians' underground water" and refuse to
permit Arab inhabitants to drill wells, even for drinking water, certainly not for irrigation. Grace Halsell, *Fort Worth News-Tribune,* October 31, 1980; see also her *Journey to
Jerusalem* (New York: Macmillan, 1980).
59. *Washington Post,* February 11, 1981.
60. Dani Rubinstein, "Grab all that you can," *Davar,* April 3, 1981.
61. Dani Rubinstein, "Save us from such legality; the new system of land seizure in the
West Bank," *Davar,* March 20, 1981. See also his "Deluxe Annexation," *New Outlook*
(June 1981), discussing the "legalistic form of sophisticated annexation" since 1967,
which is more harmful for the Arab inhabitants than real annexation and which is supported in one or another form by all major political groupings, as he shows.
62. Amnon Kapeliouk, "The robbery of the lands in the West Bank—pure and simple robbery," *Al Hamishmar,* March 17, 1981. See also "Robbery of the lands in the territories," editorial, *Ha'aretz,* March 23, 1981. Justice Cohen's comment is also cited in a
New York Times Op-Ed by Fahd Kawasmeh and Mohammed Milhem, two moderate
Arab mayors who were brutally expelled in March 1980; *New York Times,* May 31,
1981.
63. Yehuda Litani, *Ha'aretz,* March 27, 1981; March 29, 1981.
64. *Yediot Abronot,* March 16, 1976.
65. *Ma'ariv,* December 15, 1976.
66. Natan Dunvitz, "People and values go up in flames," *Ha'aretz,* March 19, 1976. See also
London *Economist,* March 20, 1976. To my knowledge, the only reference to this atrocity in the United States was in a letter of mine in the *New York Review,* March 17, 1977.
67. *Aftonbladet* (Sweden), April 22, 1971; translated in Davis and Mezvinsky, *op. cit.*

68. For references from the Israeli and British press, see Chomsky and E. S. Herman, *The Political Economy of Human Rights* (Boston: South End Press, 1979), vol. 2, p. 360.
69. Avraham Zohar, "The new feudal rulers: slavery at the Rafah Approaches," *Ha'aretz*, July 3, 1979.
70. Yossef Tzuriel, *Ma'ariv*, July 13, 1979.
71. Yerah Tal, *Ha'aretz*, September 7, 1980.
72. Avshalom Ginat, *Al Hamishmar*, September 5, September 16, 1980.
73. Avshalom Ginat, *Al Hamishmar*, April 11, 1979; Miriam Prenkel and Alex Fishman, *Al Hamishmar*, April 11, 1979.
74. Arnon Magen, "Jews are needed in the Gentile's Galilee," *Davar*, April 17, 1979.

Reporting Arab protests against land expropriation connected with the policy of "Judaization of the Galilee," Amnon Kapeliouk notes that "no Arab representative sits on the council in charge of planning Galilean development" (where Arab citizens of Israel constitute the majority of the population) and that the minister of agriculture "recently told Jewish farmers he would cut off water supplies or confiscate their property if they agreed to rent arable land to Arabs," a rather natural development since Jewish settlers are few and "while the total amount of land in Arab hands has been dropping over the years, the Arab population is constantly increasing" (*Le Monde*, June 1, 1976; translated in the *Manchester Guardian Weekly*). See also Kapeliouk's discussion of confiscation of Arab lands in *Le Monde*, December 13, 1975 (translated in *Middle East International*, February 1976), where he discusses the profoundly discriminatory policies of the State of Israel and their tragic impact on the Arab population. Recall that this is under the Labor government.

In the *New Outlook* (July 1976), Aharon Cohen pointed out that "since the state's establishment, about 3 1/4 million dunams—according to government figures—have been taken from Arab ownership"—about 800,000 acres. He notes the "false pretenses" in the claim that some of the new land assigned to the "Judaization" program is "government land," given that these lands "are none other than lands held and worked by Arabs for generations," originally called "Sultan's land" and now "state land." He protests that Arabs "are second-class citizens in their own homeland," and that in every crucial respect, the facts "are a shame and disgrace to a democratic state and to the Jewish people."

Warnings to Jewish settlers against employing Arabs are common, and are sometimes followed by direct action (see my paper "The Interim Agreement" for several examples of what is described in the Israeli press as an "energetic campaign" to eliminate the "plague" of leasing land to Arabs). *Yediot Abronot* (June 20, 1977) reports that a couple was evicted by the Jewish Agency from a moshav (collective settlement) in the Jordan Valley "because they had employed Arab workers" (note the role of the Jewish Agency, one of the "national institutions"). The Jewish Agency official in charge, who is director of the northern region, "had found three Arabs working in their fields" and explained that this is not permitted. He stated "that the instructions with regard to Jewish settlements in the Valley explicitly forbid employment of Arabs, 'and in any place under my jurisdiction—I will see that the instructions are carried out'—he commented." In response to the objection that in a neighboring moshav Arabs were employed in a packaging plant, the official stated that that would be permissible, but he did not want to see Arabs working in the fields. A year earlier the same journal had published a revealing article entitled "The gradual take-over bid by Israeli Arabs" (*Yediot Abronot*, July 16, 1976; *Israeli Mirror*, August 25, 1976). The article gave details of illegal construction by Arabs in state land, "i.e., by occupying land that belongs to the nation." Then comes the following analysis:

> *While Zionism has been declining, undergoing an ideological, political and moral degeneration, and while its creations are crumbling away, the Arab settlement movement has been growing and is about to reach its "Zionist" peak. It creates accomplished facts not only by occupying land—and especially land belonging to the nation—to erect illegal buildings, but also by occupying land for cultivation. Here and there, one can see new tobacco fields appear on stony earth and at the feet of rocks. Any removal of the cultivators will be regarded as the expulsion of Arabs from the land of their forefathers.*

There has been much concern in Israel over such "Arab Zionism." Arab citizens of Israel are cultivating the desolate land that "belongs to the nation"—that is, to the Jews of Israel and of the Diaspora. They are making the desert bloom; that must be stopped. The basic reason for this illegal Arab Zionism is the massive expropriation and lack of development opportunities within the restricted areas that remain open to Arabs, along with the reluctance of Jews to engage in such work.

American apologists for Israel regularly applaud the "legal methods" used by the state in dealing with its Arab citizens; cf. e.g., Abraham Friend in the socialist journal *New Politics* (Winter 1979), and my comments in the same issue, including the references just cited, among others. Note that these state policies are harshly criticized by a number of Israeli commentators, as noted.

75. Yosef Goell, "Small-scale summitry," *Jerusalem Post Magazine*, March 13, 1981.

76. *Ha'olam Haze*, February 7, 1979. There has been some protest in the United States over the harsh treatment of the Bedouins, often giving the impression that this is an innovation of the Begin government. That is quite untrue, however, even putting aside the brutal expulsion of Bedouins from the region south of Gaza in the early 1970s. Referring to the situation within the Green Line in the Negev, Dani Rubinstein (*Davar*, July 30, 1976) deplored the policies of the Land Development Administration (controlled by the Jewish National Fund) that grant rights to Jews while denying them to the "miserable 'Fellahs' (one should peer into the pits by the road and see in what conditions they live), who have gradually turned into a special class of vassals." Discussing the displaced Bedouins—citizens of Israel who are loyal to the state and serve in the army and border patrol—he notes that "there are no land contracts in Bedouin areas in the south, and all the 3500 constructions, including stone houses, tin shacks and tents, were built without a permit. No land agreement was ever made to determine ownership rights on land in Bedouin areas in the south. The only possibility left to the Bedouin is to build in the air." The Begin government merely extended and intensified policies of the Labor government. See also Chapter 10, note 2, below.

77. Ronny Eshel, "How Israel views its Arab citizens," *Ma'ariv*, August 19, 1980; *Israeli Mirror*, October 14, 1980.

78. *Yediot Abronot*, April 20, 1979, in an article critical of these practices. The reporter describes the case of an Arab citizen, speaking perfect Hebrew, who tried to have the name of a child registered by an official who is a recent immigrant from the USSR, un-

derstands little Hebrew, and registers the name wrongly—as he too was forced to live with an incorrect name, he complains bitterly.

79. "Israel, like the USSR, to strip 'disloyal elements' of their citizenship," *Ha'aretz*, July 31, 1980, a sharp critique of the new laws; *Israeli Mirror*, August 4, 1980.

80. *Ha'aretz*, August 1, 1980; *Israeli Mirror*, August 4, 1980.

81. *Al Hamishmar*, July 18, 1980. The reporter, Amnon Kapeliouk, regards the new laws as showing that "the Likud is trying to create an atmosphere of nationalist fanaticism in which it can win elections." Most of the Labor party voted for these laws.

82. *Yediot Abronot*, February 11, 1981; *Israeli Mirror*, n.d.

83. K. Amnon, "Daily attacks on Arab students in Jerusalem," *Al Hamishmar*, April 1, 1981. See also Danny Shapiro, "Fascism in Israeli Universities," *New Outlook* (June 1981), noting in particular that the government and police "bear their share of responsibility for these outrages by their 'see-no-evil' attitude towards campus fascism."

84. Newsletter No. 2, CAMPUS, POB 7558, Jerusalem 91074 (March 1981). The faculty senate of the Technion, however, strongly condemned the attack.

85. Statement by Issam Mahkoul, August 6, 1980.

86. Eliahu Salpeter, "Justice for the rightwing," *Ha'aretz*, August 19, 1980.

87. Released by *Al Hamishmar*, September 7, 1976. Reprinted by Americans for Middle East Understanding, Room 771, 475 Riverside Drive, New York, N.Y. 10027, as part of an undated booklet, *Palaces of Injustice.*

88. See *Leviathan* (Boston) (Spring 1977). Leibowitz added that the document and reaction to it in the community "reflect the reality of the State."

89. "After the memorandum was delivered Rabin decided that Aldorati would be his candidate to head the Arab department of the Labor party" (Ehud Yaari, *Davar;* cited in *Israleft News Service*, September 15, 1976).

90. Ran Eddelist and Kassem Zayd, "Koenig's bite: worse than his bark," *New Outlook* (January 1977).

91. If this information is not readily available to human rights organizations in the United States, it is largely as a result of their own conscious choice. Thus, the International League for Human Rights disaffiliated the Israeli League, which had been its Israeli affiliate, for the sole reason that the governing Labor party attempted a takeover of the Israeli League which was so blatant that it was barred by the courts. Despite some protest here, the International League refused to withdraw this shocking action, which is on a par with disaffiliation of a Moscow branch of an international human rights organization after it had come under attack by the Soviet government. For some discussion, including the reaction of American civil libertarians, see my *Peace in the Middle East?*, p. 197.

The Hebrew press in Israel regularly contains information on Israeli repression. The excellent reporting of Amnon Kapeliouk (*Al Hamishmar*), Yehuda Litani (*Ha'aretz*), and Dani Rubinstein (*Davar*) has been particularly noteworthy, along with the information made public by Knesset member Uri Avneri (often, in his journal *Haolam Haze*). There has also been regular reporting in the journal of the Israeli Communist Party (Rakah), *Zu Haderech.* Much of this material is published in English translation in the biweekly *Israleft* (POB 9013, Jerusalem).

92. Meir Merhav, *Jerusalem Post*, May 22, 25, 1980.

93. Note that an accurate calculation of the contribution of the U.S. taxpayer to this system would take into account not only direct government aid but also the tax-free contribu-

tions to the "national institutions" of Israel, which, as noted above, are devoted to promoting the interests of Jewish citizens of the state, in the occupied territories as well as within the Green Line.

94. "Israel: Carving a big slice of world arms sales," *Business Week*, December 8, 1980.

95. *Newsweek*, October 11, 1976.

96. Christine Dugas, "Arms from Israel," *Progressive* (June 1981).

97. *Ibid.* See also Chapter 8, note 26.

98. *New York Times*, May 8, 1981.

99. It has been a standard pretense for years that Argentina is governed by moderates who are, unfortunately (and unaccountably), unable to control their violent subordinates. For discussion, see Chomsky and E. S. Herman, *The Political Economy of Human Rights*, vol. 1.

100. *American Jewish Year Book, 1980*, published by the American Jewish Committee and the Jewish Publication Society of America (1979). The report on Argentina observes that "there was no gainsaying the fact that many thousands of people were being held without formal charges because they were suspected of being linked to left-wing underground movements." It adds that "while leading military figures stated that they were opposed to antisemitism, lower-eschelon [sic] officers and enlisted men in the police and military were notoriously antisemitic," and notes that "Jewish political prisoners were subjected to particularly cruel torture" and that prisoners report "that in many places of detention there were swastikas and portraits of Hitler." There is no comment on the Israeli government's tacit support for these practices.

101. *Ha'aretz*, August 10, 1978; cited by Israel Shahak, "Israel's global task: supplier of arms and ally to the worst among governments," *Zu Haderech* (Rakah), March 25, 1981. See his forthcoming monograph with the same title.

102. Warren Hoge, "Bolivia Regime Looks to Its Friends to Help Foil U.S.," *New York Times*, August 6, 1980.

103. Jack Anderson, *Washington Post*, December 8, 1980; *Staten Island Advance*, December 9, 1980.

104. *Economist*, November 5, 1977.

105. See Israel Shahak, "Israel's global role (3)," *Zu Haderech*, April 9, 1981, based largely on the Israeli press, and his forthcoming monograph (see note 101 above). Shahak states that the "Made in Israel" conduit for South African goods is in fact functioning. He also reports Israeli connections with Bokassa's Central African Republic and other black African dictatorships (ibid., April 1, 1981).

106. *Ha'aretz*, December 12, 1980; *Israeli Mirror*, December 19, 1980. The same article reports that Israel and South Africa have a joint economic council which has been functioning since the 1978 visit of Simha Erlich to South Africa. Israel had originally requested $250 million in South African aid; *Jerusalem Post*, December 10, 1980.

107. See Chapter 12 and references cited there.

108. On the backgrounds and development of the Lebanese civil war, see Walid Khalidi, *Conflict and Violence in Lebanon*, Center for International Affairs, Harvard University, Cambridge (1979). Some interesting information on earlier U.S. actions that heightened internal conflict is presented in Wilbur Crane Eveland, *Ropes of Sand* (New York: Norton, 1980).

109. This passage is quoted by William Claiborne and Jonathan C. Randal in the second part of a four-part series, "South Lebanon: the forgotten war," *Washington Post*, March

15–18, 1981. For extensive excerpts from the diaries and discussion of them, see Livia Rokach, *Israel's Sacred Terrorism*, Association of Arab-American University Graduates, Belmont, Mass. (1980). Sharett adds a few days later (May 28, 1954) that Dayan "supports a plan to hire a [Lebanese] officer who will agree to serve as a puppet so that the Israeli army may appear as responding to his appeal to liberate Lebanon from its Muslim oppressors." Sharett describes this as "a crazy adventure." It is now being pursued.

On February 27, Sharett describes a meeting with Ben-Gurion, Defense Minister Lavon, and Chief of Staff Dayan, in which Ben-Gurion said, according to Sharett, that this is the time "to push Lebanon, that is, the Maronites in that country, to proclaim a Christian State." Ben-Gurion reacted "furiously" to Sharett's objections, delivering a tirade on "the historical justification for a restricted Christian Lebanon" and arguing that it is worthwhile expending a million dollars on this venture, perhaps making use of the Jewish Agency if treasury funds did not suffice. In a letter the next day, Ben-Gurion wrote to Sharett that "there are various ways in which the proposed experiment can be carried out." "The creation of a Christian State is therefore a natural act; it has historical roots and it will find support in wide circles in the Christian world," though "without our initiative and our vigorous aid this will not be done."

If money is necessary, no amount of dollars should be spared. . . . This is a historical opportunity. Missing it will be unpardonable. . . . Everything should be done, in my opinion, rapidly and at full steam. The goal will not be reached, of course, without a restriction of Lebanon's borders. But if we can find men in Lebanon and exiles from it who will be ready to mobilize for the creation of a Maronite state, extended borders and a large Muslim population will be of no use to them and this will not constitute a disturbing factor.

Thus Israel can proceed to move to "restrict Lebanon's borders," how far, Ben-Gurion does not say.

110. Joseph Fitchett, *Washington Post–Boston Globe*, July 23, 1976.
111. *Time*, November 1, 1976; also August 2.
112. See Marvine Howe, "Israeli Jets Strike Lebanon"; UPI, "After the Raid, a Village Lies in Rubble Heap," *New York Times*, November 10, 1977. More than a hundred villagers were reported killed as the village of Azziye was reduced to rubble; survivors said they were Lebanese who had fled their original homes after an attack backed by Israeli artillery, and reported that there were "no guerrillas" in the town. Other villages and camps "in and around the port city of Tyre" were attacked, with many casualties, allegedly in reprisal for a rocket attack on the Israeli town of Nahariya (itself a reprisal for an earlier Israeli attack that the *Times* does not report; cf. Chapter 12). See also Chapter 12, note 4, and Introduction, note 195.
113. H. D. S. Greenway, *Washington Post–Boston Globe*, March 25, 1978.
114. Ignace Dalle, *The Times* (London), March 16, 1978.
115. *Newsweek*, March 27, 1978; *Time*, April 3, 1978. See also Richard Ben Cramer, Knight News Service, *Boston Globe*, March 19, 1978, reporting the town of Nabatiye "being blasted to bits, block by block" by the "awesome" Israeli firepower; Roger Matthews, *London Financial Times*, March 17, 1978, describing the air attack on Tyre where "there was no possible 'military' target within a couple of miles," according to doctors

tending the dead and wounded; John Cooley, *Christian Science Monitor*, March 24, 1978, David Hirst, *Manchester Guardian Weekly*, March 26, 1978.

116. Graham Hovey, *New York Times*, July 24, 1979; see also Marvine Howe, *New York Times*, July 23.

117. Christopher Bourne, *New Statesman*, August 3, 1979. For further information, see wire service reports of the shelling of six villages around Tyre "causing heavy damage and an unspecified number of casualties" (*Boston Globe*, August 4, 1979); AP, *Boston Globe*, August 26, 1979; Edward Cody, *Washington Post–Boston Globe*, August 30, 1979; *New York Times*, August 21, 1979; *New York Times*, one hundred words on "the heaviest barrage in years," August 22, 1979; Marvine Howe, *New York Times*, August 24, 1979; John Cooley, *Christian Science Monitor*, August 24, 1979.

118. E.g., Helena Cobban, "Resumed Israeli raids in Lebanon have hit civilian populace heavily," *Christian Science Monitor*, May 19, 1980; "Israelis reportedly shell southern Lebanon port," Reuter, *Boston Globe*, April 24, 1981; "Israeli warplanes strike in Lebanon," attacking areas around Sidon, killing mostly civilians, *Washington Post—Boston Globe*, April 27, 1981.

119. E.g., Pranay B. Gupte, *New York Times*, April 11, 1981, noting in passing that "according to United Nations officials, three naval vessels belonging to Israel lobbed shells into the port city of Tyre, a Palestinian center"—in fact, a Lebanese city, bombed so heavily that "if nothing is done to stop the Israeli bombing of Tyre, 6000 years of history may be wiped out, a loss not only to Lebanon but to the entire world"; Barbro Elfstrom, *Boston Globe*, October 18, 1980.

120. Jack Anderson, *Washington Post*, April 9, 1980.

121. London *Economist*, December 27, 1980.

122. Helena Cobban, *Christian Science Monitor*, June 26, 1980.

123. John Kifner, *New York Times*, July 25, 1981.

124. *Christian Science Monitor*, editorial, July 20, 1981.

125. William Beecher, "Why Israeli raids worry the White House," *Boston Globe*, July 24, 1981.

126. For discussion of this matter, see my articles "The Interim Agreement" and "Against Apologetics for Israeli Expansionism" in *New Politics, op. cit.*

Chapter Ten. Bellow, *To Jerusalem and Back*

1. *New York Times*, March 1, 1976. Cf. Chapter 12 of the present volume.

2. Cf. Kennett Love, *Suez: The Twice-fought War* (New York: McGraw-Hill, 1969). Love, who was a *New York Times* correspondent in the Middle East from 1953 to 1956, notes that as part of its general policy of incursion into the demilitarized zones established by the 1949 armistice agreement, "In 1950 Israel expelled 3,500 Azazme Bedouins from the zone with air and ground attacks. Israeli patrols burned the Bedouins' tents and shot the thirsty tribesmen and their camels and goats when they came to the wells to drink and fill their water skins. . . . UN records show that more than 7,000 Bedouins were forced out of Israel in the first five years of the Armistices" (pp. 11, 61).

In 1954, eleven Israelis were killed in an attack on a bus by members of "the Bedouin Black Hand gang, formed for purposes of robbery and revenge after the Azzazma expulsion from Israel," leading to an Israeli retaliatory attack against the completely innocent Jordanian village of Nahhaleen in which nine villagers were killed. The bus ambush was "the worst single Arab reprisal committed in Israel"; it was preceded by the Israeli attack on the al-Bureig refugee camp in the Gaza Strip in which twenty were killed (August 1953) and the Israeli army raid that killed sixty-six villagers in the Jordanian village of Qibya in October 1953. Note that Love describes the bus ambush as a "reprisal." Israel and its U.S. supporters, on the other hand, describe it as a terrorist attack that led to a reprisal. As the interplay just outlined (which is far from the whole story) indicates, the terms "terrorism" and "reprisal" are terms of propaganda, rather than descriptive categories. It all depends on whose ox is being gored. For further examples, see Chapters 11 and 12.

In both the Qibya and al-Bureig attacks, most of the victims were women and children. Both attacks were condemned by the U.N. truce teams. The Qibya attack was ordered by Ben-Gurion, who, however, publicly denied the facts, stating that "the Government of Israel rejects with all vigor the absurd and fantastic allegation that the men of the Israel Defense Forces took part in the action" (Love, *ibid.*, p. 57). The truth was later admitted. For an internal record from the diaries of Israeli Prime Minister Sharett, see Livia Rokach, *Israel's Sacred Terrorism* (Belmont, Mass.: Association of Arab-American University Graduates, 1980). An appendix includes the full statement by Ben-Gurion; *Davar*, October 20, 1953. Sharett regarded the raid as a "monstrous bloodbath" but agreed to the deception since he felt that "I couldn't seriously demand that the communiqué explicitly affirm the Army's responsibility." The attack was blamed on settlers ("mostly refugees, people from Arab countries and survivors from the Nazi concentration camps") who were enraged by "murderous attacks" (Ben-Gurion). Rokach (who was formerly a *Davar* correspondent) points out accurately that "the security of the Israeli border population could hardly be more jeopardized than by attributing to them the responsibility for a bloodbath such as Kibya's."

3. See Chapter 9, above.

4. Bellow follows a fairly common practice. See, for example, Stephen Spender, *New York Review*, March 6, 1975, who discusses the problems of Arabs in Israel very knowledgeably on the basis of information provided by Jewish government officials, Jewish Arab experts, and the inevitable taxi driver. Spender also pays tribute to the "agonized conscience" with which Israel "copes with necessity" in reconstructing the old Jewish quarter of East Jerusalem "in ways that retain its character"—though he fails to note that this reconstruction involved the expulsion of Arabs who lived there for many generations, or the fact that the old Arab quarter of Jaffa, from which Arabs were expelled in April 1948 by Irgun and Haganah in an unprovoked attack, has not been reconstructed with similar solicitude; on the contrary, the former inhabitants, driven out by these attacks, are not permitted to return.

5. Reviewing the detailed London *Sunday Times* (June 19, 1977) documentation of torture of Arabs in Israel and the Israeli response to it (but not the devastating reply of the *Sunday Times* to this rebuttal), Seth Kaplan concludes that the question of how a government should treat its people "is not susceptible to simple absolutism, such as the outright condemnation of torture. One may have to use extreme measures—call them 'torture'—to deal with a terrorist movement whose steady tactic is the taking of human life" (*New Republic*, July 23, 1977). To my knowledge, no such explicit support for torture has appeared in the West apart from ultra-right French circles during the Algerian war. It is interesting that this appears in a leading journal of American liber-

alism, without protest, when the victims are Arabs and the agents are Israelis, who are able to maintain the occupation in defiance of world opinion because of the military and economic support provided by the United States.

The remarkably high level of confessions of Arab prisoners suggests something other than humane treatment, but Israeli Supreme Court Justice Moshe Etzioni observes that this proves nothing, because "the Arabs in any case—if they are arrested—do not take much time before they confess. It's part of their nature" (Amnesty International *Newsletter*, September 1977). Whatever it is about their nature must be contagious, since by now Jewish prisoners are also confessing to crimes (which they did not commit) after police "interrogation." See, for example, Amnon Rubinstein, "This didn't happen in Sodom," *Ha'aretz*, February 27, 1981.

Commenting on the same forced confession that Rubinstein condemned, Felicia Langer reviews a series of cases in which Jewish and Arab prisoners confessed to crimes for which they were discovered to be innocent. Langer, a Rakah (Communist) lawyer who has courageously defended Arab prisoners for many years, observes that the main police investigator in the case Rubinstein discussed had long been reported to be a torturer by Arab prisoners, citing her 1974 book *Bemo Eynay* (With My Own Eyes) (London: Ithaca Press, 1974). Langer, "Ancient crimes found out," *Zu Haderech*, March 11, 1981. It had long been predicted that sooner or later the measures applied to Arabs would return home.

6. *Al Hamishmar*, December 29, 1976. See note 4.
7. *El-Shaab*, April 17, 1975 (Jerusalem).
8. British correspondent David Hirst, "Rush to Annexation: Israel in Jerusalem," *Journal of Palestine Studies* (Summer 1974). For other examples, see Israel Shahak, *Le racisme de l'état d'Israël* (Paris: Guy Authier, 1975), p. 64.
9. Cf. SWASIA, June 6, 1975 (National Council of Churches).
10. See Ehud Yaari, *Egypt and the Fedayin* (Hebrew, Givat Haviva, 1975). See Chapter 12 of the present volume, at note 34.
11. For concurring views, see *The Evasive Peace* (London: John Murray, 1968), by John Davis, the American commissioner of UNRWA.
12. Love, *op. cit.*, p. 689. Love reports that by such tactics, and with unchallenged command of the air, Israel succeeded in killing 20,000 Egyptian soldiers with 679 Israeli dead, according to the Israeli Army.

Chapter Eleven. American Foreign Policy in the Middle East

1. *New York Times*, March 14, 1977.
2. Moshe Brilliant, *New York Times*, February 13, 1977.
3. For the text, see *New York Times*, January 27, 1976. See Chapter 9 and Chapter 12, note 25, for further relevant background.
4. U.S. Department of State, *Foreign Relations of the United States*, 1945, VIII, 45; cited in Joyce and Gabriel Kolko, *The Limits of Power* (New York: Harper & Row, 1972), which provides a comprehensive analysis of the development of U.S. policy at the time. For further information with regard to petroleum policy see the important study *Multinational Oil Corporations and U.S. Foreign Policy*, report to the Committee on Foreign Relations. U.S. Senate, January 2, 1975 (henceforth, *MNOC*). Cf. Chapter 2.

5. Until 1968, North America surpassed the Middle East in oil production. Cf. John Blair, *The Control of Oil* (New York: Pantheon, 1976).

6. Edward A. Bayne, *Four Ways of Politics*, American University's Field Staff, 1965; cited by Robert B. Reppa, *Israel and Iran: Bilateral Relationships and Effect on the Indian Ocean Basin* (New York: Praeger, 1974). Reppa was a staff officer in the Defence Intelligence Agency's national intelligence analysis and estimates office, Middle East branch, from 1961 to 1966.

   While the character of the Irano-Israeli relationship remains largely unknown, nevertheless the curtain has been raised somewhat since the overthrow of the Shah's regime. Some insight into this relationship is provided by Uri Lubrani, Israeli ambassador to Iran from 1973 to 1978, in his article "Allon in the Palace of the Shah," in the Independence Day Supplement of the Labor Party journal *Davar* (April 20, 1980). According to Lubrani, "the entire upper echelon of the Israeli political leadership" visited Iran, including David Ben-Gurion, Golda Meir, Abba Eban, Yitzhak Rabin, Yigal Allon, Moshe Dayan, and Menahem Begin. Lubrani recounts in detail a secret visit by Allon in August 1976. Allon received a "very warm reception" from the director of SAVAK, who was the official host for all of these visits. He stressed to the Shah the "fundamental identity of interests between Israel and Iran" and urged that existing arrangements be perpetuated, particularly with regard to the supply of oil to Israel, in view of the "true quality of their joint interests," which goes beyond "economic calculations alone." He delivered a "fundamental lecture on the important role fulfilled, in his opinion, by the cooperation between Israel and Iran in the international arena." The Shah agreed, meanwhile complaining repeatedly about the failure of the United States to comprehend the processes at work in the world in general and the Middle East in particular. The Israeli visitors were particularly impressed by the high level of Western culture exhibited by their hosts.

   Lubrani comments further that future historians will see the Shah as a "ruler who made a fundamental contribution to the progress of Iran and to leading it out of the Middle Ages," adding that as a citizen of Israel he would regard it as his duty to respond to any request for assistance from the Shah.

   There have been occasional references to the Irano-Israeli relationship during the Shah's regime in the American press. Thus Richard Sale, in a series of reports from Iran in the *Washington Post*, observed that "innumerable Iranians, including many in a position to know, told me that the Israelis oversee SAVAK's techniques," which are well known (May 9, 1977). Perhaps this is one of the examples of cooperation between the Israeli Mossad and the CIA. The chief CIA analyst on Iran from 1968 to 1973, Jesse Leaf, alleges that "a senior C.I.A. official was involved in instructing officials in the Savak on torture techniques. . . . The C.I.A.'s torture seminars, Mr. Leaf said, 'were based on German torture techniques from World War II' " (Seymour M. Hersh, *New York Times*, January 7, 1979). See also note 17.

7. See "US trade with the Arab world," *MEMO: Middle East Money*, Beirut, February 7, 1977.

8. *New York Times*, February 15, 1977.

9. Leonard Silk, *New York Times*, October 7, 1976.

10. Don Oberdorfer, *Washington Post*, December 12, 1976.

11. Ian Smart, "Oil, the Super-Powers and the Middle East," *International Affairs* (January 1977).

12. *Business Week*, in an enthusiastic special report (May 26, 1975), applauded the new opportunities for American capital in the Middle East ("one of the few places in the world where private enterprise is making a comeback"), noting happily that Europe and Japan "are footing most of the bill for the area's prosperity" while "petrodollars coming back to the U.S. through trade offset this country's outlays for Middle Eastern oil" (not to speak of the profits of oil companies, largely U.S.-based). The opportunities for construction, investment, and trade are described in glowing terms. American businessmen report a "marked preference for American products" (*New York Times*, June 30, 1975). In Saudi Arabia, an American-designed program is expected to cost more than $17 billion, and U.S. firms and the U.S. Army Corps of Engineers are contracting for ventures that will extend over the next decade (*New York Times*, June 22, 1975).

    Subsequent developments, however, may have been less favorable. See Introduction.

13. John Saar, *Washington Post*, April 12, 1976.

14. Myra Wilkins, "The Oil Companies in Perspective," *Daedalus* (Fall 1975). See Chapter 2, note 31, above, for the rather different view of a Japanese specialist on oil politics.

15. Blair, *op. cit.* Blair provides ample evidence of the government concern to secure the profits of the energy corporations. On the international context, see Kolko and Kolko, *op. cit.* See also Robert Engler, *The Brotherhood of Oil* (Chicago: University of Chicago Press, 1977), and many other sources.

16. Reppa, *op. cit.*

17. *Congressional Record*, 21 May 1973, S9446. Cited by Joe Stork, *Middle East Oil and the Energy Crisis* (New York: Monthly Review Press, 1975). The Shah agreed. Discussing the Shah's fears of encirclement by unfriendly neighbors (the USSR, Iraq, India, Baluch in western Pakistan), Bernard Weinraub cites diplomats who "say that Israel provides a source of stable power on the Arabs' western flank." He quotes one diplomatic source who says, "Without Israeli power in the Middle East, the Shah feels that the Arabs would be difficult to control and the Russians would very much gain an upper hand in the entire area" (*New York Times*, December 30, 1973).

18. Reppa, *op. cit.* He expects the eye of the hurricane to be "followed by the ferocity of the second half of the storm," not unreasonably.

19. Jim Hoagland, *Washington Post*, February 22, 1977.

20. Rowland Evans and Robert Novak, "CIA's secret subsidy to Israel," *Boston Globe*, February 24, 1977.

21. Edward A. Behr, *Wall Street Journal*, February 22, 1977.

22. Idi Amin was originally the client of Britain and Israel. To the end of his bloody regime, he received substantial U.S. support through coffee purchases which provided "the hard currency essential to keeping Amin's repressive regime in power" (Senator Lowell Weicker, "Stop Subsidizing Amin's Murders," *Christian Science Monitor*, August 21, 1978). The CIA, the Israeli Mossad, and an Israeli entrepreneur linked to the Israeli Aircraft Industry (which is in turn closely linked to the United States) meanwhile provided Amin with an airline that he used as "a cut-rate service that transports Ugandan coffee, officials and their mistresses to Europe and brings back whiskey, machine tools, livestock, and Mercedes Benz limousines," as part of an effort to spy on Libya (Bernard Nossiter, "How the CIA keeps Idi Amin in whiskey," *New Statesman*, October 13, 1978; *Washington Post*, September 11, 1978). See Chomsky and E. S. Her-

man, *The Political Economy of Human Rights,* vol. 2 (Boston: South End Press, 1979), pp. 326–27, for further discussion.

Bokassa was overthrown by French troops in October 1979, when his massacres began to receive too much international publicity and became something of an embarrassment (the diamonds and other gifts he gave to Giscard remain an embarrassment). Basically the same government was placed in power by the French coup.

23. V. H. Oppenheim, "Why Oil Prices Go Up: The Past—We Pushed Them," *Foreign Policy* (Winter 1976–77).

24. Cf. my article "La clef de voûte du système Américain," *Le Monde diplomatique* (May 1976), for some references and discussion.

25. Emma Rothschild, "Is it time to end Food for Peace?" *New York Times Magazine,* March 13, 1977.

26. Dan Smith, "Oil—the Growing Power of Saudi Arabia," *Middle East Annual Review* (1977).

27. Henry Kissinger, *American Foreign Policy,* expanded ed. (New York: Norton, 1974). Elsewhere, Kissinger has explained that his strategy after the October 1973 war was based in part on the desire "to ensure that the Europeans and Japanese did not get involved in the diplomacy" concerning the Middle East (along with the effort "to break up the Arab united front," "to keep the Soviets out of the diplomatic arena," and to ensure continued Israeli dependency on the United States while enabling Israel "to deal separately with each of its neighbors"). "Memorandum of Conversation," Meeting with Jewish Leaders (Philip Klutznik Group), June 15, 1975, Hotel Pierre, New York; obtained under the Freedom of Information Act and published in *MERIP Reports,* May 1981; also, *Journal of Palestine Studies,* Spring 1981.

Parts of what Kissinger said in this private meeting may be attributable to the fact that his purpose was to "prevent a Jewish assault on the United States Government." Nevertheless, most of his remarks ring true, including those cited above and his emphasis on ensuring "the most massive Arab defeat possible" in 1973, his efforts "to isolate the Palestinians" so that they could be eliminated as a factor, and his "projected stall with the Arabs" in the interests of Israeli domestic politics in late 1974. Another interesting bit of information (assuming it to be true) is that in the post-1973 negotiations Hussein offered to accept a peaceful settlement if Israel would yield "about one-half of the territory called for in the old Allon Plan," i.e., a fraction of the West Bank, "but the Israelis said no." Kissinger also claims that Israel's insistence on moving settlements right up to the Syrian border in the Golan Heights prevented a settlement with Syria that would have "split the Palestinians from the Syrians." It was Israel's refusal to move towards such accommodation with Syria or Jordan, Kissinger claims, that led him to concentrate on the Sinai, though in any event he would have responded to the post-October 1973 situation by moving to accept Sadat's offer of U.S. client status, which required a Sinai settlement.

28. "Even the United States, despite Secretary Kissinger's stress on the need for the consumers to act together rather than seek individual oil producers, concluded a 5-year trade pact with Iran worth $15 billion ($12 billion of which would be spent in the U.S.)." Others entered into individual relations as well, though on a lesser scale. Robert J. Lieber, "Oil and the Middle East War," Center for International Affairs, Harvard University, 1976.

29. *Ibid.*

30. Jim Hoagland, *Washington Post,* February 19, 1977.

31. *MEMO, op. cit.*

32. *Ibid.* After the fall of the Shah and the decline of the Iranian military threat, Saudi Arabia did substantially increase production (in 1980–81), creating a temporary oil glut and thus inhibiting price increases. One consequence has apparently been to assist the United States in its efforts to bar Iranian oil from the international market. See Patrick Clawson, "Iran's Economy: Between Crisis and Collapse," *MERIP Reports,* July 1981.

33. *U.S. Military Sales to Iran,* Staff Report to the Committee on Foreign Relations, U.S. Senate, July 1976. See Chapter 12 of the present volume.

Chapter Twelve. Armageddon Is Well Located

1. *Al Hamishmar,* May 10, 1978.

2. *Ha'aretz,* May 15, 1978.

3. Nadav Safran, *Israel: The Embattled Ally* (Cambridge, Mass.: Harvard University Press, 1978). Safran provides no evidence, but Jack Anderson has reported that "locked in secret Pentagon files is startling evidence that Israel maneuvered dangerously near the edge of nuclear war after the 1973 Arab assault. The secret documents claim that Israel came within hours of running out of essential arms. At this crucial moment, 'the possibility of nuclear arms was discussed with the U.S.,' declares one report." These secret papers, Anderson claims, show that the fear that Israel might resort to nuclear weapons was "the most compelling reason" for rushing conventional weapons to Israel. *Washington Post,* March 10, 1980.

4. *Economist,* November 19, 1977.

   The question of what is a terrorist attack and what is a reprisal is more a matter of ideology than of simple fact. See., e.g., Chapter 10, note 2, and the discussion of terrorism in notes 29, 33, 39, and 40 below. In the United States, it is standard to describe Israeli attacks as "reprisals" or "preemptive," but each terror attack has its precedents, and there are differences of perception as to what counts as violence (displacing people from their ancestral lands? returning to these lands to "steal" crops? killing innocents in retaliation for earlier violence?). Few Western commentators would regard the kidnapping at Ma'alot as "retaliation" (a number of the teenage hostages were killed during an Israeli military attack attempting to free them after Israel rejected negotiation efforts). Rather, it is regarded as terrorism (as it was), unprovoked (a different question). Two days before the Ma'alot raid, an Israeli air attack on the village of El-Kfeir in Lebanon killed four civilians. This is not regarded as terrorism, but rather as "defensive." Similarly, hijackings are regarded as terrorism—in some cases; not when the hijacker is attempting to escape the Soviet Union. Or consider the capture of a Syrian civilian airliner shortly after takeoff by Israeli military aircraft in December 1954. In his personal diary, Israeli Prime Minister Moshe Sharett notes that the U.S. State Department informed him that "our action was without precedent in the history of international practice." I do not recall seeing this precedent-setting act mentioned in the history of modern terrorism. In fact, a comparison with Ma'alot would be quite to the point, as Livia Rokach points out in her study *Israel's Sacred Terrorism* (Belmont,

Mass.: Association of Arab-American University Graduates, 1980), which is based largely on Sharett's *Personal Diary* (*Yoman Ishi*, Hebrew, *Ma'ariv*, 1979). The Israeli hijacking took place the day after five Israeli soldiers were captured while installing wiretap equipment on the Syrian telephone network. Concerning the hijacking, Sharett wrote in his diary that "it is clear that [Chief-of-Staff] Dayan's intention . . . is to get [Syrian] hostages in order to obtain the release of our prisoners in Damascus," exactly the intent of the PLO terrorists at Ma'alot. The Western reaction is not exactly identical.

The same might be said about such actions as the Israeli attack on El-Kfeir. In fact, that was not reported in the U.S. media, and is known at all in the United States only because this happened to be the village of the parents of U.S. Senator James Abourezk. The regular Israeli attacks on Lebanon, with many civilian casualties, are rarely noted, or if the press reports shelling, abduction, and killing by Israeli forces (e.g., James Markham, *New York Times*, August 17, 1975), there is generally no comment. For a rare general discussion, see Judith Coburn, "Israel's Ugly Little War," *New Times*, March 7, 1975. American correspondents in Beirut report privately that the New York office of a major television network suppressed a documentary in 1975 on the effects of Israeli military actions in southern Lebanon. Some day, perhaps, a study will be done on home-office decisions on correspondents' reports, not only in the case of Lebanon. On Lebanon, see the Afterword to Chapter 9 and Introduction, note 195.

Sharett reports (secondhand) some interesting views of Moshe Dayan's on the reprisal policy (April 26, 1955; Rokach, *op, cit.*). Dayan's reported view was that "the main thing" is that reprisals "make it possible for us to maintain a high level of tension among our population and in the army. Without these actions we would have ceased to be a combative people and without the discipline of a combative people we are lost." Sharett writes that "the conclusions from Dayan's words are clear: This state . . . must see the sword as the main, if not the only instrument with which to keep its morale high and to retain its moral tension. Toward this end it may, no—it *must*—invent dangers, and to do this it must adopt the method of provocation-and-revenge. . . . And above all—let us hope for a new war with the Arab countries, so that we may finally get rid of our troubles and acquire our space." While Sharett himself strongly objected to this tendency, he was unable to prevent it from developing.

5. Henry Kissinger, *American Foreign Policy*, expanded ed. (New York: Norton, 1974). In the memorandum cited in note 27 of Chapter 11, Kissinger claims that the United States "sent an armored division down the Autobahn," "flew aircraft from the Sixth Fleet to Lod Airport in order to pick up staging plans," and "put the 82nd Airborne on alert," causing the Syrians to withdraw. He also notes that "none of this was in the newspapers." It is an open question whether it happened, or whether the story was put together to impress his audience of Jewish leaders. If the point was to "send a signal to Syria" (to adopt some Kissingerese), it is difficult to see why secrecy would have been helpful. Furthermore, others who should have known about it do not report these actions. It seems more likely that it was Israeli warnings that deterred Syria from moving to defend the Palestinians who were then being routed in Jordan. See below.
Kissinger is not noteworthy for his accuracy. See Chapter 6, above.

6. U.S. Senate, Committee on Energy and Natural Resources, Henry M. Jackson, chairman, *Assess to Oil—The United States Relationships with Saudi Arabia and Iran* (Washington, D.C.: U.S. Government Printing Office, 1977). Cf. Chapter 8, above.

7. *Ibid.,* pp. 84, 111.

8. Ibid., pp. 81, 80. Cf. Chapter 11, above.

9. William B. Quandt, *Decade of Decisions* (Berkeley: University of California Press, 1977); Bernard Reich, *Quest for Peace* (New Brunswick: Transaction Books, 1977); Safran, *op. cit.*

10. See Chapter 11, above.

11. Walter Laqueur, *The Struggle for the Middle East* (New York: Macmillan, 1969).

12. *The Middle East* (May 1978).

13. The latter fact sheds some light on the idea, occasionally voiced, that Israel's "economic miracle" can serve as a model for developing countries.

14. *New York Times,* May 19, 1978.

15. *Christian Science Monitor,* May 25, 1978.

16. Just how unstable the situation is became clear in Iran, not long after this article appeared; and shortly after, in Saudi Arabia, where a rebellion centered in Mecca in November 1979 reached threatening proportions. See "Instability and Insurrection in Saudi Arabia," *International Currency Review* (London) (January 1980), where it is claimed that there have been a dozen coup attempts in Saudi Arabia in recent years, and massive corruption and thievery.

17. *New York Times,* May 15, 1978. See Chapter 7.

18. *Boston Globe,* April 29, 1978.

19. Cf. Quandt, *op. cit.,* pp. 135–36. For the documents, see John N. Moore, ed., *The Arab-Israeli Conflict* (Princeton: Princeton University Press 1974), vol. 3, pp. 1107f. Israel agreed that Egypt had "expressed its willingness to enter into a peace agreement with Israel"—in fact, on better terms for Israel than in Sadat's subsequent trip to Jerusalem in November 1977, which was regarded as such a dramatic breakthrough, since there was no mention of Palestinian self-determination, which Israel now claims to be the main stumbling block barring a settlement. On Israel's unwillingness to accept Sadat's 1971 offer, see the comments by General Haim Bar-Lev, a cabinet member in the Meir and Rabin governments, in the Labor Party journal *Ot,* March 9, 1972: "I think that we could obtain a peace settlement on the basis of the earlier [pre-June 1967] borders. If I were persuaded that this is the maximum that we might obtain, I would say: agreed. But I think that it is not the maximum. I think that if we continue to hold out, we will obtain more." Cited by Amnon Kapeliouk, *Le Monde diplomatique* (October 1977). See also Chapter 11, note 27.

It is intriguing to see how American commentators committed to Israeli power and the denial of Palestinian national rights deal with these annoying facts. According to Theodore Draper, for example, Sadat's 1977 "program called for peace on the most extreme Arab terms, except for those Arab extremists who would be satisfied with nothing but the total destruction of the state of Israel"—we are presumably to understand that Sadat's program called for the partial destruction of Israel. Draper continues:

> *For Israel, the dilemma was excruciating. Why and how Israel came to be in the Sinai, Gaza and the West Bank are too often forgotten or ignored. They had been occupied as the result of a war openly instigated by Egypt, Syria and Jordan with the outright, boisterously proclaimed aim of doing away with the very existence of Israel. Even Mr. Sadat admittedly did not accept its existence until he decided to come to Jerusalem. Never having contemplated a victory on the scale of 1967, the*

Israelis did not know what to do with it and first thought of trading occupied territories for a peace treaty. Nasser's Egypt could have had Mr. Sadat's Jerusalem peace plan for the asking in the summer of 1967.

(Review of Ezer Weizman, *The Battle for Peace* [New York: Bantam, 1981]; *N.Y. Times Book Review*, May 17, 1981.)

Let us put aside this rather simple-minded version of the events of 1967 and the claim, for which Draper presents no particle of evidence, that Israel would have agreed to total withdrawal to the pre-June 1967 borders in 1967 (Sadat's "extremist program" of 1977, according to Draper). What is more interesting is Draper's claim that Sadat "admittedly" did not accept the existence of Israel prior to November 1977, and his complete silence concerning the plain fact, typically "forgotten or ignored," that more than six years earlier Sadat had offered Israel terms more favorable to it than those of 1977 while clearly and explicitly "accept[ing] its existence," only to meet with a complete rebuff on the part of Israel and the United States.

20. See Reich, Quandt, *op. cit.*, for details.

21. Kapeliouk, *Israël: la fin des mythes* (Paris: Albin Michel, 1975). See also Jon Kinche, *There Could Have Been Peace* (New York: Dial Press, 1973).

22. See Chapter 6, above.

23. For discussion at the time, see my paper "The Interim Agreement," *New Politics* (Winter 1975–76).

24. See *Emda*, Tel Aviv (April 1978). For an attempt to estimate the actual cost of the settlements in the occupied territories, see Zvi Sholinder, *Ha'aretz*, July 25, 1980. While much is obscure, it is clear that the sums are extremely high. For example, it appears that over 80 percent of the state budget for construction in agricultural communities is devoted to the occupied territories.

25. The U.N. session was convened at Syrian initiative; the "confrontation states" (Egypt, Jordan, and Syria) participated by invitation in the debate, as did the PLO (it was boycotted by Israel). The vetoed resolution was an adaptation of U.N. Resolution 242 to include the establishment of a Palestinian state in the West Bank and Gaza Strip. Egypt, Syria, Jordan, and the PLO denounced the American veto, Syria calling it "a betrayal" and the PLO condemning "the tyranny of the veto." Their support for the resolution, with its explicit proposal for a two-state settlement with recognized borders and guarantees for territorial integrity, security, etc., was further noted by U.N. Ambassador Malik of the USSR in his closing statement (*New York Times*, January 13, 27, 1976). Subsequently, Egypt, Syria, and Jordan "informed the United States that they would sign peace treaties with Israel as part of an overall Middle East settlement" (Bernard Gwertzman, *New York Times*, August 21, 1977). There had, in fact, been many indications on the part of the Arab states and the PLO that they would accept a two-state settlement, prior to Sadat's November 1977 offers. See Afterword to Chapter 9, above.

26. Note that this is also essentially the thesis of U.S. intelligence analysts. Cf. Chapter 11, above. See also Kimche, *op. cit.*

27. Quandt's figures are inaccurate, as Reich's more detailed account shows, but the point stands.

28. It is difficult to see why the thesis that Quandt disparages, while providing evidence to support it, should be called "Marxist." In fact, this term, like "economic determinism" or "conspiracy theory," seems to serve in mainstream scholarship merely as a device for

deflecting attention away from rational analysis of policy formation in terms of the distribution of domestic power, as noted several times in these essays.

29. Arabs constituted about 90 percent of the population of Palestine at the time of the Balfour Declaration, but as Lord Balfour explained, "Zionism, be it right or wrong, good, or bad, is rooted in age-long tradition, in present needs, in future hopes, of far profounder import than the desires and prejudices of the 700,000 Arabs who now inhabit that ancient land." Quoted in Christopher Sykes, *Crossroads to Israel* (London: William Collins, 1965).

A fact often ignored is that the Jewish inhabitants of Palestine at the time by no means generally supported the Zionist program, a fact that bears on the justification for these policies based on the persistence of Jewish settlement in Palestine, specifically, Jerusalem. I know of no careful study of their attitudes, but whatever the breakdown may have been, the threat to Zionist goals was clear and was disturbing to the early settlers. We can learn something about this from the official history of the Haganah ("self-defense" forces), the military arm of the Jewish community (*Toldot Habaganah*, vol. 2, Ma'arachot Publishing House, pp. 251f., a section on "special activities"). The section concerns a Dutch Jewish poet, Dr. Israel Jacob de Haan, who came to Israel and became involved with the Orthodox Jewish community (the "old Yishuv," the pre-Zionist Jewish settlement). He began to organize them in anti-Zionist political activities and "to construct a united front of the old Yishuv with the Arab Higher Committee against the new Yishuv and the Zionist enterprise." His activities took on a "pathological character" when, together with Rabbi Sonnenfeld, he proclaimed "the opposition of native-born Jews to Zionism" (the pathological character of his activities was further revealed, the official history states, by his homosexuality). The Central Bureau of Haganah gave an order "to remove the traitor from the land of the living," and he was duly assassinated by two Haganah agents, recent immigrants from Russia, "as he left the small synagogue in the 'Shaarey Tsedek' hospital" on June 30, 1924.

The section concludes with a description of another "special action," the placing of a bomb in the house of an Arab leader who lived near the Wailing Wall, where Arab youths were alleged to have been disturbing Jews at prayer (summer 1927).

Contrary to the impression often conveyed by the American literature, terrorism has not been a monopoly of the PLO. See notes 4, 33, 39, and 40.

30. See Chapter 9, above.

31. See the references of Chapter 9, note 55.

32. See Kennett Love, *Suez* (New York: McGraw-Hill, 1969).

33. See Livia Rokach, *Le Monde diplomatique* (April 1978). The man in charge of the Israeli terrorist group in Egypt, which bombed U.S. and British installations (as well as public buildings) in an attempt to create hostility between the United States and Nasser, describes these activities in a personal memoir: Avni el-Ad, *Decline of Honor* (Chicago: Regnery, 1976).

Israeli terrorists are reported to have carried out similar acts in Iraq in 1949, under instructions from Yigal Allon, a leading representative of the kibbutz movement: "In attempts to portray the Iraqis as anti-American and to terrorize the Jews, the Zionists planted bombs in the U.S. Information Service library and in synagogues. Soon leaflets began to appear urging Jews to flee to Israel" (Wilbur Crane Eveland, *Ropes of Sand* [New York: Norton, 1980], p. 48). Eveland, who was the military attaché of the U.S.

embassy in Baghdad and later worked for the CIA in the Middle East as well as serving on the White House and Pentagon policy planning staffs, adds that "although the Iraqi police later provided our embassy with evidence to show that the synagogue and library bombings as well as the anti-Jewish and anti-American leaflet campaigns had been the work of an underground Zionist organization, most of the world believed reports that Arab terrorism had motivated the flight of the Iraqi Jews whom the Zionists had 'rescued' really just in order to increase Israel's Jewish population." Iraqi Jews in Israel have testified to the same effect (cf. Uri Davis and Norton Mezvinsky, *Documents from Israel* [London: Ithaca Press, 1975]), but their reports received little notice. It will be a long time, no doubt, before a serious account of all of this enters the general or academic literature on Israel.

Prime Minister Sharett's personal diaries constitute another historical source that is likely to be consigned to oblivion. For informative excerpts and analysis, see Rokach, *Israel's Sacred Terrorism*. See pp. 37f. on the sabotage operations in Egypt in 1954. Though Sharett was informed of the facts immediately after the sabotage ring was broken up by Egyptian police, when the trial of the saboteurs took place he denounced "the plot . . . and the show trial . . . against a group of Jews . . . victims of false accusations," and his party's paper (*Davar*, Labor Party), accused the Egyptian government of "a Nazi-inspired policy." Privately, Sharett was much distressed; he described Defense Minister Lavon, whom he apparently regarded as bearing responsibility for this affair, in these terms, to the secretary-general of the Labor Party. "He inspired and nurtured the unworthy adventuristic army and preached the lesson that not the Arab countries but the Western Powers are the enemy, and the only way to deter them from their conspiracies is by a direct action that will terrorize them."

Sharett was no less outraged by the Gaza raid of February 1955, and by the many other acts of violence and terror initiated by Israeli military forces during the period, but did nothing about them.

After his participation in the terrorist actions in Egypt, Lavon became the secretary-general of the Histadrut (the socialist labor union, which plays a major role in Israeli society and in the economy). According to the respected Israeli journalist Nahum Barnea, Lavon gave orders that were "much more severe" than those leading to the sabotage operations in Egypt during his tenure as minister of defense, including an attempt "to poison the water sources in the Gaza Strip and the demilitarized zone on the Syrian-Israeli border." Barnea does not make explicit whether these alleged orders were executed (Nahum Barnea, *Davar*, January 26, 1979).

34. *Mitsrayim vebaFada 'in* [Egypt and the Fedayeen], Givat Haviva, 1975. See also Love, *op. cit.*; and Rokach, *op. cit.*, for important material from the Sharett diaries.

35. Uri Davis, *Israel: Utopia Incorporated* (London: Zed Press, 1977). See Chapter 9, above, note 48.

36. David Hirst, *The Gun and the Olive Branch* (New York: Harcourt Brace Jovanovich, 1977).

37. *Manchester Guardian Weekly*, April 2, 1978.

38. The public and propaganda pretense is that the Arabs fled, expecting to return after the victory of Arab armies. In internal records, the pretense is abandoned. See, e.g., the discussion in Sharett's diaries of the cabinet meetings of March 1955 discussing Ben-Gurion's proposal to attack the Gaza Strip, then held by Egypt, and to disperse its

inhabitants. In Sharett's words: "The first round would be: Israel aggressively invades the Gaza Strip. The second: Israel causes again the terrified flight of masses of Arab refugees." Sharett opposed this proposal, believing that "what we succeeded in achieving . . . in 1948, cannot be repeated whenever we desire it." For lengthy quotes, see Rokach, *Israel's Sacred Terrorism.*

39. *Al Hamishmar,* March 3, 1978; a somewhat sanitized version appeared in the *Jerusalem Post,* February 28, 1978. It is hardly possible to imagine that the history of this man, Shmuel Lahis, or the significance of the fact that he was appointed to the highest executive position in the World Zionist Organization, would be discussed in the American press or in the massive literature devoted to the country which is the prime recipient of U.S. military and economic aid. The *New York Times* had a good opportunity, however. On February 19, 1981, the *Times* reported that Lahis had resigned his position in protest over the failure of the government to act on a report he wrote urging that financial benefits be provided to induce the 500,000 Israelis who, he contends, are living in the United States to return to Israel. On the same day, the *Times* published a report by Kathleen Teltsch headed "400 Intellectuals Form 'Struggle for Freedom' Unit," describing a new organization directed by Midge Decter, who said, "The idea for the committee emerged almost two years ago after she and others attended a meeting in Jerusalem on international terrorism" from which "she came away convinced of the need for action against those who kidnap and throw bombs, many of whom are trained in the Soviet Union and Cuba." Surely the coincidence offered a fine opportunity for an editorial on terrorism and the ways in which it is viewed in various countries of the world.

For a description of the massacre in the Lebanese village of Hula for which Lahis was responsible as perceived by the victims, see Rosemary Sayigh, *From Peasants to Revolutionaries* (London: Zed Press, 1979), a study based on interviews with Palestinian refugees. She reports, for example, the case of a young Lebanese boy who later joined the Palestinian resistance; his family fled their village "because the Zionists carried out a massacre in Hula, a village near ours," he informed her. If he takes part in a terrorist attack leading to an Israeli bombing of a village, the press will denounce this unprovoked act of Arab terrorism followed by an unfortunate (but understandable) Israeli reprisal.

40. The standard interpretation is so familiar that it is perhaps superfluous to document it. The most interesting examples, in my opinion, are those produced in left-liberal circles. See, for example, Michael Walzer, "The New Terrorists," *New Republic,* August 30, 1975. He considers the evolution in patterns of terrorism in the past generation. The "new terrorists," such as the PLO, are "thugs and fanatics" who murder at random, whereas in the good old days terrorism was a political weapon (which of course we deplore) directed to specific targets, as when the Zionist Stern Gang killed Lord Moyne in 1944, taking pains not to shoot the Egyptian constable who apprehended them. Walzer might have added that, as in the cases discussed earlier, the killers are honored in Israel; in this case, one of the commanders of the operation is speaker of the Knesset, while "the Israeli Ministry of Education and Culture published a special booklet to mark the thirtieth anniversary of the execution" of the two patriots who killed Lord Moyne (*Al Hamishmar,* April 4, 1975).

History records some other incidents that go unmentioned in Walzer's account, e.g., the murder of Jacob de Haan by Haganah in 1924 (see note 29), or the exploits of

Shmuel Lahis (see note 39), or the terrorist bombings in Iraq and Egypt (see note 33; official state terrorism in this case). There are a few other examples that are similarly overlooked. Within a year of its founding in 1937, the Irgun Zvai Leumi claimed about one hundred Arab civilian dead in random terrorism (e.g., dozens killed by bombs in marketplaces). Another ninety-one civilians (British, Jewish, Arab) were killed in the Irgun bombing of the King David Hotel in 1946, and Irgun and LEHI (the Stern Gang) killed 250 civilians at Deir Yassin, among many other examples. For a grisly and rather admiring report of Irgun-LEHI atrocities, including bombing, assassination, kidnapping, arson, often with random civilian targets, see J. Bowyer-Bell, *Terror out of Zion* (New York: St. Martin's, 1977)—as history, this account, based largely on Irgun and LEHI sources, is not worth very much, but the record suffices to refute the stories about "military targets" and "warnings."

These avowedly terrorist organizations had no monopoly on atrocities in the pre-state period. Consider the sabotage of the ship *Patria* by a Haganah agent in Haifa harbor in 1940, with 240 Jewish refugees and a dozen British police killed (not intended, but then one might say the same about many terrorist acts of the PLO years later), or the Haganah atrocities at Khissas in December 1947 and Sassa the following February. Terrorism continued after the state was established, both official terrorism, as in the cases mentioned earlier (see also Chapter 10, note 1), and "retail terrorism" such as the murder of U.N. mediator Folke Bernadotte in 1948 when he was attempting to realize the U.N. provisions for an internationalized Jerusalem; one of the murderers, never prosecuted, was a close friend and fellow kibbutz member of Ben-Gurion (see *Yediot Abronot*, February 28, 1977, where it is also reported that Gideon Hausner, the Eichmann prosecutor who was then legal advisor to the prime minister, helped conceal the identity of the assassins). Or the brutal murder of innocent Bedouins in a "reprisal" by a group led by Meir Har-Tsion of Kibbutz Ein Harod in March 1955 (on the events, and Prime Minister Sharett's reaction both to the actions and to the contrasting behavior of Jordan, which arrested Arab terrorists, and Israel, which adopted the "shameful procedure" of releasing Har-Tsion and his group, see Rokach, *op. cit.*).

These examples barely touch the surface. The memoirs of the U.N. commanders give an ample record of terrorism on both sides; and Israeli terrorism, in particular, is well documented in semiofficial histories in Hebrew (e.g., Uri Milshtein's *Wars of the Paratroopers*, 1969; a Hebrew collection from these sources has been compiled by Israel Shahak: "Sefer Hateror Hatsioni," Jerusalem). Many examples also appear in the Hebrew press. See, e.g., Uri Milshtein (*Ha'aretz*, supplement, November 17, 1978), describing murderous Haganah and Palmach attacks on Arab villages and provocations that incited violence in late 1947 and early 1948, well before the engagement of armies of the Arab states in May 1948. Or Eyal Kafkafi, a kibbutz member of the Labor party (*Davar*, September 4, 1979), who deplores the "ghetto mentality" revealed in attitudes towards Israeli Arabs, which must be combated in the manner of earlier years when Arabs were simply expelled "to make room for a flourishing culture, which will help many others live," in the words of Yoseph Weitz, who was in charge of settlement in the pre-state period, referring to expulsion of Arabs in 1933. Kafkafi reports a letter written on November 8, 1948, reporting eyewitness testimony by a soldier who arrived in the Arab village of Doeima the day after it was occupied, where Brigade 89 "had killed 80–100 Arabs, women and children. They killed the children by crushing their skulls with sticks. There was not even one house without dead people." Arabs left in the village were put into houses which were then blown up, among other atrocities reported, "not during the heat of the battle" but "as a system of expulsion and elimination." There are many other examples.

It is hardly the case that old-fashioned selective terrorism has now given way to random murder by fanatical Palestinians, or that acts of Jewish terrorism are "the rare exceptions in terrible moments that cannot in any way be compared with the odious consistent terrorism of the Arabs" (David Schoenbrun, *New York Arts Journal*, September–November 1977), pretty much the standard line.

As noted above, the terrorists are now honored in Israel (e.g., Moshe Brilliant, *New York Times*, June 14, 1977: "Mr. Shamir and his associates, now acknowledged as patriots, were condemned and hounded in their time by a Jewish community that regarded them as ruthless killers"—a misleading statement, as we see from the reaction to Haganah terrorism). The reaction to earlier terrorist atrocities is also sometimes remarkable. Consider the village of Kafr Kassem, where Israeli border guards slaughtered forty-seven villagers in 1956 in a completely unprovoked attack; this was acknowledged as a crime—the military commander held responsible was fined one piaster; in 1960, a lieutenant who served a brief term in prison for the murder of forty-three Arab civilians was appointed officer for Arab affairs in the town of Ramle. At the time of the establishment of the State of Israel, 4,000 dunams, a third of the land of the village, had been expropriated. After the 1967 war, the government decided to take another 3,000 dunams, but the courts, recognizing that Kafr Kassem was something of a special case, determined that only 2,000 dunams should be expropriated (cf. Ran Kislev, *Ha'aretz*, July 27, 1976, one of a series of articles that details many examples of the real treatment of Arab citizens of Israel).

Perhaps the last word should be left for Deir Yassin, scene of the most atrocious single massacre, conducted by the armed forces commanded by the current prime minister, who is quite eloquent in his denunciations of crimes against Jews. A report in *Middle East International* (August 1, 1980) describes how bulldozers are "busily erasing the last traces of Deir Yassin" to prepare the ground for a new settlement for Orthodox Jewish families, where "streets will be named after units in both the Irgun and the Haganah"—perhaps in memory of the fact that, contrary to what is commonly assumed, the attack on Deir Yassin was authorized by Haganah, and units of Palmach (the kibbutz-based strike force of Haganah) participated in the attack (see the accounts based on eyewitness and participant reports in *Yediot Abronot*, April 4, May 5, 1972; see also [Res.] General Meir Pail, an eyewitness, who reports that the slaughter of the 250 victims by Irgun and LEHI took place after the departure of Palmach forces that "completed the capture of the village"; *Yediot Abronot*, April 20, 1972).

Further details appear in the *Ha'aretz* supplement (*Kol Ha'ir*), June 6, 1980, where it is reported that the prime minister's office had received a letter from a private citizen requesting that one of the streets in the new housing development in Deir Yassin be named after his uncle, who "was one of the commanders of the Deir Yassin operation." But "the request had to be rejected" because the Jerusalem municipality "had decided that only the names of entire units [of Palmach and the Irgun] would be immortalized on the site." Cited in *Israeli Mirror*, June 27, 1980.

41. Yehoshua Porath, *The Palestinian Arab National Movement: 1929–1939* (London: Frank Cass, 1977). See Chapter 9, above, note 74.

42. There is by now an ample literature on this shameful topic. On the U.S. role, see Arthur

D. Morse, *While Six Million Died: A Chronicle of American Apathy* (New York: Random House, 1967); David S. Wyman, *Paper Walls: America and the Refugee Crisis, 1938–1941* (Amherst: University of Massachusetts Press, 1968); Saul S. Friedman, *No Haven for the Oppressed: United States Policy toward Jewish Refugees, 1938–1945* (Detroit: Wayne State University Press, 1973). The American Jewish Community also did less than it might have. For example, in early 1941 a Polish Jewish lawyer, Zorach Warhaftig, who had managed to reach Japan through Russia, arranged with a Japanese shipping company to send as many East European Jewish refugees as could reach Japan to the United States; transit visas would be issued as soon as the money for steamship tickets was guaranteed. Warhaftig, who had been a member of the executive board of the World Jewish Congress in Warsaw and had contacts with the Joint Distribution Committee, transmitted the offer by cable to these organizations, but was informed in response that the money could not be provided until the refugees reached Japan. The proposal was aborted, and many more victims ended in crematoria. See Rabbi Marvin Tokayer and Mary Swartz, *The Fugu Plan* (New York: Paddington Press, 1979).

On the unwillingness of American Zionists to support plans for bringing European Jews to the United States in 1942, see Alfred M. Lilienthal, *The Zionist Connection* (New York: Dodd, Mead, 1978). See also Davis, *op. cit.*

43. Maurice Guernier, *An-Nabar Arab Report and Memo*, Beirut, April 17, 1978.

Chapter Thirteen. The United States and East Timor

1. For documentation bearing on the period through 1978 and much further detail, see Chomsky and E. S. Herman, *The Political Economy of Human Rights*, vol. 1 (Boston: South End Press, 1979), chapter 3, section 4.4, and references cited there. Also Arnold Kohen and John Taylor, *An Act of Genocide*, TAPOL, U.K. (1979); available from the East Timor Human Rights Committee, Box 363, Clinton Station, Syracuse, N.Y. 13201.

2. Jack Anderson, *Washington Post*, November 9, 1979. Air Force General Brent Scowcroft, President Ford's National Security Adviser, stated: "I guess it was fundamentally a matter of recognizing reality. We really had no reasonable options. . . . It made no sense to antagonize the Indonesians. . . . East Timor was not a viable entity"; Daniel Southerland, "U.S. role in plight of Timor: an issue that won't go away," *Christian Science Monitor*, March 6, 1980.

   U.S. officials have repeatedly claimed that the United States was unaware of what was happening in Timor, but it has always been obvious that this was mere pretense; cf. Chomsky and Herman, *op. cit.*, and the Afterword which follows. Anderson notes a classified U.S. intelligence report of September 19, 1975, describing an Indonesian attack that met "stiff resistance from Fretilin fighters." Another report states that Indonesian generals were "losing patience with President Suharto's go-slow approach to the Portuguese Timor problem and . . . pressing him to authorize direct military intervention." A December 3 intelligence report states that "ranking Indonesian civilian government leaders have decided that the only solution in the Portuguese Timor situation is for Indonesia to launch an open offensive against Fretilin," and another report alerted Ford and Kissinger that Suharto would bring up the Timor issue on their visit to Jakarta and would "try and elicit a sympathetic attitude" from Ford, who informed Anderson that the U.S. national interest "had to be on the side of Indonesia," while giving what Anderson calls his "tacit approval" to the invasion. In fact, there is no doubt that the United States was keeping close watch on the situation.

3. Fully aware of what they were doing, the Ford and then the Carter Administration not only provided the material support for the massacre, but placed no constraints on how U.S. equipment should be used, in clear violation of the 1958 U.S.-Indonesian bilateral arms agreement which requires that U.S. arms be used only for defensive purposes. Administration witness David Kenney stated in congressional hearings that "as long as we are giving military assistance of any sort to Indonesia we are not telling where they will or will not use it. We have not done so so far" (Hearings before the Subcommittees on Asian and Pacific Affairs and on International Organizations of the Committee on Foreign Affairs, House of Representatives, 96th Congress, 2nd session, February 1980, p. 193). Kenney was at the time Legislative Management Officer for Human Rights (sic) in the Congressional Relations Office at the State Department and is a specialist on Indonesia. From 1975 through 1979, the United States furnished over $250 million in military assistance to Indonesia, most of it after the Carter Administration accelerated the arms flow. See Scott Sidel, "The United States and Genocide in East Timor," *Journal of Contemporary Asia*, vol. 11, no. 1 (1981).

4. Daniel P. Moynihan with Suzanne Weaver, *A Dangerous Place* (Boston: Little, Brown, 1978).

5. Not for lack of effort. On December 8, 1980, the *New York Times* published a report of an address by now-Senator Moynihan (whose gall knows no limits) to the Committee for United Nations Integrity. The *Times* reports: "The conference addressed by Senator Moynihan, which was called to assess the direction of the United Nations, issued a statement signed by more than 100 scholars, scientists and artists that denounced the world body as 'no longer the guardian of social justice, human rights and equality among nations.' It said the organization is 'perverted by irrelevant political machinations' and 'is in danger of becoming a force against peace itself.' " On the same day, the *Times* carried an editorial on the Indonesian invasion of East Timor, which led to the death of "a tenth to a third" of the population in a country which "like Cambodia . . . has become synonymous with starvation and refugees." "Americans have given some emergency aid," the editorial notes, "but Washington's role has not been glorious." The actual role of Washington is not further detailed; the editorial is entitled "The Shaming of Indonesia." A letter of mine, commenting on the oversight and on the interesting conjunction of the editorial and the report of the address by the man who takes pride in rendering the U.N. ineffective in preventing the massacre while condemning it as a danger against peace because it is "perverted by irrelevant political machinations," was not published.

The Committee for United Nations Integrity was, of course, concerned not with Timor but with U.N. support for Palestinian rights, a major crime of the U.N. in American eyes. Those who might appreciate some comic relief may turn to an advertisement in the *New York Times* on October 16, 1980, where an Israeli lobbying group that operates part-time as a human rights organization denounces the U.N. for its "silence concerning human rights violations of the Kurds, Berbers and millions of beleaguered people in Cambodia, Vietnam and Timor." The U.N. has been far from silent concerning Timor, our specific concern here, though the U.S. press has effectively silenced U.N. protests as well as U.S. efforts to block them. Moynihan, incidentally, is one of the great heroes of the organization that placed this advertisement in the *Times* (the Anti-

Defamation League of B'nai B'rith, which is described in the Israeli press as "one of the main pillars" of Israeli propaganda in the U.S.; Beni Landau, *Ha'aretz*, July 28, 1981). Nineteen eighty-four approaches.

The reference to U.N. silence with regard to Cambodia and Vietnam presumably does not allude to the period when the United States was ravaging these lands. No doubt with Moynihan in mind, a State Department official conceded that our policy in Timor "has not been a policy of benign neglect. It's been a policy of malign neglect" (Southerland, *op. cit.*)—though a quarter billion dollars' worth of arms and active efforts to pervert the U.N. by irrelevant political machinations may not qualify exactly as "neglect" of any sort.

6. For extensive detail, see Chomsky and Herman, *op. cit.* U.S. efforts to "pervert" the U.N. were apparently not limited to "political machinations" of the Moynihan variety. The U.N. sent a fact-finding mission to East Timor a few weeks after the Indonesian invasion, but Indonesia prevented it from reaching the territory by such tactics as bombing areas where the mission was scheduled to land. A U.S. contribution is reported by Jack Anderson (*Washington Post*, November 8, 1979) on the basis of U.S. intelligence documents. At one point Indonesian authorities considered sinking the frigate with the U.N. observers on board. "U.S. intelligence agencies learned of the bizarre plot but buried the information deep in their files without alerting the U.N. representatives that their ship might be torpedoed."

7. Congressional Research Service, *Human Rights and U.S. Foreign Assistance*, Report for the Senate Committee on Foreign Relations (November 1979), p. 144.

8. Kathleen Teltsch, "Timor Priest, Charging Genocide, Seeks U.S. Help," *New York Times*, December 14, 1979.

9. Robert Levey, "Power play cripples E. Timor," *Boston Globe*, January 20, 1980, to date, the most accurate and comprehensive account by a professional U.S. journalist. Father Leoneto's testimony is also reported by Daniel Southerland, "East Timor's agony rivals that of Cambodia," *Christian Science Monitor*, international edition, December 17, 1979, citing his description of how "the Indonesians attacked relentlessly with infantry and with US-supplied, armed reconnaissance planes known as the OV-10 (Bronco). They concentrated people around the villages and resettlement centers. They stole at least part of the relief food and sold it."

Southerland notes that "Fr. Leoneto would have been glad to testify before the U.S. congressmen. He was not invited to do so. It might have offended the Indonesians, and it would, of course, have revived disputes about what happened in the past." He is discussing a December 4 congressional hearing. The reference to "reviving" disputes is a bit misleading, in that the disputes, far from the mainstream, were rarely noted in the U.S. media. See also Daniel Southerland, "East Timor: plight worse than Cambodia?," *Christian Science Monitor*, December 6, 1979.

10. Teltsch, *op. cit.* However, Father Leoneto's testimony did lead to a strong *New York Times* editorial ("An Unjust War in East Timor," December 24, 1979), its first condemnation of the war since 1975, noting that "although most of the weapons of suppression are American-made, Washington has muted its concern for the familiar pragmatic reasons. . . . American silence about East Timor contrasts oddly with the indignation over Cambodia; the suffering is great in both places." There is nothing odd about the contrast, however; in Cambodia, the suffering could be attributed to an official enemy, while in Timor it is the responsibility of the United States, so that the contrast is quite

predictable. The editorial also notes correctly that "Americans have only gradually become aware of the unjust war Indonesia has been waging in remote East Timor," without, however, explaining the reasons for the lack of awareness while the U.S.-backed massacre was proceeding for four years.

11. Jimmy Burns, "Indonesian troops 'taking supplies for the starving,' " *Observer,* January 20, 1980.

12. David Watts, "Relief is reaching East Timor but thousands have already died from Indonesian starvation policy," *The Times* (London), December 14, 1979.

13. For specific references and further discussion, see Chomsky and Herman, *op. cit.*

14. Henry Kamm, "War-Ravaged Timor Struggles Back from Abyss," *New York Times,* January 28, 1980. Kamm remarks that "Maj. Benny Mandalika of Indonesian military intelligence from Jakarta was always present, took notes during interviews not only with ordinary people but also with Indonesian officials of Timorese origin and often peered openly at the notes the reporter was taking. Explaining his actions when challenged, he said: 'I must stay with you so you get the right information. My boss told me to go with you wherever you go. If you interview the man in the street you may get the wrong information.' "

Kamm observes that the process of Indonesian annexation and pacification "remains enshrouded in partisan propaganda by both sides," but fails to explain on what basis he identifies "the least partisan sources," who believe "that both sides brought pressure on the population and that the savagery with which they conducted the war incited many to flee." Why, for example, is Father Leoneto not one of the "least partisan sources"? Or the many other anti-Fretilin refugees, Catholic priests, and letter-writers who smuggled out their pleas to put pressure on Indonesia to terminate the massacre, and whom the *Times* Southeast Asia correspondent studiously ignored for many years, and still does? These sources do not allege that the savagery of the war was equally divided—hardly plausible in any event, given the scale of force available and the very nature of the Indonesian attack on the civilian population. Kamm's show of evenhandedness is hardly more convincing than his parroting of the allegations of Indonesian generals in earlier years. His reference to "partisan propaganda by both sides" also fails to convey the fact that the partisan propaganda of one side, the U.S. government, completely dominated media coverage, typically presented as objective fact by the free press. See Chomsky and Herman, *op. cit.,* for extensive detail.

Alongside of Kamm's article, there is a page-long advertisement of the International Rescue Committee signed by its chairman, Leo Cherne, calling for action to compel the Vietnamese and their Russian backers to permit aid to be sent to Cambodia: "What is needed now, in addition to the expansion of humanitarian aid, is an outcry of indignation so loud that it will be heard in Vietnam and the Soviet Union. It is not true that the men in Moscow and Hanoi are impervious to world opinion. They can be shamed into action. And if they cannot, at least we will have tried. By keeping silent, we are letting them get away with murder." In Cambodia, that is; where, incidentally, international relief officials at the same time were insisting that the Vietnamese and the regime they had installed in Cambodia were successfully doing what could be done to alleviate the famine in that ravaged land.

On Cherne's solicitude for refugees, see Chapter 2, note 1.

15. James M. Markham, "Refugees from East Timor Report Famine Situation," *New York Times,* January 29, 1980. Markham reports the testimony of refugees from late 1979,

ethnic Chinese who had succeeded in bribing their way out of East Timor, which one describes in these terms: "Everyone wants to leave. It is the land of the devil." They were reluctant to speak "for fear of Indonesian reprisals against family members whose freedom they hoped to purchase." They describe beatings, executions, massive deaths from starvation, diversion of humanitarian relief by Indonesian officers, torture and disappearances, efforts to impose Indonesian nationality, regular bombing by what "appeared to be small American-made Bronco observation planes," and many Indonesian casualties "ferried to the military hospital in Dili by helicopter." One described Dili as "a world of terror." Like the other refugees in Lisbon, most seemed apolitical. One "tough-looking man" said that he had been "taken into the mountains by the guerrillas because they suspected him of being a member" of UDT: "His sentiments seemed to lie more with his one-time Fretilin captors than with the Indonesians."

Previously, American journalists had scrupulously avoided the refugees in Lisbon—or at least their testimony concerning Timor (cf. Chomsky and Herman, *op. cit.*). Refugees with tales of Communist atrocities receive a rather different treatment. In an effort to overcome this press failure to report refugee testimony, Timorese refugees were brought to the United States by private parties concerned with the issue; for example, four refugees (including three who were Markham's informants) were brought to the United States in mid-January 1980 and taken to see editors of several major newspapers, but not a word of their testimony appeared in the U.S. press, to my knowledge, and these efforts led to no notable efforts to seek out or attend to refugee testimony. One might argue that the press should be skeptical of "pre-selected" refugees, possibly a valid argument, had the press not been so careful to avoid selecting them itself.

In avoiding Timorese refugees with their unacceptable and unwanted information, the press was mimicking the behavior of the State Department. See p. 372.

16. See the articles cited above; and many important reports and comments by Alexander Cockburn in the *Village Voice;* also "Another Cambodia, with Uncle Sam in a supporting role," *New Republic*, November 3, 1979, a generally accurate article signed by editor Morton Kondracke; and a *Christian Science Monitor* editorial, "East Timor—the other famine," December 18, 1979, which calls for an "outpouring of compassion" while completely ignoring the U.S. role in bringing about the horrors it describes.

17. On the Western reaction to this massacre, see pp. 372–73.

18. Cf. Chomsky and Herman, *op. cit.*, chapter 4, section 1, for discussion and references.

19. Arnold Kohen, "The Cruel Case of Indonesia," *Nation*, November 26, 1977.

20. A. J. Langguth, review of Chomsky and Herman, *op. cit., Nation*, February 16, 1980.

21. "The New Foreign Correspondence," *Washington Journalism Review* (March 1980).

22. See, *inter alia*, the statement submitted by Father Francisco Maria Fernandes and Father Apolinario Guterres, Catholic priests "who represent the East Timor Refugee Committee in Portugal," and who state that they "were forced to leave Timor by the Indonesians because we had issued an appeal to the Royal Netherlands Ambassador in Jakarta on behalf of East Timorese in West Timor, requesting his assistance in evacuating these people to Portugal." They give an extensive account of Indonesian atrocities in East Timor, execution of many refugees in West Timor, expulsion of seven thousand refugees from West to East Timor in May 1976 to prevent them from going to Portugal in accordance with arrangements by the Netherlands ambassador, etc. "We

are talking about genocide," they say, alleging that "Indonesia's war of saturation bombing and indiscriminate killing continues unabated" while thousands of Timorese are barred from emigration and "most of the people of our country have not received any aid due to the inaccessibility of their camps and, in particular, because of widespread Indonesian official corruption." Half of the budget for the International Red Cross program is spent on helicopters to transport aid around East Timor, they observe: "This is money that will go directly to the Indonesian government. Indonesia has planes and helicopters [thanks to the United States] to kill our people, but helicopters to help them must be leased for profit."

See also the testimony of Father Fernandes at the June 10, 1980, session of the hearings before a subcommittee of the Committee on Appropriations, House of Representatives, 96th Congress, 2nd session, Subcommittee on Foreign Operations and Related Agencies, Part 6 (Washington, D.C.: U.S. Government Printing Office, 1980), also unreported in the U.S. press. Father Fernandes states here that as many as 300,000 Timorese may have died in the course of the invasion. See "Accounts of Repression in East Timor Contradict U.S. View in House Inquiry," Reuters, *International Herald Tribune,* June 13, 1980.

23. Bernard D. Nossiter, *New York Times,* October 26, November 12, 1979.
24. "Cambodia and Timor," editorial, *Wall Street Journal,* February 6, 1980.

Afterword to Chapter Thirteen

1. *Washington Journalism Review* (March 1980).
2. The terminology is that of Chomsky and Herman, *The Political Economy of Human Rights,* where numerous examples are discussed.
3. For example, the *Columbia Journalism Review.* Perhaps I may relate a personal incident. In October 1978 I testified on Timor before the United Nations General Assembly Fourth Committee, concentrating on the U.S. role and the media cover-up. A slightly revised version appeared in *Inquiry* ("East Timor: the Press Cover-up," February 19, 1979). At about that time, the *Columbia Journalism Review* suggested that I do an article on the U.S. media and Cambodia. I suggested instead the case of Timor, which was far more important both in what it reveals and for the obvious reason that exposure of the facts might, in this case, help to terminate ongoing atrocities. After some discussion, this request was denied, on the grounds that the Timor story was too obscure to arouse interest—the Nossiter-Karnow-Valeriani position. Thus the circle is complete; first, the media suppress a major story, then, a journal devoted to the performance of the media is unwilling to investigate the suppression because it has been so effective.
4. Statement by Mr. Richard Holbrooke, Assistant Secretary of State, before the House Subcommittee on Asian and Pacific Affairs, Committee on Foreign Affairs, December 4, 1979. Holbrooke did not attend the hearings, but submitted a written statement. He says that "in 1975 the collapse of Portuguese authority, civil war between the Timorese political factions and the subsequent Indonesian intervention seriously damaged the already fragile economic balance," as "is confirmed by reports of observers who visited East Timor in late 1975, before the Indonesian intervention." (On the reports of such observers, who in fact reported that the damage caused by the brief civil war was slight

and that Fretilin was carrying out constructive and apparently successful development program. See Chomsky and Herman, *The Washington Connection and Third World Fascism, The Political Economy of Human Rights*, vol. 1, section 4.4). In later years, he continues, "large numbers of the civilian population were forced to move and abandon farming, either as a result of Indonesian operations or Fretilin pressures, and the destruction of the primitive agricultural economy was completed." Compare the reports cited above, and many others like them.

Holbrooke summarized the U.S. role in later congressional hearings as follows: "In closing, I would like to emphasize that we will continue to play a constructive role in helping resolve the humanitarian problems which grew out of the tragic history of East Timor since 1975" (statement by Mr. Richard Holbrooke, Assistant Secretary of State, before the House Subcommittee on Foreign Operations, Committee on Appropriations, June 10, 1980, Draft III). Somehow, this does not seem to do justice completely to the U.S. role, for which he bore a primary responsibility.

In the December 4, 1979, hearings, U.S. Ambassador to Indonesia Edward E. Masters testified "on the basis of personal observation to the acute difficulties of poverty and malnutrition in East Timor. Much of this is the result of adverse geography and climatic conditions which will take a long time to overcome"—no other factors are mentioned, though elsewhere he does refer to "the disruption of the more recent fighting" after long Portuguese neglect.

A confidential cable from the Jakarta embassy to the State Department (March 20, 1980), reporting on a ten-day embassy visit to East Timor, explains that "the closed nature of the family system is in particular linked to the problem of continuing malnutrition," and "has created a pattern in which orphans and widows figure prominently among the acutely malnourished"; other reasons for suffering among widows and orphans—or for their existence—can be imagined. While international relief workers have found fault with Indonesian government policies, the cable continues, "they have been made aware of the extremely violent political struggle that preceded Indonesia's entry into the civil war." "The vast majority of the extremely backward population . . . have been the clear victims of [Portuguese] colonialism and civil war." On the aftermath of the three-week civil war of August–September 1975, see Chomsky and Herman, *op. cit.* It is intriguing to observe the almost fanatic level of lying in internal documents, as the government desperately tries to conceal the ugly truth from itself.

5. Benedict R. O'G. Anderson, statement delivered to the Fourth Committee of the United Nations General Assembly on East Timor, October 20, 1980. Professor Anderson of Cornell University is one of the world's leading specialists on Indonesia.

6. See my *American Power and the New Mandarins* (New York: Pantheon, 1969), pp. 33–35; *The Political Economy of Human Rights*, vol. 1, pp. 86, 217.

7. Benedict R. O'G. Anderson, testimony at the Hearings before the Subcommittees on Asian and Pacific Affairs and on International Organizations of the Committee on Foreign Affairs, House of Representatives, 96th Congress, 2nd session, February 1980, pp. 245f. (Washington, D.C.: U.S. Government Printing Office, 1980).

8. Norman Peagam, *San Francisco Chronicle*, September 13, 1978. Peagam was reporting for the *New York Times*, which was then on strike. For further reports on this visit, see *The Political Economy of Human Rights*, vol. 1, chapter 3, section 4.4.

9. *Far Eastern Economic Review*, September 29, 1978.

10. Henry Kamm, *New York Times*, January 28, 1980. The details of the "sordid delay" in

admitting the ICRC are discussed in Arnold S. Kohen and Roberta A. Quance, "The Politics of Starvation," *Inquiry,* February 18, 1980.

11. Jill Jolliffe, "Timorese tell of executions," *The Australian,* April 9, 1980.

12. "Amnesty fears for Fretilin," *The Australian,* May 5, 1980.

13. Brian Eads, "Timorese struggle back to life," *Observer* (London), May 2, 1980.

14. Confidential cable from the Jakarta embassy to the State Department (March 1980); see note 4 above. On the facts concerning the preparation of the "extremely backward population" for self-government, prior to the dose of benevolence administered by the U.S. government and its Indonesian associates, see, *inter alia,* the statement before the Fourth Committee of the U.N. General Assembly, October 17, 1980, by Elizabeth Traube, an anthropologist who worked in East Timor, who concludes that "the people of East Timor are fully capable of determining their own political future."

15. James M. Markham, "Refugees Say Rebels in East Timor Are Still Fighting the Indonesians," *New York Times,* July 29, 1980. See also the *Times* editorial "Tears for Timor," July 25, 1980.

16. Cameron Forbes, "Indons herd 'confused' Timor tribes," *Age* (Melbourne), November 19, 1980.

17. Edward Girardet, "East Timor: more food but repressive rule lingers," *Christian Science Monitor,* November 19, 1981.

18. Benedict Anderson, statement before Fourth Committee (see note 5). In the *Far Eastern Economic Review,* May 23, 1980, David Jenkins claims that the army is returning the expropriated coffee plantations to former Portuguese or Timorese owners after having cleared about $20 million in coffee earnings, allegedly "to offset the heavy costs of its military operations against the Fretilin independence movement there."

The *Review* is often a valuable source of information, but on Indonesia particularly its reports have to be taken with a grain of salt. The *Review* has been highly protective of the Indonesian generals, even resorting, in one instance, to a disgraceful Stalinist-style attack on a human rights organization concerned with Indonesia (Derek Davies, editor, *Far Eastern Economic Review,* September 12, 1980). Davies comments that "most such organisations [namely, "pressure groups and campaigning organisations devoted to humanitarian causes"] which profess themselves concerned with human rights largely confine their targets to non-communist countries," which demonstrates their insincerity—just as the same logic demonstrates the insincerity of the groups (which in fact constitute the vast majority in the West) that confine their targets to Communist countries—a standard charge in the Communist press. The specific target of his attack, TAPOL, "is remarkable for the few names of people who have any known connection with Indonesia or knowledge of conditions there. (Indeed it seems possible that some of them have never visited the country)." Again, the argument is familiar from analogous complaints in the Communist press. The attack continues in the same familiar vein.

19. Henry Kamm, "Jakarta Ending Foreign Famine Aid to Annexed Land," *New York Times,* December 9, 1980.

20. Pieter Luteyn, "East Timor: Indonesia Plays with the Lives of the Survivors," *Bijeen* (April 1980).

21. For some references and discussion, see Chomsky and Herman, *op. cit.,* vol. 2, chapter 5, note 67. On the CRS and Timor, see Mark Winiarski, "CRS 'Political Link'; Aid scarce in strife-torn East Timor," *National Catholic Reporter,* November 16, 1979; also George

Cotter and Sue Nichterlein, "CIA net reaches Catholic relief," *National Times* (Australia), September 7–13, 1980. Winiarski cites (secondhand) a "very well informed Indonesian source" who is reported to have said: "The CRS program should not be described as a church program. CRS is just functioning as a link between the U.S. Agency for International Development and the Indonesian army." Cotter and Nichterlein observe that Cotter's visits to thirty-three countries, where he has worked with numerous voluntary agencies and church leaders as a Catholic priest of the Maryknoll mission assigned to assist Third World church workers in poverty projects, "have brought him to the conviction that CRS is more an instrument of the US Government than an agency of the Catholic Church." They report that local social action groups have "resolved not to participate in aid programs with CRS in the Philippines because they felt that 'the nature of most so-called development aid handled by US/AID-CRS is paternalistic, and palliative at the most.' " They also note that USAID has contributed more than six times as much to CRS as to the ICRC for Timor relief, and cite former CRS employees who hold that AID is "using private organisations such as CRS to feed CIA agents into situations such as Vietnam or East Timor, and for extracting intelligence from levels and parts of society where military and political agents can't reach." The record in Vietnam reviewed by Richard Rashke in the *National Catholic Reporter* (December 1976) after a year's investigation of the CRS role there, which they review, lends credibility to this charge, at least in the case of Vietnam.

22. Father Pat Walsh, "Notes on the East Timor Issue; based on an international visit, 7.6.80–18.8.80," Christmas 1980, Action for World Development, 183 Gertrude Street, Fitzroy 3065, Australia.

23. Father Walsh notes that "the detailed ACFOA [Australian Council for Overseas Aid] report *Aid and East Timor* released in July 1979 charged that thousands of East Timorese died because aid supplied to the army-controlled Indonesian Red Cross failed to reach them owing to corruption." Furthermore, "an army supplies manager who regularly visited East Timor, informed me he had resigned his position because of the high level of corruption pre-1979."

24. On the civilizing role of Israel in the Middle East, see Chapters 9 to 12, above.

25. *Kompas* (Jakarta), March 26, 1981. Introduced into the *Congressional Record*, May 21, 1981, E2518, by representative Don Edwards of California.

26. On this initiative, a Portuguese request for a U.N. commission to examine the East Timor question, see Jill Jolliffe, *Age* (Melbourne), April 28, 1981 (*Congressional Record*, May 21, 1981, E2519). Jolliffe observes that in September 1980 the Portuguese government had proposed talks among "all interested parties" over the future of East Timor. "Indonesia never officially responded, and Portugal failed to win support from any senior Western nation."

27. Tom Harkin, "Our proxy war in East Timor: the U.S. abets a brutal annexation," *Progressive*, December 1980.

28. The laws, however, are not applied to the abuses of client states.

29. Paul Tsongas, *Congressional Record-Senate*, April 29, 1981, S 4094–5.

30. J. R. Walsh and G. J. Munster, *Documents on Australian Defence and Foreign Policy, 1968–1975* (Sydney: Hale & Iremonger, 1980). See "Controversial Book on Australia Appears Despite Court Injunction," *International Herald Tribune*, November 11, 1980; "Defence secrets book still on sale," *Manchester Guardian*, November 11, 1980; "Kissinger's personal instructions," *New Statesman*, November 21, 1980; "Australia's

'Pentagon Papers,' " *Newsweek*, November 24, 1980; Daniel Southerland, "US might have averted tragic Timor takeover," *Christian Science Monitor*, December 17, 1980; Jack Anderson, "Tiny Nation, Lost in a Grand Strategy," *Washington Post*, December 21, 1980; Robert Levey, "Cables show US watched as E. Timor was invaded," *Boston Globe*, December 22, 1980. See Arnold Kohen, "Invitation to a Massacre in East Timor: the U.S. involvement," *Nation*, February 7, 1981, for a review of the most important documents relating to East Timor. As Kohen observes, it was these that primarily concerned the Australian government, as it attempted to have the book suppressed and to prevent major newspapers from publishing excerpts.

The articles cited report the major documents, apart from *Newsweek*, which has only this to say: "Lengthy sections of the 430-page volume deal with Jakarta's military take-over of East Timor in 1975 and the record is filled with unflattering references to Indonesian leaders—many of them still in office. In fact, officials said, it was to spare the Indonesians public humiliation that the injunction was sought. If the documents were widely circulated, said Foreign Affairs Secretary Peter Henderson, Jakarta might show Australia 'a different pattern of behavior.' " True enough, as far as it goes, but what is significant is what *Newsweek* chooses to suppress for its American audience.

31. Chomsky and Herman, *op. cit.*, pp. 144, 156–57. The Australian press noted that "a Gilbertian touch" was given to the controversy in the courts when the publisher pointed out that the cable that the government had described as having "overriding sensitivity" had already appeared in this book, which was reviewed by the mainstream press in Australia (not in the United States) and "had been on sale quite openly for some time and is the kind of publication which, normally, one could expect to be read by foreign affairs gurus" (Trevor Sykes and Alan Reid, "Why gag was unnecessary," *The Bulletin*, November 25, 1980). In his review of this book in the *Nation* (see note 20 of main chapter), A. J. Langguth, formerly bureau chief of the *New York Times* in Saigon, complained that it was unfair for us to criticize the working journalist on the basis of hindsight. This is one of a great many examples that illustrate that the true story is rather different. See also the reference of note 3.

Shortly after the "Australian 'Pentagon Papers' " affair erupted, "a mystery fire which yesterday gutted an eight-storey office block in Sydney, destroyed stocks of two of the most politically sensitive books in Australia," one of them, *The Political Economy of Human Rights*, and another, a book on American installations in Australia. The former "is said to contain a cable which the Federal Government claims is extremely sensitive and directly affected relations with Indonesia." "Arson squad detectives are investigating the blaze" (" 'Sensitive books' in Fire," *Sunday Mail*, November 16, 1980).

32. Further evidence appeared prior to Kamm's article. In Daniel Southerland's report of his interview with Ford's National Security Adviser Brent Scowcroft in March (see note 2 of main chapter), he states that according to Scowcroft, Ford and Kissinger "did not encourage the invasion but also did not oppose it," adding that "we really had no reasonable options," thus implying that the invasion was indeed discussed. In his article in the *Nation* (February 7, 1981), Kohen cites the 1980 book *Suharto's Indonesia* by Hamish MacDonald, former *Washington Post* Jakarta correspondent, where it is asserted that "an attack on Dili was to have been made on 5 December, the day U.S. President Gerald Ford and his Secretary of State, Henry Kissinger, were due to arrive in Jakarta from China. American intelligence learnt of this highly compromising

timetable, and successfully demanded that the operation be postponed until after Ford left on 6 December."

33. On this topic, see Chomsky and Herman, *op. cit.,* vol. 2, chapter 2, section 2, and sources cited there. Note that the relevant sense of "political" does not involve familiarity with John Locke, but rather commitment to independence.

34. This prediction was fulfilled all too soon. Church sources in Timor and Indonesia report that in September 1981, the Indonesian occupying forces launched a new offensive in an effort to destroy the Fretilin resistance. Timorese males from fifteen to fifty have been forced to join the army to participate in this campaign, undertaken just before the rainy season, depriving villages of their normal labor force at the planting season. They predict that this will lead to another famine, with the threat of full-scale genocide, now that the ICRC has been compelled to terminate its relief program. Relatives of Fretilin are being rounded up by the Indonesian military and sent to prison islands. It is alleged that one island, Atauro, now holds 60,000 prisoners. The reports of mass conscription are confirmed in letters from East Timor and by refugees in Australia. See Father Pat Walsh, "Urgent Memorandum on the Situation Inside East Timor," Action for World Development, 183 Gertrude Street, Fitzroy, Victoria 3065, Australia; Statement by Mr. José Ramos-Horta before the Fourth Committee of the General Assembly by the U.N., October 21, 1981; Peter Wise, *Boston Globe,* November 26, 1981, p. A26.

The U.N. correspondent for the *New York Times,* Bernard Nossiter, reports (November 23, 1981) that in the General Assembly session, "Mr. Ranos-Horta [*sic*] won by a tidy majority, 58 to 40," referring to the vote supporting self-determination for East Timor. He reports that Indonesia had invaded East Timor in 1975, "with soldiers, planes, napalm and tanks." There is no mention of the U.S. role. He does not mention the U.S. vote against the resolution, or earlier U.S. efforts to provide diplomatic cover for the Indonesian aggression and massacre. His note is devoted to the hypocrisy of the Arab states, which (with other Third World states) "lead the cry for the rights of the Palestinians against Israel and Namibians against South Africa," but which voted for the most part with Moslem Indonesia, proving that "religion was thicker than principle." There is no word on the contents of Ramos-Horta's statement. Perhaps in five years some crusading journalist for the *Times* will report the current actions that threaten to wipe out the remnants of the population, perhaps even noting that the U.S. role was less than glorious, but surely not commenting on the role of the press.

35. Perhaps the French government may desist from its disgraceful contributions to Indonesian atrocities with the complicity of most of the intelligentsia when it mattered most (see Chomsky and Herman, *op. cit.,* vol. 1, pp. 192–93). François Mitterand has stated that "a whole people was killed in Cambodia, and another is being killed in Timor" (see *Time,* May 25, 1981). It remains to be seen whether this concern for the people of Timor will be translated into policy.

36. Ross Waby, *Australian,* January 22, 1976, reporting from New York; cited in Chomsky and Herman, *op. cit.*

INDEX

ABOUT THE AUTHOR

Noam Chomsky is Professor at the Department of Linguistics and Philosophy at MIT. He is the author of numerous books, including *American Power and the New Mandarins, For Reasons of State, Problems of Knowledge and Freedom, On Language,* and *Understanding Power: The Indispensable Chomsky* (edited by Peter R. Mitchell and John Schoeffel), all of which have been published by The New Press. He is also the author, most recently, of *Hegemony or Survival, Middle East Illusions, 9-11, Pirates and Emperors, Old and New, Rogue States, On Nature and Language,* and *The Minimalist Program.*